On DS2401 with some claimed reports (10.20.87)
(nt invoiced)

D0534919

On DS24401 with some claimed reports (10.20.87)
(nt invoiced)

International
Whaling
Commission

Right Whales: Past and Present Status

PROCEEDINGS OF THE WORKSHOP ON THE STATUS OF RIGHT WHALES

New England Aquarium,
Boston, Massachusetts
15–23 June 1983

Edited by

Robert L. Brownell, Jr.

P.O. Box 70, San Simeon, CA. 93452, USA

Peter B. Best

Mammal Research Institute
University of Pretoria, Pretoria 0002, South Africa

and

John H. Prescott

New England Aquarium, Central Wharf, Boston, MA. 02110, USA

Reports of the International Whaling Commission
Special Issue 10

Cambridge 1986

The Workshop was funded by the International Whaling Commission, the New England Aquarium, the US Marine Mammal Commission and the World Wildlife Fund. The publication of this volume was made possible by the International Whaling Commission, the US National Marine Fisheries Service (Southwest, Northwest, Southeast and Northeast Fisheries Centers), the US Marine Mammal Commission, the US Minerals Management Service, the Australian National Parks and Wildlife Service, Sohio Alaska Petroleum Company and the Windstar Foundation.

Cover photo: Right whale (*Eubalaena glacialis*) breaching, Peninsula Valdes, Argentina. Courtesy of K. Payne.

ISBN 0 906975 16 6
ISSN 0255-2760

Preface

It is never easy to assist in publishing the Proceedings of a Workshop you did not attend. In this instance the quality of the work in the volume has made me sorrier than ever that I did not manage to participate in what was clearly a fascinating workshop. I would like to thank the editors of the volume for making my task easier by diligently adhering to unfamiliar guidelines and the authors for agreeing to unreasonable deadlines. I believe the finished product justifies the many hours we have all spent over the last three years, and is a most valuable addition to our special issue series.

G. P. DONOVAN
Series Editor
Cambridge, December 1986

OTHER VOLUMES IN THE SPECIAL ISSUE SERIES
(ISSN 0255-2760)

1 [1977]—Report of the Special Meeting of the Scientific Committee on Sei and Bryde's Whales.
i–v+150 pp.; ISBN 0 906975 03 4

2 [1980]—Sperm Whales.
i–iv+275 pp.; ISBN 0 906975 01 8

3 [1980]—Age Determination of Toothed Whales and Sirenians.
Eds W. F. Perrin and A. C. Myrick.
i–viii+229 pp.; ISBN 0 906975 05 0

4 [1982]—Aboriginal/Subsistence Whaling (with special reference to the Alaska and Greenland Fisheries).
Ed. G. P. Donovan.
i–v+86 pp.; ISBN 0 906975 09 3

5 [1983]—Special Issue on Historical Whaling records.
Eds M. F. Tillman and G. P. Donovan.
i–v+490 pp.; ISBN 0 906975 11 5

6 [1984]—Reproduction of Whales, Dolphins and Porpoises.
Eds W. F. Perrin, R. L. Brownell, Jr and D. P. DeMaster.
i–xii+490 pp.; ISBN 0 906975 07 7

7 [1986]—Bibliography of Whale Killing Techniques.
By E. D. Mitchell, R. R. Reeves, A. Evely and M. Stawsky.
i–v+161 pp.; ISBN 0 906975 14 X

8 [1986]—Behaviour of Whales in Relation to Management.
Ed. G. P. Donovan.
i–v+282 pp.; ISBN 0 906975 15 8

9 [1987]—The Biology of the Genus *Cephalorhynchus*.
Eds R. L. Brownell Jr and G. P. Donovan.
Ca. 200 pp.; ISBN 0 906975 17 4

Available from the office of the Commission, The Red House, Station Road, Histon, Cambridge CB4 4NP, United Kingdom.

Introduction

Right whales were first protected internationally by the League of Nations Convention in Geneva in 1931, which came into force in 1935. This protection was continued in the Principal Agreement of 1937 and has been continued by the International Whaling Commission (IWC) since the signing of the Convention for the Regulation of Whaling in 1946.

The holding of a special meeting on right whales thus might seem an unusual departure for the IWC, which has normally concerned itself with whale species that are currently exploited. However, in 1981 the Commission asked its Scientific Committee to assess the degree to which IWC actions in extending protection had resulted in the intended recovery of the species. Besides right whales, legal protection from commercial whaling had been afforded to gray whales (1937), humpback whales (North Atlantic 1955, Southern Hemisphere 1963, all oceans 1966) and blue whales (North Atlantic 1960, Antarctic 1965, all oceans 1966). Apart from the Eastern Pacific stock of gray whales (e.g. see Reilly, 1984, *Rep. int. Whal. Commn* (special issue 6): 389–99), none of these has shown any demonstrable recovery in spite of up to 45 years of official protection.

In its response to the Commission's request, the Scientific Committee drew attention to the fact that relatively few stocks of protected species were being systematically monitored, and most of these had been surveyed for five years or less. The chances of detecting a population response in such a short interval were slim. Nevertheless, the subject was clearly an important one and its consideration at the 1981 meeting prompted the Committee to call for the analysis of available historical or recent data for any protected stock that would clarify initial unexploited levels, trends in population size or current population levels (*Rep. int. Whal. Commn* 32: 57–8).

Although this appeal for information was non-specific, the Scientific Committee's sub-committee on protected species and aboriginal whaling recommended that consideration should be given first to right whale stocks, particularly those in the Okhotsk/Sea of Japan, the Northwest Atlantic, the South Atlantic and around Australasia. These stocks were chosen because it was believed that data existed and was being or could be analysed to provide the information required. Right whales were also of special interest because of their close systematic relationship with the bowhead whale, a species subject to aboriginal exploitation and of particular concern to the Commission because of its depleted status (see *Rep. int. Whal. Commn* (special issue 4)).

Right whales were a particularly appropriate choice for other reasons. The first victims of a regular whaling industry (by the Basques in the 12th century), they were also the first species to be given international protection, and yet they still remained among the rarest of the large whales. They seemed to represent an extreme example of the inability of whale stocks to recover from excessive depletion. And yet pioneering studies by Payne and others in the Southwest Atlantic had shown that right whales could be individually identified through the pattern of natural callosities on the head, a technique which meant that the dynamics of the surviving populations could perhaps be studied in some detail without destructive sampling. There was the exciting prospect therefore, that by getting the appropriate people together, some conclusions could be reached not only about what right whale populations had done in the past, but also about their current status and how future trends might develop.

A list of proposed projects on right whales was drawn up and 25 people approached for their co-operation in providing written submissions on the topics, or at least extended abstracts, by the 1982 meeting. The response was sufficient to recommend a special workshop meeting in 1983, finally scheduled for the New England Aquarium, Boston from 15–23 June for which Brownell acted as convenor, Best as chairman and Prescott as local coordinator.

A total of 34 participants attended the workshop, with an extremely high proportion of invited participants covering a wide spectrum, from biologists to historians and archaeologists. In retrospect the meeting would have had a better balance if there had been more input from historians and (perhaps unexpectedly) from mathematicians. Nevertheless, the meeting was a milestone in the IWC's approach to a species not subject to even aboriginal whaling, and the report of the workshop plus associated papers as published here will form a major source of information on right whales for many years to come.

A total of 29 papers were available at the workshop of which 28 were submitted for publication and an additional four were submitted after the workshop. Eight of the final 32 were subsequently rejected or withdrawn.

Special thanks are due to the following people who reviewed the various manuscripts in the volume: A. N. Baker, J. L. Bannister, L. G. Barnes, R. Bastida, J. E. Bird, H. W. Braham, P. J. H. van Bree, J. M. Breiwick, H. J. Brockmann, S. G. Brown, D. G. Chapman, R. Clarke, W. H. Dawbin, C. de Jong, G. P. Donovan, E. M. Dorsey, T. du Pasquier, M. A. Fraker, D. E. Gaskin, R. N. P. Goodall, P. S. Hammond, S. K. Katona, S. Kraus, R. Kugler, K. Martin, S. A. McLeod, J. G. Mead, E. D. Mitchell, S. Ohsumi, H. Omura, R. S. Payne, M. C. Pinedo, C. A. Price, K. Ralls, G. B. Rathbun, D. W. Rice, R. R. Reeves, C. J. Rørvik, G. J. B. Ross, V. Rowntree, W. E. Schevill, S. Taber, P. O. Thomas, H. E. Winn, B. Würsig.

In addition to the staff of the New England Aquarium, Martin Harvey and Ray Gambell of the IWC assisted with financial and practical arrangements for the invited participants. W. E. Evans, D. G. Chapman, R. J. Hoffman and J. R. Twiss Jr proved invaluable in assisting us to find funds to publish the volume. Greg Donovan saw the production through the printers and assisted with many stages of preparation, editing and artwork, while Stella Bradley and Anne-Florence Dujardin tirelessly typeset the tabular matter and read proofs. Susan Wright retyped a number of the manuscripts before they were sent to Cambridge.

Robert L. Brownell Jr
Pt Piedras Blancas
Peter B. Best
Cape Town
John H. Prescott
Boston

December 1986

Contents

Section IV – Historical Whaling

Flensing whales in open waters, probably in the 18th century [Reproduced from Sañez Reguart, A. (1791) *Diccionario Histórico de los Artes de la Pesca Nacional* (Madrid): 330–453]

Report of the Workshop on the Status of Right Whales

1. ARRANGEMENTS FOR MEETING

Following a two-day open symposium on right whales held at the New England Aquarium on 15–16 June, a workshop on the status of right whales was held at the same venue from 17 to 23 June 1983. A list of the participants is given in Appendix 1.

2. ELECTION OF CHAIRMAN

Best was elected Chairman. He described the origins of the meeting and its purpose and objectives. These could be summarised as two questions:
  (a) To what extent were original right whale stocks depleted?
  (b) What is the evidence for the current status of these stocks?

The management procedures for aboriginal/subsistence whaling adopted by the IWC in 1982 (*Rep. int. Whal. Commn* 33:29, 40) included a minimum population level below which no whaling could be allowed. This population level had not yet been defined, but it was felt that the answers to the two critical questions posed above for right whales were very relevant in this regard.

3. APPOINTMENT OF RAPPORTEUR

Reeves agreed to act as rapporteur.

4. ADOPTION OF AGENDA

The agenda as revised and adopted is given as Appendix 2.

5. REVIEW OF DOCUMENTS AND AVAILABLE DATA

A list of the documents presented to the meeting is given as Appendix 3.

Mitchell suggested that the series of papers and charts on whale distribution by Bolau (1885 – North Atlantic; 1892 – Indian Ocean; 1895 – Pacific Ocean) would be useful in interpreting right whale distribution and stock identity, but he could make available to the workshop only the North Pacific chart.

Kugler (see Appendix 4) reported that the long abstracts of all the logbooks and journals (more than 1,000) used in the preparation of Maury's (1852) charts are available in the National Archives, Washington, DC. Thus, many of the questions pertaining to Maury's charts can be resolved. Kugler estimated that about 75% of the original manuscripts represented in this collection of 'abbreviated logbooks' do not survive.

Winn referred to the handwritten compilations (extracted from logbooks and journals) used by Townsend (1935) in plotting nineteenth-century Yankee catches. It was agreed that these valuable documents, only a portion of which is known to be extant, would be of considerable value in clarifying the dates and positions

of catches and that they should therefore be made more widely available.

Dawbin pointed out that a revised and expanded index to the Pacific Manuscripts Bureau Collection, including some 3,800 American whaling logbooks, is due to become available late in 1983.

6. DISTRIBUTION AND SPECIES/STOCK IDENTITY

The questions of how many species of right whales should be recognized and what nomenclature to use for them were referred to W. E. Schevill (Appendix 5).

While recognising the distinction between bowheads (*Balaena*) and right whales (*Eubalaena*), the workshop recommended that the morphological distinctions between *E. glacialis* and *E. australis* be further examined. A table was prepared (Appendix 6) listing places where skulls and other hard parts of balaenids are available for examination. Blood grouping, karyology, and other analysis of soft tissues should also be carried out to the extent possible, given the obvious limits to the availability of specimen material.

Because of geographical barriers, differences in timing of northern and southern breeding seasons and an apparent discontinuity in distribution across the Equator, there appears to be no significant mixing between North Atlantic, North Pacific and Southern Ocean populations of right whales. The few records near the Equator (e.g. off Gabon – Budker, 1952) cannot be attributed to either Northern or Southern Hemisphere stocks.

The following discussions of stock identity were organized by ocean basin (Fig. 1).

6.1. North Atlantic

The distribution of right whales in the western North Atlantic is generally in coastal waters from Florida to southeast Labrador. There are a few recent records (SC/35/RW17) and some historical evidence (SC/35/RW23) of right whales in the Gulf of Mexico. One sighting of a pair of animals involved in courtship behaviour at Bermuda in mid-April 1970 (Payne, pers. comm.) is of interest.

Right whales were a major target of the early Basque fishery in the Strait of Belle Isle region (SC/35/RW1; SC/35/RW13; SC/35/RW11), but much of the evidence involves problems of distinguishing records of *E. glacialis* from those of *Balaena mysticetus*. Similar problems apply to summer records along the Labrador coast, north to the mouth of Davis Strait (SC/35/RW23). Right whales were hunted east of the Grand Bank and possibly in an area charted by Maury (1853) in mid-ocean. Calving grounds appear to be along the southeast US coast (SC/35/RW17; SC/35/RW29) and near Cape Cod (SC/35/RW27).

Right whales were formerly hunted during summer in an area east of Cape Farewell centred at 60–62° N, 33–35° W, around the coasts of Iceland, off North Cape, and off the British Isles (SC/35/RW8; SC/35/RW1;

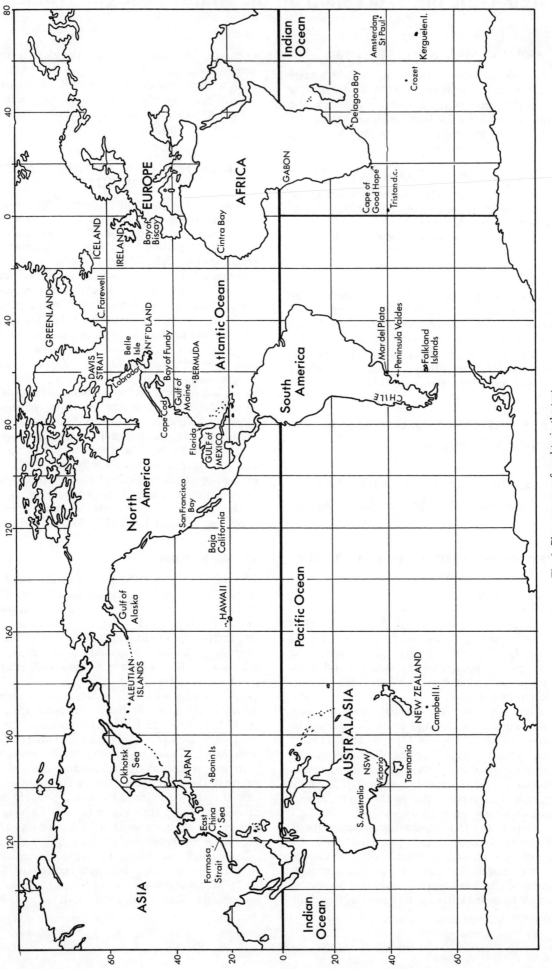

Fig. 1. Place names referred to in the text.

SC/35/RW13; SC/35/RW23). The Bay of Biscay was an important winter ground (SC/35/RW1) and right whales were hunted off the northwest coast of Africa in an area centred at Cintra Bay (23° N, 16° 15′ W) (SC/35/RW23). Calving grounds were probably in these last two areas.

Three hypotheses concerning stock identity were presented and discussed (SC/35/RW23). However, the only direct evidence of movements by individuals pertains to the Gulf of Maine and Scotian Shelf areas (SC/35/RW15; SC/35/RW29), which represent a small proportion of the species' range. The indirect evidence (e.g. exploitation patterns and trends, hiatuses in distribution, and inferences from timing of arrival on various grounds), while inconclusive, suggests there are at least separate eastern and western North Atlantic stocks. By analogy with the proposal by Payne (SC/35/RW21) for Southern Hemisphere populations that perhaps right whales do not migrate long distances and thus can be separated into relatively small stock units, Braham suggested there may be several such stock units on either side of the North Atlantic. Observations off Cape Cod in winter might help elucidate the migrations off eastern North America. The statement in SC/35/RW1 that the Spanish Basques abandoned the Grand Bay (Strait of Belle Isle) fishery because of a dramatic decline in the availability of whales by 1610–20, or well before the colonial right whale fishery began in the eastern USA, is taken to suggest a discontinuity between the whales hunted in the two areas. To facilitate further research pertaining to stock identity in the North Atlantic, Aguilar, Du Pasquier and Cumbaa compiled a table showing important dates or periods in the activities of the Basque whalers (Appendix 7).

The workshop participants provisionally agreed to divide the North Atlantic, for statistical purposes, into eastern and western sectors and to treat the 60–62° N, 33–35° W area separately. Some of the unspecified catches by the Basques, French and others during early years have been assigned to a fourth grouping – 'northern areas' – because of a possible confusion with bowheads.

6.2 North Pacific

Due to a lack of expertise among participants regarding North Pacific and especially Northwest Pacific right whale catch history, Richard Kugler and David Henderson of the New Bedford Whaling Museum were asked to make presentations and answer questions. Henderson was nearing completion of a major study of the nineteenth-century whale fishery in the Sea of Okhotsk. Kugler's report is summarized in Appendix 4.

Right whale distribution in the North Pacific east of 180° and south of 50° N was reviewed in SC/35/RW26 and SC/35/RW6. The main former summer whaling ground for right whales on the east side was in the Gulf of Alaska (50–58° N, 140–152° W). Right whales have been caught or sighted during winter and early spring (February–April) along the west coast of North America as far south as Baja California. There is only one record for Hawaii (Rountree et al., 1980). The few records along the west coast south of Canada suggest that this is not now, nor was during the last 150 years the site of major winter concentrations of right whales.

The Maury (1852) charts show a continuous distribution across the North Pacific north of 35° N, calling into question stock separation in the North Pacific. They show a high concentration of right whales along the 180° line between 35° N and the Aleutian Islands, a region for which Townsend shows little evidence of their presence.

Klumov (1962) replotted some northwest Pacific right whale kills mapped by Townsend (1935) and sightings of a few right whales observed between 1951 and 1957. He 'supposed', on the basis of these data, that there were two 'herds' with separate wintering grounds (west and southwest as versus south and southeast of Japan) but with partly overlapping summer feeding grounds (one occurring exclusively in the Okhotsk Sea). He took differing response to exploitation as evidence of separate 'herd' identity, the Okhotsk herd having been nearly extirpated. However the Committee noted that adequate quantitative data were not available to support Klumov's reasoning and that winter calving grounds have not been identified for two such 'herds'.

Although no evidence of coastal calving grounds could be identified, workshop participants were reluctant to speculate that right whales calve in pelagic rather than coastal waters of the North Pacific. Such behaviour would be contrary to what appears to be true in all other oceans, although it cannot be certain that all calving in the Southern Hemisphere and North Atlantic takes place near shore. The possibility that inshore waters of the Pacific Northwest (of North America) may have served as calving grounds cannot be dismissed. Large numbers of nearly weaned calves were taken on the Kodiak Ground, but this was in summer (Bowles, 1845). All of the February and March sightings of right whales shown in Maury's (1852) charts are far offshore, while Townsend's (1935) show some catches in February and March in Formosa Strait and the East China Sea. Right whales were hunted from December to March along the south and west coasts of Japan (Omura, 1958), and around the Bonin Islands in February (Rowntree et al., 1980).

Mitchell suggested that the timing of exploitation of humpback (Townsend, 1935, chart D) and gray whales along the California, Baja California and mainland Mexico coasts comprises evidence that right whales were not abundant and did not calve in bays from San Francisco Bay south to 20° N and the Mexican coast. The Northwest (Kodiak) Ground population supported a peak fishery in 1845–46, when the winter gray whale (and humpback) coastal and lagoon fishery began. The 'Kodiak' population persisted after 1856 as a minor fishery for approximately one or two more decades; if that population migrated coastwise south of San Francisco Bay, then the gray and humpback whalers would have preferentially taken the commercially more desirable right whales and their calves.

It was felt that, as for the North Atlantic, it would be convenient to consider the right whale populations on the east and west sides of the North Pacific as separate stock units for statistical purposes. However, in the absence of direct evidence, no conclusion can be reached concerning the identity of different biological populations. It was noted that the Japanese and Russian sightings and effort data for the North Pacific are difficult to use in their present, published form. The workshop recommends that these data be made available in original form for closer analysis, or at least that effort be made available on a monthly basis for 5° squares, and the latitude, longitude and date be made available for each sighting, including sightings by catcher boats since 1969. The workshop also *recommends* that historical catch and archaeological data for the North Pacific be examined for evidence of calving grounds.

6.3 South Pacific/Indian Ocean

The information available on right whale distribution off the Chilean coast (mainly the Townsend and Maury charts; SC/35/RW19; SC/35/RW21) indicates that the population there is disjunct from that near New Zealand and from those along the east coast of South America. Such an interpretation is based mainly on an apparent hiatus in distribution between *ca* 130° W and 90° W which might, however, be influenced to some extent by sighting or catch effort. The workshop provisionally recognized a separate Chilean stock of right whales.

Dawbin urged that, for the present, the right whale population found near the Campbell and Auckland Islands groups be treated as distinct from others, on the grounds that it has a separate catch history from the New Zealand stock. Dawbin referred to shore whalers at Campbell Island making peak catches from mid-May to the end of September, which corresponds with the breeding season. The timing in appearance of animals at Campbell Island overlaps considerably with that of the more northerly grounds near New Zealand. It may be useful to consider this stock as an analogue to others centred on small mid-ocean island groups (e.g. Tristan da Cunha).

Dawbin proposed that the whales found near New Zealand and the Kermadecs be considered one stock unit, based on a compatible seasonality of occurrence between the two areas and the discontinuity in catches between them and the Australia/Tasmania region. Calves are found in bays along the New Zealand coast, especially either side of Cook Strait.

It was agreed to group the whales occurring in coastal waters of Tasmania, Victoria, eastern Australia, New South Wales and South Australia into a single stock unit (Southeast Australia Stock) with calving taking place in coastal embayments and with summer movements offshore. There is no discontinuity in distribution or catch records to suggest a partitioning of stocks between this region and the coast of western Australia (the coast of New Holland Ground), but it was considered useful to adopt 135° W as an arbitrary boundary for statistical purposes and to score catch records separately for areas east and west of this line.

Bannister proposed a westward limit of 90° E in the Indian Ocean for the 'Southwest Australian Stock' (based on Townsend and Maury).

The only available approach to identifying stocks in the central and western Indian Ocean was by reference to the Townsend and Maury charts. Although no information was available on calving grounds, catches were concentrated near sub-Antarctic island groups. Three statistical areas (provisional stocks) were identified on the basis of catch records plotted by Townsend: (1) Crozet, (2) Kerguelen (summer), and (3) Amsterdam/St Paul/Central Indian Ocean (late spring). Participants agreed that populations concentrated around these islands probably are not connected to Delagoa Bay and other known calving areas, but logbooks and other sources should be examined to determine the seasonality and age and sex composition of the catches on these grounds.

6.4 South Atlantic

Lack of matches in callosity patterns between samples of right whales off South Africa and off eastern South America is taken as evidence that there are separate stocks on either side of the South Atlantic (SC/35/RW21). Best did not agree with Payne's proposal to separate South African right whales into two separate stocks, with the dividing line at *ca* 20° E. He (Best) felt that although Townsend's plotted catches may support an argument for splitting them, there is at present a generally continuous string of calving bays linking the populations on the east and west sides of the Cape of Good Hope. However, for statistical purposes, it was agreed to divide catches at 20° E longitude, possibly corresponding to Townsend's (1935) distinction between Indian and South Atlantic oceans.

The well-documented offshore whaling grounds in the South Atlantic present interpretive problems. Best believes Tristan is a separate calving area, but this means catches between there and South Africa can be attributed to either a Tristan or a South African stock. Payne considered the Tristan and Pigeon grounds (i.e. 10–30° W) to involve the same stock. In Payne's view, the Falklands Ground is associated with the calving grounds along and south of Peninsula Valdes, and the animals on False and Brazil banks calve along the Brazil coast (SC/35/RW21) where females and calves have been caught in recent years (SC/35/RW20). However, Bastida reported that two right whales (one a male) identified at Peninsula Valdes have been resighted off Mar del Plata (38° 57′ S) (Bastida and Bastida, in press), suggesting that females missing in a 2-year period from Peninsula Valdes may be found farther north along the South American coast. It was noted that the hypothesis of one stock along the South American east coast (Bastida) is based on biological evidence while the alternate hypothesis that there is more than one stock (Payne) is based on analysis of Townsend's historical catch data. The lack of recent sightings along the coast south of Peninsula Valdes suggests that whales in Subpopulation 1 are depleted (SC/35/RW21).

Mitchell emphasized that plotted concentrations of whale kills on the Townsend (1935) charts give information on seasonal whale occurrence but that other biological data, and tagging or comparable evidence, are necessary to demonstrate genetic relationships between and within groupings. Two or more biological populations might be represented on some Townsend whaling 'grounds' where records occur throughout the year.

Mitchell and Martin expressed concern about over-reliance upon the Maury (1851, 1852, 1853), Townsend (1931, 1935), and Clark (1887) charts as sources of information on whale distribution. These charts are useful for addressing such large-scale matters as catch areas and effort, but finer-scale questions relating to population or stock identity require that documentary sources be examined directly. Whenever the charts alone are used, it is important to bear in mind possible biases in the data.

7. HISTORICAL CATCHES BY AREA OR STOCK*

A table of known and estimated catches of right whales, by area, was compiled by Du Pasquier (Appendix 7). For most areas, the reconstruction of catch history is incomplete. This is particularly true of the North Atlantic, where the highest catches occurred before 1800. Even for the North Atlantic, however, it is of interest to note that high catches by the Basques and the collapse of their Newfoundland/Grand Bay fishery preceded the colonial shore fisheries along the US coast.

Estimated total catches for other oceans, based as they are on catch histories with more nearly complete documentation, are: 38,000–39,000 in the South Atlantic from 1785 to 1939; 12,000–13,000 in the Indian Ocean from 1830 to 1939; 38,000–39,000 in the South Pacific from 1815 to 1969; and 15,000–16,000 in the North Pacific from 1840 to 1969. These figures do not include an adjustment to account for hunting loss. The workshop wishes to call attention to the fact that for some areas and periods, the cumulative catch figures are greatly underestimated. For example, shore-based catches along the US coast north and south of Long Island have not been listed. Also, the catches made by the large number of British vessels that cleared for the southern whale fishery from 1776 to 1843 are not included.

7.1 Struck and lost rates, associated mortality

All fisheries for right whales in which pre-modern whaling technology was used involved a substantial amount of hunting loss. Thus, data on secured catch must be corrected to account for whales killed or mortally wounded but not processed or reported in the catch statistics. The following categories of struck whales were identified:
  (1) struck, killed and processed;
  (2) struck but escaped (and presumably survived);
  (3) struck but escaped, moribund,
      (a) lanced and/or spouting blood,
      (b) whaling gear attached;
  (4) struck, killed, but not processed,
      (a) recovered later as a drift whale or stinker,
      (b) not recovered (due to sinking, rough seas, etc.).
There are significant differences in loss rates by whaling area, time period and technology in use. These should be recognised in any reconstruction of catch history. Efforts to quantify loss rates in fisheries for other large whales have been published by Bannister *et al.* (1981), Mitchell (1983) and Mitchell and Reeves (1983). Some new data on mortality factors in right whale fisheries were presented at the workshop (Appendix 8). Losses seem to have been higher on the open seas than they were in bay whaling. An average mortality factor, pertaining to fisheries in which hand harpoons and lances (non-explosive) were used, would be between 1.2 and 1.5.

---

* Provisional figures estimated by Best (Appendix 12) and used at the meeting and hence in the report have been extensively re-worked since the meeting (see the explanatory note to Appendix 12). Total figures used here should thus be interpreted with caution as the final revised values are not yet available and thus we cannot adjust the values accordingly for this report.

8. BIOLOGICAL PARAMETERS (FOR NORTHERN AND SOUTHERN RIGHT WHALES)

8.1 Age and growth

An age-length curve for ages 0–10 years (with wide confidence intervals) is available for the Argentine population, developed using data on known-length individuals and allometry equations (Whitehead and Payne, 1981). Mean length at birth is 5.5 m. This figure is lower than published estimates of 6 m for animals off South Africa (Best, 1981) and in the North Pacific (Ohsumi, 1981). An estimate of 4.5 m for mean birth length in the North Atlantic (SC/35/RW17), based on measurements of three stranded specimens, could be biased downward because stranded neonates are not necessarily representative of a healthy newborn population. (This should be tested by comparing lengths of stranded calves in Argentina and elsewhere with those of living calves.) Two calves, believed to have been seen within two weeks of being born in Cape Cod waters, were estimated to be 6 m long or slightly less (SC/35/RW27).

Calves of the year observed in the Bay of Fundy in summer are 6.1–7.3 m long and are believed to be 3–8 months old (S. Kraus, pers. comm.), assuming that birth occurs mainly in the period December–April (SC/35/RW17; SC/35/RW27; SC/35/RW29). A second size-class of whales in the Bay of Fundy consists of animals 8.5–9.8 m long which are thought to be in their second year. However, in judging the relative age of animals in this size range, it is necessary to use behavioural and other clues in addition to body lengths. There appears to be no distinct mode in length of animals one year or older that can be used to estimate relative age, although a 'juvenile' or 'subadult' class is sometimes used in behavioural studies (e.g. SC/35/RW21).

Maximum reported lengths of female specimens, by area, are:
Southern Hemisphere: 53.7 ft (16.5 m) (SC/35/RW5, Table 4) or 15.6 m (Whitehead and Payne, 1981, Table 3-3);
North Atlantic: 59 ft (18 m) (Thompson, 1928, p. 7; probably measured along body contour) or 16.5 m (Andrews, 1908);
North Pacific: 18.3 m (Klumov, 1962).
Maximum reported lengths for males are:
Southern Hemisphere: 15.2 m (Lönnberg, 1906);
North Atlantic: 12.9 m (Allen, 1916);
North Pacific: 16.4 m (Omura *et al.*, 1969) or 17.1 m (Klumov, 1962).

North Pacific right whales are consistently larger than those in other oceans.

8.2 Mortality rates

An estimate of natural mortality for sexually mature right whales in the Argentine population is $4 \pm 10\%$ (SC/35/RW28). This estimate is within the range of those for other mysticetes of recruited age but near the lower end of that range (SC/35/RW7, Table 1). It should be possible to derive a more rigorous estimate of natural mortality using resight data collected over a long period of time for the Argentine population. To estimate infant mortality, it is important to count and estimate sizes of stranded calves at the breeding grounds and to estimate

Table 1

Data on calves and non-calves in the Bay of Fundy and near Browns Bank. Except for the 46 animals seen on Browns Bank in 1980 (Winn, 1982), figures represent number of individuals identified during the entire summer season. See Kraus and Prescott (1983) for details. Information on calves of the year is from SC/35/RW22. In 1982 an additional (6th calf was seen but it was impossible to judge whether it was a first- or second-year animal.

Year	Calves of year	Non-calves		% calves
		Bay of Fundy	Browns Bank	
1980	4	22	46	5.9
1981	5	56	16	6.9
1982	5	64	45	4.4

the total numbers and average residence times of cows and calves on these grounds. There are a few records of stranded neonates, possibly premature, in South Africa (Best, pers. comm.), in the southeast USA (SC/35/RW17) and in the Peninsula Valdes region (R. Payne, pers. comm.). R. Bastida (pers. comm.) reported strandings in Golfo San Jose and Golfo Nuevo but none along the eastern outer coast of Peninsula Valdes: 1981 (2 calves, one adult) and 1982 (3 calves, one adult) (Appendix 9).

8.3 Reproductive parameters

8.3.1 *Age at sexual maturity*

The smallest measured cow with a calf in the Argentine population was 12.4 m long, and the estimated mean length at sexual maturity (defined as first calving) is 12.5–13 m (Whitehead and Payne, 1981). Estimates of length at sexual maturity in females – 13–15.5 m – and males – 14–15 m – were made by Klumov (1962) and Omura et al. (1969) (summarised in (SC/35/RW7)).

The age of female southern right whales at sexual maturity is estimated as 2.5–6 years from Whitehead and Payne's (1981) growth curve. There is, however, a discrepancy between this theoretical range and the fact that during eight years of study, no identified first-year calf at Peninsula Valdes has been observed to mature and give birth to a calf of its own (SC/35/RW21; Appendix 10). Thus the estimate by Whitehead and Payne may be too low for this population.

No information was available on age at sexual maturity in males.

8.3.2 *Pregnancy rate*

Payne's data from Argentina indicate the majority of adult females give birth every third year (SC/35/RW21), the average calving interval being 3.26 years (SC/35/RW6). Rowntree (pers comm.) reported that the apparent tendency of females with calves to remain close to shore for weeks at a time makes it unlikely that a female with a calf would be missed in the Peninsula Valdes study area. However the possibility cannot be discounted that some females in Payne's sample calved elsewhere, aborted or lost calves from predation or perinatal complications in years when they were seen without a calf.

One identified cow from the western North Atlantic is known to have had a 3-year calving interval on one occasion (SC/35/RW27). This is the only direct biological evidence of the length of the calving interval outside Argentina.

Payne attempted to apply a 3-year calving interval (and

an associated 3-year cycle of visitation by mature females to inshore calving grounds) to sightings data and catch data in other areas. Best's sightings data from South Africa (SC/35/RW4) were interpreted by Payne to suggest medium abundance in Year 1, low abundance in Year 2 and high abundance in Year 3 during each successive 3-year cycle (SC/35/RW21). Best and Payne cautioned against using Best's sightings data to demonstrate such periodicity in occurrence without rigorous statistical testing to account for random year-to-year variability (e.g. Cole, 1954).

Payne pointed out that catch data from bay whaling could be used as corroborative, albeit indirect, evidence of a 3-year cycle. If whaling effort were intensive and consistent for a series of years in a particular calving bay, then one could expect relatively high catches during the first three years, as the three subpopulations of adult females successively entered the bay to calve, followed by an abrupt decline in catches during the 4th, 5th, and 6th years, reflecting depletion of the three subpopulations. Dawbin presented some catch (but no effort) data demonstrating such a pattern for some bays in New Zealand, but there were also other bays for which the catches showed no such trend (SC/35/RW12).

8.3.3 *Possible changes over time*

There are no data available which demonstrate a change in reproduction parameters over time.

8.3.4 *Gross annual reproductive rate*

Gross Annual Reproductive Rate (GARR) is the total number of first-year calves as a proportion of the entire population. Kraus tabulated three years of sightings data from the Bay of Fundy and Browns Bank in summer (Table 1). If it is assumed that this sample of sighted individuals is an unbiased sample of the population as a whole, then the mean percentage of calves is 5.7. However, there are several problems with the above assumption. The calf count does not include calves that died before reaching the summer feeding grounds (SC/35/RW17) or that did not summer in one of the two areas surveyed. Also, right whale populations are apparently segregated in summer. From July to October in each year from 1980 to 1982, only one of 15 identified cow/calf pairs was observed outside the Bay of Fundy that did not later appear in the bay. Calves were not reported in right whale sightings made on the Scotian Shelf by the Blandford, Nova Scotia whalers, although this may have been an artifact of data collection procedures (SC/35/RW18). The Basque fishery in the Bay of Biscay in winter included about 30% calves (SC/35/RW1).

Bannister noted that of 406 right whales caught on the Coast of New Holland Ground in summer, only one cow/calf pair was reported, whereas 50% of bay whaling catches were cow/calf pairs (see Appendix 11). The high proportion of mature females observed in the inshore Argentine population suggests that mature males are under-represented inshore (SC/35/RW28). This evident population segregation would tend to bias estimates of calf percentages in only partial surveys of the population.

Segregation of this nature means that sex ratios in the adult population are difficult to estimate. The sex ratio at birth is believed to be roughly equal (7 males and 6 females amongst identified calves in Argentina – Payne, pers. comm.).

Payne was encouraged to analyse his data in a way that would permit an estimate of calves as a percentage of the entire population. Mitchell suggested an approach for such an analysis by taking the cumulative total of calves from three year-classes as a percentage of total non-calf females observed and estimated to be present in those three year-classes and an equal number of males:

$$\frac{N_c}{[N_{Fx}+N_{Fy}]+N_M} = \% \text{ calves of non-calf population,}$$

where:

N_c = number of calves in year-classes 1, 2, 3;

N_{Fx} = number of females, seen as cows with calves, in year-classes 1, 2, 3;

N_{Fy} = number of immature and mature females in non-cow/calf population, derived from a combination of behavioural evidence, observations of genital slits, photo-identifications and occurrence as in a cow/calf pair in other years;

N_M = number of males in entire biological population, estimated as equal to $[N_{Fx}+N_{Fy}]$.

Lack of time prevented such calculations being done at this meeting.

In the absence of unbiased empirical evidence for GARR, the group asked Breiwick to attempt to calculate a theoretical GARR, using the following assumptions about right whales:

(1) mean calving interval of 3.2 years (crude birth rate of 0.31);
(2) age at female sexual maturity of 10 years (first parturition at age 11);
(3) survival rate (for sexually mature animals) of 0.96;
(4) equal sex ratio.

Juvenile survival can be calculated for a stable population from the following balance equation:

$$\tfrac{1}{2}bs_0{}^a s^{m-a}[1-(s/\lambda)^{w-m-1}] = \lambda^m(\lambda-s),$$

where b = crude birth rate (reciprocal of calving interval) s_0 = juvenile survival rate, s = adult survival rate, λ = eigenvalue or 'population multiplier', a = number of years for which s_0 applies, m = age at sexual maturity and w = maximum age (taken as 50 years). Given the above parameters, the expected proportion of mature animals in a stable population (p) can be calculated (see Breiwick, Eberhardt and Braham, 1984) and the gross annual reproduction rate:

$$\text{GARR} = (\tfrac{1}{2})bp.$$

Juvenile survival rates calculated from the above balance equation, the proportion of mature animals in the population, and GARR are shown in Table 2 for several values of λ, m and a.

GARR was calculated for a stable population using mean calving intervals of 3.2 and 2.5 years. In both cases, a stationary population resulted in first-year survival rates that were unrealistically low when $a = 1$ was used in the balance equation. The workshop agreed to use the range of GARR values between 0.07 and 0.09 for extrapolations to the total population. The reason for this was that, on the basis of empirical evidence from Peninsula Valdes, an age at sexual maturity greater than six years and first-year survival rates of 0.732 or greater (Appendix 10) were thought to be more realistic.

There is a discrepancy between the model's results and observed trends in abundance from surveys (see Section

Table 2

Calculation of GARR (for definition of symbols see text). An asterisk denotes an estimated survival rate greater than one.

b	λ	m	a=1			a=m		
			s_0	p	GARR	s_0	p	GARR
1/3.2	1.00	10	0.46	0.59	0.091	0.89	0.51	0.079
		8	0.42	0.64	0.100	0.87	0.56	0.087
		6	0.38	0.70	0.109	0.82	0.63	0.097
	1.05	10	*			0.99	0.46	0.071
		8	*			0.98	0.51	0.080
		6	0.96	0.58	0.090	0.96	0.58	0.090
1/2.5	1.00	10	0.36	0.57	0.114	0.87	0.47	0.093
		8	0.32	0.63	0.125	0.84	0.52	0.104
		6	0.29	0.68	0.136	0.79	0.58	0.117
	1.05	10	*			0.97	0.42	0.084
		8	0.90	0.48	0.096	0.95	0.47	0.095
		6	0.75	0.57	0.114	0.92	0.54	0.109

9). The results from the model indicate unrealistically high survival rates of juveniles to get a 5% rate of increase. This could mean that the estimated recovery rates in SC/35/RW4 and SC/35/RW28 are too high or that some of the values for the biological parameters used in calculating GARR are incorrect. The estimated rate of increase off Argentina does have wide confidence limits which include 0, whereas the estimated rate off South Africa has narrower confidence limits. Possible biases in the South African data include: (1) increased efficiency in detecting whales over time, (2) increased circling time in more recent surveys and (3) immigration from outside the surveyed area (although less likely).

Because of its importance in directly estimating GARR, the question of the duration and peak of the calving season was considered. Payne stated that calves are born in the waters of Peninsula Valdes between late July and mid-November. The peak incidence of calves off Australia is in August–September (SC/35/RW3). Best (1981) estimated the mean birth date to be in mid-August off South Africa, assuming a mean length at birth of 6.1 m; calving was estimated to be completed by the end of November. Neonates (including stranded calves, possibly premature) have been reported off eastern North America from 30 December through 6 April (SC/35/RW17; SC/35/RW27).

The assumed gestation period of 12 months for right whales is based on little data and on analogy with other mysticetes. Payne stressed that the timing of observations of courtship behaviour is difficult to reconcile with a 12-month gestation period.

9. TRENDS IN SIGHTINGS DATA

9.1 North Atlantic

It was agreed that the sightings data from the east coast of North America show no trend in abundance that can be considered unrelated to observational effort. SC/35/RW27 pointed out an interesting but inconclusive comparison between present and historic populations off Cape Cod. There is no information on trends in sightings in other parts of the North Atlantic.

9.2 North Pacific

No trends unrelated to effort were noted for the available sightings from the North Pacific.

9.3 South Atlantic

Sightings from annual systematic aerial surveys of the South African coast show a positive trend in number of whales sighted and number of calves sighted from 1971 to 1982 (SC/35/RW4). Because cow-calf pairs are considered to have higher sightability than unaccompanied adults, the observed annual rate of increase in calves (7.3 ± 1.3%) is believed to be the more reliable estimate of the true rate of increase. Kraus pointed out that in the Bay of Fundy in summer, cow-calf pairs appear to be less easy to detect than other whales because of their more consistent response to aircraft.

Bastida and Bastida (in press) reported an apparent increase in the number of incidental sightings made from shore in northern Argentina and Uruguay, but this may be an artifact of increased observational effort. Based on mark-recapture techniques using resightings of known individuals, the rate of increase for the Argentine population ('Subpopulation 2' – SC/35/RW21) was estimated as 6.8%, with 95% confidence limits of 0–13.6% (SC/35/RW28).

9.4 South Pacific/Indian Ocean

Incidental sightings off Australia (SC/35/RW3) show an increase, particularly since 1975, but effort cannot be standardized. Aerial survey results from the south coast of western Australia (SC/35/RW3) seem to indicate an overall increase since 1976. However, a statistically significant increase is only obtained (at the 5%, not the 1% level), when all the data points are included, giving an annual rate of increase of 38.6%. Omitting those points for which only one month's data are available (1976, 1977, 1981) gives a rate of increase of 12.7%, but it is not significant at the 5% level.

There has been an apparent increase in sightings off New Zealand and the Auckland Islands, but the nonsystematic nature of the effort prevents any definite conclusion about trends in stock size (SC/35/RW10).

No information was available for the central Indian Ocean.

Japanese sightings data from the Southern Hemisphere, while providing interesting information on summer distribution (SC/35/RW19), do not provide definite evidence of any trends in abundance.

9.5 General

There was discussion concerning the degree to which apparent rates of increase in South Africa and Argentina are feasible, given the known or assumed biological parameters for right whales (Agenda Item 8, above). It was suggested that either natural mortality of juveniles is unexpectedly low, age at sexual maturity for females is substantially less than 10 years and/or there is a significant amount of immigration occurring in areas being surveyed.

10. POPULATION MODELS

Because catch histories for right whale populations are generally incomplete, it was agreed that the most useful approach to modelling would consist of extrapolation backward from estimates of present population size to obtain estimates of population size at the time of protection. Since estimates of present population size were to play a key role, the various methods available for estimating right whale numbers are discussed below.

The Seber–Jolly method of mark–recapture was used in Argentina (SC/35/RW28). In this method, marking consisted of photo-documentation, and capture of resighting (and photo-documenting) known individuals (Payne et al., 1981). It was suggested that a standard Seber–Jolly table showing the number of animals marked and recaptured during each sampling period be included in SC/35/RW28. This mark–recapture method depends critically on the accuracy and efficiency of re-identification techniques. Some northwest Atlantic workers felt that movements of cyamids may modify the features used for identification, especially when aerial photographs are used. Payne noted that cyamid movements may be seasonal (Payne et al., 1981). The workshop agreed that the value of this technique was dependent on good-quality photographs.

A second method is to extrapolate from calf counts, on the assumption that calves comprise a certain percentage of the population. It is assumed that aerial surveys are efficient at counting calves and that it is possible to distinguish first-year from second-year calves. Population segregation could clearly bias results from this method if surveys did not cover all areas where calves were present. Also, surveys made before the calving season is complete would cause a downward bias in estimates. The accuracy of this method can be tested at Peninsula Valdes, where independent estimates have been made using other methods. A special problem must be borne in mind for data from the western North Atlantic, where the sampling period for calf totals occurs in summer, i.e. approximately 4–6 months after the peak of calving. Therefore, it can be assumed that half of the first-year mortality has already occurred by the time the calf counts are made.

Extrapolations from calf counts depend on the value of GARR discussed above (Agenda Item 8.3.4). A question was raised as to whether the figure of 32.4% mature females in the population reported for Peninsula Valdes in SC/35/RW28 is valid, considering that it contradicts the proportions of the whole population given by theoretical calculations. The figure of 32.4% may be too high because many males remain offshore and do not occur in the sampled portion of the population. Payne indicated that there may be a large absenteeism of males in the Peninsula Valdes coastal sample. On the other hand, if mean age at sexual maturity of females is much less than 10 years, then the proportion of mature females given by the theoretical model may be too low. Breiwick stated that the model used is relatively sensitive to age at sexual maturity of females. The workshop felt that Payne's data on calves reidentified for a long series of years give no indication that mean age at sexual maturity is much less than 10 years (Appendix 10).

Total counts of individuals that have been identified with photo-documentation techniques provide another means of estimating minimum population size. Although this approach is being used in several areas, the most complete record at present is for Peninsula Valdes, where data are available from 1971 to 1981 (SC/35/RW21). Payne noted that identified individuals which have died during the interim need to be subtracted from the total.

Investigators in various areas have made one-day

counts which provide minimum estimates of population size. Although very conservative, such estimates are of value in demonstrating when estimates (or confidence limits) resulting from other methods are unrealistically low. It was noted that the assumption of 3 kts to be the mean swimming speed of right whales on their feeding grounds, as used in SC/35/RW18 to eliminate possible duplicate sightings in one-day counts, may not be acceptable. Single right whales may swim at speeds as high as 6–10 kts (SC/35/RW18, 21).

Line-transect techniques were used by CETAP to estimate the western North Atlantic right whale population (Scott and Gilbert, 1982; Winn, 1982). There is probably a downward bias in some estimates from aerial surveys because a key assumption – that the probability of detecting animals on the trackline is 1 – may be violated because animals may be submerged. It was noted that CETAP estimates were corrected to account for animals below the surface and unavailable to be sighted, using dive and surface times measured at the same season and in the same area as the surveys. However, the workshop felt that the assumption that all whales at the surface and on the trackline were seen may not necessarily hold true.

11. ESTIMATES OF INITIAL AND PRESENT POPULATION SIZES

Because the catch histories for most areas are incomplete, no attempt was made to estimate initial population sizes. However, for all areas where we have evidence of trends in abundance, the populations of right whales appear to be greatly depleted from what they were in historic times. As an example, at least 17,400 right whales were taken

in the South Atlantic during the 10-year period 1830–1839 (Appendix 7). If this were taken to indicate an initial population of at least 17,000 whales, then the combined best estimates of present population size off South America and South Africa would be a small fraction of initial. For the Indian Ocean, approximately 9,000 right whales were taken between 1835 and 1844 by US pelagic vessels alone, which represents 72% of the estimated catch by these vessels between 1830 and 1939 (Appendix 7). A rapid rise to a peak catch from the Southeast Australian/New Zealand stock of more than 3,500 whales in 1841 was followed by a rapid decline thereafter (SC/35/RW12). Detailed historical studies are needed to develop more useful estimates of initial population size.

Estimates of present population size, by area, are given in Table 3. Methods used to obtain these estimates are described under Item 10. It should be noted that the population estimates in Table 2 do not necessarily represent all of the world's right whales. Populations may remain undiscovered in remote areas, and for such areas as Tristan da Cunha where right whales are known to be present, no current population estimates are available. In other areas, the estimates given are obviously minimum figures, as they are based on maximum one-day counts.

In the case of the Argentine coastal stock, for which three different methods of estimation are available, agreement between them is good. Discrepancies were found between estimates for the western North Atlantic using different estimation methods. The workshop gave special attention to the extrapolations from GARR which did not agree with direct estimates based on empirical data. Possible reasons why the two types of estimate, one based on field observations and the other on theoretical

Table 3

Estimates of current population size for right whales. Line-transect values are for 95% confidence limits. The GARR extrapolation method is discussed in the text. Notes: * = pers. comm.; [1] 131 estimated as seen in one year (SC/35/RW27); [2] from incidental sightings.

Area (year)	Maximum 1-day count	Total identified individuals	Modified line-transect	Jolly Seber mark-recapture	GARR extrapolation Calves	GARR extrapolation Population	Sources
Northeast Atlantic	1	–	–	–	–	–	SC/35/RW8
Northwest Atlantic							
Nova Scotia to Cape Hatteras (1979–81)	–	85	380 + 688 493 + 1100	–	–	–	Winn, 1982
Cape Cod Area (through 1983)	–	45	–	–	–	–	Watkins*
Cape Cod Area (1970)	70[1]	–	–	–	–	–	Watkins & Schevill, 1983
Nova Scotia to Cape Cod (1980–82)	–	150+	–	–	–	–	S. Krauss*
Scotian Shelf (1971)	67	–	–	–	–	–	SC/35/RW18
Nova Scotia to Florida (1980–82)	–	–	–	–	5	55 – 71	See Table 1
Northeast Pacific (1959)	8	–	–	–	–	–	SC/35/RW26
South Atlantic							
Argentine coast ('Subpop. 2', 1981–82)	–	–	–	–	36	400 – 514	Bastida & Bastida, in press
Argentine coast ('Subpop. 2', 1971–76)	–	–	–	450 – 600	–	–	SC/35/RW28
Argentine coast ('Subpop. 2', 1971–77)	–	580+	–	–	–	–	SC/35/RW21
Argentine coast ('Subpop. 2', 1979)	155	–	–	–	–	–	Payne*
South Africa (1980–82)	–	–	–	–	43	478 – 614	SC/35/RW4
South Africa (1981)	256 (2 days)	–	–	–	–	–	SC/35/RW4
Tristan (1971)	3	–	–	–	–	–	Best, 1974
South Pacific/Indian Ocean							
New Zealand incl. Campbell I. (1981)	20	–	–	–	–	–	SC/35/RW10
SW Australia, Coast of New Holland Gd (1981)	40	–	–	–	–	–	SC/35/RW3
SW Australia, Coast of New Holland Gd (1980–82)	–	–	–	–	6	67 – 86	SC/35/RW3
Southeast Australian Stock (1982)	15	–	–	–	–	–	SC/35/RW3
Southeast Australian Stock (1980–82)	–	–	–	–	3[2]	33 – 43	Bannister*
Southeast Pacific							
Chilean coast (1966)	2	–	–	–	–	–	Aguayo, 1974

calculations from a model, are sometimes difficult to reconcile are given below.

(1) There may be some degree of duplication in the counting of identified individuals, which would inflate estimates from this method.

(2) Calves may be present in the population but not in the areas surveyed. This would bias downward population estimates made using GARR. However, population segregation is documented for the calving grounds (Appendix 10) and suspected for the Bay of Fundy, the only summer feeding ground that has been studied (Kraus and Prescott, 1982), so it is possible that few calves are being missed. Workers in South Africa, Southwest Australia, and Argentina nevertheless suspect there are some calves being born in bays outside the sampled coastal areas.

(3) There may be a higher calf mortality rate in the western North Atlantic in comparison to other areas, possibly because of a higher level of ship traffic and industrial activity in coastal waters of the USA.

(4) Mean age at sexual maturity of females may be greater than 10 years, and this would give a lower value for GARR and result in larger population estimates.

(5) Parameter values used to obtain GARR were derived from a single area (Argentine coast) and may not be applicable elsewhere.

Although the workshop had intended to back-calculate from estimates of present population size to estimate population sizes at the time of protection, it was decided that doing so would not be justified at present due to uncertainty about rates of increase.

12. TROPHIC RELATIONSHIPS

12.1 Feeding behaviour

Moore summarized available information on right whale feeding behaviour from Watkins and Schevill (1972; 1976; 1979). These observations apply to right whales feeding in waters near the Massachusetts coast.

(1) Right whales feed on *collected* food – slicks at the surface and patches underwater.

(2) For the most part, they do not feed at the surface, except on calm days.

(3) Evidence for feeding at depth is:

(a) repeated surfacings in one or two locations,

(b) sounds recorded on 3-dimensional hydrophone arrays at constant depths and on repeated tracks, often at the depth of a thermocline.

(4) Right whales have been observed feeding on zooplankton with *Balaenoptera borealis* while ignoring abundant fish being eaten in the same vicinity by *B. physalus* and *Megaptera novaeangliae*.

(5) Two individual right whales of equal size have been seen to maintain constant positions with respect to each other while feeding for a total of six hours during two days. One always remained about $\frac{1}{3}$ of a body length behind and to the side of the other.

(6) Plankton tows in areas near feeding right whales (in Cape Cod Bay) demonstrated that *Calanus finmarchicus* was the main species present.

In relation to point (3) above, evidence for deep feeding by right whales in Argentina is also based on direct observations during diving (R. and V. Bastida, pers. comm.) and during aerial observations of baleen-washing producing visible yellow clouds of presumed plankton after prolonged dives (SC/35/RW21).

In relation to point (5), right whales in the Argentine population also maintain constant positions during feeding but for lesser periods. Such feeding whales also pass very close to each other on opposite courses (SC/35/RW21).

Winn (1982) also found *C. finmarchicus* to be abundant in plankton tows made near feeding right whales in Great South Channel, and Kraus and Prescott (1982) identified this species in right whale faeces collected in the Bay of Fundy. Kraus (pers. comm.) noted that surface feeding has been observed in the Bay of Fundy only three times in as many years and that most feeding in this area occurs underwater. Collett (1909) reported *Thysanoessa inermis* in the stomach contents of whales killed in the Northeast Atlantic. Prey species in the North Pacific, based on stomach contents, include *Calanus plumchrus, C. cristatus, Euphausia pacifica*, and *Metridia* sp. (Omura, 1958; Klumov, 1962; Omura *et al.*, 1969).

There is relatively little information on right whale food and feeding behaviour in the Southern Hemisphere. The only two prey species identified in the literature are *Euphausia superba* (Matthews, 1938) and *Munida gregaria* (Matthews, 1932). Lönnberg (1906) referred to 'krill' in the diet of southern right whales. Several recent observations have been made of right whales believed to be feeding on *Munida gregaria* and ichthyoplankton at Campbell Island (Cawthorn, pers. comm.), *Calanus* sp. at Peninsula Valdes (SC/35/RW21, p. 70) and *Munida gregaria* larvae and ctenophores in Golfo Nuevo (Bastida and de Bastida, pers. comm.).

12.2 Interspecific competition

The problem before the workshop was to consider whether the status of right whales had been (or was being) affected by interspecific competition, especially as regards the sei whale (*Balaenoptera borealis*). It has been suggested that the depletion of right whale stocks allowed the sei whale, a copepod specialist, to expand its range and increase its population size, effectively preventing the right whale from recovering from overexploitation as rapidly as it otherwise might have. In recent decades, sei whales have themselves been heavily exploited in the Southern Hemisphere and off Nova Scotia, a factor which may partly account for an apparent increase in right whale numbers in some areas (e.g. Southern Hemisphere).

Little overlap in distribution between sei and right whales has been observed in continental shelf waters off the eastern USA, except in Great South Channel (Winn, 1982). However, there is considerable overlap on the two species' feeding grounds on the Scotian Shelf (SC/35/RW18) and in the Southern Hemisphere (SC/35/RW19). It is of interest that no sei whales have been seen during recent surveys of the Bay of Fundy and Browns Bank, where concentrations of right whales are found in summer.

Winn (1982) has made a preliminary effort to develop an energetics model for right whales.

The workshop concluded that although there is some information on right whale feeding strategies (based on observations off eastern North America and Argentina), very little information was before the workshop on sei whale feeding strategies. A hypothesis exists for competition between the two species in the Southern Hemisphere, but more data are needed, especially on the feeding strategy of the sei whale, before the question of interspecific competition can be properly addressed.

13. ENVIRONMENTAL FACTORS POTENTIALLY AFFECTING RECOVERY

Because many populations of right whales occur in coastal waters of temperate regions and appear to depend on inshore areas for reproductive activities, they may be more vulnerable to the detrimental effects of human activity than are many other cetaceans. There is some direct evidence of factors contributing to right whale mortality or serious injury and this is given below.

(1) *Interactions with fisheries.* Off eastern North America, five instances have been reported since 1976 in which right whales have become entangled or trapped in fishing gear (SC/35/RW17). Kraus (pers. comm.) referred to three more entanglements, one of which may have resulted in the whale's death. In US and Canadian waters, gill nets, lobster lines and herring weirs have been involved.

Best and Carter mentioned that a right whale was entangled in, but escaped from, a crayfish trapline off South Africa in 1981, and a calf was accidently taken in a shark net off Durban in 1982 (Best, pers. comm.). The entanglement of a mother and calf in a fishing net off Brazil on 8 September 1981 was reported by Bastida (pers. comm.); both escaped alive. Bannister noted one record off South Australia: an 11 m right whale was caught in a shark net in May 1982.

(2) *Collisions with ships or ship propellors.* Mead reported that two stranded right whales from the eastern USA had severed tail stocks. He was uncertain as to whether this wounding had occurred before or after the whales' death.

Bannister reported a carcass of a whale possibly hit by a ship that came ashore in South Australia in March 1981.

Scars, of unknown origin but presumed from their nature (large slices) to have been caused by ship propellors, have been observed on right whales in the Northwest Atlantic.

(3) *Strikes by harpoons or lances.* Wounds thought to have been made by harpoons or hand lances are occasionally seen on right whales off Argentina and Brazil (SC/35/RW20; SC/35/RW21).

(4) *Loss of inshore habitat.* Right whales may now be effectively excluded by shipping from some bays which are known or suspected to be former calving areas. These include Table Bay in South Africa, Delaware Bay in eastern North America, Wellington Harbour in New Zealand, and Derwent River in Tasmania. An alternative assumption was that populations using some of these areas were exterminated by whaling, and that their absence from those areas does not necessarily reflect exclusion caused by other human activities.

Aguilar noted that certain lagoons along the coasts of southern France, Spain and North America, once possibly used as calving grounds by whales of unknown species, have disappeared due to geological change.

An additional series of factors were identified which the workshop felt might potentially have an adverse effect on right whales. These are discussed below.

(1) *Oil and gas development and production activities.* Spillage of oil may represent a greater threat to right whales than to other mysticetes because their skim-feeding behaviour may result in fouling of the baleen. Acoustic disturbance is a cause for concern as well. The actual effects on right whales of activities associated with offshore oil and gas development remain largely unknown, but they are the subject of various studies presently under way for other species.

The workshop identified the following geographic areas off North America that are of special concern in this regard.
(1) Northwest Atlantic
  (a) Gulf of Maine, Georges Bank and Great South Channel
  (b) Southeast US coast off the Carolinas, Georgia and Florida
(2) North Pacific
  (a) Gulf of Alaska, especially Fairweather Ground, Kodiak-Shumagin Islands (including Albatross and Portlock Banks)
  (b) Southern Bering Sea, especially St George (Pribilof Islands to Unimak Pass) and Navarin (SW of St Matthew Island) Basins.

The Peninsula Valdes area may eventually be developed, but efforts at oil and gas exploitation there are not yet under way.

Kraus noted that the proposed development of an oil refinery which has been pending for the last 12 years at Eastport, Maine, in the lower Bay of Fundy, is no longer being actively pursued by its proponents.

(2) *Military activities.* Best reported that a missile testing range is being planned by the South African government for an area immediately adjacent to a right whale ground in which 25–30% of the known calving off South Africa occurs. Details of planned activities have not yet been divulged.

Bastida stated that annual shelling exercises on Peninsula Valdes have recently been modified to prevent disturbances of right whales during the calving season. Bastida pointed out that the entire coast of Peninsula Valdes was recently designated as a provincial nature reserve.

(3) *Power plants.* Because they would involve damming of bays important to right whales, tidal generating plants as proposed in the past for the Bay of Fundy and Peninsula Valdes regions are potential threats.

Kraus also expressed concern about thermal pollution associated with the nuclear power plant at Pt Lepreau, New Brunswick, adjacent to an important right whale summering ground.

(4) *Boat traffic.* Although the exact magnitude and nature of disturbance from increasing levels of boat traffic cannot be assessed, the workshop was concerned particularly about the potential impact of ship and small-boat traffic in Cape Cod Bay, in certain South African bays and in the waters of Peninsula Valdes.

14. FURTHER RESEARCH

Recommendations for further research were grouped into three categories of priority:

Category I – First priority

(1) *Photo-identification*
Further research on individual whale recognition using photo-documentation techniques is desirable for all stocks, and where possible, throughout a stock's range.

Such studies provide critical information on calving interval, age at sexual maturity, movements (including between calving and feeding grounds), population segregation by sex and age, and behaviour.

(a) Wherever possible, national groups and individuals involved in such work should cooperate in comparing photos from different areas to evaluate stock identity and movements. Publication of catalogues is an important aspect of this approach. We note and encourage plans underway for catalogues of this nature in the western North Atlantic and Argentina.

(b) Because very reliable matching techniques are required if the data are to be used for quantitative calculations, a rigorous set of guidelines should be developed to provide confidence that the data are unbiased.

The value of data from ongoing long-term studies based on repeated sightings of identified individuals was noted throughout the workshop. Inasmuch as the information they afford becomes increasingly valuable over time, the workshop noted that funding for such studies should be given a high priority.

(2) *Radio-tracking*

The right whale workshop has given a great deal of time and effort to ingenious conjecture about distribution and species/stock identity in the oceans, for the most part founded on insufficient or even unavailable data. We cannot do much better about the past, but we could go to sea for data of the present. Radio tracking techniques are now sufficiently well advanced.

The workshop recognised that a pilot project could test the effectiveness of radio-tracking of right whales. Such work would be particularly useful, for example, for finding the wintering grounds in the western North Atlantic, as well as for following individual whale movements and obtaining physiological information.

(3) *Sex determination*

Studies of the Argentine population are well advanced but contain a major omission – there are no data on the sex ratio. There is, however, good historical evidence that other coastal populations were strongly skewed towards females with calves. In order to make any determination of assessment of stocks, it is therefore important to understand what segments of the population use such areas. Studies that allow for determination of sex are thus a high priority.

The problem of determining the sex of individual right whales during field studies can be solved by several techniques, e.g. through chromatin work with skin biopsies.

(4) *Biochemical studies*

The problem of determining stock discreteness might be addressed by applying biochemical techniques to tissue samples.

Category II – Second priority

(1) *Systematic surveys*

The workshop reviewed several reports of recent increases in incidental sightings, but was unable to evaluate them because effort could not be quantified. It recommends that standardized surveys, e.g. using spotter aircraft, be continued and expanded to provide quantifiable estimates of population trends.

The value of data from such ongoing long-term studies was noted throughout the workshop. Inasmuch as the information they afford becomes increasingly valuable over time, the workshop noted that funding for such studies should be given a high priority.

In other unsurveyed areas where right whales are known to exist, particularly possible calving grounds, similar systematic surveys should be instigated. Examples include:

(a) The exact status of the very few right whales sighted in recent years in the eastern North Atlantic is unclear. They may be survivors of a much reduced eastern stock. A probable calving ground on the north west African coast in Cintra Bay (23° N, 16° 15′ W) was frequented by American whalers in the 1850s. It is possible that right whales still calve in this area, and a systematic survey in the months November–April would give valuable evidence as to the continued existence of the eastern stock.

(b) Right whale concentrations in the Northwest Atlantic have been identified off Cape Cod, the lower Bay of Fundy, and Browns Bank south of Nova Scotia during the spring, summer and early fall. While winter calving has been reported from north Florida to Cape Cod Bay, Massachusetts, no discrete calving ground has been identified. The workshop recommends right whale research efforts in the northwest Atlantic be expanded to determine calving grounds and the incidence of calves in the total population, including surveys on the summer feeding grounds.

(2) *Reconstruction of historical catch*

Work with logbooks and other manuscript sources should continue, as it provides important information on stock identity, initial population size, and locations of calving grounds. Some specific examples recommended are:

(a) *British and other southern whale fisheries.* There are substantial existing sources in Governmental Department archives, Parliamentary papers, consular records, etc. that should be further located and extracted for data relating to past right whale distribution. Because of the scarcity of British logbook data relating to the southern whale fishery, such a programme is especially needed for British catch estimates. Further searches should also be made of Australian and other sources to collate Southern Hemisphere data.

(b) *North Pacific.* Studies on population identity and catch history of North Pacific right whales are encouraged. Particularly, a search of a small sample of appropriate logbooks and journals should be undertaken to confirm or refute the reputed absence of concentrations of right whales, and especially inshore or coastal calving areas, along the North American west coast from Mexico to northern California during the period the 'Kodiak Ground' population survived as a biological entity (*ca* 1830s–*ca* 1870s).

(c) *North Atlantic.* Workers investigating Dutch Arctic whaling records should be encouraged to separate catches of right and Greenland (bowhead) whales. Additional logbook research should be carried out to document duration, peak catch, and composition of catch in the Cintra Bay region in the Northeast Atlantic to confirm its importance as a calving area. Especially for the Northwest Atlantic, efforts should be made to reconstruct catch history to identify biological populations and to estimate initial population size.

(3) *Calving interval*

The workshop recognised from South American work that most adult females return to the calving areas only every third year, but it was felt that further confirmation of a 3-year calving interval is necessary.

Category III – Third priority

(1) *Feeding strategies*

Feeding strategies of right whales and their potential competitors (e.g. sei whales) should be investigated. The importance of feeding on calving grounds to the energetics of right whales should be investigated.

(2) *Effects of underwater sound*

Experiments are needed to study the effects of man-made underwater sound (seismic exploration, drilling, commercial and private vessel traffic, marine construction, etc.) on the behaviour and distribution of right whales.

15. OTHER BUSINESS

Arrangements for publication of meeting documents were discussed and referred to a sub-committee of Best, Brownell and Prescott.

The workshop acknowledged the work of the Chairman and the rapporteur. It also expressed its heartfelt thanks to the New England Aquarium, especially John Prescott, Eleanor Jensen, and Liz Gorham, for their timeless hospitality and assistance. The group was also grateful to the three historians – Richard Kugler, David Henderson, and Ken Martin – who came at short notice to provide expert advice.

16. CONCLUSION/RECOMMENDATIONS

With regard to the extent to which original right whale stocks were depleted, the workshop agreed that current stocks range in size from less than 100 to 500 or 600 animals. The degree of depletion for individual stocks is hard to evaluate without a more adequate historical record. However, what data there are on catches in the Southern Hemisphere make it clear that stocks there are very considerably depleted.

With regard to the current status of right whales, there are signs of an increase in recent years for certain Southern Hemisphere populations (e.g. South Africa and Argentina). However, no exact rate of increase has yet been established. For Northern Hemisphere stocks, the data are inadequate to demonstrate the presence of any trend.

The workshop classified stocks for which it had any recent information into three groups:

(1) those with population sizes in the range of at least 400–600 (South Africa, Argentina);

(2) those with populations of probably *ca* 100–200 (northwest Atlantic, northwest Pacific, southwest Australia, southeast Australia/New Zealand); and

(3) those believed to be near extinction, possibly represented by no more than a few individuals (northeast Atlantic, northeast Pacific).

The following recommendations were made:

(1) That no killing of right whales from any stock should be permitted, because even the largest stocks have so few individuals that even a small kill would adversely affect the rate of recovery. The workshop recommends that the Commission obtain further information from the Brazilian government on the recent reported catches of right whales in southern Brazil.

(2) That, because their coastal distribution makes right whales especially vulnerable to industrial and other man-caused disturbances, areas critical to their survival and continued recovery (e.g. calving and feeding grounds) should be managed to exclude the effects of such disturbances.

(3) That research be continued and expanded as recommended under Item 14, above.

REFERENCES

Aguayo L. A. 1974. Baleen whales off continental Chile. pp. 209–17. *In*: W. E. Schevill (ed.) *The Whale Problem: a status report.* Harvard Univ. Press, Cambridge, Mass. 419 pp.

Allen, G. M. 1916. The whalebone whales of New England. *Mem. Boston Soc. Nat. Hist.* 8(2): 107–322.

Andrews, R. C. 1908. Notes upon the external and internal anatomy of *Balaena glacialis* Bonn. *Bull. Am. Mus. Nat. Hist.* 24: 171–82.

Bannister, J. L., Taylor, S. and Sutherland, H. 1981. Logbook records of 19th century American sperm whaling: a report on the 12-month project, 1978–79. *Rep. int. Whal. Commn* 31: 821–33.

Bastida, R. and de Bastida, L. (In press.) Informe preliminar sobre los estudios de ballena franca austral (*Eubalaena australis*) en la zona de la Peninsula Valdes (Chubut-Argentina). Actas IIIa Reunion Iberoamericana sobre Conservacion y Zoologia de Vertebrados.

Bastida, R. and de Bastida, V. L. (In press.) Sightings of right whales (*Eubalaena australis*) off the coast of Buenos Aires Province (Argentina) and Uruguay. INIDEP contributions.

Best, P. B. 1981. The status of right whales (*Eubalaena glacialis*) off South Africa, 1969–1979. *Investl Rep. Div. Sea Fish Inst. S. Afr.* 123: 1–44.

Bolau, H. 1885. Ueber die wichtigsten wale des Atlantischen Ozeans und ihre verbreitung in demselben. Segelhandbuch f. d. Atlantischen Ozean herausg. v. d. Deutschen Seewarte, Hamburg, pp. 353–65.

Bolau, H. 1892. Die wichtigsten wale des Indischen Ozeans und ihre verbreitung in demselben, Hamburg, Segelhandbuch für dem Indischen Ozean Herausgegeben von dem Deutschen Seewarte. pp. 415 etc.

Bolau, H. 1895. Die geographische verbreitung der wichtigsten wale des Stillen Ozeans. *Abh. Gebiete Naturw.* 13: 1–22.

Bowles, M. E. 1845. Some account of the whale-fishery of the west coast of Kamchatka. *The Polynesian* [Honolulu], 2 October 1845.

Breiwick, J. M., Eberhardt, L. L. and Braham, H. W. 1984. Population dynamics of western Arctic bowhead whales (*Balaena mysticetus*). *Can. J. Fish. Aquat. Sci.* 41(3): 484–96.

Budker, P. 1952. Quelques considérations sur la campagne baleinière 1951 au Cap Lopez (Gabon). *Mammalia* 16: 1–16.

Clark, A. H. 1887. History and present condition of the (whale) fishery. pp. 3–218. *In*: G. B. Goode (ed.) *The Fisheries and Fishery Industries of the United States.* sec. 5, vol. 2, part 15.

Cole, L. C. 1954. Some features of random population cycles. *J. Wildl. Manage.* 18: 1–24.

Collett, R. 1909. A few notes on the whale *Balaena glacialis* and its capture in recent years in the North Atlantic by Norwegian whalers. *Proc. Zool. Soc. Lond.* 1909: 91–8.

Klumov, S. K. 1962. Gladkiye (Yaponskiye) kity Tikhogo Okeana [The right whales (*Eubalaena sieboldi*) in the Pacific Ocean]. *Tr. Inst. Okeanol.* 58: 202–97. [in Russian].

Kraus, S. D. and Prescott, J. H. 1982. The North Atlantic right whale (*Eubalaena glacialis*) in the Bay of Fundy, 1981, with notes on distribution, abundance, biology and behaviour. Paper SC/34/PS14, presented to the IWC Scientific Committee, June 1982 (unpublished).

Lönnberg, E. 1906. Contributions to the fauna of South Georgia. 1. Taxonomic and biological notes on vertebrates. *K. Svenska VetenskAkad. Handl.* 40(5): 41–9.

Matthews, L. H. 1932. Lobster krill: anomuran crustaceans that are the food of whales. *Discovery Rep.* 5: 467–84.

Matthews, L. H. 1938. Notes on the southern right whale, *Eubalaena australis. Discovery Rep.* 17: 169–82.

Maury, M. F. 1851. Whale chart (preliminary sketch) constructed by Lts. Leigh, Herndon, and Fleming and Pd.Midn. Jackson, Series F. Natl. Observatory, Washington DC. 1 sheet.

Maury, M. F. 1852. Whale chart of the world. [The wind and current charts], Series F. Washington DC. 4 sheets.

Maury, M. F. 1853. A chart showing the favorite resort of the sperm and right whale by M. F. Maury, L.L.D, Lieut US Navy. Constructed from Maury's Whale Chart of the World (Maury 1852), by R. H. Wyman, Lt US Navy, Bureau of Ordnance and Hydrography, Washington DC. 1 sheet.

Mitchell, E. D. 1983. Potential of whaling logbook data for studying aspects of social structure in the sperm whale (*Physeter macrocephalus*), with an example – the ship *Mariner* to the Pacific, 1836–1840. *Rep. int. Whal. Commn* (special issue 5): 63–80.

Mitchell, E. D. and Reeves R. R. 1983. Catch history, abundance and present status of northwest Atlantic humpback whales. *Rep. int. Whal. Commn* (special issue 5): 153–212.

Omura, H. 1958. North Pacific right whale. *Sci. Rep. Whales Res. Inst., Tokyo* 13: 1–52.

Omura, H., Ohsumi, S., Nemoto, T., Nasu, K. and Kasuya, T. 1969. Black right whales in the North Pacific. *Sci. Rep. Whales Rep. Inst., Tokyo* 21: 1–78.

Payne, R., Brazier, O., Dorsey, E., Perkins, J., Rowntree, V. and Titus, A. 1981. External features in southern right whales (*Eubalaena australis*) and their use in identifying individuals. US Dept Commer., NTIS No. PB81-161093. US Govt Printing Office, Springfield, Va. 77 pp.

Rowntree, V., Darling, J., Silber, G. and Ferrari, M. 1980. Rare sighting of a right whale (*Eubalaena glacialis*) in Hawaii. *Can. J. Zool.* 58(2): 309–12.

Scott, G. P. and Gilbert, J. R. 1982. Problems and progress in the US BLM-sponsored CETAP surveys. *Rep. int. Whal. Commn* 32: 587–600.

Thompson, D'Arcy W. 1928. On whales landed at the Scottish whaling stations during the years 1908–1914 and 1920–1927. *Fish. Bd Scot. Sci. Invest.* 3, 39 pp.

Townsend, C. H. 1931. Where the nineteenth century whaler made his catch. *Bull. N.Y. Zool. Soc.* 34(6): 173–9.

Townsend, C. H. 1935. The distribution of certain whales as shown by logbook records of American whaleships. *Zoologica, N.Y.* 19(1): 3–50.

Watkins, W. A. and Schevill, W. E. 1972. Sound source location by arrival times on a non-rigid three-dimensional hydrophone array. *Deep-Sea Res.* 19: 691–706.

Watkins, W. A. and Schevill, W. E. 1976. Right whale feeding and baleen rattle. *J. Mammal.* 57: 58–66.

Watkins, W. A. and Schevill, W. E. 1979. Aerial observations of feeding behavior of four baleen whales: *Eubalaena glacialis, Balaenoptera borealis, Megaptera novaeangliae, Balanenoptera physalus. J. Mammal.* 60: 155–63.

Whitehead, H. and Payne, R. 1981. New techniques for measuring whales from the air. Report to the US Marine Mammal Comm., contract MM6AC017, No. MMC-76/22. 36 pp.

Winn, H. E. 1982. A characterization of marine mammals and turtles in the mid- and north Atlantic areas of the US Outer Continental Shelf. Final report of CETAP contract No. AA551-CT8-48 to the Bureau of Land Management, US Dept Interior, 18th and C. St, N.W., Room 2455, Washington, DC. 20240.

Appendix 1
LIST OF PARTICIPANTS*

Alex Aguilar (M)
Department of Zoology (Vertebrates)
Faculty of Biology
University of Barcelona
Diagonal 645
Barcelona 08028
SPAIN

Thomas F. Albert (M)
Department of Wildlife Management
P.O. Box 69
Barrow
Alaska 99723, USA

John L. Bannister (M)
Director
Western Australian Museum
Francis Street
Perth
AUSTRALIA

Ricardo Bastida (E)
Instituto Nacional de Investigacion
    y Desarrollo Pesquero (INIDEP)
Playa Grande
Casilla de Correo 175
7600 Mar del Plata
ARGENTINA

Peter B. Best
c/o Department of Oceanography
University of Cape Town
Rondebosch 7700
SOUTH AFRICA

James E. Bird
Weston Road
Lincoln
MA 01773, USA

Howard W. Braham
National Marine Mammal Laboratory
National Marine Fisheries Service, NOAA
7600 Sand Point Way, NE
BIN C15700, Seattle
WA 98115, USA

Jeff M. Breiwick
National Marine Mammal Laboratory,
Seattle (as above)

Sidney G. Brown
24 Orchard Way
Oakington
Cambridge CB4 5BQ, ENGLAND

Robert L. Brownell, Jr (M)
US Fish and Wildlife Service
Piedras Bancas Field Station
P.O. Box 70
San Simeon
CA 93452, USA

L. A. Carter
P.O. Box 227
Fish Hoek 7975
Cape
SOUTH AFRICA

Martin Cawthorn
Ministry of Agriculture
    and Fisheries
P.O. Box 297
Wellington
NEW ZEALAND

Steven L. Cumbaa (E)
Zoological Identification Centre
National Museum of Natural Sciences
491 Bank Street
Ottawa, Ontario
CANADA K1A 0M8

William H. Dawbin
3 Owen Street
Lindfield
New South Wales
AUSTRALIA

Thierry du Pasquier
6 rue de la Mission Marchand
75016 Paris
FRANCE

David A. Henderson
New Bedford Whaling Museum
18 Johnnycake Hill
New Bedford
MA 02740, USA

V. Michael Kozicki (E)
Arctic Biological Station
555 St Pierre Blvd
Ste Anne de Bellevue, Quebec
CANADA H9X 3R4

Scott D. Kraus (E)
New England Aquarium
Central Wharf
Boston
MA 02110, USA

Victoria Lichtschein (E)
Instituto Nacional de Investigacion y
    Desarrollo Pesquero (see Bastida
    address above)

Richard Kugler (E)
Old Dartmouth Historical Society
Whaling Museum
18 Johnnycake Hill
New Bedford
MA 02740, USA

* M = member, E = invited expert.

Kenneth Martin (E)
P.O. Box 248
Woolwich
Maine 94579, USA

James G. Mead (E)
Division of Mammals
NHB Stop 180
National Museum of Natural History
Smithsonian Institution
Washington DC 20560, USA

Edward Mitchell (E)
Arctic Biological Station
555 St Pierre Blvd
Ste Anne-de-Bellevue
Quebec
CANADA H9X 3R4

Karen Moore (E)
Woods Hole Oceanographic Institution
Woods Hole
MA 02543, USA

P. Michael Payne (E)
Manomet Bird Observatory
Manomet
MA 02345, USA

Roger Payne (E)
Weston Road
Lincoln
MA 01773, USA

John H. Prescott (E)
New England Aquarium
Central Wharf
Boston
MA 02110, USA

Carol Price (E)
Northeast Fisheries Center
National Marine Fisheries Service
R.R.7, South Ferry Road
Narragansett
RI 02882, USA

Randall R. Reeves
Arctic Biological Station
555 St Pierre Blvd
Ste Anne-de-Bellevue
Quebec
CANADA H9X 3R4

Victoria Rowntree
Weston Road
Lincoln
MA 01773, USA

James Scarff (E)
1248 8th Avenue No. 3
San Francisco
CA 94122, USA

William E. Schevill (E)
Woods Hole Oceanographic Institution
Woods Hole
MA 02543, USA

William A. Watkins (E)
Woods Hole Oceanographic Institution
(as above)

Howard E. Winn (E)
University of Rhode Island
Graduate School of Oceanography
Narrangansett
RI 02881, USA

Appendix 2

AGENDA

1. Arrangements for Meeting
2. Election of Chairman
3. Appointment of Rapporteurs
4. Adoption of Agenda
5. Review of documents and available data
6. Distribution and species/stock identity
7. Historical catches by area or stock
    7.1 Struck/lost rates, associated mortality
8. Biological parameters
    8.1 Age and growth
    8.2 Mortality rates
    8.3 Reproductive parameters
        8.3.1 Age at sexual maturity
        8.3.2 Pregnancy rate

        8.3.3 Possible changes over time
        8.3.4 Gross annual reproductive rate
9. Trends in sightings data
10. Population models
11. Estimates of initial and present population sizes
12. Tropic relationships
    12.1 Feeding behavior
    12.2 Interspecific competition
13. Environmental factors potentially affecting recovery
14. Further research
15. Any other business
16. Conclusion/Recommendations
17. Adoption of report

Appendix 3
LIST OF DOCUMENTS

SC/35/RW

1 AGUILAR, A. A review of old Basque whaling and its effect on the right whales of the North Atlantic.

2 BANNISTER, J. L. Notes on the 19th century catches of southern right whales off Western Australia.

3 BANNISTER, J. L. Status of southern right whales in Australian waters, 20th century.

4 BEST, P. B. Current status of right whales off South Africa.

5 BEST, P. B. and ROSS, G. J. B. History of right whale catches from southern African shore stations.

6 BRAHAM, H. W. An annotated bibliography of right whales, *Balaena glacialis*, for the North Pacific.

7 BRAHAM, H. W. Concerning certain life history parameters for large whales: a supplemental list to Lockyer.

8 BROWN, S. G. Twentieth century records of right whales (*Eubalaena glacialis*) in the North-East Atlantic Ocean.

9 BROWN, S. G. Preliminary notes on sources for right whale catches in the British southern whale fishery.

10 CAWTHORN, M. W. Current status off New Zealand – 20th century sightings and trends.

11 CUMBAA, S. L. Archaeological evidence of the 16th century Basque right whale fishery at Red Bay, Labrador (Abstract only).

12 DAWBIN, W. Provisional estimates of the number of right whales caught in waters around south eastern Australia and New Zealand.

13 DuPASQUIER, T. Catch history of French right whaling mostly in the South Atlantic.

14 KASAMATSU, F. Sightings and natural markings of three southern right whales in the waters south of 60° S near Antarctic Peninsula in 1982 and 1983.

15 KRAUS, S. D. and PRESCOTT, J. H. The use of callosity patterns and natural markings to determine distribution, abundance and movements of the North Atlantic right whale, *Eubalaena glacialis*.

16 KRAUS, S. D. and PRESCOTT, J. H. A note on the efficiency of aerial surveys for North Atlantic right whales, *Eubalaena glacialis* (Abstract only).

17 MEAD, J. D. Twentieth century records of right whales (*Eubalaena glacialis* in the northwestern Atlantic Ocean.

18 MITCHELL, E. D., KOZICKI, V. M. and REEVES, R. R. Sightings of right whales, *Eubalaena glacialis*, on the Scotian Shelf, 1966–1972.

19 OHSUMI, S. Recent status of off-shore distribution patterns of the southern right whales in summer.

20 PALAZZO, J. T., Jr and CARTER, L. A. Projecto Baleia Franca (Right Whale Project).

21 PAYNE, R. Behavior of southern right whales (*Eubalaena australis*).

22 PRESCOTT, J. H. and KRAUS, S. D. Preliminary notes on cow/calf associations and growth rates in *E. glacialis* with information on right whale behavior during the summer and fall.

23 REEVES, R. R. and MITCHELL, E. D. American pelagic whaling for right whales in North Atlantic.

24 REEVES, R. R. and MITCHELL, E. D. The Long Island (New York) right whale fishery, 1650–1924.

25 RICE, F. H., CARTER, L. A. and SAAYMAN, G. S. The behaviour and movements of right whales (*Eubalaena australis*) off the coasts of South Africa, 1977–1982.

26 SCARFF, J. E. Historic and present distribution of the right whale (*Eubalaena glacialis*) in the eastern North Pacific south of 50° N and east of 180° W.

27 SCHEVILL, W. E., WATKINS, W. A. and MOORE, K. E. Status of *Eubalaena glacialis* off Cape Cod.

28 WHITEHEAD, H., PAYNE, P. M. and PAYNE, R. Population estimate for the right whales off Peninsula Valdes, Argentina, 1971–1976.

29 WINN, H. E. and PRICE, C. A. A model (scheme) of the annual activities of the northern right whale in the western North Atlantic.

Appendix 4
RANDOM NOTES ON THE HISTORY OF RIGHT WHALING ON THE 'NORTHWEST COAST'

Richard C. Kugler

The first documented whaling voyage to the Northwest Coast right whale grounds was made in 1835 by the French whaleship *Gange* of Le Havre. Scammon (1874), citing a Nantucket newspaper, attributes this initial voyage to an American whaleship *Ganges*, an error repeated by Starbuck (1878), Clark (1887) and most subsequent writers on the subject. Both Scammon and Starbuck further confuse the matter by stating that the American *Ganges* took the first right whale on the 'Kodiak

ground'. The logbook of the French *Gange* records its most northerly position as 48°39′, reached on June 7–8, 1835 at 159°20′ W. The position would not qualify as being within the Kodiak ground, but the use of that name by Scammon and Starbuck is clearly a case of applying a later terminology retroactively. What can be said from the present evidence is that the *Gange* of Le Havre was the first known whaleship to take a right whale on the Northwest Coast.

Until 1843–44, the term Northwest Coast appears to have been applied to all whaling activity in the Pacific above 50° N even though a few vessels were being reported 'on Kamchatka' in 1840–42. The northern limit of the North Pacific right whale range was considered by whalemen to be 61° N or approximately in the latitude of Saint Matthew's Island. The indications of right whale sightings across the central North Pacific which appear on Maury's 1852 Whale Chart (most continuously on the 30, 35, 40 and 45° latitudes) are difficult to explain and may possibly result from erroneous readings or recordings of data abstracted from logbooks.

An interesting contemporary report, 'Some Account of the Whale-Fishery of the N. West Coast and Kamchatka', by M. E. Bowles, appeared in *the Polynesian*, 2 October 1845, and included the following:

It has often been queried, the probable duration of this fishery. We can only arrive at any reasonable conclusion by comparing the extent of this cruising ground with others already run out, never losing sight of the fact, however, that here are all the ships of all nations who hold a share in the fishery, and their number has already doubled within five years, (right whalers) whereas they were formerly divided each upon their favorite grounds, as Brazil, South Atlantic, New Zealand, New Holland, and Chili. Each of these furnished good encouragement to the whaler for about 10 or 12 years – Brazil and South Atlantic holding out the longest, and New Zealand and Chili (less in extent) the shortest time. Now this Northern fishery embraces an extent of ocean greater than all these put together, and I think we may safely assert there will be found good fishing for at least half a century from its commencement. From the fact that there is not, nor is likely there ever will be, any 'bay whaling' in this fishery, the whales are less constantly hunted, and nearly all the calves arrive at an age when they can take care of themselves, before the old whales encounter their sworn enemy, man. Attempts have been made to prosecute the fishery during the winter months, in the bays upon the coast, but none other than the Scrag Whales have ever visited these bays, and it is now generally supposed that the cow whales repair to the deep bight towards Behring's Straits, or Sea of Kamschatka, in the calving season and here they will remain undisturbed, protected by the rigors of a climate severe enough in winter to cool even the ardor of a yankee whale-fisherman.

Before 1840, only a handful of whaleships had ventured beyond 40° N in search of whales in the North Pacific. After 1840, an increasing number of vessels began to cruise along the North Pacific rim, exploiting the already discovered right whale grounds on the so-called Northwest Coast and opening new areas along the Kuriles, 'on Kamchatka' and, in 1845, venturing for the first time into the Okhotsk Sea. In 1848, this northward expansion came to a climax with Roys' penetration of Bering Strait and the shift of the Okhotsk fleet into the Upper Sea, north of 55°, in pursuit of bowheads.

The descent on the Arctic following the news of Roys' discovery drew off most of the vessels previously active on the American and Asian sides of the North Pacific rim. In 1851 and 1852, the huge Arctic fleet (170 ships in 1851; 220 in 1852) fared poorly, with the result that many masters elected to return to the older grounds, particularly in the Okhotsk. In 1854, for example, 160 ships headed for the Okhotsk, compared to 45 bound for Bering Strait. From 1854 to 1857, the Okhotsk remained the center of all North Pacific whaling activity.

During the temporary withdrawal from the Arctic between 1854 and 1857, whaling on the Northwest Coast never resumed on its former scale, probably reflecting the widespread belief that those grounds – Kodiak, Gulf of Alaska – were largely 'fished out'.

The intensity of whaling effort on the Northwest Coast between 1840 and 1848 was rarely equalled on any other whaling grounds, except for those of Baja California and the western Arctic. Even the 12 years suggested by Bowles in *The Polynesian* article (1845) as the productive period for other right whale grounds was not approached in this area. After 1848, most of the Northwest Coast fleet headed for the bowhead grounds beyond Bering Strait, and even during the slump in that fishery from 1852 to 1856, few returned to the Northwest Coast, preferring to chance their luck in the Okhotsk. Catch figures for Alaskan waters for the period 1912–1929 records the taking of 18 right whales and suggest the failure of the stock to recover during more than half a century of respite.

Without the kind of intensive analysis carried out by Bockstoce and Botkin on the western Arctic bowheads, our knowledge of the right whale stocks of the North Pacific is rudimentary and impressionistic. Henderson's work on Okhotsk whaling will correct some of this deficiency, but whaling on the Northwest Coast remains poorly charted. No evidence is presently available as to the size, age or sex characteristics, and even the crudest figures on returns of oil and bone have yet to be compiled for this fishery. No suggestions as to calving areas of the Northwest stock(s) have been noted in an (unsystematic) reading of logbooks or other accounts.

Contemporary accounts:

Friend (Honolulu), 24 September 1844:

'From what we can learn, the number of ships (on the Northwest ground) must exceed two hundred. Many of these have already arrived at the Islands...'

Friend, 24 September 1844, prints an article, 'Notices of the Whale Fishery in the Chinese Seas, as Conducted by the Inhabitants of the Coasts', which contains the following:

'during the months of January and February, whales and their young resort to the coast of China,...in great numbers;...The fish are, I believe, what whalers call the right whale, and were calculated by those on board to yield on an average of 50 barrels of oil each'.

Friend, 2 June 1845:

'...of the total number of ships at Lahaina, 173 have sailed to cruise on the Northwest, 8 on Japan and 1 on the Off Shore Ground'.

Friend, 1 October 1845:

'...it appears that vessels on the N.W. cruised between 50 and 60° North latitude and 139° West and 170° East longitude...The past season on the N.W. has not been so favorable for taking oil, as some former years have been. Some report that whales are becoming more scarce, while others assert that there are now as many as formerly, but that they are more difficult to capture'.

Logbook of *Roman*, 26 May 1854:

'Capt. Sowle says that right whales first make their appearance of Petropavlovski in May and gradually work over to St Paul's Island, then down through the Fox Islands into the Okhotsk in August.'

Polynesian, 15 January 1848:

'How nearly exhausted the great fishing grounds to the north of the islands (Hawaiian) are, it is impossible for anyone to judge. Still it is not to be doubted that the cream of the business is over, and that 1846 for this kingdom will prove the climax of prosperity from that source...We believe the result from the United States and Europe will show, that we will never see afloat again so large a whaling fleet as existed in 1845 and 1846. The reasons for this are obvious. The opening of the North West and Kamschatka grounds operated upon those engaged in this business as does the discovery of a rich vein in a gold mine. It draws all the laborers and speculators to the spot...The whaling vein at the north is not exhausted, but the ground has been thoroughly hunted over.'

Polynesian, 9 September 1848:

'The whalers arrived arrived from the Japan sea have met with good success, while those from the north-west coast have taken little or no oil. From all we can gather we are inclined to think that the great northwest whaling ground is about exhausted. Such a fleet of enemies appearing in their waters has probably induced the monsters of the deep to change their habitation.'

Appendix 5
RIGHT WHALE NOMENCLATURE

W. E. Schevill

The International Code of Zoological Nomenclature is the system of rules and recommendations authorized and from time to time amended by the International Congresses of Zoology. The Preamble states: 'The object of the Code is to promote (1) stability and (2) universality (i.e., same names used in all languages) for the scientific names of animals and (3) to ensure that each name is unique and distinct. All its provisions are subservient to these ends...Priority is the basic principle of zoological nomenclature.'

The datum for this policy is the binomial system as published by the Swedish naturalist Linnaeus in the 10th edition of his *Systema Naturae* of 1758. 'The date of 1 January 1758 is arbitrarily assigned in this Code as the date of publication of that work and as the starting point of zoological nomenclature. Any other work published in 1758 is to be treated as having been published after that edition.' From this it is clear that this is an *ex post facto* sort of legal system; its major codification dates from the mid-19th century.

The rule of priority (later names giving way to older) has had to be controlled, as its unrestricted application has over the years considerably undermined the goal of stability. Workers who should have pursued biology have become bibliographical archaeologists, and their excavations have given taxomony a bad name among zoologists. Continuing discussion and arbitration have accumulated many volumes of *Opinions of the International Commission on Zoological Nomenclature*, constituting case law.

In this workshop we are concerned with the large balaenids (right whales), leaving aside *Caperea marginata* (Gray) 1846, the pygmy right whale. The technical names from which we must choose are:

Balaena Linnaeus 1758
Included species: *B. mysticetus, physalus, boops, musculus* Linnaeus 1758.
Type (by subsequent designation): *B. mysticetus* Linnaeus 1758.

Eubalaena Gray 1864
Type (by monotypy): *Balaena australis* Desmoulins 1822.
Other species: *Balaena glacialis* Borowski 1781.
Balaena japonica Gray 1846.
There is no problem with the technical name of the bowhead or Greenland (right) whale. It is *Balaena mysticetus*. The species *B. physalus* (finback) and *B. musculus* (blue whale) have been transferred to the genus *Balaenoptera* Lacépède 1804. *B. boops* is happily submerged.

The lower latitude right whales have been referred to *Eubalaena* Gray 1864. For several years conservative writers continued to use *Balaena* for these whales, but the use of *Eubalaena* increased, and has been predominant over the last sixty or seventy years. Since the 17th century, whalers have recognized the conspicuous distinction between the bowhead and the more southern right whales, and ultimately zoologists caught on. By now they have recognized morphological differences greater than those separating the several species of *Balaenoptera* and it would be a step backward to put the lower latitude right whales in *Balaena* thus obscuring obvious differences useful in zoology and management legislation. The people who wish to drop *Eubalaena* have simply resumed the use of *Balaena* without formally proposing and justifying the change. Such arbitrary changes undermine the efforts for nomenclative stability.

Therefore I recommend the continued use of *Eubalaena* for the species *E. australis* (Desmoulins) and *E. glacialis* (Borowski). I accept Dr H. Omura's conclusion that *E. japonica* (Gray) is a junior synonym of the latter.

I further recommend study of specimens of *Balaena mysticetus* and of the southern and northern *Eubalaena*, including skeletal material in and out of museums, to evaluate any differences between them (for example, the report of J. Muller (1954), *Zool. Mededelingen* 32(23): 279–90). As available material and analytical techniques permit, non-skeletal parts should be investigated toward this same end.

Appendix 6
LIST OF INSTITUTIONS POSSESSING SPECIMENS OF WHALES OF THE FAMILY BALAENIDAE

Donald R. Patten[1], Scott D. Kraus[2], John Zoeger[1] and Sidney G. Brown[3].

Bowhead (*Balaena mysticetus*) and black right whales (genus *Eubalaena*) have been exploited for several centuries, but relatively few specimens have been retained for scientific study. Pygmy right whales (*Caperea marginata*) have not been commercially exploited, and little is known of the biology of these cetaceans (Ross, Best and Donnelly, 1975). Because of the paucity of data, it is especially important that the existence and deposition of specimens be known to potential investigators. Accordingly, this survey reports on extant recent specimens of the genera *Balaena*, *Eubalaena* and *Caperea* as well as incidental information on some fossil specimens. Undoubtedly, this survey remains incomplete, and readers are requested to report additions and corrections.

METHODS

One hundred and seventy one institutions (museums, oceanaria, educational and governmental agencies) were surveyed, either directly or indirectly. A five-page typescript list of *Eubalaena* and *Balaena* skeletal material by Kraus and Brown provided the starting point, which was merged with an independent survey of slightly wider scope begun by Patten and Zoeger. Institutions were located by consulting published lists of mammal collections (e.g., Genoways and Schlitter, 1981; Hansen, Perrin and Mead, 1979; van Veneden, 1868), publications on particular collections or specimens (see references) and personal communication with knowledgeable individuals. One hundred and seventy five questionnaires were mailed to curators and directors of known and suspected collections, of which 133 (76%) were returned.

RESULTS

Of the 171 institutions surveyed, 98 (57%) had specimens (Table 1) and 73 (43%) did not (Table 2). For our purposes, anything from a single blade of baleen, fluid-preserved sample, or a single bone to a complete skeleton constituted a specimen. The term complete skeleton indicates a skull plus all postcranial skeletal elements. A complete skull includes the cranium and both mandibles. Anatomical terms with quotation marks in Table 1 are listed as reported whenever ambiguity existed. Nomenclature used in Table 1 is listed as reported, except that *Eubalaena* sp. is used for those holdings reported as distinct from the bowhead or Greenland right whale or under the common names 'right whale' or 'black right whale.' Geographic origin of the specimens, in general terms and whenever reported, is included in Table 1, but additional specimen information (e.g., sex, length and catalogue number) is not included because it was not consistently provided to us. Miscellaneous information on whaling stations and frequent stranding sites where right whale (*sensu lato*) specimens might be obtained are listed in Table 3.

ACKNOWLEDGEMENTS

For information on their respective collections, we are extremely grateful to all the respondents listed in Tables 1, 2 and 3. Additional information, suggested contacts, and reports on the holdings of institutions, other than their own, were provided by the following people: Dr Alex Aguilar, Universidad de Barcelona; Dr Thomas F. Albert, North Slope Borough, Barrow; Dr Alan Baker, National Museum of New Zealand; Ricardo Bastida, Instituto Nacional de Investigacion y Desarrollo Pesquero, Argentina; Dr Howard Braham, National Marine Mammal Laboratory, Seattle; Dr Robert L. Brownell, Jr., U.S. Fish and Wildlife Service, San Simeon; Dr Ingvar Byrkjedal, University of Bergen; Dr R. Duguy, Musee Oceanographique, La Rochelle; Dr Carl Edelstam and Professor B. Fernholm, Naturhistoriska Riksmuseet, Stockholm; Mr Hermann R. Hansen, Commander Chr. Christensen's Whaling Museum, Sandefjord; Gordon Jarrell, University of Alaska Museum, Fairbanks; Zhou Kaiya, Nanjing Normal University; Mr S. Kannemeyer, South African Museum, Capetown; Dr Toshio Kasuya, Far Seas Fisheries Research Laboratory, Shimizu; Dr I. H. J. Lyster, Royal Museum of Scotland, Edinburgh; Diana R. McIntyre, Natural History Museum, Los Angeles; Dr James G. Mead, National Museum of Natural History, Washington D.C.; Dr Edward D. Mitchell, Arctic Biological Station, Ste. Anne de Bellevue; Dr Nobuyuki Miyazaki, National Science Museum, Tokyo; Charles Pettitt, University of Manchester; Prof. Dr G. Pilleri, Hirnanatomisches Institute der Universitat Bern; Dr Roberto Poggi, Museo Civico Di Storia Naturale 'Giacomo Doria', Genova; Ricardo Praderi, Museo Nacional de Historia Natural, Montevideo; Dr Graham J. B. Ross, Port Elizabeth Museum; Dr C. Smeenk, Rijksmusseum van Natuurlijke Historie, Leiden; and Dr Alex Yeoman, Edinburgh University Medical School. Considerable correspondence was typed by Terri Togiai. Judy Astone entered the information and produced the computer printout.

REFERENCES

Albert, T. F. 1985. Scientific research activities concerning the collection and distribution of marine mammal specimen materials under authority of Permit # 345 issued by the National Marine Fisheries Service. Department of Conservation and Environmental Protection, North Slope Borough, Barrow, [iv]+56 pp.

Allen, J. A. 1908. The North Atlantic right whale and its near allies. *Bull. Amer. Mus. Nat. Hist.*, 24: 277–329+6 pls.

Angst, R., Kohler H. and Schuppiser, R. 1979 [for 1978]. Die Skelettmontage eines Nordkapers (*Eubalaena glacialis*) in den Landessammlungen fur Naturkunde in Karlsruhe. *Der Praparator*, 24(4): 297–303.

[1] Natural History Museum, 900 Exposition Blvd., Los Angeles, CA 90007.

[2] New England Aquarium, Central Wharf, Boston, Ma 02110.

[3] 24 Orchard Way, Oakington, Cambridge CB4 5BQ, England.

Anonymous. 1979. *Guidebook to the Whale Museum of Taiji.* [In Japanese] Taiji Whale Museum, Taiji, 30 pp.

Broekema, J. W. 1983. Catalogue of Cetacea in the collection of the Rijksmuseum van Natuurlijke Historie, Leiden. *Zool. Meded.* 57(7): 67–79.

Cameron, A. W. 1951. Greenland right whale recorded in Gaspe County, Quebec. *Bull. Nat. Mus. Can.*, 123: 116–119.

Castello, H. P. and Pinedo, M. C. 1979. Southern right whales (*Eubalaena australis*) along the southern Brazilian coast. *J. Mammal.*, 60(2): 429–430.

Cumbaa, S. L. 1986. Archaeological evidence of the 16th century Basque Right Whale Fishery in Labrador. (Published in this volume.)

Gasco, F. 1878. Intorno alla balena presa in Taranto nel Febbrajo 1877. *Atti della Reale Accademia delle Scienza Fisiche e Matematiche*, [Napoli], 7 (16): 1–47+9 pls.

Genoways, H. H. and Schlitter, D. A. 1981. Collections of recent mammals of the world, exclusive of Canada and The United States. *Ann. Carneg. Mus.*, 50: 47–80.

Goodall, R. N. P. and Galaezzi, A. R. 1986. Recent sightings and strandings and Southern Right whales off subantartic South America and the Antarctic Peninsula. (Published in this volume.)

Hansen, L. J., Perrin, W. F. and Mead, J. G. 1979. A list of U.S. Institutions possessing collections of marine mammal osteological specimens. National Marine Fisheries Service, Southwest Fisheries Center Administrative Report LJ-79-10, La Jolla, 3 pp.+2 tables.

Holder, J. B. 1883. The Atlantic right whales: a contribution, embracing an examination of (1) the exterior characters and osteology of a cisarctic right whale—male, (2) the exterior characters of a cisarctic right whale—female, (3) the osteology of a cisactic right whale—sex not known, to which is added a concise resume of historical mention relating to the present and allied species. *Bull. Amer. Mus. Nat. Hist.*, 1(4): 99–137+[2]+pls. x–xiii.

Maul, G. E. and Sergeant, D. E. 1977. New Cetacean records from Madiera. *Bocaqiana*, 43: 1–8.

Munday, B. L., Green, R. H. and Obendorf, D. L. 1982. A pygmy right whale *Caperea marginata* (Gray, 1846) stranded at Stanley, Tasmania. *Pap. Roy. Soc. Tasm.*, 116: 1–4.

Nishiwaki, M. 1982. The mandible of bowhead in Kathmandu. *Sci. Rep. Whales Res. Inst., Tokyo*, 34: 49–57.

Omura, H., Ohsumi, S., Nemoto, T., Nasu, K. and Kasuya, T. 1969. Black right whales in the North Pacific. *Sci. Rep. Whales Res. Inst., Tokyo* 21: 1–78+18 pls.

Omura, H., Nishiwaki, M. and Kasuya, T. 1971. Further studies on two skeletons of the black right whale in the North Pacific. *Sci. Rep. Whales Res. Inst., Tokyo*, 23: 71–81.

Patten, D. R. 1981. Floyd E. Durham, 1901–1980. *Whalewatcher*, 15(4): 16–18.

Pilleri, G. 1984. Morphologie des Gehirns des 'Southern Right Whale', *Eubalaena australis* Desmoulins 1822 (Cetacea, Mysticeti, Balaenidae). *Acta Zoologica*, 46: 245–272.

Ross, G. J. B., Best, P. B. and Donnelly, B. G. 1975. New records of the pygmy right whale (*Caperea marginata*) from South Africa, with comments on distribution, migration, appearance, and behavior. *J. Fish. Res. Bd Can.*, 32(7): 1005–1017.

Slijper, E. J., 1938. Die Sammlung Rezenter Cetacea des Musée Royal d'Historie Naturelle de Belgique. *Bull. Mus. Hist. nat. Belg.*, 14(10): 1–33.

Tomilin, A. G. 1957. *Zveri SSSR in prilezhaschilkh Stran. Zveri vostochnoi Evropy i sevomoi Azii. IX. Kitoobraznye.* Akad. Nank Moscow, 756 pp. Translated in 1967 as *Mammals of the U.S.S.R. and adjacent countries. Vol. IX. Cetacea* by the Israel Program for Scientific Translations, Jerusalem, xxii+717 pp.

Turner, W. 1912. *The Marine Mammals in the Anatomical Museum of the University of Edinburgh.* Macmillan and Co., Ltd., London, frontis.+xvi+207 pp.

van Beneden, P. J. 1868. Les squelettes de cétacés et les musées qui les renferment. *Bull. Acad. Roy. Sci. Belgique*, 2nd Ser., 25: 88–125.

van Bree, P. J. H. and Duguy, R. 1977. Catalogue de la collection des Mammifères marins du Muséum de Bordeaux. *Ann. Soc. Sci. Nat. Charente-Maritime*, 6(4): 289–307.

Woodhouse, C. D., Jr., and Strickley, J. 1982. Sighting of northern right whale (*Eubalaena glacialis*) in the Santa Barbara Channel. *J. Mammal.*, 63: 701–702.

Table 1

Institutions possessing specimens of whales of the family Balaenidae (genera *Balaena*, *Eubalaena* and *Caperea*) as of 15 January 1986, based upon survey. * = No direct confirmation.

Institution (Respondent)	Holdings/Origin	References
Argentina		
Collection of R.N.P. Goodall, Sarmiento 44, 9410 Ushuaia, Tierra del Fuego.	Eubalaena sp. (Argentina): 'cervicals', photos & baleen of 3 animals. C. marginata (Argentina): 1 complete skeleton incl. bullae.	
Museo Argentina de Ciencias Naturales, Laboratory de Mamiferos Marinos, Avda. Angel Gallardo 470, Casilla de Correro 220, Sucursal 5, 1405 Buenos Aires. (Lic. H. P. Castello)	E. australis (S. Georgia): 1 complete adult skull.	R. Bastida (pers. comm.)
Universidad Nacional de la Plata, Facultad de Ciencias Naturales y Museo, Division Palaeontologia Vertebrados, Paseo del Bosque, 1900, La Plata. (Dr R. Pascual & Lic. M.A. Cozzuol)	Eubalaena sp.: 1 complete skull, 1 vertebra, 2 ribs.	
Australia		
Australian Museum, 6–8 College St, Sydney, NSW 2000. (Ms L. Gibson, Collection Manager)	C. marginata: 4 complete skeletons (2 display), 1 baleen.	
Museum of Victoria, 328 Swanston St, Melbourne, Victoria Australia 300. (J.M. Dixon)	Eubalaena sp.: 1 plate baleen, 1 vertebra. C. marginata: 2 plates baleen.	
Queen Victoria Museum, B.M. Munday Collection, Wellington Street, Launceston, Tasmania 7250 (R.H. Green)	C. marginata: 1 complete skull, 1 fetus.	Munday et al., 1982.
South Australia Museum, North Terrace, Adelaide 5000, South Australia. (Dr J.K. Ling)	Eubalaena sp.: 1 complete skull. C. marginata: 2 complete skeletons (1 display), 1 complete skull, 5 incomplete skulls, 2 incomplete post-cranial skeletons, 3 bullae, 1 'part skin', baleen.	
Tasmanian Museum, GPO Box 1164 M, Hobart, Tasmania, Australia 7001. (Mr A.P. Andrews)	C. marginata (Tasmania): 1 complete skull, 1 fused cervical vertebrae, 1 incomplete 'skeleton', 2 incomplete series of baleen plates.	
Western Australia Museum, Francis St, Perth, Western Australia 6000. (J.L. Bannister, Director)	C. marginata: 1 complete skeleton (buried & awaiting exhumation), 1 'nearly' complete skull, 1 baleen.	
Austria		
Naturhistorisches Museum Wien, Burgring 7, A-1014 Wien, Postfach 417, Austria. (Dr K. Bauer, Curator)	B. mysticetus: 1 cranium (N. Atlantic), 1 vertebra & 1 scapula (identification uncertain). C. marginata (New Zealand): 1 complete skeleton (display).	
Belgium		
Institut Royal des Sciences Naturelles de Belgique, 31 rue Vautier, B-1040, Bruxelles, Belgium. (Dr W. De Smet)	B. mysticetus: 1 complete skeleton (in prep. for display). C. marginata: 2 complete skeletons (1 fetal).	Slijper, 1938.

Table 1. (*cont.*)

Institution (Respondent)	Holdings/Origin	References
Brazil		
Fundacao Universidade do Rio Grande Unidade: Depto. Oceanografia, Lab. Mamiferos Marinhos, Novo Campus: Av. Italia, Km8, Caixa Posta 474, Rio Grande - RS, Brazil. (Profa. M.C. Pinedo)	E. australis (S. Atlantic): 1 disarticulated skeleton (with incomplete skull & flippers, 31 vertebrae).	Castello & Pinedo, 1979.
Canada		
Arctic Biological Station, Dept of Fisheries & Oceans, 555 St. Pierre Blvd, Ste. Anne de Bellevue, Quebec, Canada H9X 3L6. (Dr E.D. Mitchell)	B. mysticetus (Thule sites over Canadian Arctic): Approx. 150+ periotics (singles & pairs), 2-3 bullae. [All to be deposited in National Museums of Canada and/or US National Museum Nat. History]	
McGill University, Redpath Museum, 859 Sherbrooke St. W, Montreal, PQ, Canada H3A 2K6. (D. Allison)	B. mysticetus: 1 partial cranium (N. Atlantic), 2 bullae, misc. mandible fragments, 1 scapula, 3 vertebrae. E. glacialis: 1 bulla.	Cameron, 1951.
National Museum of Natural Sciences, National Museums of Canada, Ottawa, Canada K1A 0M8.	B. mysticetus (Canadian Arctic): 5 crania (brain-case portions only).	E.D. Mitchell & J. Mead (pers. comm.)*
University of Guelph, Dept. of Pathology, College of Veterinary Medicine, Guelph, Ontario, Canada.	B. mysticetus: baleen plates & soft tissue samples.	Albert, 1985.
Denmark		
Zoologisk Museum, Universitetsparken 15, DK 2100, Kobenhavn O, Danmark. (Dr H.J. Baagoe, Curator)	B. mysticetus: 4 articulated skeletons (1 display; 1 incomplete; 3 juvenile; Greenland-3, Davis Strait-1), 1 incomplete skull, 4 sets(?) baleen, 20 bullae, 2 cervical vertebrae, 5 sterna, 6 pelves, 10 scapulae, 11 flippers. E. glacialis: 3 complete articulated skeletons (none on display; San Sebastion-1 juvenile, Iceland-2), 2 baleen, 2 bullae (casts), 1 cervical vertebra. "Eubalaena sieboldii" (Taxon uncertain, either B. mysticetus or E. glacialis): 1 head of fetus (fluid-preserved).	
England		
British Museum (Natural History), Cromwell Rd, London SW7 5BD, England. (Dr I.R. Bishop & M.C. Sheldrick, Curator of Marine Mammals)	B. mysticetus: 1 complete skeleton (display; Arctic), 1 complete skull, 1 mandible ("Greenland Sea"), 12 bullae, 1 pelvis & bone of hind limb. E. australis: 2 complete skeletons (N. Zealand-1, S. Georgia Is-1), 2 skulls (Campbell Is-1, S. Shetland Is-1), 14 bullae. E. glacialis: 2 complete skeletons (1 display; Shetland Is-1, Iceland-1), 1 set cervicals, 1 set forlimb bones. C. marginata: 2 complete skeletons (1 formerly on display; N. Zealand), 5 bullae.	
Town Docks Museum, Queen Victoria Sq., Kingston upon Hull, England, HU1 3DX. (A.G. Credland, Keeper)	E. glacialis (Long Is, NY): 1 skeleton (display). [Received in 1908 by Zool. Museum, Cambridge from American Museum of Natural History, New York. Transferred to Hull in 1933.]	Allen, 1908.
University Museum of Zoology, Dept. Zoology, Downing St, Cambridge, CB2 3EJ, England. (Dr A.E. Friday & Dr K.A. Joysey, Director)	B. mysticetus: 2 bullae, 1 vertebra, 2 pelves, misc. baleen. Eubalaena sp.: 4 "tympanics" (incl. 2 casts), 1 sternum (cast), 1 plate baleen. C. marginata: 1 complete skeleton (display).	
Whitby Museum, Pannett Park, Whitby, N. Yorks YO21 3ET, England. (Mrs C. Stamp, Hon. Curator, Scoresby Section)	B. mysticetus (?): baleen, skin (small piece).	
Federal Republic of Germany		
Forschungsinstitut Natur-Museum, Senckenberg, Senckenberganlage 25, 6000 Frankfurt Am Main 1, Federal Republic of Germany. (Dr H. Felten, Curator)	B. mysticetus: 1 incomplete skull (no bullae).	
Landessammlungen für Naturkunde, Erbprinzenstrasse 13, Postfach 4045, D 75 Karlsruhe 1, Federal Republic of Germany. (Dr R. Angst, Curator of Vertebrates)	Eubalaena sp. (N. Pacific): 1 incomplete skeleton (display; lacks sternum & some left limb bones).	Omura et al., 1969 & 1971. Angst et al., 1979.
Staatliches Museum fur Naturkunde, Saugetier Abteilung, Schloss Rosenstein, D-7000 Stuttgart, Federal Republic of Germany. (Dr F. Dieterlen)	B. mysticetus: 1 bulla. E. glacialis: 2 bullae.	
Uber-see Museum, Bahnhofsplatz 13, 2800 Bremen, Federal Republic of Germany.	E. glacialis: 1 complete skeleton (display).	A.N. Baker (pers. comm.)*
Finland		
University of Helsinki, Zoological Museum, P. Rautatiekatu 13, 00100 Helsinki 10, Finland. (Dr A. Forsten)	"Balaena sp.": some tympanic bullae.	
France		
Museum de Bordeaux, Bordeaux, France.	B. mysticetus: right auditory bulla. E. glacialis: left auditory bulla.	Van Bree & Duguy, 1977.
Museum National d'Histoire Naturelle, Lab. d'Anatomie Comparée, 55 rue de Buffon, 75005 Paris, France. (Dr D. Robineau)	B. mysticetus (Greenland): 1 complete skeleton (display). E. glacialis australis: 3 complete skeletons (display; New Zealand-1, S. Africa-2), 1 vertebral column (New Zealand). C. marginata: 1 complete skull.	
Museum National d'Histoire Naturelle, Zoologie Mammifères et Oiseaux, 55 rue de Buffon, 75005 Paris, France. (Dr F. Petter)	B. mysticetus: 1 fetus (fluid preserved).	
Musée Océanographique, Centre National d'Etude des Mammifères Marins, Port des Minimes, 28 rue Albert 1er, 17000 La Rochelle, France. (Dr R. Duguy)	B. mysticetus: 1 incomplete cranium (basioccipital portion), 2 blades baleen. E. glacialis: 2 incomplete crania (basioccipital portions); France-1, Spain-1, 1 bulla, 2 blades baleen.	

Table 1. (*cont.*)

Institution (Respondent)	Holdings/Origin	References
German Democratic Republic Staatliches Museum fur Tierkunde, Augustusstrasse 2, DDR 8010 Dresden, German Democratic Republic. (A. Feiler)	*E. australis*: "os tympanicum".	
India National Zoological Collection, Zoological Survey of India, 8 Lindsay St, Calcutta, 700087, India. (Dr S. Chakraborty)	*B. mysticetus*: 1 incomplete skull (display), 1 blade baleen. *E. glacialis*: 1 incomplete skull (display), 3 vertebrae, 1 scapula.	
Italy Instituto E. Museo Di Zoologia, Universita Degli Studi Di Napoli, Facolta Di Scienze, Via Mezzocannone 8, 80134 Napoli, Italy. (Prof. O. Picariello)	*E. glacialis*: 1 complete skeleton.	Gasco, 1878.
Japan Ayukawa Whale Museum, Ayukawa, Oshika, Miyagi, Japan.	*E. glacialis*: 1 complete skeleton (display).	Kasuya (pers. comm.)*
National Science Museum, Hyakunin-Cho 3-23-1, Shinjuku-Ku, Tokyo, 160 Japan. (Dr N. Miyazaki, Senior Curator of Marine Mammals)[1]	*B. mysticetus* (N. Pacific): 2 plates baleen. *E. glacialis*: 1 complete skeleton (display), 1 caudal vertebra, 1 left rib (N. Pacific).	
Taiji Whale Museum, Taiji-Cho Higashimuro-Gun, Wakayama, Japan. (T. Saiga, Curator)	*B. mysticetus* (N. Pacific): 1 complete skeleton (display). *E. glacialis*: 1 skeleton (display; N. Pacific), baleen, cervical vertebrae, body cast, fluid preserved materials (incl. ecto-parasites), ethnographic materials, photographs.	Anon., 1979. Omura et al., 1971.
Tokyo University of Fisheries, Kasuhinagawa, Tokyo.	*E. glacialis* (N. Pacific): 1 complete skeleton (display).	Kasuya (pers. comm.)*
Nepal National Museum, Kathmandu, Nepal.	*B. mysticetus*: 2 mandibles.	Nishiwaki, 1982.*
New Zealand Auckland Institute & Museum, Private Bag, Auckland 1, New Zealand. (A.B. Stephenson, Marine Biologist)	*C. marginata*: 1 cranium (one-half, sagittal section, on display), 1 pair mandibles.	
Canterbury Museum, Rolleston Av., Christchurch 1, New Zealand. (G.A. Tunnicliffe, Curator of Vertebrates)	*C. marginata*: "neurocranium".	
National Museum of New Zealand, Private Bag, Wellington, New Zealand. (Dr A.N. Baker, Assistant Director)	*Eubalaena* sp.: 11 "earbones and parts", 3 sets cervical vertebrae, 2 pelves, 1 scapula (holotype, *Balaena hectori*, Gray 1874), 2 plates baleen. *C. marginata*: 4 skeletons (3 incomplete), 3 skulls (1 missing mandible), 7 pairs bullae, "baleen plates".	
Otago Museum, Dunedin, New Zealand. (J.T. Darby)	*C. marginata*: 1 complete skull, "bullae", misc. vertebrae, "sternum (part)", pelves.	
Norway Stavanger Museum, N-4000 Stavanger, Norway. (K. Skipnes, Curator)	*B. mysticetus*: 1 cranium.	
University of Bergen, Museum of Zoology, Bergen, Norway. (Dr I. Byrkjedal, Curator of Vertebrates)	*E. glacialis* (Iceland): 1 complete skeleton (display).	
Universitetets Zoologisk Museum, Sarsgt. 1, Oslo, 5 Norway. (J.A. Pedersen, Mammologisk & Osteologisk avd. Konservator)	*B. mysticetus*: 2 bullae (1 subfossil).	
Vestfold Fylkesmuseum, Farmannsveien 30, Postgironr. 3 57 83 58, 3100 Tonsberg, Norway. (H. Ostmoe)	*E. glacialis*: "head and flippers".	
People's Republic of China Dalian Museum of Natural History, 3 Yantai St., Xigang Dist., Dalien, People's Republic of China. (Mr Shi Youren)	*E. glacialis*: 2 complete skeletons (W.N. Pacific), 2 "skin samples".	
Portugal Museu Municipal do Funchal, Funchal, Ilha Da Madeira, Portugal.	*E. glacialis*: 1 skull.	Maul & Sergeant, 1977.
Republic of South Africa Port Elizabeth Museum, 6013 Humewood, Posbus 13147, Port Elizabeth, Republic of South Africa. (Dr G.J.B. Ross, Deputy Director)	*E. australis*: 1 skeleton (display; lacking bullae), external measurements; photographs. *C. marginata*: 1 incomplete skeleton, 1 fluid-preserved specimen & measurements.	Ross et al., 1975.
South African Museum, P.O. Box 61, Capetown, South Africa 8000. (S.X. Kannemeyer)	*Eubalaena* sp.: 1 complete skeleton (display), 1 complete skull, 5 bullae. *C. marginata*: 1 complete skeleton (display), 5 skulls (2 lacking mandibles), 9 bullae, 2 complete vertebral columns, 1 sternum, 2 pair pelves, 2 pair scapulae, 2 pair forelimbs.	
Scotland Aberdeen University, Natural History Museum, Dept. of Zoology, Tillydrone Av., Aberdeen AB9 2TN, Scotland. (Mr K. Watt (via I.H.J Lyster))	*B. mysticetus*: baleen plate, model, pelvic bone.	

Table 1. (*cont.*)

Institution (Respondent)	Holdings/Origin	References
Royal Museum of Scotland, Edinburgh, EH1 1JF, Scotland. (Dr I.H.J Lyster, Deputy Keeper & Dr A.S. Clarke, Keeper)	B. mysticetus (N. Atlantic): 1 skeleton (articulated, young animal), 1 skull lacking mandible, 1 fetus (stuffed & dried with skeleton), misc. elements & soft parts. [Constitute 2 syntypes of B. mysticetus borealis, Knox 1838.] E. australis: misc. vertebrae & tympano-periotics. "B. biscayensis": 1 skull including tympano-periotics (right only?). C. marginata: baleen. [Surviving material of the Turner cetacean collection was transferred from the Dept Anatomy, Univ. Edinburgh to the Roy. Mus. Scotland in 1956.]	Turner, 1912.
University of Glasgow, Hunterian Museum, Zoology Section, Glasgow, G12 8QQ, Scotland. (M.M.T. Reilly)	B. mysticetus: 2 plates baleen.	
Spain El Acuario Museo Oceanografico, Paseo de Jose Antonio on Monte Urgull, San Sebastian, Spain.	E. glacialis: 1 skeleton (display; lacking some caudal vertebrae, bullae & pelvics; N. Atlantic), baleen plates (from skeleton now at Zoologisk Museum, Copenhagen). Eubalaena sp.: 1 incomplete cranium (occipital area).	D.R. McIntyre (pers. comm.).
Museo Do Pabo Galego, Cuesta Santo Domingo 3, Santiago de Compostela, La Coruna, Spain.[2]	E. glacialis: 1 skeleton (temporarily off display; possible lacking baleen, bullae & one flipper).	D.R. McIntyre (pers. comm.)
Sweden Lund University, Museum of Zoology, S-223, 62 Lund, Sweden. (L. Cederholm, Curator)	B. mysticetus: 1 scapula. Taxon undetermined: misc. cetacean bones.	
Natural History Museum, Gothenburg, Sweden.	B. mysticetus: 1 skeleton (subfossil, display), 1 skull. "Odd items of both Balaena and Eubalaena."	Prof. B. Fernholm (pers. comm.)* C. Edelstam (pers. comm.)*
Naturhistoriska Riksmuseet, Sektionen for Vertebrat-zoologi, 104 05 Stockholm, Stockholm, Sweden. (Dr C. Edelstam & Prof B. Fernholm)	B. mysticetus: 1 skeleton (display; includes baleen, but lacks pelves, sternum, & minor limb bones; N. Atlantic), 1 incomplete cranium, 1 right maxilla, fragments – cranium, vertebrae & ribs, small fetus (possibly Balaena). E. glacialis: 3 skeletons (display; incl. 1 subfossil of young animal; N. Atlantic), misc. elements.	
Uppsala Universitet, Zoologiska Museet, Box 561, S-751 22 Uppsala, Sweden. (L. Wallin)	B. mysticetus: 2 vertebrae. E. glacialis: 1 bulla. Eubalaena sp.: 2 bullae, 2 subfossil specimens, including type of Hunterius swedenborgii, Lilljeborg 1867.	
Switzerland Hirnanatomisches Institute der Universitat Berne, Untere Zollgasse 71 (Waldau), CH-3072 Ostermundigen, Switzerland. (Prof. Dr G. Pilleri, Director)	E. australis: 1 incomplete skull (braincase), periotic + bulla, baleen, brain (all from 1 animal; Natal Waters).	Pilleri, 1964
The Netherlands Rijksmuseum van Natuurlijke Historie, Raamsteeg 2, Leiden, Nederland. (Dr C. Smeenk)	B. mysticetus: 1 skull (presumably neonate). E. glacialis: 1 complete skeleton (display), 1 skull.	Broekema, 1983.
Universiteet van Amsterdam, Zoologisch Museum, Adres Afd. Mammalia, Plantage Kerklaan 36, NL 1018 CZ Amsterdam, The Netherlands. (Dr P.J.H. van Bree)	B. mysticetus: vertebrae, scapulae (from 16th & 17th century tryworks of Dutch whalers). E. glacialis australis (S. Africa): 1 complete skull.	
USA American Museum of Natural History, Central Park West at 79th St, New York, New York 100241, USA. (W.K.H. Fuchs)	B. mysticetus: 1 partial skeleton, bulla (right, damaged). E. glacialis: 1 skeleton, 1 incomplete skeleton, 1 bulla (left). Eubalaena sp.: "whalebone". C. marginata: 1 skeleton.	Holder, 1883. J.A. Allen, 1908.
California Academy of Sciences, Dept. of Birds & Mammals, Golden Gate Park, San Francisco, CA 94118-9961, USA. (M. Marcussen, Curatorial Assistant)	B. mysticetus (N. Pacific): 1 plate baleen.	
Carnegie Museum of Natural History, Annex, Section of Mammals, 5800 Baum Blvd, Pittsburg, Pennsylvania 15213, USA. (S.B. McLaren, Collection Manager)	"Balaenidae" (N. Pacific): 1 fossil bulla.	
The Charleston Museum, 360 Meeting St, Charleston, South Carolina 29403, USA. (A.E. Saunders)	E. glacialis (N. Atlantic): 1 complete skeleton (display).	
College of the Atlantic, Bar Harbor, Maine 04609, USA.	E. glacialis (N. Atlantic): 1 incomplete skeleton (lacking some caudal vertebrae).	S. Katona (pers. comm.)*
East Hampton Marine Museum, East Hampton, Long Island, New York, USA.	E. glacialis: 1 skull.	J. Mead (pers. comm.)*
Field Museum of Natural History, Roosevelt Road at Lake Shore Drive, Chicago, Illinois 60605-2496, USA. (Dr R.M. Timm, Curator & R.J. Izor, Collection Manager)	E. glacialis (N. Atlantic): 1 complete skeleton (display, some damage & reconstruction).	
Harvard University, Museum of Comparative Zoology, Cambridge, Massachusetts 02138, USA. (J. Winchell & M.E. Rutzmoser, Curatorial Assistant)	B. mysticetus: 2 vertebrae, 1 forelimb, 2 plates baleen. Eubalaena sp.: 1 skeleton (display), 1 "tympanic", 1 vertebra, 1 forelimb, 2 plates baleen.	
Humboldt State University, Vertebrate Museum, Arcata, California 95521, USA. (Dr T.E. Lawlor)	E. glacialis: "baleen".	
Louisiana State University, Dept. of Veterinary Anatomy, School of Veterinary Medicine, Baton Rouge, Louisiana 70803-8408, USA. (Dr J.R. Haldiman)	B. mysticetus: 1 cranium & partial nasal passages, 11 baleen (small filaments & "beginnings of small plates"), 3 vertebrae, brain, eyes, larynges & numerous other soft tissue samples.	Albert, 1985.
Nantucket Whaling Museum, Nantucket Historical Assoc., P.O. Box 1016, Nantucket, Massachusetts 02554, USA. (R.A. Stackpole, Curator)	E. glacialis: 3 mandibles (incl. pair).	

Table 1. (*cont.*)

Institution (Respondent)	Holdings/Origin	References
National Marine Mammal Lab. (NOAA), 7600 Sand Point Way, Bldg 32, Seattle, Washington 98115, USA. (M. Nerini & D.W. Rice)	B. mysticetus: 1 incomplete skull, 10 bullae, 2 vertebrae.	
National Museum of Natural History, Smithsonian Inst., Washington, D.C. 20560, USA. (Dr J.G. Mead, Curator of Marine Mammals)	B. mysticetus: 1 skull, 20 "skeletal elements" (W. Arctic-2 & W.+C. Arctic), 10 "baleen". E. glacialis: 3 complete skeletons (1 with baleen; N. Atlantic-2; N. Pacific-1), 3 skulls (1 with baleen; N. Atlantic-1, S. Atlantic-1, & N. Pacific-1), 5 "skeletal elements" (N. Atlantic & N. Pacific), 9 "baleen", 4 "casts, models, photographs & 'fluid-preserved' samples". C. marginata: 1 skull (N. Zealand), 1 "baleen", 4 "casts, models, photographs" (N. Zealand).	
Natural History Museum of Los Angeles County, 900 Exposition Blvd, Los Angeles, California 90007. (D.R. Patten, Curator)	B. mysticetus: 8 complete skulls with partial postcranial skeletons, 6 skulls (4 complete; 2 with single mandible), numerous misc. baleen, skeletal elements & photographs, fetal & fluid-preserved materials (all W. Arctic). E. glacialis (N. Atlantic): 1 complete skeleton (neonate).	Patten, 1981.
Naval Arctic Research Lab. (NARL), Point Barrow, Alaska.	B. mysticetus: 3 skulls, "few skeletal elements". [Some specimens originally at NARL transferred to Univ. Alaska Museum, Fairbanks (G. Jarrell, pers. comm.)]	H. Braham (pers. comm.)* T. Albert (pers. comm.)*
New England Aquarium, Central Wharf, Boston, Massachusetts 02110, USA. (S. Kraus, Research Associate)	E. glacialis: 1 skeleton (display).	
North Carolina State Museum of Natural History, P.O. Box 27647, Raleigh, North Carolina 27611. (M.K. Clark)	Eubalaena sp.: 1 skeleton (display).	
Old Dartmouth Historical Society, Whaling Museum, 18 Johnny Cake Hill, New Bedford, Massachusetts 02740. (Dr R.C. Kugler, Director)	B. mysticetus: "baleen". E. glacialis: "baleen".	
Philadelphia Academy of Sciences, 19th St and Parkway, Philadelphia, Pennsylvania 19103.	Eubalaena sp.: 1 "skull/skeleton", 3 misc. "skeletal elements".	J.G. Mead (pers. comm.)*
San Diego Natural History Museum, P.O. Box 1390, San Diego, California 92112. (S. Breisch, Curatorial Asst)	B. mysticetus: 2 pieces baleen, 1 bulla (left).	
Santa Barbara Museum of Natural History, 2559 Puesta de Sol Rd, Santa Barbara, California 93105. (Dr C. Woodhouse, Curator)	E. glacialis (N. Pacific): 1 plate baleen. Balaenidae (Taxon uncertain): 1 mandible, 1 bulla.	Woodhouse & Strickley, 1982.
Texas A & M University, Dept of Veterinary Anatomy, College of Veterinary Medicine, Texas A & M University, College Station, Texas 77843. (Dr R.J. Tarpley)	B. mysticetus: 1 fetus (fluid preserved), vertebrae & flipper elements, larynges, ovaries, testes & numerous other soft tissue samples.	Albert, 1985.
University of Alaska Museum, Fairbanks, Alaska 99701. (G. Jarrell)	B. mysticetus: 1 incomplete skeleton (cranium on display: W. Arctic), 1 partial skeleton (occipital portion of cranium, scapula, 7 vertebrae, 1 flipper, plus 1 mandible on display; W. Arctic), 5 bullae, 5 vertebrae, 2 humeri.	
University of California, Museum of Paleontology, Berkeley, California 94720. (J.H. Hutchison, Research Paleontologist)	Balaenidae: 2 skulls, 1 cranium, 1 periotic, 1 periotic + bulla, 2 bullae (all fossil).	
University of Colorado Museum, Campus Box 315, Boulder, Colorado 80309. (L.D. Ivy)	Eubalaena sp.: 1 incomplete skull, "baleen".	
University of Florida, Florida State Museum, Museum Rd, Gainsville, Florida 32611. (L. Wilkins, Collections Manager)	Eubalaena sp.: 1 pair mandibles (imm.), 1 mandible (display; N. Atlantic).	
University of Georgia, Dept of Medical Microbiology, College of Veterinary Medicine, Athens, Georgia.	B. mysticetus: various soft tissue samples.	Albert, 1985.
University of Iowa, Museum of Nat. Hist., Iowa City, Iowa 52242. (G.D. Shrimper, Director)	Eubalaena sp. (N. Atlantic): 1 complete skeleton (display).	
University of New Orleans, Center for Bio-Organic Studies, New Orleans, Louisiana 70148.	B. mysticetus: various soft tissue samples.	Albert, 1985.
University of Puget Sound, J.R. Slater Museum of Nat. Hist., Thompson Hall, Tacoma, Washington 98416-0360. (E.B. Kritzmann, Curator)	B. mysticetus (N. Atlantic): 2 complete skulls, 4 bullae.	
University of Washington, Dept of Microbiology & Immunology, School of Medicine, Seattle, WA 98195.	B. mysticetus: various soft tissue samples.	Albert, 1985.
Yale University, Peabody Museum, P.O. Box 6666, New Haven, Connecticut 06511. (F.C. Sibley)	"B. mysticetus" (Newfoundland): 1 mandible, ribs, vertebrae, scapula, humerus. Eubalaena sp. (New Jersey): skeleton (cataloged as "B. mysticetus").	
USSR		
Museum of Arkhangel'sk.	B. mysticetus: 1 mandible.	Tomilin, 1957
Novosibirsk Museum.	B. mysticetus: 1 rib.	Tomilin, 1957
Riga Nature Museum, Latvia.	B. mysticetus: 2 mandibles, 1 plate baleen.	Tomilin, 1957
Zoological Museum, Moscow State University, Moscow.	B. mysticetus: 2 mandibles, 2 "cervical units", 3 plates baleen. E. glacialis: baleen.	Tomilin, 1957
Zoological Museum of the USSR, Academy of Sciences, Leningrad.	B. mysticetus: 1 mandible, vertebrae & flipper bones, 6 plates baleen, fetal baleen (fluid), "tympanic bones".	Tomilin, 1957

Notes to the table:
1. Kasuya (pers. comm.) reports bullae of both species at NSM. Miyazaki makes no note of bullae for either species.
2. A. Aguilar (pers. comm.) reports the baleen plates but McIntyre was unable to confirm during on-site visit (D.R. McIntyre, pers. comm.).

Table 2
Surveyed institutions reporting no specimens of whales of the Family Balaenidae.

Australia
University of Queensland, Dept of Anatomy, St Lucia, Queensland 4067, Australia. (Dr M.M. Bryden)

Brazil
Universidade Federal da Paraiba, Dept Sistematica e Ecologia, Campus Universitario, 58000 Joao Pessoa – PB, Brazil. (Dr A. Langguth)

Canada
British Columbia Provincial Museum, Parliament Bldgs, Victoria, B.C., Canada V8V 1X4. (D. Nagorsen, Curator of Mammals)
Provincial Museum of Alberta, 12845 102nd Av, Edmonton, Alberta, Canada T5N OM6. (H. Smith)
University of British Columbia, Cowan Vertebrate Museum, Dept of Zoology, Vancouver, British Columbia, Canada V6T 1W5. (Dr I. McTaggart Cowan)

Denmark
Naturhistorisk Museum, DK–8000 Aarhus, Copenhagen, Denmark. (B. Jensen)

England
City of Bristol Museum & Art Gallery, Queens Rd, Bristol, Avon BS8 1RL. (Mrs A.F. Hollowell, Curator of Natural History (via C.W.A. Pettitt)).
Merseyside County Museums, William Broun St., Liverpool L3 8EN. (Dr M.J. Largen, Keeper of Vertebrate Zoology (via I.H.J. Lyster)).
The University of Manchester, Manchester Museum, Oxford Rd, Manchester M13 9PL. (Dr M.V. Hounsome, Keeper of Zoology (via I.H.J. Lyster)).

Federal Republic of Germany
Universitat Hamburg, Zoologisches Institut und Zoologisches Museum, Martin–Luther–King–Platz 3, 2000 Hamburg 13. (Prof Dr H. Schliemann)
Zoologische Staatssammlung, Maria–Ward–Strasse 1b, D–8000 Munchen 19, Federal Republic of Germany. (Dr R. Kraft, Curator of Mammology)

France
Musee Guimet d'Histoire Naturelle, 28 Bd. des Belges, 69006 Lyon, France. (Mr J. Clary, Assistant de Zoologie (via D.R. Patten))
Museum d'Histoire Naturelle, 12 rue Voltaire, 44000 Ville de Nantes, France. (Mme J. Baudouin)

German Democratic Republic
Zoologisches Museum, Invalidenstrasse 43, Berlin 104, Democratic Republic of Germany. (D.R. Patten, pers. comm.)

Iceland
Icelandic Museum of Natural History, P.O. Box 5320, 125 Reykjavik, Iceland. (A. Petersen, Curator of Zoology)

Ireland
National Museum of Ireland, Natural History Division, Kildare Sreet, Dublin 2, Ireland. (Dr C.E. O'Riordan)
Trinity College Zoology Museum, Dept of Zoology, Dublin 2, Ireland. (M. Linnie)
University College, Zoology Dept, Galway, Ireland. (Dr J.S. Fairley)

Italy
Museo Civico di Storia Naturale "Giacomo Doria", Via Brigata Liguria, N.9, I–16121 Genova, Italy. (Dr R. Poggi)

Korea
National Fisheries, University of Busan, Busan, Korea 608. (Dr Chan–il Chun)

Malaysia
Sarawak Museum, Kuching, Sarawak, Malaysia. (C. Leh, Zoologist)

Namibia
State Museum, P.O. Box 1203, Windhoek 9100, Namibia. (Dr C.G. Coetzee)

Northern Ireland
Ulster Museum & Botanic Gardens, Dept of Zoology, Belfast BT9 5AB, N. Ireland. (T. Bruton, Scientific Officer of Vertebrates)

Norway
Kommander Chr. Christensens Hvalfangstmuseum, Museumsgf. 39, N–3200 Sandefjord, Norway. (Mr H.R. Hansen, Librarian)

Poland
Polish Academy of Science, Mammals Research Inst., 17–230 Biatowieza, Poland. (Dr A.L. Ruprecht)

Portugal
Museu e Laboratorio Zoologico, Universidade de Coimbra, Centro de Sistematica e Ecologia, 3049 Coimbra Codex, Portugal.
  (M.M. da Gama F. Assalino)

Republic of South Africa
Kaffrarian Museum, Post 1434, King William's Town 5600, South Africa. (L.R. Wingate, Curator of Mammals)

Scotland
Airdrie Museum, Wellwynd, Airdrie, Lanarkshire ML6 OAG, Scotland. (via C.W.A. Pettitt, pers. comm.)
Art Gallery and Museum, Kelvingrove, Glasgow G8 8AG, Scotland. (Mr C. Hancock, Keeper of Natural History (via I.H.J. Lyster))
Daniel Stewart and Melville College, Dept of Biology, Queensferry Rd, Edinburgh EH4 3EZ, Scotland. (E. Campbell (via C.W.A. Pettitt))
Dundee Museum & Art Gallery, Albert Sq., Dundee DD1 1DA, Scotland. (Mr R.K. Brinklow, Keeper of Natural History (via I.H.J. Lyster))
Inverness Museum & Art Gallery, Castle Wynd, Inverness IV2 3ED. (Mr S. Morgan, Curator (via C.W.A. Pettitt & I.H.J. Lyster, pers. comm.))
Kircaldy Museum & Art Gallery, War Memorial Gardens, Kirkcaldy, Fife KY1 17G, Scotland. (Miss A.J. Kerr, Curator (via I.H.J. Lyster))
Montrose Museum & Art Gallery, Panmure Place, Montrose, Angus DD1O 8HE, Scotland. (M.N. Atkinson, Curator (via I.H.J. Lyster))
Peterhead Arbuthnot Museum, St Peter St., Peterhead, Aberdeenshire AB4 6QD, Scotland. (Miss J. Chamberlain–Mole, Curator (via I.H.J. Lyster))
Shetland Museum, Lower Hillhead, Shetland ZE1 OEL, Scotland. (Mr T. Watt, Assistant Curator (via I.H.J. Lyster))
Stirling Smith Art Gallery & Museum, 30 Albert Place, Dumbarton Rd, Stirling FK8 2RQ, Scotland. (Mr M. McGinnes, Assistant Curator)
University of Edinburgh, Dept of Anatomy, Edinburgh, Scotland. (Dr Yeoman) [Surviving materials from the Turner cetacean collection are now at the Royal Museum of Scotland]

Singapore
National University of Singapore, Dept of Zoology, Zoological Reference Collection, Upper Jurong Rd, Singapore 2263.
  (Mrs Yang Chang Man, Scientific Officer)

Spain
Santander Museum, Santander, Spain. (A. Aguilar, pers. comm.)
Universidad de Barcelona, Catedra de Zoologica (Vertebrados), Barcelona 08071, Spain. (Dr A. Aguilar)

Uruguay
Museo Nacional de Historia Natural, Casilla de Correo 399, Montevideo, Uruguay. (Mr R. Praderi)

USA
Alaska Dept of Fish & Game, 1300 College Rd, Fairbanks, Alaska 99701. (K.J. Frost, Marine Mammals Biologist)
Alaska State Museum, Pouch FM, Juneau, Alaska 99811–0507. (L. Wallen, Curator)
Bishop Museum, P.O. Box 19000–A, Honolulu, Hawaii 96819. (A. Engilis, Jr., Curatorial Assistant)
Bowdoin College, Peary–Macmillan Arctic Museum, Hubbard Hall, Brunswick, Maine 04011. (Dr S.A. Kaplin)
California Polytechnic State University, San Luis Obispo, California 93407. (Dr A.I. Roest)
California State University, Dept of Biological Science, 6000 J. St., Sacramento, California 95819. (J. Tilley)
Clemson University, Dept of Biological Sciences, Vertebrate Collections, 338 Long Hall, Clemson, South Carolina 29631.
Cornell University, Mammal Collection, Ecology & Systematics, Div. Biol. Sciences, Corson Hall, Ithaca, New York 14853–0239. (Dr R.G. Bauer)

Table 2. (*cont.*)

Denver Museum of Natural History, City Park, Denver, Colorado 80205. (B. Webb, Curator of Zoology)
Florida State University Museum, Dept of Biological Science, Tallahassee, Florida 32306-2043. (F.C. James)
Louisiana State University, Museum of Zoology, Baton Rouge, Louisiana 70893. (Dr M. Hafner, Curator of Mammals)
Milwaukee Public Museum, Milwaukee, Wisconsin 53233. (Dr M. Tuttle, Curator of Mammals)
Moss Landing Marine Laboratories, P.O. Box 223, Moss Landing, California 95039-0223. (Dr B. Wursig)
New York State Museum, Science Service, The State Education Dept, Cultural Education Center, Albany, New York 12230.
  (Dr D.W. Steadman, Senior Scientist (Zoology))
North Carolina State University, Dept of Zoology, Box 7617, Raleigh, North Carolina 27695-7617. (Dr R.A. Powell)
North Slope Borough, Conservation and Environmental Protection Office, P.O. Box 69, Barrow, Alaska 99723. (Dr T.F. Albert, Senior Scientist)
Oregon Institute of Marine Biology, University of Oregon, Charleston, Oregon 97420. (M. Graybill)
Oregon State University, Marine Science Center, Newport, Oregon 97365. (Dr B. Mate)
San Jose State University, Museum of Birds and Mammals, Dept of Biological Sciences, 1 Washington Sq, San Jose, California 95192-0100.
  (J. Vollenweider-Geary, Assistant Curator)
Texas Cooperative Wildlife Collection, Texas A & M University, College Station, Texas 77843-2258. (P.S. Cato)
University of California, Center for Coastal Marine Studies, Div. of Natural Sciences, Santa Cruz, California 95064. (T.P. Dohl)
University of California, Museum of Vertebrate Zoology, 2593 Life Sciences Bldg, Berkeley, California 94720.
  (Dr J.L. Patton, Curator of Mammals)
University of California, Zoology Dept, Collection of Milton Hildebrand, Davis, California 95616. (Dr M. Hildebrand)
University of Connecticut, Museum of Natural History, Room 314, 75 North Eagleville Rd, Storrs, Connecticut 06282. (R.E. Dubos)
University of Miami, School of Marine & Atmospheric Science, Div. of Biology & Living Resources, 4600 Rickenbacker Causeway, Miami, Florida
  33149-1098. (Dr D.K. Odell)
University of Michigan, Museum of Zoology & Museum of Paleontology, Ann Arbor, Michigan 48109. (Dr L.R. Heaney, Curator of Mammals)
University of Oregon, Condon Museum of Geology, Dept of Geology, Eugene, Oregon 97403-1272. (Dr W.N. Orr, Curator)
University of Rhode Island, Graduate School of Oceanography, Narragansett Bay Campus, Narragansett, Rhode Island 02882-1197.
  (Dr H.E. Winn)
University of Washington, Burke Museum, Zoology Division, Seattle, Washington 98195. (J. Rozdilsky)
Washington State University, Charles R. Conner Museum, Pullman, Washington 99164-4220. (J.D. Reichel, Assistant Curator)
The Whaling Museum, Box 25, Cold Spring Harbor, Long Island, New York 11724. (R.D. Farwell, Director)
Wales
National Museum of Wales, Cathys Park, Cardiff CF1 3NP, Wales. (Mr P.J. Morgan, Keeper of Zoology (via I.H.J. Lyster))

Table 3

Whaling and stranding sites where specimens of right whales (*sensu lato*) might be obtained.

Locality	Material	Source
Peninsula Valdes, Argentina.	Approx. 3 specimens of *E. australis* strand per year.	R. Bastida (pers. comm.)
Whaling station, Imbituba (28°15'S) south of Florianopolos, Brazil.	Several skulls and bone of *E. australis* (30 yrs of whaling).	L. Carter (pers. comm.)
Red Bank, Labrador, Canada.	Few crania (weathered basicranial portions only) of Balaenidae on west shore of bay.	D.R. Patten (see SC/35/RW11)
Cabo Espiretu Santo, Chile.	Skeleton of *Eubalaena* sp. from stranded specimen.	Goodall & Galeazzi, this vol.
Whaling station, 8-12 mi. inland, south of Ugab River, ca. 120 mi. (?) north of Swakopmund, Namibia.	Old skulls and bones of *E. australis*.	L. Carter via B. Loutit
St Lawrence Island, Alaska, USA.	100+ skulls (weathered) of *B. mysticetus*.	H. Braham (pers. comm.)

Appendix 7
HISTORICAL CATCHES OF RIGHT WHALES BY AREA

The following catch figures have been obtained by a combination of recorded catches and estimates using oil or whalebone yields, depending on the source of information. Thus most 'U.S. Whalers' catches are estimates from oil yields (see Appendix 12 and particularly the note of caution about its use), whereas most French catches have been obtained from records of catches actually obtained. Users of this information should consult the sources listed for details of estimation.

Summarized from tables prepared by T. Du Pasquier.

NORTH ATLANTIC RIGHT WHALE CATCHES FROM ELEVENTH CENTURY

A. Basque Fishery

1. Bay of Biscay (SC/25/RW1)

French Basque Country   1059-1688, peak 1251-1300
Spanish Basque Country   1150-1893, peak 1451-1600
Santander   1190-1720, peak 1601-1650
Asturias   1232-1722, peak 1601-1650
Galicia   1371-1720, peak 1601-1640
Possible catch: some dozens, less than 100 per year (only 4 whales caught during the twentieth century).

2. Newfoundland and Labrador

From *ca.* 1530 to *ca* 1610–20, with small catches up to 1713.

Estimated catch of Spanish whalers: 10–12 per voyage, or 300–500 per season. In small sample of 17 individuals from the Basque whaling station at Red Bay, Labrador, bone evidence indicates that approximately 50% were bowheads and 50% right whales (SC/35/RW11).

Estimated total catch from 1530 to 1610: 25,000–40,000 whales (of which an unknown but possibly significant percentage may have been bowheads).

3. Spitsbergen and seas around Iceland (SC/35/RW13)

These values refer to the minimum number of voyages by French whalers and the minimum estimated right whale catch.

The average number of 'right whales' for nine voyages was four. The main catch was bowhead or Grand Bay whales, near Spitsbergen or in the ice; but if they did not fill up the ship, the whalers fished Sardes (right whales) around Iceland, very likely what we later call 60–35 Ground. As certain whalers only took bowheads, estimates of the catch have been made with an average of 3 right whales per voyage from 1613 to 1718.

To these figures should be added the small number of Spanish vessels, and also captures by Dutch, German and English whalers, although according to Dr C. de Jong (pers. comm.) and Dutch took almost only bowheads.

Period	Voyages	Catches	Period	Voyages	Catches
1613–18	10	30	1669–78	202	606
1619–28	8	24	1679–88	143	429
1629–38	32	96	1689–98	68	204
1639–48	45	135	1699–1708	40	120
1649–58	19	57	1709–18	93	279
1659–68	78	234	Total	738	2,214

4. Davis Strait

These values refer to the exact number of voyages by French whalers and the estimated right whale catch.

After 1719, French whalers went mostly to Davis Strait. They apparently took a much smaller number of right whales, probably on their return trip, as Appendix 4 (in (SC/35/RW13) shows an average catch of 1.2 right whales for 18 voyages from 1737–1754. Thus this average has been applied from 1719 to 1758: after 1758 no right whales were taken.

The take by Dutch, German, Danish and English vessels is unknown.

Period	Voyages	Catches	Period	Voyages	Catches
1719–28	193	231	1749–58	21	25
1729–38	230	276	1759–66	4	0
1739–48	55	66	Total	503	598

B. Dutch, English, Danish and German fisheries, 17th to 19th centuries

Greenland and Spitsbergen waters, later Davis Strait, incidentally around Iceland. No data available differentiating right whales from bowheads. Presumably mostly bowheads captured.

C. Long Island (New York) Fishery (SC/35/RW24)

The estimated annual catch from 1650–99 was 20–25, from 1700–25. Although whaling continued, no data are available from 1750–1820 (see 'D' below).

Year	Catch	Year	Catch	Year	Catch
1656	1	1688	8–9	1708	17
1669	12–13	1699	12–13	1711	*ca* 27
1687	100	1707	111	1721	40
				1732/33	11

D. Massachusetts Coast

Records are scanty and imprecise, but shore-based right whaling along the Massachusetts coast began in the early 17th century, reaching a peak in the early 18th century. The record season's catch of Nantucket was 86 in 1726. Allen (1916) found records of only 9 whales taken along the coast between 1800 and 1850, and at least 63 between 1850 and 1900. From available records, the average catch from 1620 to 1913 was three whales per year. In this century, in addition to the values in the Table 1, one right whale was taken at Madeira in 1959 and two in 1967.

Period	Long Island (SC/35/RW24)	US whalers N. Atlantic (Appendix 12)	US whalers N. Atlantic (SC/35/RW23)[1]	20th C, NE Atlantic (SC/35/RW8)	Total
1820–4	20	0		–	20
1825–9	2	0		–	2
1830–4	6	0		–	6
1835–9	6	0		–	6
1840–4	1	0		–	1
1845–9	20	0		–	20
1850–4	25	0		–	25
1955–9	5	24		–	29
1860–4	7	45	[65]	–	52
1865–9	7	8		–	15
1870–4	4	4	[3]	–	8
1875–9	8	39		–	47
1880–4	2	19	[38–43]	–	21
1885–9	18	30		–	48
1890–4	3	0	[28]	–	3
1895–9	2	6		–	8
1900–4	0	0	[6]	7	7
1905–9	4	0		82–83	86–87
1910–4	1	–		38–40	39–41
1915–9	2	–		1	3
1920–4	1	–		5	6
1925–9	–	–		1	1
Total	144	175	[140–145]	134–137	453–456

[1] Periods actually 1855–65, 1866–75, 1876–85, 1886–95, 1896–1905.

SOUTH ATLANTIC RIGHT WHALE CATCHES, 1785–1939

South Atlantic right whale catches by five-year period, 1785–1939. The South Atlantic ground was opened in 1775 – catches prior to 1785 are unknown. US catches prior to 1805 are underestimates. To the totals below should be added to catches of British whalers. The following numbers of British whalers are known to have been in the South Atlantic: 1775 – 10; 1788 – 13; 1793 – Brazil and Patagonia – 7, South Georgia – 4, Africa – 6, east coast of Africa – 3 (SC/35/RW9). The total catch figures for French vessels have been divided proportionally according to the number of vessels on each ground, assuming that unknown catches are equal to the average catch of the other vessels in the same year; as whales were usually present on the grounds immediately before and after the calendar year end, catches have been assigned to the latter year.

There was also a Brazilian fishery from at least 1950–73 (1957 – 10; 1973 – 1). The average catch at Santa Catarina Is. was 5–6 yearly. The possible total kill from 1952–73 was 350 (SC/35/RW20).

| Period | Southern African shore whaling (SC/35/RW5) | French whalers (SC/35/RW13) | | | | US whalers Appendix 12 | Modern whaling, Antarctic(IWS, 1942) | Total |
		Southern Africa	Tristan da Cunha	Brazil Banks, Falklands	Unspecified			
1785–9	14	147	–	205	–	4	–	370
1790–4	70	425	–	238	360	86	–	1,179
1795–9	87	0	–	0	–	6	–	93
1800–4	150	–	–	–	–	–	–	150
1805–9	81	0	–	0	–	(4,339)	–	(4,420)
1810–4	148	0	–	0	–	–	–	148
1815–9	144	46	–	119	11	177	–	497
1820–4	191	75	–	505	111	3,742	–	4,624
1825–9	105	0	–	559	93	3,739	–	4,496
1830–4	214	340	320	536	49	8,959	–	10,418
1835–9	56	219	62	207	–	6,477	–	7,021
1840–4	33	–	–	–	–	484	–	517
1845–9	31	–	–	–	–	400	–	431
1850–4	25	–	–	–	–	722	–	747
1855–9	24	–	–	–	–	319	–	343
1860–4	9	–	–	–	–	555	–	564
1865–9	15	–	–	–	–	443	–	458
1870–4	9	–	–	–	–	176	–	185
1875–9	7	–	–	–	–	351	–	358
1880–4	6	–	–	–	–	362	–	368
1885–9	10	–	–	–	–	318	–	328
1890–4	20	–	–	–	–	293	–	313
1895–9	21	–	–	–	–	10	–	31
1900–4	11	–	–	–	–	44	–	55
1905–9	4	–	–	–	–	34	–	38
1910–4	11	–	–	–	–	26	202	239
1915–9	6	–	–	–	–	–	115	121
1920–4	11	–	–	–	–	–	39	50
1925–9	9	–	–	–	–	–	26	35
1930–4	1	–	–	–	–	–	2	3
1935–9	7	–	–	–	–	–	2	9
Total	1,530	1,252	382	2,369	624	32,066	386	38,609

NORTH PACIFIC RIGHT WHALE CATCHES, 1840–1969

Pacific right whale catches by five-year period, 1840–1969. The Japan ground, East China Sea opened around 1822, mainly for sperm whaling, are available but low catches would have been involved – whaling countries were Britain, USA and France. The north east coast, Kodiak opened in 1835 with a peak from 1840–48 – the USA, France, Britain, Germany and Hawaii were involved. The Okhotsk Sea ground opened in whaling ended in 1907. The total catch was 2,400–2,800 with a total kill perhaps as high as 3,600 – the USA, Britain (colonial France, Germany, Russia and Hawaii were involved.

Period	Okhotsk Sea (SC/35/RW26)	Shore whaling, US west coast (SC/35/RW26)	Japan, Korea, Kuriles & Kamchatka (SC/35/RW26)	Alaska, Bering Sea (SC/35/RW26)	British Columbia (SC/35/RW26)	US Whalers (Appendix 12)	Total
1840–4	–	–	–	–	–	2,985	2,985
1845–9	[820]	–	–	–	–	8,044	8,044
1850–4	[536]	–	–	–	–	1,370	1,370
1855–9	[593]	[2]	–	–	–	1,369	1,369
1860–4	[40]	[1]	–	–	–	585	585
1865–9	–	[1]	–	–	–	439	439
1870–4	[8]	[2]	–	–	–	60	60
1875–9	–	[1]	–	–	–	85	85
1880–4	–	[1]	–	–	–	5	5
1885–9	[21]	[6]	–	–	–	228	228
1890–4	–	–	–	–	–	23	23
1895–9	[11]	–	–	–	–	24	24
1900–4	–	–	–	–	–	24	24
1905–9	–	–	–	–	–	3	3
1910–4	–	–	7	–	–	–	7
1915–9	–	–	22	3	–	–	25
1920–4	–	1	25	2	3	–	31
1925–9	–	–	39	11	1	–	51
1930–4	–	–	30	–	–	–	30
1935–9	–	–	8	2	–	–	10
1940–4	–	–	24	–	–	–	24
1945–9	–	–	2	–	–	–	2
1950–4	–	–	–	–	1	–	1
1955–9	–	–	12	–	–	–	12
1960–4	–	–	3	9	–	–	12
1965–9	2	–	–	–	–	–	2
Total	[2,029] 2	[14] 1	172	27	5	15,244	15,451

SOUTH PACIFIC RIGHT WHALE CATCHES, 1815–1969

South Pacific right whale catches by five-year period, 1815–1969. The coast of Chile ground opened in 1790 (for sperm whales) and French whalers were estimated to take 7 right whales in 1791 and 2 in 1792 (SC/35/RW13). Other countries involved were the USA and Britain. By 1790–93, 41 vessels were operating in the Pacific (23 British, 8 French, 10 American), mostly sperm whaling (SC/35/RW9). The approximate opening of the Australian ground was 1793 and the New Zealand in 1801 (Dawbin, pers. comm.). To the totals below should be added the British and German vessels.

Period	Coast of Chile French (SC/35/RW13)	Chile & Peru (IWS, 1942; Aguayo, 1974)	S. Australia Victoria, N.S. Wales (SC/35/RW12)	Bay whaling Tasmania (SC/35/RW12)	New Zealand (SC/35/RW10, 12)	Campbell Is. (SC/35/RW12)	US whalers (Appendix 12)	French whalers (SC/35/RW13)	Total
1815–9	31	–	–	–	–	–	1,298	–	1,329
1820–4	51	–	–	188	–	–	–	–	239
1825–9	18	–	5	587	24	–	–	–	634
1830–4	862	–	536	1,388	610	–	675	–	4,071
1835–9	1,349	–	2,282	3,512	1,015	–	3,026	2,723	13,907
1840–4	46	–	1,686	2,799	787	–	4,808	1,148	11,274
1845–9	24	–	316	597	624	–	2,568	–	4,129
1850–4	–	–	170	92	76	–	282	–	620
1855–9	–	–	10	9	168	–	431	–	618
1860–4	–	–	42	28	29	–	520	–	619
1865–9	–	–	26	3	25	–	103	–	157
1870–4	–	–	28	1	18	–	68	–	115
1875–9	–	–	7	8	56	–	7	–	78
1880–4	–	–	5	6	56	–	122	–	189
1885–9	–	–	5	6	56	–	432	–	499
1890–4	–	–	–	–	–	–	100	–	100
1895–9	–	–	–	–	–	–	–	–	–
1900–4	–	–	–	–	–	–	–	–	–
1905–9	–	–	–	–	–	13	20	–	33
1910–4	–	–	–	–	–	50	–	–	50
1915–9	–	12	–	–	14	–	–	–	26
1920–4	–	7	–	–	12	–	–	–	19
1925–9	–	26	–	–	6	–	–	–	32
1930–4	–	48	–	–	3	–	–	–	51
1935–9	–	56	–	–	–	–	–	–	56
1940–4	–	1	–	–	–	–	–	–	1
1945–9	–	0	–	–	1	–	–	–	1
1950–4	–	0	–	–	1	–	–	–	1
1955–9	–	7	–	–	1	–	–	–	8
1960–4	–	1	–	–	–	–	–	–	1
1965–9	–	3	–	–	–	–	–	–	3
Total	2,381	161	5,118	9,224	3,582	63	14,460	3,871	38,860

INDIAN OCEAN RIGHT WHALE CATCHES

The Table shows catches in the Indian Ocean by five-year periods from 1830–1939, but does not include catches by British and French whalers. In addition there was some local whaling at Madagascar in the mid-1750s. The Delagoa Bay fishery opened in 1789 and the following French results are known for this ground (du Pasquier, pers. comm.). 1789: 2 vessels; 29 whales; 1,430 bbls oil. 1790: 4 vessels; est. 58 whales; 2,620 bbls oil. 1791: 2 vessels; est. 16 whales; 773,55 bbls. 1792–3: 9 vessels. 1803: 2 vessels. In addition, Townsend (1935) reports 18 right whales taken by US whalers in 1793.

Period	South Africa (Natal) (SC/35/RW5)	W. Australia bay whaling (SC/35/RW2)	US whalers (Appendix 12)	Total	Period	South Africa (Natal) (SC/35/RW5)	W. Australia bay whaling (SC/35/RW2)	US whalers (Appendix 12)	Total
1830–4	–	–	684	684	1885–9	–	–	18	18
1835–9	–	50	4,055	4,105	1890–4	–	–	–	–
1840–4	–	45	4,697	4,742	1895–9	–	–	12	12
1845–9	–	76	955	1,031	1900–4	–	–	8	8
1850–4	–	27	398	425	1905–9	–	–	269	269
1855–9	–	57	484	541	1910–4	18	–	25	43
1860–4	–	3	240	243	1915–9	5	–	–	5
1865–9	–	8	176	184	1920–4	8	–	–	8
1870–4	–	–	184	184	1925–9	2	–	–	2
1875–9	–	–	85	85	1930–4	5	–	–	5
1880–4	–	–	–	–	1935–9	2	–	–	2
					Total	40	266	12,290	12,596

Appendix 8
MORTALITY FACTORS IN RIGHT WHALE FISHERIES

In nearly all the campaigns in the Table the technique used was hand harpoon and lance. The mortality factor seems to have been higher in open seas than in bays (e.g. 1834–64) and an average mortality factor 1.2–1.5 seems likely. In the Table mortality factor 'one' = a/d and mortality factor 'two' = (d + 0.5c + b)/d.

Period	Region	Struck (a)	Struck, killed and not processed (b)	Struck and escaped (c)	Struck, killed and processed (d)	Mortality factor		Source
						'one'	'two'	
1783–1794	South Atlantic	294	41.5	70	182.5	1.61	1.42	SC/35/RW13
1804–1869	Bay whaling, South Africa	84	8	20	56	1.50	1.32	SC/35/RW5
1817–1837	South Atlantic	1,330	–	388	942	1.41	1.21	SC/35/RW13
1838–1839	New Holland ground	112	–	29	83	1.35	1.18	SC/35/RW2
1855–1858	Cintra Bay	25	5	–	20	(1.25)	1.25	SC/35/RW22
1834–1864	S. Atlantic, N. Pacific, Indian Ocean	170	22	55	93	1.83	1.53	SC/35/RW22
1868–1898	60/35 ground	19	6	1	13	1.46	1.50	
Total		2,034	82.5	563	1,389.5	1.46	1.26	

Appendix 9
RIGHT WHALE SURVIVORSHIP AROUND PENINSULA VALDES, ARGENTINA

R. L. Brownell, Jr.

Data are rarely available to directly estimate calf survivorship in baleen whales.

Two sets of observations were available on the number of live and dead calves around Peninsula Valdes, Argentina for five years (Table 1). The pooled calf survivorship was calculated to be 0.945 for the mean period females are present with their calves in the Peninsula Valdes area (44.3 days, R. S. Payne, pers. comm.). The pooled calf survivorship using just the Payne data from 1971 to 1973 was 0.952 and using the data from Bastida and Bastida for 1981 and 1982 was 0.935. Observed calf survivorship may be high because currents are particularly strong almong the eastern outer coast of the Valdes Peninsula and stranded calves could have been washed out to sea before they were discovered.

An annual calf survivorship of 0.627 results from these data if this same rate prevailed throughout the year. This is unrealistically low, because calf mortality would be highest soon after birth. Payne (Appendix 10) calculated a calf survivorship in the first year for returning known right whales at 0.732. The actual annual calf survivorship is probably between 0.732 and 0.945.

Table 1

Observed strandings and counts of right whale calves at Peninsula Valdes with calf survivorship for the period females are present with calves (see text). It is assumed that all calves were born alive. Data from 1971–3 from R. Payne and from 1981–82 from R. and V. Bastida.

Year	Number calves	Dead calves	Survivorship	Year	Number calves	Dead calves	Survivorship
1971	19	2	0.905	1981	35	2	0.946
1972	27	1	0.964	1982	37	3	0.925
1973	37	1	0.974				

Appendix 10
AGE AT SEXUAL MATURITY AND CALF MORTALITY AS DETERMINED FROM IDENTIFIED CALVES

R. Payne

Although the callosity patterns of right whales remain constant (within the limits necessary for individual identification) throughout the life of an individual, the identification of calves from aerial photographs is difficult owing to their small head size and to a dense cover of cyamids in the first months of life (Payne et al., 1981). However, we have been able to identify a few individuals each year and to follow their subsequent reappearance at Peninsula Valdes, Argentina.

Table 1 lists the number of all identified individuals

Table 1

Number of identified calves born each year (n) and numbers of these potentially available for reidentification each year. Assumptions: 1 year gestation period; 1:1 calf sex ratio. YTM = maximum number of years to sexual maturity; NTM = maximum number of animals potentially observable for each assumed age at sexual maturity (the number in parenthesis is the maximum number of females).

Year of birth	n	YTM	NTM	Year of birth	n	YTM	NTM
1971	8	7	8 (4)	1974	3	4	42 (20)
1972	17	6	25 (12.5)	1975	6	3	48 (24)
1973	14	5	39 (19.5)	1976	8	2	56 (28)

Table 2

Numbers of identified calves born each year (n) and numbers of not resighted in subsequent years. 1st = calves seen only in their first year, 2nd = animals last seen in their 1st year, 3rd = calves last seen in their 2nd year, etc. N–M = total number available minus deaths in earlier years; % mortality = deaths per number of animals alive at the start of a year.

Year of birth	n	1st	2nd	3rd	4th	5th	6th
71	8	0	0	0	0	1	1
72	17	5	1	2	2	1	–
73	14	5	1	1	2	–	–
74	3	1	0	0	–	–	–
75	6	2	1	–	–	–	–
76	8	2	–	–	–	–	–
Totals	56	15	3	3	4	2	1
N–M		56	35	29	24	15	7
% mortality		26.8	8.6	10.3	16.7	13.3	14.3

(grade B or better; Payne *et al.*, 1981) first seen in their calf year. Because none of these animals had been seen with a calf of its own by the end of 1979 we cannot yet fix an age at sexual maturity for females. We can, however, comment on what the minimum age may be by noting the numbers of animals that reappear each year without calves of their own.

Table 1 shows that there are eight animals which we might have seen over eight years. Assuming a gestation period of one year, and calf sex ratio of 50–50, there were only four animals which might have been seen with calves of their own had they become sexually mature by age seven (assuming that they returned to calve at Peninsula Valdes and were photographed with their calves). Both assumptions seem safe considering that known females seen for several years before being seen with a calf at Valdes are usually present each year prior to calving (SC/35/RW21); and females with calves are the animals with highest sightability (Payne *et al.*, 1981; Best, 1981).

Table 1 indicates that the number of identified calves old enough to be sexually mature within our sighting period is low. Thus, the chances seem relatively poor that sexual maturity is reached between the ages of 2.5 and 6 years (as proposed by Whitehead and Payne, 1981).

Table 2 gives a further breakdown of data on the individuals in Table 1 in order to get a maximum figure for calf mortality. In this case we assume that any animal permanently absent in our records from Valdes between the years 1971 and 1977 (the years with best coverage) has died. This assumption, though unrealistic, gives an upper limit on mortality. It is clear that calves born in

later years are more likely to be alive even when considered dead than calves born in the first years of the study (the latter group being animals for which we have more years of absence to confirm the assumption that they have died).

The year 1974 was a year of very poor photographic coverage, meaning that all data affected by that year are suspect. For example, an apparent mortality of five calves in their first year from the class of 1973 is probably high (the return of these individuals in 1974 might well have been missed).

Nevertheless, it seems safe to conclude that mortality in the first year is higher than in subsequent years.

REFERENCES

Best, P. B. 1981. The status of right whales (*Eubalaena glacialis*) off South Africa, 1696–1979. *Investl. Rep. Sea. Fish. Inst. S. Africa* 123: 1–44.
Payne, R., Brazier, O., Dorsey, E., Perkins, J., Rowntree, V. and Titus, A. 1981. External features in southern right whales (*Eubalaena glacialis*) and their use in identifying individuals. US Dept of Commer., NYIS No. PB81-161093. 77 pp.
Whitehead, H. and Payne, R. 1981. New techniques for measuring whales from the air. Rep. to the US Marine Mammal Comm., Contract MM6ACO17, No. MMC-76/22. 36 pp.

Appendix 11

TO WHAT EXTENT HAVE RIGHT WHALE CALVES BEEN RECORDED AWAY FROM THE COAST?

J. L. Bannister

Examination of 18 American logbooks, mainly from the 'New Holland Ground', gives the following information. For pelagic whaling for the years 1836–48 and months August to March (mainly 1838–42, October to December), 406 whales were killed and only one calf recorded. For bay whaling by American vessels for the years 1839, 1840 and 1842 and months June to October (mainly July to September), 68 whales were killed and 17 calves recorded.

The single pelagic whaling calf record is from the vessel *Condor* on 19 October 1840, in 36°52′ S, 117°27′ E, i.e., fairly close to the south coast of Western Australia.

In extracting the above data, some logs were only skimmed, seeking whale stamps (where whale stamps did not occur in the log at all, it was read fully). In one log at least, special small 'calf' stamps were used. Some pelagic calf catches may therefore have been missed, but certainly only very few. It is, of course, possible that for some unknown reason the logkeeper did not record calves when at sea, but only when bay whaling; however, this seems unlikely. It is also possible, but unlikely, that calves might have been ignored by pelagic harpooners, as well as in the records.

An associated question is the extent to which adult male right whales occur in coastal waters in winter. Catches are not often recorded by sex, except as 'cow and calf', but for one bay whaling period in 1839, the *Emerald* records details of most of the catch. Of 21 animals taken in Doubtful Island Bay, on the south coast of Western Australia, between 1 July and 5 October, there are four records of 'cows and calves', five of single cows, one of a bull, one of a cow and bull, one 'dryskin', one 'small' and four unspecified. At least in that instance, bulls accounted for almost 10% of the bay whaling catch.

Appendix 12

AN ATTEMPT TO RECONSTRUCT THE CATCH HISTORY OF RIGHT WHALES IN THE AMERICAN FISHERY, 1805–1909

P. B. Best

Note that these calculations were extensively reworked following the meeting and supplemented with an independent analysis based on the catch per voyage (Best, in prep., 'Estimates of the landed catch of right (and other whalebone) whales in the American fishery, 1805–1909'; submitted to Fishery Bulletin). The tables given here should therefore be considered only as a preliminary version prepared for the purposes of the meeting.

Table 1

Mean yield per whale for the US fishery. Values were calculated (except for the gray whale where the value was taken from Henderson, 1972) from voyages listed by Townsend (1935) on which only one species of baleen whale was taken (North Pacific right whales were considered as a different 'species'). Only voyages on which ten or more individuals were landed were included in the calculation. Production figures for each voyage were obtained from Starbuck (1878) or Hegarty (1959) and include oil sent home or sold abroad when known.

	Number voyages	Catch	Oil landings (barrels)	Oil/whale (barrels)		Number voyages	Catch	Oil landings (barrels)	Oil/whale (barrels)
Bowhead whales	39	987	80,888	82.0	Humpback whales	29	1,137	27,797	24.5
North Pacific right whales	17	341	41,645	122.1	Gray whales	–	–	–	35
Other right whales	130	3,247	213,903	65.9					

Table 2

Preliminary estimate of numbers of baleen whales taken by US whalers, 1805–1909. The species composition of the catch was obtained from the logbook sample examined by Townsend (1935) for each period. This sample was pro-rated using US import figures for whale oil from Starbuck (1878) and Hegarty (1959), and mean oil yields per whale for each species from Table 1.

Period	Bowhead	Right, North Atl.	Right, North Pacific	Right, South Atl.	Right, South Pacific	Right, South Indian	Humpback	Gray	Period	Bowhead	Right, North Atl.	Right, North Pacific	Right, South Atl.	Right, South Pacific	Right, South Indian	Humpback	Gray
1805–09	–	–	–	(4,339)	–	–	–	–	1860–64	3,260	45	585	555	520	240	965	960
1810–14	–	–	–	–	–	–	–	–	1865–69	2,943	8	439	443	103	176	508	882
1815–19	295	–	–	177	1,298	–	118	–	1870–74	1,812	4	60	176	68	184	3,016	276
1820–24	–	–	–	3,742	–	–	–	–	1875–79	676	39	85	351	7	85	2,470	52
1825–29	–	–	–	3,739	–	–	14	–	1880–84	550	19	5	362	122	–	2,900	–
1830–34	–	–	–	8,959	675	684	48	–	1885–89	564	30	228	318	432	18	1,110	6
1835–39	–	–	2,985	6,477	3,026	4,055	816	–	1890–94	662	–	23	293	100	–	169	–
1840–44	–	–	2,985	484	4,808	4,697	614	–	1895–99	366	6	24	10	–	12	20	–
1845–49	688	–	8,044	400	2,568	955	659	–	1900–04	296	–	24	44	–	8	4	–
1850–54	9,130	–	1,370	722	282	398	697	50	1905–09	112	–	3	34	20	269	–	–
1855–59	7,310	24	1,369	319	431	484	1,422	389	Total	28,664	175	15,244	27,605	14,460	12,265	15,550	2,615

Cow and calf (*E. glacialis*), Peninsula Valdes, Argentina (Photo courtesy R. Payne)

History of Right Whale Catches in the Waters around Japan

HIDEO OMURA

Whales Research Institute, 3-32-11, Ojima, Koto-Ku, 136, Japan

ABSTRACT

Two populations of right whales migrated in the waters around Japan, at least prior to the present century. One migrated through the waters south of Mie, Wakayama and Kochi prefectures (the Pacific population), the other through the waters north of Kyoto to Yamaguchi prefectures and then to the west of Kyushu (the Sea of Japan population). Both populations moved southwards in winter and northwards in spring. The calving grounds of these populations are not known, but presumably lie further south and around the Ryukyu Islands.

The northerly migration of the Pacific population went further north along the coast of Japan, reaching the waters near the Kuril Islands in summer; some would enter the Bering Sea. The Sea of Japan population also undertook long migrations and is thought to have entered the Okhotsk Sea in summer.

Annual catches of right whales by net whaling in the nineteenth century were estimated as about 50 at their highest from each of the two populations in the former half of the century, but the catches greatly decreased in the latter half. It is thought this was attributable to the operation of American whale ships working in the Sea of Japan, Okhotsk Sea and eastward of the Kuril Islands as far as 170° E.

Results of the catches of right whales by Japanese modern whale catchers since 1910 indicate that the Sea of Japan population was more heavily reduced than the Pacific population.

SHORT HISTORY OF WHALING IN JAPAN

Whaling in the waters around Japan has a very long history. Catching of whales using boats and primitive gear possibly dates back prior to the tenth century. Some tools made of baleen plates of the right whale, *Eubalaena glacialis*, are kept at the Shosoin, the storehouse in Nara where many articles and ornaments used in the Nara palaces have been preserved for 1,200 years (Shindo, 1978). This shows that as early as the Nara period (A.D.710–784) carcasses of some right whales were utilized by man, even by the royal families. It is uncertain as to whether active hunting occurred or if only stranded whales were used.

In the years of Genki (1570–73), whaling was conducted by villagers of Mikawa and Owari (now Aichi prefecture), facing Ise Bay, who formed teams of 7–8 vessels and used hand harpoons (Otsuki, 1808). The centre of this whaling was Morosaki, the southernmost village of Chita peninsula. This is the oldest Japanese whaling known to history. The species of whales taken are not known, but it is probable that gray whales, *Eschrichtius robustus*, were the most commonly caught species.

This hand harpoon whaling spread to the south along the coast of Ise and Kumano districts (present Mie and Wakayama prefectures), and then to the western parts of Japan, including Shikoku and Kyushu. In the 11th year of Keicho (1606), Yorimoto, head of the then powerful Wada clan, established five whaling groups at Taiji, Kumano. He took command of the operation, assisted by a fisherman named Denji from Morosaki, possibly a skilled harpooner (Hashiura, 1969).

In 1675 Yoriharu Wada, later renamed Kakuemon Taiji, a grandson of Yorimoto, invented a new method of whaling using nets; whales entangled by many folds of nets were easily harpooned. At first straw nets were used but they were too weak and were replaced in subsequent years by hemp nets.

The use of nets was a revolutionary event in the history of whaling in Japan, allowing the taking of humpback whales, *Megaptera novaeangliae*, and other balaeno-pterids; right whales also became easier prey than before. However, the net method required more fishing boats, more manpower and a cooperative operation of many fishermen. At Taiji, five whaling groups were reorganized into one and Yoriharu Wada took command.

One operating group consisted of 15–20 *Seko-bune* or beater boats for driving and killing whales, 6 *Ami-bune* or netting boats and 4 *Mosso-bune* or tug boats, or in total 25–30 boats with about 400 crew. From a hillside hut with a wide view, watchmen scanned the sea surface for whale blows. When a whale was sighted within range, the watchmen sent signals with flags or rockets informing the boat crew of the species, position and swimming direction of the whale. When the commander gave the order the boats moved into action in an orderly fashion.

The beater boats surrounded the whale from a distance and drove it towards the netting boats which moved into proper position to set their nets. The netted whale was harpooned from the beater boats. Several types of harpoon were used. Each whale was initially harpooned with a light harpoon of about 200 g in weight, 55 cm in length, and attached to a wooden shaft of about 3.8 m. The weight of harpoon was then increased gradually, and finally a harpoon of about 3 kg was thrown (Taiji, 1937).

When the whale was sufficiently weakened by a number of harpoons, a sailor jumped into the water and climbed on to the head of the whale to make a hole with his knife in the septum of the blowholes, through which a rope was passed. Another hole was made in a similar way in the back blubber near the tail. In both cases the sailor stayed on the slippery surface of the whale body by grasping the handle of a struck harpoon. These harpoons also prevented the nets from slipping off. Then the whale was tied between two tug boats and stabbed in the heart with long swords.

The invention of net whaling was a major event in the economy of Japanese fishing villages. Whaling supported many hundreds of people, including workers who processed the whale carcass, made nets or engaged in other related activities, as well as sailors at sea. A whaling operation needed large amounts of money for preparation as well as operation; so net whaling was mostly

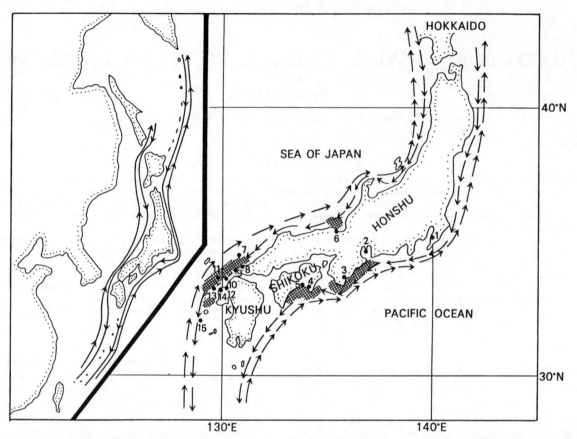

Fig. 1. Chart showing migration routes of right whales around Japan and places where they were taken by net-whaling (shaded). Place names appearing in the text are indicated by numerals as follows: 1. Katsuyama, Chiba prefecture; 2. Morosaki, Aichi pref; 3. Taiji, Wakayama pref; 4. Tsuro, Kochi pref; 5. Ukitsu, Kochi pref; 6. Ine, Kyoto pref; 7. Mishima, Yamaguchi pref; 8. Kayoi, Yamaguchi pref; 9. Kawajiri, Yamaguchi pref; 10. Ogawajima, Saga pref; 11. Iki, Nagasaki pref; 12. Yobuko, Saga pref; 13. Ikitsuki, Nagasaki pref; 14. Hirado, Nagasaki pref; 15. Goto, Nagasaki pref.

conducted by powerful clans like the Wada family in Taiji.

Net whaling was soon introduced at Koza, a town close to Taiji, and at other places in Kumano district (part of the present Mie and Wakayama prefectures). In 1683 this method was transferred to Tosa (present Kochi prefecture), where the two whaling groups of Ukitsu and Tsuro were already in operation. In the following year a whaling boss named Gidayu Fukazawa from Omura, west Kyushu, came to Taiji and learned this method from Yoriharu (Hashiura, 1969). Upon Fukazawa's return to Kyushu, net whaling soon spread over the west coast of Kyushu and the north coast of Yamaguchi prefecture.

Whaling was also conducted in other places in Japan. The most famous of these was the whaling conducted at Katsuyama (present Chiba prefecture) by the Daigo Clan (Yoshihara, 1976a). This whaling started as early as the years of Meireki (1655–57) and lasted towards the end of the Edo or Tokugawa era (1867). Baird's beaked whale, *Berardius bairdii* and other small toothed whales were taken by hand harpoon. Nets were never used in this whaling and no baleen whales were taken.

CATCHES OF RIGHT WHALES

Right whales were taken in two different regions of Japan by net whaling: the south coast (the Mie, Wakayama and Kochi prefectures) which took animals from the Pacific population; and the waters north of the prefectures from Kyoto to Yamaguchi and to the west of Kyushu which took animals from the Sea of Japan population.

Pacific population

Off the south coast of Japan, right whales were taken in a season lasting from winter to spring. Other species taken were humpback, gray, Bryde's (*Balaenoptera edeni*), fin (*B. physalus*) and blue whales (*B. musculus*). At Taiji, Wakayama, sperm whales (*Physeter catodon*) were also taken. Gray and sperm whales were taken by hand harpoon and nets were not used. In Mie prefecture, right and other baleen whales were also taken, usually by harpoon.

Practically no catch statistics exist for Wakayama and Mie prefectures. At Taiji, whaling continued after the Meiji Revolution (1868) until a tragic disaster on 24 December 1878 (Hashiura, 1969) when more than 100 people were killed by a heavy storm while chasing a right whale accompanied by a calf. This incident was practically the end of the old whaling at Taiji.

In Kochi prefecture, whaling with hand harpoon dates from the years of Kanei (1624–43) (Izukawa, 1943), and net whaling from 1683 when it was introduced from Taiji. Two groups of whalers, Ukitsu and Tsuro, operated on the coast of Kochi, splitting their activities between the east and west whaling grounds. There are two peninsulas in Kochi, the Muroto Peninsula in the east, and the Ashizuri Peninsula in the west. The east whaling grounds were on the east (in winter or from the end of September until December), and west side (in spring or from February to April) of the Muroto Peninsula. The west ground was on the east side of the Ashizuri Peninsula, both in winter (southbound whales) and spring (northbound whales).

Table 1

Catches of whales by net-whaling in Kochi prefecture (summarized from Appendix Table 1). * Recorded as *Iwashi kujira*, which usually means sei whales, but in this case Bryde's whales (Omura, 1977).

	Group	Gray	Right	Hump-back	Bryde's*	Others	Total
1800–1835	Ukitsu	144	259	521	5	10	959
1849–1865	Tsuro	101	19	209	35	6	370
1874–1896	Tsuro	99	23	134	72	56	384
1875–1896	Ukitsu	64	21	126	81	78	370
Average per year							
1800–1835	Ukitsu	4.0	7.2	14.5	0.1	0.8	26.6
1849–1865	Tsuro	5.9	1.1	12.3	2.1	0.4	21.8
1874–1896	Tsuro	4.3	1.0	5.8	3.1	2.4	16.7
1875–1896	Ukitsu	2.9	1.0	5.7	3.7	3.5	16.8

Table 2

Catches of whales at Ine, 1656–1913 (prepared from Yoshihara, 1976b) * Possibly includes minke whale.

Years	Humpback	Fin*	Right	Total
1656–1700	42	25	6	73
1701–1750	36	35	3	74
1751–1800	33	26	14	73
1801–1850	34	28	10	72
1851–1900	22	31	7	60
1901–1913	–	3	–	3
Total	167	148	40	355
%	47.0	41.7	11.3	100.0

Table 3

Catches of whales by net-whaling at Kawajiri (summarized from Appendix Table 2)

	Gray	Right	Humpback	Fin	Others	Total
Total catch						
1699–1768	110	166	591	22	28	917
1769–1818	?	?	?	?	?	582
1819–1858	73	119	229	28	109	558
1859–1888	97	9	138	227	7	478
1894–1901	7	0	28	55	9	99
Average per year						
1699–1768	1.6	2.4	8.4	0.3	0.4	13.1
1769–1818	?	?	?	?	?	11.6
1819–1858	1.8	3.0	5.7	0.7	2.7	13.9
1859–1888	3.2	0.3	4.6	7.6	0.2	15.9
1894–1901	0.9	0.0	3.5	6.9	1.1	12.4

The Ukitsu and Tsuro whaling groups operated alternately on the east and west grounds each year; in the year of operation on the west ground, the crew and other people concerned with the operation also moved to the west and stayed there during the period of operation. Both groups left good catch records by species, from which general trends of the whaling in Kochi can be detected. These are summarised in Table 1 (detailed catch figures of whales in Kochi prefecture are shown in Appendix Table 1).

Table 1 shows that humpback and right whales comprised the major part of the catch in the first half of the nineteenth century, accounting for about 80% of the total catch. Thereafter catches of these two species, especially right whales, decreased considerably to as little as only one per year for both groups.

It can safely be assumed that the catch and its composition for the Ukitsu and Tsuro groups were nearly the same (cf. Appendix Table 1, c and d). The total catch of right whales by them is estimated as about 15 whales per year before 1850. Further if it is assumed that nearly equal numbers of right whales were taken in Wakayama and Mie prefectures, then about 50 or fewer right whales were taken annually on the south coast of Japan prior to the latter half of the nineteenth century. In Wakayama prefecture the intensity of whaling was thought to be at the same level as that in Kochi prefecture, but in Mie prefecture fishermen were more dependent on fishing than whaling.

Sea-of-Japan population

On the Sea of Japan coast whaling was conducted at several villages and right whales were taken. At Ine, Kyoto prefecture, whaling was conducted from ancient times, probably as early as the Tenmon years (1532–54). The village of Ine is located on a small inlet called Inewan, into which whales occasionally swam. When this happened fishermen of Ine blocked the entrance of the inlet and caught the whale by using hand harpoons and nets.

Catch records of the Ine whaling during a period from 1656 to 1913 are available by species (Yoshihara, 1976b). These are given in Table 2 which shows that humpback and fin whales were the major catch; right whales comprised about 11% of the total. No gray whales were taken and 'fin whales' possibly included the minke whale, *Balaenoptera acutorostrata*. It is possible that minke whales migrated into the Sea of Japan, but I cannot find either Japanese name for minke whale in any of the old Japanese literature on whales. This is perhaps not surprising as one of the current Japanese names for minke

whale is *minku*, which without doubt is derived from minke, and another name is *koiwashi-kujira*, a translation of 'little piked whale'.

Whaling was conducted in several villages on the north coast of Yamaguchi prefecture, including Kayoi in the east and Kawajiri in the west (Tokumi, 1957; Tada, 1978). At Kayoi, presently Nagato city, there is a temple named Koganji where records contain the Buddhist names of each whale taken, from which catch figures by species were obtained (Kimura, 1956). During a period from 1802 to 1850 a total of 308 whales was taken, including 116 fin, 105 humpback, 59 right and 28 gray whales. The average catch per year was 6.3 animals, and right whales comprised 19% of the catch.

For Kawajiri, catch statistics arranged by species and by 10 year increments, are available from 1699, when whaling was started, until 1901 (Anon., 1890; Tada, 1978). These figures are shown in Appendix Table 2 and summarised in Table 3. Catches at Kawajiri consisted primarily of humpback and right whales until the middle part of the nineteenth century, but after 1859 catches of both species, especially right whales, decreased considerably and no right whales were taken after 1884 (Tada, 1978). Catches of fin whales increased after 1859 compensating for the decreased catches of other species.

In addition to that at Kayoi and Kawajiri, whaling was also conducted at several villages in Yamaguchi prefecture, including Mishima a small island village about 45 km northwest of Hagi city (Tada, 1968). Whaling at these villages began around 1680 and lasted until near the end of the nineteeth century, although on rather a small scale. Unfortunately, no details of the catches are available.

Whaling was conducted at various places on the west coast of Kyushu. In Kyushu whaling was started as a small enterprise using hand harpoons. After the invention of net whaling this technique spread over the west coast of Kyushu, which became the most flourishing whaling

Table 4

Average price in year per whale, Kawajiri, 1879–1888 (Anonymous, 1890). For the Index, the humpback = 1. No distinction to species is made for calves

Species	Price	Index	Species	Price	Index
Right	4,362	3.09	Gray	479	0.34
Humpback	1,411	1.00	Calves	44	0.03
Fin	1,044	0.74			

Table 5

Catch ratio against total number of right whales sighted by Ukitsu whaling group in years 1880, 1882 and 1883 (Hattori, 1887–1888)

	1880	1882	1883	Total
Total number sighted	7	9	1	17
Catch	1	0	1	2
Escaped, breaking net	0	0	0	0
Escaped, beneath net	2	4	0	6
Escaped, round net	0	1	0	1
Sighted, but not operated	4	4	0	8
Sighted, rough weather	4	4	0	8
Sighted, offshore	0	0	0	0

region (Anon., 1980). Whaling in Kyushu was carried out by several clans or groups, e.g. the Nakao clan of Yobuko and Ogawajima (Saga prefecture), the Toi clan of Iki Island (Nagasaki prefecture) and the largest, the Masutomi clan of Hirado and Ikitsuki (Nagasaki prefecture). From 1725, when the group was formed by the powerful clan Matazaemon Masutomi, to 1874 when operations ceased, a total of 21,790 whales was taken (Yoshihara, 1977), a yearly average of 150 whales for all locations combined. The group operated at several locations in Kyushu, and sometimes at Mishima and Kayoi (both in Yamaguchi prefecture) as well. It was said this whaling group employed 3,000 people and about 200 fishing vessels when in operation.

The breakdown by species of the average yearly catch of 150 whales by the Masutomi group is not known, but if an assumption is made that 18% were of right whales (percentage figure at Kayoi, 1699–1768), the annual catch of right whales would have been 27. There is no further material to estimate the annual catch of right whales on the coasts of Kyushu and Yamaguchi combined, but it is thought that it never exceeded 50 whales.

Whaling operations by the Masutomi group were well explained and illustrated in a book entitled *Isanatori Ekotoba*, published in 1829. According to Hawley (1958) this book was published in 1832, but the date has been recently corrected. An English translation of this book recently published (Yamada, 1983), unfortunately contains some mistakes in translation. The correct name of this book is *Isanatori Ekotoba*, not *Yogiotoru Eshi*, and the name of the author is 'Oyamada Tomokiyo', not 'Yamada Yosei'. In recent years it has become clear that the book was compiled by Matazaemon Masutomi, the operator of the whaling at Hirado and Ikitsuki in 1829 (Anon., 1980). In the book it is stated that 'the whale migrating from south to north was called the Up-going whale and that coming from north to south the Down-going whale'. It is clear from this that the right whales on the coast of west Kyushu were migrating and that the calving ground lay further south.

As in Yamaguchi prefecture, right, humpback, fin and gray whales were the main species taken by net whaling. Of these the right whale was the most important species because of the large amount of meat and oil produced. The average prices per whale of each species at Kawajiri during the 10 years from 1879 to 1888 are shown in Table 4; the right whale had a value three times higher than that of a humpback whale.

Net whaling in Kyushu had nearly finished towards the end of the 19th century as in the case of Wakayama and Kochi prefectures.

DISCUSSION AND CONCLUSION

It is clear, from the above accounts, that two populations of right whales migrated in the waters around Japan in

the days of net whaling. The Pacific population migrated on the south side of Mie, Wakayama and Kochi prefectures and the Sea-of-Japan population migrated on the north coast from Kyoto to Yamaguchi prefectures and then to the west coast of Kyushu. Both populations moved southwards in winter and northwards in spring. At Taiji, Wakayama prefecture, the southerly migration took place towards the end of September until December and the northerly migration from February to April (Hashiura, 1969). The calving ground is unknown, but lay further south, probably around the Ryukyu Islands. No sightings of copulation recorded by the lookouts on the top of hills remain.

The northern migration of this population would continue further north along the coastline of Japan. Omura, Ohsumi, Nemoto, Nasu and Kasuya (1969) showed sightings of black right whales in the North Pacific by Japanese whale catchers (1941–68) and those of the USSR (1951–57) cited from Klumov (1962). According to these, the Pacific population would reach the southeastern side of Hokkaido in April and then move in a northeasterly direction and reach the waters around the Kuril Islands, some entering the Bering Sea. It is not clear whether this population or a part of it entered into the Gulf of Alaska.

The Sea of Japan population also followed a long migration route, in spring probably moving to the north and spending summer in the Okhotsk Sea, although I have no evidence to support this assumption. In winter it moved further south to its calving ground, probably near the Ryukyu Islands.

The maximum annual catch of right whales from either of the two populations was estimated as 50 in the years before the middle of the nineteeth century. No exact data about total sightings and the number caught therefrom remain, but Hattori (1887–88) reports results for three years (1880, 1882 and 1883) of right whaling by Ukitsu whaling group in Kochi prefecture (Table 5). A total of 17 right whales was sighted and two whales or 12% of the total were killed. Seven whales escaped from being netted, but probably some of them were struck by harpoons. There is no information on the mortality of animals that so escaped.

As already stated, catches of right whales dropped heavily in the latter half of the nineteenth century, both on the western and southern coasts of Japan. It is thought that this is attributable to the operation of American whale ships. The Japan Ground (for sperm whales) was discovered about 1820 and whaling for the northern right whale, off the Asiatic coast, extended from the Sea of Japan into the head of the Okhotsk Sea, and along the east side of the Kamchatka peninsula, with considerable

Table 6

Catches of right whales by modern whaling in waters around Japan and Korea (rearranged and corrected from Kasahara, 1950). The areas* referred to are: A – Kuril Islands, south coasts of Hokkaido, and Sanriku (northeast coast of Honshu); B – South coast of Honshu, Shikoku and east coast of Kyushu; C – Bonin Islands; D – Okhotsk Sea; E – West Coast of Kyushu; F – Coast of Korea. In addition, one right whale and three right whales were taken in 1940 and 1941 respectively by pelagic operations in the North Pacific.

Year	Area*							Year	Area*						
	A	B	C	D	E	F	Sum		A	B	C	D	E	F	Sum
1911	–	2	–	–	–	–	2	1929	5	–	–	–	–	–	5
1912	–	3	–	–	–	–	3	1930	5	–	–	–	–	–	5
1913	–	–	–	–	–	1	1	1931	–	–	–	8	–	–	8
1914	1	–	–	–	–	–	1	1932	14	–	–	–	–	–	14
1915	5	1	–	–	1	–	7	1933	1	–	2	–	–	–	3
1916	5	3	–	–	–	–	8	1934	–	1	1	–	–	–	2
1917	2	1	–	–	–	–	3	1935	2	–	–	–	–	–	2
1918	2	–	–	–	–	–	2	1936	4	–	–	–	–	–	4
1919	4	1	–	–	–	–	5	1937	2	1	2	–	–	–	5
1920	1	3	–	–	–	–	4	1938	2	–	–	–	–	–	2
1921	1	3	–	–	2	–	6	1939	–	–	–	–	–	–	–
1922	1	3	–	–	–	–	4	1940	–	–	–	–	–	–	–
1923	4	2	–	–	1	–	7	1941	–	–	2	–	–	–	2
1924	3	1	–	–	–	–	4	1942	5	–	–	–	–	–	5
1925	9	–	–	–	–	–	9	1943	12	–	1	–	–	–	13
1926	7	–	–	–	–	–	7	1944	1	–	–	–	–	–	1
1927	9	–	–	–	–	–	9	1945	1	–	–	–	–	–	1
1928	4	1	–	–	–	–	5	1948	1	–	–	–	–	–	1
								Total	113	26	8	8	4	1	160

offshore hunting to the east of the Kuril Islands as far as 170° E, as clearly shown in Chart C of Townsend (1935).

According to Kashiwabara (1891), whaling in Kyushu flourished most in the years from the beginning of Tempo (1830) to Koka and Kaei (1844–48), but catches decreased from Ansei (1854) and reached their lowest in the years around Keio (1865) and Meiji (1868). This decrease was caused by the operation of foreign whale ships in the north. In the years of Kaei and Ansei, carcasses which had been struck by harpoons of a foreign country or those which were already flensed of their blubber drifted to the Goto Islands in Kyushu. Records of foreign whalers operating in the immediate vicinity of the Japanese coast do not exist.

Japanese modern-style whaling began in 1893 when the whale boat *Saikai-maru*, built of wood, caught three whales (Akashi, 1910; Tønnessen and Johnsen, 1982). Modern whaling first operated in the waters east of Korea, west of Kyushu and off the south coast of Honshu, but gradually it shifted to Sanriku (northeast of Honshu), the south coast of Hokkaido and then around the Kuril Islands, i.e. from the winter to the summer grounds.

Kasahara (1950) gave catch statistics for all whales taken in the waters around Japan since 1911, dividing whaling grounds into 16 areas. In Table 6 the catches of right whales are shown in more simplified areas. Right whales were mostly taken in an area from the Kuril Islands to Sanriku, followed by the area south of Honshu and Shikoku. Some right whales were also taken in the waters around the Bonin Islands. These all belong to the Pacific population.

In the Okhotsk Sea the only catch was of eight right whales in 1931, apart from two animals taken in 1968 for scientific research. Off the west coast of Kyushu, only four right whales were taken. Off the coast of Korea one right whale was caught, but between 1955 and 1963, two right whales were caught near Hai Yang Island in the Yellow Sea by a Chinese whale catcher (Wang, 1978). From the above it is concluded that the Sea-of-Japan population of right whales was more heavily reduced than the Pacific population.

Between 1956–68, the Whales Research Institute was permitted to take a total of 13 right whales for scientific research. Research results were reported by Omura (1958) and Omura *et al.* (1969). One of these whales was taken at Ayukawa, Sanriku, one at Kiritappu, south coast of Hokkaido, and two at Wakkanai or in the Okhotsk Sea. Of the remainder three were taken in the Gulf of Alaska and six in the Bering Sea.

All whales taken in the Japanese fishery were fully utilised locally and no trade in whale products with other nations is known, so that these catches are independent of any derived from production figures for other nations.

ACKNOWLEDGEMENTS

I am much indebted to Drs P. B. Best (Sea Fisheries Institute, Cape Town, South Africa) and R. L. Brownell, Jr (US Fish and Wildlife Service, San Simeon, California) for their kind encouragement and help in this work. I am also indebted to Mr Dale W. Rice (National Marine Fisheries Service, Seattle, Washington) and Mr James E. Scarff (1248 8th Avenue 3, San Francisco, California) for their critical comments on an earlier draft of this manuscript.

REFERENCES

Akashi, K. 1910. *Hompo no Norway-shiki Hogeishi* [History of Norwegian-type Whaling of Japan]. Toyo Hogei Kabushikigaisha, Osaka. 280 pp. [In Japanese]

Anonymous. 1890. Hogei Tokei [Whale catch statistics]. *Dainihon Suisankai Hokoku, Tokyo* 104: 142–5 [In Japanese].

Anonymous. 1937. *Tsuro hogeishi* [Whaling History of Tsuro]. Tosataro Yamaji, Tokyo. 314 pp. [In Japanese]

Anonymous. 1980. *Genkai no Kujiratori* [Whaling in the Western Sea]. Saga-kenritsu hakubutsukan, Saga. 174 pp. [In Japanese]

Hashiura, Y. 1969. *Kumano Taijiura Hogeishi* [A History of Whaling at Taiji, Kumano]. Heibonsha, Tokyo. 662 pp. with 6 scrolls. [In Japanese]

Hattori, T. 1887–1888. *Nihon Hogei Iko* [Studies of Whaling of Japan] Dainihon Suisankai, Tokyo. I, 110 pp.; II, 210 pp. [In Japanese]

Hawley, F. 1958. *Whales and Whaling in Japan*. Miscellanea Japonica II, Vol. 1, Part 1. MCMLVIII-MCMLX, Kyoto. i–xviii + 354 pp.

Izukawa, A. 1943. *Tosa Hogeishi* [Whaling History of Tosa]. Nihon Jomin Bunka Kenkyujo, Tokyo. 638 pp. [In Japanese]

Kasahara, A. 1950. Nihon Kinkai no Hogeigyo to sono Shigen [Whaling in the Waters around Japan and Its Stock]. *Nihonsuisan Kenkyujo Hokoku* No. 4, i–xv + 103 pp. with 95 figures. [In Japanese]

Kashiwabara, C. 1891. Kyushu Geiryo no Seisui ni tsuite [On the rise and fall of whaling in Kyushu]. *Dainihon Suisankai Hokoku* 116: 759–61. [In Japanese]

Kimura, S. 1956. Kujira no Kakocho [Buddhistic records of dead whales]. Whales Res. Inst. *Geikentsushin, Tokyo* 63: 144–50 [In Japanese]

Klumov, S. K. 1962. Gladkiye (Yaponskiye) Kity Tikhovo Okeana. *Inst. Okeanol.* 58: 202–97. [In Russian]

Omura, H. 1958. North Pacific right whale. *Sci. Rep. Whales Res. Inst, Tokyo* 13: 1–52.

Omura, H. 1977. Review of the occurrence of Bryde's whale in the northwest Pacific. *Rep. int. Whal. Commn* (special issue 1): 88–91.

Omura, H., Ohsumi, S., Nemoto, T., Nasu, K. and Kasuya, T. 1969. Black right whales in the North Pacific. *Sci. Rep. Whales Res. Inst., Tokyo* 21: 1–78.

Otsuki, K. 1808. *Geishiko* [A draft of a history of the whale]. 1951 edition, Japan Whaling Association, Tokyo. 169 pp. [In Japanese].

Shibusawa, K. 1939. Tosa Muroto Ukitsugumi Hogei Shiryo [Records of the Ukitsu whaling group, Tosa Muroto]. *Attique Museum Iho*, Tokyo. 36: 1–371 [In Japanese].

Shindo, H. 1978. *Kujira no Bunkashi* (Cultural History of Whales). Aotani Shobo, Kobe. 186 pp. [In Japanese]

Tada, H. 1968. *Mishima no Kujira* [Mishima Island and whales]. Mishima to Kujira Henshukai, Toyokitamachi, Yamaguchi prefecture. 230 pp. [In Japanese]

Tada, H. 1978 *Meijiki Yamaguchiken Hogeishi no Kenkyu* [Studies of whaling history in Yamaguchi Prefecture in Meiji period]. Matsuno Shoten, Tokuyama, Yamaguchi Prefecture. 256 pp. [In Japanese]

Taiji, G. 1937. *Kumano Taijiura Hogei no Hanashi* [Story of Whaling at Taijiura, Kumano]. Kishujinsha, Osaka. 138 pp. [In Japanese]

Tokumi, K. 1957. *Choshu Hogeiko* [Studies of whaling in Yamaguchi prefecture]. Kanmon Mingeikai, Shimonoseki, Yamaguchi prefecture. 317 pp. [In Japanese]

Townsend, C. H. 1935. The distribution of certain whales as shown by logbook records of American whaleships. *Zoologica*, N.Y. 19 (1): 1–50.

Tønnessen, J. N. and Johnsen, A. O. 1982. *The History of Modern Whaling*. Hurst, for London and Australian National University Press, Canberra. 789 pp.

Wang, P. 1978. Studies on the baleen whales in the Yellow Sea. *Acta Zoologica Sinica* 24(3): 269–277. [In Chinese]

Yamada, Y. 1983. Yogiotoru Eshi. In: G. Pilleri (ed.) *Investigation on Cetacea*. Vol. XIV, Supplementum. 119 pp. Berne, Switzerland.

Yoshihara, T. 1974. Kujira Golunjo Hikae niyoru Bakumatsu no Tosa niokeru Hogei nitsuite [On whaling in Kochi prefecture in the late Edo era, known from whale tax records]. Whales Res. Inst. *Geiken Tsushin*, Tokyo. 278: 77–84. [In Japanese]

Yoshihara, T. 1976a. History of the whale fishery off Kanto district. *Tokyo Suisan Daigaku Ronshu*. 11: 145–184. [In Japanese].

Yoshihara, T. 1976b. On the whaling at Ine, Kyoto prefecture. *Tokyo Suisan Daigaku Ronshu*. 11: 145–184. [In Japanese]

Yoshihara, T. 1977. Tomb of whale. *Tokyo Suisan Daigaku Ronshu*. 12: 15-101. [In Japanese]

Appendix 1
CATCHES OF WHALES BY NET-WHALING IN KOCHI PREFECTURE

Key: G = gray; R = right; H = humpback; B = Bryde's; O = other; T = total.
Sources: a, from Yoshihara, 1974; b and c, from Anon., 1937; d, from Shibusawa, 1939.

a. Ukitsu group, 1800–1835

Year	G	R	H	B	O	T
1800	5	2	4	–	1	12
1801	0	1	5	–	2	8
1802	5	2	6	1	3	17
1803	1	4	17	–	–	22
1804	2	4	29	–	1	36
1805	0	11	17	–	–	28
1806	3	3	23	–	1	30
1807	2	5	15	–	–	22
1808	5	5	29	–	1	40
1809	4	11	11	–	–	26
1810	3	2	11	–	–	16
1811	1	7	20	–	–	28
1812	4	7	14	–	–	25
1813	6	5	10	–	–	21
1814	5	8	5	2	2	22
1815	6	3	41	–	–	50
1816	2	4	8	–	–	14
1817	4	5	13	–	–	22
1818	4	8	12	–	1	25
1819	4	3	10	–	6	23
1820	6	7	6	–	1	20
1821	4	5	9	–	5	23
1822	5	10	3	1	1	20
1823	5	7	18	–	2	31
1824	3	8	20	–	–	31
1825	3	11	27	–	–	41
1826	1	16	8	–	–	25
1827	4	10	17	–	–	31
1828	2	5	12	–	–	19
1829	4	9	15	–	–	28
1830	7	9	25	–	2	43
1831	6	10	21	–	–	37
1832	7	12	16	1	–	36
1833	6	11	10	–	–	27
1834	7	15	4	–	2	28
1835	8	14	10	–	–	32
Total	144	259	521	5	30	959
Av.	4.0	7.2	14.5	0.1	0.8	26.6
%	15.0	27.0	54.3	0.5	3.1	100

b. Tsuro group, 1849–1865

Year	G	R	H	B	O	T
1849	4	–	10	3	–	17
1850	8	4	14	4	–	30
1851	6	1	25	–	–	32
1852	5	–	11	1	–	17
1853	5	1	22	–	–	28
1854	5	1	9	5	–	20
1855	8	2	10	2	–	22
1856	5	–	7	3	–	15
1857	2	–	14	1	–	17
1858	9	–	9	3	2	23
1859	6	1	8	1	1	17
1860	5	1	21	–	2	29
1861	9	1	3	1	1	15
1862	10	–	14	2	–	26
1863	6	3	7	5	–	21
1864	7	4	18	1	–	30
1865	1	–	7	3	–	11
Total	101	19	209	35	6	370
Av.	5.9	1.1	12.3	2.1	0.4	21.8
%	27.3	5.1	56.5	9.5	1.6	100

c. Tsuro group, 1874–1896

Year	G	R	H	B	O	T
1874	9	2	4	4	2	21
1875	5	–	5	2	–	12
1876	4	1	6	2	4	17
1877	5	3	6	–	2	16
1878	5	–	14	1	1	21
1879	7	–	5	2	–	14
1880	9	2	13	3	1	28
1881	4	2	–	1	3	10
1882	8	7	9	4	–	28
1883	3	–	1	3	3	10
1884	9	–	10	3	2	24
1885	2	1	2	1	1	7
1886	2	1	11	7	1	22
1887	3	1	5	2	5	16
1888	5	1	8	4	3	21
1889	1	–	2	–	3	6
1890	1	–	7	2	2	12
1891	2	2	3	4	3	14
1892	3	–	3	8	2	16
1893	2	–	–	1	4	7
1894	4	–	7	2	8	21
1895	4	–	4	3	4	15
1896	2	–	9	13	2	26
Total	99	23	134	72	56	384
Av.	4.3	1.0	5.8	3.1	2.4	16.7
%	25.8	6.0	34.9	18.7	14.6	100

d. Ukitsu group, 1875–1896

Year	G	R	H	B	O	T
1875	1	1	2	4	3	11
1876	2	–	6	5	4	17
1877	11	–	19	3	–	33
1878	1	6	4	4	3	18
1879	7	3	9	2	1	22
1880	6	1	2	8	6	23
1881	5	2	10	5	1	23
1882	3	–	4	2	3	12
1883	3	1	7	3	–	14
1884	1	2	1	2	6	12
1885	3	2	5	4	5	19
1886	1	–	6	3	10	20
1887	4	–	13	4	5	26
1888	1	–	6	4	4	15
1889	2	–	4	7	2	15
1890	1	–	–	4	3	8
1891	1	–	9	–	5	15
1892	1	1	1	3	2	8
1893	4	1	3	1	4	13
1894	1	1	3	4	1	10
1895	3	–	6	5	3	17
1896	2	–	6	4	7	19
Total	64	21	126	81	78	370
Av.	2.9	1.0	5.7	3.7	3.5	16.8
%	17.3	5.7	34.0	21.9	21.1	100

Appendix 2
CATCHES OF WHALES BY NET-WHALING AT KAWAJIRI, YAMAGUCHI PREFECTURE

Years	Gray	Right	Humpback	Fin	Others	Total	Years	Gray	Right	Humpback	Fin	Others	Total
a. 1699–1888 (Anonymous, 1890)													
1699–1708	11	29	94	2	7	143	1819–1828	8	19	55	–	37	119
1709–1718	17	17	103	14	9	160	1829–1838	10	29	27	–	72	138
1719–1728	21	29	103	3	9	165	1839–1848	18	48	59	4	–	129
1729–1738	12	31	92	3	2	140	1849–1858	37	23	88	24	–	172
1739–1748	21	26	93	–	–	140	1859–1868	34	2	55	32	7	130
1749–1758	13	20	48	–	–	81	1869–1878	44	4	34	65	–	147
1759–1768	15	14	58	–	1	88	1879–1888	19	3	49	130	–	201
Total	110	166	591	22	28	917	Total	170	128	367	255	116	1,036
Average	1.6	2.4	8.4	0.3	0.4	13.1	Average	2.4	1.8	5.2	3.6	1.7	14.8
%	12.0	18.1	64.4	2.4	3.1	100	%	16.4	12.4	35.4	24.6	11.2	100
1769–1778	species not recorded for the years 1769–1818					140	**b. 1894–1901 (Tada, 1978)**						
1779–1788						136	1894	0	0	3	10	1	14
1789–1798						117	1895	0	0	0	4	1	5
1799–1808						84	1896	4	0	1	7	1	13
1809–1818						105	1897	0	0	4	9	2	15
Total						582	1898	1	0	4	10	1	16
Average						11.6	1899	0	0	2	8	0	10
							1900	2	0	1	4	1	8
							1901	0	0	13	3	2	18
							Total	7	0	28	55	9	99
							Average	0.9	0	3.5	6.9	1.1	12.4
							%	7.0	0	28.3	55.6	9.1	100

Historic and Present Distribution of the Right Whale (*Eubalaena glacialis*) in the Eastern North Pacific South of 50° N and East of 180° W

JAMES E. SCARFF

1248 8th Avenue 3, San Francisco, California 94122, USA

ABSTRACT

This paper is a review and analysis of all records of right whales (*Eubalaena glacialis*) in the North Pacific south of 50° N and east of 180° W. The location and season of 786 records from Maury's (1852 *et seq.*) chart of sightings by early 19th-century whaling ships are described. The sightings and catch of right whales by both the shore-based and pelagic whalers during the 19th and 20th centuries are reviewed along with the available information on whaling effort. Between 1855 and 1900 there were 14 sightings of at least 19 whales along the California coast. Between 1900 and 1982 there are 9 reliable records from the coast of California, 1 from Baja California, 5 from the coast of Washington, 1 from Hawaii, and 12 from mid-ocean. Between 1910 and 1930 a minimum of 123 right whales was taken in the North Pacific. Between 1931 and 1982, another 101 right whales were killed. The searching effort for whales in the study area is described for the period 1950–82 and the records analyzed in the context of that searching effort. There are no published records which indicate any calving grounds historically or presently for right whales in the eastern North Pacific. It is hypothesized that right whales that summer in the eastern North Pacific mate, calve, and overwinter in the mid-Pacific or in the western North Pacific. Ecological factors which might be affecting population recovery are reviewed. The data in this study suggest that the population in the eastern North Pacific is still very small. There is no evidence of population recovery.

INTRODUCTION

The winter distribution of the right whale (*Eubalaena glacialis*) in the eastern North Pacific has been a subject of much speculation and controversy for more than a century (Van Beneden, 1868; Gray, 1868). Scammon (1874, p. 67) wrote: 'It has ever been a matter of mysterious conjecture with the most philosophical whalemen, where the northern Right Whales go to bring forth their young, and whither they migrate during the winter months'.

Historically, there were major concentrations of right whales in the Gulf of Alaska (50–58° N, 140–152° W) at least during the summer months. This area, known to the 19th-century whalers as 'the Northwest Coast' or the 'Kodiak Ground', became a major focus of the pelagic whaling industry for a brief period during the middle of the 19th century. It is from these early whaling records that most of our knowledge about the distribution of right whales in the eastern North Pacific derives (Maury, 1851; 1852 *et seq.*; Townsend, 1935).

In other regions there are conspicuous local winter populations of right whales in inshore waters. These local populations have been described off Argentina (Payne, 1972; 1976; 1983; Payne, Brazier, Dorsey, Perkins, Rowntree and Titus, 1981), off Chile (Townsend, 1935), off South Africa (Best, 1981), off central Africa (Townsend, 1935), in the western North Pacific (Townsend, 1935; Omura, Ohsumi, Nemoto, Nasu, and Kasuya, 1969), off Australia (Townsend, 1935; Bannister, 1986) and off New Zealand (Townsend, 1935; Cawthorn, 1983). In the western North Atlantic a similar pattern of nearshore wintering concentrations is not as evident (Reeves, Mead and Katona, 1978; Mead, 1986). Instead, inshore summer populations appear to have occurred historically in the Cape Cod area and presently in the Bay of Fundy (Reeves, Kraus and Turnbull, 1983; Kraus, Prescott, Turnbull and Reeves, 1982).

There is little recent data on the winter distribution of

right whales in the eastern North Pacific. What data exist do not show a clear pattern of inshore concentrations of right whales in winter along the western coast of North America. The question remains: where do the whales that summer in the Gulf of Alaska go in winter? The most prevalent hypothesis is well expressed by Berzin and Rovnin (1966, p. 128) who state that although 'virtually nothing is known about the migration paths of the right whale in the Northeastern Pacific, in the opinion of the majority of the researchers, the whales from the American population migrate south along the western coast of North America'. Similar comments appear in Gilmore (1956; 1978) and Banfield (1974). A recent review of the species concludes that 'The normal winter range was from Washington State south to northern California, with stragglers occasionally reaching southern California and northern Baja' (Reeves and Brownell, 1982, p. 416).

The present population of right whales in the eastern North Pacific is so small that the species is rarely sighted. The few recent records make generalizations about current migration patterns particularly speculative. The most numerous records of right whales in the eastern North Pacific remain those of the 19th-century whalers. These records, particularly those contained in Maury's map no. 1 (1852 *et seq.*) represent a previously lightly tapped source of information about the species (Best, 1981). This paper examines the 19th-century whaling records from pelagic and coastal whaling operations as well as all recent catch and sighting records of right whales in the eastern North Pacific south of 50° N and east of 180° W.

Rather than representing a real biological barrier, the 50° N limit of the study area is a convenient boundary widely used historically (Maury, 1851, 1852 *et seq.*; Scammon, 1874; Townsend, 1935). There has been little whaling or searching effort north of 50° N in winter. The summer records of right whales north of 50° N are so numerous, at least in the 19th-century data, that inclusion of that data in this analysis would be more burdensome than helpful given resource and time constraints. The 180° W western boundary of the study area is a convenient arbitrary line chosen simply to divide the North Pacific into eastern and western sections.

ABORIGINAL WHALING

Native Americans killed whales in the eastern North Pacific for many years prior to the coming of the Yankee whalers in the mid-19th century. Although the geographic regions in which such whaling occurred are fairly well known, the number of whales taken, particularly right whales, is not. Mitchell (1979) reviews the literature on aboriginal takes of gray whales (*Eschrichtius robustus*) and concludes that the total number of gray whales removed annually from the population was probably substantially more than the 225 estimated by Ohsumi (1976), although a note of caution in accepting Mitchell's estimate is given by O'Leary (1984).

The three main areas of aboriginal whaling in the eastern North Pacific were (1) the west and northwest coasts of Alaska, (2) the Aleutian Islands and the Alaska peninsula, and (3) the coasts of Vancouver Island and Washington (Mitchell, 1979). The Eskimos (Inuit) of the Bering Sea coast of Alaska have been whalers for centuries. However, they live at the edge of the right whale's range and beyond (Maury, 1852 *et seq.*; Townsend, 1935). In historical times the primary targets of their hunt have been bowhead whales (*Balaena mysticetus*) and gray whales. The extent of their catch of right whales is unknown, but probably small.

The Aleuts of the Aleutian Islands and the Alaska peninsula hunted whales with hand-thrown spears tipped with the poison aconitum. Mitchell (1979, p. 309) points out that the distribution of these whalers

> matches precisely the shorewards summer distributions of the east and west North Pacific stocks of the right whale…and straddles the distribution of the gray whale…The right whale probably was taken, although other species were clearly involved.

He also notes that the loss rate of struck animals may have been as high as 90–95%.

The native Americans of the Nootka, Makah, Quilleute, and Quinault tribes inhabiting Vancouver Island and the coast of Washington were highly skilled whalers. Their main quarry was the gray whale; however, they did take some right whales.

Swan (1870) visited the Nootka in 1855, only 10 years after the peak of pelagic right whaling in the eastern North Pacific, and again in 1861. He reports that the gray whale was the species usually taken, although not the only species hunted. He notes that the natives had a word for the right whale: *yakh'-yo-bad-di*. Regarding this species, his only comment is

> there are several varieties [of whale] which are taken at different seasons of the year. Some are killed by the Indians; others, including the right whale, drift ashore, having been killed either by [white?] whalemen, swordfish, or other casualties. (Swan, 1870, p. 49).

Drucker (1951) also recorded whaling by the Nootka. He notes that the primary whales taken were gray whales and humpbacks (*Megaptera novaeangliae*), but that the whalers recognised another whale, the *quotsxi* which was like the gray whale, but larger 'with something growing on the back of its head' (Drucker, 1951, p. 49). This appears to refer to the callosities on the rostrum of the right whale.

Archaeological research of prehistoric aboriginal whaling cultures along the northwest coast of North America reveals clues as to the distribution of right whales prior to the arrival of European and Yankee pelagic whalers in the mid-19th century. Researchers from Washington State University, excavating at the Ozette site, 14 miles south of Cape Flattery, Washington, have uncovered substantial evidence of aboriginal whaling during a continuous period of approximately 1,500 years. Gray and humpback whale bones appear most frequently among the whale bones. However, recent digs have revealed 20 right whale bones from a minimum of 11 individual whales. Right whale bones constitute only 2.3% of the total number of identified bones. The identifications were made primarily from scapulas and judging from the size of these, there was one small whale, 3 medium-sized whales, 3 large whales, and 3 very large whales (D. Huelsbeck, Univ. Santa Clara, pers. comm.).

Although the historical record is very sparse, it appears that aboriginal whaling for right whales involved much smaller takes than 19th-century commercial whaling. As the right whale population declined, so did the aboriginal take of this species in the eastern North Pacific.

PELAGIC WHALING 1835–1900

The first whaling ships rounded Cape Horn and began whaling in the South Pacific in 1789. Within a couple of years more than 40 whalers were operating in the South Pacific (Whipple, 1979). By 1800, some whalers had ventured as far north as Baja California. In 1818, whalers first landed at Hawaii. Two years later they found the productive grounds for sperm whales (*Physeter macrocephalus*) off Japan and were exploring other areas of the North Pacific. By 1823, over 60 whaling ships were hunting off Japan (Stackpole, 1953).

By the early 1820s, both English and American whaling ships were stopping at the then Mexican ports of San Francisco and Monterey to obtain fresh supplies. These visits to the California coast usually occurred during the whalers' return from the Japan grounds. After leaving California, the whalers usually headed to the equatorial sperm whaling grounds then back to New England via Cape Horn (Huff, 1957). The coast of California was not yet a primary hunting ground.

In 1835, a French whaler discovered the 'Northwest Coast' ground in the Gulf of Alaska (50–61° N, 140–152° W). At approximately the same time the whalers discovered the right whale grounds off Kamchatka (Stackpole, 1953; R. C. Kugler, pers. comm.). Previously the whalers in the North Pacific had focused their efforts on the more tropical sperm whales. Having found a major concentration of summering right whales, many whalers made the right whale their primary summer target (Stackpole, 1953). The relative scarcity of sperm whales on these northern grounds and the danger and difficulty of catching the large male sperm whales further concentrated the whalers' attention on right whales (Maury, 1851, 1852 *et seq.*; Townsend, 1935; R. C. Kugler, pers. comm.).

The speed with which the whaling fleet responded to the discovery of these two northern grounds is remarkable. According to Starbuck (1878, p. 104), the number of American whaling ships operating north of 50° N in the Pacific increased from 2 in 1839 to 108 in 1843 and 292 in 1846. More than 150 American whaling ships hunted in the North Pacific north of 50° nearly every year between 1844 and the outbreak of the American civil war in 1861. To the above numbers must be added the large number of French, British, German and Hawaiian ships also hunting right whales on these grounds (R. Kugler, pers. comm.). Table 3 shows the distribution by 5-year intervals of the right whale catch in the entire North Pacific reported by Townsend (1935) and estimated by DuPasquier (1986). In each case, over half of this catch was made between 1845 and 1849. This pattern appears to be real rather than an artifact of the logbooks selected (R. C. Kugler, pers. comm.).

In their tabular descriptions of the right whales landed per voyage, neither Townsend (1935) nor DuPasquier (1986) distinguish between whales caught in the eastern and western North Pacific. Thus, it is not possible from these sources to determine the catch per decade for each whaling ground.

The minimum total number of right whales processed by 19th century pelagic whalers operating in the North Pacific has been estimated by DuPasquier (1986) as 15,244 (see Table 3). Considering the animals struck with a harpoon which were not processed, the total removals from the North Pacific population(s) were approximately 19,207 (1.26 × 15,244) (see DuPasquier, 1986). Berzin and Doroshenko (1981) state that from 1850 to 1873 American whalers 'took more than 20,000 right whales'. It is unclear from the context whether this refers to the catch in the North Pacific or worldwide, and no source for this number is given.

American whalers in the early and mid-1800s played a major role in the charting of the lands, winds and currents of the Pacific (Stackpole, 1953). One of the earliest oceanographers, Matthew Fontaine Maury, sought to use the wealth of information being gathered by 19th-century American whalers to map the oceans. In exchange for use of their logbooks, Maury promised the whalers information which would help them locate the best whaling grounds.

The results of this collaboration were numerous charts by Maury published at various times under the general title 'Wind and Current Charts'. Included among these are several charts which map the distribution of right and sperm whales. The first of these 'Whale Charts', entitled 'Preliminary Sketch, Series F' (Maury, 1851), is a map of the world showing the distribution of these two species by 5° of latitude and longitude in the Southern Hemisphere and North Pacific. The occurrence of right and sperm whales in each quadrant as well as the species' relative abundance are depicted by pictorial symbols of the species and seasonal notes. A portion of this map has been reproduced as Fig. 1. The entire map has been republished at a much reduced scale as the endpapers in Starbuck (1878) and also in Whipple (1979, pp. 70–1).

The other, lesser-known charts are part of a set entitled series F, nos. 1, 2, 3 and 4 (Maury, 1852 et seq.). These also show the distribution of right and sperm whales in the same oceans, but with far more detail than in the more widely known Preliminary Sketch. Done on a larger scale, the maps show for each 5° of latitude and longitude by month both the number of days on which right whales were seen and the number of days whaling ships spent in that quadrant. The data are displayed in histograms in each quadrant. Map no. 1 covers the North Pacific east of 180° W and north of 20° N. A portion of this map is reproduced at actual size in Fig. 2.

The information in all these charts is derived from the logbooks of about 1,000 whaling voyages as explained more fully in Kugler (1981) and Bannister and Mitchell (1980) and the references listed therein. The latter article

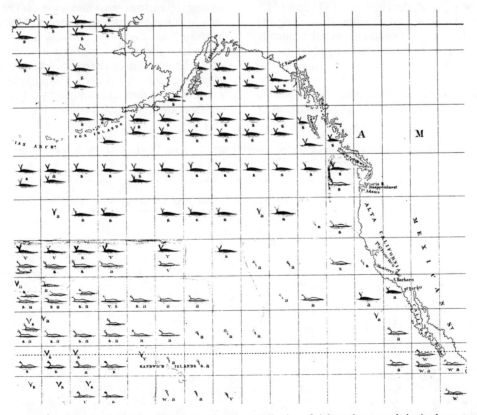

Fig. 1. Part of the Maury (1851) Series F, Preliminary Sketch showing the distribution of right and sperm whales in the eastern and central North Pacific. Dark whales with v-shaped spouts are right whales; v-shaped spouts alone are "straggling" right whales; light whales with single spouts are sperm whales; and single spouts alone are "straggling" sperm whales.

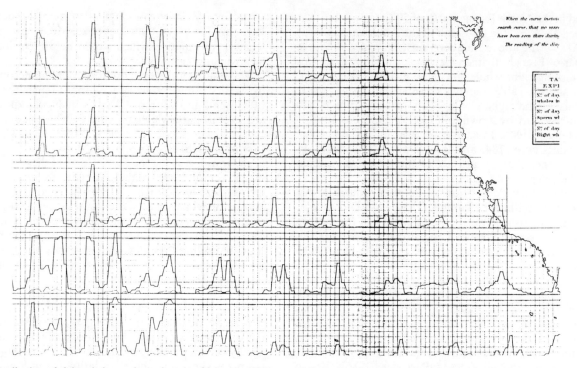

Fig. 2. Distribution of right whales as shown in part of Maury's (1852 *et seq.*) Series F, Map No. 1. The top line of each histogram shows the number of days whaling ships were in that sector by month. The second line (usually) represents the number of days by month right whales were seen in the sector. The third line (usually) represents the number of days by month sperm whales were seen in the sector.

includes extensive bibliographic information about both sets of charts, important because of the rarity of the later Maury (1852 *et seq.*) charts.

Several general comments can be made regarding the information on both sets of these charts. Most of the right whale sightings in the eastern North Pacific were made during summer on the Kodiak ground, the principal ground used by the right whalers between 1835 and 1852. These charts show that the small whaling effort along the west coast of California and Oregon occurred primarily in the fall. There was very little effort anywhere in the eastern North Pacific during the winter months of January–March.

Map no. 1 contains records in the eastern North Pacific south of 50° N of approximately 786 days on which right

whales were reported seen. (The number of days on which the species was seen and number of searching days were determined only approximately because of the difficulty of reading the small scale histograms with precision.) The distribution of these sightings by latitude and longitude is shown in Table 1. This table must be interpreted with great caution because of the variability of searching effort among the various areas and seasons. The number of days on which right whales were seen and the searching effort by month are presented in Table 2.

Because map no. 1 contains both sighting and effort data it is possible to derive indices of abundance which may be used to test different hypotheses regarding right whale distribution and migration patterns. However, the highly nonrandom nature of the searching effort, the very

Table 1.

Number of days on which right whales were seen in the eastern North Pacific between 20–50° N by season for 5° squares (from Map No. 1, Maury 1852 *et seq.*)

		175–180	170–175	165–170	160–165	155–160	150–155	145–150	140–145	135–140	130–135	125–130	Total	Grand total
45–50 N	Jan–Mar	9	–	–	–	3	–	–	–	–	–	–	12	
	Apr–June	27	7	13	65	27	43	34	9	–	–	–	225	
	July–Sept	4	2	–	9	16	18	38	25	13	7	3	134	371
40–45 N	Jan–Mar	–	–	–	–	2	–	–	–	–	–	–	2	
	Apr–June	5	3	11	22	17	5	8	–	–	–	–	71	
	July–Sept	21	5	5	–	–	9	5	13	2	–	–	60	
	Oct–Dec	5	3	–	–	–	–	–	–	–	–	–	8	141
35–40 N	Jan–Mar	2	–	–	–	–	8	–	–	–	–	–	10	
	Apr–June	8	12	12	3	34	21	–	–	2	–	–	92	
	July–Sept	17	4	–	–	–	–	–	–	3	–	–	24	
	Oct–Dec	14	8	3	–	–	–	–	–	–	–	–	25	151
30–35 N	Jan–Mar	4	–	3	–	–	4	–	–	–	–	–	11	
	Apr–June	10	5	19	2	3	–	4	–	–	–	–	43	
	July–Sept	13	–	–	–	–	–	–	–	–	–	–	13	
	Oct–Dec	2	–	–	–	–	3	8	4	–	–	–	17	84
25–30 N	Jan–Mar	3	–	–	–	–	–	–	–	–	–	–	3	
	Apr–June	5	–	–	–	6	–	–	–	–	–	–	11	
	July–Sept	5	–	–	–	–	–	–	–	–	–	–	5	
	Oct–Dec	4	–	–	–	–	–	–	–	–	–	–	4	23
20–25 N	Jan–Mar	5	6	–	4	–	–	–	–	–	–	–	15	15

Table 2.

Number of days right whales seen and total number of searching days by pelagic whalers in the eastern North Pacific between 20–50° N prior to 1852 (from Map No. 1: Maury 1852 et seq.)

Month	No. of days right whales seen	Searching days	
		35–50 N	20–50 N
January	0	3	198
February	3	26	278
March	35	126	802
April	119	520	1,939
May	212	952	2,051
June	126	457	1,276
July	81	407	1,148
August	95	722	1,726
September	61	744	2,471
October	44	256	2,443
November	5	76	1,538
December	5	34	671
Total	786	4,323	16,541

Table 3.

Approximate numbers of right whales removed from North Pacific populations by pelagic whalers by five year periods as reported in Townsend (1935) and DuPasquier (1986). L (no. of whales landed) represents the number secured and processed; it has not been adjusted to include whales struck but lost. The figures for Townsend (L_t) are crude estimates of the whales taken per interval. He reported catches by voyage which in some cases lasted for four or five years. Catches from multi-year voyages were allocated to five year intervals in a fairly arbitrary manner.

Period	L	Du Pasquier			Period	L	Du Pasquier		
		L	%	Cumm. %			L	%	Cumm. %
1754–39	0	0	0.0	0.0	1875–79	9	85	0.6	98.1
1840–44	407	985	19.6	19.6	1880–84	5	5	0.03	98.1
1845–49	1,057	8,044	52.8	72.4	1885–89	29	228	1.5	99.6
1850–54	144	1,370	9.0	81.4	1890–94	5	23	0.16	99.7
1855–59	264	1,369	9.0	90.4	1895–99	8	24	0.16	99.8
1860–64	58	585	3.8	94.2	1900–04	5	24	0.16	99.9+
1865–69	107	439	2.9	97.1	1905–20	1	3	0.02	100.0
1870–74	19	60	0.4	97.5	Total	2,118	15,244		100.0

small sample sizes in many quadrants, and the variability in the sightability of whales due to environmental factors associated with season and latitude may prevent the statistical testing of some, or all, of these hypotheses. A statistical analysis of these data is planned and will be presented in a later paper.

It should be noted that the information in the Preliminary Sketch (Maury, 1851) and map no. 1 (Maury, 1852 et seq.) are not in complete agreement. For example, the preliminary sketch (Fig. 1) shows right whales occurring in the autumn off the coast of southern California near San Diego (20–35° N, 125–135° W) with 'stragglers' occurring off Baja California (25–30° N, 130–135° W). Map no. 1 shows no right whale ever being reported in these waters.

In 1848, a few years before Maury published his series of whale charts, Yankee whaling ships ventured through the Bering Straits and discovered concentrations of bowhead whales. The latter, being larger and yielding much greater quantities of both whale oil and baleen than the right whales, rapidly became the prime quarry of at least the more daring whalers (Bockstoce, 1977). However, right whales in the Eastern North Pacific continued to be taken in small numbers until the early part of the 20th century (see Table 3) (R. Kugler, pers. comm.).

Pelagic whaling in the North Pacific is also described by Townsend (1935). Townsend's assistants reviewed over 1,600 log-books of whaling ships. On 249 of these voyages between 1839 and 1906, 2,118 right whales were reported caught in the North Pacific, at most, one-seventh of the total catch during this period (DuPasquier, 1986).

Townsend (1935) plotted much of this data on a series of famous maps showing the geographic location of most of the right whales caught as recorded in the logbooks. Chart C includes the locations of many of the 2,118 right whales caught in the North Pacific. The records are plotted by month, each month represented by a different colored circle. The actual densities of the whale catches cannot be determined because some dots represent more than one whale killed.

Chart C shows that approximately half the right whales recorded were caught east of 180° W. Of these, approximately 68 records are from locations south of 50° N. The precise number of records south of 50° N cannot be readily determined because of the large number of records from the area immediately around this

latitude. Fifty-four of the records east of 180° W are from between 45 and 50° N. None of the records is from locations south of 35° N. In contrast, the chart shows hundreds of records of right whales in the western North Pacific south of 50° N and perhaps 100 records south of 40° N in the Sea of Japan. Fifty-four of the 68 records east of 180° W and south of 50° N are from the area between 145–160° W. The monthly distribution of these records is shown in Table 9.

Townsend's chart shows only one record of a right whale taken in winter east of 180° W. It shows no records in this area during the months of November, January, February and March, and only one apparent record for December. As in the case of Maury's charts, the scarcity of winter records in Townsend's chart probably reflects the greatly reduced whaling effort during this season. However, it should be noted that Townsend's Chart B shows that about 80 sperm whales were taken around the main Hawaiian Islands, around Midway Island, and northeast of the Hawaiian Islands during the months of October–March. No right whales are recorded from these same areas on Chart C.

Several additional comments should be made regarding Townsend's chart. First, there is almost certainly some overlap in the logbooks consulted by Maury (1852 et seq.) and Townsend (1935), but the extent of the overlap is not known. Thus, there is some overlap in the data presented in Table 9. Second, there appears on the Townsend chart to be a discrete summer population of right whales in the Gulf of Alaska and another two in the west Pacific on both sides of the Kamchatka peninsula. There are few whales reported between 175° W and 170° E, although this may simply be an artifact of biased searching effort. Third, the southern-most records of right whales in the western North Pacific are 7 records off Taiwan (25° N) and 20 off China (ca 30° N) during February and March. Fourth, the chart shows extensive latitudinal dispersion of right whales in the eastern North Pacific, particularly during spring and fall. For example, Townsend shows right whales in both May and October being recorded from 38° N to 62° N. Because of the nonrandom nature of the searching effort and the possible misidentification of bowhead whales as right whales, too much emphasis should not be placed on the above patterns.

As early as the 1870s, commentators were noting the

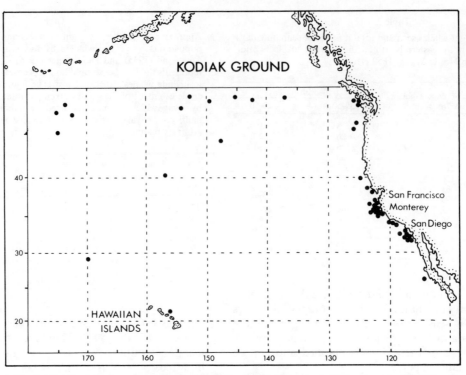

Fig. 3. Distribution of previously unmapped right whale landings and sightings south of 50° N and east of 180° W (from Table 4, this study).

relative rarity of right whales off the west coast of North America. Scammon (1874, p. 66) suggested that their contemporary scarcity may have been the result of heavy catches made by the early whalers: 'In former years, the Right Whales were found on the coast of Oregon, and occasionally in large numbers...' Scammon's comment appears to be the basis for a similar comment by Starks (1922 p. 35). It is unclear how much weight should be afforded Scammon's comment about the species' former abundance off the coast of Oregon. Scammon is usually a highly reliable source, but his statement conflicts with the paucity of catch records from the coasts of Oregon, Washington, and California. Considering the very small amount of whaling effort made along the coasts of Oregon and Washington during the mid-19th century and Scammon's lack of personal involvement in this whaling, his comment may simply be the repetition of unreliable reports of other whalers. Researchers operating further south along the California coast in the 1880s reported no direct evidence that right whales had recently been more common off that coast (Townsend, 1886; Jordan, 1887; Collins, 1892).

SHORE WHALING 1854–1900

Commercial whaling from shore-based stations began along the west coast of North America soon after the influx of settlers, including whalers, to California during the gold rush of 1849. During this early period of shore whaling, the whales were generally spotted by lookouts stationed on cliffs or other shore-based observation platforms. Thus the whales detected were those within 10–15 km of shore. Once whales were spotted, the whalers rowed or sailed out to the whales in traditional whaleboats and killed the animals with hand-thrown harpoons, or in later years small darting guns or cannon-fired harpoons, in the same manner as the contemporary pelagic whalers. The whales were hauled back to shore to be flensed.

The shore whaling operations are described at various times during this period in Scammon (1874), Townsend (1886), Jordan (1887), Collins (1892), Starks (1922), and Sayers (1984). Information regarding period of operation and seasons of individual stations and catch records is fragmentary. The best summary is contained in Sayers (1984).

Whaling from shore occurred at 17 different locations from Crescent City, California (42° N) to Punta Eugenia, Baja California, Mexico (28° N) (Fig. 3). Most stations were active for less than a decade; only four operated for more than 25 years.

The main target of the southern shore stations, at least during the early years, was the gray whale which occurs off California during the months of December through April (Rice, 1963b). The northern stations, and later the southern stations, devoted much of their effort to hunting humpback whales which were taken during the months of March through October (Rice, 1963b).

During the period 1854–1900 there are records of only 10 right whales being landed by these shore stations. There are records of additional sightings involving 13 animals. One record warrants a comment. The San Diego Union for 2 March 1871 reports that on about 17 February of that year 'a right whale appeared within a quarter of a mile of [the whaling] camp [at Punta Banda, California]; immediately all the boats were set in motion and chase given; the whale received two harpoons, but got away'. The article goes on immediately to report that two days later a large 'cow whale', one of the largest of the season, was caught which 'will fill from 50 to 60 barrels' and would have yielded 10 barrels more if it had been captured near the better tryworks at Point Loma. This oil yield would be very large for a gray whale, but small for an adult right whale. Humpback whales are

Table 4.

Records of right whales in the eastern North Pacific south of 50° N and east of 180° W, 1855–1982. NMFS POP = US National Marine Fisheries Platforms of Opportunity Program. *Group size unknown.

Year	Date	No. whales	Location	Comments	References
1855	Mar	2	36°30'N 122°0'W, nr Monterey, Ca	Seen in harbor	Anon. (1855)
1856	Mar 22	1*	" "	Landed	Anon. (1856)
1859	?	1*	" "	Landed	Starks (1922)
1861	Mar	1*	33°40'N 118°20'W, nr San Pedro, Ca	Landed	Anon. (1861)
1866	Feb	1*	32°30'N 117°20'W, nr San Diego, Ca	Landed	Davis (1929)
1871	Feb 17	1	32°40'N 117°20'W, Punta Banda, Ca	Seen, 0.25 mi. from shore	Anon. (1871)
1873	?	1*	36°30'N 122°0'W, nr Monterey, Ca	Landed, male 21.5m, 175bbls oil, 682kg baleen	Starks (1922); Watkins (1925, p.221)
'78/9	Winter	1*	36°20'N 121°55'W, Pt Sur, Ca	Landed	Jordan (1887)
'79/80	Sep–Apr	1*	36°30'N 122°0'W nr Monterey, Ca	Landed	Jordan (1887)
'79/80	Oct–Mar	3*	36° 'N 122° 'W, nr. Carmel, Ca	Seen by whalers	Jordan (1877)
'84/5	?	1*	34°30'N 120°30'W, Cojo Viejo, Ca	Landed	Townsend (1886); Starks (1922)
'84/5	?	1*	32°30'N 117°20'W, nr San Diego, Ca	Landed	Townsend (1886)
'84/5	Dec–Apr	3*	35°40'N 121°20'W, nr San Simeon, Ca	Landed	Townsend (1886)
1886	Mar 8	1*	32°30'N 117°20'W, nr San Diego, Ca.	Landed, 150 bbls oil	Anon. (1886)
1916	?	1*	34°0'N 119°40'W, Santa Cruz I., Ca.	Stranding, 1 baleen plate only	Woodhouse & Strickley (1982)
1924	Apr 19	1*	38°N 123°W, nr Farallon Is, Ca.	Landed, 12m female, empty stomach	Gilmore (1956); Szczepaniak (pers. comm.)
'41–'68	Jun	3+*	45–50°N 170–175°W	3 sightings by catcher boats	Omura et al. (1969)
1955	Jan 14	(4)	32 50'N 117 30'W, La Jolla, Ca.	Possible sighting	Gilmore (1956)
1955	Mar 31	1	" "	Length = 13m, very close to shore	Gilmore (1956)
'55–'58	Jun	4	40–50°N 170–180°W	Opportunistic sighting by Dutch vessels	Slijper et al. (1964)
1959	Apr 8	3	45°55'N 125°25'W, 80mi W Tillamook Hd, Wa	Seen during fur seal research cruise	Fiscus & Niggol (1965)
1959	Apr 10	3	46°54'N 124°56'W, 33mi W Tillamook Hd, Wa	Seen during fur seal research cruise	Fiscus & Niggol (1965)
1959	Apr 19	(8)	47°35'N 124°46'W, 13mi SW Destruction I, Wa	See text	Fiscus & Niggol (1965)
1959	Apr 19	(8)	47°37'N 124°42'W, 9mi SW Destruction I, Wa	See text	Fiscus & Niggol (1965)
1959	May 13–5	1	37°25'N 122°48'W, 16mi SW Pt Montara, Ca	Seen, length = 13m, depth = 100–110m	Rice & Fiscus (1968)
1963	Apr 11	1	37°08'N 123°05'W, 61mi SW Pigeon Pt, Ca	Seen, length = <9m, depth = 730–910m	Rice & Fiscus (1968)
1963	May 10	1	37°20'N 123°10'W, 44km SSW Farallon I, Ca	Seen by catcher, length =14m, depth = 1100m	Rice & Fiscus (1968)
1964	Jan.	(1)	40°N 157°W	No details	Berzin & Doroshenko (1982)
1965	Mar 11	2	26°39'N 113°40'W, 12km SW Punta Abreojos, Baja California	Seen, length = 15m, depth = 54m, photos	Rice & Fiscus (1968)
1965	Summer?	1	45–50°N 170–180°W	Japanese sighting cruise	Wada (1975)
1967	Jan 17	3	48°20'N 125 06'W, 28km WSW C Flattery, Wa	2 large, 1 small, depth = 110m, heading N	Rice & Fiscus (1968)
1969	Summer?	1	45–50°N 170–180 W	Japanese sighting cruise	Wada (1975)
1973	Mar 20	(6+1)	48°29'N 124 57'W, nr C Flattery, Wa	Made by NMFS employee	NMFS POP
1973	Summer?	1	45–50°N 140–150 W	Japanese sighting cruise	Wada (1975)
1974	Summer?	1	40–50°N 140–160 W	Japanese catcherboat sighting	Anon. (1976)
1974	Sep 13	1	39°35'N 124 45'W, 60km W Ft Bragg, Ca	Seen from NOAA ship Fairweather	NMFS POP
1975	?	(1)	22° 158°W, N Oahu, Hawaii	Possible sighting	DeBus (1975)
1976	Summer?	1	45–50°N 150–155°W	Japanese sighting cruise	Wada (1978)
1977	Summer?	1	45–50°N 150–155°W	Japanese sighting cruise	Wada (1979)
		1	45–50°N 140–145°W		
		2*	45–50°N 135–140°W		
1977	Summer?	2*	20–30°N 160–180°W	Japanese catcherboat sighting	Anon. (1979)
1979	Mar 25	1	20°40'N 156°53'W, between Maui and Kahoolawe, Hawaii	Length = 15–16m, schooling with humpback whales, depth = 145–160m	Rowntree et al. (1980) Herman et al. (1980)
1979	Apr 10	1	21°03'N 157°30'W, SW Molokai, Hawaii	Same animal as on Mar 25, depth = 55m	Herman et al. (1980)
1979	Summer	1	40–45°N 145–150°W	Japanese sighting cruise	Wada (1981)
1981	Apr 17	1	34°07'N 119°18'W, nr Santa Barbara, Ca	Length = 14m	Woodhouse & Strickley (1982)
1982	Mar 20	1	37°30'N 122°30'W, nr Half Moon Bay, Ca	Length = 15m	Johnson (1982)

usually not found off the California coast during February. Because there is no mention in the article of the captured whale being the animal struck two days earlier or of the captured whale being a right whale, I have treated the record as a right whale sighting only, not as a capture.

All the known catches and three of the sightings are described in all known detail in Table 4. The other sightings are reported in Starks (1922, p. 35) who writes that the captain of the San Simeon whaling station reported seeing only 9 right whales in his 17 years at the station. Three of these nine are presumably the whales in the winter of 1884–85 reported in Townsend (1886).

The few records of right whales contrast with far larger numbers of gray whales reported in the catch. For only a few years are the catch records detailed and comprehensive enough to allow a fair comparison. Jordan (1887) reports only one right whale landed and three sighted during 1878–80 in contrast to 57 gray whales landed during the same period. Townsend (1886) reports 5 right whales landed during 1884 and 1885 in contrast

to 121 gray whales landed during the 1884–5 and 1885–86 seasons.

The ratio of right to gray whales in the catch reported by Townsend (1886) and Jordan (1887) may not be an appropriate ratio for use in trying to estimate the total right whale catch from shore stations during this period. By 1878, gray whales were becoming much rarer than they had been twenty years earlier (Townsend, 1886). It is probable that the right whales are relatively over-represented in the catch data compared to gray whales for years in which the data are fragmentary. The rarity of the right whale during this entire period made the capture of one notable. More important is that the taking of a right whale usually represented a major windfall for the station. Right whales typically yielded an average of 130 barrels of oil (Scammon, 1874; Allen, 1916), in contrast to the gray whale which yielded only 25–30 barrels (Henderson, 1972). In addition, the amount of baleen yielded by a right whale, 1,000–1,500 pounds, was both vastly greater than that from a gray whale and also of higher quality. Starks (1922, p.12) writes that 'The right whale was the only one of the region that had whalebone of much value, and it was seldom taken. When it was, its whalebone very materially increased the income of the fortunate station that secured it'. The several newspaper reports of right whales being landed, or even just being seen, support the idea that the take of right whales was disproportionately reported compared to the take of gray whales.

If the few records of right whales landed represent a reasonably complete listing of the number of this species that was in fact taken, then the contrast with gray whales is particularly striking. Henderson (1972) estimates that during the period 1855–1865 shore stations operating along the California and Baja coasts landed 1,200 gray whales. He estimates that between 1866 and 1874 the shore stations landed 960 gray whales. This information supports the conclusion that right whales were rare along the California coast as early as the 1850s.

SHORE WHALING AND RECORDS OF RIGHT WHALES 1900–1930

Catch records for shore stations operating in the North Pacific between 1900 and 1931 are fragmentary. Records which describe the catch by species were reviewed for stations in Alaska (1912–37) (Tønnessen and Johnsen, 1982; Brueggeman, Newby and Grotefendt, in press), British Columbia and Washington (1919–30) (Kellogg, 1931; Pike and McAskie, 1969; Scheffer and Slipp, 1948), California (1919–29) (Starks, 1922; Kellogg, 1931), Mexico (1925–29) (IWS., 1933), and Japan, Korea, Kamchatka, and the Kurile Islands (1910–30) (Tønnessen and Johnsen, 1982; IWS, 1933). The catch of right whales taken during this period is presented in Table 5.

A Norwegian factory ship operated off the coast of Baja California, Mexico, between 1925 and 1929. The catch during this period was 3,043 whales, consisting of humpback, blue (*Balaenoptera musculus*), and 222 gray whales. No right whales were reported caught (Kellogg, 1931).

There is only one record of a stranding of a right whale on the west coast of North America. This is represented by a single baleen plate in the Santa Barbara, California, Museum of Natural History (SBMNH cat. no. 1570).

Table 5.

Minimum catch (N) of right whales in the N. Pacific, 1910–30. The whaling grounds are: J = Japan; K = Korea; Ka = Kamchatka; A = Alaska; BC = British Columbia; C = California. The sources (in parentheses) are: a = IWS (1933); b = Tonnesen and Johnsen (1982); c = Brueggeman *et al.* (in press); d = Omura (1986); e = Kellogg (1931); f = Gilmore (1956).

Year	N	Ground(source)	Year	N	Ground(source)
1910	0	J, K+Ka (a)	1921	6	J (b)
1911	2	J, K+Ka (a)	1922	4	J (b)
1912	3	J, K+Ka (a)	1923	9	J7 (b); A2 (c)
1913	1	J, K+Ka (a)	1924	10	BC3 (e); A1 (c);
1914	1	J, K+Ka (a)			C1 (f); J5 (d)
1915	7	J, K+Ka (a)	1925	10	A1 (c); J9 (b)
1916	9	J, K+Ka8 (a);A1 (b)	1926	10	BC1 (e); A2 (c); J7 (b)
1917	3	A1* (c);J2 (d)	1927	11	A1 (c); J10 (b)
1918	2	J, K+Ka (a)	1928	15	A6 (c); J9 (b)
1919	5	J, K+Ka (a)	1929	6	A1 (c); J5 (b)
1920	4	J, K+Ka (a)	1930	5	J (b)

* Tonnesen & Johnson (1982:734) report two right whales taken in Alaska in 1917. This may include one or two bowheads.

This plate is labeled as having been salvaged from a dead specimen on Santa Cruz Island on 14 November 1916. A mandible of a balaenid whale is also in the collection, but no information is available concerning the date or location of its collection (Woodhouse and Strickley, 1982). Although those authors state that it is from a right whale, the specific identity of the whale has not yet been determined (E. Mitchell, pers. comm.).

At California shore stations between 1919 and 1930, 3,459 whales were landed. Between 1919 and 1924, the catch was primarily made up of humpback whales taken in summer. Between 1925 and 1929 the catch consisted primarily of blue and fin whales (*Balaenoptera physalus*), species found in the area mainly during summer and early fall (Dohl, Norris, Guess and Bryant, 1981a, Dohl, Norris, Dunman and Helm, 1982). Only 9 gray whales were landed during this period which is probably a good indication of the minimal whaling effort expended in winter and early spring (Starks, 1922; Kellogg, 1931). Gilmore (1956) reports a right whale caught near the Farallon Islands in 1924 by catcher boats out of the Moss Landing, California shore station. Review of the logbook of the station which is at the California Academy of Sciences confirms that a 12.1 m female was caught on 19 April. The animal appeared in good condition. Its stomach was empty. No data were collected regarding its reproductive condition. For unknown reasons, this catch was not reported in the official catch figures (Starks, 1922; Kellogg, 1931).

Shore whaling was conducted along the coast of Washington from 1911 to 1925. Four catcher boats operated out of one shore station at Bay City at the south side of Grays Harbor. Catch records by species are available for the period 1911–25 (Kellogg, 1931; Tønnessen and Johnsen, 1982). No right whales were ever reported landed or seen by catcher boats operating out of this station. Detailed records are available for only five years, during which period the station operated from 14 to 27 April, continuing until 13 September to 19 October, although in 1912 a humpback was reported taken on 14 March. The above information comes from Scheffer and Slipp (1948, p. 265), who state that 'whaling during the winter months was not practiced because whales were scarce and the weather uncertain'. During the whaling season, the catcher boats typically operated within 135 miles of the station, although occasionally they would travel as far south as southern Oregon.

Shore whaling began in British Columbia in 1905 (Tønnessen and Johnsen, 1982). Catch records by species are available only for the period 1919–30 (Pike and McAskie, 1969; Tønnessen and Johnsen, 1982). During this period, 3,890 whales were landed, consisting primarily of fin, sperm, and humpback whales. Four right whales were taken during this period and no gray whales. Of the right whales, none was caught south of 50° N.

Pike and McAskie (1969) report that whalers operating out of the Queen Charlotte Islands (52–54° N) took two right whales in 1924 and another one in 1926. Andrews and Larssen (1959, p. 162) include a photograph of a large right whale labeled as having been taken by the Kyuquat whaling station on the west coast of Vancouver Island (50° N, 127° W). No date for the photograph or catch is given. A drawing made from the photograph appears in Foster (1974, p. 97). The Kyuquat station operated from 1907 to 1925 (Pike and McAskie, 1969). This right whale may have been taken in 1924, for Kellogg (1931) reports three right whales landed by British Columbia stations in 1924 whereas Pike and McAskie (1969) report only two.

The absence of records of right whales from the Washington shore station and the few records from California and British Columbia stations are remarkable considering the lack of legal protection for this species during the entire period and the considerable amount of shore whaling that occurred. The minimum known catch of right whales throughout the North Pacific during this period is given in Table 5.

THE CATCH OF RIGHT WHALES 1931–82

Legal protection for the right whale came very late. The first protection the North Pacific right whale received came in 1931 when most of the major whaling nations signed the International Convention for the Regulation of Whaling. Article four of this convention prohibited the taking of right whales world-wide. However, the treaty did not come into effect until 1935. The United States, Canada, and Mexico all ratified the treaty. The Soviet Union and Japan did not, and thus were not bound by the restrictions contained in the treaty (Leonard, 1941; Scarff, 1977).

Japan's decision not to sign the 1931 treaty resulted in continued take of the species in the North Pacific by that country's whalers. The catch of right whales taken by Japan and other nations in the North Pacific since 1931 is shown in Table 6. As can be seen from this table, a minimum of 43 right whales were captured in the North Pacific between 1931 and 1938.

Japan did sign the Final Act to the 1938 Protocol to the (1937) Agreement for the Regulation of Whaling (Leonard, 1941; Scarff, 1977), but the Soviet Union did not. While Japan's signing did not legally bind its whalers to comply with the Protocol's prohibition on the taking of right whales, the Act reflected its intent to seek

immediate compliance with the Protocol. At the Informal Conference on the International Regulation of Whaling held in London in 1939, Japan reiterated its commitment to adopting the necessary legislation to allow it to adhere to the Protocol by the opening of the next whale season. The protection offered by Japan's informal efforts at compliance was short-lived. By 1940, the growing military conflicts in the Pacific made further agreements between major whaling countries infeasible. In the absence of such agreements, Japanese whalers began taking right whales again. During the period 1940–45, they caught 26 more right whales in the North Pacific.

After World War II, most of the major whaling nations signed the 1946 Convention for the International Regulation of Whaling which came into effect in 1949. From the date the convention became effective until the present, right whales in all oceans have been declared protected species which commercial whalers were generally prohibited from capturing (Scarff, 1977). According to official records, this prohibition has generally been effective.

In 1951, whalers from Coal Harbour in Quatsino Sound, Vancouver Island, British Columbia (51° 30′ N, 128° W) 'accidentally' captured a right whale off the northwest coat of Vancouver Island. The animal was described as a sexually mature 12.5 m male. Photographs of this animal appear in Pike and McAskie (1969) and Reeves and Brownell (1982, p. 417).

The 1946 convention contained a provision whereby nations were allowed to grant their whaling operations scientific permits to take species otherwise protected (Scarff, 1977). Under this provision, the Soviet Union captured 10 right whales in 1955 (Klumov, 1962), and Japanese whalers caught 13 more between 1956 and 1968 (Omura, 1958; Omura et al., 1969). No scientific permits for the capture of right whales in the North Pacific have been issued since 1968.

SIGHTING RECORDS 1931–82

I have found no sighting records of right whales in the eastern North Pacific south of 50° N between 1924 and 1955. Between 1955 and 1982 there are apparently reliable sightings of 32 individuals plus 6 unconfirmed sightings of 20 more whales. These sightings are summarized in Table 4.

Gilmore (1956, p. 22) reports a possible sighting of four right whales near San Diego, California in January 1955. He states:

On January 14 two volunteer gray whale-watchers, atop the look-out at Ritter Hall on the Scripps [Oceanographic Institute] campus, saw four whales at a distance of 3 to 4 miles going southeastward. These whales were described as showing a distinct double spout. a smooth black back, and pointed, broad flukes. They were logged as 'gray whales', a species which was then migrating south in numbers... The double condition of the observed spouts in this case was too great for the gray whale, however, and the back and tail stock were without the slight, but easily visible ridge and sharp knuckles, and no clear patches of light, discolored areas were present.

No more details are given of this sighting.

Gilmore (1956) also reports a single whale that was observed for about 2 hours on 31 March 1955, also near San Diego. The whale was initially spotted from land and came so close to shore that it 'almost struck the piles of the pier'. The whale was initially seen coming from the north and last seen heading southwest. Gilmore suggests

Table 6.

Minimum catch of right whales in the North Pacific, 1931–1982* The whaling grounds are: J = Japan; CJ = Coast of Japan; K = Korea; Ka = Kamchatka; A = Alaska; GA = Gulf of Alaska; BC = British Columbia; BS = Bering Sea; YS = Yellow Sea; OS = Okhotsk Sea; KI = Kurile Islands. The sources (in parentheses) are: a = IWS (1936); b = IWS (1941); c = Brueggeman et al. (in press); d = Omura (1986); e = IWS (1953); f = IWS (1959); g = IWS (1963); h = Omura (1958); i = Pike and McAskie (1969); j = Klumov (1962); k = Omura et al. (1969); l = IWS (1968); m = Wang (1978); n = Morast et al. (1985).

Year	N	Ground (source)	Year	N	Ground (source) & comment
1931	8	J+K (a)	1944	3	J+K (f)
1932	16	J+K14 (a); A2 (c)	1945	1	J+K (f)
1933	3	A1 (a); J+K2 (a)	1948	1	J+K (g)
1934	2	J (d)	1951	1	BC (i)	"Accident"
1935	4	J2 (d); A2 (c)	1955	10	KI (j)	Soviet research
1936	4	J (d)	1956	2	CJ (k)	Japanese research
1937	6	J+K5 (b); Ka1 (b)	1961	3	GA (k)	Japanese research
1938	2	J+K (f)	1962	3	BS (k)	Japanese research
1939	1	J (d)	1963	3	BS (k)	Japanese research
1940	1	BS (e)	1964	1	Ka (l)	–
1941	3	E side of Ka (h)	1965	2	YS (m)	Chinese whalers
1942	5	J+K (f)	1968	2	OS (k)	Japanese research
1943	13	J+K (f)	1968	1	K (n)	Korean whalers

* I was able to review an early draft of Omura (1986). The relation between the catch figures in that paper and the figures reported in the International Whaling Statistics was ambiguous. The above total includes the larger figure from one or the other source as a minimum catch. In some cases it may be more accurate to include the sum of the figures in Omura (1986) and IWS.

that the animal's behavior of sticking its head out of the water to look over the nearby shore-line may signify that the whale was confused regarding its location and perhaps lost. When initially detected, the whale was travelling in a normal manner. While being followed by Gilmore in a small boat the animal breached 13 times, repeatedly showed its flukes, and waved a flipper in the air. Three photographs of this animal, two of it breaching, appear in Gilmore (1956).

The next four reported observations of right whales were made during pelagic fur seal investigations. Most of the published information about these sightings appears in Table 4. The two reported sightings on 19 April 1959 deserve special comment. Niggol (Fiscus and Niggol, 1965) reported seeing two groups of eight right whales apiece at 0610 h and 0715 h 13 and 9 miles south-west of Destruction Island, Washington respectively (H. Kaji-mura, pers. comm.). He also reported seeing two groups of eight humpback whales apiece at the same locations on the same day. Finally, at the same date and location of the first of these observations but not the second he reported seeing eight gray whales. The observational conditions on 19 April were recorded as excellent, with calm seas throughout the day (H. Kajimura, pers. comm.).

The published data are not consistent with other records and are highly anomalous. The rough data sheets at the National Marine Mammal Laboratory state only: 'school of 25–30 whales: gray, right, and humpbacks. 5–10 miles N of Destruction Island feeding'. Note that this record has the whales north of Destruction Island whereas the published account has them southwest of the island. For unexplained reasons the National Marine Fisheries Service Platforms of Opportunity data bank lists only one sighting of five right whales on 19 April at this location (M. Tillman, pers. comm.).

No other confirmed sightings of right whales in the south-eastern North Pacific have been of more than three animals together. Omura (1958) reports that of 94 sightings of right whales in the western North Pacific there are only two records of four right whales together and none of more than four. Omura et al. (1969) report that of 126 sightings of right whales by Japanese whalers in the North Pacific between 1961 and 1968, only 12 sightings involved three animals, and none involved more than three (see Table 10). These Japanese data illustrate the low probability of encountering one aggregation of eight whales, let alone two such groups accompanied by similar numbers of humpback whales on the same day.

Considering the inconsistencies in the above reports, the improbable number of right whales in each group, the remarkable coincidence of eight humpback whales being with each pod of right whales, the close proximity of the two locations, and the lack of detailed documentation accompanying the reports, it is hard to completely accept the published account. No additional information regarding these sightings is available (K. Niggol, pers. comm). The most plausible scenario is that one mixed group of an undetermined number of right, humpback, and gray whales was seen twice on the same day near Destruction Island. The data has been treated this way in the tables of this report.

Berzin and Doroshenko (1982) report an unspecified number of right whales observed by a TINRO vessel in 1964 at 40° N, 157° W. No further information is provided concerning this sighting; there is no indication whether

photographs exist or what fieldmarks were used for identification. The authors also report that in 1963 'TINRO vessels observed about 200 right whales at 51° N, 145° W'. Apparently in reference to this latter sighting, Berzin and Rovnin (1966) imply that the whales were distributed over a wide area. They state that 'in the majority of instances they were found in pairs or alone, and very rarely in groups of 4–5 animals'. It is unfortunate that no detailed information about this extraordinarily large number of sightings has been published.

Off central California, three sightings of right whales were made in 1959 and 1963 by captains of whaling catcher boats operating out of Richmond, California (38° N) (Rice and Fiscus, 1968). They also report two sightings made during a whale-marking cruise and a pelagic fur seal investigation. The 1965 record of two right whales off Punta Abreojos, Baja California at 26° 39′ N, is the southernmost record of a right whale in the eastern North Pacific in recent times. A photograph of one of the whales seen off Baja California appears in Rice and Fiscus (1968) and Gilmore (1978). This is the only published report of right whales along the west coast of North America south of San Diego (32° N) other than Scammon's (1874, pp. 66–7) statement that some right whales had been taken 'as far south as the Bay of San Sebastian Viscaino, and about Cedros or Cerros Island, both places being near the parallel of 29° north latitude'.

There have been nine right whales observed south of 50° N and east of 180° W by Japanese sighting boats between 1965 and 1979. What has been published about these sightings is set forth in Tables 4 and 8. All but one of these sightings occurred between 45–50° N in the mid-Pacific. Unfortunately, the sources do not describe the dates on which the sightings were made, although it appears that all the sightings were made during the summer months.

Two sightings of right whales were made during 1973 and 1974 as part of the NMFS's Platforms of Opportunity program. Both sightings are formally described by NMFS as 'tentative' which NMFS defines as meaning they are probably valid records, but unverified (L. Actor, pers. comm.). Both sightings are listed in Table 4.

In 1981, a single right whale was seen off Santa Barbara, California (Woodhouse and Strickley, 1982). This animal was encountered during a recreational whale-watching cruise. Photographs and behavioral observations appear in the report.

On 20 March 1982, one right whale about 15 m in length was observed by the author and approximately 100 others near Half Moon Bay, California. For a two hour period this whale repeatedly approached to within 5 m of the three 15–20 m party-fishing boats idling in the water nearby (Scarff, 1986; Johnson, 1982). Comparisons by Woodhouse and this author of photographs of this animal and the whale seen off Santa Barbara in 1981 have not been conclusive in eliminating the possibility that the two sightings were of the individual.

SIGHTINGS NEAR HAWAII 1820–1983

Despite the presence of whalers in Hawaiian waters since 1818 (Stackpole, 1953), there is only one well-documented record of a right whale near the islands. An unconfirmed sighting was reported from north of Oahu in 1975. The observer, Harold Stanley, described the whale as having

no dorsal fin, no mottling as in the gray [whale], smooth...and slow...about 50 feet long, and with a long slow ten-second spout. It had a very large head and a broad smile. (DeBus, 1975).

I was unable to discover any photographs of this animal or any researcher in Hawaii who had any further information regarding this sighting.

In 1979 a single right whale, individually identifiable due to a white blaze on its back, was observed twice on 25 March off Maui and again on 10 April off Molokai (Rowntree, Darling, Silber and Ferrari, 1980; Herman, Baker, Forestell and Antinoja, 1980). On all three occasions the right whale was seen swimming and interacting with humpback whales. Good photographs and behavioral observations are contained in each article.

The possible historic occurrence of right whales in the vicinity of the Hawaiian Islands was discussed in both Rowntree et al. (1980) and Herman et al. (1980). Both sets of authors reviewed the Maury (1851) Preliminary Sketch and Townsend's (1935) chart as well as reports of right whales in Hawaiian waters contained in Eschricht and Reinhardt (1866) and Tomilin (1957). Rowntree et al.'s (1980) argument that the reports of right whales near Hawaii in the latter two references were actually distorted reports of gray whales off California is persuasive. These authors also note that the nearest record on the maps they observed is of 'straggling' right whales 250 nautical miles west of Hawaii. Herman et al. (1980) reviewed much of the same material, but came to the opposite conclusion that the Hawaiian Islands may have been an important wintering ground for right whales during the last 100 years. The latter's argument for this conclusion is unconvincing.

Maury (1851) shows 'straggling right whales' occurring in summer in a wide area west and southwest of the Hawaiian Islands (15–25° N, 160–165, 170–180° W) (see Fig. 1). Maury's more detailed map no. 1 (1852 et seq.) extends south only to 20° N. This latter chart was not discussed by either Rowntree et al. (1980) or Herman et al. (1980). Analysis of this chart supports Rowntree et al.'s conclusion that right whales were not common near the islands during the last 160 years. Map no. 1 contains no reports of right whales among, or just north of, the Hawaiian Islands (20–25° N, 155–160° W) despite the relatively large amounts of searching effort in the area during winter months (Dec. = 130 days, Feb. = 45 days, Mar. = 200 days). However, as Table 7 shows, Maury's map no. 1 does contain records of a few sightings west of Hawaii in April and May and a few more north of the islands in May and June. These locations are so far south so late in the spring, that I suspect they may reflect errors of identification or transcription. Indices of abundance calculated from this chart show the heaviest concentrations of right whales north of 35° N by April and north of 40° N by May. Even if the reported sightings between 20 and 25° N are reliable, the whales observed represent stragglers rather than concentrations of wintering right whales as suggested by Gilmore (1978) and Herman et al. (1980).

SEARCHING EFFORT 1950–82

The few records of right whales in the eastern North Pacific shown in Table 4 must be viewed in the context

Table 7.

Reported sightings of right whales near the Hawaiian Islands in Maury Map No. 1 (1852 et seq.). NR = no. days right whales seen, NE = no. days searching effort.

Location	Month	NR	NE	Location	Month	NR	NE
20–25 N, 160–165 W	May	4	25	20–25 N, 175–180 W	May	5	35
20–25 N, 170–175 W	April	4	10	25–30 N, 155–160 W	May	4	100
20–25 N, 170–175 W	May	2	13	25–30 N, 155–160 W	June	2	28

Table 8.

Number of right whales seen and effort (in miles) during Japanese sighting cruises in the North Pacific, 1965–1979 (from Wada 1974–1981).

	East of 180 W				Entire North Pacific	
	40–50 N		North of 50 N			
Year	Whales	Effort	Whales	Effort	Whales	Effort
1965	1	2,855	2	42,950	3	52,982
1966	0	3,449	5	42,376	6	60,549
1967	0	6,869	3	14,676	3	37,876
1968	0	21,413	0	11,548	7	67,397
1969	1	43,139	1	16,654	7	107,167
1970	0	57,017	2	30,637	5	118,010
1971	0	48,935	0	12,663	6	104,714
1972	0	33,687	0	3,623	10	110,442
1973	1	24,877	1	4,902	2	73,754
1974	0	16,084	0	3,190	0	55,855
1975	0	–	0	–	0	–
1976	1	4,711	1	2,371	3	18,541
1977	4	6,631	0	1,313	4	22,143
1978	0	4,706	2	1,249	2	17,980
1979	1	1,816	0	79	1	11,384
Total	9	276,189	17	188,231	59	858,794

of the searching effort that has occurred in the region during the last 30 years. The range and extent of this searching effort, particularly along the coast of California, is persuasive evidence of the scarcity of this species throughout the region and particularly in the nearshore waters of the west coast of North America. The major surveys are summarized below.

The most extensive searching effort for right whales has been the Japanese sighting cruises (Wada, 1975–81; Ohsumi and Yamamura, 1982). These cruises, extending over nearly all the North Pacific, have led to sightings of 59 right whales between 1965 and 1979, nine of which were in this study area. Unfortunately, the published material does not describe the amount of searching effort by month, limiting the usefulness of the data to detect migratory patterns. It is probable that most, if not all, of the searching effort in the study area took place during the summer when right whales are least expected in the area. Both the sighting and effort data are summarized in Table 8. The greater density of whales north of 50° N is consistent with the data on Maury's map no. 1 (1852 et seq.).

Whale sightings were carried out by whale catcherboats and other ships off the coast of British Columbia between 1958 and 1969 (Pike and McAskie, 1969). Other than the single right whale landed at Coal Harbour in 1951, the authors report no other records of right whales south of, or near, 50° N.

Catcherboats operating out of shore stations at Richmond, California (38° N) between 1956 and 1971 routinely searched the area within 230 km of the station. Most of the searching effort occurred during the months of April through November (Rice, 1963a, b; 1974).

During this time there was also considerable searching effort between mid-December and mid-April close to shore as part of the catch of gray whales under a scientific research permit (Rice and Wolman, 1971). Three right whales were reported by the catcher boats during this period (Rice and Fiscus, 1968) (see Table 4).

Slijper, Van Utrecht and Naaktgeboren (1964) describe opportunistic observations of whales in the North Pacific between 0 and 50° N made by Dutch naval and merchant vessels during the years 1955–58. They include as the measure of searching effort the number of daylight hours participating ships spent in each 10° of latitude and longitude by month. The eastern North Pacific was not heavily travelled by Dutch ships during this period and the searching effort is low, ranging from 9 to 130 hours per 10° square during the winter months of December through April. During the summer months some of the squares received as much as 326 hours of potential observation. Only one group of four right whales was observed, that in June as reported in Table 4. The authors expressed general confidence in the identification of right whales during this study but mention no field marks seen for any individual sighting.

Considerable searching effort has been conducted by the National Marine Fisheries Service (NMFS) Northwest Fisheries Center during ship surveys for its pelagic fur seal investigations (32–62° N, shore to 180° W) and whale-marking cruises (18–35° N, mostly within 150 n. miles of shore). These cruises have been generally described by Rice (1963a, b; 1974) and Fiscus and Niggol (1965), but the searching effort is not quantified in a manner that would allow the development of indices of abundance. Right whales observed during these cruises (nine reported sightings), are reported in Fiscus and Niggol (1965) and Rice and Fiscus (1968) and included in Table 4.

Aerial and ship surveys conducted by the Naval Ocean Systems Center (NOSC) between 1965 and 1976 are summarized in Leatherwood and Walker (1979; 1982). Aerial surveys were flown over an area of the southern California bight from 32 to 34° N extending from shore to 120° W. Searching effort is summarized by month. During the months of December through March total effort during the period 1968–1976 averaged more than 2,000 n. miles per month. A total of 4,475 n. miles were flown during April. Ship surveys were conducted from 1965 through 1975 within 150 n. miles of shore from 22° N to 35° N principally during winter and spring. No right whales were reported as observed during either the aerial or ship surveys.

Further intensive surveys of the southern California Bight area are described in Dohl *et al.* (1981a). This latter study involved both aerial and ship surveys between 1975 and 1978. Thirty-five flights were made at 300 m altitude and approximately 170 km/hr along 15 transect lines extending southwest from Pt. Arguello (34° 30′ N) south along the coast to the Mexican border (32° 35′ N). Attempts were made to identify all marine mammals seen. During the months of January, February and March, 428 gray whales, 13 fin whales and 5 unidentified whales longer than 12.2 m were observed, but no right whales. Approximately 24,000 transect miles were flown over the three years during the first quarter of the year. Twenty-nine nearshore and 5 offshore ship surveys covering 26,400 km were conducted in the same area. During the first quarter of the year 241 gray whales, 2

humpback whales and 4 unidentified whales longer than 12.2 m were observed, but no right whales.

Observations of cetaceans have been systematically made by NMFS observers on American tuna boats operating in the south-eastern North Pacific. This searching effort is located almost entirely south of 35° N and east of 160° W. Although most of the effort is concentrated south of 25° N, a considerable amount did occur north of that latitude during the first quarter of the year. Searching effort between 1974 and 1979 is summarized in Dahlheim, Leatherwood and Perrin (1982). The searching effort continued after 1979, but since the inception of the program to date no right whales have been observed (W. Perrin, pers. comm., May 1983).

Intensive surveys have recently been conducted in the coastal waters off central and northern California. Dohl *et al.* (1981b, 1982) describe aerial and ship surveys conducted between January 1980 and December 1981. Each month one high-altitude (300 m ASL) and low-altitude (65 m ASL) aerial survey was made. Flights were made over standard transects extending from the coast out to 120′ longitude (ca. 185 km) from shore between Pt. Conception (34° 27′ N) and the California/ Oregon border (42°0′ N). Approximately 3,600 km of transects were flown on each of these surveys each month. Five ship surveys were conducted in 1981 from Monterey Bay to Bodega Bay extending 100 km offshore. During the first quarter of the year, a total of 1,590 gray whales, 3 minke whales and 18 sperm whales were observed. No right whales were observed during either the aerial or ship surveys. Continuing aerial surveys through spring 1983 did not detect any right whales (T. Dohl, pers. comm.).

Two other surveys of local central California coastal waters also failed to detect any right whales. Barham (1982) reports marine mammal sightings made during 239 weekly vessel voyages in Monterey Bay between 1950 and 1955. Huber, Ainley and Morrell (1982) report sightings of cetaceans made during 236 vessel surveys in the Gulf of the Farallones near San Francisco between 1971 and 1979.

Reilly, Rice and Wolman (1980) review the shore-based censuses for gray whales that were made each year from 1967 to 1979 near Monterey, California (36° 29′ N). In each of those years intensive observations were made from shore each day, typically from 10 December through 6 February. Whales passing within 2+ miles of shore were counted. During the period 1967/68 through 1978/79 an average of 3,031 gray whales were counted each year. These shore-based observations were conducted in the same general area where there had been at least seven observations of right whales during the period 1855–80. However, the known dates of records of right whales off central California are generally from late February or March, after the end of these censuses.

In January 1978, Reilly *et al.* (1980) conducted aerial transects in this same area to determine the extent to which the gray whales migrated off-shore. Between 2 and 13 January they flew 14 flights at 1,000 feet altitude and 190 m.p.h. along 16 transects perpendicular to shore from Pt Lobos to Pt Sur, each extending 16 km out to sea. Total air time was approximately 32 hours, during which time 529 gray whales were seen as well as many small cetaceans and pinnipeds. No right whales were observed during either the land-based or aerial observations.

Recently there has been a significant amount of searching effort conducted off the California coast in connection with recreational whale- and bird-watching (Kaza, 1982). Recreational cruises directed to observing gray whales have increased in number tremendously since the late 1970s. Both of the two most recent observations of right whales off the California coast (Woodhouse and Strickley, 1982; Johnson, 1982) were made during the course of recreational whale-watching cruises. During almost every weekend from the beginning of January through March and sometimes through April, commercial party fishing boats and other larger vessels sail from San Diego, San Pedro, Long Beach, Santa Barbara, Morro Bay, Monterey, Half Moon Bay, San Francisco, and Bodega Bay in search of gray whales. The typical pattern is for trips of half-day length or less with the ship following the first group of whales encountered until time to return. Ships generally stay within 5 miles of shore except in bay areas like Monterey, Half Moon Bay, and San Francisco where they may go up to 10 miles offshore. On weekdays, many of these same boats go out on charter whale-watching trips. Usually each group of whale-watchers is accompanied by a trained naturalist who could identify a right whale and would be likely to report such a sighting.

In recent years there has also been a growing interest in observing the gray whales in their calving lagoons in Baja California. Most weeks during the winter one or more whale-watching cruises sail from San Diego. Beside being at sea for a longer period, these cruises generally travel further offshore searching for humpback whales and small cetaceans. No right whales have yet been reported from these cruises.

Finally, some additional early surveys of the waters off California and Mexico are reported in Norris and Prescott (1961) and Leatherwood, Perrin, Rowntree, Hubbs and Dahlheim (1980). No additional right whale observations were made during the course of these surveys.

SIGHTABILITY FROM AIRCRAFT AND BOATS

All recorded observations of right whales in the eastern North Pacific have been made by shipboard observers, none by observers in airplanes. On one occasion (Johnson, 1982; Scarff, 1986), a right whale was detected by shipboard observers in the general study area, but not detected during the twice monthly aerial surveys or during a special attempt to relocate the whale from an airplane only two hours after shipboard contact with the whale had been voluntarily broken off (Dohl et al., 1982; T. Dohl, pers. comm.; this author, unpublished data). Increasing wind velocity and large numbers of gray whales in the immediate area added to the difficulty of relocating the right whale.

Aerial surveys for right whales have been successful in the Bay of Fundy (Kraus et al., 1982), off Argentina (Payne et al., 1981), off South Africa (Best, 1981), off Australia (Bannister, 1986) and in the Okhotsk Sea (Berzin and Doroshenko, 1981). Right whales' reactions to aircraft are discussed in detail in Payne et al. (1981). They found a variety of responses with solitary animals and animals in transit being the most difficult to observe due to both behavioural and environmental factors. Both Best (1981) in surveys off the coast of South Africa and Kraus and Prescott (1981) in surveys in the Bay of Fundy conclude that there is a high probability of sighting a right whale from an aircraft. However, after further surveys, Kraus and Prescott (1983) now believe that the sightability of right whales from aircraft may be lower than from boats and may be less than for other species. During 1981 and 1982 shipboard surveys using photo-identification techniques they identified nearly twice as many individuals as would have been predicted based on the aerial surveys.

In deep offshore waters of the eastern North Pacific, right whales are probably significantly harder to detect during aerial surveys than they are in the shallow nearshore waters off Argentina (Payne, 1983), South Africa (Best, 1981; pers. comm.) and Australia (Bannister, pers. comm.), where the whales are detected by the contrast of their dark body against a light-colored seabed. The environmental conditions would presumably not affect the relative sightability of right whales compared to other whale species, paticularly those such as sei whales (*Balaenoptera borealis*), which also have a relatively low,

Table 9.

Number of sightings (or days on which whales sighted) of right whales in the North Pacific 20–50° N, by 5° latitude and month from Maury (1852, *et seq.*), Townsend (1935), and Table 4. In Table 4, some sightings were only identified as 'summer' or 'winter'.

Latitude	Source	J	F	M	A	M	J	J	A	S	O	N	D	Summer	Winter	Total
45–50 N	Maury	–	–	12	81	104	83	59	60	16	–	–	–	–	–	371
	Townsend	–	–	–	–	12	13	10	–	1	–	–	1	–	–	37
	Table 4	1	–	1	3*	–	1	1	–	–	–	–	–	7(+4)	–	14
40–45 N	Maury	–	–	2	8	32	31	9	20	31	7	1	–	–	–	141
	Townsend	–	–	–	1	3	1	1	–	1	–	–	1	–	–	8
	Table 4	–	–	–	–	–	–	–	–	–	–	–	–	1(+2)	–	1
35–40 N	Maury	–	–	10	39	49	4	9	9	6	25	–	–	–	–	151
	Townsend	–	–	–	–	4	–	–	–	–	1	–	–	–	–	5
	Table 4	–	–	4	2	2	–	–	–	1	–	–	–	–	4	13
30–35 N	Maury	–	–	11	25	12	6	4	6	3	8	4	5	–	–	84
	Townsend	–	–	–	–	–	–	–	–	–	–	–	–	–	–	0
	Table 4	–	2	2	1	–	–	–	–	–	–	–	–	–	–	5
25–30 N	Maury	–	3	5	5	4	2	–	–	5	4	–	–	–	–	23
	Townsend	–	–	–	–	–	–	–	–	–	–	–	–	–	–	0
	Table 4	–	–	1	–	–	–	–	–	–	–	–	–	–	–	1
20–25 N	Maury	–	–	–	4	11	–	–	–	–	–	–	–	–	–	15
	Townsend	–	–	–	–	–	–	–	–	–	–	–	–	–	–	0
	Table 4	–	–	1	1	–	–	–	–	–	–	–	–	–	–	2

* Only 3 of 4 sightings by Fiscus and Niggol (1965) included.

Table 10.

Records of right whales by pod size in the North Pacific and off South Africa. Confirmed records are those sightings for which pod size is clearly known. Best (1981) defines "unaccompanied whales" as pods which do not contain mother and calf pairs.

Area/Source	Number of whales in pod								(n)	Mean
	1	2	3	4	5	6	7	8		
Eastern N. Pacific (this study, Table 4)										
Confirmed records	18	2	3	0	0	1	0	0	24	1.35
All records	18	2	3	2	0	1	0	2	28	2.18
Entire N. Pacific										
Pelagic										
Omura (1958)	58	30	4	2	0	0	0	0	94	1.48
Omura et al.(1969)	79	35	9	0	0	0	0	0	123	1.36
Coastal stations										
Omura (1958)	53	15	2	0	0	0	0	0	70	1.27
South Africa Best (1981)										
Unaccompanied whales	228	161	46	21	2	2	0	1	461	1.74
Total	228	429	52	25	3	4	0	1	742	1.87

Table 11.

Length of right whales landed or sighted in the eastern North Pacific south of 50° N.

"Small"	9m	12m	13m	14m	15m	>15m	"Large"
1	1	1	2	2	3	1	3

dispersed blow (Leatherwood, Goodrich, Kinter and Truppo, 1982).

Right whales have a reputation of allowing close approaches by observers in boats (Payne, 1972, 1976; Payne et al. 1981; Reeves and Brownell, 1982). However, Scammon (1874) reported that toward the end of the period of extensive exploitation in the eastern North Pacific right whales were wild and difficult to approach. Recent observations of right whales in this region by Gilmore (1956), Rice and Fiscus (1968), Johnson (1982) and Scarff (1986) discussed above, support a conclusion that right whales are at least as, if not more, approachable than gray whales.

SUMMARY OF SIGHTING DATA

The records of right whales in the eastern North Pacific have been summarized in various ways in the following tables and in Fig. 3. As a general comment, it should be noted that the reliability of apparent trends in these data are untested. The apparent patterns should be treated generally as nothing more than working hypotheses until appropriate adjustments have been made to correct for biases in searching effort.

The overall sighting records described by month and latitude in Table 1 do not manifest a clear migratory pattern as has been reported for the western North Pacific (Omura et al., 1969). However, there have been only 17 recorded sightings of right whales for which the month is known between November and February, plus four other sightings made in 'winter'. The southern-most sightings occurred in March and April, which is consistent with patterns in the northwest Pacific (Townsend, 1935; Omura et al., 1969). Of note are the surprising number of sightings (23) of right whales south of 30° N during the period March–October.

Despite the depletion of the population, there does not appear to be any decrease in the size of the right whale's range south of 50° N. It might be expected that a depleted population would shrink its range to concentrate on those areas most ecologically beneficial to the species. However, because of the paucity of data, any comments on change in distribution of the species in this area are speculative.

The number of right whales per pod has been reported for only 27 sightings in the eastern North Pacific. These data, along with the much larger samples of Omura (1958) and Omura et al. (1969) from the western North Pacific and Best (1981) from South Africa, are reported in Table 10. Although right whales are known to form large breeding aggregations off Argentina (Payne et al., 1981; Payne, 1983) the more typical pattern in the Northern Hemisphere is for right whales to occur singly or in groups of two or three whales (Reeves and Brownell, 1982).

Scammon (1874, p. 68) wrote that during most of the season single right whales were most frequently encountered but pairs and trios were not uncommon. However, by late summer and early autumn the whales were 'scattered over the surface of the water as far as the eye can discern from the mast-head'. There are no comparable sightings of large aggregations reported by other observers in this region.

No reported sighting of four or more right whales in the eastern North Pacific is confirmed by photographs or detailed field notes. I consider the pod size estimates for all of these sightings to be unreliable.

The length of the right whales landed or sighted in the eastern North Pacific is known for only 14 individuals (Table 11). Omura et al. (1969) conclude that right whales in the North Pacific probably reach sexual maturity at a body length of 14.5–15.5 m for males and 15–16 m for females, and that this corresponds to an age of approximately 10 years. Pike and McAskie (1969) report that a 12.5 m male landed in 1951 was sexually mature.

The largest right whales recorded in the North Pacific are an 18.3 m female (Klumov, 1962) and a 16.4 m male (Omura et al., 1969). From the data in Table 11, it appears that about half of the animals seen in the North Pacific south of 50° N were immature animals. This is a conservative estimate because 19th-century whalers probably noted the size of a right whale more frequently when it was large, so mature animals are probably over-represented in the early data. The report of a 70 foot long (21.3 m) right whale taken in Monterey in 1873 (Starks, 1922) appears to be an error.

DISCUSSION

Extent of Migration

The extent to which right whales in the eastern North Pacific engage in north–south migrations is not known. It has generally been assumed that right whales migrate long distances south from their summering grounds in the Gulf of Alaska and near the Aleutian Islands. However, as Table 9 reveals, there are extremely few records of right whales in winter to support or deny this hypothesis. There are records of right whales south of 25° N in March and April, but it appears from the table that some right whales spend all summer south of 30° N, so the records from April and May may represent the periphery of a summer population.

Calving Grounds

I have discovered no records of newborn or very young calves in the eastern North Pacific. Earlier commentators do not discuss this anomaly. They apparently assumed that the population was depleted before significant effort was spent to find calving grounds or record sightings of calves. These assumptions appear unwarranted, and the lack of records of calves along the west coast of North America appears to reflect a true absence of coastal calving grounds at least within historic times.

There was a substantial amount of aboriginal and pelagic whaling effort in the eastern North Pacific prior to the depletion of the right whale population in the 1840s and 1850s. However, the literature on the aboriginal whaling cultures makes no suggestion that these whalers knew of any calving areas along the west coast of North America. The most extensive contemporary account of this whaling is that of Swan (1870) who visited the Nootka first in 1855, only 15 years after the beginning of Yankee whaling on the Kodiak ground, and he refers to the right whale as being rare.

There was also a substantial amount of non-aboriginal settlement and whaling along the west coast of North America prior to and during the early period of pelagic whaling for right whales. Yet these sources also fail to reveal any calving grounds for right whales along the coast. The substantial harvest of right whales by the non-aboriginal pelagic whaling fleets did not commence in the eastern North Pacific until after the discovery of the Kodiak Ground in 1840. The pelagic fishery remained productive until at least 1850 (see Table 3). Spanish colonists had been inhabiting the areas near potential calving areas such as Drake's Bay, San Francisco Bay and Monterey Bay since the 1770s. American and British pelagic whalers had been operating along the coast of California since 1840 (Huff, 1957). Coastal whaling began in California in 1845. Neither the Spanish colonists, the early pelagic whalers, nor the early coastal whalers refer to the right whale having a coastal calving ground. It seems highly unlikely that nearshore mating or calving grounds along the California coast would have remained unnoticed over such a long period.

Thus, the location of the calving grounds for the right whales that summer in the Gulf of Alaska remains more of a mystery than ever. This study suggests that neither the west coast of North America nor the Hawaiian Islands constituted a major calving ground for right whales within the last 200 years. The mid-ocean records of right whales in winter in Maury map no. 1 (1852 *et seq.*) and the late fall records in Townsend (1935) suggest that right whales may have wintered and calved far off shore in the North Pacific. Such pelagic calving would appear to be inconsistent with the records of nearshore calving grounds off Argentina, Australia and South Africa, and the recent sightings of female right whales and calves in nearshore waters off the southeastern United States. However, no coastal calving grounds for right whales have been found in the western North Pacific. Offshore calving grounds for North Pacific right whales would be consistent with the pattern of most other whale species.

One possibility is that some right whales which summer in the Gulf of Alaska migrate west or southwest and bear their young near the coast of Kamchatka or further south. Non-breeding whales may winter near the Emperor seamount, or, on rare occasions, off the west coast of North America. This hypothesis is consistent with Payne's (1986) finding that only one third of the adult female population returns to the coastal area around Peninsula Valdes, Argentina each year.

Stock Identity

Klumov (1962, p. 297) writes that the right whales in the North Pacific constitute three discrete stocks, one which summers in the waters south of Alaska and winters between the Hawaiian Islands and the west coast of North America, and two others which summer in the western North Pacific – one in the Sea of Okhotsk and the other in the western North Pacific east of the Kurile Islands. He states that the Asiatic and American populations 'are independent and do not mingle'. Berzin and Rovnin (1966) also conclude that there is an eastern North Pacific stock and at least one western North Pacific stock. However, their figure 6 suggests that right whales winter over a broad longitudinal band in the eastern North Pacific. Gilmore's (1956, 1978) charts also suggest a discrete population that winters close to the west coast of North America.

The sighting data summarized in Table 1 from Maury's map no. 1 are more ambiguous. They suggest that the population was not significantly more dense close to shore, and indicate no near-shore migration along the west coast of North America. Indeed, the data suggest that at least some of the right whales may have migrated south far offshore near the 180° meridian.

Recent sighting data summarized in Table 4 are strongly biased toward nearshore sightings. However, this probably reflects a nearshore bias in the searching effort. The few reports of right whales landed by the early shore whaling stations between 1855 and 1900 do not support the hypothesis of major nearshore concentrations.

The recent concentrations of scientific investigations on nearshore populations of right whales off South America, South Africa, eastern North America and Australia may have led to an exaggerated view of the species' coastal tendencies.

The hypothesis that right whales form a more or less continuous interbreeding band across the North Pacific rather than two discrete stocks has not received the rigorous testing necessary to corroborate or reject it. Future analysis of indices of abundance derived from Maury's maps nos. 1 and 2 (1852 *et seq.*) may help resolve this question.

Population Estimates and Extent of Depletion

The very few sightings of right whales in the North Pacific in the last 25 years when compared with the many records of other whale species strongly suggests that the population(s) is very small. Berzin and Yablokov (1978, *in* Berzin and Vladimirov, 1981) estimated a population of 200–500 whales in the entire North Pacific. Rice (1974) stated that there may be 'only a few individuals' in the eastern North Pacific. Certainly, the population in the eastern North Pacific appears smaller than that in the western North Pacific based on the far greater number of recent sightings in the latter area (Omura *et al.*, 1969; Wada, 1975–81).

Data from Maury's map no. 1 (1852 *et seq.*) give an indication of how depleted the population in the eastern region is. Whalers operating in sailing ships in the 1840s reported seeing right whales on approximately 40% of the days they searched from April through September. In contrast, between 1965 and 1979 the much swifter Japanese scouting boats operating in much the same area saw right whales on average only once every 11,072 miles of cruising. Although the data are not strictly comparable, they suggest a greatly depleted population.

Excessive whaling by the nineteenth-century whalers combined with continued whaling in the 20th century on the remnant survivors is the most probable cause for the severe depletion. However, due to our ignorance regarding the ecology of the species, it is impossible to rule out changes in the environment as significant factors.

Population Trends

A basic tenet of population biology is that nearly all populations of wildlife species will show an increase in size after a short-term disturbance which reduces the population without radically altering the availability and quality of resources available to the population. This tenet forms the basis for sustained yield management of whales. Whaling is assumed to affect whale populations like other short-term disturbances. In response to decreased population density, the net recruitment rate of the population is expected to increase.

This theory has proven difficult to verify regarding the recovery of depleted whale populations after the cessation of whaling. This is due in part to the low reproductive potential of whales which causes the expected increases in the population to be relatively small compared with the high variability in population estimates based on sighting data. The possibility that changes in local abundance are the result of an overall population increase rather than a change in the species' geographic distribution makes interpretation of trends in local sighting data difficult.

The only convincing example of population recovery after depletion is the eastern North Pacific population of gray whales. This population appears to have increased from approximately 4,400 in 1875 (Ohsumi, 1976) to a minimum of 16,500 in 1978 (Reilly et al., 1980), even though substantial numbers of gray whales continued to be taken after the species was 'protected' by treaty in 1938 (Storro-Patterson, 1977). Other protected stocks which appear to be increasing include blue whales off Iceland and in the Antarctic, and Southern Hemisphere humpbacks (FAO ACMRR, 1978).

Probably more relevant to the population dynamics of the right whale are the observed trends in the closely related bowhead. Recent studies on the bowhead suggest that once a population has been reduced to extremely low levels, population recovery may not occur, or occur only slowly (Mitchell and Reeves, 1982a, b; Reeves, 1980; Jonsgård, 1981).

Regarding right whales there is evidence of population increases in some areas, but not others. The most persuasive data suggesting population increases are for stocks off South Africa (7% per year) (Best, 1981), Argentina (Whitehead, Payne and Payne, 1986) and in the Bay of Fundy in the western North Atlantic (Kraus et al., 1982; Reeves et al. 1983). In contrast, there is no indication of significant increases in right whale populations in the eastern North Atlantic (Brown, 1986).

For the right whale in the North Pacific, there is no

Table 12.

Number of right whales sighted in the North Pacific by Japanese catcher boats, 1941, 1948–1967 (from Omura, 1958 and Omura et al., 1969). A dash (–) signifies data not available.

Year	Pelagic	Coastal	Total	Year	Pelagic	Coastal	Total
1941	6	–	6	1958	17	–	17
1948	–	1	1	1959	50	–	50
1949	–	–	–	1960	106	–	106
1950	–	4	4	1961	31	–	31
1951	–	11	11	1962	106	–	106
1952	–	4	4	1963	–	–	–
1953	–	6	6	1964	–	–	–
1954	37	13	50	1965	–	102	102
1955	10	2	12	1966	13	34	47
1956	78	3	81	1967	9	83	92
1957	70	45	115	Total	533	308	841

persuasive indication of an increase in the population(s) in the last century. Omura (1958) and Omura et al. (1969) summarize sightings of right whales by month for the months of April through September made from Russian (1951–57) and Japanese catcherboats (1941, 1948–67) operating with the factory ship fleets. Total sightings per year are also given and reproduced here in Table 12 for the Japanese sightings. Three of these latter sightings were made in June just south of 50° N in the study area. One of the sightings may be the same as that reported from a Japanese sighting boat in 1965 (Wada, 1975). Omura et al. (1969) do not provide a measure of searching effort associated with these sightings. It does not appear that there was any searching effort north of 20° N in the eastern North Pacific during winter.

Omura (1958) correctly notes that these sighting data do not form a good basis for developing population estimates or detecting trends:

> Further it occurs without doubt that the same whale or the same school of whales may be sighted by different catchers, thus increasing the numbers of sighting records considerably. It is obvious, therefore, that these data have little value for the study of relative abundance in different years.

Wada (1981) concludes from his analysis of Japanese sighting data in the North Pacific between 1968 and 1979 that no trend can be statistically shown for changes in the observed right whale population. This is primarily due to the small number of sightings.

Nothing in this current study suggests persuasively that the population is increasing. The increase in reported sightings during the last 30 years over the preceding 60 years is probably the result of greatly increased searching effort and greater reporting of the sightings that were made. A conservative hypothesis useful for management purposes is that, in the absence of better data, the population in the eastern North Pacific should clearly continue to be classified as a Protection Stock.

Factors Affecting Population Recovery

In reviewing the status of right whales in the western North Atlantic, Reeves et al. (1978) identified eight possible factors which singly or in combination may have prevented the species from having recovered (faster) in that region. These are examined below.

(1) Critical population size. Allen (1974) contrasts the right whale's apparent failure to recover in the Northern Hemisphere with the readily apparent recovery of the eastern North Pacific population of the gray whale. He

suggests that the right whale's apparent failure to recover may be the result of either or both a greater level of depletion by whalers or a greater difficulty in locating members of the opposite sex for breeding due to the more dispersed breeding distribution of the right whale. Ohsumi (1976) suggests that the gray whale population may not have been reduced below 4,400 animals. This is as much as 20 times some current estimates of the right whale population in the same area.

Allen (1974) contrasts the concentrations of mating gray whales near the calving lagoons with the less concentrated mating populations of right whales. Reeves *et al.* (1978) suggest that aboriginal whaling in the western North Atlantic may have driven right whales from traditional coastal calving before the arrival of European whalers. A similar occurrence in the eastern North Pacific seems less likely because of the apparent absence of an aboriginal whaling culture south of the Puget Sound area (48° N).

(2) *Natural predation.* Reeves *et al.* (1978) conclude that predation by killer whales (*Orcinus orca*) on right whales is probably not a significant factor in the western North Atlantic. Their conclusion is based in part on the lack of observations of killer whales attacking right whales anywhere in the world and partly on their relative scarcity in the western North Atlantic.

There are no published records of right whales being attacked by killer whales in the North Pacific. However, there are several records from the North Pacific of them attacking large baleen whales (Baldridge, 1972; Tarpy, 1979). There are several old records of them attacking right whales in the North Atlantic and Southern Hemisphere summarized in Mitchell and Reeves (1982a) and several recent records of their having predatory interest in right whales (Cummings *et al.*, 1972; Payne, 1983).

Killer whales are probably more common in the eastern North Pacific than in the western North Atlantic (Dahlheim, 1981; Dahlheim *et al.*, 1982; Braham and Dahlheim, 1982). A recent study (Dohl *et al.*, 1981b, 1982) reveals that they are fairly common as far south as central California at least in autumn. However, the species' conspicuousness and high densities in the nearshore waters from Washington to Alaska (Braham and Dahlheim, 1982) does not necessarily mean there are high densities in offshore waters south of Alaska or in the mid-Pacific where right whales are more likely to be found.

In conclusion, killer whale predation may cause significant mortality in the eastern North Pacific. However, given the lack of data on killer/right whale interactions, it is impossible to evaluate the magnitude of this predation.

(3) *Competition for food with other species.* Several researchers have suggested that the slow observed rates of recovery of right whale populations in the Northern Hemisphere may reflect interspecific competition for food. Mitchell (1975) analyzed trophic relations among baleen whales in the western North Atlantic and noted that right and sei whales were sympatric on their feeding grounds and both preferred copepods as food (see also Watkins and Schevill, 1979). Right whales in the North Atlantic had been depleted by centuries of whaling before the development of steam-driven catcher boats permitted the capture of the sei whales. Mitchell hypothesized that the sei whale population grew as a result of increased food

availability resulting from the reduction in the right whale population. He further suggested that the increased sei whale population may have slowed or prevented the recovery of the right whale population.

Possible competition between right and sei whales in the Southern Hemisphere has been analyzed by Kawamura (1978). He suggests that the euryphagous sei whale is more of an *r*-selected species than the stenophagous right whale. (See also Omura *et al.*'s [1969] discussion for the North Pacific.)

Similar patterns can be seen in the eastern North Pacific. Sei whales are generally sympatric with right whales (Masaki, 1977). The few records of right whale feeding habits show feeding almost entirely on copepods (*Metrida lucens, Calanus plumchrus, C. cristatus*) (Omura, 1958; Klumov, 1963; Omura *et al.*, 1969). Although they are far more opportunistic feeders than right whales, sei whales show a strong preference for the same copepods in the north-eastern North Pacific (Nemoto and Kasuya, 1965; Nemoto and Kawamura, 1977), but not off the California coast (D. Rice, pers. comm.). The whalers depleted the right whale population in the North Pacific over a century before they began to take sei whales in substantial numbers in the early 1960s (Rice, 1974). The sei whale population in the eastern North Pacific was recently estimated to have been stable at about 40,000 until 1963 after which time it was reduced to about 8,000 in 1974 (Tillman, 1977).

Reeves *et al.* (1978) and Reeves and Brownell (1982) both comment that several species in addition to right and sei whales feed on copepods, and therefore the population interactions which may affect the right whale's food supply are likely to be more complex than the simple competitive model suggests.

(4) *Accidental net and fish-trap entanglement.* Reeves *et al.* (1978) conclude that although several right whales have been killed in entanglements with fishing gear in the western North Atlantic, this circumstance does not occur often enough to be a major cause of mortality. I have found no records of right whales entangled in fishing gear in the eastern North Pacific. I doubt that this is a significant cause of mortality of this species in this area.

(5) *Increased turbidity.* Reeves *et al.* (1978) suggest that the right whale is dependent on its eyesight to locate food and to navigate. Increased turbidity of the water column might hinder the whale's ability to do either task. Because of the apparently greater offshore distribution of right whales in the eastern North Pacific than in the western North Atlantic, it seems unlikely that increased turbidity, if it exists at significant levels in the former area, would affect the right whale population.

(6) *Noise.* Reeves *et al.* (1978) suggest that increased ambient noise levels in the ocean, due primarily to increased shipping traffic and other human activities, may hinder communication among right whales necessary for their normal social behavior. Considering the relatively greater offshore distribution of right whales in the eastern North Pacific, the density of shipping traffic may be less than in other former right whale habitats, but the pelagic nature of the distribution may make the existence of quiet channels for long-distance communication more important.

Herman *et al.* (1980) suggest a variant of this hypothesis. Specifically they suggest that in the Hawaiian Islands the highly vocal humpback whales acoustically crowded the right whales out of the region. Because of the scarcity of sightings of right whales in the immediate vicinity of the Hawaiian Islands during the last 130 years, if such an interaction occurred, it must have happened before 1820. Considering the extensive dispersion of the few humpback whales in the Hawaiian Islands, the idea of right whales currently being crowded out seems implausible.

(7) *Pollution.* Reeves *et al.* (1978) hypothesize that right whales may be especially vulnerable to pollution, and in particular oil spills, because of the species' habit of feeding near, or at, the surface skimming larger volumes of water through its baleen than other whales (Watkins and Schevill, 1979). There are no recorded strandings of right whales in the North Pacific where pollution has been identified as a contributing cause. However, this may merely reflect the very small population size and an offshore distribution. No tissue or baleen samples from the whales captured under scientific permits during the 1950s and 1960s were closely examined for contamination by pollutants. Although there is no data which implicate pollution as a significant mortality factor on right whales in the North Pacific, the species does appear particularly vulnerable, and increased amounts of pollution associated with development of offshore oil resources and the mid-ocean dumping of oil by ships will not benefit the species.

(8) *Ship collisions.* There are no published records of right whales being injured or killed in collisions with ships in the eastern North Pacific. There are records from the North Atlantic (Schmitt, 1979; Reeves and Brownell, 1982) and Southern Hemisphere (IWC, 1986). Because nearly any source of mortality is significant on a very small population, this might be important in the North Pacific.

(9) *Continued catch by whalers.* A factor suggested by Gilmore (1978) as preventing recovery is the possible continued catch of right whales by commercial whalers. This could occur either as (1) whales taken under scientific permit, (2) whales illegally taken by IWC-member nations but not reported, or (3) whales taken by non-IWC-member nations. As shown in Table 6, between 1955 and 1968, 23 right whales were taken in the North Pacific under scientific permits. No whales have been so taken since then. Since 1979 the Scientific Committee has instituted a policy requiring its review of such permits prior to their issuance by a member nation (IWC, 1980; Mitchell and Tillman, 1978). Although there are scientific questions which can be most easily answered through the examination of whales captured as part of the fishery, considering the very small size of the population in the North Pacific, the ease of answering those questions by the examination of right whale carcasses does not justify the taking of any more animals.

Gilmore (1978) suggests that the unreported catch of right whales in the North Pacific by IWC member nations may be a significant factor preventing population recovery. There is enough evidence concerning such illegal whaling in the South Atlantic near Tristan da Cunha in 1963 and 1967 (Flint, 1967; Payne *et al.*, 1981) to suggest that such actions may have also occurred in the North Pacific. Since the inception of the IWC's international observer scheme in 1972 (Scarff, 1977), the chances of such illegal catches occurring undetected have been greatly reduced.

The extent of the catch of right whales by non-IWC member nation whalers in the North Pacific is probably slight. Prior to 1965, two right whales were taken by Chinese whalers (Wang, 1978). At least one right whale was landed by Korean whalers, reported to be in 1982 according to Morast, Forkan and Nielsen (1985). Activity by whaling ships flying flags of convenience of non-IWC nations as documented by Van Note (1979) and Carter (1979) seems primarily to have occurred in the Atlantic. It may continue to be a significant source of mortality for right whales there considering the number of animals observed off Argentina with scars apparently caused by harpoons (Payne *et al.* 1981; Payne, 1983; Palazzo and Carter, 1983). Considering the lack of reports of pelagic whalers operating under flags of convenience in the eastern North Pacific, it seems unlikely that this has been a significant source of mortality during the last several decades.

RECOMMENDATIONS REGARDING FURTHER RESEARCH

(1) A statistical analysis should be done of the sighting and effort data contained in Maury's (1852 *et seq.*) maps nos 1 and 2. Such an analysis should provide further information regarding the extent of north–south migration in the North Pacific and the longitudinal distribution of the species during migration. Such a study is planned by this author.

(2) As recommended in 1980 by the IWC Scientific Committee (IWC, 1981), an analysis of 19th- and early 20th-century logbooks should be carried out for the North Pacific. Such an analysis could provide further useful information regarding the timing and extent of exploitation by early pelagic whalers by area and provide further data on the species' distribution. A useful model is the study of sperm whaling in the northwest Pacific carried out by Bannister, Taylor and Southerland (1981).

(3) The NMFS's Platforms of Opportunity program should be modified to focus more on sightings of right whales. Although there are considerable problems associated with the uncertain reliability of sighting records obtained from untrained observers, the distinctiveness of the right whale's form and behaviour make it a relatively easy species to identify (Slijper *et al.*, 1964). The more intensive collection of opportunistic sightings by merchant and naval vessels in the Gulf of Alaska and other areas in the eastern North Pacific represents the best opportunity to accumulate more complete data on the species's distribution and abundance.

(4) Attempts should be made to obtain high-quality photographs of all right whales observed. The whale's natural markings of callosities and colored blazes allow for the identification of individual animals (Payne *et al.*, 1981) and such identification can provide useful information about stock size and migration patterns. Photographs should particularly be taken of the head and callosities, preferably from above or in front of the whale.

(5) A catalog of all photographs of right whales in the North Pacific should be maintained at one location as an aid for further research.

(6) Given the extremely low population level of the species in the North Pacific, the need for complete protection outweighs the value to science of any more right whales harvested for research purposes. At the current population levels, any mortality may be significant. As a corollary, there is little value in marking right whales with Discovery tags because the risk of injury

probably outweighs the value of the tag given the very low probability of the tag being recovered and the redundancy of the tag and natural markings.

ACKNOWLEDGEMENTS

I thank Hazel Sayers for providing me with unpublished material on 19th-century California shore whaling and the catch of right whales during that period. I also thank Dr Dave Huelsbeck for allowing me to use his unpublished data on the Ozette archaeological site. Dale Rice, National Marine Mammal Laboratory, 7600 Sand Point Way N.E., Bldg 32, Seattle, WA 98115 and Dr Hideo Omura, Whales Research Institute, Tokyo, Japan, reviewed the manuscript and offered many wise comments. I owe much to Ed Mitchell, Dale Rice, Steve Leatherwood, and the late Ray Gilmore for their help and encouragement in this project. Barbara McCorkle of the Yale University Library was most helpful in providing me with copies of the Maury charts (1851 and 1852 et seq.). I thank Denise Mann for her invaluable assistance in gathering references. Finally, I thank my parents for their continuing support and encouragement.

REFERENCES

Allen, G. M. 1916. The whalebone whales of New England. *Mem. Boston. Soc. nat. Hist.* 8 (2) : 107–322.

Allen, K. R. 1974. Recruitment to whale stocks, pp. 352–358. *In :* W. E. Schevill (ed.). *The whale problem: A Status Report*, Harvard University Press, Cambridge, Mass. 419 pp.

Andrews, R. W. and Larssen, A. K. 1959. *Fish and Ships*. Bonanza Books, New York. 173 pp.

Anonymous. 1855. Monterey, California *Sentinel*, 10 November.

Anonymous. 1856. Monterey, California *Sentinel*, 22 March.

Anonymous. 1861. Los Angeles, California *Star*, 9 March.

Anonymous. 1871. San Diego, California *Union*, 2 March, p. 3.

Anonymous. 1886. San Diego, California *Daily Union*, 9 March, p. 3.

Anonymous. 1976. Japan progress report on whale research. *Rep. int. Whal. Commn*. 26 : 416–24.

Anonymous. 1979. Japan progress report on cetacean research June 1977–May 1978. *Rep. int. Whal. Commn* 29: 117–20.

Baldridge, A. 1972. Killer whales attack and eat a gray whale. *J. Mammal.* 53: 898–900.

Banfield, A. W. F. 1974. *The Mammals of Canada*. University of Toronto Press (2nd printing 1977). 438 pp.

Bannister, J. 1986. Southern right whales: status off Australia from twentieth century 'incidental' sightings and aerial survey. (Published in this volume.)

Bannister, J. L. and Mitchell, E. D. 1980. North Pacific sperm whale stock identify: distributional evidence from Maury and Townsend charts. *Rep. int. Whal. Commn* (special issue 2): 219–30.

Bannister, J. L., Taylor, S. and Sutherland, H. 1981. Logbook records of 19th century American sperm whaling: a report on the 12 month project, 1978–1979. *Rep. int. Whal. Commn* 31: 821–33.

Barham, E. G. 1982. Marine mammals in Monterey Bay, California, during the years 1950–1955. *Calif. Fish and Game* 68: 213–23.

Berzin, A. A. and Doroshenko, N. V. 1981. Right whales of the Okhotsk Sea. *Rep. int. Whal. Commn* 31: 451–5.

Berzin, A. A. and Doroshenko, N. V. 1982. Distribution and abundance of right whales in the North Pacific. *Rep. int. Whal. Commn* 32: 381–3.

Berzin, A. A. and Rovnin, A. A. 1966. The distribution and migrations of whales in the northeastern part of the Pacific, Chuckchee and Bering seas. *Izv. TINRO* 58: 179–207 (in Russian) [Transl. by US Dept. Inter., Bur. Commer. Fish., Seattle, Washington, 1966, pp. 103–36 *In:* K. I. Panin (ed.), *Soviet Research on Marine Mammals of the Far East.*]

Berzin, A. A. and Vladimirov, V. L. 1981. Changes in the abundance of whalebone whales in the Pacific and the Antarctic since the cessation of their exploitation. *Rep. int. Whal. Commn.* 31: 495–8.

Best, P. 1981. The status of right whales (*Eubalaena glacialis*) off South Africa, 1969–1979. *Investl Rep. Sea Fish. Inst. S. Afr.* 123: 1–44.

Bockstoce, J. R. 1977. *Steam Whaling in the Western Arctic*. Old Dartmouth Hist. Soc., New Bedford, Mass. 127 pp.

Bowles, M. E. 1845. Some account of the whale-fishery of the N. west coast and Kamchatka. Honolulu, Hawaii *Polynesian*, 2 October, 1845.

Braham, H. W. and Dahlheim, M. E. 1982. Killer whales in Alaska documented in the platforms of opportunity program. *Rep. int. Whal. Commn* 32: 643–5.

Brown, S. G. 1986. Twentieth century records of right whales (*Eubalaena glacialis*) in the Northwest Atlantic Ocean. (Published in this volume.)

Brueggeman, J. J., Newby, T. and Grotefendt, R. A. In press. Catch records of twenty North Pacific right whales between 1917 and 1937. *Arctic.*

Carter, L. A. 1979. *Pirate Whaling*. People's Trust for Endangered Species, Guildford, Surrey, England. 52 pp.

Cawthorn, M. W. 1983. Current status off New Zealand – 20th century sightings and trends. Paper presented to the Workshop on the Status of Right Whales, June 1983.

Collins, J. W. 1892. Report on the fisheries of the Pacific coast of the United States, pp. 3–269. *In: Rep. Cmmr for 1888, US Commn Fish and Fisheries.* US House of Rep. Misc. Doc. No. 274. 902 pp.

Convention for the Regulation of Whaling, September 24, 1931, 49 Stat. 3079, T.S. No. 880, 155 LNTS 349.

Cummings, W. C., Fish, J. F., and Thompson, P. O. 1972. Sound production and other behavior of southern right whales, *Eubalaena glacialis*. San Diego Soc. Nat. Hist. Trans. 17(1): 1–14.

Dahlheim, M. E. 1981. A review of the biology and exploitation of the killer whale, *Orcinus orca*, with comments on recent sightings from Antarctica. *Rep. int. Whal. Commn* 31: 541–546.

Dahlheim, M. E., Leatherwood, S. and Perrin, W. F. 1982. Distribution of killer whales in the warm temperate and tropical eastern Pacific. *Rep. int. Whal. Commn* 32: 647–653.

DeBus, B. (ed.) 1975. [News] *Whalewatcher* 9(7): 10–11. [Am. Cetacean Soc., San Pedro, Ca.].

Dohl, T. P., Norris, K. S., Guess, R. C., Bryant, J. D. 1981a. Cetacea of southern California bight. *In: Summary of Marine Mammal and Seabird Surveys of the Southern California Bight Area 1975–1978* vol. III (2), NTIS PB81-248189. 434 pp.

Dohl, T. P., Norris, K. S., Dunman, M. L., and Helm, R. C. 1981b. Marine mammal and seabird study, central and northern California. Ann. Prog. Rep. Center for Coastal Marine Studies, University of California, Santa Cruz.

Dohl, T. P., Norris, K. S., Dunman, M. L. and Helm, R. C. 1982. Marine mammal and seabird study central and northern California. Ann. Prog. Rep. USDI POCS Tech. Pap. No. 82–1.

Drucker, P. 1951. The northern and central Nootkan tribes. *Smithson. Inst. Bur. Am. Ethnol.*, Bull. 144: 480 pp.

Du Pasquier, T. 1986. Historical catches of right whales by area. Appendix to Workshop Report. (Published in this volume.)

Eschricht, D. F. and Reinhardt, J. 1866. On the Greenland right whale (*Balaena mysticetus*, Linn.), pp. 1–150. *In:* W. H. Flower (ed.). *Recent memoirs on the Cetacea.* Ray Soc. London. 312 pp.

FAO ACMRR. 1978. Report of the Working Party on Marine Mammals. *FAO Fish. Ser.* 5 (1): 1–264.

Fiscus, C. H. and Niggol, K., 1965. Observations of cetaceans off California, Oregon, and Washington. *US Fish and Wildl. Serv. Spec. Sci. Rep. Fish.* No. 498.

Flint, J. H. 1967. Conservation problems on Tristan da Cunha. *Oryx* 9(1): 28–32.

Foster, L. 1974. The whale object: a portfolio of drawings. pp. 97–103. *In:* J. McIntyre (ed.) *Mind in the Waters.* Charles Scribner's Sons, New York. 240 pp.

Gilmore, R. M. 1956. Rare right whale visits California. *Pac. Discovery* 9(4): 20–5.

Gilmore, R. M. 1978. Right whale, pp. 62–9. *In:* D. Haley (ed.) *Marine Mammals of the Eastern North Pacific and Arctic Waters.* Pacific Search Press, Seattle. 256 pp.

Gray, J. E. 1868. On the geographical distribution of the Balaenidae or right whales. *Ann. Mag. Nat. Hist.* 4th ser. 1 (April): 242–7.

Henderson, D. A. 1972. *Men and Whales at Scammon's Lagoon.* Dawson's Book Shop, Los Angeles. 313 pp.

Herman, L. M., Baker, C. S., Forestell, P. H. and Antinoja, R. C. 1980. Right whale *Balaena glacialis* sightings near Hawaii: a clue to the wintering grounds? *Mar. Ecol. Prog. Ser.* 2: 271–5.

Huber, H. R., Ainley, D. G. and Morrell, S. H. 1982. Sightings of cetaceans in the Gulf of the Farallones, California, 1971–1979. *Calif. Fish Game* 68: 183–90.

Huff, B. 1957. *El Puerto de los Balleneros. Annals of the Sausalito Whaling Anchorage.* Glen Dawson, Los Angeles. 47 pp.

International Whaling Commission. 1980. Chairman's report of the thirty-first annual meeting. *Rep. int. Whal. Commn* 30: 25–41.

International Whaling Commission. 1981. Report of the subcommittee on other protected species and aboriginal whaling. *Rep. int. Whal. Commn* 31: 133–39.

International Whaling Commission. 1982. Report of the subcommittee on protected species and aboriginal whaling. *Rep. int. Whal. Commn* 32: 104–12.

International Whaling Commission. 1983. Report of the subcommittee on protected species and aboriginal whaling. *Rep. int. Whal. Commn* 33: 142–51.

I.W.S. International Whaling Statistics. Edited and Published by the Committee for Whaling Statistics, Sandefjord, Norway, 1930–.

Jenkins, J. T. 1932. *Whales and Modern Whaling*. Witherby, London. 239 pp.

Johnson, T. 1982. A survivor at sea. *Oceans* 15(5): 52.

Jonsgård, A. 1981. Bowhead whales, *Balaena mysticetus*, observed in Arctic waters of the eastern North Atlantic after the second world war. *Rep. int. Whal. Commn* 31: 511.

Jordan, D. S. 1887. Coast of California. pp. 52–64. *In*: A. H. Clark (ed.) The history and present condition of the fishery. *In* G. B. Goode (ed.), *The Fisheries and Fishery Industries of the United States*, Vol. II, Section V (History and methods of the fisheries).

Kawamura, A. 1978. An interim consideration on a possible inter-specific relation in southern baleen whales from the view-point of their food habits. *Rep. int. Whal. Commn* 28: 411–19.

Kaza, S. 1982. Recreational whalewatching in California: a profile. *Whalewatcher* 16(1): 6–8.

Kellogg, R. 1931. Whaling statistics for the Pacific coast of North America. *J. Mammal.* 12: 73–7.

Klumov, S. K. 1962. Gladkie (Yaponskie) kity Tikhogo Okeana [The right whales in the Pacific Ocean]. *Trudy Inst. Okeanol.* 58: 202–97. [In Russian with English summary.]

Klumov, S. K 1963. Pitanie i gelmintofauna usatykh (Mystacoceti) v osnovnykh promyslovykh raionakh mirovogo okeana [Food and helminth fauna of whalebone whales (Mystacoceti) in the main whaling regions of the world ocean]. *Tr. Inst. Okeanol.* 71: 94–194. [Translated from Russian as *Fish. Res. Board Can. Trans. Ser.* no. 589, 1965.]

Kraus, S. D. and Prescott, J. H. 1981. Large cetaceans of the Bay of Fundy. Rep. to US Dept. of Comm. Natl Mar. Fish. Serv. *cited in* Kraus and Prescott (1983).

Kraus, S. D. and Prescott, J. H. 1983. A note on the efficiency of aerial surveys for right whales *Eubalaena glacialis*. Paper presented to the Workshop on the Status of Right Whales, June 1983.

Kraus, S. D., Prescott, J. H., Turnbull, P. V. and Reeves, R. R. 1982. Preliminary notes on the occurrence of the North Atlantic right whale, *Eubalaena glacialis*, in the Bay of Fundy. *Rep. int. Whal. Commn* 32: 407–11.

Kugler, R. C. 1981. Historical records of American sperm whaling. Mammals of the sea. *FAO Fish. Ser.* 5(3): 321–6.

Leatherwood, S. and Walker, W. A. 1979. The northern right whale dolphin, *Lissodelphis borealis* Peale, in the eastern North Pacific, pp. 85–141. *In*: H. E. Winn and B. L. Olla (eds.) *Behavior of Marine Animals, Vol. 3: Cetaceans*. Plenum Press, New York 438 pp.

Leatherwood, S. and Walker, W. A. 1982. Population biology and ecology of the Pacific white-sided dolphin *Lagenorhynchus obliquidens* in the northeastern Pacific. Part 1. NOAA NMFS SWFC Admin. Rep. LJ-82-18C. 76 pp.

Leatherwood, S., Perrin, W. F., Rowntree, V. L., Hubbs, C. L. and Dahlheim, M. 1980. Distribution and movements of Risso's dolphin, *Grampus griseus*, in the eastern North Pacific. *Fish. Bull., US* 77: 951–63.

Leatherwood, S., Goodrich, K., Kinter, A. L. and Truppo, R. M. 1982. Respiration patterns and 'sightability' of whales. *Rep. int. Whal. Commn* 32: 601–13.

Leonard, L. L. 1941. Recent negotiations toward the international regulation of whaling. *Am. J. Intl Law* 35: 90–113.

Masaki, Y. 1977. The separation of the stock units of sei whales in the North Pacific. *Rep. int. Whal. Commn* (special issue 1): 71–79.

Maury, M. F. 1851. *Whale Chart (Preliminary Sketch)*. Series F. Natl Observatory, Washington, DC 1 sheet.

Maury, M. F. 1852 *et seq. Whale Chart of the World*. (The Wind and Current Charts), Series F. Washington, DC 4 sheets, No. 1 (North Atlantic, NE Pacific) 1852. Whale Sheet No. 2 (NW Pacific) n.d.

Mead, J. G. (1986. Twentieth century records of right whales (*Balaena glacialis*) in the northwestern Atlantic ocean (Published in this volume.)

Mermoz, J. F. 1980. Preliminary report on the southern right whale in the southwestern Atlantic. *Rep. int. Whal. Commn* 30: 183–6.

Mitchell, E. 1975. Trophic relationships and competition for food in northwest Atlantic whales. *Proc. Can. Soc. Zool. (Ann. Mtg.)*: 123–132.

Mitchell, E. 1979. Comments on magnitude of early catch of east Pacific

gray whale (*Eschrichtius robustus*). *Rep. int. Whal. Commn* 29: 307–14.

Mitchell, E. D. and Reeves, R. R. 1982a. Factors affecting the abundance of bowhead whales (*Balaena mysticetus*) in the eastern Arctic of North America, 1915–1980. *Biol. Cons.* 22: 59–78.

Mitchell, E. D. and Reeves, R. R. 1982b. Catch history and cumulative catch estimates of initial population size of cetaceans in the eastern Canadian Arctic. *Rep. int. Whal. Commn* 31: 645–82.

Mitchell, E. and Tillman, M. F. 1978. Scientific review of IWC scientific permits. *Rep. int. Whal. Commn* 28: 269–70.

Morast, D. J., Forkan, P. and Nielsen, M. 1985. Pirate whaling in the Republic of Korea. The Human Society of the U.S., Washington, D.C., 3pp.

Nemoto, T. and Kasuya, T. 1965. Foods of baleen whales in the Gulf of Alaska of the North Pacific. *Sci. Rep. Whales Res. Inst., Tokyo* 19: 45–51.

Nemoto, T. and Kawamura, A. 1977. Characteristics of food habits and distribution of baleen whales with special reference to the abundance of North Pacific sei and Bryde's whales. *Rep. int. Whal. Commn* (special issue 1): 80–87.

Norris, K. S. and Prescott, J. H. 1961. Observations on Pacific cetaceans of California and Mexican waters. *Univ. Calif. Publ. Zool.* 63: 291–402.

Ohsumi, S. 1976. Population assessment of the California gray whale. *Rep. int. Whal. Commn* 25: 350–9.

Ohsumi, S. and Yamamura, K. 1982. A review of the Japanese whale sightings. *Rep. int. Whal. Commn* 32: 581–6.

O'Leary, B. L. 1984. Aboriginal whaling from the Aleutian Islands to Washington State, pp. 79–102. *In*: M. L. Jones, S. L. Swartz and S. Leatherwood (eds) *The Gray Whale, Eschrichtius robustus*, Academic Press, Inc, Orlando and London, i–xxiv + 600 pp.

Omura, H. 1958. North Pacific right whale. *Sci. Rep. Whales Res. Inst., Tokyo* 13: 1–52.

Omura, H. 1986. History of right whale catches in the waters around Japan (Published in this volume.)

Omura, H., Ohsumi, S., Nemoto, R., Nasu, K. and Kasuya, T. 1969. Black right whales in the North Pacific. *Sci. Rep. Whales Res. Inst., Tokyo* 21: 1–78.

Palazzo, J. T., Jr and Carter, L. A. 1983. Projecto baleia francia (Right Whale Project). Paper presented at the Workshop on the Status of Right Whales, June 1983.

Payne, R. 1972. Swimming with Patagonia's right whales. *Nat. Geogr.* 142: 576–87.

Payne, R. 1976. At home with right whales. *Nat. Geogr.* 149: 322–39.

Payne, R. 1986. Long term behavioral studies of the southern right whale (Eubalaena australis). (Published in this volume.)

Payne, R., Brazier, O., Dorsey, E., Perkins, J., Rowntree, V. and Titus, A. 1981. External features in southern right whales (*Eubalaena australis*) and their use in identifying individuals. USDC NTIS PB81-161093. 77 pp.

Pike, G. C., and McAskie, I. B. 1969. Marine mammals of British Columbia. *Fish. Res. Bd Can. Bull.* 171: 1–54.

Reeves, R. R. 1980. Spitzbergen bowhead stock: a short review. *Mar. Fish. Rev.* 42(9–10): 65–9.

Reeves, R. R. and Brownell, R. L., Jr. 1982. Baleen whales (*Eubalaena glacialis* and allies), pp. 415–444. *In*: J. A. Chapman and G. A. Feldhamer (eds.), *Wild Mammals of North America: Biology, Management, and Economics*. Johns Hopkins University Press, Baltimore. 1147 pp.

Reeves, R. R., Mead, J. G. and Katona, S. 1978. The right whale, *Eubalaena glacialis* in the western North Atlantic. *Rep. int. Whal. Commn* 28: 303–12.

Reeves, R. R., Kraus, S. and Turnbull, P. 1983. Right whale refuge? *Nat. Hist.* 92(4): 40–45.

Reilly, S. B., Rice, D. W. and Wolman, A. A. 1980. Preliminary population estimate for the California gray whale based upon Monterey shore censuses, 1967/68 to 1978/79. *Rep. int. Whal. Commn* 30: 359–68.

Rice, D. W. 1963a. Progress report on biological studies of the larger cetacea in the waters off California. *Norsk Hvalfangsttid.* 52(7): 181–7.

Rice, D. W. 1963b. The whale marking cruise of the Sioux City off California and Baja California. *Norsk Hvalfangsttid.* 52(6): 105–7.

Rice, D. W. 1974. Whales and whale research in the eastern North Pacific, pp. 170–95. *In*: W. Schevill (ed.). *The Whale Problem: A Status Report*, Cambridge, Mass., Harvard University Press, 419 pp.

Rice, D. W. 1977. Synopsis of biological data on the sei whale and Bryde's whale in the eastern North Pacific. *Rep. int. Whal. Commn* (special issue 1): 92–7.

Rice, D. W. and Fiscus, C. H. 1968. Right whales in the south-eastern North Pacific. *Norsk Hvalfangsttid.* 57(5): 105–7.

Rice, D. W. and Wolman, A. A. 1971. The life history and ecology of the gray whale (*Eschrichtius robustus*). *Am. Soc. Mammal. Spec. Publ.* No. 3. 142 pp.

Rowntree, V., Darling, J., Silber, G. and Ferrari, M. 1980. Rare sighting of a right whale (*Eubalaena glacialis*) in Hawaii. *Can. J. Zool.* 58: 309–12.

Sayers, H. 1984. Shore whaling for gray whales along the coasts of the Californias, pp. 121–57. *In*: M. L. Jones, S. L. Swartz and S. Leatherwood (eds) *The Gray Whale, Eschrichtius robustus.* Academic Press, Inc., Orlando and London. i–xxiv + 600 pp.

Scammon, C. M. 1874. *The Marine Mammals of the Northwestern Coast of North America* (John M. Carmany and Co., San Francisco), 319 pp. [Reprinted in Dover edn, 1968.]

Scarff, J. E. 1977. The international management of whales, dolphins, and porpoises, an interdisciplinary assessment. *Ecol. Law Quart.* 6: 323–427, 574–638.

Scarff, J. E. 1986. Occurrence of the barnacles *Coronula diadema, C. reginae* and *Cetopirus complanatus* (Cirripedia) on right whales. *Sci. Rep. Whales Res. Inst., Tokyo* 37: 129–53.

Scheffer, V. B. and Slipp, J. W. 1948. The whales and dolphins of Washington state. *Am. Midl. Nat.* 39: 257–334.

Schmitt, F. P. 1979. Vessels vs. whales. *Sea Frontiers* 25(3): 141–4.

Slijper, E. J., Van Utrecht, W. L. and Naaktgeboren, C. 1964. Remarks on the distribution and migration of whales, based on observations from Netherlands ships. *Bijdr. Dierkd.* 34: 1–93.

Stackpole, E. A. 1953. *The Sea-Hunters, the New England Whalemen during the Two Centuries 1635–1835.* Lippincott, New York. 510 pp.

Starbuck, A. 1878. History of the American whale fishery from its earliest inception to the year 1876. *Rep. U.S. Comm. Fish* (4) 1875–76, Appendix A, 768 pp. (Reprinted; 1964, Argosy-Antiquarian Ltd, New York, 2 vols.)

Starks, E. C. 1922. A history of California shore whaling. *Calif. Fish Game Commn Fish Bull.* 6: 1–38.

Storro-Patterson, R. 1977. Gray whale protection; how well is it working? *Oceans* 10(4): 45–9.

Swan, J. C. 1870. The Indians of Cape Flattery. *Smithson. Contrib. Knowl.* 16(8): 1–108.

Tarpy, C. 1979. Killer whale attack. *Nat. Geogr.* 155: 542–5.

Tillman, M. 1977. Estimates of population size for the North Pacific sei whale. *Rep. int. Whal. Commn* (special issue 1): 98–106.

Tomilin, A. G. 1957. *Mammals of the USSR and adjacent countries Vol. 9, Cetacea.* Izdatel'stvo Akademi Nauk SSSR, Moskva, 756 pp. [Translated from Russian in 1967 by the Israel Program for Sci. Trans., Jerusalem. 717 pp].

Tønnessen, J. N. and A. O. Johnsen. 1982. *The History of Modern Whaling*, (trans. from Norwegian by R. I. Christophersen). University of California Press, Berkeley. 798 pp.

Townsend, C. H. 1886. Present condition of the California gray whale fishery. *Bull, US Fish Commn* 6: 346–50.

Townsend, C. H. 1935. The distribution of certain whales as shown by logbook records of American whaleships. *Zoologica* N.Y. 19: 1–50.

Van Beneden, P. J. 1868. Les baleines et leur distribution géographique. *Bull. Acad. R. Belg.* 2 ser. 25(1): 9–25.

Van Note, C. 1979. *Outlaw Whalers.* Whale Protection Fund, Washington, DC 28 pp.

Wada, S. 1975. Indices of abundance of large-sized whales in the North Pacific in the 1973 whaling season. *Rep. int. Whal. Commn* 25: 129–65.

Wada, S. 1976. Indices of abundance of large-sized whales in the North Pacific in the 1974 whaling season. *Rep int. Whal. Commn* 25: 382–91.

Wada, S. 1977. Indices of abundance of large-sized whales in the North Pacific in the 1975 whaling season. *Rep. int. Whal. Commn* 27: 189–93.

Wada, S. 1978. Indices of abundance of large-sized whales in the North Pacific in the 1976 whaling season. *Rep. int. Whal. Commn* 28: 319–24.

Wada, S. 1979. Indices of abundance of large-sized whales in the North Pacific in the 1977 whaling season. *Rep. int. Whal. Commn* 29: 253–64.

Wada, S. 1980. Japanese whaling and whale sighting in the North Pacific 1978 season. *Rep. int. Whal. Commn* 30: 415–24.

Wada, S. 1981. Japanese whaling and whale sighting in the North Pacific 1979 season. *Rep. int. Whal. Commn* 31: 783–92.

Wang, P. 1978. Studies on baleen whales in the Yellow Sea. *Acta Zool. Sinica* 24(3): 269–77 [In Chinese.]

Watkins, W. A. and Schevill, W. E. 1979. Aerial observation of feeding behavior in four baleen whales: *Eubalaena glacialis. Balaenoptera borealis, Megaptera novaeangliae*, and *Balaenoptera physalus. J. Mammal.* 60: 155–63.

Whipple, A. B. C. 1979. *The Whalers.* Time-Life Books, Alexandria, Virginia. 176 pp.

Whitehead, H., Payne, R. and Payne, P. M. 1986. Population estimate for the right whales off Peninsula Valdes, Argentina 1971–1976 (Published in this volume.)

Woodhouse, C. D. Jr and Strickley, J. 1982. Sighting of northern right whale in the Santa Barbara channel. *J. Mammal.* 63: 701–2.

An Annotated Bibliography of Right Whales, *Eubalaena glacialis*, in the North Pacific

HOWARD W. BRAHAM

National Marine Mammal Laboratory, Northwest and Alaska Fisheries Center, NMFS, NOAA,
7600 Sand Point Way, N.E., Seattle, Washington 98115

ABSTRACT

An annotated bibliography (108 items plus an appendix of 21 unseen references) has been compiled for right whales in the North Pacific. Annotations include information primarily concerning sightings, distribution, abundance, migration, historical catches, life history data and prey items.

INTRODUCTION

This bibliography was written to give an overview of the available published and unpublished material (located) on right whales (*Eubalaena glacialis*) in the North Pacific Ocean. Annotations were provided, first, to inform users of the nature, scope and level of detail found in each reference so they might judge for themselves its utility and, second, because much information is either not readily available in most libraries or is found buried in lengthy or obscure volumes. For example, of the over 100 annotations herein, approximately 48% are (1) from 'grey literature' sources (3%); (2) in a foreign language as originally published (13%); (3) in hard-to-locate annual reports (e.g. early volumes of the International Whaling Commission) and some older whaling references (e.g. Townsend, 1886 and Tower, 1907) (31%); or (4) simply unpublished (1%). Several foreign language articles were unavailable to me for annotation and therefore appear in the appendix. In a few instances (e.g. Allen, 1974) information regarding other geographic areas was included where the references contained indirect material relevant to right whales in the North Pacific. Annotations include information primarily concerning sighting records, distribution, abundance, migration, historical catches and whaling, life history summaries, or prey items. In some cases (e.g., IWC, 1976; 1977; Wada, 1979) I further interpreted or analyzed raw data where no discussion was provided by the author(s) of the original paper.

Although the records reflected in this bibliography are probably not complete, it appears that about 149–163 right whale sightings have been reported in the past three decades (1958–1982) divided between four geographic areas: 42 in Japan-northwest Pacific waters; 54–59 in the Okhotsk Sea; 32–36 for the central North Pacific-Bering Sea; and 21–26 from the west coast of North America south of Kodiak, Alaska. The 164 sightings reported by Omura (1958) for the period 1941–1957 are about equal to those since 1957. For the past 45 years, then, approximately 300 reports of right whales have occurred. These sightings came from many vessel and aerial surveys conducted by Japan, the Soviet Union and the United States but do not account for duplicate sightings or sightings made of the same animal over several years.

The size of the North Pacific population(s) is unknown and no statistically reliable estimate is possible given the limited sighting information. The sighting records suggest, however, that there are probably only a few hundred survivors today, an estimate frequently seen in the current literature. They also suggest that the North Pacific population or regional populations of right whales were severely depleted by commercial whaling. A complete analysis of available whaling records is needed to help determine how abundant right whales were before commercial whaling began. An analysis and review of the published information on right whales in the North Pacific south of 50°N is summarized by Scarff (1986).

Referencing for this bibliography came from a variety of sources. I relied initially on N. Severinghaus (1979, Selected annotated references on marine mammals of Alaska. NWAFC Proc. Rep. 79–15, National Marine Mammal Laboratory, Seattle, Wash., 178 p.), and in a few cases after verifying the material, simply edited her annotations (e.g. Nemoto, 1957, 1959; Sleptsov, 1955). For most citations however greater information specifically concerning right whales was inserted. All citations were found in the National Marine Mammal Laboratory (NMML) library book, journal or reprint collection; the library of the University of Washington; Severinghaus (1979); J. E. Bird (1983, An annotated bibliography of the published literature on the humpback whale (*Megaptera novaeangliae*) and the right whale (*Eubalaena glacialis/australis*) from 1864 to 1980, p. 467–625. *In*: R. Payne (ed.), *Communication and Behaviour of Whales*. AAAS Selected Symposia Series, 76 Westview Press, Boulder, Colo.); the personal libraries of Dale W. Rice, National Marine Mammal Laboratory, R. R. Reeves, Arctic Biological Station, Ste.-Anne-de-Bellevue, Quebec, or my own. Publication titles and abbreviations were derived from BioSciences Information Service (1984. *Serial Sources for Biosis Data Base*. Volume 84, BioSciences Information Service, 2100 Arch St., Philadelphia, PA 19103–1399) except for certain unlisted periodicals (e.g. Report of the International Whaling Commission, Whale Watcher, and NOAA Technical Memorandum NMFS F/AKR series). Foreign language transliteration referencing followed that adopted by the US Library of Congress.

ACKNOWLEDGEMENTS

I thank Dale Rice, Richard Kugler, David Henderson, Randall Reeves, Sherry Pearson, Michele Eames, Kathy Strickland, Nancy Pagh, Leola Hietala and three anonymous reviewers for their assistance.

ANNOTATED BIBLIOGRAPHY

Allen, J. A. 1908. The North Atlantic right whale and its near allies. *Bull. Am. Mus. Nat. His.* 24(18): 277–329.
Interesting account of the history and taxonomy of right whales in general, with small mention of Pacific right whales (pp. 305, 307–8). Includes information that North Pacific right whales have longer body lengths and longer baleen than their North Atlantic counterpart.

Allen, K. R. 1974. Current status and effect of a moratorium on the major whale stocks. *Rep. int. Whal. Commn* 24: 72–5.
Projects the possible effects on six species, including right whales, of a complete and protracted moratorium on killing. Brief text explains use of terms in table and methods of estimation used.

Berzin, A. A. and Doroshenko, N. V. 1981. Right whales of the Okhotsk Sea. *Rep. int. Whal. Commn* 31: 451–55.
Results of two vessel surveys (1967 and 1974) and one aerial survey (1979) are reported: 14 right whales were seen in July 1967 near the Kuril Islands; 40–45 were seen in the central and northeast region of the Okhotsk Sea in 1974; and none was seen in August 1979 in southwest Okhotsk Sea, where 55 bowheads were sighted primarily in Academy Bay. Bowheads were also seen in southwest Okhotsk Sea in 1967(54) and 1974(35).

Berzin, A. A. and Doroshenko, N. V. 1982. Distribution and abundance of right whales in the North Pacific. *Rep. int. Whal. Commn* 32: 381–83.
Right whale and bowhead whale distributions are discussed with liberal use of commercial records from Townsend (1935), the recent literature and Soviet data. The authors report right whales once occurred south to 20°N (no data provided) and in the Sea of Japan but may not now. Most recent records (this half century) occurred in waters from northern Japan to Kamchatka Peninsula and Commander Islands. They suggest that a sighting at 58°30′N is perhaps a northern record, and report that right whales are now found mostly in the southeast Bering Sea and Gulf of Alaska.

Berzin, A. A. and Kuz'min, A. A. 1975. Serye i gladkie kity okhotskogo moria (Gray and right whales of the Okhotsk Sea), pp. 30–32. *In*: G. B. Agarkov and I. V. Smelova (eds.) Morskie mlekopitayushchie (Marine mammals), Part 1, (Materials from 6th All-Union Conf. (on Studies on Marine Mammals)), Kiev, 1–3 Oct. 1975. Min. Rybn. Khoz. SSSR, Ikhtiol. Kom., VNIRO, Akad. Nauk SSSR. Inst. Evol. Morfol. Ekol. Zhivotn., Inst. Biol. Razvit., Zool. Inst., Akad. Nauk USSR, Inst. Zool. Izd. 'Naukova Dunka', Kiev. In Russian. (Transl. avail. Natl. Mar. Fish. Serv., Off. Int. Fish., Lang. Serv. Branch, Washington, D.C., 2 pp.)
Pacific right whales are present in the central and northeast areas of the Okhotsk Sea in summer. Bowhead whales are found in the western areas in the summer. No further details given.

Berzin, A. A. and Rovnin, A. A. 1966. Raspredelenie i migratsii kitov v severo-vostochnoi chasti Tikhogo okeana, v Beringovom i Chukotskom moryakh (Distribution and migration of whales in the northeastern part of the Pacific Ocean, Bering and Chukchi Seas). *Izv. Tikhookean. Nauchno-issled. Inst. Rybn. Khoz. Okeanogr.* (TINRO) 58: 179–207. In Russian. (Transl. by U.S. Dep. Inter., Bur. Commer. Fish.,

Seattle, Washington, 1966, pp. 103–6. *In*: K. I. Panin (ed.), Soviet Research on Marine Mammals of the Far East.)
Information on sperm, humpback, finback, blue, gray, and Pacific right whales has been gathered by Russian research vessels and whaling fleets, and is presented here. Three oceanographic factors are discussed as they relate to whale distribution: salinity of water, cyclonic current systems, and distribution of preferred food species. In the Bering Sea, right whales were only encountered in the southeastern 'corner' within a line connecting Atka, St Matthew and Nunivak islands. Sightings were also made north of Amukta Strait (52° 30′ N, 171° 30′ W about 150 km west of Atka Island), between the Pribilof Islands, Nunivak Island and Bristol Bay. Only 'rare single right whales were observed by our vessels as far as Chichagov Island' (southeast Alaska). Plots of whales suggest that 200 to 450 right whale sightings (possibly including whales taken) were made between 1958–1964 in the southeast Bering Sea and Gulf of Alaska. No numbers, positions or dates are given. The authors suggest that right whales move in a broad front from the North Pacific to the Bering Sea. Pelagic sightings reported were: May (no year) at 50–51° N, 140–150° W (whales moving north); January (1964) at 40° N, 157° W; and October (1962) at 45° N, 161° E (whales moving south). In 1963 'only 200 right whales were encountered', usually as singles or pairs, and rarely 4–5 together.

Birkeland, K. B. 1926. *The Whalers of Akutan*. An account of modern whaling in the Aleutian Islands. Yale Univ. Press, New Haven, Conn. 171 pp.
Two visits by the author to the southeastern Bering Sea in 1914 and 1915 are chronicled; discussed in particular is his stay at the Akutan Whaling Station, which he helped establish on Akutan Island in the eastern Aleutian Islands. In 1911, the Alaska Whaling Company (in 1912 renamed the North Pacific Sea Products Company) was formed from money contributed by Norway and the United States. The Alaska Whaling Station was built from the money raised and two whaling boats (*Kodiak* and *Unimak*) were commissioned. He reported that only two right whales were killed at the station during his two summers' stay (page 26), and one whale produced 300 barrels of oil. (Dates whales taken are not given.) Photos of a right whale and baleen are included (pages 89 and 82, respectively). Frequent discussion is made of whales being taken (primarily humpback and sperm) but the details are not reported. From the discussion (e.g. page 111), the struck and lost rate may at times have been high.

Braham, H. W., Oliver, G. W., Fowler, C., Frost, K., Cowles, C., Costa, D., Schneider, K. and Calkins, D. 1982. Marine Mammals, pp. 55–81, Chapter 4. *In*: M. J. Hameedi (ed.) *The St George basin environment and possible consequences of planned offshore oil and gas development*. US Dep. Commer., Natl. Oceanic Atmos. Admin., Off. Mar. Pollut. Assess., Outer Cont. Shelf Environ. Assess. Program, Juneau, Alaska.
Reviews the natural history and biology of marine mammals in the southeastern Bering Sea including distribution, migrations, food species and possible effects of industrial activities. Right whales, because of their low population size, may be particularly vulnerable to industrial activity; others include fur seals, sea otters, and humpback whales.

Braham, H. W. and Rice, D. W. 1984. The right whale, *Balaena glacialis*. *Mar. Fish. Rev.* 46(4): 38–44.
Summarizes current information from the literature on the stocks of right whales worldwide covering distribution and migration, life history and ecology, exploitation and population size, and management, including two early 20th century photographs of whaling stations at Akutan, Alaska, and Kyvoquot, Vancouver Island, British Columbia.

Brueggeman, J. J., Grotefendt, R. A. and Erickson, A. W. 1984. Endangered whale abundance and distribution in the Navarin Basin of the Bering Sea during the ice-free period, pp. 201–36. *In*: B. R. Melteff and D. H. Rosenberg (eds.), *Proceedings of the Workshop on Biological Interactions among Marine Mammals and Commercial Fisheries in Southeastern Bering Sea, October 18–21, 1983, Anchorage, Alaska.*

Alaska Sea Grant Report 84–1, University of Alaska. 300 pp.

Three joint aerial (helicopter)/vessel surveys in May–June, July–August and October–November 1982 were conducted across deep water to over continental shelf waters east of the US–USSR convention line in the Central Bering Sea from approximately 58° N to 63° N west of St Matthew Island in an area considered for oil development called the Navarin Basin. Two right whales were observed from the vessel, together, southwest of St Matthew Island (exact position not given) in August 1982 at water depths of 104 m. From a coverage of approximately 2% of the Navarin Basin, the authors estimate the density of right whales to be 1.1 animal per 1,000 nmi², and an abundance estimate of 57 ± 118 animals for the summer period.

Brueggeman, J., Newby, T. and Grotenfendt, R. A. 1986. Catch records of the twenty North Pacific right whales from two Alaska whaling stations, 1917 to 1937. *Arctic* 39(1): 43–6.

'The North Pacific right whale population was hunted commercially between 1835 and 1935, at which time the species received protection. Commercial whalers harvested over 15,000 North Pacific right whales during this period, so reducing the population that today there are an estimated 100–200 right whales in the North Pacific. The American Pacific Whaling Company operated in the Gulf of Alaska and eastern Bering Sea from 1917 through 1939. We report the distribution, sexes, and lengths of 20 right whales recorded in the company logbooks and ledgers. These records identify that right whale catches were widely distributed on the whaling grounds and tended to decrease over the May to October whaling season. Of the 17 whales for which sex and length data were documented, 11 were females. Their average length exceeded that of males. Lengths of the whales indicated that 41% of the catch was sexually mature; two females carried fetuses. Although the sample size is small, these results suggest that the North Pacific right whale population was inhabiting its prehistoric summering grounds after the period of heavy exploitation in the 1800s, reproducing as late as 1926, and supporting a subadult cohort at least until the species was protected.' (Author's abstract; cited with permission from the author.)

Clark, A. H. 1887. The American whale-fishery, 1877–1886. *Science* 9(217): 321–4.

Describes whale fisheries for sperm, right, bowhead, gray and humpback whales worldwide. Data are provided by years for oil yields (including walrus oil added to yields for arctic whales) and whale bone. Only a passing mention is made of the right whale whaling grounds ('Kodiak', or 'North-west coast', and Japan and Okhotsk seas). At one point 'upwards' of 200 American vessels were used to take right whales (as well as sperm whales) in the North Pacific; most turned their attention to bowheads and had abandoned the right whale fishery before 1877.

Dall, W. H. 1874. Catalogue of the cetacea of the North Pacific Ocean, with osteological notes, and descriptions of some new forms; with special reference to the forms described and figured in the foregoing monograph of Pacific cetacea, by Captain C. M. Scammon, U.S.R.M., pp. 281–307. *In*: C. M. Scammon, 1874. *The marine mammals of the North-western coast of North America, described and illustrated: together with the account of the American whale-fishery*. John H. Carmany and Company, San Francisco, and G. P. Putnam's Sons, New York. 319 p. +i–v.

Lists the right whale as in the genus *Balaena*, from Gray 1866, but also uses *Eubalaena* Gray 1866, and classifies the species as *Balaena sieboldii* with other names appearing *Eubalaena sieboldii*, var *Japonica*, Gray 1866, and *Balaena cullamach*? Cham., Cope, Proc. Phil. Acad. 1869. Gives its range as Arctic, Bering, and Okhotsk Seas, Lower California and perhaps Japan. Dall believed the name *Japonica* to be a misnomer.

Fiscus, C. H. and Niggol, K. 1965. Observation of cetaceans off California, Oregon and Washington. *US Fish Wildl. Serv., Spec. Sci. Rep. Fish.*, 498: 1–27.

Twenty-two sightings of right whales are reported, all in 1959: (1) three at 45° 55′ N, 125° 55′ W on 8 April; (2) three at 46° 54′ N, 124° 56′ W on 10 April; (3) eight at 47° 35′ N, 124° 46′ W on 19 April; and (4) eight at 47° 37′ N, 124° 42′ W on 19 April. (Because of the proximity of sightings, I believe these represent two groups of 3 and 8 individuals, totaling 11 animals.) See discussion in Scarff, this volume.

Gilmore, R. M. 1956. Rare right whale visits California. *Pac. Discovery* 9(4): 20–6.

Description is made of a right whale sighted heading south near Scripps Institution of Oceanography, La Jolla, and followed by boat in the San Diego, California, area. A history of the species is also given. Data from California shore whalers show only a handful of right whales were taken. One animal was killed in April 1924 off the Farallon Islands (about 37° 40′ N, 124° W). A map shows its 'original' distribution in the North Pacific and Bering Sea. Mention is made of the Kodiak Gyre and Kodiak Ground as important whaling areas.

Gilmore, R. M. 1978. Right whale, pp. 62–9. *In*: D. Haley (ed.) *Marine Mammals of Eastern North Pacific and Arctic Waters*. Pac. Search Press, Seattle, Washington. 256 pp.

This is a general paper on the biology and natural history of the species and includes personal anecdotal accounts of several sightings of right whales such as Gilmore's (1956), nearshore off southern California on 31 March 1955. Other sightings were for the South Atlantic. A distribution chart for the species in the eastern North Pacific is presented showing the winter range from Oregon to Baja California, Mexico, and summer range extending nearshore from British Columbia to the Aleutian Islands and north into the eastern Bering Strait. The location of calving and mating is unknown.

Gray, J. E. 1868. On the geographical distribution of the Balaenidae or right whales. *Ann. Mag. Nat. Hist.*, 4A Series, 1(4, page 31): 242–7.

Gray is critical of the hypothesis of Van Beneden (*Les Balaeines*, first 1868 issue, Royal Academy of Belgium bulletin); concerning the distribution of right whales worldwide, as being unsupported by Maury's whale charts. Gray goes on to discuss current 'theories' by scientists and accounts of whales (e.g. Capt. Thomas Welcome Roys, famed 'discoverer' of the Bering Sea bowhead whaling grounds). He acknowledges, for example, that right whales from the China Sea, and Kamchatka (presumably Okhotsk Sea and perhaps North Pacific-southwestern Bering Sea) and the 'Northwest Whale' (from the northwest coast of North America) are the same species (*Balaena glacialis*) and different from the 'right whale' found north to the Bering Strait and in Baffin Bay (*B. mysticetus*). A brief discussion is given of evidence for right whales in various oceans, but for the North Pacific he describes only *B. japonica*, finding evidence of the occurrence of the species in and around Japan in Maury (1852) and in the 'extensive whale-fishery' carried out and published by the Japanese. (He cites no Japanese literature however. A review of 19th century (and earlier) Japanese literature would be instructive in re-creating the early whale fisheries in the Japan and China seas where right whales may have once been abundant; c.f. Webermann, 1914).

Harrison, J. P. 1954. An 1849 statement on the habits of right whales by Captain Daniel McKenzie of New Bedford. *American Neptune* 14(2): 139–41.

A letter dated February 5, 1849, from Captain Daniel McKenzie to Lt. Matthew F. Maury is published in its entirety. McKenzie was Maury's agent who collected logbooks and records from his colleagues, other whalemen, to help Maury plot whale sightings and catches throughout the world for Maury's now famous 'Whale Chart of the World' (see Maury, 1851; 1852). McKenzie makes some general comments about right whales (from his experience in the Atlantic) for example, females with calves leave the 'bulls' and move into coastal temperate waters in autumn, then in spring head south and out to sea to meet the bulls, while the calves remain nearshore for some time before joining the remainder of the whales. He suggests that right whales along the northwest coast of North America might not live long; or, perhaps, they might not have been in large numbers [this I take from the comments by McKenzie which state 'to what age they live I cannot tell – my opinion is they are a short lived animal or the Sea (which is quite narrow) on the N. West coast would be filled with them – since they have ever remained undisturbed till within ten years.']

Hegarty, R. B. 1959. *Returns of Whaling Vessels Sailing*

From American Ports. A continuation of Alexander Starbuck's 'History of the American Whale Fishery' 1876–1928. The Old Dartmouth Historical Society, and Whaling Museum, New Bedford, Mass. 58 pp.
Hegarty extends the data reported by Starbuck (1878) on American whaling vessel activities from the last year (1876) of Starbuck, but also includes some additional information for the period 1868 and 1876. From the index, Hegarty reports separately on average prices and import amounts (sperm and 'whale' oil by barrels and whale-bone by pounds, in US dollars), 1877–1932. In addition, he reports returning vessel information separately by 'American' ports and 'Hawaiian' ports. The latter, titled 'Honolulu' (pp. 48–50), reports the first voyage in 1832 to the last in about 1880. Most vessels from Honolulu were bound for the Arctic, presumably in search of bowhead whales. Only one specific mention is made of the 'NW coast' fishery (see Starbuck, 1878, for other details).

Herman, L. M., Baker, C. S., Forestell, P. H. and Antinoja, R. C. 1980. Right whale *Balaena glacialis* sightings near Hawaii: a clue to the wintering grounds? *Mar. Ecol. Prog. Ser.* 2: 271–5.
On 25 March 1979 and 10 April 1979, approximately 122 km apart, two sightings of the...right whale *Balaena glacialis* were made during regular surface and aerial observations of the winter assembly of humpback whales *Megaptera novaengliae* in Hawaiian waters. Markings, together with ancillary observations of others, suggest that the two sightings were of the same animal...The location of the wintering grounds of the North Pacific right whale have long been a mystery. Speculations from whalers' records that Hawaii may have been a wintering ground are strengthened by the current sightings...(Author's abstract paraphrased; see Rowntree *et al.*, 1980, for the same sighting.)

International Commission on Whaling. 1965. Report of the working group on the North Pacific whale stocks. *Rep. int. Whal. Commn* 15: 40–6.
In 1963, and January, March and April 1964, six right whales were marked with Discovery tags in the North Pacific, three by the USSR and three by Japan. No details are given. These may be the same Soviet marks described in Ivashin and Rovnin (1967). No original reference was found for the Japanese marking operations.

International Whaling Commission. 1976. Japan progress report on whale research June 1974 to May 1975. *Rep. int. Whal. Commn* 26: 416–24.
During 1974 scouting boat surveys, five right whales were sighted in the northwestern Pacific; four between 30°–50° N, 160° E–180°, and one between 40°–50° N and 140° W–160° W (dates not specified). Along the Japan coast, 32 right whale sightings were made. No further details were provided.

International Whaling Commission. 1977. Japan progress report on whale research June 1975 to May 1976. *Rep. int. Whal. Commn* 27: 88–91.
During whaling operations in 1975, four right whales in groups of one and three were sighted in the northwestern Pacific between 30°–50° N, 160° E–180° (dates not specified). No further details were provided.

International Whaling Commission. 1979. Japan progress report on cetacean research June 1977–May 1978. *Rep. int. Whal. Commn* 29: 117–20.
From Table 2, two right whales were sighted during 24 catcher days whaling (CDW) by catcher boats in an area 20°–30° N, 180°–160° W in summer 1977. Another right whale was sighted from a Japan coastal catcher boat during 1,282 CDW.

International Whaling Commission. 1980. Japan progress report on cetacean research June 1978–May 1979. *Rep. int. Whal. Commn* 30: 155–60.
From Table 4, two right whales were sighted during 1,249 nmi of scouting boat surveys in an area 50°–60° N, 160°–140° W in early summer 1978. No right whales were seen from coastal or pelagic catcher boats.

International Whaling Commission. 1981. Japan progress report on cetacean research June 1979–May 1980. *Rep. int. Whal. Commn* 31: 195–200.

From Tables 1 and 5, one right whale was sighted from a scouting boat during 936 nmi survey in an area 40°–50° N, 160°–140° W in early summer 1979, and one right whale was marked with a Discovery tag in the 10° square 'N27' (approximately 40°–50° N, 150°–160° W). No right whales were seen from coastal or pelagic catcher boats.

International Whaling Commission. 1982. Japan progress report on cetacean research June 1980 to May 1981. *Rep. int. Whal. Commn* 32: 179–83.
Although greater survey effort was extended by Japanese scouting boats in summer 1980 (13,222 nmi) than in 1979 (12,137 nmi), no right whales were sighted in the North Pacific between 20°–50° N, 135° W–130° E (one right whale was seen in 1979). No right whales were seen in coastal waters of Japan.

International Whaling Commission. 1983. Japan progress report on cetacean research June 1981–May 1982. *Rep. int. Whal. Commn* 33: 213–20.
From Table 5, three right whales were sighted in 10° square sector 'M21' (coastal Japan, 30°–40° N, 140°–150° E) during 482.5 'catcher days whaling' (CDW) from Japanese catcher boats in summer 1981. (No right whales were seen by Japanese whalers in 1982, as reported in *Rep. int. Whal. Commn* 34: 203–9.)

International Whaling Commission. 1985. Japan progress report on cetacean research June 1983 to April 1984. *Rep. int. Whal. Commn* 35: 168–71.
From Table 9, four right whales were sighted, two each in areas 30°–40° N, 140°–160° E and 30°–40° N, 120°–140° E during 790 nmi and 3,232 nmi, respectively, of scouting boat surveys of the North Pacific.

Ivanova, E. I. 1961a. K morfologii yaponskogo kita (*Eubalaena sieboldi* Gray) (The morphology of the Japanese right whale (*Eubalaena sieboldi* Gray)). *Trudy Inst. Morfol. Zhivot.* 34: 216–25. In Russian. (English abstract translation in *Biological Abstracts*, General and Systematic Zoology – Chordata., 1963, Vol. 42, No. 3, abstract number 26737.)
According to the author, various measurements from the Pacific right whale demonstrate its close anatomical similarity to the Atlantic and 'Biscay right whale' (*E. glacialis*). The longest baleen plate measured was 260 cm, with 217–250 plates per side.

Ivanova, E. I. 1961b. Proportsii tela i kharakter rosta kitov Dal' nego vostoka (Proportions of the body and the nature of growth in whales from the Far East). *Trudy Soveshch. Ikhtiol. Kom.* 12: 72–8. In Russian. (English abstract translation in *Biological Abstracts*, General and Systematic Zoology–Chordata., 1963, Vol. 42, No. 3, abstract number 12443.)
Using biological and morphological characters from 10 right whales (*Eubalaena glacialis sieboldii*) from the Kuril Islands region, the author suggests that taxonomic differences exist between Southern and Northern Hemisphere right whales. No details given in abstract.

Ivashin, M. V. and Rovnin, A. A. 1967. Some results of the Soviet whale marking in the waters of the North Pacific. *Norsk Hvalfangsttid.* 56(6): 123–35.
Soviet whale marking in the North Pacific began in 1954. Marking was first done only in the northwestern Pacific but expanded to cover the entire North Pacific (and Bering Sea) north of Lat. 40° N. The Soviets marked 20 Pacific right whales. Location and dates not given.

Jenkins, J. T. 1921. *A History of the Whale Fisheries.* H. F. & G. Witherby, London 336 p.
Discusses individual whale fisheries from 17th century Basque to early 20th century steam whaling, along with some information on the natural history of related species and economics and the regulation of whaling. An account of the northwest coast fishery for right whales is given. American whalers took right whales along the northwest coast (Oregon to the Aleutian Islands to 150° W) from April to September, then gray whales from February to April south of 29° N off Baja California (Bahia San Sebastian Viscaino and 'Cerres Islands' – presumably Cedros Island). American whalers first entered the Pacific in 1781, but because of the depleted market and the War of 1812, little commerce resulted. In 1818, the 'offshore

grounds' of the Pacific were visited, e.g. the Sandwich (Hawaiian) Islands, and in 1820 American whalers first reached Japan; two years later, coastal whaling off Japan was conducted by 30–40 vessels. By 1835 over 400 vessels were operating in the Pacific, visiting 30 ports. The American whale fishery in the Pacific reached its zenith between 1835 and 1855, with Nantucket and New Bedford the principal home ports for most vessels, along with New London, Sag Harbour, Fairhaven, Stonington, Warren, Provincetown, and Mystic. Increasing use of long whale bone (baleen from right and bowheads) and great quantities and new uses for oil (e.g. sperm candles and whale oil lamps) fueled the whaling industry. In 1859, the discovery of petroleum oil as a substitute for whale oil, along with rapidly dwindling right and bowhead whale populations, triggered the demise of the fishery. Even so, from 1835–1860, the annual revenue from the approximately 600 vessels involved in Pacific whaling exceeded $8,000,000. The high price of oil and continuing or new use of whale products meant the whale fishery held on as an important industry till near the end of the 19th century. From 1869 to 1880, San Francisco rose to be the leading west coast port, taking away much business from the American east coast ports by 1890. A good catch of bowhead or right whales would average 10 whales yielding more than 1,000 barrels (30 gal. each) of oil and 10,000 lbs of whalebone (baleen). Starbuck (1878) mentions (p. 249) that a small Russian whale fishery took place in the late half of the 19th century in the North Pacific, but gives no details. Much of the book discusses various aspects of bowhead, gray and sperm whaling, and little else about right whaling in the North Pacific.

Johnson, T. 1982. Rare northern right whale sighting off northern California coast. *Whale Newsl.* 5(2): 1, 7.
One right whale was sighted '10 min' out of Pillar Point Harbor, near San Francisco, 21 March 1982. (A photograph by Johnson and unauthored comments concerning this rare sighting are also reported in *Oceans* 15(5): 52.)

Kamiya, T. 1958. How to count the renculi of the cetacean kidneys, with special regard to the kidney of the right whale. *Sci. Rep. Whales Res. Inst., Tokyo* 13: 253–67.
The renculi (bindles forming the lobulations on mammalian kidneys) from one right whale (female, 11.65 m long; see Omura, 1958, page 3) were compared to 'other cetacean species.' This right whale had 5,377 renculi, intermediate in number to the blue whale (about 3,000) and fin whale (about 6,000), and thus near the highest of any cetacean recorded.

Kellogg, R. 1931. Whaling statistics for the Pacific coast of North America. *J. Mammal.* 12(1): 73–7.
Catch data by species and location from 1919–1929 are tabulated. Species are blue, finback, humpback, sei, gray and sperm whales, plus 'miscellaneous' whales inlcuding beluga, bowhead, right, bottlenose, sharp-headed finback (minke), and Bryde's whales. Locations described for right whales include Alaska, British Columbia, Washington, and California. A total of 18 right whales was reported taken between 1923 and 1929, 17 of which were from an unspecified area in Alaska.

Klumov, S. K. 1962. Gladkiye (Yaponskiye) Kity Tikhogo Okeana (The right whales in the Pacific Ocean). *Trudy Inst. Okeanol.* 58: 202–97. [In Russian.]
Whaling and research vessels conducted observations of right whales in the northwest Pacific from 1952 to 1957. The results of this work describe two stocks: the Pacific stock is larger than the Okhotsk stock and population growth of the Pacific stock was reported to be faster. The author speculates that puberty comes when the animals are 14–15 m long and weaning takes place 6–7 months after parturition. The weight of adult whales is more than 100 tons at a length of 16–17 m. All data are reported 'preliminary'. Analysis of food showed that right whales are stenophagous; their main food in the Northern Hemisphere being copepods. (Unauthored English translation also available.)

Kugler, R. C. 1984. Historical survey of foreign whaling: North America, pp. 149–57. *In*: H. K. s'Jacob, K. Snoeijing and R. Vaughan (eds.), *Arctic Whaling: proceedings of the international symposium, Arctic Whaling, February 1983.* Arctic Centre, University of Groningen. 181 pp.
Recent analyses of whaling for right and bowhead whales is

presented, based upon whaling records for the 19th century. (Credit for the information is given to D. Henderson, *Whaling in the Okhotsk Sea*, '…scheduled for publication in 1984'.) Between 1841 and 1844 the price of baleen had doubled, for use in women's skirts. In 1845 the first whales were landed in the Okhotsk Sea and by the end of 1846, 341 right whales had been taken. From 1847 to 1867, approximately 3,600 right whales were killed (2,400 landed; 1,200 more killed but lost) and 18,240 bowheads killed (15,200 landed; 3,040 killed but lost) in the Okhotsk Sea. An analysis of such whaling records provides, in addition, information of geographical distribution: bowheads occurred in the northern Okhotsk Sea, above a line drawn between the northern end of Sakhalin Island (54° N) to the southern tip of Kamchatka (52° N) whereas right whales were south of this line.

Kuz'min, A. A. and Berzin, A. A. 1975. Raspredelenie i sovremennoe sostoianie chislennosti gladkikh i serykh kitov v dal'nevostochnykh moriakh. (Distribution and current numbers of right and gray whales in the far-east seas), pp. 121–2. *In*: Papers of the All-Union conference, Oct. 1975, Vladivostok – Biologicheskie resursy morei dal'nego vostoka. (Biological resources of the far-east seas). Ichthyol. Comm., Min. Fish. USSR, Pac. Ocean Res. Inst. Fish. Oceanogr. (TINRO). [In Russian.] (Transl. avail. Natl. Mar. Fish. Serv., Off. Int. Fish., Lang. Serv. Branch, Washington, D.C., 2 pp.)
Vessel cruises were conducted August to October 1974. Pacific right whales (40–45) were found in an area of presumed major upwelling, northeastward from the Kashaverov shoal, Okhotsk Sea. No details given.

Leatherwood, S., Reeves, R. R., Perrin, W. F. and Evans, W. E. 1982. Whales, dolphins, and porpoises of the eastern North Pacific and adjacent Arctic waters: A guide to their identification. US Dep. Commer., *NOAA Tech. Rep. NMFS Circ.* 444, 245 pp.
A general summary is made of recent sightings and areas in the eastern North Pacific where right whales were once taken, and a brief comparison is given of sighting characteristics of right whales and other large cetaceans (e.g. bowheads) where they overlap in range. Numerous photographs are presented to aid in field identification.

Leatherwood, S., Bowles, A. E. and Reeves, R. R. 1983. Endangered whales of the eastern Bering Sea and Shelikof Strait, Alaska; results of aerial surveys, April 1982 through April 1983 with notes on other marine mammals seen. *Hubbs-Sea World Res. Inst. Tech. Rep.* 83–159, 322 pp.
No right whales were sighted during eight aerial surveys of the southeastern Bering Sea (Aleutian Islands at 174° W, north to 62° N east to the Alaska coast) and Shelikof Strait (approximately 156° W, 56° 30′ N) to the southwest end of Cook Inlet to approximately a line drawn between the northern tips of Augustine Island and Barren Islands, Alaska. The monthly surveys covered 3,696 nmi², or approximately 1–2% of the total area; April, June and December 1982 were essentially missed. The available records are summarized for the eastern North Pacific, and in particular, provide a record of the take of right whales from the Alaskan whaling stations at Akutan and Port Hobron: a total of at least 25 whales were landed between 1916 and 1935, as compared to more than 2,118 landed between 1839 and 1906 (40% from the Kodiak ground). Other records of 'incidental' takes, strandings and early sightings are presented.

Martin, K. R. 1979. Whalemen of letters. *Oceans* 12(1): 20–9.
First-hand accounts of day-to-day whaling activities during the 1840s is provided from three logbooks now in the Kendall Whaling Museum, Sharon, Massachusetts, reported as being particularly illustrative of the toils of whaling – for sperm and right whales. One account is reproduced from the logbook of John F. Martin on board the *Lucy-Ann* of Wilmington, Delaware, in pursuit of right whales along the northwest coast of North America. Martin concludes that right whales from the northwest coast are more difficult to catch than elsewhere (e.g. from Australian waters) as the whales take evasive action, perhaps being able to detect (i.e. hear and see) the whalers better than southern right whales.

Maury, M. F. 1851. *Whale chart* (preliminary sketch). Series F. Bureau of Ordnance and Hydrography, United States Navy, Washington, 1 sheet. H. O. Miscel. No. 8514.
Maury's initial attempt to depict, in qualitative fashion, the seasonal distribution (in 5° squares) of sperm and right whales around the world based upon incidental sighting records and (primarily) whaling records reported by vessel captains, whose logbooks had been stored in the US Navy's National Observatory since the American Revolutionary War. Records reported in this chart (see Maury 1852 for greater details) are principally from whaling records in the 1840s. In the central North Pacific, the southern distribution of right whales is approximately 32–35° N, along the Japan coast 35° N, and west coast of Baja California at 30° N. His chart suggests (again qualitatively) that the species was most abundant in the Gulf of Alaska, at the entrance to the Okhotsk Sea (45–50° N) and due west to about 175° W in the North Pacific Ocean. Maury is the first to show that right whales are geographically isolated in the Northern and Southern Hemispheres.

Maury, M. F. 1852. *Whale Chart of the World.* (The Wind and Current Charts.) Series F. United States Hydrographic Office, Washington, 4 sheets.
The final charts after Maury (1851). These four charts provide greater quantitative evidence for the distribution of right whales in North America than Maury's (1851) single chart, representing a much larger sampling of whaler's logbooks than that reported by Townsend (1935). (Maury also published Maury, M. F. 1853. A Chart of the Favorite Resorts of the Sperm and Right Whale by M. F. Maury, L. L. D. Lieut. US Navy. Constructed from Maury's Whale Chart of the World, by Robert H. Wymann, Lieut. U.S.N. by Authority of Commo. Charles Morris U.S.N. Chief of Bureau of Ordnance and Hydrography. Washington, 1 sheet.) (Charts not available at NMML for detailed review; information supplied by R. Kugler and R. R. Reeves.) Also see Bannister and Mitchell (1980) *Rep. int. Whal. Commn* (special issue 2): 219–30 for detailed bibliography of Maury charts.

Maury, M. F. 1863. *The Physical Geography of the Sea*, 6th ed. T. Nelson and Sons, London, Edinburgh and New York. 493 pp. XIII pl.
Sixth edition of the 1855 foundation modern text on the world's oceanography. On plate IX Maury depicts the drift patterns of the oceans and has drawn in lines of the 'polar limits' of the sperm whale (as this is a tropical to subarctic species) and 'equatorial limits' of right whales (as this is a temperate to arctic species group). Maury's depiction of the 'mean' geographic limits is based upon thousands of whaling records and sightings by ship captains during the first half of the 19th century, and reported in Maury (1851, 1852). In the North Pacific, Maury proposes that the 'mean' southern edge of the distribution of right whales in Asia is approximately 32° N south of the coast of Japan and China, and on the North American coast at 52° N near the Queen Charlotte Islands, Canada. In the western North Pacific this mean limit arcs up to about 46° N, drops to 32° N (approximately 600 nmi north of the Hawaiian Islands), then extends directly to the North American coast at 52° N.

Morris, B. F., Alton, M. S. and Braham, H. W. 1983. Living marine resources of the Gulf of Alaska, a resource assessment for the Gulf of Alaska/Cook Inlet proposed oil and gas lease Sale 88. US Dep. Commer., *NOAA Tech. Memo. NMFS* F/AKR-5, 232 pp.
Briefly describes the distribution, ecology, and life history of marine mammals in the North Pacific. Using the available literature, three 'tentative' (unconfirmed) sightings of right whales were reported, totaling six animals: (1) one animal in July 1977 at 56° 27.5′ N, 135° 38.4′ W, about 75 km northwest of Cape Ommaney, Baranof Island, Alaska; (2) four animals on 27 March 1979 at 59° 35.8′ N, 139° 55.8′ W in Yakutat Bay, Alaska; and (3) one animal on 16 October 1980 at 58° 48.1′ N, 145° 00.3′ W, about 56 km south southwest of Cape St Elias, Alaska.

Murie, O. J. 1959. Fauna of the Aleutian Islands and Alaska Peninsula, pp. 1–364. *In*: Fauna of the Aleutian Islands and Alaska Peninsula with notes on invertebrates and fishes collected in the Aleutians, 1936–38. US Fish Wild. Serv., *North American Fauna*, No. 61, 406 pp.
Short account of the occurrence of the 'Pacific right whale' (*Eubalaena sieboldii*) in the Aleutian Islands, formerly present but 'exceedingly rare' today (page 333). The author reports from the literature (Osgood, 1904 – not available; see Appendix) that a possible right whale stranded between Kanatak and Wide Bay (57° 22–34′ N, 156° 02–11′ W) in 1902; also cites Birkeland (1926, page 26) concerning two right whales killed by the Akutan whalers dating from 1914. Murie saw no right whales during his two year biological survey of the Aleutian Islands.

Nasu, K. 1960. Oceanographic investigation in the Chukchi Sea during the summer of 1958. *Sci. Rep. Whales Res. Inst., Tokyo* 15: 143–57.
An oceanographic and whale sighting survey was conducted in the Chukchi Sea 16–20 August 1958 south of 69° 30′ N. Fin (1), right (2), and gray (82) whales were sighted. The 'right whale' sightings (two individuals) were at approximately 68° 25′ N, 172° W (no date given) about 120 nmi west of Point Hope, Alaska and at about 40 nmi northeast of Northeast Cape, St Lawrence Island (63° 40′ N, 168° W in the Bering Sea). Nasu does not say whether these sightings were of *Eubalaena glacialis* or *Balaena mysticetus* (he implies the former). He cites Nikulin, P. G. (1947) [actually published in 1946] O raspredelenii kitoobraznykh v moriakh, omyvaiushikh Chukotskii poluostrov [Distribution of cetaceans in seas surrounding the Chukchi Peninsula]. Izv. Tikhookean. Nauchno-issled. Inst. Rybn. Khoz. Okeanogr. (TINRO) 22: 255–7. [In Russian.] Transl. by US Navy Oceanogr. Office, Washington, D.C., 1969, Transl. No. 28, 3 pp.) as identifying *E. glacialis* as occurring in the Chukchi Sea; however Nikulin (1946) makes no mention of *E. glacialis* (he discussed only gray, humpback, fin, greenland [bowhead], killer and belukha whales). Were these sightings by Nasu of right whales or bowheads?

Nasu, K. 1963. Oceanography and whaling ground in the subarctic region of the Pacific Ocean. *Sci. Rep. Whales Res. Inst., Tokyo* 17: 105–55.
Data were obtained by whaling factory and whale marking ships in the North Pacific Ocean and Bering and Chukchi seas. Extensive oceanographic data were collected. Annual catches by species 1940–1962 are tabulated (6 right whales). Areas north and south of Unalaska are particularly productive for all species (including right whales) except perhaps blue whales. No empirical data are presented.

Nemoto, T. 1957. Foods of baleen whales in the northern Pacific. *Sci. Rep. Whales Res. Inst., Tokyo* 12: 33–89.
Analyses of stomach samples collected 1954–56 and of the whaling grounds along the Aleutian Islands chain are discussed. Food preference among species is discussed, including hour of feeding as related to diurnal migration of plankton, depth of whale dives, fluctuation of food abundance from year to year and corresponding presence of whales, and feeding by 'skimming' (sei and right whales) versus 'gulping' (blue, fin and humpback whales). Prey included euphausiids, copepods, fish, and squid. Zooplankton biology is discussed in reference to large whales such as the right whale. No right whales were taken, and none was reported seen.

Nemoto, T. 1959. Food of baleen whales with reference to whale movements. *Sci. Rep. Whales Res. Inst., Tokyo* 14: 149–290.
Discusses blue, sei, Bryde's, fin, right, Greenland (bowhead), gray, humpback, and little piked (minke) whales. Data come from whales caught in three areas: the northern North Pacific, the waters adjacent to Japan, and the Antarctic. In addition to food items found in the stomachs of each species, the author discusses: 'feeding apparatus' in relation to food preference; hours of feeding; natural history of *Euphausia superba*; yearly fluctuations in abundance and location of prey in North Pacific; quantity of stomach contents; previous publications on feeding; and congregation, diurnal migration and depth of food species. A description of baleen and general whale anatomy related to food type is presented. No right whales were taken, but the author discusses the importance of some prey species (e.g. *Euphausia* species) to right whales in other oceans using information from the literature. Concerning the following information on the takes of right whales in the North Pacific by Pacific whaling centers from 1910 to 1945: 67 right whales were landed, 1 from the 'Arctic' (north of 65° N); 3 from the 'Eastern side' (Alaska to Mexico); and 63 from the 'Western side' (Kamchatka, USSR to Formosa, i.e., Republic of China).

Nemoto, T. 1964. School of baleen whales in the feeding areas. *Sci. Rep. Whales Res. Inst., Tokyo* 18: 89-110.

Details 'school' patterns of single species and two-species groupings of baleen whales (fin, blue, sei, humpback, right and gray whales) in the North Pacific and Antarctic waters based on marking, sighting and catch data. Right whale data from the North Pacific for 1941–63 show that they are predominantly found as single animals; four per group is the largest school reported. Of a total of 197 groups or schools recorded, 67% (132) were single animals, 26.9% (53) were in pairs, 5.1% (10) were in groups of three and 1.0% (2) were in groups of four, for a total of 276 animals. (Does not account for repeat sightings of the same animal within seasons or in several years.)

Nemoto, T. and Kasuya, T. 1965. Foods of baleen whales in the Gulf of Alaska of the North Pacific. *Sci. Rep. Whales Res. Inst., Tokyo* 19: 45–51.
Right whales take *Calanus plumchrus* (Copepoda) in coastal waters of Kodiak Island. No details are given.

Nichols, J. T. 1926. Impressions of Alaska, – where east and west approximate. *Nat. Hist.* 26(6): 605–13.
Description of his vessel cruise (aboard the S.S. *Victoria*) to the southern Bering Sea, including a brief discussion of whaling in the Aleutian Islands for fin, blue, humpback, sperm and right whales. Four photographs of the whaling operation at Akutan are presented, including a right whale (page 609) presumably taken on Nichols' trip (possibly summer 1926).

Ohsumi, S. 1964. Comparison of maturity and accumulation rate of corpora albicantia between the left and right ovaries in Cetacea. *Sci. Rep. Whales Res. Inst., Tokyo* 18: 123–48.
Three adult female right whales (taken from the North Pacific by special scientific permit) were examined for presence of *corpora albicantia* (c.a.); two whales were pregnant and one was considered entirely immature. One animal had 1 corpus luteum (c.l.) in the right ovary and no c.a. in either ovary, the other had 1 c.l. in the left ovary and 2 c.a. in the right, and the last whale had 1 follicle (left ovary). The appearance of approximately equal *corpora* counts between ovaries within the same whales, the author suggests, is similar to other mysticete whales.

Ohsumi, S., Shimadzu, Y. and Doi, T. 1971. The seventh memorandum on the results of Japanese stock assessment of whales in the North Pacific. *Rep. int. Whal. Commn* 21: 76–89.
Index of abundance tables are presented using CPUE (catch per unit effort) and whale sightings for fin, sei, sperm, blue, humpback and right whales. Maximum sustainable yield and changes in population size are discussed.

Ohsumi, S. and Wada, S. 1974. Status of whale stocks in the North Pacific, 1972. *Rep. int. Whal. Commn* 24: 114–26.
Gives catch of seven large whale species by three Japanese and two Soviet expeditions and eight Japanese land stations in 1972. Indices of abundance for the North Pacific (roughly 35°–65° N) were calculated from Japanese sighting data, 1965–1972, for fin, sei, sperm, minke, blue, humpback, and right whales. Right whale abundance was estimated at 120–540 for the areas surveyed. The estimate for 1972 was 230. The authors conclude that no trend in population growth is apparent for right whales.

Omura, H. 1957. Report on two right whales caught off Japan for scientific purposes under Article VIII of the International Convention for the Regulation of Whaling. *Norsk Hvalfangsttid.* 46(7): 374–90.
Biological description and accounts of two right whales taken off Japan on 23 May and 30 June 1956, respectively: a 38 ft female at 38° 33′ N, 143° 40′ E; and a 41 ft male at 41° 46′ N, 148° 55′ E. The female was sexually immature; the male could not be examined (gonads putrefied). Estimates of total weight (weighing body parts) in pounds were 22,866 (female) and 22,247 (male), excluding blood and some body fluids and tissues. Numerous photographs of parts, etc., are included. Further details are given in Omura (1958).

Omura, H. 1958. North Pacific right whale. *Sci. Rep. Whales Res. Inst., Tokyo* 13: 1–52.
Black right whales appear in the Bering Sea in June and stay all summer. Sightings from 1941–57 are mapped by months; April, May, June and July–September. Numerous sightings occurred between the

Pribilof Islands and Aleutian Islands in July. In June and July a few whales were seen as far east as the Shumagin Island region west of Kodiak Island. Whales sighted near the Aleutian Islands are thought perhaps to belong to a 'Kodiak Ground' stock. Of all sightings, 68% were of single individuals; the largest group seen was four. The total number of schools observed from 1941 to 1957 from northern Japan to the Shumagin Islands, Alaska, was 164. Complete physical descriptions are given of two right whales taken near Japan in 1956 (see Omura, 1957). Also compares data on two right whales taken in 1941 (reported in Matsuura, 1942 – see Appendix): a 58 ft 5 in female on June 10 at 48° 27′ N, 157° 51′ E and a 44 ft 7 in male on June 11 at 48° 23′ N, 159° 29′ E. He reports that the former was the largest right whale ever appearing in a scientific paper.

Omura, H. 1964. A systematic study of the hyoid bones in the baleen whales. *Sci. Rep. Whales Res. Inst., Tokyo* 18: 149–70.
Compares the hyoid bones of five right whales taken in 1962–63 in the North Pacific-Bering Sea (details lacking) and compares these to blue, fin, sei, Bryde's, minke and humpbacks, formulating an approximate phylogenetic key to the species.

Omura, H. and Ohsumi, S. 1964. A review of Japanese whale markings in the North Pacific to the end of 1962, with some information on marking in the Antarctic. *Norsk Hvalfangsttid.* 53(4): 90–112.
Marking of whales by species is discussed including actual data on the marking process, marking and recovery locations, marking experiments on carcasses, etc., principally for blue, fin, sei and Bryde's, humpback and sperm whales. Mention is made of right whales being marked: one in 1961 in the Gulf of Alaska ('Area III B'), and one in 1962 in the Bering Sea ('Area IV A') (Table 9 footnote). In Table 10, two right whales are reported as marked in the 'total' column, however, no further information provided; presumably they are the same reported above in Table 9.

Omura, H., Ohsumi, S., Nemoto, T., Nasu, K. and Kasuya, T. 1969. Black right whales in the North Pacific. *Sci. Rep. Whales Res. Inst., Tokyo* 21: 1–78.
Thirteen right whales were collected and analyzed: three just south of Kodiak Island, Alaska in 1961 (about 56° N, 153° W); six north of the eastern Aleutian Islands in the southern Bering Sea, Alaska in 1962–63 (about 53°–54° N, 170°–173° W); two off the east coast of Japan in 1956 (between 38°–42° N, 143°–149° E); and two in the Okhotsk Sea in 1968 (about 48°–49° N, 145°–147° E). Sightings from Japanese catcher boats are plotted. These plots suggest that the species is most numerous off the Kuril Islands, south Okhotsk Sea and between the eastern Aleutian Islands and Kodiak Island, with records extending from the east-central coast of Japan to central Gulf of Alaska north to southwestern Chukchi Sea. In May, right whales appear north of 57° N, and by June they have moved into the Bering Sea. A detailed description of morphology is presented. Principal food items included calanoid copepods and euphausiids. Data first reported by Klumov (1962) are summarized.

Omura, H., Nishiwaki, M. and Kasuya, T. 1971. Further studies on two skeletons of the black right whale in the North Pacific. *Sci. Rep. Whales Res. Inst., Tokyo* 23: 71–81.
Describes two right whale skulls, along with two others from Omura (1958) and two from Omura *et al.* (1969), above, indicating that as right whales age, the proportional width of the skull decreases, while the rostral length increases with greater downward curvature. 'Sexual difference in the form and size of the pelvic bone is suggested.'

Pike, G. C. 1956. Guide to the whales, porpoises and dolphins of the north-east Pacific and Arctic waters of Canada and Alaska. *Fish. Res. Board Can.*, Circ. No. 32 (revised), 14 pp.
Brief anatomical description and natural history of right whales, with reference to their 'former habitat' being waters from the Bering Sea south occasionally to California.

Pike, G. C. 1962. Canadian whaling off British Columbia and progress of research, 1948 to 1959. Document C1 submitted to the June 1963 meeting of the International Whaling Commission's working group on North Pacific whale stocks (unpublished).

Concerns current and historical whaling operations principally for blue, fin, humpback, sei, bottlenose and sperm whales. From a total of 18,483 whales landed between 1905 and 1959 (Table 1), 10 gray whales (1953 at Coal Harbour) and four right whales (1924, 2; 1926, 1; 1951, 1) were also reported (see Pike and MacAskie, 1969). Land station operations were located on Vancouver Island (Sechart, 1905–1914; Page's Lagoon, 1906–1909; Kyuquot, 1907–1925; Coal Harbour, 1948–1959) and Queen Charlotte Island (Naden Harbour, 1911–1941; Rose Harbour, 1911–1943). No other details on right whales are given.

Pike, G. C. and MacAskie, I. B. 1969. Marine mammals of British Columbia. *Bull. Fish. Res. Bd. Can.* 171: 1–54.

A complete review of all marine mammals from inshore to offshore waters of British Columbia, Canada to 1967 is assembled. One text page (p. 38) is devoted to the right whale, and Appendix I lists four right whales taken: two in 1924 and one in 1926 at Queen Charlotte Islands whaling station, and one in May 1951 at Coal Harbour whaling station on Vancouver Island. The Coal Harbour whale was a 41-foot male, young but sexually mature. Three offshore sightings are reported, all between 1958 and 1967 in July or August: two at 50° N, 145° W (weathership); and one at 54° N, 155° W.

Reeves, R. R. and Leatherwood, S. 1985. Sightings of right whales (*Eubalaena glacialis*) in the eastern North Pacific. Document SC/37/PS3 submitted to the June 1985 meeting of the International Whaling Commission (unpublished).

Four unpublished sightings are reported, one of which is most probably a confirmed right whale, *Eubalaena glacialis* (R. R. Reeves, pers. comm.). The sighting occurred about noon 28 August 1983 at Swiftsure Bank on the Canadian side near the mouth of the Strait of Juan de Fuca (at approximately 48° 33′ N, 124° 39′ W). Two whales were present, one estimated to be 40 to 50 feet long. The observer is a trained ecologist and university professor who has observed right whales off South Africa. The other three sightings, thought to be of less probable identity, were: (1) two 'right whales', 4 April 1856, off Guadalupe Island, Mexico (at 28° 30′ N, 117° W) made by an unidentified San Francisco-based whaler; (2) one right whale, 7 June 1984, on the outer bank of Fairweather Grounds, about 100 km southwest of Cape Fairweather, Alaska, made by a fisherman; and (3) one right whale (or bowhead whale? as suggested by authors), 30 August 1982 at 64° 50.1′ N, 168° 25.4′ W (approximately 30 nmi north and 4 days later than Brueggeman *et al.*, 1984) observed from the NOAA R/V *Discoverer*. (Cited with permission of the author.)

Reeves, R. R., Leatherwood, S., Karl, S. A. and Yohe, E. R. 1985. Whaling results at Akutan (1912–39) and Port Hobron (1926–37), Alaska. *Rep. int. Whal. Commn* 35: 441–57.

Modern whaling stations operated at Akutan, Alaska (Bering Sea and North Pacific Ocean) from 1912 to 1939 and at Port Hobron, Alaska (Gulf of Alaska) from 1926 to 1937. Unpublished records of the American Pacific Whaling Company, deposited in the manuscript and University Archives Division of the University of Washington libraries (Seattle, Washington, USA), together with a variety of other sources, were used to compile information on the catch at these two stations... Right whales (*Eubalaena glacialis*) were rarely encountered on the whaling grounds but were chased at every opportunity before 1935... Twenty-one right whales were landed at Port Hobron and Akutan from 1916 to 1935. (Authors' abstract paraphrased). A thorough account of early 20th century whaling in Alaska is given including details of early whaling activities and records, monthly charts of whale sizes (lengths) by species (i.e. blue, fin and humpback whales), monthly locations taken by species, struck-but-lost ('a loss factor of 1.02 was calculated'; the killed-but-lost percentage was estimated to be 1.8% of those landed), and a brief discussion of some vital rates.

Rice, D. W. 1963. Progress report on biological studies of the larger Cetacea in the waters off California. *Norsk Hvalfangsttid.* 52(7): 181–7

An examination and biological critique is given for 737 whales including blue, fin, sei, humpback, gray, sperm and giant bottlenose whales landed by California shore-based whalers between 36° 30′ N and 39° N out to 124° 50′ W (Monterey Bay to Pt. Arena) between 1959 and 1962. Also mentioned is that only one right whale was seen

in the area, in May 1959. No other details given. See Rice and Fiscus (1968) for further details.

Rice, D. W. 1974. Whales and whale research in the eastern North Pacific, pp. 170–95. *In:* W. E. Schevill (ed.), *The Whale Problem – a Status Report.* Harvard Univ. Press, Cambridge, Mass.

The 11 large cetaceans of the eastern North Pacific are discussed, with particular regard to distribution and population. Five of the species are considered endangered; their populations are estimated as follows: black right, a few dozen; humpback, a few hundred; blue, 2,000; bowhead, a few thousand; gray, 11,000. Population data are summarized from catch statistics and other authors. The Kodiak whaling ground (Vancouver Island, Gulf of Alaska and eastern Aleutian Islands) was well known as the favored whaling area for right whales in summer months. Between 1905 and 1937 (the year right whales became completely protected), 24 animals were killed by whalers at stations in Alaska and British Columbia.

Rice, D. W. 1984. Cetaceans, pp. 447–90 (Chapter 14). *In:* S. Anderson and J. K. Jones, Jr. (eds.) *Recent Mammals of the World.* John Wiley & Sons, Inc., New York.

General description of all Cetacea, including characteristics and natural history, range and distribution with some charts, fossil groupings (with references to four extinct genera) and list of selected references. The genus *Balaena* is used here for the species *glacialis* (right whale) and *mysticetus* (bowhead) following Linnaeus, 1758, but Rice recognizes *Eubalaena* Gray, 1864 as a later inclusion for the right whale. The family name Balaenidae follows Gray, 1825. The geologic range for both species is middle Miocene to Pleistocene in western North America, and Recent in all oceans.

Rice, D. W. and Fiscus, C. H. 1968. Right whales in the southeastern North Pacific. *Norsk Hvalfangsttid.* 57(5): 105–7.

Right whales, *Balaena glacialis*, since being afforded complete protection by the IWC in 1937, have been recorded only 10 times in the eastern North Pacific south of 50° N. Five of these records are newly reported, including the southernmost known occurrence off Punta Abreojos, Baja California, Mexico. (Author's abstract paraphrased.) The article lists these records as: (1) an estimated 13 m animal on 13–15 May 1959 at 37° 25′ N, 122° 48′ W, 30 km southwest of Point Montara, Califonia; (2) an estimated 9 m animal on 11 April 1963 at 37° 08′ N, 123° 05′ W, 61 km west of Pigeon Point, California; (3) an estimated 14 m animal on 10 May 1963 at 37° 20′ N, 123° 10′ W, 44 km south southwest of the Farallon Islands, California; (4) two whales estimated at 15 m each on 11 March 1965 at 26° 39′ N, 113° 40′ W, 12 km southwest of Punta Abreojos, Baja California; and (5) one small and two large whales on 17 January 1967 at 48° 20′ N, 125° 06′ W, 28 km west southwest of Cape Flattery, Washington.

Rowntree, V., Darling, J., Silber, G. and Ferrari, M. 1980. Rare sighting of a right whale (*Eubalaena glacialis*) in Hawaii. *Can. J. Zool.* 58(2): 309–12.

Reports the sighting of two right whales in Hawaiian waters. The most recent occurred in Auau Channel off West Maui (20° 49′ N, 156° 45′ W) at 1045 on 25 March 1979. Body length was estimated at 15–16 m (about 51 ft). Underwater photographs are provided including one of the dorsal aspect of the whale's head showing the callosity pattern. A second record (reported first in *The Whalewatcher* 9(7): 10–11, 1975) was of an estimated 50 ft right whale north of Oahu, Hawaii in 1975. The authors report one earlier record at about 465 km (250 nmi) west of Maui first reported or plotted by Maury (1851). Other information from Maury (1851) is discussed and the authors conclude that right whales are rare visitors to the Hawaiian Islands. They dispute Tomilin's (1957) record of right whales in Hawaii. The authors discuss the subject of where calving and mating take place in the North Pacific based on Japan and US published coastal winter sighting records. See Herman *et al.* (1980) for the same whale sighting

Ruud, J. T. 1942. A review of the investigations on whales and whaling in recent years. *Int. Whal. Stat.* (Oslo) 16: 67–77.

One shortcoming of the IWS series, according to Ruud, is that several species of whales (including the right whale) are reported as 'Other whales' in the text statistics, which thus on occasion provide few details of catches. Ruud focuses on life history, plankton, migration, and effects of whaling on whale stocks primarily for blue, fin, humpback, sei and sperm whales from the literature and whaling records.

Following Ruud's article, beginning on page 78, list of the catches of these five species, plus 'Others' (nine other species including right whales) are summarized by year (1910–1939) by areas of the world. The 80 known right whales reported landed in the North Pacific were taken as follows: 'pelagic whaling in the Arctic,' 1931, 4; 'Pacific (north),' 1923, 1 and 1935, 2; 'Japan and Korea,' 1911, 2, 1912, 3, 1913, 1, 1914, 1, 1915, 7, 1916, 8, 1918, 2, 1919, 5, 1928, 9, 1930, 2, 1931, 8, 1932, 14, 1933, 3, 1937, 5, 1938, 2; and 'Kamchatka' 1937, 1. The mention of several thousand whales with 'no specification' suggests that many more right whales were landed than reported.

Scammon, C. M. 1869. On the cetaceans of the western coast of North America. *Proc. Acad. nat. Sci. Philad.*, April 1869, pp. 13–63.

A short description of whaling and the occurrence of right whales. The first west coast shore party for whaling was established in Monterey, California in 1852. Right whales were few in number along the upper California coast, as compared to their abundance near Kodiak Island, Alaska. They were primarily found from Vancouver Island to the Aleutian Islands out to 150° W; a few were taken in Baja California waters from Sebastian Vizcaino Bay (outside Scammon's Lagoon) to Cedros Island (about 27°–29° N). They were usually seen from February to April. Early whalers did not know where right whales migrated to in winter, nor where they gave birth. Most sailors agreed that the species did not go to tropical waters, and some speculated that they wintered over near the Kuril (USSR) and adjacent islands. Scammon includes a brief discussion of bowheads with right whales. He refers to whales moving into the bays, etc., when the 'small ice comes,' but it is unclear whether these are bowheads only or right whales moving north in spring into the Bering Sea–Aleutian Islands passes. Whalers reported seeing large right whales near St Paul Island, Bering Sea in October during the whales' southbound migration. In the Okhotsk Sea, right whales were found in the northern waters, then late in the season (presumably in late summer–autumn) in southern waters near the Kuril Islands. Near the end of the northern whaling season, right whales were reported to gather in large groups (called 'gams'), an indication they were about ready to leave the whaling ground. The remainder of the article refers to methods of chasing and dispatching the animals, and the acknowledgement that the whales had been nearly annihilated or driven to other unknown feeding grounds.

Scammon, C. M. 1871. Northern Whaling. *Overland Mon.* 6(6): 548–54.

The two North Pacific whale species principally pursued by 19th century whalers were the right whale (*Balaena cullamach*, now known as *Eubalaena glacialis*) and the great polar whale (*Balaena mysticetus*). The former 'haunts' of the right whale were 'north-west coast' of North America (Vancouver Island to Gulf of Alaska), southern Bering Sea, coast of Kamchatka, Sea of Japan, Kuril Islands, and southern Okhotsk sea. The remainder of the article on right whales is virtually the same as Scammon's 1869 paper in Proceedings of the Academy of natural Sciences of Philadelphia; bowhead whaling is also discussed in some detail.

Scammon, C. M. 1874. *The Marine Mammals of the North-Western Coast of North America, Described and Illustrated: Together with an account of the American Whale-Fishery.* John H. Carmany and Company, San Francisco, and G. P. Putnam's Sons, New York. 319 pp. + i–v.

A general account is given of the occurrence of the right whale, '*Balaena Sieboldii*? Gray', of the 'north-western' coast and a comparison made with related baleen whales. The author reports right whales were once 'occasionally in large numbers' off Oregon, but were only 'stragglers' (from their northern grounds) off California. Known universally by the American whalers as the 'North-west Whale', this species was early on considered distinct from the southern right whale. Scammon reports that gestation is one year, the calf one-fourth the length of the 'dam' at birth, but the calving grounds are unknown and no calving bays have been identified along the eastern shores (Japan, USSR, etc.) or west coast of North America, as has been discovered for bays in the Southern Hemisphere. This article is virtually the same as Scammon (1869; 1871); for greater details see Scammon (1869).

Scheffer, V. B. 1972. Marine mammals in the Gulf of Alaska, pp. 175–207. *In*: D. H. Rosenburg (ed.), *A review of the Oceanography and Renewable Resources of the Northern Gulf of Alaska.* Inst. Mar. Sci., Univ. Alaska, Fairbanks. 10 + 690 pp.

Discusses the history of regulations, uses of marine mammals and threats to particular species. A summary of the take of right whales in Alaska this century is provided, from the literature of (cf. Kellogg, 1931): 13 landed, 1919–29; and 9 landed 1960–69 (3 each year, 1961–63; presumably by Japanese pelagic whalers although not cited in this paper). Population estimates are tabulated; the right whale population is estimated at 50. Large whale estimates are considered rough and procedures used to arrive at them are explained.

Seki, Y. 1958. Observations on the spinal cord of the right whale. *Sci. Rep. Whales Res. Inst., Tokyo* 13: 231–51.

An extensive description with drawings and photographs (15 plates) is given of the spinal cord of a female right whale (*Eubalaena glacialis*), 11.65 m (38 ft) body length taken on 23 May 1956 'off Kinkazan' (probably the same whale reported on page 3 of Omura, 1958). The author comments that this whale had a 'remarkably' short spinal cord (174 cm) for its body length (about 15% of body length compared to 24% in fin whales). Nerve cells in the region of the lower spinal column are much larger than in the upper body (in humans they are about the same size), and the author suggests this is because the spinal nerves must run a much longer distance in *Eubalaena* than *Homo*.

Sleptsov, M. M. 1955. Biologiya i promysel kitov dalnevostochnykh morei (Biology of whales and the whaling fishery in Far Eastern seas). 'Pishch. Prom.', Moscow. In Russian. (Transl. with comments and conclusions only by Fish. Res. Board Can., Transl. Ser. 118, 6 pp.)

The Russian version reports on species composition of cetaceans (including right whales) in the northwestern Pacific; food of whales; studies of the regions in which whales feed; distribution and migrations; reproduction; and analysis of age and sex composition of whale stocks. Includes contour maps of plankton abundance seaward from the Kuril Islands, at various times in 1953 and compared with the distribution of cephalopod molluscs, sauries and the various whales. The North Pacific whale catch is given by species and region, with data on mean length and size distribution. Sleptsov concludes that right whales are increasing in number and suggests they will recover from whaling in 5–10 years. No data are presented.

Sokolov, V. E. 1961. Stroenie i prichiny vozniknoveniya kozhnykh narostov u yaponskikh kitov (*Eubalaena glacialis sieboldii* Gray) (Structure and reasons for the formation of cutaneous excrescences in the Japanese whale (*Eubalaena glacialis sieboldii* Gray)). *Zool. Zh.* 40(9): 1,427–9. [In Russian.] (English abstract in *Biological Abstracts*, General and Systematic Zoology – Chordata, 1962, No. 16I320.)

Abstract states that callosities are '...formed basically by thickening of the epidermis...and dermis...formed from small nodules from which hairs grow.' 'The subsequent pathological growth...is secondary, a result of the parasitization...by lice which can easily stay on the body of the whale in those places.'

Starbuck, A. 1878. History of the American whale fishery from its earliest inception to the year 1876. *U.S. Comm. Fish and Fisheries. Part IV. Rep. Commnr 1875–76*, Appendix A, 779 pp.

Lengthy discourse on the background and effort of the whale fishery in the Atlantic and, to a lesser extent, Pacific and Indian Oceans, along with annual records of ships' names, owners, voyage dates, oil (sperm and 'whale') and whalebone taken, and whaling grounds (e.g., 'Pacific Ocean', 'Cape de Verdes', 'South Seas', 'West Indies', 'Brazil', 'Patagonia', 'New Zealand', 'Bay of Mexico', 'Falkland Islands', 'Chili', 'NW coast' and many others). The principal species taken were sperm and right whales, but it is known that some humpback and gray and many bowhead whales are also included in these data. The total estimated catch for the period 1804–1876 is 225,521 sperm whales, and 193,522 right whales (footnote, page 661). The latter figure for 'right whales' also included some bowhead, humpback and gray whales for some years. American whalers fitted out from Nantucket first sailed for the Pacific Ocean in 1789 (preceded by the British in 1787) but mostly whaled in the South Atlantic. It was not until 1791 that the first American whaling vessel (the *Beaver*) actually reached the (south) Pacific whaling grounds. And it was not until 1819–22 that whaling in the North Pacific (China to Hawaiian Islands) became active; this whaling was mostly for sperm whales. In 1835, the first right whale was taken off the Kodiak ground by B. T. Folger of the *Ganges*, commencing the 'Northwest Coast' fishery (page 98). Starbuck's records do not specifically reflect whaling effort in the northwest coast fishery until 1841. Between 1841 and 1856, he reports nearly 500 voyages to the northwest coast of America which took place (pages 382–511) primarily for right whales. One anecdotal comment from this book is of interest: according to Starbuck, more than one whaling captain reported that a considerable number of right whales sank after being killed (cf. footnotes page 129). This is a different story from the one commonly held that right whales got their name, in part, because they float once dead.

Starks, E. C. 1922. A history of California shore whaling. *Fish. Bull.*, Sacramento No. 6, 38 pp.

A rather detailed account of related whaling activities along the coast of California, beginning with some comments by Sebastian Vizcaino in 1602. Much of the text is of course on gray whaling, however in several places mention is made of right whales: (1) Page 8, 25 bomb lances were fired into a 'huge' (right) whale by whalers from the San Simeon shore station. The whale smashed one boat and got away. (2) Page 10, pelagic whalers (not shore whalers) usually confined their whaling to the more valuable right and sperm whale, but on occasion took 'finner' (fin) or humpback whales as well. Seldom did shore whalers take right (see footnote page 12) and sperm whales; they concentrated on gray and humpback whales. (3) Page 18, one right whale was taken in 1859 (no details given). Several other land stations are mentioned (e.g. Crescent City, Bolivar Bay, Goleta, and two stations at San Pedro) which are not mentioned by Scammon, Townsend, Tower or other authors. (4) Page 27, repeats Townsend's (1886) records of three right whales taken in 1884–85. (5) Page 35, right whales were never taken during modern California shore station operations, but a few were taken during the early years (presumably between 1855 and about 1880s); they were fairly common south to Oregon; and only nine right whales had been seen during the 17 years Captain Clark operated at San Simeon/San Luis Obispo Stations (1865–82). Numerous valuable historic references are cited in the text, but in the (xerox) copy available to me (original publication not read), no literature citation section is given.

Tillman, M. F. 1975. Assessment of North Pacific stocks of whales. *Mar. Fish. Rev.* 37(10): 1–4.

Modern whaling in the North Pacific is reviewed. Stocks of whales are assessed giving 'original population', 'maximum sustainable yield level', and 'current population'. Black right whales are severely depleted, now fluctuating near 200. No estimate is available for the size of the North Pacific right whale population(s) before commercial whaling began in the mid-1850s.

Tomilin, A. G. 1957. Kitoobraznye (Cetacea). Vol. IX. *In*: V. G. Heptner (ed.) of *Zveri SSSR i prilezhashchikh stran* (Mammals of the USSR and adjacent countries). *Zveri vostochnoi Evropy i severnoi Azii* (Mammals of eastern Europe and adjacent countries). Izd. Akad. Nauk SSSR, Moskva, 756 p. In Russian. (Transl. by Israel Program Sci. Transl., 1967, 717 pp.)

Detailed description of right whales from all sources given. Reports that Reinhardt (1866) (reference not cited by Tomilin) stated that right whales once occurred near Hawaii (see Rowntree *et al.*, 1980, who question this). Tomilin reports from the early literature (late 1800s) that the southern distribution in the east is 28° N ('American coast') and in the west to 25° N ('Asian coast'). Right whales were found in summer and autumn (June to October) near Kamchatka and Sea of Okhotsk, and in winter adjacent to the islands near Japan and in the Yellow Sea. Interesting account of seasonal movement patterns along the coast of Japan is given; several possible useful references are provided in text (e.g. Möbius, 1893; Slyunin, 1895) but not listed in his literature cited sections. See Appendix for several references cited by Tomilin.

Tower, W. S. 1907. A history of the American whale fishery. *Publications of the Univ. Pennsylvania, Series in Political Economy and Public Law*, No. 20. 145 pp.

Broadly chronicled and (often) critical summary of the history of American whaling, principally using the earlier literature of the 19th century (e.g. Starbuck, 1878). Includes not only a description of whaling by area and nation, but also a summary of whale products, shipping activities, etc. by year, methods of capture, and future prospects for whaling and whalers. A separate chapter is included on 'The Rise of Pacific Whaling.' The northwest coast fishery (dominated by right whaling to 1848 and later by gray whaling) was at its height between 1838 and 1843–8, after which rights and bowheads were discovered in the Okhotsk and Bering Seas. San Francisco was established as a whaling port in 1850, partially replacing east coast ports, followed shortly by 11 other stations from Half Moon Bay (south of San Francisco) to 'Point Abanda' (probably Punta Banda at the south end of Ensenada Bay, Baja California, Mexico). No specific mention is made of right whales sighted or landed along the northwest coast of North America. Factors which contributed in varying degree to the decline in whaling in the North Pacific by the early 20th century were falling prices for oil and bone (e.g. replacement of whale oil with petroleum oils and natural gas); use of cheap coal; invention of metals and rubber products; demise of most target whale species (over-fishing); the high cost of outfitting a whaling vessel; the Civil War; discovery of gold in California; several disasters in the Arctic (numerous boats being lost in the ice); and others. The majority of the whale products (oil and whalebone) reported by other authors (c.f. Starbuck, 1878 and others) came from right whales and bowheads, especially after 1838 to perhaps the early 1880s (right whale 1838–1848; bowhead 1843–1880s probably). Interpretation of 'whale oil' reported by most authors is confounded by the fact that a variety of whalebone (baleen) whales were taken, as well as some porpoises (e.g. 'blackfish' or, probably, pilot whale) and walrus.

Townsend, C. H. 1886. Present condition of the California gray whale fishery. *Bull. US Fish Comm.* 6: 346–50.

By 1884, only five Californian whaling stations remained of the 11 mentioned by Scammon (1874); at Monterey, San Simeon, San Luis Obispo (Port Hanford), Point Conception, and San Diego. Besides gray whales being taken in winter and spring, humpback whales were taken in 'summer' (September to December), primarily from the Monterey station. Although not taken from San Simeon or San Luis Obispo stations, Townsend reports humpback whales (by then scarce) were once common (along the central coast of California). In 1884–85, five right whales were landed, one each at San Diego and Point Conception, and three at the San Simeon whaling station. (The locations taken from shore were not reported.)

Townsend, C. H. 1935. The distribution of certain whales as shown by logbook records of American whaleships. *Zoologica, NY* 19(1): 1–50.

Records from 744 vessels and 1,665 voyages carried out from 1785 to 1916 are presented. Tables of the catches are given for six species of whales (sperm, bowhead, northern right, southern right, humpback and California gray) and those for right whales in three oceans (Atlantic, Pacific, and Indian). Whaling data presented for the North Pacific and Bering Sea involved principally right and bowhead whales; whaling activity occurred almost exclusively during the summer months. Maps include seasonal catches of right whales primarily in the Gulf of Alaska and near Kodiak Island. From whaling records, right whales were formerly distributed to St Lawrence and St Matthew Islands and Cape Prince of Wales (Bering Strait) in the central and northern Bering Sea.

True, F. W. 1904. The whalebone whales of the western North Atlantic compared with those occurring in European waters, with some observations on the species of the North Pacific. *Smithson. Contrib. Knowl.* 33, 332 pp. + 50 pl.

In Chapter IX, 'Whalebone whales of the eastern Pacific Ocean', pages 220–71, True recounts comments made by Scammon (1874), and reports one right whale was killed in 1871 near the Aleutian Islands as reported by Pechuel (Pechuel-Loesche, M. E. 1871. *Wale und Walfang*. Ausland, Vol. 4, pp. 985–1,234, and Vol. 45, pp. 6–11). He also reports on baleen in the National Museum from whales taken near Japan (two pieces) and the northwest coast of North America (two pieces) (longest lengths ranging from 7 ft. 2 inch to 8 ft. 6 in.). An anatomical description is provided (page 298) as well as photos of specimens taken (plates 42–46 and 50).

Tsuyuki, H. and Naruse, U. 1963. Studies on the oil of black right whale in the Northern Pacific Ocean. *Sci. Rep. Whales Res. Inst., Tokyo* 17: 171–90.

Reports on the properties of oils (e.g. percent oil, specific gravity, acid value, saponification and iodine value) from muscle tissue, blubber and 11 organs from three right whales (male 17.1 m, > 12 yr; male 17.0 m, > 12 yr; male 15.1 m, > 9 yr) killed on 22 August 1961 at approximately 55° 53′ N, 153° 4′ W (south of Kodiak Island, Alaska). The various properties for right, fin, blue, humpback, sei and gray whale oil are given. The component saturated fatty acids of right whales are reported to be about 30% in the samples, about 10% higher than in fish, and about twice that of *Calanus plumchrus*, the North Pacific right whale's principal prey.

Tsuyuki, H. and Naruse, U. 1964. Studies on the lipids in brain of black right whale in the Northern Pacific Ocean. *Sci. Rep. Whales Res. Inst., Tokyo* 18: 173–80.
The yield of acetone-soluble lipids from the brain of a 15.1 m male right whale (see Tsuyuki and Naruse, 1963) was reported as 1.26%. The yield of phospholipids from frozen brain tissue was 0.42%. Palmitic, stearic and arachidic saturated fatty acids were found in both lipids, as were the component acids of the unsaturated fatty acid group.

Tsuyuki, H. and Itoh, S. 1970. Fatty acid components of black right whale oil by gas chromatography. *Sci. Rep. Whales Res. Inst., Tokyo* 22: 165–70.
Quantitative fatty acid analysis was conducted on stomach, liver, tongue, and blubber at nine locations on the body from one adult 17.1 m male right whale taken near Kodiak Island, Alaska in 1962 (see Tsuyuki and Naruse, 1963, for details of catch). About 25 kinds of fatty acids were identified, principally consisting of monoenoic and polyenoic types. No 'remarkable differences' were observed in fatty acid components among the body parts tested.

Wada, S. 1975. Indices of abundance of large-sized whales in the North Pacific in 1973 whaling season. *Rep. int. Whal. Commn* 25: 129–65.
Effort and catch for 1973 are tabulated by species and area. Indices of abundance, calculated from Japanese catch and effort data and Japanese sighting data and presented the previous year, are updated and revised. Area of operation was extended southward to about 25° N. In addition to indices, appendices give species raw data from Japanese catches from 1966–1973 tabulated by 10° squares, and sightings from 1965–1973 by 5° (Lat.) × 10° (Long.) squares. Thirty-two right whales were seen in the western North Pacific (west of 180°). Estimates of abundance using 1965–1973 data were 150–530, including a minimum estimate for 1973 of 220.

Wada, S. 1976. Indices of abundance of large-sized whales in the North Pacific in the 1974 whaling season. *Rep. int. Whal. Commn* 26: 382–91.
Effort and catch for 1974 are tabulated by species and area. Japanese catch and sighting data and indices of abundance for 1974 are tabulated, updating previous tabulations. No right whales were found by Japanese scouting boats in the North Pacific in 1974. A minimum estimate of abundance for 1974 was 60.

Wada, S. 1977. Indices of abundance of large-sized whales in the North Pacific in the 1975 whaling season. *Rep. int. Whal. Commn* 27: 189–94.
Effort and catch for 1975 are tabulated by area. Japanese catch and sighting data and indices of abundance for 1975 are tabulated, updating previous tabulations. Distance covered in sighting activities has decreased steadily since 1972. Two right whales were seen in the square N8S2 (40°–45° N, 140°–150° W). A minimum estimate of abundance for 1975 was 200.

Wada, S. 1978. Indices of abundance of large-sized whales in the North Pacific in the 1976 whaling season. *Rep. int. Whal. Commn* 28: 319–24.
Effort and catch data for 1976 are tabulated by species and area. Three right whales were seen from scouting boats, one each in: 40°–45° N, 170°–175° E; 50°–55° N, 155°–160° W; and 45°–50° N, 150°–155° W.

Wada, S. 1979. Indices of abundance of large sized whales in the North Pacific in the 1977 whaling season. *Rep. int. Whal. Commn* 29: 253–64.
Summarizes whale sightings and catch and effort data primarily for the area encompassing 40°–50° N, 160° E–130° W. No detectable increase in right whale abundance was noted for the years 1965–1977, although a steady increase in sightings occurred from 1973 to 1977 based on a small data set. Sightings by 5° square area are summarized; in 1977 four right whales were observed which constituted 1% of all baleen whales sighted. On the basis of sightings indices of abundance were 50–650 (1965–77 data set), depending upon the estimation method used. Most whales were seen between 160° E–180° in the 1960s, and between 160° W–140° W in the 1970s. A comparison of effort and vessel coverage between areas and years was not given.

Wang, P. 1978. Studies on the baleen whales in the Yellow Sea. *Acta Zoo. Sin.* 24(3): 269–77. [In Chinese.]
(From English abstract.) 'Two right whales were caught near Hai Yang Island, the female being 18 m and the male 13.8 m in body length. The morphometric and skull data are listed in Tables 9 and 10.' The morphology, ecology and distribution of right, gray, blue, fin, sei, minke and humpback whales are described. [This paper was reprinted as: Wang, P. 1980. Studies on the baleen whales in the Yellow Sea. *Collected Oceanic Works* 3(2): 71–81.]

Wang, P. 1984. Distribution of cetaceans in Chinese waters. *Chinese J. Zool.* 6: 52–6. [In Chinese.] [In: Wang, P. 1985. Distribution of cetaceans in Chinese waters, trans. C. H. Perrin, editor W. F. Perrin, NMFS, Southwest Fisheries Center. Admin. Rep. No. LJ-85-24, 11 p.]
(From LJ-85-24.) 'Very few right whales migrate through Chinese waters. Japan captured 2 in 1944 in the Yellow Sea. Captures also have been made in Taiwan. In January 1973, two right whales were sighted in the Hai Iang Dao in the northern Yellow Sea. One more sighting was made in southeastern waters of Hai Iang Dao in December 1977.'

Webermann, E. C. 1914. Kitoboinyi promysel' v Rossii. Chast 1: Istoriya promysla (The whale fishery in Russia. Part 1: A history of the whale fishery). Moscow. Izv. Moskovskago Kommercheskago Inst. Kommerchesko-tekhn. otdelenie. Kn. II. 312 pp. [In Russian].
Describes pre-20th century historical whaling conducted by coastal Japanese villages and commercial whaling carried out along the coast of China and Korea. 'Balaena glacialis, Linne' is described on pages 268–70, and figures 43–4 appear to be old reproductions of right whales.

Williams, H. (ed.) 1964. *One Whaling Family*. The Riverside Press, Cambridge and Houghton Mifflin Co., Boston. 401 pp.
A chronological account of the voyage of the whaling vessel *Florida* into the Indian and Pacific Oceans, 1858–1861, from the diary of Eliza Azelia Williams written during the voyage. Specific references are made on a daily basis to various species of whales sighted, associated with approximate locations. For example, while in the Sea of Japan and southern Okhotsk Sea, right whales were reported on numerous occasions, some were chased, some harpooned. The Okhotsk Sea was entered on 12 June 1861, near the southeast tip of Sakhalin Island. Right whales were immediately pursued. Reference is made to this area being called 'Weed Ground' by the whalers, a place where whales were plentiful. Kamchatka was also visited. The whaling season ended on 1 October 1861, when the *Florida* departed for San Francisco.

Woodhouse, C. D. Jr. and Strickley, J. 1982. Sighting of northern right whale (*Eubalaena glacialis*) in the Santa Barbara channel. *J. Mammal.* 63(4): 701–2.
Reports the observation of an estimated 14 m (45 ft) right whale at 34° 07′ N, 119° 18′ W (about 18.5 km [10 nmi] ENE of Anacapa Island, California) at 1230 hr on 17 April 1981. A photograph is provided. Also mentioned was a baleen plate from a stranded right whale from Santa Cruz Island, California obtained on 14 November 1916. Authors indicate that these are the only two known documented cases of right whales occurring in the Northern Channel Islands area this century.

Yablokov, A. V. and Andreyeva, T. V. 1965. Age determination in baleen whales (mystacoceti). *Nature, Lond.* 205(4,969): 412–3.
An unspecified number of baleen plates from 'Balaena glacialis' (along with four other mysticetes) taken near the Kuril Islands or

(not specified in paper) by Chukotsk Eskimos were examined for historical use in ageing. Stratified tubules were visible in greater quantities than younger ones. No conclusions could be drawn from the small sample size whether a relationship exists between ageing and tubule formation.

Yamamoto, Y. and Hiruta, H. 1978. Stranding of a black right whale at Kumomi, southwestern coast of Izu Peninsula. *Sci. Rep. Whales Res. Inst., Tokyo* 30: 249–51.
On 15 April 1977 at about 2000 hr an 11.5 m (37 ft) male right whale stranded at approximately 34° 40′ N, 138° 45′ E, near the southwest tip of Izu Peninsula, Japan (southwest of Tokyo). The authors report on 16 body measurements; no internal examination was made.

Zenkovich, B. A. 1934. Kitoboinyi promysel v Kamchatskom i Beringovom moryakh, sezoh 1933. (Whaling in the Kamchatka and Bering Seas during the 1933 season). *Ryb. Khozy. Dal'nego Vostoka* 1–2: 113–8. [In Russian.]
In October 1933, while whaling off Kronotskiy Bay (about 54° N, 161° E) in the *Aleut*, a probable Japanese smooth whale (*Balaena japonica*), or right whale, was observed swimming in a southwesterly direction along the west coast of Kamchatka. This paper describes whaling activities and the occurrence of humpback, fin, sperm, bottlenose and gray whales along the far east coast. No other details on right whales except this probable sighting. (Unauthored English translation.)

Zenkovich, B. A. 1955a. Kratkaia istoriia kitoboingo promysla: soremennoe ego sostoianie v SSSR (A brief history of whaling in pre-revolutionary Russia and an account of present-day whaling in the USSR) Chapter 1. *In*: S. E. Kleinenberg and T. I. Makarova (eds.), *Kitoboiny Promysel Sovetskogo Soyuza* (*The Whaling Industry of the Soviet Union*). Minister Rybnoi. Promy. SSSR, Vses. Nauchno-issled. Inst. Rybn. Khoz. Okeanogr. Izdatel'stvo. [In Russian.] (Transl. by Israel Program for Sci. Transl. in 1968.)
Details of the early whaling history and catches in the western North Pacific and Bering Sea are reported for the period of 1932 to 1954. A total of 9 right whales was taken: 1935, 1; 1937, 1; 1939, 2; 1944, 3; 1945, 1; and 1946, 1, of a total of 23,368 whales including blue (138), fin (4,534), sei (742), minke (58), humpback (658), gray (624), sperm (16,342), beaked (98), and killer whales (169). A photograph of 'Pacific right whales' is included.

Zenkovich, B. A. 1955b. O migratsiiakh kitov. Promyslove raiony v dal'nevostochnykh vodakh (The migration of whales, whale fishing in the waters of the Soviet far east), pp. 51–68. *In*: S. E. Kleinenberg and T. I. Makarova (eds.) *Kitoboiny Promysel Sovetskogo Soyuza* (*The Whaling Industry of the Soviet Union*) (107 pp.), Vses. Nauchno-issled. Inst. Rybn. Khoz. Okeanogr. [VINRO] Izdatel'stvo, Part One, Chapter III. [In Russian.] (Transl. by Israel Program Sci. Transl., 1968, for US Dep. Inter. and Sci. Found., 14 pp.)
The effect of a weakening of the warm Japan current in the 1940s on abundance of whales' prey species and thence upon distribution is described. Segregation by age during migration is reported. Baleen whales of the Soviet far eastern seas, including right whales, move south in mid-September, gravid females leaving first. These regions are discussed individually: (1) The 'southern' region, i.e., Pacific shore of southern Kamchatka Peninsula; (2) Commander Islands; (3) Olyutorski Gulf; (4) Glubokaya-Severnaya Bay north to Cape Navarin, 'The region of the young of the gray California whales'; (5) Anadyr Gulf; (6) Bering Strait; and (7) Kuril Islands.

Zhirnov, L. V., Vinokurov, A. A. and Bychkov, V. A. 1975. *Redkie mlekopitayushchie, ptitsy i ikh okhrana v SSSR* (Rare mammals, birds and their protection in the USSR). Moscow: Ministry of Agriculture. 82 pp. [In Russian.] (Chapter 3, Marine Mammals, pp. 27–38

plus accompanying references, translated by Francis H. Fay, Univ. Alaska, Fairbanks, 1977, 17 pp.)
Over the years 1968–1973, fourteen species of marine mammals have been identified as rare and vanishing, including the 'Japanese right whale (*Eubalaena glacialis seiboldii* Gray)'. The status of cetacean stocks are briefly described. In many cases recommendations include establishing refuge areas or complete protection from harvesting.

APPENDIX

The following are original references not available to me but which are likely to contain some information relevant to right whales (*Eubalaena glacialis*) in the North Pacific.

Anonymous. Ms. 1855–56. Logbook of unidentified whaling vessel (Schooner William S. La[rsen] or La[wrence] of San Francisco), 1 July 1855–12 November 1856. Private collection. (Cited in Reeves and Leatherwood, 1985.)

Bowles, M. E. 1845. Some account of the whale-fishery of the N. West Coast and Kamchatka. *Polynesian* 2 October 1845.

Chapskii, K. K. 1941. Morskie zveri Sovetskoi Arktiki (Marine animals of the Soviet Arctic). Izdatel'stvo Glavsevmorputi, Moskva-Leningrad, p. 175. (A Pacific right whale hauled onto the whaling factory ship *Aleut*; from Tomilin, 1957, page 45 in Tomilin, 1967, translation edition.)

Dukul', I., Ergomyshev, N. and Tolstoi, V. 1929. Zveroboinyi promysel i utilizatsiya rybnykh otbrosov (Utilization of fishing industry waste in hunting). Tekhizdat, p. 6. Moskva. (From Tomilin, 1957, page 44 in Tomilin, 1967, translation edition.)

Egorov, I. 1940. Den'na 'Aleute' (A day aboard the '*Aleut*'). *Rybnoe khozyaistvo* 3: 18. (Photograph of a Pacific right whale; from Tomilin, 1957, page 45 in Tomilin 1967 translation edition.)

Fraser, F. C. 1937. Early Japanese whaling. *Proc. Linn. Soc. Lond.* 150th Session, part 1. 31(7): 19–20.

Gelett, C. W. 1917. *A Life on the Ocean*. Hawaiian Gazette Co., Ltd., Honolulu, Hawaii. (Brief mention is made of right whales in the southern Okhotsk Sea as well as the west coast of Kamchatka, 1847–1852. source, Richard Kugler, Director, Old Dartmouth Historical Society Whaling Museum, New Bedford, Massachusetts. Also available at the Hawaii State Library, 478 S. King St., Honolulu, HI.)

Gray, J. E. 1864. *Proc. Zool. Soc. London*, (Title unknown) pp. 170, 349, 587. (Mention is made of the excrescence on the head of a right whale from the Hawaiian Islands; from Tomilin, 1957, page 43 in Tomilin, 1967, translation edition).

International Whaling Statistics. Edited by the Committee for Whaling Statistics. (Det Norske Hvalrads Statistiske Publikasjoner). Grøndahl and Son, Oslo, No. 1 (1928) to No. 94 (1984).

Iwasa, M. 1934. Two species of whale lice parasitic on a right whale. *J. Faculty Sci., Hokkaido Imper. University*, Series 6, Zoology. 3(1): 33–9. (*Cyamus ovalis* and *C. erraticus* reported presumably from a Pacific right whale; from Tomilin 1957, page 44 in Tomilin, 1967, translation edition.)

Kleinenberg, S. E. and Makarova, T. I. 1955. *Kitoboiny: promysel Sovetskogo Soyuza* (The whaling industry of the Soviet Union). Moscow, Izdatel'stvo 'Rybnoe Khozyaistvo,' 118 p.

Leatherwood, S., Reeves, R. R. and Karl, S. A. 1985. Trends in catches at the Akutan, and Port Hobron (Alaska) whaling stations, 1912–39. Document SC/37/O 1 submitted to the June 1985 meeting of the International Whaling Commission (unpublished).

Marsh, M. C. and Cobb, J. N. 1911. The fisheries of Alaska in 1910. Dep. of Commerce and Labor, Bureau of Fisheries Doc. No. 746, 72 pp. (From Reeves *et al.*, 1985.)

Matsuura, Y. 1936. Studies on the right whale, *Balaena glacialis* Bonnaterre, in the adjacent waters of Japan. *Shokubutsu oyobi Dobutsu* (Flora and Fauna) 4(4): 24–30. [In Japanese.] (Also reported as vol. 4, pages 696–703).

Matsuura, Y. and Maeda, K. 1942. Kita-taiheiyo-san geizoku no sei butsugaku-tek: Chosa (Biological investigations of whales from the North Pacific). Senis-kujira. *Hogei-shiryo* 9: 1–59. [In Japanese.]

Mikhailov, S. 1936. O kitoboinom promysle na Murmane (On the whaling industry of Murman). Karelo-Murmanskii Krai, No. 3, p. 31 (From Tomilin, 1957, page 44 in Tomilin 1967 translation edition.)

Osgood, W. H. 1904. A biological reconnaissance of the base of the Alaska Peninsula. *North American Fauna* No. 24, US Biological survey, Washington, D.C.

Schmidt, P. Y. 1905. Morskie promysly Ostrova Sakhalina (Marine fishing and hunting grounds of Sakhalin Island). Rybnye promysly Dal'nego Vostoka, Vol. 3, Sankt-Peterburg. (Concerns a whaling net and whaling station in Aniwa Bay; from Tomilin, 1957, page 44 in Tomilin, 1967, translation edition.)

Sleptsov, M. M. 1952. Kity dal'nevostochnykh morei (Whales of the far eastern seas). *Izvest. Tikh. inst. morsk. rybnof. khozy. Okean. (TINRO)* 38: 128. (From Tomilin 1957, page 45 in Tomilin 1967 translation edition.)

Temminck, C. J. 1842. Fauna Japonica, Mammiferes. (Referenced in Tomilin, 1957, page 43 in Tomilin, 1967, translation edition.)

Vinogradov, M. P. 1949. Morskie mlekopitayushchie Arktiki (Marine mammals of the Arctic). *Trudy Arkti. Inst.* 202, Leningrad-Moskva. (From Tomilin, 1957, page 45 in Tomilin, 1967, translation edition.)

Adult right whale off Florida (Photo courtesy E. D. Asper)

Status of *Eubalaena glacialis* off Cape Cod

WILLIAM E. SCHEVILL, WILLIAM A. WATKINS AND KAREN E. MOORE

Woods Hole Oceanographic Institution, Woods Hole, Massachusetts 02543

ABSTRACT

Historic and recent records of abundance and distribution of *Eubalaena glacialis* near Cape Cod are scanty and imprecise, and cannot be considered a census. The historical records since 1620 and ours from 1955 to 1981 both show a seasonal peak in April and few sightings in summer months. During the last quarter century our counts show up to 131 individuals in one year; 70+ were the most seen in one day. We have seen 21 calves, up to 4 in one year, with an indication of a 3-year reproductive cycle. Individual whales usually remain in the area only a few days at a time. The evidence available does not demonstrate that *E. glacialis* in our waters nowadays are really very much fewer than they were in 1620. Our sightings off Massachusetts since 1955 show neither an increase nor a decrease in right whales.

INTRODUCTION

There is little firm information about North Atlantic right whales (*Eubalaena glacialis*). Knowledge of their distribution and any stock assessment is based on scant whaling and sighting records. Some recent sightings from the North Atlantic were compiled by Watkins and Schevill (1976), Reeves, Mead and Katona (1978), Winn (1982), Reeves and Brownell (1982), Watkins and Schevill (1983) and Kraus, Prescott and Stone (1984). These scattered occurrences demonstrate the general lack of detailed information about *Eubalaena*, which enhances the importance of any local history of catches and sightings. By examining observations of behavior and recent occurrence together with historical records in the vicinity of Cape Cod (roughly between 41° and 43° N, 69° and 71° W), some understanding can be gained about *Eubalaena* in at least one area of the western North Atlantic. This paper deals with this one small region.

HISTORICAL OBSERVATIONS

The right whale was the first whale to be hunted by the New England colonists. Shore-based right whaling began along the Massachusetts coast (Massachusetts Bay, Cape Cod, Martha's Vineyard, and Nantucket) in the 17th century, and was carried on in late fall, winter and spring (Macy, 1835; Allen, 1916). Right whales were reported as numerous in these waters when Europeans came in the sixteenth century. Just how numerous seems impossible to determine. Even after the English settlement of New England, the best we can do is to utilize the chronicles painstakingly compiled by Allen (1916, 131–41, 146, 158–60), although they contain little information on actual numbers of whales. In 1620 during the six weeks (21 November–26 December) that the *Mayflower* lay in Cape Cod Harbor (Provincetown), Bradford reported that

'we saw daily great whales, of the best kind for oil and bone, come close aboard our ship, and, in fair weather, swim and play about us.'

Shore whaling began soon after the settlement. Not much in the way of actual numbers turns up until January 1700, when it was stated that 'all the boates round [Cape Cod Bay] killed twenty nine whales in one day'. This implies that a considerably larger number was there, but no figure for this is even hinted at, nor do we know the number of boats involved; we have the catch, but no data on the effort. The maximum caught in a single day at Nantucket was 11 and the record season's catch there was 86 whales in 1726, shared by some 28 boats. Soon after this the New England coastal right whale fishery declined. Contributing factors may have been the use of larger vessels and the lure of more rewarding, although distant, prey – bowheads, *Balaena mysticetus*, to the north, and sperm whales, *Physeter catodon*, offshore to the east and south.

During the second half of the 19th century, whalers from New England were still taking right whales in the North Atlantic. In the course of his major study of Yankee whaling logbooks, Townsend (1935) counted 35 North Atlantic right whales taken during 15 voyages. Examining 12 of these original sources (3 logbooks not found), Schevill and Moore (1983) counted 32 *E. glacialis* struck, from more than 56 sighted between 1853 and 1898, none of which was encountered along the New England coast, even though these ships sailed out of and into their Massachusetts ports in all seasons. During this same period (1850–1900), Allen (1916, pp. 136–41) notes at least 63 right whales along the Massachusetts coast, while he had found records of only 9+ between 1800 and 1850, which may be partly due to fewer written accounts from the earlier years.

PRESENT DAY OBSERVATIONS

Sightings data

Our aerial and shipboard observations since 1955 in Cape Cod waters (mostly within about 25 km of the shore) indicate the occasional occurrence of *Eubalaena* in all months but September, November and December (Watkins and Schevill, 1983). To the whales there listed we add for 1981: 3 seen in April, 2 (cow and calf) in June and 1 in October. From 1955 through 1981 we made 764 sightings of *Eubalaena*, including at least 117 seen on more than one day during a year. In most cases identification of individuals seen in different years is not certain, so these sightings may represent fewer whales. A maximum of 131 individuals were seen in one year, 1961, with the next highest only 70+ (all seen in one day!) in 1970. Because of our acoustic interest, we prefer quiet weather for our boat work; rough seas, wind and rain all interfere noisily with listening. Quiet weather is also favorable for aerial observation and photography. As a result, we have few sightings in bad weather, which further skews our counts away from a proper census.

Reproduction

Information about reproduction, including numbers of calves, cow/calf behavior and sexual activity, is important for understanding populations. We have seen 21 different small calves in Cape Cod waters. Several were observed on more than one day, resulting in a total of 29 calf sightings in 12 years: 3 in March (1975, 1977), 14 in April (1959, 1961, 1963, 1973, 1974, 1976, 1977, 1980), 11 in May (1960, 1961, 1966, 1973, 1976, 1980) and 1 in June (1981), with up to 4 calves in one year (1976). There were 10 years scattered between 1955 and 1981 in which only adult right whales were seen. At least two calves appeared to be born here, because adults seen clearly without calves (March and April) were resighted within a week with very small (about 6 m) calves. During four successive years, we saw the same cow, identified by her callosity pattern, with two successive calves, indicating a 3-year reproductive cycle. This cow was seen in April and May 1973 with a very small (6 m) calf. On 1 April 1974 the 2 were seen again; the calf was larger but still with the cow. In March 1975 the cow was with 3 other large whales and 1 slightly smaller, possibly the same calf. Then in 1976 the cow was seen 4 times from 24 March to 10 May with a newborn calf. Identification was based on the cow's distinctive arrangement of callosities; the outlines of newborn calves' callosities are not clearly marked. If a 3-year calving cycle, also noted in the Bay of Fundy by Kraus *et al.* (1984), and for southern right whales, *E. australis*, by Payne (1976; p. 331), is typical for *E. glacialis*, it is not surprising that stock recovery would be as slow or slower than for other baleen whales.

Calves are sometimes difficult to see and photograph because they often remain close to, and sometimes beneath, the cows. We have observed cows apparently placing themselves between the calf and an approaching vessel or low-flying aircraft [also noted by Payne and Payne (1971, p. 164) for *E. australis*]. Whalers often took advantage of this protective tendency by first harpooning the calf, in the hope that the cow would remain nearby and be easier to take.

> Lowered three boats...Larb boat struck the calf and Waist boat struck...the cow but lost her by the line parting and she went off to windward spouting good blood after much trouble killed the calf and took him alongside by 2 P.M. as the cow and calf kept together, the calf being first one side of the cow and then the other and then on top of her the lines got in awful fix...cow swam off ship couldn't fall in with her. (Yield of calf about 20 barrels. From logbook of barque *Daniel Webster*, 17 June 1877, near 60° N, 34° W).

The wasteful practice of killing both calves and cows continued into the twentieth century. It was forbidden by the International Whaling Commission at its establishment in 1946.

New England colonial whalers considered a one-year-old calf a good catch (fat and yielding up to 50 bbl of oil), while a two-year-old after weaning yielded only 24 to 28 bbl (Dudley, 1726, p. 257). Allen (1916) found no record of young calves off New England in the late months of the year, so he suggested that calving occurred in January and February to the south of New England. He cited incidents of calves being taken off New England in March through June.

In Cape Cod Bay we have observed sexual activity in groups of 2 to 5 right whales in March, April and July. These behaviors were difficult to follow because they were only partly visible and the surface was churned up by the activity. Sex of the group members could be confirmed only when penises were visible or when a whale rolled onto its back, raising the genital area out of water. Activity was defined as sexual, not merely social, when an extruded penis was seen. Sexual activity included much rolling and physical contact, like some of the behavior described for *E. australis* by Donnelly (1967), Saayman and Tayler (1973) and Payne (1976). Similar social/sexual activity in *E. glacialis* was reported by Collett (1909) in July west of the British Isles, in the spring in the Great South Channel area east of Cape Cod (Winn 1982, p. 60) and from July through October in the Bay of Fundy, where Kraus *et al.* (1984, pp. 25, 26) recorded intromission three times during four years. Sexual activity, and presumably copulation, of *E. glacialis* occurs at least from March through October, while newborn calves appear in late winter and early spring. Assuming that gestation is about a year (Klumov, 1962, pp. 258–60), it appears that sexual activity occurs over a longer period than does conception.

Distribution and abundance

From identifications based on callosity patterns and body markings, we note that individual right whales are not usually found in Cape Cod waters for more than a few successive days (Watkins and Schevill, 1983). The repeated sightings in 1976 of a cow and calf over a 7-week period represent the longest time that we know of individual whales staying near Cape Cod. Usually right whales seem to pass through in small groups. This sort of movement may have facilitated exploitation in the 17th and 18th centuries by allowing the shore-based whalers to spread the harvest over many components of the population, including calves.

Right whales are still seen within a few kilometers of shore in all seasons, although irregularly. In recent years they have seldom been seen to seaward of Nantucket, where from the mid 17th to mid 18th centuries they were taken by shore whalers in small boats. By about 1730 right whales were reported as scarce in Cape Cod waters, supposedly from excessive hunting. Even after the whaling effort was reduced (and nearly stopped), *E. glacialis* remained scarce, as they still are now after some 75 years of essentially no hunting. They have probably never been totally absent from our waters, even though we had not heard of them here between 1916 and 1955. It was undoubtedly a mistake to speak as we did of the 'return of the right whale to New England waters' (Schevill, 1959). It is tantalizing not to know how many whales had to be present to allow the Cape Cod whalers of 1700 to kill 29 in one day. Their efficiency was surely not great enough to have made comparably large catches from the 25 or so that evaded the schooner *Glide* near Nantucket in April 1886 (Allen, 1916, p. 138), or from the 30 we saw in less than an hour in April 1959, and again on 4 May 1961, but perhaps they might have if faced with the more than 70 that we had on 13 April 1970.

Both the older records presented by Allen (1916) and our experience since 1955 show the greatest abundance of right whales in Massachusetts waters in April, with few, if any, in the warmer months (Fig. 1). Allen notes that the colonial whalers began their catches in October and

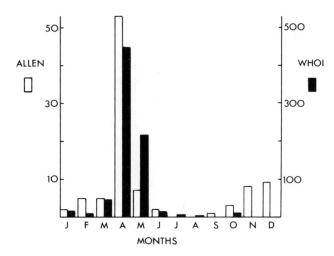

Fig. 1. *Eubalaena* encountered off the Massachusetts coast from 1620 through 1913 (Allen, 1916) are compared with WHOI sightings from 1955 through 1981. Although the WHOI total is greater than Allen's by a factor of about 10, the distribution agrees in the April peak and in the low numbers in summer.

continued to find whales throughout the winter and spring months. Doubtless the small number of our sightings in fall and early winter reflects our irregular effort. Although one tends to expect an annual migration cycle poleward in summer and equatorward in winter, in our local experience near Cape Cod we have seen little hint of it. When we see these whales swimming on the same heading for an hour or more, it may be in any direction, including south in the spring. Increasing evidence of north–south annual migration is accumulating; researchers working over longer distances have identified several individuals in winter on the east coast of Florida and Georgia which were also seen in summer off southern Nova Scotia (Kraus *et al.*, 1984, pp. 11–12).

DISCUSSION

Because the incomplete records of early shore whaling do not confirm with numbers the oft-stated abundance of whales, it may be that when the colonists began whaling, the whale population in this area may not have been as large as has been supposed. There is a possibility, not yet supported by recognition of individual whales, that the New England right whale stock hunted by the English colonists after 1620 may range past Newfoundland, and so may have been reduced in the sixteenth century by the Biscayan whalers based in the Straits of Belle Isle ('Grand Bay', Newfoundland). They seem to have taken both *B. mysticetus* and *E. glacialis*: we have no estimate of their catch of *Eubalaena* (Aguilar, (1986), offers estimates of the combined catch), but Barkham (1977, p. 78) points out that the great reduction and near termination of the Basque fishery was due not to scarcity of whales, but rather to the absorption of the whalers and their ships by the Spanish naval enterprises culminating in the disastrous attack on England in 1588.

Throughout our observations beginning in 1955 we may have been seeing about as many right whales per year as did the colonial coastal whalers. If we compare our numbers with Allen's (1916), we find about 30 per year for us and about 3 per year for him (Fig. 1). Our yearly totals have ranged from 2 to 131. We assume that many whales were missed, both by us and the early settlers. The

numbers of *Eubalaena* that we have seen close to shore in recent years would perhaps not have consistently supported the whaling that was carried on by the early colonials, although sizeable catches could still occasionally be taken. We cannot rule out the possibility that the whales may have changed their routes, as have the Hawaiian humpbacks, *Megaptera novaeangliae*, in historic times (Herman, 1979).

Our sightings since 1955 do not demonstrate either an increase or decrease in numbers of *Eubalaena* seen in Massachusetts coastal waters, and the record back to 1620 is not really very different. Given these imprecise data, we suggest that the population of right whales passing near Cape Cod is at worst only slightly smaller now than it was in the 17th century.

ACKNOWLEDGEMENTS

Many people have participated in these observations, including Stanley E. Poole, Robert G. Weeks, Jay Bercaw, and A. D. Colburn. This work was funded mostly by the Oceanic Biology Program of the Office of Naval Research (Contract N00014-82-C0019 NR 083-004). This is Contribution No. 5419 from the Woods Hole Oceanographic Institution.

REFERENCES

Aguilar, A. 1986. A review of old Basque whaling and its effect on the right whales *Eubalaena glacialis* of the North Atlantic. (Published in this volume.)

Allen, G. M. 1916. The whalebone whales of New England. *Mem. Boston Soc. Nat. Hist.* 8(2): 107–322, plates 8–16.

Barkham, S. H. 1977. Guipuzcoan shipping in 1571 with particular reference to the decline of the transatlantic fishing industry. Desert Res. Inst., Publs. in the Social Sciences, no.13: 73–81. University of Nevada, Reno.

Collett, R. 1909. A few notes on the whale *Balaena glacialis* and its capture in recent years in the North Atlantic by Norwegian whalers. *Proc. Zool. Soc. Lond.* 1909: 91–8, plates 25–27.

Daniel Webster, barque, Gilbert D. Borden, master. Voyage 1877–1879. Logbook in Providence Public Library, Providence, Rhode Island.

Donnelly, B. G. 1967. Observations on the mating behaviour of the southern right whale *Eubalaena australis*. *S. Afr. J. Sci.* 63(5): 176–81.

Dudley, P. 1726. An essay upon the Natural History of Whales, with a particular Account of the Ambergris found in the *Sperma Ceti* Whale. *Phil. Trans. Lond.* 33: 256–69.

Herman, L. M. 1979. Humpback whales in Hawaiian waters: a study in historical ecology. *Pacif. Sci.* 33(1): 1–15.

Klumov, S. K. 1962. Gladkie (yaponskie) kity Tichogo Okeana. (Japanese) right whales in the Pacific Ocean.] *Tr. Inst. Okeanol.* (*Akad. Nauk SSSR*) 58: 202–297. [In Russian]

Kraus, S. D., Prescott, J. H. and Stone, G. S. 1984. Right whales (*Eubalaena glacialis*) in the western North Atlantic: a summary of research conducted from 1980 to 1984. Report to the U.S. Dept. of Commerce, NOAA, National Marine Fisheries Service, 49 pp. (Unpublished.)

Macy, O. 1835. *The History of Nantucket*. Hilliard, Gray, and Co., Boston, 300 pp. Reprinted by Research Reprints, New York, 1970.

Payne, R. S. 1976. At home with right whales. *Natl Geogr. Mag.* 149: 322–39.

Payne, R. and Payne, K. 1971. Underwater sounds of southern right whales. *Zoologica* 56: 159–65.

Reeves, R. R. and Brownell, R. L., Jr. 1982. Baleen whales, *Eubalaena glacialis* and allies. pp. 415–44, *In:* J. Chapman and G. Feldhamer (eds.), *Wild Mammals of North America*. Johns Hopkins, Baltimore.

Reeves, R. R., Mead, J. G. and Katona, S. 1978. The right whale, *Eubalaena glacialis*, in the western North Atlantic. *Rep. int. Whal. Commn* 28: 303–12.

Saayman, G. S. and Tayler, C. K. 1973. Some behaviour patterns of the southern right whale *Eubalaena australis*. *Z. Säugetierkunde* 38(3): 172–83.

Schevill, W. E. 1959. Return of the right whale to New England waters. *J. Mammal.* 40(4): 639.

Schevill, W. E. and Moore, K. E. 1983. Townsend's unmapped North Atlantic right whales (*Eubalaena glacialis.*) *Breviora*, No. 476, 8 pp.

Townsend, C. H. 1935. The distribution of certain whales as shown by logbook records of American whaleships. *Zoologica*, N.Y. 19(1): 1–50, pls. 1–4.

Watkins, W. A. and Schevill, W. E. 1976. Right whale feeding and baleen rattle. *J. Mammal.* 57(1): 58–66.

Watkins, W. A. and Schevill, W. E. 1983. Observations of right whales (*Eubalaena glacialis*) in Cape Cod waters. *Fish. Bull.* 80(4): 875–80.

Winn, H. E. 1982. A characterization of marine mammals and turtles in the Mid- and North Atlantic areas of the U.S outer continental shelf. Final report of the Cetacean and Turtle Assessment Program to the U.S. Dept. Of Interior, Bureau of Land Management. (Unpublished). 450 pp. + 'Special Topics'.

Sightings of Right Whales, *Eubalaena glacialis*, On The Scotian Shelf, 1966–1972

EDWARD MITCHELL, V. MICHAEL KOZICKI AND RANDALL R. REEVES

Arctic Biological Station, Ste-Anne-de-Bellevue, Province of Québec, Canada H9X 3R4

ABSTRACT

We present and analyze all available data on right whales, *Eubalaena glacialis*, from the Canadian east-coast whaling industry (e.g. sightings and tagging by catcher boats) and a series of whale census and tagging cruises in the Northwest Atlantic between 1966 and 1972. 'Sightings' provided by the whalers are sometimes records of encounters as they occurred, but more often they are cumulative totals of whales seen during an hour or half-hour of searching.

Only one right-whale sighting was made by Newfoundland catcher vessels, of one animal east of Bonavista Bay on 6 June 1970. Blandford (Nova Scotia) catcher vessels reported 1,786 whale sightings between 1966 and 1972, 70% of which involved one or more fin whales, *Balaenoptera physalus*. Right whales were the fourth most commonly seen whale. There were 313 sightings of right whales, of which 11 did not involve any other species. The maximum number of right whales reported in one sighting was 30. Up to six sightings of right whales made on one day were analyzed for repetitive sightings, and we conclude that the maximum number of different individuals observed on one day was 70 whales.

The trends in these data are related to sighting effort; thus, the data cannot be used to give an index of population abundance. No calves were reported, but this may be an artifact of data collection. Right whales were concentrated around Roseway Basin between Browns Bank and Baccaro Bank; only 51 of 313 sightings were east of 64° W, and four of these were east of 62° W. There was no clear correlation between right whale occurrence and surface water temperature or weather conditions. Eight right whales were tagged with 'Discovery' type tags from catcher vessels and survey vessels. One winter sighting of two right whales was made on 13 March 1971 off Cape Cod.

Analysis of associated species in whale sightings indicates that on the Scotian Shelf right whales occurred 20% more frequently with fin whales, *Balaenoptera physalus*, than with any other species (53.5%; with sei, *B. borealis*, 31.9%).

INTRODUCTION

The North Atlantic right whale (*Eubalaena glacialis*) was the main target of an early colonial whale fishery off eastern North America (Dudley, 1725). According to Allen (1908), by the end of the 18th century its 'incessant pursuit' had accomplished the 'commercial extinction' of the right whale in the North Atlantic. American shore whalers (True, 1904; Allen, 1916; Edwards and Rattray, 1932; 1956; Lipton, 1975; Reeves and Mitchell, 1986a) and pelagic whalers (Clark, 1887; Starbuck, 1878; Reeves and Mitchell, 1986b) continued to take small numbers of right whales in the western North Atlantic until the early 20th century, and there is no evidence that the population was able to recover fully from the depleted condition it had reached by about 1750.

The 'rediscovery' of surviving North Atlantic right whales began with some sightings off northeast Florida (Moore, 1953; Layne, 1965), in the Gulf of Mexico (Moore and Clark, 1963) and off Cape Cod (Schevill, Moore and Watkins, 1981; Watkins and Schevill, 1982) during the 1950s and early 1960s. By the late 1970s, individuals and small groups had been reported in much of the species' known former range off eastern North America (Reeves, Mead and Katona, 1978).

Mention was made by Mitchell (1974; 1975a) of right whale sightings by whalers operating out of the Blandford, Nova Scotia, land station during the late 1960s, and Sutcliffe and Brodie (1977) published data tables containing information on some of these sightings. During recent years, concentrations of right whales have been found during summer and fall months (July to October) in the lower Bay of Fundy (Arnold and Gaskin, 1972; Gaskin and Smith, 1979; Kraus, Prescott, Turnbull and Reeves, 1982) and on or near Browns Bank (Winn, Goodale, Hyman, Kenney, Price and Scott, 1981).

In this paper, we present and analyze all available data on right whales from the Canadian east-coast whaling industry and from a series of whale sighting and tagging cruises between 1966 and 1972. The new information presented here pertains to an area with a meager historic record of whaling activity and where virtually no cetacean research had taken place previously. It should be of particular use in constructing hypotheses about right whale migration on or along the North American continental shelf, and in interpreting abundance estimates and other results from ongoing research in the Bay of Fundy and Gulf of Maine.

STUDY AREA

The Scotian Shelf is defined as the area bounded on the north by the outer coast of Nova Scotia, on the east by the deep Laurentian Channel, on the south by the continental shelf, and on the west by the Fundian Channel (Hachey, 1961). It is generally less than 100 fathoms deep. Sable Island is the only island on this shelf, but there are numerous offshore ledges and banks (Fig. 1). The water column on the Scotian Shelf is sharply stratified. A thick (as much as 40 fathoms) surface layer has temperatures ranging between 5°C and 20°C, with salinities of less than 32.0‰. The cold intermediate layer, 17–80 fathoms thick, determines the water characteristics on most of the offshore banks. Temperatures range between 0°C and 4°C; the salinity of this layer is 32.0–33.5‰. The bottom layer at 50–110 fathoms of depth can reach temperatures as high as 12°C, due to incursions of slope water.

The slope water which forms a well-defined band between the coastal waters on the shelf and the Gulf Stream offshore has salinities of 33.0–33.5‰ and temperatures of 5°C to 20°C (McLellan, Lauzier and

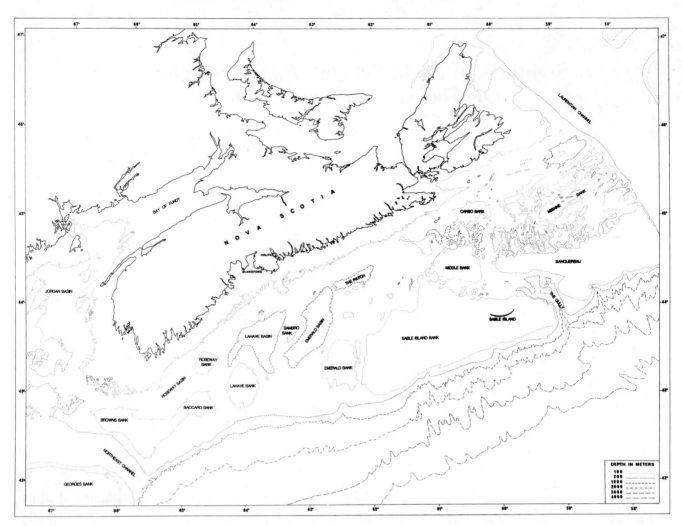

Fig. 1. Chart of study area off eastern Canada. Key to bathymetry as illustrated.

Bailey, 1953; Hachey, 1961). Circulation on the shelf is generally anti-clockwise.

Blandford whaling activities, and most of the observations reported here, took place on the Scotian Shelf and in adjacent slope waters, including Northeast Channel. A few catches were made on the northeast corner of Georges Bank. Because meat was an important product of the fishery, it was necessary for catcher vessels to operate relatively close to the whaling station in order to deliver carcasses in fresh condition. This meant that they usually worked within a radius of about 150 mi. of Blandford (Mitchell, 1974, Fig. 5–1).

PREVIOUS RECORDS OF RIGHT WHALES IN EASTERN CANADIAN WATERS

Ample evidence has accumulated during recent years demonstrating that right whales regularly summer in nearshore waters of the northern Gulf of Maine, the lower Bay of Fundy and the vicinity of Browns Bank (Neave and Wright, 1968; Arnold and Gaskin, 1972; Reeves *et al.*, 1978; Gaskin and Smith, 1979; Kraus and Prescott, 1981 Ms, 1982 Ms, 1983 Ms; Kraus *et al.*, 1982; Winn *et al.*, 1981; Winn, 1982). In contrast, there is little definite evidence of right whales reaching more northern areas along the eastern Canadian coasts.

Two right whales were killed in the St. Lawrence River in 1850 and another in 1912 (Wakeham, Bernard and

Riendeau, 1913). An 11–12 m specimen stranded alive at Pugwash, Nova Scotia (45°52′N, 63°40′W), in the southern Gulf of St. Lawrence, in October 1954 (Sergeant, Mansfield and Beck, 1970). Sears (1979) reportedly saw 3–4 right whales in Moisie Bay (50°18′N, 65°57′W), in the St. Lawrence Estuary, on 13–16 September 1976. There was another unsubstantiated sighting somewhere in the Gulf of St. Lawrence in 1980 (IWC, 1982, p. 106).

There are also a few records of right whales in Newfoundland waters. Millais (1907, pp 162–83) considered the species 'an irregular visitor' there before about 1830; the last capture of which he knew took place in 1850 near Gaultois, on the south coast. A right whale killed in Placentia Bay in mid-August 1937 was the first of its kind taken at the Rose-au-Rue whaling station during more than 19 years of operation (Anon., 1937a,b; Fig. 2). Another right whale was taken 'in error' from a Newfoundland shore station in 1951, and an animal 'probably of this species' was seen in Dildo Arm, Trinity Bay, in July 1959 (Sergeant, 1966, Ms). The most recent published Newfoundland sighting was in Bonavista Bay on 31 August 1981 (Beamish, 1981).

The early Basque whale fishery off Newfoundland and Labrador and in the Strait of Belle Isle and Gulf of St. Lawrence appears to have been principally a balaenid fishery (Tuck and Grenier, 1981), as was the Yankee 18th century fishery in these areas (Starbuck, 1878; Allen,

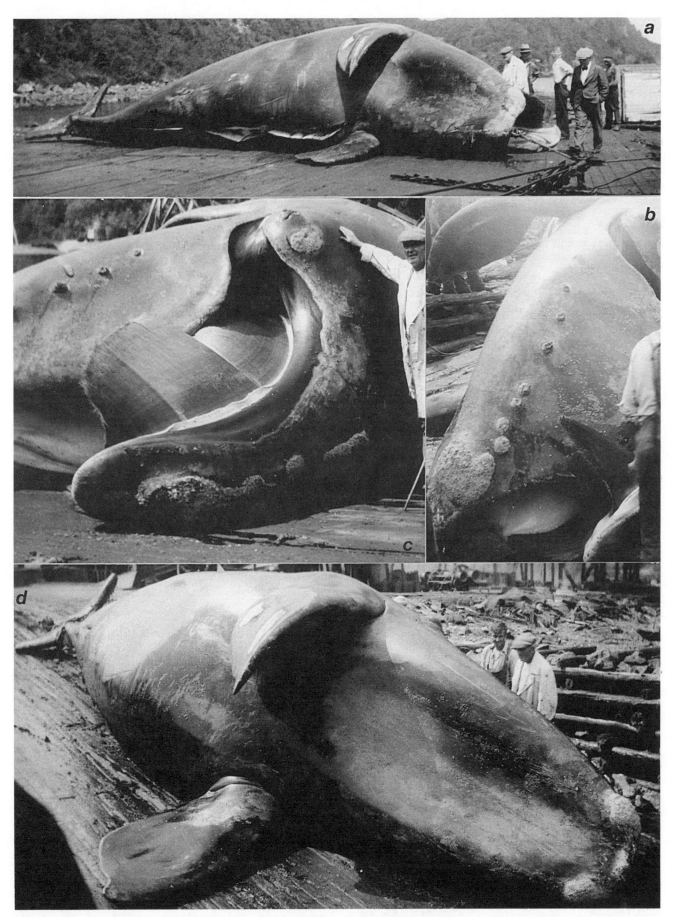

Fig. 2. Views of a right whale killed in Placentia Bay in mid-August 1937 and processed at Rose-au-Rue whaling station, south coast of Newfoundland (Anon., 1937a, b). (Courtesy of J. G. Mead)

1908; Reeves and Mitchell, 1986b). We agree with Eschricht and Reinhardt (1866) that the animals hunted there in summer were likely right whales, whereas those hunted amongst the ice early and late in the whaling season could have been bowheads (*Balaena mysticetus*). Starbuck (1878, p. 158) mentioned a record of a large whale taken near Cape Cod in March 1736 allegedly worth £1,500. This would mean, according to Starbuck, that the whale produced about 290 bbls of oil and 2,500 lbs of baleen — 'either a very remarkable whale, or an equally surprising inaccuracy.' If it were a stray bowhead, the yield, while still large, would be less difficult to believe. Allen (1916, p. 135) in fact suggested that a whale killed off Cape Cod in May 1843, which purportedly produced 300 bbls of oil and 1½ tons of baleen (max. length of 14 ft.), may have been 'a stray specimen of the Arctic Bowhead.'

MATERIALS AND METHODS

The most recent episode of commercial whaling for large whales in eastern Canada began in 1964 and ended in 1972, when the federal Minister of Fisheries declared a moratorium on commercial whaling in Canadian waters. The principal targets of this modern fishery were fin (*Balaenoptera physalus*) and sei (*B. borealis*) whales (Mitchell, 1974; Mitchell and Chapman, 1977); bottlenose whales (*Hyperoodon ampullatus*) (Mitchell, 1975b), minke whales (*Balaenoptera acutorostrata*) (Mitchell and Kozicki, 1975) and sperm whales (*Physeter catodon*) (Mitchell, 1975c; Mitchell and Kozicki, 1984) were also taken sporadically.

During the period 1966–72, the industry was required to report on a daily basis, data on all whales seen as well as caught by crews of the catcher boats. Although the instructions given to vessel captains specified that sightings be logged at the time of occurrence, in many cases they were logged only on the hour or half-hour. Consequently, many of the one-line entries on the data sheets represent an accumulation of sightings made over 30- or 60-minute periods. In this paper, the term 'sighting' should be understood to mean a single one-line entry on a data sheet. It may refer to encounters with whales or groups of whales as much as 55 minutes (or 10–12 n. miles) apart.

The sightings data were entered on Canadian catch-effort forms and subsequently verified, corrected and coded for computer entry and analysis (Breiwick, Mitchell and Kozicki, 1980, Ms.). Although not a requirement, gunners were asked to tag (with standard Discovery-type tags) any whale encountered on or *en route* to the whaling grounds.

In addition to the whaling operations, Mitchell (1974; 1975d) conducted research cruises throughout much of the western North Atlantic including, in particular, areas thought to be inhabited by whale stocks being fished from Canada's Atlantic whaling stations. Strip-census procedures followed on each of these cruises involved the recording of data on all sightings of cetaceans. Where possible, quantitative data were collected on surfacing and diving characteristics of whales observed. Tagging with Discovery-type and other experimental tags was attempted.

For this paper, we retrieved records from the commercial whaling data base pertaining to sightings of right whales (Appendix 1). Sighting times and positions

reported by the whaling industry were checked for accuracy. For all days when more than one sighting was reported, distances between pairs of sightings were divided by times elapsed between the sightings to calculate the catcher vessel's apparent speed. Only ten pairs of sightings resulted in calculated vessel speeds greater than 16 knots, considered the maximum cruising speed. Calculated speeds in all ten instances were less than 20 knots. Such error is trivial, and thus we made no allowance for it in our analysis.

Table 1.

Sightings by Blandford catcher vessels, 1966–72, in which right whales were not reported to be present. Key: F-fin, S-sei, H-Humpback, B-blue, Sp-sperm, Bo-bottlenose. The percentage frequency is expressed as a percentage of the total number of sightings made, 1,786, i.e. including those 313 with right whales in Table 2.

F	S	H	B	Sp	Bo	Freq	%	F	S	H	B	Sp	Bo	Freq	%
1	0	0	0	0	0	701	39.25	1	0	0	0	0	1	5	0.28
1	0	0	1	0	0	169	9.46	1	0	1	1	1	0	4	0.22
0	1	0	0	0	0	96	5.38	0	1	0	1	0	0	3	0.16
1	0	1	0	0	0	90	5.04	0	0	1	0	1	0	2	0.11
1	1	0	0	0	0	88	4.93	0	0	1	1	0	0	2	0.11
1	0	1	1	0	0	80	4.48	1	0	0	1	0	1	2	0.11
0	0	0	0	1	0	62	3.47	1	1	0	0	0	1	2	0.11
1	0	0	0	1	0	40	2.24	0	0	0	0	0	1	1	0.06
0	0	0	1	0	0	25	1.40	0	0	0	1	1	0	1	0.06
1	1	0	1	0	0	21	1.18	0	0	1	0	0	1	1	0.06
0	0	1	0	0	0	18	1.01	0	1	0	0	0	1	1	0.06
0	1	0	0	1	0	11	0.62	0	1	1	0	0	0	1	0.06
1	1	1	0	0	0	11	0.62	1	0	0	0	1	1	1	0.06
1	0	0	1	1	0	10	0.65	1	0	1	1	0	1	1	0.06
1	1	1	1	0	0	9	0.50	1	1	0	1	1	0	1	0.06
1	1	0	0	1	0	7	0.40	1	1	1	1	1	0	1	0.06
1	0	1	0	1	0	6	0.34								

Table 2.

Sightings by Blandford catcher vessels, 1966–72, in which right whales were reported to be present. Key: R-right, F-fin, S-sei, H-humpback, B-blue, Sp-sperm, Bo-bottlenose. The percentage frequency is expressed as a percentage of only the 313 sightings here, for which right whales were reported.

R	F	S	H	B	Sp	Bo	Freq	%	R	F	S	H	B	Sp	Bo	Freq	%
1	1	0	0	0	0	0	103	32.91	1	1	1	0	1	0	0	2	0.64
1	1	1	0	0	0	0	80	25.56	1	0	0	0	1	0	0	1	0.32
1	0	1	0	0	0	0	44	14.06	1	0	0	1	0	0	0	1	0.32
1	1	0	1	1	0	0	20	6.39	1	0	1	0	0	1	0	1	0.32
1	1	0	0	1	0	0	18	5.75	1	0	1	1	0	0	0	1	0.32
1	1	0	1	0	0	0	17	5.43	1	1	0	0	0	0	1	1	0.32
1	0	0	0	0	0	0	11	3.51	1	1	0	0	0	1	0	1	0.32
1	1	1	1	0	0	0	7	2.24	1	1	0	1	0	1	0	1	0.32
1	1	1	1	1	0	0	3	0.96	1	1	1	1	1	1	0	1	0.32

RESULTS AND DISCUSSION

Summary of sightings, by species

The Blandford catcher vessels reported a cumulative total of 1,786 sightings, involving seven cetacean species, between 1966 and 1972 (Tables 1 and 2). Fin whales were included in 1,249 (70%) of the sightings, 701 times by themselves and 548 times in the general vicinity of at least one other species. The other six species were, in order of their sighting frequencies: sei (391 sightings; of which 96 times alone), blue (*Balaenoptera musculus*) (373; 3 alone), right (313; 11 alone; Fig. 3), humpback (*Megaptera novaeangliae*) (267; 18 alone), sperm (150; 40 alone) and bottlenose 17; 1 alone). For reasons not clear to us, minke, pilot (*Globicephala melaena*) and killer whales (*Orcinus orca*) and other cetaceans were not reported by the

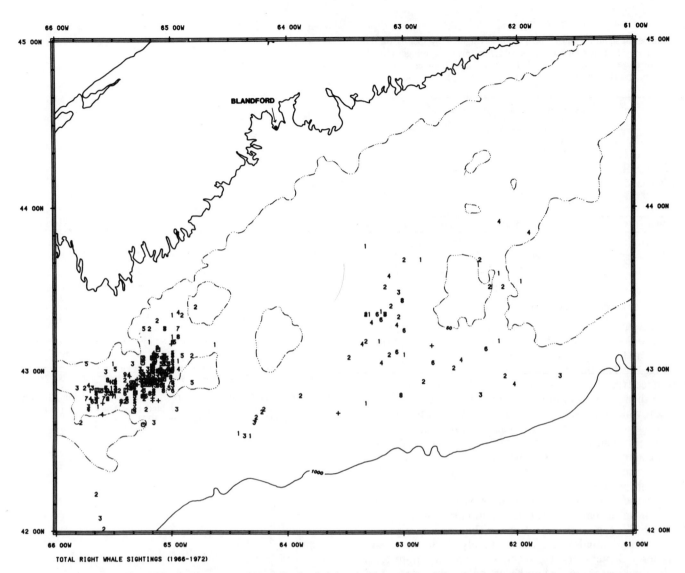

TOTAL RIGHT WHALE SIGHTINGS (1966-1972)

Fig. 3. Computer-generated chart of seas around Nova Scotia, showing positions where right whales were sighted by Blandford catcher vessels, 1966–1972. Numbers represent number of whales in a sighting, from 1 to 9. Symbols represent: + = 10–14 whales, □ = 15–9 whales, ⊕ = 20–24 whales, ★ = 25–30 whales.

catcher vessels, although we know that these species occur on the whaling grounds during the whaling season of May to December.

As noted above, only 11 of the 313 sightings of right whales (3.5%) made from Blandford catcher vessels involved right whales alone (Table 2). The most frequently observed combination of species was right whales with fin whales (103 times, or 32.9% of total right whale sightings), followed by right, fin and sei together (80 times, or 25.6%), sei and right together (44 times, or 14.1%), and right, fin, humpback and blue together (20 times, or 6.4%). These and other interspecies associations are shown in Tables 1–4.

Among the observations of individuals and small groups of right whales were the following combinations: a single right whale with 22 sei and two fin whales; two right whales with 30 fin and six blue whales: two right whales with four fin and 56 sperm whales; and four right whales with 65 fin, 12 humpback, and six blue whales. Large numbers of right whales were sometimes reported with other species as well, such as: 10 right whales with two fin, 30 sei, four humpback, 10 blue, and two sperm whales; 15 right whales with two fin and 20 sei whales; and 27 right whales with four sei whales.

Table 3.

Number of sightings and number of whales sighted, by the species, on the Nova Scotian whaling grounds, 1966–72. Also, ratios between species for fin, sei, and right whales.

	Number of sightings	% of total	Number sighted	% of total
Fin	1503	49.7	8558	57.1
Sei	391	12.9	1972	13.2
Blue	373	12.3	1108	7.4
Humpback	277	9.1	842	5.6
Right	313	10.4	1889	12.6
Sperm	150	5.0	571	3.8
Bottlenose	16	0.53	51	0.3

Ratios	From number of sightings	From number sighted
Fin : sei	3.84 : 1	4.34 : 1
Fin : right	4.80 : 1	4.53 : 1
Sei : right	1.25 : 1	1.04 : 1

We examine some of these associations in detail below, particularly the putative association of right whales with sei whales, and the general question of the species composition of sightings.

Table 4.

Number of sightings and number of whales sighted, by species, on the Nova Scotian whaling grounds, 1966–72, but only for sightings in which one or more right whale was included. Also, ratios between species for fin, sei, and right whales.

	Number of sightings	% of total	Number sighted	% of total
Fin	254	51.4	1612	53.5
Sei	139	28.1	968	31.9
Blue	45	9.1	190	6.3
Humpback	51	10.3	161	5.3
Sperm	4	0.81	78	2.6
Bottlenose	1	0.20	10	0.3

Ratios	From number of sightings	From number sighted
Fin : sei	1.76 : 1	1.68 : 1
Fin : right	0.81 : 1	0.85 : 1
Sei : right	0.44 : 1	0.51 : 1

Number of right whales per sighting

The number of right whales reported in a sighting ('school size') ranged from one to 30, although sightings of more than eight right whales together were exceptional (Fig. 4). The mean school size over the years 1966–72 ranged from 1.7 in 1966 to 14.7 in 1972, with the majority of other years around 6.0. The mode of the number of right whales per sighting was three whales (Fig. 5). This is generally in accord with whalers' knowledge of school size, although we emphasize that these data do not prove that actual social units of whales were involved. There were a number of sightings in 1972 in which the number of right whales reported exceeded 16.

The scatter-plots of these data by year do not indicate much of a pattern, but the summary for all years (1966–72; Fig. 3) shows a trend in that the larger groups (> 10 individuals) were seen relatively late in the season (after 1 September). However, substantially more total sightings were recorded in the last half of the season, and this could be due to the fact that the catcher boats were operating in different areas.

Although the instructions called for the whalers to report sightings as they occurred, as we have noted many of the 'sightings' appear to be cumulative totals of whales seen during a half-hour or hour of watch. Of 31 sightings involving 15 or more right whales, 93.6% were recorded exactly on the hour or half-hour. Thus it is probably fair to assume that school sizes are overestimated. This is certainly true if 'school' is understood as a pair or group of whales within less than, say, a mile of one another. However, if a 'school' is understood as a loose aggregation of whales, perhaps fanned out to feed across an area of several square miles, then the school sizes reported by the whalers could in fact be underestimates. The imprecision of the term 'school' as understood and used by the men who gathered the data limits the usefulness of the analysis.

Right whale distribution

Right whale sightings were concentrated in Roseway Basin between Browns Bank and Baccaro Bank, generally within the area of 64°35′–65°45′W and 42°35′–43°20′N. Only 51 of 313 sightings were east of 64°00′W.

One sighting of one right whale was reported by the

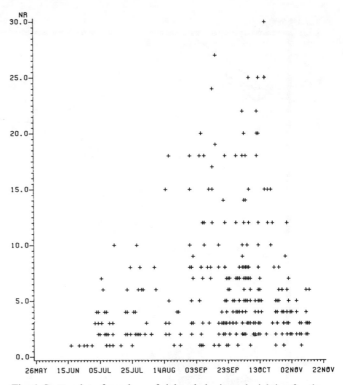

Fig. 4. Scatterplot of numbers of right whales in each sighting for the period when right whales were sighted by catcher boats operating from Blandford shore station, 1966–1972.

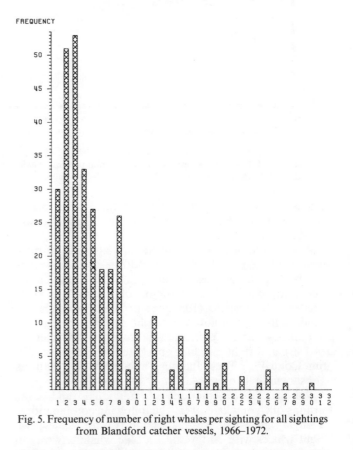

Fig. 5. Frequency of number of right whales per sighting for all sightings from Blandford catcher vessels, 1966–1972.

catcher vessel *Westwhale 8* (Captain A. Borgen) from the South Dildo, Trinity Bay, Newfoundland, whaling station. It was seen on 6 June 1970 east of Bonavista Bay (48°55′N, 51°55′W) near 12 humpbacks and 6 fin whales. Surface water temperature at the site was 1.1°C. This was the only sighting reported from the Newfoundland whaling grounds for the period 1966–72.

Calf sightings

No right whales seen in the study area were reported by the whalers to be calves. This does not necessarily mean that no calves were present. Gunners on the Blandford catcher boats appear to have systematically failed to report calves for any species other than the fin whale. We assume they had an incentive to specify the presence of fin whale calves. Regulations prohibiting the capture of fin whales accompanied by calves were in force at the time, so by noting the presence of a calf the whalers could justify their failure to attempt a shot at a nearby adult. However it is of course possible that no calves were reported because the right whales sighted in the study area were not accompanied by calves.

Multispecies sightings

We examined sightings involving more than one species, called herein 'multispecies sightings', to determine whether associations of right whales with other species could be demonstrated quantitatively. The term 'association' is used in this section, and elsewhere in the paper, in a spatial and not necessarily a social sense. Because of the nature of 'sightings' reported by the whalers (see above), we cannot be certain that whales listed in the same sighting were closer than about 10–12 n. miles of one another. Considering the scale of distances traversed by whales in a short time (e.g. Watkins, Moore, Wartzok and Johnson, 1981; Watkins, Moore, Sigurjónsson, Wartzok and di Sciara, 1984), it is by no means unreasonable to consider whales found within 10–12 n. miles of one another to be part of one feeding aggregation and thus 'associated' in at least a limited sense. However it should be remembered that the Watkins et al. (1981; 1984) papers refer to fin whales leaving the feeding grounds. Right whales are generally believed to be slower swimmers than fin whales and later we assume (c.f. Watkins and Schevill, 1976) that they do not average net speeds greater than 3 knots, although as later discussed, during chasing for tagging purposes some animals approached speeds of 11 knots.

Overall, fin whales were sighted more frequently and in greater cumulative numbers than any other species on the whaling grounds (Tables 1 and 3; Fig. 6). Right whales were seen more often with fin whales than with any other species (103 times) (Tables 2 and 4; Figs 7 and 8). However, this association is probably largely an artifact of the effort directed towards the commercial target species, the fin whale, by the Blandford whalers and of the fin whale's general abundance and wide distribution. The ratios of fin whales to sei whales on all grounds in all years were 3.84:1 (number of sightings) and 4.34:1 (number of whales sighted) (Table 3). When only the 313 sightings involving right whales are considered, fin whales were again seen more frequently and in greater cumulative numbers than any other species (Table 4). However, the fin:sei ratios were reduced to 1.76:1 (sightings) and 1.68:1 (whales sighted). This pattern is shown graphically in Figs 9–11. The fin:right ratio decreased from 4.80:1 (sightings) and 4.53:1 (sighted) on all grounds to 0.81:1 (sightings) and 0.85:1 (sighted) on the 'right whale grounds' only; whereas, the sei:right ratio decreased much less, from 1.25:1 (sightings) and 1.04:1 (sighted) to 0.44:1 (sightings) and 0.51:1 (sighted). From these ratios, we can infer that

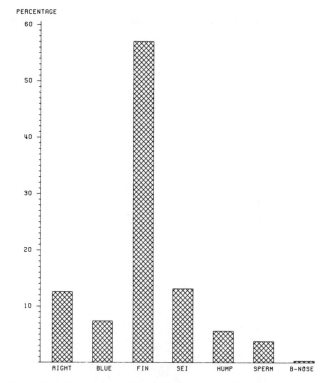

Fig. 6. Cumulative percentage of all whales sighted by species, in all sightings by Blandford catcher vessels, 1966–1972.

there is a closer association between right and sei whales than there is between right and fin whales.

Fig. 10 shows the percentage of sightings of right whales with other species. This figure was derived by looking at all multispecies sightings and scoring those including right whales. Sightings comprising two or more species were then allocated to each species (thus inflating the number of 'sightings' [313] to 494), and percentages calculated. This figure represents the relative abundance of these four baleen species in the study area when right whales were seen (excluding sperm and bottlenose whales as not typical for banks and basins on the continental shelf).

When right whales were sighted with only one other species, it was almost always with either fin (103 instances) or sei (44 instances) whales (Fig. 12a). When right whales were sighted with two other species, fin whales were included in all but two of the sightings, and the fin-sei-right combination accounted for more than 67% of the sightings (Fig. 12b). When there were three different species with right whales, the fin-humpback-blue combination was most prevalent (20 times or 66.7%; Fig. 12c).

There were 825 sei whales taken in the fishery (Table 5) and about half (403) of these were killed in the Roseway Basin area (Table 5). Of these 403, more than half were sighted with right whales (Table 5). More than half the total sei whale sightings, and most of the right whale sightings (89%) after 15 August in any year, were in Roseway Basin (Table 5). After the largest sei whale catch of 235 whales in 1971, the total sightings of sei whales from all grounds dropped, but the number of right whale sightings increased (Table 5).

The occurrence of right whales in Roseway Basin coincides with the 'second run' of sei whales on the Scotian Shelf (Mitchell, 1975e; see below). Right whales essentially remain in the Roseway Basin area for some

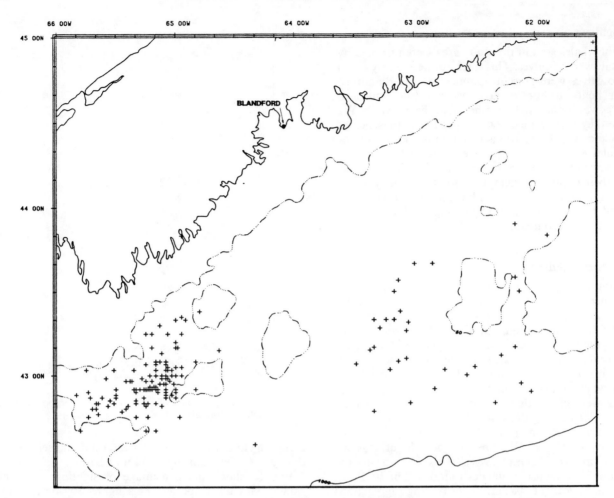

Fig. 7. Computer-generated chart of seas around Nova Scotia, showing positions where right whales were sighted near fin whales. Note that only sightings in which sei whales were not also reported to be present are included on this chart.

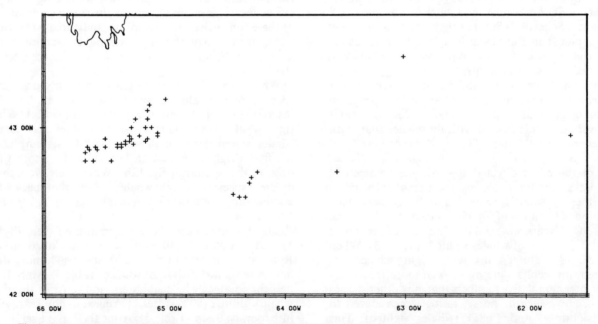

Fig. 8. Computer-generated chart of seas around Nova Scotia, showing positions where right whales were sighted near sei whales. Note that only sightings in which fin whales were not also reported to be present are included on this chart.

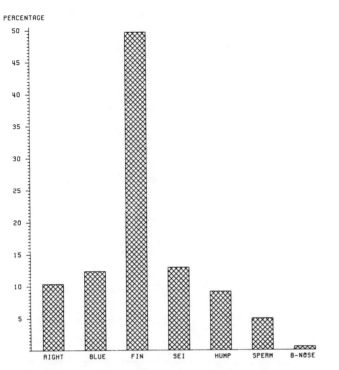

Fig. 9. Percentage occurrence of whales by species, in sightings where sightings comprising two or more species are counted as separate sightings and allocated to each species, for catcher vessels from Blandford, 1966–1972.

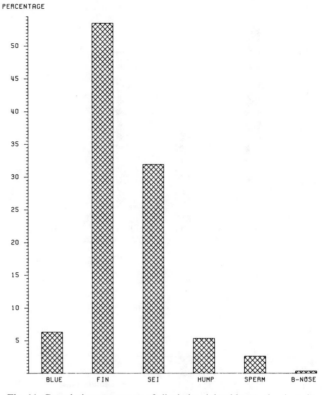

Fig. 11. Cumulative percentage of all whales sighted by species, in only those sightings where right whales were present, by Blandford catcher vessels, 1966–1972.

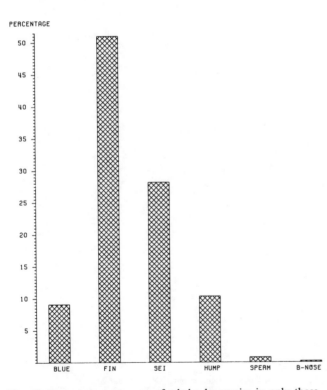

Fig. 10. Percentage occurrence of whales by species in only those sightings where right whales were present, and the sightings are counted in the compilation for each species represented, by Blandford catcher vessels, 1966–1972.

time, while the sei whales are 'on passage', migrating southwards through the Basin. For example, in 1972 from 12 October to 13 November only five sei whales were sighted while 190 right whales were sighted (and resighted?). Other statistics (Table 5) show the same trends – the preponderance of sei and right whale

sightings occurring together in the Roseway Basin area, and with a ratio of 1:1 right whales to sei whales outside the Basin (Table 5), 1.15:1 in favor of right whales inside the Basin (Table 5).

In 1969, 1971 and 1972 the whaling company directed much effort to catching sei whales, but because of a managerial policy of attempting to reach the fin whale quota as quickly as possible, sei whales were not taken during the first half of the 1970 season. In the years 1969, 1971, and 1972, combined, there were 831 sightings of all species made by Blandford catcher vessels, and only 25 of these were made on the 'sei whale grounds' (Fig. 1, area between 42°00′N and the coast, and 64°20′W and 66°00′W), during the period when sei whales generally were absent from these grounds – ca 25 July to 13 September. Right whales were sighted 5 times, while fin whales, sometimes in large numbers (up to 30), were included in all 25 sightings.

The two largest concentrations of sei whales reported by the Blandford whalers were both near groups of right whales – 40 sei with six fin and three right at 42°58′N, 65°13′W; and 30 sei with 10 right at 43°09′N, 62°45′W.

Trends in right whale sightings related to changes in whaling effort

In the early years of the Nova Scotia fishery, fin whales were hunted preferentially; later, as the fin whale quota was reduced (from 325 in 1967 to 95 in 1972), effort was redirected toward sei whales (Mitchell and Kozicki, 1974, Ms.) There was no quota for sei whales at any time during the fishery, and the catch of this species steadily increased from 11 in 1966 to a peak of 235 in 1971. A dramatic increase in the number of right whale sightings occurred from 1969 to 1972 (Fig. 13). This corresponded closely

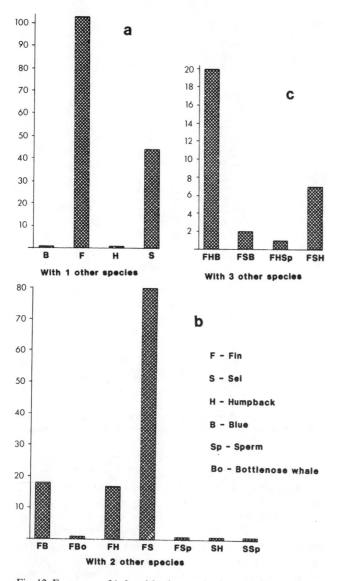

Fig. 12. Frequency of 1, 2 and 3 other species, in multispecies sightings which included right whales.

with the increase in catches of, and increase in sighting effort directed towards, sei whales (Mitchell, 1975e). There is no reason to believe there was any major change in reporting procedures which might otherwise account for these trends in right whale sightings.

The effort directed towards right whales can be taken as the total number of hours for each day when the catcher was involved in getting to the grounds (HG), hunting whales (HH), chasing whales (HC) and towing carcasses (HT) (Appendix 1). This effort did not change significantly between 1967 and 1972 (Fig. 14), except in 1970 when two catcher vessels operated simultaneously from the Blandford land station between 11 June and 28 August (the season lasted from 1 June to 28 November). Thus a marked increase in total whaling effort resulted in only a moderate increase in right whales sighted (Fig. 14) in this instance – which in any event occurred later in the season when only one catcher was in operation. The dramatic increase of right whale sightings in 1971 and 1972 (Figs 15 and 16), with overall effort levels similar to those in 1967–1969, we attribute to the transfer of effort from fin to sei whales (Figs 17, 18). With a larger proportion of working hours spent on the 'sei whale

Table 5.

Comparisons of sightings of right and sei whales throughout total whaling grounds, and on restricted grounds. Se = sei, Ri = right.

A. All grounds, all years, all seasons.

	Sightings	Sighted	Sei killed
Sei	391	1,972	825
Right	313	1,888	–
Sei + right together	139	968 Se – 960 Ri	287

B. Roseway Basin area, 42 35'N to shore and 64 40'W–65 35'W, all years, after 15 August.

	Sightings	Sighted	Sei killed
Sei	199	1,083	403
Right	249	1,688	–
Sei + right together	119	771 Se – 890 Ri	241

C. Sightings of right whales and sei whales in area of Roseway Basin, and on all grounds combined, after 15 August.

	Roseway Basin		All grounds	
	Sei	Right	Sei	Right
1966	9	–	30	6
1967	47	1	71	36
1968	41	14	134	66
1969	100	9	246	65
1970	101	223	176	251
1971	379	408	726	415
1972	406	1,033	588	1,050

D. Kills of sei whales in area of Roseway Basin, and on all grounds.

	Roseway Basin	Per cent	All grounds
1966	3	27	11
1967	27	47	57
1968	24	24	100
1969	54	36	149
1970	64	69	93
1971	123	52	235
1972	115	63	183

E. Sei whales and right whales sighted together.

	Roseway Basin			All grounds		
		Sighted			Sighted	
	Sightings	Sei	Right	Sightings	Sei	Right
1966	–	–	–	2	5	4
1967	–	–	–	3	12	24
1968	2	7	12	3	12	15
1969	–	–	–	2	31	16
1970	19	65	68	20	66	69
1971	53	332	282	56	392	289
1972	45	367	528	53	444	543
Total	119	771	890	139	968	960

F. Sei killed when sei and right sighted together.

	Roseway Basin	All grounds		Roseway Basin	All grounds
1966	–	–	1970	42	42
1967	–	7	1971	95	109
1968	5	9	1972	99	120
1969	–	–	Total	241	287

grounds' (Fig. 19), more sightings (and resightings) of right whales resulted.

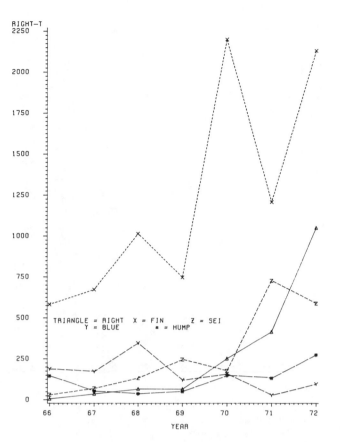

Fig. 13. Total whales sighted by species and by year, by Blandford catcher vessels, 1966–1972.

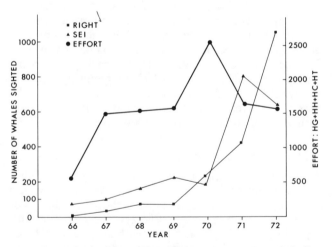

Fig. 14. Number of right and sei whales sighted per year and effort expressed as the sum of hours to grounds (HG), hours hunting (HH), hours chasing (HC), and hours towing (HT), Blandford, 1966–1972.

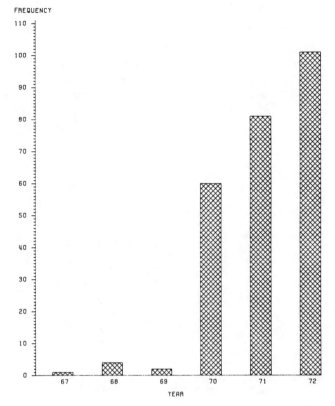

Fig. 15. Frequency of right whale sightings in the area of Roseway Basin, for catcher vessels from Blandford 1967–1972.

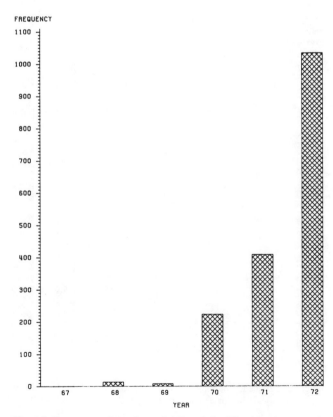

Fig. 16. Frequency of numbers of right whale sighted in the area of Roseway Basin, for catcher vessels from Blandford 1966–1972.

Sei whales appeared on the Blandford whaling grounds in two distinct 'runs' (Mitchell, 1975e). The early run began in mid-June and lasted through July; the later run was from early September to mid-November. There were two major areas of concentration in distribution during the early run: (1) along the edge of the continental shelf centered at 42°30′N, 64°20′W; and (2) in Northeast Channel between Browns and Georges Banks centered at 42°00′N, 64°40′W. The second run took place farther inshore, between Baccaro and Browns Banks in Roseway Basin, generally from 42°34′N, 64°34′W to 43°20′N, 65°35′W.

All right whales sighted during the 'late run' of sei whales were in Roseway Basin (Table 5). The portion of right whales sighted here comprised 89% of the right whales sighted on all grounds. More than half the sei

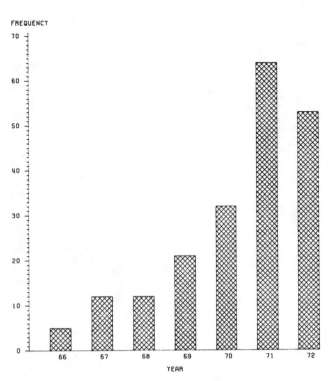

Fig. 17. Frequency of sei whale sightings in the area of Roseway Basin, for catcher vessels from Blandford 1966–1972.

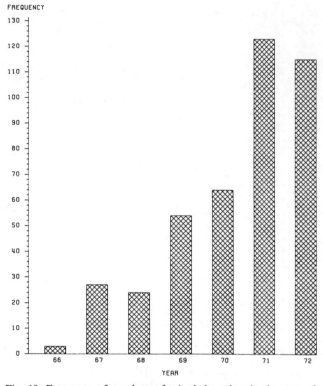

Fig. 19. Frequency of numbers of sei whales taken in the area of Roseway Basin by catcher vessels from Blandford 1966–1972.

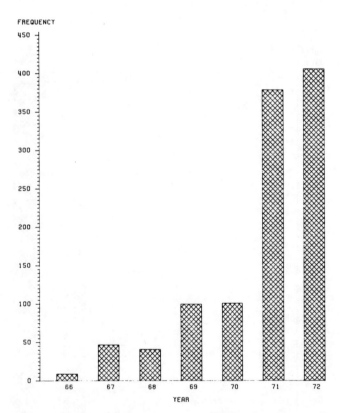

Fig. 18. Frequency of numbers of sei whales sighted in the area of Roseway Basin, for catcher vessels from Blandford 1966–1972.

Sighting conditions

Sighting effort is much affected by sighting conditions. Our term 'AVSD'–Average Whale Sighting Distance – represents a whaler's summary of conditions such as sea state, visibility, humidity, illumination, etc. This parameter's value ranged from 0 miles to 4–10 miles (Appendix 1). The range of average values for each year for the period 1966–1972 is 3.83 to 4.22, representing visibility for whales around $1\frac{1}{2}$ miles in any direction from the vessel, with very little fluctuation over the years and rather considerable variation in any given year.

Surface water temperature

Mean surface water temperatures recorded at the times and positions of sightings of right whales with fin whales (Fig. 20) are essentially the same as those at sightings of right whales with sei whales (Fig. 21). The mean for 'with fin' was 13.8±2.06°C and for 'with sei', 13.5±1.13°C, with corresponding minimums and maximums of 10°–21°C for 'with fin' and 10°–18°C for 'with sei'. The average sea surface temperature on the 'right whale grounds' (defined as positions where right whales were sighted) did not fluctuate more than 2°C from year to year in the period 1966 to 1972. In the course of a single season, right whales were seen in waters ranging in surface temperature from 10°C to 21°C (Fig. 22).

Multiple sightings of right whales on one day

No attempt was made by the catcher vessels to census right whales, and all sightings were made incidentally during the search for target species – fin and sei whales. The catcher vessels did not cover the study area systematically; rather, they concentrated their effort on relatively small areas occupied by the target species.

whales sighted, and 50% of those killed in the fishery, were in the same area (Table 5). Fig. 4 shows an increase in number of sightings and number of whales per sighting, from the beginning of September until early November.

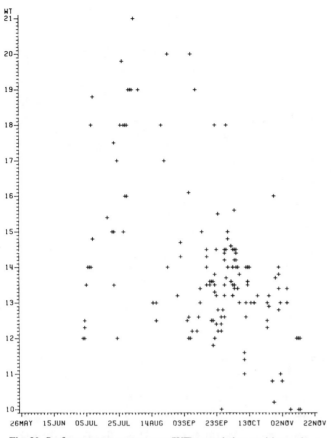

Fig. 20. Surface water temperatures (WT) recorded at positions where right whales and fin whales were sighted by Blandford catcher vessels, 1966–1972.

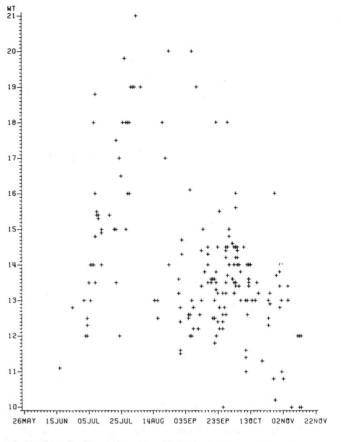

Fig. 22. Surface water temperatures (WT) recorded at positions where right whales were sighted by Blandford catcher vessels, 1966–1972.

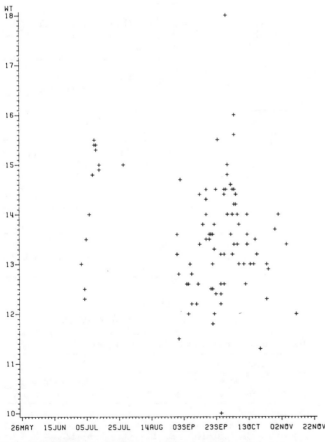

Fig. 21. Surface water temperatures (WT) recorded at positions where right whales and sei whales were sighted by Blandford catcher vessels. 1966–1972.

Thus, these sightings are not useful as a basis for population estimation. Mitchell (1975a, p. 127) emphasized that 'apparent abundance' represented by the whalers' sightings was likely due to recurrent sightings of a few individual right whales, not that 'the whaler's sightings off Nova Scotia for 1966–1972 represent migration of only a few individuals' (Winn, 1982, p. 'R/W.MODEL 6–7').

The cumulative total of right whales reported – 1889 in 313 sightings over a seven-year period – is obviously an overestimate of the number of different whales seen, since repeat sightings undoubtedly occurred. In 29 of the 59 cases in which right whales were sighted on two consecutive days, the last sighting of day 1 was made within 10 nautical miles of the first sighting of day 2. In this subsample, the number of right whales reported for the day 1 and day 2 sightings was identical in only three cases, and it varied widely, with differences of from −6 to +10.

For certain days when there was more than one sighting of right whales, it is possible to add together the numbers seen in some or all of the sightings, and to attempt to omit duplicate sightings (Fig. 23; Tables 6–11). (Note that plots in Fig. 23 are quite distorted. For the 42nd to 43rd parallel the ratio of latitude to longitude should be 1:36 while the computer made it 1:2.34; however, the calculation of distances is accurate.) In this attempt we assumed that right whales do not travel at average net speeds greater than three knots, particularly while on their feeding grounds (c.f. Watkins and Schevill, 1976). Distance:time ratios were calculated for all pairs of sightings on a given day. For those pairs in

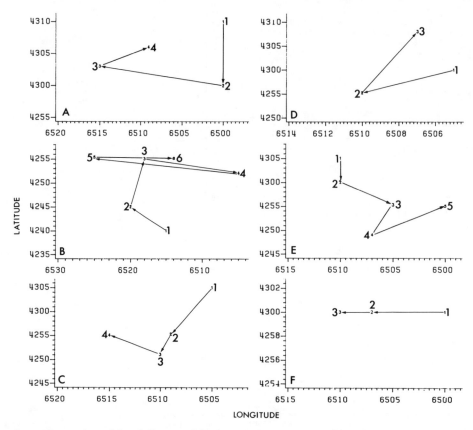

Fig. 23. Plots of co-ordinate where right whales were sighted on 13 September (A), 2 Oct. (B), 6 Oct. (C), 11 Oct. (D), 12 Oct. (E), and 16 Oct. (F), all in 1972. Numbers indicate chronological order of the sightings. (See Tables 6–11).

Table 6

Details of sightings of right whales on 13 September 1972 (see Fig. 23a). Key: WT = water temperature; NR, NF, NS = numbers of right, fin and sei whales respectively; distance (s, in miles) and time elapsed between pairs of sightings (t, in hours) were used to calculate speed required to cover the distance between the two positions in that time (v in knots). Sighting no. 4 was omitted from the calculation (less than 3·0 kts). Total number of right whales for the day = 51.

No.	Time	Position °N	°W	WT	NR	NF	NS	Nos	s	t	v
1	1000	4310	6500	13.0	12	3	0	1–2	10.0	1	10.0
2	1100	4300	6500	13.4	15	2	2	1–3	13.0	2	6.5
3	1200	4303	6515	13.4	24	0	12	1–4	7.7	5	1.5
4	1500	4306	6509	14.4	17	0	8	2–3	11.3	1	11.3
								2–4	8.9	4	2.2
								3–4	5.3	3	1.8

Table 7.

Details of sightings of right whales on 2 October 1972 (see Fig. 23b). Key as in Table 6. Sightings and 5 and 6 omitted from calculation (less than 3·0 kts). Total number of right whales for the day = 58.

No.	Time	Position °N	°W	WT	NR	NF	NS	Nos	s	t	v
1	1100	4240	6515	13.6	22	12	0	1–2	6.2	1	6.2
2	1200	4245	6520	13.6	18	10	0	1–3	15.2	2	7.6
3	1300	4255	6518	13.6	10	8	0	1–4	14.0	3	4.7
4	1400	4252	6505	13.6	8	10	0	1–5	19.4	5	3.9
5	1600	4258	6525	13.6	9	8	0	1–6	16.0	6.5	2.4
6	1730	4256	6514	13.6	4	3	2	2–3	10.1	1	10.1
								2–4	13.0	2	6.5
								2–5	13.5	4	3.4
								2–6	11.8	5.5	2.2
								3–4	9.9	1	9.9
								3–5	5.9	3	2.0
								3–6	3.1	4.5	0.7
								4–5	15.8	2	7.9
								4–6	7.7	3.5	2.2
								5–6	8.3	1.5	5.5

which an implied traveling speed of more than 3 knots would be required for an individual whale to be involved in both sightings, we considered the sightings to be non-duplicative. This procedure produced one-day counts of 42, 45, 51, 58, 67 and 70 right whales. In all cases, the whales were reported as changing direction, not swimming on one heading.

The highest one-day count from the above procedure – 70 whales – was on 16 October 1972 (Table 11, Fig. 23f). Although the calculated catcher-boat speed between sightings 2 and 3 on this day was only 2.2 knots, we considered the whales in sighting 3 as 'new' because the catcher boat was proceeding due west in a straight line along the 43rd parallel. For this and the other sightings on this day all whales were reported as 'milling around'.

Table 8.

Details of sightings of right whales on 6 October 1972 (see Fig. 23c). Key as in Table 6. Sighting no. 4 omitted from calculation (less than 3·0 kts). Total number of right whales for the day = 45.

No.	Time	Position °N	°W	WT	NR	NF	NS	Nos	s	t	v
1	1400	4305	6505	14.0	25	8	0	1–2	8.5	0.75	11.4
2	1445	4257	6509	13.4	12	3	8	1–3	14.5	2	7.2
3	1600	4251	6510	14.0	8	15	3	1–4	12.4	4.5	2.8
4	1830	4255	6515	13.4	15	12	0	2–3	6.0	1.25	4.8
								2–4	4.8	3.75	1.3
								3–4	5.4	2.5	2.2

Table 9.

Details of sightings of right whales on 11 October 1972 (see Fig 23d). Key as in Table 6. Sighting no. 3 omitted (less than 3.0 kts). Total number of right whales for the day = 42.

		Sighting information						Between sightings			
		Position									
No.	Time	°N	°W	WT	NR	NF	NS	Nos	s	t	v
1	0745	4300	6505	13.0	22	3	0	1–2	4.7	0.75	6.3
2	0830	4257	6510	12.6	20	2	10	1–3	8.1	10.25	0.8
3	1800	4308	6507	14.0	18	3	0	2–3	11.2	9.5	1.2

Table 10.

Details of sightings of right whales on 12 October 1972 (see Fig. 23e). Key as in Table 6. Sighting no. 5 omitted (less than 3.0 kts). Total number of right whales for the day = 67.

		Sighting information						Between sightings			
		Position									
No.	Time	°N	°W	WT	NR	NF	NS	Nos	s	t	v
1	1230	4305	6510	14.0	12	3	0	1–2	5.0	0.75	6.7
2	1315	4300	6510	13.6	20	4	1	1–3	8.8	2	4.4
3	1430	4257	6505	13.6	25	12	0	1–4	16.1	2.5	6.5
4	1500	4249	6507	13.6	10	8	0	1–5	12.4	3.5	3.5
5	1600	4255	6500	13.6	8	7	0	2–3	4.7	1.3	3.8
								2–4	11.2	1.8	6.4
								2–5	8.8	2.8	3.2
								3–4	8.1	0.5	16.3
								3–5	4.2	1.5	2.8
								4–5	7.9	1	7.9

Table 11.

Details of sightings of right whales on 16 October 1972 (see Fig. 23f). Key as in Table 6. Sighting no. 3 was not omitted even though it was less than 3.0 kts (see text). Total no. of right whales for the day = 70.

		Sighting information						Between sightings			
		Position									
No.	Time	°N	°W	WT	NR	NF	NS	Nos	s	t	v
1	0900	4300	6500	13	30	7	0	1–2	5.1	1	5.1
2	1000	4300	6507	13	25	9	0	1–3	7.3	2	3.7
3	1100	4300	6510	13	15	3	4	2–3	2.2	1	2.2

Average Whale Sighting Distance at the time was 1–2 mi (Appendix 1). By the very definition of a 'sighting', the catcher boat's crew should not have reported the same (1000 hr) sighting again at 1100 hr, even if they had the 1000-hr whales in sight when reporting the 1100-hr whales. Their instructions for completing the sighting forms included a caution against recording the same whales more than once, and we accepted the judgment of these experienced whalemen as to whether a group of whales encountered on a straight-line course should be considered 'new' or 'old'.

Stomach contents of fin and sei whales taken in proximity to right whales

There is no direct evidence of feeding behavior or food of right whales within the study area. However, we considered it useful to report the stomach contents of fin and sei whales killed in proximity to right whales, in order to indicate the availability of potential prey. By 'proximity' we mean that the whalers assigned the same time and position for a right whale sighting as for a kill

of a fin or sei whale. We assume the whales were all less than 10–12 mi. from one another.

Our subsample of whales killed in proximity to right whales included 117 fin and 134 sei whales (Table 12). Of the 87 fin whales with food in their stomachs, most (86%) had recently fed on 'krill'; of the 54 sei whales with food in their stomachs, most (87%) had recently fed on 'copepods', as judged from field observations. These results are similar to those for the fishery as a whole (Mitchell, 1975a). Field identification of stomach contents is usually only possible when the material is recovered from the forestomach in relatively fresh condition. Because none of the identifications reported here was made using feces or food in an advanced stage of digestion, we conclude that the whales had been feeding within a few hours before death.

Table 12.

A subsample of fin and sei whale stomach contents, for whales that were killed on the Nova Scotian whaling grounds at the same time and position as one or more right whales were sighted. All fin whales fitting this criterion are included here, but only those sei whales that were killed in 1972 are included. Descriptions of stomach contents are based on field identifications only.

A. Fin whales (N = 117)			B. Sei whales killed (N = 134)		
30	empty or cut at sea	– 26%	80	empty or cut at sea	– 60%
75	krill	– 64%	47	copepods	– 35%
8	fish	– 7%	4	krill	– 3%
2	krill and fish	– 2%	3	krill and copepods	– 2%
1	squid	– 1%			
1	squid and krill	– 1%			

As a check on what we believe to be a well-established preference by fin and sei whales for euphausiids and copepods, respectively, on these grounds, we also examined a sample of fin and sei whales taken near one another but not near right whales.

During the whaling period 1966–1972 there were 30 sightings of fin and sei whales when specimens of both species were taken (Table 13). In 11 of these instances, the stomachs of both the fin and the sei whales contained large quantities of 'krill'. On one occasion both species had eaten copepods, and in 10 cases the sei whales had copepods while the fin whales had 'krill' or fish remains in their stomachs. On one occasion when two fin and three sei whales were taken, four animals had eaten 'krill' while one sei had traces of fish in its stomach. On another occasion when one fin and two sei whales were taken, the fin and one sei had eaten 'krill', and this sei whale's stomach also contained one 'digested squid'. (The other sei whale's stomach was empty.) The remaining 43 animals' stomachs were either empty or had been cut at sea.

Table 13.

Stomach contents (field identification) of 50 fin and 69 sei whales killed from the same (30) sightings by Blandford 1966–72. * = or cut at sea.

	Fin	Sei	Total		Fin	Sei	Total
Krill	36	21	57	Squid	–	1	1
Copepods	1	11	12	Empty*	9	34	43
Fish	4	1	5	Total	50	68	118

Table 14.

Down times of right whales being chased for tagging, 28 July 1966, near Emerald (43° N, 62°40′W). Minutes: seconds. a = 14:45 elapsed without detailed times of some short dives and two long dives, one of which exceeded 7:45. b = including one exhalation underwater? c = may include one blow. d = tagged here. e = first three long dives consecutive, interspersed with untimed short dives; last two long dives not consecutive.

Whale	Dive times
1	:20, :25, 1:25, :30, ca :25, :15, :20, 4:30, :18, 2:15, :15, ca :20, :20, :20, [14:45a], :45 (2 "dives"?), ca :30, ca :45, 7:45, :18, :30b, :15, :10, :55, :20, 2:00, 3:00c, :18, :17, 2:35, :14, :30, :30, :25d, 2:00.
2e	——, 5:45, ——, 4:35, ——, 4:40, —— ——, 5:30, —— ——, 4:45

Sighting and tagging of 28 July 1966 on Emerald Bank

On 28 July 1966, Mitchell and K. Kariya observed three, and tagged two, single, large right whales in the vicinity of Emerald Bank from the *William S*, a 165 ft long, 613 gross ton freighter (corvette) used for whale tagging and census work. The *William S* has a maximum speed of 11 knots.

Six dolphins (*Lagenorhynchus acutus*) were sighted at 0730 h., then four single fin whales were seen at 0815 h. and chased for tagging (at 43°35′N, 62°44′W). One fin whale was tagged at 0845 h. (10–15 *L. acutus* were sighted), another at 0940 h. A fifth whale was observed from a distance at 1005 h., and on steaming to its position farther east on Emerald Bank at approximately 1015 h., it was identified as a 17–18 m long right whale. The first 12 ga. Discovery whale tag shot at this whale was a protrude. On chasing the now running whale, dive times were obtained (Table 14) before it was tagged effectively with a .410 Discovery-type mark (Table 15). After tagging this whale, no other whales were in sight. These dive times are from a whale not unduly spooked and which was not chased at maximum speed.

The *William S*'s noon position was 43°11′N, 62°40′W (surface temperature 16.4°C). We lost sight of the tagged whale, but another ('new') right whale was seen at 1300 h. While unsuccessfully chasing this large whale, at maximum speed, the short dives were not timed, but some long dives were (Table 14). We lost this whale in steadily deteriorating weather.

A third 17–18 m long right whale was sighted at 1540 h. It was chased at maximum speed and tagged (Table 15). We jogged off and on Emerald Bank all night, and although we remained in the same area on 29 July, heavy weather precluded searches for additional right whales.

An analysis of this hunt at day's end led us to conclude that three rather than two right whales had been sighted. The three whales were about the same size, had no major distinguishing marks, were dispersed in the vicinity of Emerald Bank a few miles from fin whales and *L. acutus*, and did not form into a tight school on being chased. The data on respiration show a pattern of an average of three blows 27 seconds apart between each long dive of 4:07 minutes (N = 15). The second and third whales sometimes fluked up highly for short dives, and sometimes showed no peduncle and did not raise flukes above the surface for long dives. The first whale carries a .410 tag; the last, a 12 ga. tag in the left side. Large stranded carcasses of North Atlantic right whales should be examined with a

Table 15.

Results of tagging right whales 28 July 1966 near Emerald Band with Discovery-type tags.

Whale	Tag	Time	Range	Result	Surface temp. (°C)	Position
1	12ga./no.95	1020h	20m	Protrude, dorsal midline	16.2	43°11′N 62°50′W
1	.410/no.19	1125h	30–40m	Hit, right (?) side	16.4	43°11′N 62°50′W
2	12ga./no.96	1605h	35m	Hit, left side midway down	16.25	43°12′N 62°42′W

metal detector and dissected in a search for these tags (Mitchell, 1970).

March sighting off Cape Cod

On 13 March 1971 at 1425 h., Mitchell, Kozicki and other observers (J. G. Mead, A. Pivorunas, B. B. Osborne, P. Beamish) saw two large right whales off Cape Cod from the *Westwhale 8*, a whale catcher vessel under charter for tagging and census work. The whales were moving generally southwest. While following them, two fin whales were sighted. The right whale chase was suspended at 1642 h in order to listen with a hydrophone to the right and fin whales. The right whales were then lost. While hunting for them, a single sei whale was sighted and chased for tagging. One right whale had an irregular white spot on the ventral surface of a fluke, near the tip. Both whales were estimated at about 50 ft in length, but one was slightly larger than the other.

Table 16

Results of attempts to tag right whales in the Northwest Atlantic, by commercial whaling vessels operating out of eastern Canadian shore whaling stations, 1966–72. No other tags were shot at these whales. The Captain of the *Chester* was E. Abrahamsen and Captain of the *Thorarinn* was P. Stokke.

Date	Vessel	Tag no.	Tag type	Result	Position Lat.	Position Long.	Est. size (ft)
02.8.68	Chester	15483	12Ga	Hit	43°20′N	63°04′W	55
10.9.68	Chester	15488	12Ga	Hit	43°00′N	62°30′W	55
10.9.68	Chester	15487	12Ga	Hit	43°00′N	62°30′W	50
10.9.68	Chester	15499	12Ga	Hit	43°00′N	62°30′W	60
21.9.71	Thorarinn	1758	12Ga	Hit	43°10′N	65°00′W	60
26.9.71	Thorarinn	1768	12Ga	Hit	43°05′N	64°55′W	65

Tagging from catcher vessels

We asked captains and gunners of whaling-station catcher boats to tag protected species of large cetaceans with Discovery-type tags in the late 1960s, partly in response to suggestions from the International Whaling Commission that such work be carried out. All captains and gunners responded and were cooperative in recording their attempts at tagging. The work was conducted during periods of inactivity in the hunt for commercially important species (i.e. fin, sei and sperm on these grounds). Six right whales were reported as tagged (Table 16), and the records indicate there was only one shot per whale, with no misses or protrudes reported.

Speed of right whales

Although we used 3 knots as a mean swimming speed of feeding right whales in the calculations above, it is of interest to consider the maximum swimming speed of this species, both in undisturbed conditions and in disturbed conditions while being chased by catcher or tagging vessels. In the sighting of 28 July 1966, the second and third whales were chased at or near the maximum speed of the *William S*, for approximately 30 mins each. Although no stopwatch or other timing device was used to measure the whales' rate of movement, we suspect that, at least for periods during the chase, their speeds were approaching 11 kts. This is greater than the maximum swimming speed of right whales reported by Cummings, Fish and Thompson (1972).

Association between right and sei whales

Several earlier workers have commented on the coincidence in timing of the appearance of right whales and sei whales on the whaling grounds (e.g. Collett, 1909; Thompson, 1919). More recently, other investigators have emphasized the convergence between the balaenid right whale and the balaenopterid sei whale in feeding behavior and food preferences (Nemoto, 1959, 1970; Nemoto and Kawamura, 1977; Kawamura, 1978; Mitchell, 1975a). Omura (1974; partial translation *in* Mitchell, 1975a) suggested the possibility that the two species compete for prey. An observation of a sei whale feeding with several right whales was made by Watkins and Schevill (1979).

We have found a relationship between the occurrence of right whales and sei whales in the restricted area of Roseway Basin, from approximately the 50-fathom line along the Nova Scotian coast to 42°34′N, and between 64°34′W and 65°35′W. Our analysis of the Nova Scotia sightings has shown:

(1) Both sei whales and right whales have a more restricted distribution in the study area than do fin whales.

(2) Sei whales and right whales are closely sympatric on the Scotian Shelf.

(3) Fin whales are generally more abundant than either sei whales or right whales in the study area as a whole. Therefore, when right whales are associated with other whales, fin whales would be expected to be the dominant associated species. Although right whales were seen near fin whales more often than they were seen near any other species, the ratio of fin whale sightings to sei whale sightings was much lower on the 'right whale grounds' than it was in the study area as a whole (1.8:1 vs 3.8:1). Therefore, we believe there is a closer association between right and sei whales than there is between right and fin whales.

Right and sei whales have broadly sympatric distributions during the feeding season, and on the whaling grounds they associate more closely and regularly than would be expected by chance, assuming random distribution of whales of all species on the grounds.

Separate evidence (not from the sightings data base) was provided by the stomach contents of fin whales and sei whales killed near where right whales were seen. Results showed that sei whales usually had eaten copepods, while fin whales had eaten 'krill' predominantly, followed by fish and other organisms. This suggests some partitioning of prey resources by the fin and sei whales, with the latter favoring the same kind of prey as right whales are known to take elsewhere (Reeves and Brownell, 1982, Table 19.1).

In spite of extensive survey coverage in recent years, no sei whales or blue whales have been seen in the lower Bay of Fundy during summer and fall months (Kraus and Prescott, 1981 Ms, 1982 Ms, 1983 Ms; Winn, 1982). These findings contradict those of Neave and Wright (1968), who reported four sightings of sei whales and one sighting of blue whales made in the Bay by ferry-boat operators. Schevill (1968) questioned the validity of Neave and Wright's species identifications, arguing that the subtle differences in behavior and appearance among the large balaenopterids at sea cannot always be detected and correctly interpreted by untrained observers. Regardless of whether sei whales (and blue whales) occur at all in the Bay of Fundy, it is clear that they are not common there. This appears to be one difference between the summer right whale grounds in this protected embayment and the more exposed offshore right whale grounds on the Scotian Shelf discussed above.

ACKNOWLEDGEMENTS

Karl Karlsen of the K. Karlsen Shipping Co. supplied the catcher-vessel data. The captains and gunners on the *Chester* (E. Abrahamsen and P. Lyngvaer) and the *Thorarinn* (P. Stokke) made the observations and filled out the forms which made this compilation possible. We also thank B. Osborne, J. G. Mead, P. Beamish, A. Pivorunas and Capt. A. Borgen for assistance in documenting the *Westwhale 8* sighting. The SAS statistical package at McGill University Computer Centre was used, with the aid of H. Brodie. J. Breiwick and S. Mizroch generously provided the computer-generated charts. J. G. Mead kindly provided the photographs of the Placentia Bay right whale.

REFERENCES

Allen, G. M. 1916. The whalebone whales of New England. *Mem. Boston Soc. Nat. Hist.* 8(2): 107–322 + pls. 8–16.

Allen, J. A. 1908. The North Atlantic right whale and its near allies. *Bull. Amer. Mus. Nat. Hist.* 24 (18): 277–329 + pls. 19–24.

Anon.
1937a. Newfoundland Whaling Records Go Back More Than 200 Years. Monster caught at Fortune Harbor probably a 'Right'whale. *Evening Telegram*, St. John's, Newfoundland, 24 August 1937.

Anon.
1937b. Unusual whale Caught in Placentia Bay. *Evening Telegram*, St. John's, Newfoundland, 17 August 1937, p. 4. (Also repeated in issue of 21 August 1937, p. 7.)

Arnold, P. W. and Gaskin, D. E. 1972. Sight records of right whales (*Eubalaena glacialis*) and finback whales (*Balaenoptera physalus*) from the Lower Bay of Fundy. *J. Fish. Res. Bd. Can.* 29(10): 1,477–78.

Beamish, P. 1981. Rare sighting of a right whale. Trinity, Nfld. *J. Ceta-Res.* 2:2.

Breiwick, J. M., Mitchell, E. and Kozicki, V. M. Ms. 1980. Analysis of Newfoundland (Williamsport and Dildo) fin whale abundance from catch and effort data. Paper [SC/32/Ba5] submitted to the Scientific Committee of the International Whaling Commission, Cambridge, July 1980. 41 pp. + Appendix, 30pp. (unpublished).

Clark, A. H. 1887. 1. – History and Present Condition of the Fishery. pp. 3–218 *of* Part XV. The Whale Fishery. *In* G. B. Goode [Ed.], *The Fisheries and Fishery Industries of the United States.* Section V. History and Methods of the Fisheries. In two volumes, with an atlas of two hundred and fifty-five plates. Volume II. Washington, Government Printing Office, pp. i–xx + 1–881.

Collett, R. 1909. A few notes on the whale *Balaena glacialis* and its capture in recent years in the North Atlantic by Norwegian whalers. *Proc. Zool. Soc. Lond.* 1909: 91–8 + pls. 25–7.

Cummings, W. C. Fish, J. F. and Thompson, P. O. 1972. Sound production and other behavior of southern right whales, *Eubalena glacialis. Trans San Diego Soc. Nat. Hist.* 17 (1): 1–14.

Dudley, P. 1725. An Essay upon the Natural History of Whales, with a particular Account of the Ambergris found in the *Sperma Ceti* Whale. In a Letter to the Publisher from the Honourable *Paul Dudley*, Esq; F.R.S. *Roy. Soc. Lond., Phil. Trans.* 33 (387): 256–69.

Edwards, E. J. and Rattray, J. E. 1932. '*Whale Off!*' *The Story of American Shore Whaling.* New York: Frederick A. Stokes Company, pp. i–xvi + 1–285 + frontis + 17 pls.

Edwards, E. J. and Rattray, J. E. 1956. '*Whale Off!*' *The Story of American Shore Whaling.* New York: Coward-McCann, Inc., p. frontis + i–xxiv + 1–285 + 15 pls.

Eschricht, D. F. and Reinhardt, J. 1866. On the Greenland Right-Whale. (*Balaena mysticetus*, Linn.), with especial reference to its geographical distribution and migrations in times past and present, and to its external and internal characteristics. pp. 1–150 *in* Flower, W. H. [Ed.], *Recent Memoirs on the Cetacea by Professors Eschricht, Reinhardt and Lilljeborg.* London: Published for the Ray Society by Robert Hardwick, 192, Piccadilly. p. i–xii + 1–312 + 6 pls.

Gaskin, D. E. and Smith, J. D. 1979. Observations on marine mammals, birds and environmental conditions in the Head Harbour Region of the Bay of Fundy. pp. 69–86 *In* D. J. Scarratt, [Ed.], Evaluation of Recent Data Relative to Potential Oil Spills in the Passamaquoddy Area. Fisheries and Environment Canada, *Fisheries and Marine Service Technical Report* 901: i–iv + 1–107.

Hachey, H. B. 1961. Oceanography and Canadian Atlantic Waters. *Bull. Fish. Res. Bd Can.* 134, 120pp. + 6 pls.

International Whaling Commission. 1982. Report of the sub-committee on protected species and aboriginal whaling. *Rep. int. Whal. Commn* 32: 104–12.

Kawamura, A. 1978. An interim consideration on a possible interspecific relation in southern baleen whales from the viewpoint of their food habits. *Rep. int. Whal. Commn* 28: 411–20.

Kraus, S. D. and Prescott, J. H. Ms. 1981. Distribution, abundance and notes on the large cetaceans of the Bay of Fundy Summer and Fall 1980. Final Report to U.S.D.C., NOAA, National Marine Fisheries Service in fulfillment of Contract NA-80-FA-2-00048, pp. [i–viii] + 1–87.

Kraus, S. D. and Prescott, J. H. Ms. 1982. The North Atlantic right whale (*Eubalaena glacialis*) in the Bay of Fundy, 1981, with notes on distribution, abundance, biology and behavior. Final Report to US Dept. Commerce, National Marine Fisheries Service in fulfillment of Contract NA-81-FA-C-00030, and to the World Wildlife Fund – U.S., Washington, D.C., p. [i–vi] + 1–105 + [i] Errata typescript.

Kraus, S. D. and Prescott, J. H. Ms. 1983. Summary of 1982 research on the North Atlantic right whale *Eubalaena glacialis*, with notes on seasonal distribution and abundance, and significant resightings of individuals. Final Report to US Dept. Commerce, National Marine Fisheries Service in fulfillment of contract NA-81-FA-C-00030, and to the WWF-US, Washington D.C. pp. [1] + 1–39.

Kraus, S., Prescott, J. H., Turnbull P. and Reeves R. R. 1982. Preliminary notes on the occurrence of the North Atlantic right whale, *Eubalaena glacialis*, in the Bay of Fundy. *Rep. int. Whal. Commn* 32: 407–11.

Layne, J. N. 1965. Observations on marine mammals in Florida waters. *Fla State Mus. Bull. (Biol. Sci.)* 9 (4): 131–81.

Lipton, B. 1975. Whaling Days in New Jersey. *Newark Mus. Quart.* 26 (2 & 3): 1–72 + map [inside back cover].

McLellan, H. J., Lauzier. L. and Bailey, W. B. 1953. The Slope Water off the Scotian Shelf. *J. Fish. Res. Bd Can.* 10 (4): 155–76.

Millais, J. G. 1907. *Newfoundland And Its Untrodden Ways.* Longmans, Green and Co., 39 Paternoster Row, London, New York, Bombay, and Calcutta. p. frontis + [i]–xvi + [1]–340 + 85 pls. + 2 maps.

Mitchell, E. 1970. Request for information on tagged whales in the North Atlantic. *J. Mammal.* 51 (2): 378–81.

Mitchell, E. 1974. Present status of northwest Atlantic fin and other whale stocks. pp 108–69 *In:* W. E. Schevill, [Ed.], *The Whale Problem. A Status Report.* Harvard University Press, Cambridge, pp. i–x + 1–419 + /pls 1–7.

Mitchell, E. 1975a. Trophic Relationships and Competition for Food in Northwest Atlantic whales, pp 123–33 *In:* M.D.B. Burt, (Ed.), *Proceedings of the Canadian Society of Zoologists Annual Meeting,* June 2–5, 1974.

Mitchell, E. 1975b. *Porpoise, Dolphin and Small Whale Fisheries of the World. Status and problems.* International Union for Conservation of Nature and Natural Resources, Morges, Switzerland. IUCN Monograph No. 3, p. 1–129.

Mitchell, E. 1975c. Preliminary report on Nova Scotia fishery for sperm whales (*Physeter catodon*). *Rep. int. Whal. Commn* 25: 226–35.

Mitchell, E. 1975d. Canada progress report on whale research, May 1973–May 1974. *Rep. int. Whal. Commn* 25: 270–82.

Mitchell, E. 1975e. Preliminary report on Nova Scotia fishery for sei whales (*Balaenoptera borealis*). *Rep. int. Whal. Commn* 25: 218–25.

Mitchell, E. and Chapman, D. G. 1977. Preliminary assessment of stocks of Northwest Atlantic sei whales (*Balaenoptera borealis*). *Rep. int. Whal. Commn* (special issue 1): 117–20.

Mitchell, E. D. and V. M. Kozicki. 1974. Ms. The sei whale (*Balaenoptera borealis*) in the Northwest Atlantic Ocean. Paper SC/SP74/Doc.32 submitted to the IWC Special Meeting of the Scientific Committee on Sei and Bryde's Whales, La Jolla, California, 3–13 December, 1974. 65pp + 49figs. + Suppl.

Mitchell, E., and Kozicki, V. M. 1975. Supplementary information on minke whale (*Balaenoptera acutorostrata*) from Newfoundland fishery. *J. Fish. Res. Bd Can.* 32 (7): 985–94.

Mitchell, E. and Kozicki, V. M. 1984. Reproduction in Northwest Atlantic male sperm whales, *Physeter macrocephalus. Rep. int. Whal. Commn* (special issue 6): 243–52.

Moore, J. C. 1953. Distribution of marine mammals to Florida waters. *Amer. Mid. Nat.* 49 (1): 117–58.

Moore, J. C. and Clark, E. 1963. Discovery of right whales in the Gulf of Mexico. *Science* 141 (3577): 269.

Neave, D. J. and Wright, B. S. 1968. Seasonal migrations of the harbor porpoise (*Phocoena phocoena*) and other Cetacea in the Bay of Fundy. *J. Mammal.* 49 (2): 259–64.

Nemoto, T. 1959. Food of baleen whales with reference to whale movements. *Sci. Rep. Whales Res. Inst., Tokyo* 14: 149–290–pl. 1

Nemoto, T. 1970. Feeding pattern of baleen whales in the ocean. pp. 241–52 *In:* J. H. Steele (Ed.), *Marine Food Chains.* University of California Press, Berkeley and Los Angeles, 552 pp.

Nemoto, T. and Kawamura. A. 1977. Characteristics of food habits and distribution of baleen whales with special reference to the abundance of North Pacific sei and Bryde's whales. *Rep. int. Whal. Commn* (special issue 1): 80–7.

Omura, H. 1974. *Kujira No Seitai. (Ecology of the Whale.)* Kyoritsu Shippan K. K., p. i–vi + 1–186.

Reeves, R. R. and Brownell, R. L. Jr. 1982. Baleen whales. *Eubalaena glacialis* and allies. pp. 415–44 *In:* J. A. Chapman, and Feldhamer G. A. (eds.), *Wild Mammals of North America: Biology, Management, and Economics.* Baltimore, MD: The Johns Hopkins University Press, 1,147 pp.

Reeves, R. R., Mead, J. G. and Katona, S. 1978. The right whale, *Eubalaena glacialis*, in the western North Atlantic. *Rep. int. Whal. Commn* 28: 303–12.

Reeves, R. R. and Mitchell, E. 1986 a. History of the Long Island, New York, fishery for right whales, 1644–1924. (Published in this volume).

Reeves, R. R. and Mitchell, E. 1986 b. American pelagic whaling for right whales in the North Atlantic. (Published in this volume).

Schevill, W. E. 1968. Sight records of *Phocoena phocoena* and of cetaceans in general. *J. Mammal.* 49: 794–6.

Schevill, W. E., Moore, K. E. and Watkins, W. A. 1981. Right whale, *Eubalaena glacialis*, sightings in Cape Cod waters. Technical Report. Prepared for the Office of Naval Research under Contract N00014-79-C-0071; NR 083-004. Woods Hole Oceanographic Institution Technical Report WHOI-81-50, p. [i–iv] + 1–16 + [i–iv].

Sears, R. 1979. An occurrence of right whales (*Eubalaena glacialis*) on the North Shore of the Gulf of St. Lawrence. *Naturaliste canadien* 106 (5–6): 567–68.

Sergeant, D. E. Ms. 1966. Populations of large whale species in the western North Atlantic with special reference to the fin whale. Fisheries Research Board of Canada, Circular No. 9, p. [i–ii] + 1–13 + Tables 1–9 + Figs. 1–9 [mimeo].

Sergeant, D. E., Mansfield, A. W. and Beck, B. 1970. Inshore records of cetacea for Eastern Canada, 1949–68. *J. Fish. Res. Bd Can.* 27 (11): 1,903–15 + Figs. 4–5.

Starbuck, A. 1878. History of the American Whale Fishery from its earliest inception to the year 1876. *Report of the US Commission on Fish and Fisheries*, Part 4, Washington, p. 1–768 + pls. 1–6.

Sutcliffe, W. H. Jr. and Brodie, P. F. 1977. Whale distributions in Nova Scotia waters. Fisheries and Environment Canada, *Fish. Mar. Serv. Tech. Rep* 722: i–vi–1–83.

Thompson, D. W. 1919. On whales landed at the Scottish whaling stations, especially during the years 1908–1914 – Part VII. The Sei-whale. *Scottish Nat.* 87 & 88: 37–46.

True, F. W. 1904. *The Whalebone Whales of the Western North Atlantic compared with those occurring in European waters with some observations on the species of the North Pacific.* City of Washington, Published by the Smithsonian Institution, Smithsonian Contributions to Knowledge, Vol. 33, p. i–xii + i–viii + 1–332 + pls. 1–50.

Tuck, J. A. and Grenier, R. 1981. A 16th-Century Basque whaling station in Labrador. *Sci. Am.* 245(5): 180–84, 186–8 + 190.

Wakeham, W., C. A. Bernard and J. Riendeau. 1913. Appendix No. 6. Quebec. *Forty-Sixth Annual Report of the Department Of Marine And Fisheries* 1912–13. *Fisheries*. Printed by order of Parliament. Ottawa: C. H. Parmelee, Printer to the King's Most Excellent Majesty, pp. 221–253.

Watkins, W. A., Moore, K. E., Sigurjónsson, J., Wartzok, D. and di Sciara, G. N. 1984. Fin whale (*Balaenoptera physalus*) tracked by radio in the Irminger Sea. *Rit Fisk.* 8 (1): 1–14.

Watkins, W. A., Moore, K. E., Wartzok, D. and Johnson, J. H. 1981. Radio tracking of finback (*Balaenoptera physalus*) and humpback (*Megaptera novaeangliae*) whales in Prince William Sound, Alaska. *Deep-Sea Res.* 28A, (6,): 577–88.

Watkins, W. A. and Schevill, W. E. 1976. Right whale feeding and baleen rattle. *J. Mammal.* 57 (1): 58–66.

Watkins, W. A. and Schevill, W. E. 1979. Aerial observation of feeding behavior in four baleen whales: *Eubalaena glacialis, Balaenoptera borealis, Megaptera novaeangliae,* and *Balaenoptera physalus*. *J. Mammal.* 60 (1): 155–63.

Watkins, W. A. and Schevill, W. E. 1982. Observations of right whales, *Eubalaena glacialis*, in Cape Cod waters. *Fish. Bull. U.S.* 80 (4): 875–80.

Winn, H. E. 1982. A characterization of marine mammals and turtles in the Mid- and North Atlantic area of the U.S. Outer Continental Shelf. Final Report of the Cetacean and Turtle Assessment Program, University of Rhode Island, Graduate School of Oceanography, Kingston, Rhode Island 02881. Prepared for: U.S. Department of the Interior, Bureau of Land Management, Washington, DC 20240, Under Contract AA551–CT8–48. [i–x]+[1]–450pp+Special Topics [4 additional papers, variously paginated]+ 2 transparencies [contained in back cover pocket].

Winn, H. E., D. R. Goodale, M. A. M. Hyman, R.D. Kenney, C. A. Price and G. P. Scott. 1981. Right whale sightings and the right whale minimum count. pp. 49–51 in A Characterization of Marine Mammals and Turtles in the Mid- and North-Atlantic Areas of the U.S. Outer Continental Shelf. Executive Summary for 1979 Cetacean and Turtle Assessment Program, University of Rhode Island, Sponsored by the Bureau of Land Management under contract AA551–CT8–48, 75pp (mimeo).

Appendix 1

SIGHTING AND EFFORT DATA FROM BLANDFORD, NOVA SCOTIA, WHALE CATCHER VESSELS, RELATING TO ENCOUNTERS WITH RIGHT WHALES, 1966–72

The data (Appendix 1) are arranged into two files:

First file (149 observations) – *Effort Card* describes effort and weather conditions for the days when right whales were sighted. Vessels were required to report their activity for each day of whaling season.

Second file (313 observations) – *Sighting Card* gives details of each individual sighting of right and other whales. Each line in that file represents a separate sighting as judged by the captain/gunner. Omitted from these data are sightings without presence of right whales.

Definition of variables in first file: *Effort Card* (*pp. 102–103*)

OBS = Observation number.

ASD = Asdic on board. 0 – No, 1 – Yes.

V3 = Catcher vessel. This variable refers to the various vessels used in Blandford, N.S.: 1 – Chester, 2 – Polarfish, 3 – Minna, 4 – Thorarinn, 5 – Brandal, 6 – Tem, 7 – Haryfjord.

DA3 = Day. The actual day for which the C/E form was filled in. Coded 01–31.

MO3 = Month. Coded 01–12.

YR3 = Year. The year is identified, using only the last 2 digits.

VER = Version of C/E form used. Coded: 1 – early, 2 – modified, 3 – final, 4 – information obtained from other than C/E form such as IWS Reports and Fisheries Department Reports.

LS3 = Landstation. 1 – Blandford, NS.

Next eight variables describe the type, and duration, of effort involved in killing whales, by catcher and associated vessels. Only daylight hours* are taken into consideration. All times are expressed as whole hours. Fractions of an hour are founded off to the nearest whole hour.

HG = Hours to grounds;

HH = Hours hunting;

HC = Hours chasing;

HT = Hours towing;

HB = Hours bunkering;

HR = Hours repairing;

HIP = Hours in port;

HL = Hours lost at sea.

To grounds, hunting, chasing and towing are considered to occur consecutively in this respective order. They are also dealt with as mutually exclusive events, except when a given a catcher-boat was hunting or chasing whale(s) with whale(s) already in two. This time was then entered as hunting or chasing time and subtracted from hours towing.

*Daylight hours on Blandford whaling ground (nautical sunrise and sunset for middle day of the month, and mean latitude (43 00′N):

May 15	0400–2000	16 hrs
June 15	0330–2030	taken as 17 hrs
July 15	0400–2030	taken as 17 hrs
August 15	1430–2000	taken as 16 hrs
September 15	0500–1830	taken as 14 hrs
October 15	0600–1800	12 hrs
November 15	1630–1700	taken as 11 hrs
December 15	0700–1700	10 hrs

[From: The Nautical Almanac 1976, NP 314–76 HMSO London, England.]

WSV = Working with other vessels. 0 – no other vessel(s) involved, 1 – other vessel(s) towing, 2 – other vessel(s) scouting, 3 – other vessel(s) hunting.

SVID = Other vessel(s) identification. Vessels coded as in V3.

HW = Hours worked by other vessel(s).

BN = Beaufort number. 1 – less than 4, 2–4 to 6, 3 – greater than 6, 4 – gale.

WS = Wind speed. 1 – less than 11 knots, 2 – 11–16 knots, 3 – greater than 16 knots.

WD = Wind direction. 1 – north, 2 – northeast, 3 – east, 4 – southeast, 5 – south, 6 – southwest, 7 – west, 8 – northwest, 9 – variable or changing through the day.

WHT = Wave height. 1 – less than 2 ft, 2 – 2 to 3.5 ft, 3 – greater than 3.5 ft.

AC = Atmospheric conditions. 1 – clear, 2 – haze, 3 – rain, 4 – haze and rain, 5 – fog, 6 – intermittent fog.

SC = Sighting conditions. 1 – good, 2 – moderate, 3 – poor.

AVSD = Average whale sighting distance. 1 – 0 visibility, 2 – less than half a mile, 3 – half to 1 mile, 4 – 1 to 2 miles, 5 – 2 to 4 miles, 6 – 4 to 10 miles.

TOTS = Total number of sightings made for day. This parameter serves as a cross-reference with second file (*Sighting card*), which lists these sightings in detail.

Definition of variables pertaining to second file:
Sighting Card (pp. 104–107)

First six variables same as in first file – (*Effort Card*).

TIME4 = Time of sighting. The time is expressed in hours and minutes on a 24-hour clock.

LAT4 = Position, Latitude (North).

LONG4 = Position, Longitude (West).

WT = Water temperature. Generally this is surface water temperature, taken by some on-board instrument such as an automatic thermograph or by the bucket and thermometer method. The temperature is given in degrees Celsius.

NF = Number of fin whales sighted.

FDT = Direction of travel. This parameter is expressed by the cardinal points of the compass, and is coded like variable WD (wind direction) in the first file. (In the case of "milling around" while in sight, the code is 9).

NS to

DDT = These parameters enumerate the number of sightings and direction of travel of ten species of whales, and are treated in the same fashion as fin. NS – sei, NM – minke, NSP – sperm, NH – humpback, NB – blue, NBO – bottlenose, NP – pilot, NR – right, DO – dolphins.

NW = Number of whales killed for the day. The total number of whales killed that day by the catcher-vessel, regardless of species. This parameter acts as a cross-reference to next Data file (V), where the biological data is entered for all whales killed and landed at a whaling station.

Computer Table 1
Effort card

OBS	LS3	V3	DA3	MO3	YR3	VER	ASD	HG	HH	HC	HT	HB	HR	HIP	HL	WSV	SVID	HW	BN	WS	WD	WHT	AC	SC	AVSD	TOTS
1	1	1	6	9	66	1	0	0	2	4	8	0	0	0	0	0	.	.	2	2	5	2	1	1	5	1
2	1	1	28	9	66	1	0	0	5	5	4	0	0	0	0	0	.	.	2	2	6	2	6	3	2	1
3	1	1	29	9	66	1	0	0	4	10	0	0	0	0	0	0	.	.	3	3	2	3	4	3	3	1
4	1	1	4	10	66	1	0	0	3	8	1	0	0	0	0	0	.	.	2	2	6	2	1	1	5	1
5	1	1	27	6	67	1	0	6	6	2	3	0	0	0	0	0	.	.	1	1	3	1	1	1	5	1
6	1	1	30	6	67	1	0	0	7	1	9	0	0	0	0	0	.	.	1	1	3	2	6	3	2	1
7	1	1	14	7	67	1	0	0	1	1	5	0	0	0	10	0	.	.	2	2	6	2	6	3	2	1
8	1	1	8	8	67	1	0	0	12	4	0	0	0	0	0	0	.	.	1	1	6	1	2	2	3	1
9	1	1	9	8	67	1	0	0	10	6	0	0	0	0	0	0	.	.	1	1	5	1	4	2	3	1
10	1	1	22	8	67	1	0	0	4	4	0	0	0	0	8	0	.	.	1	1	6	1	6	3	2	1
11	1	1	23	8	67	1	0	0	1	1	2	0	0	0	12	0	.	.	1	1	6	1	6	3	2	1
12	1	1	24	8	67	1	0	0	6	5	5	0	0	0	0	0	.	.	1	1	5	1	1	1	5	1
13	1	1	2	7	68	2	0	0	8	2	7	0	0	0	0	0	.	.	1	1	6	1	2	2	4	1
14	1	1	9	7	68	2	0	4	10	3	0	0	0	0	0	0	.	.	1	1	6	1	1	1	5	2
15	1	1	13	7	68	2	0	0	7	1	9	0	0	0	0	0	.	.	1	1	3	1	5	3	2	2
16	1	1	22	7	68	2	0	0	5	10	2	0	0	0	0	3	3	6	1	1	6	1	1	1	5	1
17	1	1	24	7	68	2	0	0	12	2	3	0	0	0	0	0	.	.	1	1	6	1	6	3	2	1
18	1	1	26	7	68	2	0	0	4	5	5	0	3	0	0	0	.	.	1	1	2	1	1	1	5	1
19	1	1	28	7	68	2	0	0	6	3	8	0	0	0	0	3	3	2	1	1	6	1	1	1	5	1
20	1	1	29	7	68	2	0	0	9	3	5	0	0	0	0	3	3	4	1	1	6	1	6	3	3	1
21	1	1	30	7	68	2	0	0	6	4	7	0	0	0	0	0	.	.	1	1	6	1	1	1	5	1
22	1	1	31	7	68	2	0	0	5	3	9	0	0	0	0	0	.	.	1	1	6	1	1	1	5	1
23	1	1	1	8	68	2	0	0	9	2	5	0	0	0	0	0	.	.	2	2	5	2	2	2	3	1
24	1	1	2	8	68	2	0	0	8	4	0	0	0	0	4	3	3	5	2	2	7	2	3	2	3	1
25	1	1	6	8	68	2	0	3	8	5	0	0	0	0	0	0	.	.	1	1	5	1	1	1	4	1
26	1	1	10	9	68	2	0	0	11	3	0	0	0	0	0	0	.	.	1	1	4	1	1	1	5	1
27	1	1	22	9	68	2	0	0	8	3	3	0	0	0	0	0	.	.	2	2	6	2	2	2	3	1
28	1	1	29	9	68	2	0	0	11	3	0	0	0	0	0	0	.	.	2	2	8	2	1	1	5	1
29	1	1	4	10	68	2	0	0	10	2	0	0	0	0	0	0	.	.	3	3	6	3	4	3	2	1
30	1	1	28	10	68	2	0	0	7	3	2	0	0	0	0	0	.	.	1	2	6	2	2	2	3	1
31	1	1	3	7	69	2	0	3	8	4	2	0	0	0	0	0	.	.	1	1	6	1	1	1	5	1
32	1	1	4	7	69	2	0	0	10	6	1	0	0	0	0	0	.	.	1	1	8	1	3	2	4	2
33	1	1	6	7	69	2	0	0	11	5	1	0	0	0	0	0	.	.	2	1	8	2	1	1	5	1
34	1	1	7	7	69	2	0	0	6	5	6	0	0	0	0	0	.	.	1	1	6	1	1	1	5	2
35	1	1	8	7	69	2	0	0	11	1	5	0	0	0	0	0	.	.	2	2	6	2	1	1	5	1
36	1	1	21	7	69	2	0	4	9	4	0	0	0	0	0	0	.	.	1	1	4	1	2	2	4	2
37	1	1	22	7	69	2	0	0	12	1	4	0	0	0	0	0	.	.	1	1	2	1	2	2	4	1
38	1	1	24	7	69	2	0	0	11	1	1	0	0	0	4	0	.	.	1	1	2	1	6	3	3	2
39	1	1	28	7	69	2	0	0	10	2	5	0	0	0	0	0	.	.	1	1	4	1	1	1	6	1
40	1	1	29	7	69	2	0	0	7	2	8	0	0	0	0	0	.	.	3	2	4	3	4	2	4	1
41	1	1	30	7	69	2	0	0	15	1	1	0	0	0	0	0	.	.	1	2	4	1	2	2	4	1
42	1	1	24	8	69	2	0	0	10	4	2	0	0	0	0	0	.	.	1	1	6	1	1	1	6	1
43	1	1	7	9	69	2	0	0	10	2	2	0	0	0	0	0	.	.	2	2	6	2	2	2	4	1
44	1	1	17	6	70	2	0	0	15	2	0	0	0	0	0	0	.	.	1	1	5	1	1	1	5	8
45	1	1	6	7	70	2	0	0	5	4	2	0	0	0	6	0	.	.	1	1	6	1	6	3	2	5
46	1	1	9	7	70	2	0	0	9	1	7	0	0	0	0	0	.	.	1	1	6	1	6	3	2	4
47	1	4	22	6	70	2	1	3	14	0	0	0	0	0	0	0	.	.	1	1	5	1	6	3	2	2
48	1	4	25	6	70	2	1	0	15	0	0	0	0	0	0	1	1	2	1	1	5	1	6	3	3	3
49	1	4	8	7	70	2	1	3	8	1	5	0	0	0	0	0	.	.	1	1	5	1	2	4	3	2
50	1	4	9	7	70	2	1	0	10	0	1	0	0	0	6	0	.	.	1	1	3	1	2	2	3	2
51	1	4	22	7	70	2	1	0	15	2	0	0	0	0	0	0	.	.	2	2	7	2	1	1	5	9
52	1	4	27	7	70	2	1	0	11	2	4	0	0	0	0	0	.	.	1	1	6	1	1	1	5	3
53	1	4	3	8	70	2	1	0	12	4	0	0	0	0	0	1	.	8	2	2	6	2	1	1	5	3
54	1	4	6	8	70	2	1	0	14	0	2	0	0	0	0	0	.	.	1	1	6	1	6	3	2	2

Computer Table 1 (*continued*)

OBS	LS3	V3	DA3	MO3	YR3	VER	ASD	HG	HH	HC	HT	HB	HR	HIP	HL	WSV	SVID	HW	BN	WS	WD	WHT	AC	SC	AVSD	TOTS
55	1	4	20	8	70	2	1	3	10	1	2	0	0	0	0	0	.	.	1	1	6	1	1	1	5	2
56	1	4	14	9	70	2	1	3	10	1	0	0	0	0	0	0	.	.	1	1	6	1	1	1	5	3
57	1	4	17	9	70	2	1	0	12	2	0	0	0	0	0	0	.	.	3	3	8	3	1	2	4	10
58	1	4	20	9	70	2	1	0	11	2	1	0	0	0	0	0	.	.	2	2	3	2	1	3	3	4
59	1	4	21	9	70	2	1	3	8	2	1	0	0	0	0	0	.	.	2	2	6	2	4	2	3	3
60	1	4	23	9	70	2	1	0	3	2	0	0	0	0	9	0	.	.	2	2	6	2	6	3	3	1
61	1	4	24	9	70	2	1	3	6	3	2	0	0	0	0	0	.	.	1	1	8	1	1	1	5	5
62	1	4	29	9	70	2	1	3	5	1	5	0	0	0	0	1	6	1	2	2	1	3	4	2	4	1
63	1	4	30	9	70	2	1	0	4	5	5	0	0	0	0	1	6	.	1	1	1	1	1	1	5	3
64	1	4	2	10	70	2	1	0	2	10	0	0	0	0	0	0	.	.	1	1	3	1	1	1	5	5
65	1	4	5	10	70	2	1	0	4	5	3	0	0	0	0	0	.	.	2	2	7	2	1	2	3	3
66	1	4	6	10	70	2	1	0	4	8	0	0	0	0	0	0	.	.	1	1	8	1	1	1	5	7
67	1	4	7	10	70	2	1	3	6	0	3	0	0	0	0	0	.	.	1	1	7	1	1	1	5	5
68	1	4	9	10	70	2	1	0	5	1	2	0	0	0	4	0	.	.	1	1	3	1	6	2	2	7
69	1	4	12	10	70	2	1	0	8	1	3	0	0	0	0	0	.	.	1	1	9	1	1	2	4	7
70	1	4	13	10	70	2	1	0	8	1	3	0	0	0	0	0	.	.	1	1	6	1	1	1	5	7
71	1	4	21	10	70	2	1	3	6	2	1	0	0	0	0	0	.	.	1	1	7	1	1	1	5	6
72	1	4	22	10	70	2	1	0	8	2	2	0	0	0	0	0	.	.	1	1	5	1	1	1	5	6
73	1	4	23	10	70	2	1	0	9	1	2	0	0	0	0	0	.	.	2	2	5	2	1	1	5	10
74	1	4	27	10	70	2	1	0	12	0	0	0	0	0	0	0	.	.	2	2	1	3	1	1	4	6
75	1	4	28	10	70	2	1	0	6	2	4	0	0	0	0	0	.	.	1	1	1	1	1	1	5	9
76	1	4	30	10	70	2	1	0	11	1	0	0	0	0	0	0	.	.	2	2	1	3	1	1	5	10
77	1	4	8	11	70	2	1	0	9	2	0	0	0	0	0	0	.	.	2	2	1	2	1	2	4	7
78	1	4	4	7	71	3	1	0	4	4	9	0	0	0	0	0	.	.	1	1	6	1	1	1	5	2
79	1	4	5	7	71	3	1	9	2	3	3	0	0	0	0	0	.	.	1	1	6	1	1	2	4	2
80	1	4	17	9	71	3	1	0	3	3	0	0	0	0	8	0	.	.	1	1	8	1	6	3	2	3
81	1	4	19	9	71	3	1	0	4	4	6	0	0	0	0	0	.	.	1	1	1	1	1	1	5	2
82	1	4	20	9	71	3	1	2	4	2	6	0	0	0	0	0	.	.	1	1	1	1	1	1	5	2
83	1	4	21	9	71	3	1	0	3	3	3	0	0	0	5	0	.	.	1	1	5	1	2	3	4	2
84	1	4	22	9	71	3	1	0	5	5	4	0	0	0	0	0	.	.	1	1	1	1	1	1	5	7
85	1	4	23	9	71	3	1	4	6	4	0	0	0	0	0	0	.	.	1	1	1	1	1	1	5	4
86	1	4	26	9	71	3	1	0	8	5	1	0	0	0	0	0	.	.	1	1	7	2	1	1	5	4
87	1	4	27	9	71	3	1	4	6	3	1	0	0	0	0	0	.	.	1	1	8	1	1	1	5	3
88	1	4	28	9	71	3	1	4	5	4	1	0	0	0	0	0	.	.	1	1	7	1	1	1	5	5
89	1	4	29	9	71	3	1	3	4	3	4	0	0	0	0	0	.	.	2	2	6	2	1	1	5	2
90	1	4	30	9	71	3	1	3	6	4	1	0	0	0	0	0	.	.	2	2	7	2	4	2	4	3
91	1	4	3	10	71	3	1	0	5	5	2	0	0	0	0	0	.	.	2	2	1	2	1	2	4	4
92	1	4	4	10	71	3	1	4	5	0	3	0	0	0	0	0	.	.	1	1	1	1	1	1	5	6
93	1	4	5	10	71	3	1	0	2	4	6	0	0	0	0	0	.	.	1	1	6	1	1	2	4	2
94	1	4	7	10	71	3	1	0	5	4	3	0	0	0	0	0	.	.	2	2	7	2	1	2	4	2
95	1	4	10	10	71	3	1	0	2	9	1	0	0	0	0	0	.	.	1	1	5	1	1	2	4	4
96	1	4	12	10	71	3	1	0	2	8	2	0	0	0	0	0	.	.	2	2	6	3	1	2	4	5
97	1	4	14	10	71	3	1	0	1	5	6	0	0	0	0	0	.	.	1	1	5	1	1	2	4	3
98	1	4	17	10	71	3	1	0	4	1	7	0	0	0	0	0	.	.	3	3	1	3	1	2	4	2
99	1	4	18	10	71	3	1	0	7	4	1	0	0	0	0	0	.	.	2	2	1	2	1	2	4	4
100	1	4	20	10	71	3	1	0	3	4	5	0	0	0	0	0	.	.	2	2	3	2	1	2	4	2
101	1	4	24	10	71	3	1	0	7	4	1	0	0	0	0	0	.	.	2	2	1	2	1	2	4	5
102	1	4	25	10	71	3	1	4	5	3	0	0	0	0	0	0	.	.	1	1	1	1	1	2	4	5
103	1	4	29	10	71	3	1	0	1	2	0	0	0	0	9	0	.	.	1	1	7	1	6	3	2	1
104	1	4	31	10	71	3	1	0	5	3	4	0	0	0	0	0	.	.	2	2	1	3	1	2	4	5
105	1	4	1	11	71	3	1	5	3	1	2	0	0	0	0	0	.	.	1	1	5	1	4	3	4	2
106	1	4	5	11	71	3	1	4	5	1	1	0	0	0	0	0	.	.	2	2	7	2	1	2	4	4
107	1	4	11	11	71	3	1	5	3	2	1	0	0	0	0	0	.	.	1	1	7	1	1	2	4	3
108	1	4	12	11	71	3	1	6	5	0	0	0	0	0	0	0	.	.	2	2	8	3	1	2	4	4
109	1	4	13	11	71	3	1	0	9	1	0	0	0	0	0	0	.	.	1	1	8	2	1	2	4	5
110	1	4	9	7	72	3	1	0	5	3	9	0	0	0	0	0	.	.	1	1	8	1	1	1	5	3
111	1	4	10	7	72	3	1	2	3	3	9	0	0	0	0	0	.	.	1	1	6	1	1	1	5	3
112	1	4	11	7	72	3	1	0	5	3	9	0	0	0	0	0	.	.	1	1	6	1	1	2	3	4
113	1	4	13	7	72	3	1	4	3	5	1	0	0	0	4	0	.	.	1	1	6	1	6	3	2	4
114	1	4	18	7	72	3	1	5	4	3	5	0	0	0	0	0	.	,	1	1	7	1	1	2	4	3
115	1	4	25	7	72	3	1	5	5	3	4	0	0	0	0	0	.	.	1	1	6	1	1	1	5	5
116	1	4	15	8	72	3	1	4	8	0	4	0	0	0	0	0	.	.	1	1	8	1	1	1	5	7
117	1	4	17	8	72	3	1	2	10	2	2	0	0	0	0	0	.	.	1	1	6	1	1	1	5	9
118	1	4	30	8	72	3	1	0	8	4	4	0	0	0	0	0	.	.	1	1	8	1	1	1	5	5
119	1	4	31	8	72	3	1	5	2	4	5	0	0	0	0	0	.	.	1	1	6	1	1	2	4	6
120	1	4	1	9	72	3	1	4	2	3	5	0	0	0	0	0	.	.	1	1	2	1	1	2	3	4
121	1	4	5	9	72	3	1	0	5	4	5	0	0	0	0	0	.	.	1	1	7	1	1	2	4	4
122	1	4	6	9	72	3	1	2	4	3	5	0	0	0	0	0	.	.	1	1	7	1	1	1	5	4
123	1	4	7	9	72	3	1	2	5	2	5	0	0	0	0	0	.	.	1	1	7	1	1	2	3	3
124	1	4	8	9	72	3	1	0	4	3	7	0	0	0	0	0	.	.	1	1	6	1	2	2	3	3
125	1	4	11	9	72	3	1	0	4	3	7	0	0	0	0	0	.	.	2	2	8	3	1	2	3	2
126	1	4	12	9	72	3	1	0	3	3	8	0	0	0	0	0	.	.	1	1	7	2	2	3	3	2
127	1	4	13	9	72	3	1	2	5	5	2	0	0	0	0	0	.	.	2	2	8	2	1	2	4	4
128	1	4	15	9	72	3	1	0	4	5	5	0	0	0	0	0	.	.	1	1	8	1	1	1	5	3
129	1	4	17	9	72	3	1	5	6	3	0	0	0	0	0	0	.	.	1	1	6	1	2	3	3	3
130	1	4	21	9	72	3	1	0	3	5	6	0	0	0	0	0	.	.	1	1	2	1	1	1	5	4
131	1	4	24	9	72	3	1	0	6	5	3	0	0	0	0	0	.	.	1	1	7	1	1	2	4	6
132	1	4	26	9	72	3	1	0	4	2	8	0	0	0	0	0	.	.	1	1	6	1	1	2	4	1
133	1	4	28	9	72	3	1	0	4	4	6	0	0	0	0	0	.	.	1	1	2	1	1	2	4	2
134	1	4	2	10	72	3	1	0	10	1	1	0	0	0	0	0	.	.	2	2	2	2	1	1	5	7
135	1	4	3	10	72	3	1	3	5	2	2	0	0	0	0	0	.	.	1	1	8	1	1	1	5	7
136	1	4	4	10	72	3	1	4	3	3	2	0	0	0	0	0	.	.	1	1	1	1	1	1	5	6
137	1	4	5	10	72	3	1	4	3	3	2	0	0	0	0	0	.	.	1	1	6	1	1	1	5	6
138	1	4	6	10	72	3	1	6	3	2	1	0	0	0	0	0	.	.	1	1	2	1	1	1	5	4
139	1	4	11	10	72	3	1	0	3	3	6	0	0	0	0	0	.	.	1	1	6	1	1	1	5	3
140	1	4	12	10	72	3	1	4	5	1	2	0	0	0	0	0	.	.	2	2	6	2	4	2	4	6
141	1	4	13	10	72	3	1	0	3	0	0	0	0	0	9	0	.	.	3	3	7	3	1	3	3	3
142	1	4	16	10	72	3	1	0	4	6	2	0	0	0	0	0	.	.	2	2	6	3	1	2	4	3
143	1	4	27	10	72	3	1	2	6	3	1	0	0	0	0	0	.	.	1	1	7	1	1	1	5	6
144	1	4	28	10	72	3	1	2	3	2	5	0	0	0	0	0	.	.	1	1	6	1	1	1	5	4
145	1	4	1	11	72	3	1	0	9	1	1	0	0	0	0	0	.	.	2	2	2	2	1	2	4	7
146	1	4	2	11	72	3	1	0	5	1	5	0	0	0	0	0	.	.	1	1	4	1	1	1	5	6
147	1	4	7	11	72	3	1	0	5	0	0	0	0	0	6	0	.	.	3	3	1	3	4	3	3	3
148	1	4	12	11	72	3	1	0	4	1	6	0	0	0	0	0	.	.	2	2	1	2	2	2	3	3
149	1	4	13	11	72	3	1	3	8	0	0	0	0	0	0	0	.	.	2	2	1	3	2	3	3	2

Computer Table 2
Sightings card

OBS	LS4	V4	DA4	MO4	YR4	TIME4	LAT4	LONG4	WT	NF	FDT	NS	SDT	NM	MDT	NSP	SPDT	NH	HDT	NB	BDT	NBO	BODT	NP	PDT	NK	KDT	NR	RDT	ND	DDT	NW
1	1	1	6	9	66	715	4335	6210	16	7	.	0	.	0	.	0	.	4	.	2	.	0	.	0	.	0	.	1	.	0	.	3
2	1	1	28	9	66	950	4330	6215	.	6	.	2	.	0	.	0	.	2	.	2	.	0	.	0	.	0	.	2	.	0	.	4
3	1	1	29	9	66	1005	4310	6210	.	6	.	0	.	0	.	0	.	2	.	3	.	0	.	0	.	0	.	1	.	0	.	4
4	1	1	4	10	66	905	4340	6220	16	21	4	3	4	0	.	0	.	2	4	8	4	0	.	0	.	0	.	2	4	0	.	6
5	1	1	27	6	67	1845	4340	6251	.	6	.	0	.	0	.	0	.	3	.	4	.	0	.	0	.	0	.	1	.	0	.	1
6	1	1	30	6	67	1145	4302	6504	.	3	.	0	.	0	.	0	.	0	.	0	.	10	.	0	.	0	.	1	.	0	.	1
7	1	1	14	7	67	1440	4244	6334	.	0	.	2	.	0	.	0	.	0	.	0	.	0	.	0	.	0	.	10	.	0	.	2
8	1	1	8	8	67	1700	4325	6301	.	0	.	6	.	0	.	0	.	0	.	0	.	0	.	0	.	0	.	8	.	0	.	5
9	1	1	9	8	67	1545	4314	6300	.	4	.	4	.	0	.	0	.	1	.	4	.	0	.	0	.	0	.	6	.	0	.	4
10	1	1	22	8	67	1400	4350	6154	17	6	3	0	.	0	.	0	.	0	.	2	3	0	.	0	.	0	.	4	3	0	.	4
11	1	1	23	8	67	1730	4354	6210	.	2	.	0	.	0	.	0	.	2	.	2	.	0	.	0	.	0	.	4	.	0	.	1
12	1	1	24	8	67	1000	4330	6208	20	7	4	0	.	0	.	0	.	1	4	3	4	0	.	0	.	0	.	2	4	0	.	5
13	1	1	2	7	68	1100	4257	6138	13	0	.	5	.	0	.	1	.	0	.	0	.	0	.	0	.	0	.	3	.	0	.	4
14	1	1	9	7	68	1230	4345	6320	16	0	.	0	.	0	.	0	.	0	.	0	.	0	.	0	.	0	.	1	.	0	.	5
15	1	1	13	7	68	1500	4250	6354	14	0	.	0	.	0	.	0	.	0	.	0	.	0	.	0	.	0	.	2	5	0	.	3
16	1	1	22	7	68	1000	4320	6320	14	14	2	0	.	0	.	0	.	0	.	6	2	0	.	0	.	0	.	4	2	0	.	5
17	1	1	24	7	68	1500	4320	6320	17	6	.	0	.	0	.	0	.	0	.	2	.	0	.	0	.	0	.	2	.	0	.	3
18	1	1	26	7	68	1000	4334	6308	18	16	2	0	.	0	.	0	.	0	.	4	2	0	.	0	.	0	.	4	2	0	.	6
19	1	1	28	7	68	1000	4330	6310	18	12	.	0	.	0	.	0	.	0	.	10	.	0	.	0	.	0	.	2	.	0	.	4
20	1	1	29	7	68	830	4323	6307	18	10	4	0	.	0	.	0	.	0	.	8	4	0	.	0	.	0	.	2	4	0	.	4
21	1	1	30	7	68	1000	4320	6310	18	20	6	0	.	0	.	0	.	4	6	8	6	0	.	0	.	0	.	8	6	0	.	5
22	1	1	31	7	68	900	4320	6314	19	16	6	0	.	0	.	0	.	4	6	12	6	0	.	0	.	0	.	6	6	0	.	4
23	1	1	1	8	68	1200	4306	6304	19	8	6	0	.	0	.	0	.	4	6	4	6	0	.	0	.	0	.	6	6	0	.	2
24	1	1	2	8	68	1600	4305	6308	19	10	.	0	.	0	.	0	.	2	.	6	.	0	.	0	.	0	.	2	.	0	.	4
25	1	1	6	8	68	1500	4340	6300	19	20	5	0	.	0	.	0	.	2	5	4	5	0	.	0	.	0	.	2	5	0	.	4
26	1	1	10	9	68	1400	4250	6302	19	5	4	0	.	0	.	0	.	0	.	0	.	0	.	0	.	0	.	8	4	0	.	3
27	1	1	22	9	68	1200	4302	6531	18	6	7	0	.	0	.	0	.	1	7	0	.	0	.	0	.	0	.	1	7	0	.	2
28	1	1	29	9	68	1500	4306	6510	18	1	4	3	4	0	.	0	.	0	.	0	.	0	.	0	.	0	.	4	4	0	.	3
29	1	1	4	10	68	1000	4248	6527	16	0	.	4	5	0	.	0	.	0	.	0	.	0	.	0	.	0	.	8	5	0	.	3
30	1	1	28	10	68	1300	4320	6500	16	8	6	0	.	0	.	0	.	0	.	0	.	0	.	0	.	0	.	1	6	0	.	3
31	1	1	3	7	69	1600	4309	6322	12	10	.	0	.	0	.	0	.	3	.	2	.	0	.	0	.	0	.	4	.	0	.	2
32	1	1	4	7	69	1700	4317	6317	12	6	.	0	.	0	.	0	.	2	.	4	.	0	.	0	.	0	.	4	.	0	.	5
33	1	1	6	7	69	1400	4320	6310	14	30	3	0	.	0	.	0	.	6	3	8	3	0	.	0	.	0	.	7	3	0	.	2
34	1	1	7	7	69	1150	4318	6312	14	12	.	1	.	0	.	0	.	0	.	4	.	0	.	0	.	0	.	6	.	0	.	6
35	1	1	8	7	69	1400	4302	6312	14	12	.	0	.	0	.	0	.	0	.	6	.	0	.	0	.	0	.	4	.	0	.	2
36	1	1	21	7	69	800	4257	6207	15	4	.	0	.	0	.	0	.	0	.	1	.	0	.	0	.	0	.	2	.	0	.	6
37	1	1	21	7	69	1200	4254	6202	15	8	.	0	.	0	.	0	.	0	.	4	.	0	.	0	.	0	.	4	.	0	.	6
38	1	1	22	7	69	1610	4307	6217	15	30	.	0	.	0	.	0	.	4	.	6	.	0	.	0	.	0	.	6	.	0	.	1
39	1	1	24	7	69	1950	4350	6457	12	30	.	0	.	0	.	0	.	2	.	8	.	0	.	0	.	0	.	8	.	0	.	2
40	1	1	28	7	69	1150	4309	6245	15	2	.	30	.	0	.	2	.	4	.	10	.	0	.	0	.	0	.	10	.	0	.	2
41	1	1	29	7	69	800	4302	6245	16	20	.	0	.	0	.	0	.	0	.	7	.	0	.	0	.	0	.	6	.	0	.	3
42	1	1	30	7	69	1900	4255	6250	16	30	.	0	.	0	.	0	.	0	.	6	.	0	.	0	.	0	.	2	.	0	.	1
43	1	1	24	8	69	1350	4303	6457	14	6	.	0	.	0	.	0	.	0	.	0	.	0	.	0	.	0	.	1	.	0	.	4
44	1	1	7	9	69	1000	4247	6320	20	12	.	0	.	0	.	0	.	1	.	2	.	0	.	0	.	0	.	1	.	0	.	2
45	1	1	17	6	70	1140	4310	6313	11	0	.	0	.	0	.	0	.	0	.	0	.	0	.	0	.	0	.	1	.	0	.	2
46	1	1	6	7	70	1350	4328	6303	13	0	.	0	.	0	.	0	.	0	.	0	.	0	.	0	.	0	.	3	.	0	.	1
47	1	1	9	7	70	1410	4321	6312	14	0	.	0	.	0	.	0	.	0	.	1	.	0	.	0	.	0	.	1	.	0	.	1
48	1	4	22	6	70	1400	4320	6318	.	3	.	1	.	0	.	0	.	0	.	2	.	0	.	0	.	0	.	1	.	0	.	0
49	1	4	25	6	70	900	4305	6300	13	0	.	0	.	0	.	0	.	1	.	0	.	0	.	0	.	0	.	1	.	0	.	1
50	1	4	8	7	70	1600	4319	6303	18	4	4	0	.	0	.	0	.	0	.	0	.	0	.	0	.	0	.	2	5	0	.	3
51	1	4	9	7	70	1420	4316	6304	19	1	4	0	.	0	.	0	.	0	.	0	.	0	.	0	.	0	.	4	4	0	.	0
52	1	4	22	7	70	1140	4304	6329	18	4	6	0	.	0	.	56	6	0	.	0	.	0	.	0	.	0	.	2	6	0	.	3
53	1	4	27	7	70	1530	4300	6234	20	4	3	0	.	0	.	0	.	2	3	1	3	0	.	0	.	0	.	2	3	0	.	4
54	1	4	27	7	70	1600	4303	6230	20	1	3	0	.	0	.	0	.	0	.	0	.	0	.	0	.	0	.	4	3	0	.	4
55	1	4	3	8	70	1500	4250	6220	21	1	4	0	.	0	.	0	.	0	.	0	.	0	.	0	.	0	.	3	4	0	.	3
56	1	4	6	8	70	1900	4310	6320	.	3	6	0	.	0	.	0	.	0	.	2	6	0	.	0	.	0	.	2	6	0	.	0
57	1	4	20	8	70	1730	4458	6131	18	3	3	0	.	0	.	0	.	0	.	0	.	0	.	0	.	0	.	1	3	0	.	2
58	1	4	14	9	70	1015	4309	6438	15	5	5	0	.	0	.	0	.	0	.	0	.	0	.	0	.	0	.	1	5	0	.	2
59	1	4	17	9	70	1720	4253	6532	14	3	1	8	1	0	.	0	.	1	1	0	.	0	.	0	.	0	.	1	1	0	.	2
60	1	4	20	9	70	915	4304	6515	13	1	5	0	.	0	.	0	.	5	5	0	.	0	.	0	.	0	.	2	5	0	.	3
61	1	4	20	9	70	1500	4248	6525	13	2	.	0	.	0	.	0	.	1	.	0	.	0	.	0	.	0	.	2	.	0	.	3
62	1	4	20	9	70	1700	4259	6516	13	2	.	2	.	0	.	0	.	1	.	0	.	0	.	0	.	0	.	3	.	0	.	3
63	1	4	21	9	70	1500	4245	6514	13	1	6	0	.	0	.	0	.	0	.	0	.	0	.	0	.	0	.	2	6	0	.	2
64	1	4	21	9	70	1630	4250	6520	13	6	.	1	.	0	.	0	.	5	.	0	.	0	.	0	.	0	.	3	.	0	.	2
65	1	4	21	9	70	1750	4256	6525	13	2	.	1	.	0	.	0	.	0	.	0	.	0	.	0	.	0	.	2	.	0	.	2
66	1	4	23	9	70	1715	4250	6530	15	2	8	4	8	0	.	0	.	0	.	0	.	0	.	0	.	0	.	1	8	0	.	2
67	1	4	24	9	70	1300	4259	6535	16	2	.	0	.	0	.	0	.	4	.	0	.	0	.	0	.	0	.	3	.	0	.	9
68	1	4	24	9	70	1340	4249	6534	16	1	.	6	.	0	.	0	.	0	.	0	.	0	.	0	.	0	.	2	.	0	.	9
69	1	4	24	9	70	1530	4252	6534	16	0	.	4	.	0	.	0	.	0	.	0	.	0	.	0	.	0	.	2	.	0	.	9
70	1	4	29	9	70	1800	4249	6536	15	2	6	7	6	0	.	0	.	0	.	0	.	0	.	0	.	0	.	7	6	0	.	2
71	1	4	30	9	70	730	4243	6537	14	3	.	3	.	0	.	0	.	0	.	0	.	0	.	0	.	0	.	4	.	0	.	9
72	1	4	30	9	70	1000	4249	6545	14	1	.	6	.	0	.	0	.	0	.	0	.	0	.	0	.	0	.	7	.	0	.	9
73	1	4	30	9	70	1200	4251	6540	14	0	.	3	.	0	.	0	.	0	.	0	.	0	.	0	.	0	.	5	.	0	.	9
74	1	4	2	10	70	730	4248	6540	15	0	.	5	6	0	.	0	.	0	.	0	.	0	.	0	.	0	.	2	6	0	.	8
75	1	4	2	10	70	900	4246	6544	15	1	.	3	.	0	.	0	.	0	.	0	.	0	.	0	.	0	.	3	.	0	.	8
76	1	4	2	10	70	1200	4249	6543	15	5	.	2	.	0	.	0	.	0	.	0	.	0	.	0	.	0	.	4	.	0	.	8
77	1	4	2	10	70	1400	4253	6542	15	2	.	1	.	0	.	0	.	0	.	0	.	0	.	0	.	0	.	3	.	0	.	8
78	1	4	2	10	70	1800	4253	6546	15	1	.	3	.	0	.	0	.	0	.	0	.	0	.	0	.	0	.	2	.	0	.	8
79	1	4	5	10	70	900	4250	6540	15	2	5	0	.	0	.	0	.	0	.	0	.	0	.	0	.	0	.	3	5	0	.	4
80	1	4	6	10	70	1010	4257	6501	.	3	.	0	.	0	.	0	.	0	.	0	.	0	.	0	.	0	.	8	.	0	.	6
81	1	4	6	10	70	1030	4254	6505	.	2	.	0	.	0	.	0	.	0	.	0	.	0	.	0	.	0	.	3	.	0	.	6
82	1	4	6	10	70	1130	4253	6522	.	0	.	2	.	0	.	0	.	0	.	0	.	0	.	0	.	0	.	7	.	0	.	6
83	1	4	7	10	70	1715	4249	6524	.	4	.	0	.	0	.	0	.	0	.	0	.	0	.	0	.	0	.	6	.	0	.	0
84	1	4	7	10	70	1755	4250	6531	.	3	.	0	.	0	.	0	.	0	.	0	.	0	.	0	.	0	.	7	.	0	.	0
85	1	4	7	10	70	1900	4245	6544	.	2	.	0	.	0	.	0	.	0	.	0	.	0	.	0	.	0	.	1	.	0	.	0
86	1	4	9	10	70	1310	4252	6528	15	0	.	0	.	0	.	0	.	0	.	0	.	0	.	0	.	0	.	2	3	0	.	2
87	1	4	9	10	70	1400	4255	6520	.	2	.	0	.	0	.	0	.	0	.	0	.	0	.	0	.	0	.	3	.	0	.	2
88	1	4	9	10	70	1800	4249	6515	.	3	.	0	.	0	.	0	.	0	.	0	.	0	.	0	.	0	.	2	.	0	.	2
89	1	4	12	10	70	1220	4254	6524	.	0	.	3	.	0	.	0	.	0	.	0	.	0	.	0	.	0	.	4	.	0	.	3
90	1	4	12	10	70	1530	4252	6530	.	7	.	0	.	0	.	0	.	0	.	0	.	0	.	0	.	0	.	2	.	0	.	3

Computer Table 2 (*continued*)

OBS	LS4	V4	DA4	MO4	YR4	TIME4	LAT4	LONG4	WT	NF	FDT	NS	SDT	NM	MDT	NSP	SPDT	NH	HDT	NB	BDT	NBO	BODT	NP	PDT	NK	KDT	NR	RDT	ND	DDT	NW
91	1	4	12	10	70	1745	4302	6521	.	4	.	0	.	0	.	0	.	0	.	0	.	0	.	0	.	0	.	3	.	0	.	3
92	1	4	13	10	70	1115	4255	6521	.	4	.	0	.	0	.	0	.	1	.	0	.	0	.	0	.	0	.	7	.	0	.	1
93	1	4	13	10	70	1440	4254	6506	.	5	.	1	.	0	.	0	.	2	.	0	.	0	.	0	.	0	.	6	.	0	.	1
94	1	4	13	10	70	1610	4257	6508	.	4	.	0	.	0	.	0	.	1	.	0	.	0	.	0	.	0	.	3	.	0	.	1
95	1	4	21	10	70	1610	4259	6505	.	10	.	0	.	0	.	0	.	0	.	0	.	0	.	0	.	0	.	12	.	0	.	2
96	1	4	21	10	70	1650	4300	6513	.	12	.	0	.	0	.	0	.	0	.	0	.	0	.	0	.	0	.	3	.	0	.	2
97	1	4	21	10	70	1715	4305	6510	.	8	.	0	.	0	.	0	.	0	.	0	.	0	.	0	.	0	.	3	.	0	.	2
98	1	4	22	10	70	1400	4250	6516	.	18	.	0	.	0	.	0	.	2	.	0	.	0	.	0	.	0	.	8	.	0	.	3
99	1	4	23	10	70	1150	4258	6503	.	12	.	0	.	0	.	0	.	0	.	0	.	0	.	0	.	0	.	2	.	0	.	2
100	1	4	23	10	70	1220	4255	6509	.	5	.	0	.	0	.	0	.	0	.	0	.	0	.	0	.	0	.	4	.	0	.	2
101	1	4	23	10	70	1345	4250	6514	.	11	.	0	.	0	.	0	.	0	.	3	.	0	.	0	.	0	.	5	.	0	.	2
102	1	4	23	10	70	1450	4258	6523	.	10	.	0	.	0	.	0	.	0	.	0	.	0	.	0	.	0	.	4	.	0	.	2
103	1	4	23	10	70	1610	4310	6512	.	4	.	0	.	0	.	0	.	0	.	0	.	0	.	0	.	0	.	1	.	0	.	2
104	1	4	27	10	70	1400	4252	6516	.	6	.	0	.	0	.	0	.	0	.	0	.	0	.	0	.	0	.	4	.	0	.	0
105	1	4	27	10	70	1430	4251	6520	.	4	.	0	.	0	.	0	.	0	.	0	.	0	.	0	.	0	.	2	.	0	.	0
106	1	4	27	10	70	1630	4254	6520	.	6	.	0	.	0	.	0	.	0	.	0	.	0	.	0	.	0	.	6	.	0	.	0
107	1	4	28	10	70	715	4252	6543	.	3	.	0	.	0	.	0	.	0	.	0	.	0	.	0	.	0	.	1	.	0	.	2
108	1	4	28	10	70	745	4252	6537	.	4	.	0	.	0	.	0	.	0	.	0	.	0	.	0	.	0	.	3	.	0	.	2
109	1	4	28	10	70	935	4246	6539	.	6	.	0	.	0	.	0	.	0	.	0	.	0	.	0	.	0	.	1	.	0	.	2
110	1	4	28	10	70	1115	4249	6534	.	7	.	0	.	0	.	0	.	0	.	0	.	0	.	0	.	0	.	4	.	0	.	2
111	1	4	30	10	70	1110	4250	6539	.	7	.	0	.	0	.	0	.	0	.	0	.	0	.	0	.	0	.	12	.	0	.	0
112	1	4	30	10	70	1130	4248	6542	.	4	.	0	.	0	.	0	.	0	.	0	.	0	.	0	.	0	.	6	.	0	.	0
113	1	4	30	10	70	1200	4245	6544	.	6	.	0	.	0	.	0	.	0	.	0	.	0	.	0	.	0	.	4	.	0	.	0
114	1	4	30	10	70	1400	4250	6520	.	6	.	0	.	0	.	0	.	0	.	0	.	0	.	0	.	0	.	3	.	0	.	0
115	1	4	30	10	70	1600	4253	6505	.	8	.	0	.	0	.	0	.	0	.	2	.	0	.	0	.	0	.	2	.	0	.	0
116	1	4	8	11	70	1545	4256	6513	.	3	.	0	.	0	.	0	.	0	.	0	.	0	.	0	.	0	.	2	.	0	.	0
117	1	4	8	11	70	1610	4258	6512	.	2	.	0	.	0	.	0	.	0	.	0	.	0	.	0	.	0	.	3	.	0	.	0
118	1	4	8	11	70	1625	4259	6517	.	3	.	0	.	0	.	0	.	0	.	0	.	0	.	0	.	0	.	1	.	0	.	0
119	1	4	4	7	71	715	4204	6538	12	3	9	20	9	0	.	0	.	0	.	0	.	0	.	0	.	0	.	3	9	0	.	8
120	1	4	4	7	71	1200	4200	6536	13	2	9	15	9	0	.	0	.	0	.	0	.	0	.	0	.	0	.	2	9	0	.	8
121	1	4	5	7	71	1800	4213	6540	14	3	1	25	1	0	.	0	.	1	1	0	.	0	.	0	.	0	.	2	1	0	.	8
122	1	4	17	9	71	1530	4255	6506	14	3	9	2	9	0	.	0	.	0	.	0	.	0	.	0	.	0	.	3	9	0	.	7
123	1	4	17	9	71	1555	4258	6504	14	0	.	7	9	0	.	0	.	0	.	0	.	0	.	0	.	0	.	2	9	0	.	7
124	1	4	17	9	71	1910	4258	6504	14	0	.	6	9	0	.	0	.	0	.	0	.	0	.	0	.	0	.	1	9	0	.	7
125	1	4	19	9	71	730	4305	6500	14	2	9	7	9	0	.	0	.	0	.	0	.	0	.	0	.	0	.	3	9	0	.	6
126	1	4	19	9	71	800	4300	6503	14	3	9	12	9	0	.	0	.	0	.	0	.	0	.	0	.	0	.	4	9	0	.	6
127	1	4	20	9	71	1000	4301	6506	14	2	9	12	9	0	.	0	.	0	.	0	.	0	.	0	.	0	.	14	9	0	.	6
128	1	4	20	9	71	1400	4305	6504	14	5	9	8	9	0	.	0	.	0	.	0	.	0	.	0	.	0	.	3	9	0	.	6
129	1	4	21	9	71	900	4310	6500	13	0	.	5	9	0	.	0	.	0	.	0	.	0	.	0	.	0	.	8	9	0	.	5
130	1	4	21	9	71	1540	4304	6503	14	4	9	4	9	0	.	0	.	0	.	0	.	0	.	0	.	0	.	5	9	0	.	5
131	1	4	22	9	71	930	4306	6500	14	4	9	2	9	0	.	0	.	0	.	0	.	0	.	0	.	0	.	5	9	0	.	8
132	1	4	22	9	71	1020	4303	6504	14	2	9	0	.	0	.	0	.	0	.	0	.	0	.	0	.	0	.	7	9	0	.	8
133	1	4	22	9	71	1100	4302	6506	13	5	9	2	9	0	.	0	.	0	.	0	.	0	.	0	.	0	.	5	9	0	.	8
134	1	4	22	9	71	1200	4259	6507	12	7	9	0	.	0	.	0	.	0	.	0	.	0	.	0	.	0	.	4	9	0	.	8
135	1	4	22	9	71	1230	4258	6513	12	6	9	40	9	0	.	0	.	0	.	0	.	0	.	0	.	0	.	3	9	0	.	8
136	1	4	22	9	71	1800	4302	6503	13	3	9	4	9	0	.	0	.	0	.	0	.	0	.	0	.	0	.	3	9	0	.	8
137	1	4	23	9	71	1300	4304	6510	13	4	9	0	.	0	.	0	.	1	9	0	.	0	.	0	.	0	.	6	9	0	.	8
138	1	4	23	9	71	1755	4253	6521	12	2	9	15	9	0	.	0	.	1	9	0	.	0	.	0	.	0	.	7	9	0	.	8
139	1	4	26	9	71	800	4305	6455	10	3	9	2	9	0	.	0	.	0	.	0	.	0	.	0	.	0	.	5	9	0	.	6
140	1	4	26	9	71	835	4301	6500	12	4	9	3	9	0	.	0	.	0	.	0	.	0	.	0	.	0	.	3	9	0	.	6
141	1	4	26	9	71	1100	4300	6506	13	3	9	2	9	0	.	0	.	0	.	0	.	0	.	0	.	0	.	4	9	0	.	6
142	1	4	26	9	71	1215	4256	6517	13	0	.	2	9	0	.	0	.	3	9	0	.	0	.	0	.	0	.	3	9	0	.	6
143	1	4	27	9	71	1630	4254	6509	13	9	9	0	.	0	.	0	.	3	9	0	.	0	.	0	.	0	.	5	9	0	.	7
144	1	4	28	9	71	1500	4305	6500	15	5	6	3	6	0	.	0	.	0	.	0	.	0	.	0	.	0	.	4	6	0	.	6
145	1	4	28	9	71	1535	4302	6502	14	4	6	0	.	0	.	0	.	0	.	0	.	0	.	0	.	0	.	3	6	0	.	6
146	1	4	28	9	71	1635	4259	6507	13	5	6	3	6	0	.	0	.	0	.	0	.	0	.	0	.	0	.	2	6	0	.	6
147	1	4	28	9	71	1730	4259	6511	14	7	6	10	6	0	.	0	.	0	.	0	.	0	.	0	.	0	.	7	6	0	.	6
148	1	4	29	9	71	1600	4300	6502	14	12	9	0	.	0	.	0	.	0	.	0	.	0	.	0	.	0	.	1	9	0	.	3
149	1	4	30	9	71	1130	4303	6500	15	5	9	0	.	0	.	0	.	0	.	0	.	0	.	0	.	0	.	8	9	0	.	7
150	1	4	30	9	71	1230	4257	6504	15	4	9	3	9	0	.	0	.	0	.	0	.	0	.	0	.	0	.	7	9	0	.	7
151	1	4	30	9	71	1500	4256	6515	15	3	6	7	6	0	.	0	.	0	.	0	.	0	.	0	.	0	.	5	6	0	.	7
152	1	4	3	10	71	900	4255	6508	15	4	6	3	6	0	.	0	.	0	.	0	.	0	.	0	.	0	.	2	6	0	.	6
153	1	4	3	10	71	1000	4252	6520	14	2	9	5	9	0	.	0	.	0	.	0	.	0	.	0	.	0	.	7	9	0	.	6
154	1	4	3	10	71	1045	4251	6525	14	3	9	8	9	0	.	0	.	0	.	0	.	0	.	0	.	0	.	6	9	0	.	6
155	1	4	3	10	71	1630	4248	6524	14	3	9	8	9	0	.	0	.	0	.	0	.	0	.	0	.	0	.	5	9	0	.	6
156	1	4	4	10	71	1530	4315	6457	15	12	6	0	.	0	.	0	.	0	.	0	.	0	.	0	.	0	.	7	6	0	.	0
157	1	4	4	10	71	1600	4310	6459	15	10	6	0	.	0	.	0	.	0	.	0	.	0	.	0	.	0	.	5	6	0	.	0
158	1	4	4	10	71	1700	4300	6502	15	7	6	2	6	0	.	0	.	0	.	0	.	0	.	0	.	0	.	8	6	0	.	0
159	1	4	4	10	71	1830	4256	6507	14	5	6	3	6	0	.	0	.	0	.	0	.	0	.	0	.	0	.	4	6	0	.	0
160	1	4	5	10	71	715	4256	6507	14	3	9	5	9	0	.	0	.	0	.	0	.	0	.	0	.	0	.	5	9	0	.	6
161	1	4	5	10	71	1130	4252	6515	14	4	5	1	5	0	.	0	.	0	.	0	.	0	.	0	.	0	.	3	5	0	.	6
162	1	4	7	10	71	1000	4300	6530	13	3	6	3	6	0	.	0	.	2	6	0	.	0	.	0	.	0	.	5	6	0	.	8
163	1	4	7	10	71	1240	4251	6535	14	2	3	15	3	0	.	0	.	0	.	0	.	0	.	0	.	0	.	3	3	0	.	8
164	1	4	10	10	71	830	4302	6545	11	4	9	0	.	0	.	0	.	0	.	0	.	0	.	0	.	0	.	5	9	0	.	4
165	1	4	10	10	71	920	4254	6544	12	3	9	0	.	0	.	0	.	0	.	0	.	0	.	0	.	0	.	4	9	0	.	4
166	1	4	10	10	71	1300	4248	6540	11	3	9	0	.	0	.	0	.	1	9	0	.	0	.	0	.	0	.	3	9	0	.	4
167	1	4	10	10	71	1430	4252	6538	13	0	.	4	9	0	.	0	.	0	.	0	.	0	.	0	.	0	.	2	9	0	.	4
168	1	4	12	10	71	800	4248	6520	14	3	9	3	9	0	.	0	.	0	.	0	.	0	.	0	.	0	.	5	9	0	.	6
169	1	4	12	10	71	1100	4255	6530	14	2	9	0	.	0	.	0	.	0	.	0	.	0	.	0	.	0	.	8	9	0	.	6
170	1	4	12	10	71	1430	4253	6535	13	0	.	5	9	0	.	0	.	0	.	0	.	0	.	0	.	0	.	5	9	0	.	6
171	1	4	12	10	71	1700	4253	6535	13	0	.	15	9	0	.	0	.	0	.	0	.	0	.	0	.	0	.	6	9	0	.	6
172	1	4	14	10	71	800	4256	6530	13	0	.	3	6	0	.	0	.	0	.	0	.	0	.	0	.	0	.	4	6	0	.	8
173	1	4	14	10	71	1300	4252	6530	13	2	6	18	6	0	.	0	.	0	.	0	.	0	.	0	.	0	.	5	6	0	.	8
174	1	4	17	10	71	830	4253	6530	14	0	.	3	9	0	.	0	.	0	.	0	.	0	.	0	.	0	.	2	9	0	.	1
175	1	4	18	10	71	1320	4259	6502	13	1	9	3	9	0	.	0	.	0	.	0	.	0	.	0	.	0	.	12	9	0	.	4
176	1	4	18	10	71	1500	4257	6504	13	0	.	6	9	0	.	0	.	0	.	0	.	0	.	0	.	0	.	15	9	0	.	4
177	1	4	20	10	71	900	4253	6539	11	0	.	10	9	0	.	0	.	0	.	0	.	0	.	0	.	0	.	15	9	0	.	8
178	1	4	20	10	71	1330	4248	6536	11	0	.	15	9	0	.	0	.	0	.	0	.	0	.	0	.	0	.	10	9	0	.	8
179	1	4	24	10	71	1000	4300	6500	13	3	9	2	9	0	.	0	.	0	.	0	.	0	.	0	.	0	.	5	9	0	.	5
180	1	4	24	10	71	1200	4250	6516	13	14	9	0	.	0	.	0	.	0	.	0	.	0	.	0	.	0	.	4	9	0	.	5

Computer Table 2 (*continued*)

OBS	LS4	V4	DA4	MO4	YR4	TIME4	LAT4	LONG4	WT	NF	FDT	NS	SDT	NM	MDT	NSP	SPDT	NH	HDT	NB	BDT	NBO	BODT	NP	PDT	NK	KDT	NR	RDT	ND	DDT	NW
181	1	4	24	10	71	1330	4255	6514	12	3	9	0	.	0	.	0	.	0	.	0	.	0	.	0	.	0	.	3	9	0	.	5
182	1	4	24	10	71	1800	4254	6516	12	0	.	4	9	0	.	0	.	0	.	0	.	0	.	0	.	0	.	3	9	0	.	5
183	1	4	25	10	71	1500	4304	6505	13	6	9	0	.	0	.	0	.	0	.	0	.	0	.	0	.	0	.	8	9	0	.	4
184	1	4	25	10	71	1540	4258	6510	13	4	6	3	6	0	.	0	.	0	.	0	.	0	.	0	.	0	.	5	6	0	.	4
185	1	4	25	10	71	1630	4256	6511	13	3	9	0	.	0	.	0	.	0	.	0	.	0	.	0	.	0	.	6	9	0	.	4
186	1	4	29	10	71	1530	4255	6522	14	8	9	7	9	0	.	0	.	0	.	0	.	0	.	0	.	0	.	9	9	0	.	5
187	1	4	31	10	71	800	4305	6508	13	3	6	0	.	0	.	0	.	0	.	0	.	0	.	0	.	0	.	5	6	0	.	4
188	1	4	31	10	71	900	4256	6512	14	4	6	5	6	0	.	0	.	0	.	0	.	0	.	0	.	0	.	7	6	0	.	4
189	1	4	31	10	71	1200	4253	6502	13	8	6	0	.	0	.	0	.	0	.	0	.	0	.	0	.	0	.	5	6	0	.	4
190	1	4	31	10	71	1430	4254	6500	14	4	6	0	.	0	.	0	.	0	.	1	6	0	.	0	.	0	.	3	6	0	.	4
191	1	4	1	11	71	1500	4300	6457	13	3	9	0	.	0	.	0	.	0	.	0	.	0	.	0	.	0	.	4	9	0	.	1
192	1	4	5	11	71	1200	4305	6500	13	5	9	1	9	0	.	0	.	0	.	0	.	0	.	0	.	0	.	5	9	0	.	1
193	1	4	5	11	71	1400	4300	6510	13	10	9	0	.	0	.	0	.	0	.	0	.	0	.	0	.	0	.	4	9	0	.	1
194	1	4	5	11	71	1600	4300	6500	13	8	9	0	.	0	.	0	.	0	.	0	.	0	.	0	.	0	.	2	9	0	.	1
195	1	4	11	11	71	1315	4302	6510	12	8	9	0	.	0	.	0	.	0	.	0	.	0	.	0	.	0	.	2	9	0	.	3
196	1	4	11	11	71	1400	4258	6515	12	4	9	2	9	0	.	0	.	0	.	0	.	0	.	0	.	0	.	6	9	0	.	3
197	1	4	11	11	71	1530	4254	6511	12	5	9	6	9	0	.	0	.	0	.	0	.	0	.	0	.	0	.	4	9	0	.	3
198	1	4	11	11	71	1630	4250	6515	12	3	9	3	9	0	.	0	.	0	.	0	.	0	.	0	.	0	.	3	9	0	.	3
199	1	4	12	11	71	1400	4302	6505	12	4	7	0	.	0	.	0	.	0	.	0	.	0	.	0	.	0	.	3	7	0	.	0
200	1	4	12	11	71	1500	4255	6510	12	8	7	0	.	0	.	0	.	0	.	0	.	0	.	0	.	0	.	2	7	0	.	0
201	1	4	13	11	71	900	4252	6500	12	5	9	0	.	0	.	0	.	0	.	0	.	0	.	0	.	0	.	6	9	0	.	1
202	1	4	13	11	71	1000	4256	6510	12	4	9	0	.	0	.	0	.	0	.	0	.	0	.	0	.	0	.	3	9	0	.	1
203	1	4	9	7	72	900	4245	6413	15	2	9	8	9	0	.	0	.	0	.	0	.	0	.	0	.	0	.	2	9	0	.	7
204	1	4	9	7	72	1230	4241	6417	15	2	9	22	9	0	.	0	.	0	.	0	.	0	.	0	.	0	.	1	9	0	.	7
205	1	4	10	7	72	800	4244	6414	15	0	.	7	9	0	.	0	.	0	.	0	.	0	.	0	.	0	.	2	9	0	.	7
206	1	4	10	7	72	1200	4242	6417	16	0	.	18	9	0	.	0	.	0	.	0	.	0	.	0	.	0	.	2	9	0	.	7
207	1	4	11	7	72	900	4240	6418	15	0	.	3	7	0	.	0	.	0	.	0	.	0	.	0	.	0	.	3	7	0	.	7
208	1	4	11	7	72	1230	4235	6420	15	0	.	8	9	0	.	0	.	0	.	0	.	0	.	0	.	0	.	1	9	0	.	7
209	1	4	13	7	72	1500	4235	6423	15	0	.	4	9	0	.	0	.	0	.	0	.	0	.	0	.	0	.	3	9	0	.	7
210	1	4	13	7	72	2030	4236	6426	15	0	.	7	9	0	.	0	.	0	.	0	.	0	.	0	.	0	.	1	9	0	.	7
211	1	4	18	7	72	1500	4235	6420	15	7	9	0	.	0	.	0	.	0	.	0	.	0	.	0	.	0	.	1	9	0	.	4
212	1	4	25	7	72	1445	4332	6158	17	0	.	0	.	0	.	0	.	0	.	0	.	0	.	0	.	0	.	1	9	0	.	1
213	1	4	15	8	72	1440	4318	6508	13	2	9	0	.	0	.	0	.	0	.	0	.	0	.	0	.	0	.	2	9	0	.	0
214	1	4	15	8	72	1630	4305	6510	13	5	9	0	.	0	.	0	.	0	.	0	.	0	.	0	.	0	.	15	9	0	.	0
215	1	4	15	8	72	1730	4255	6512	13	8	9	0	.	0	.	0	.	0	.	0	.	0	.	0	.	0	.	3	9	0	.	0
216	1	4	17	8	72	900	4315	6515	13	2	9	0	.	0	.	0	.	0	.	1	9	0	.	0	.	0	.	5	9	0	.	2
217	1	4	17	8	72	1030	4255	6513	13	7	9	0	.	0	.	0	.	0	.	0	.	0	.	0	.	0	.	18	9	0	.	2
218	1	4	17	8	72	1130	4253	6530	13	9	9	0	.	0	.	0	.	0	.	0	.	0	.	0	.	0	.	3	9	0	.	2
219	1	4	17	8	72	1230	4245	6520	13	7	9	0	.	0	.	0	.	0	.	0	.	0	.	0	.	0	.	2	9	0	.	2
220	1	4	30	8	72	1130	4253	6524	13	0	.	4	9	0	.	0	.	0	.	0	.	0	.	0	.	0	.	18	9	0	.	7
221	1	4	30	8	72	1445	4257	6513	14	0	.	3	9	0	.	0	.	0	.	0	.	0	.	0	.	0	.	8	9	0	.	7
222	1	4	30	8	72	1930	4302	6510	13	6	9	8	9	0	.	0	.	0	.	0	.	0	.	0	.	0	.	15	9	0	.	7
223	1	4	30	8	72	2000	4305	6508	13	7	9	12	9	0	.	0	.	0	.	0	.	0	.	0	.	0	.	10	9	0	.	7
224	1	4	31	8	72	1330	4308	6508	12	0	.	4	9	0	.	0	.	0	.	0	.	0	.	0	.	0	.	8	9	0	.	6
225	1	4	31	8	72	1400	4304	6511	12	0	.	0	.	0	.	0	.	0	.	0	.	0	.	0	.	0	.	5	9	0	.	6
226	1	4	31	8	72	1430	4302	6510	12	0	.	0	.	0	.	0	.	0	.	0	.	0	.	0	.	0	.	3	9	0	.	6
227	1	4	31	8	72	1500	4301	6511	12	0	.	0	.	0	.	0	.	0	.	0	.	0	.	0	.	0	.	2	9	0	.	6
228	1	4	31	8	72	1630	4258	6517	12	0	.	0	.	0	.	0	.	0	.	0	.	0	.	0	.	0	.	3	9	0	.	6
229	1	4	31	8	72	1720	4254	6520	13	0	.	5	9	0	.	0	.	0	.	0	.	0	.	0	.	0	.	8	9	0	.	6
230	1	4	1	9	72	1200	4315	6504	14	12	9	0	.	0	.	0	.	0	.	0	.	0	.	0	.	0	.	7	9	0	.	3
231	1	4	1	9	72	1300	4303	6509	15	0	.	5	9	0	.	0	.	0	.	0	.	0	.	0	.	0	.	9	9	0	.	3
232	1	4	1	9	72	1400	4305	6509	15	2	9	2	9	0	.	0	.	0	.	0	.	0	.	0	.	0	.	3	9	0	.	3
233	1	4	5	9	72	800	4312	6500	13	2	9	0	.	0	.	0	.	0	.	0	.	0	.	0	.	0	.	1	9	0	.	7
234	1	4	5	9	72	1000	4254	6522	13	0	.	12	9	0	.	0	.	0	.	0	.	0	.	0	.	0	.	18	9	0	.	7
235	1	4	5	9	72	1230	4253	6522	13	0	.	10	9	0	.	0	.	0	.	0	.	0	.	0	.	0	.	5	9	0	.	7
236	1	4	5	9	72	1700	4300	6510	13	0	.	8	9	0	.	0	.	0	.	0	.	0	.	0	.	0	.	5	9	0	.	7
237	1	4	6	9	72	900	4320	6455	12	9	1	0	.	0	.	0	.	0	.	0	.	0	.	0	.	0	.	2	1	0	.	7
238	1	4	6	9	72	930	4315	6504	12	7	9	0	.	0	.	0	.	2	9	0	.	0	.	0	.	0	.	8	9	0	.	7
239	1	4	6	9	72	1100	4254	6520	13	2	9	18	9	0	.	0	.	0	.	0	.	0	.	0	.	0	.	20	9	0	.	7
240	1	4	6	9	72	1800	4312	6457	12	5	9	17	9	0	.	0	.	0	.	0	.	0	.	0	.	0	.	8	9	0	.	7
241	1	4	7	9	72	1000	4305	6505	12	2	9	0	.	0	.	0	.	0	.	0	.	0	.	0	.	0	.	3	9	0	.	5
242	1	4	7	9	72	1100	4257	6518	13	0	.	5	9	0	.	0	.	0	.	0	.	0	.	0	.	0	.	12	9	0	.	5
243	1	4	7	9	72	1130	4255	6520	13	0	.	12	9	0	.	0	.	0	.	0	.	0	.	0	.	0	.	7	9	0	.	5
244	1	4	8	9	72	830	4255	6510	13	0	.	3	9	0	.	0	.	0	.	0	.	0	.	0	.	0	.	10	9	0	.	5
245	1	4	8	9	72	900	4255	6518	13	0	.	22	9	0	.	0	.	0	.	0	.	0	.	0	.	0	.	12	9	0	.	5
246	1	4	8	9	72	1500	4305	6515	12	2	9	15	9	0	.	0	.	0	.	0	.	0	.	0	.	0	.	18	9	0	.	5
247	1	4	11	9	72	900	4255	6512	12	2	9	20	9	0	.	0	.	0	.	0	.	0	.	0	.	0	.	15	9	0	.	4
248	1	4	11	9	72	1130	4300	6517	12	0	.	10	9	0	.	0	.	0	.	0	.	0	.	0	.	0	.	3	9	0	.	4
249	1	4	12	9	72	800	4259	6505	13	2	9	3	9	0	0	0	.	0	.	0	.	0	.	0	.	0	.	8	9	0	.	5
250	1	4	12	9	72	845	4256	6509	13	0	.	15	9	0	.	0	.	0	.	0	.	0	.	0	.	0	.	7	9	0	.	5
251	1	4	13	9	72	1000	4310	6500	13	3	9	0	.	0	.	0	.	0	.	0	.	0	.	0	.	0	.	12	9	0	.	7
252	1	4	13	9	72	1100	4300	6500	13	2	9	2	9	0	.	0	.	0	.	0	.	0	.	0	.	0	.	15	9	0	.	7
253	1	4	13	9	72	1200	4303	6515	13	0	.	12	9	0	.	0	.	0	.	0	.	0	.	0	.	0	.	24	9	0	.	7
254	1	4	13	9	72	1500	4306	6509	14	0	.	8	9	0	.	0	.	0	.	0	.	0	.	0	.	0	.	17	9	0	.	7
255	1	4	15	9	72	900	4303	6509	14	0	.	4	9	0	.	0	.	0	.	0	.	0	.	0	.	0	.	27	9	0	.	5
256	1	4	15	9	72	1300	4300	6507	14	0	.	10	9	0	.	0	.	0	.	0	.	0	.	0	.	0	.	19	9	0	.	5
257	1	4	17	9	72	1400	4304	6510	14	3	9	2	9	0	.	0	.	0	.	0	.	0	.	0	.	0	.	8	9	0	.	4
258	1	4	17	9	72	1500	4257	6516	15	2	9	4	9	0	.	0	.	0	.	0	.	0	.	0	.	0	.	10	9	0	.	4
259	1	4	21	9	72	700	4256	6532	12	2	9	10	9	0	.	0	.	0	.	0	.	0	.	0	.	0	.	12	9	0	.	6
260	1	4	21	9	72	800	4256	6530	12	3	9	8	9	0	.	0	.	0	.	0	.	0	.	0	.	0	.	18	9	0	.	6
261	1	4	21	9	72	1000	4256	6534	12	3	9	5	9	0	.	0	.	0	.	0	.	0	.	0	.	0	.	8	9	0	.	6
262	1	4	24	9	72	1300	4247	6527	12	15	9	0	.	0	.	0	.	0	.	0	.	0	.	0	.	0	.	7	9	0	.	6
263	1	4	24	9	72	1400	4249	6534	13	3	9	0	.	0	.	0	.	0	.	0	.	0	.	0	.	0	.	6	9	0	.	6
264	1	4	24	9	72	1500	4252	6535	13	0	.	0	.	0	.	0	.	0	.	0	.	0	.	0	.	0	.	3	9	0	.	6
265	1	4	26	9	72	830	4251	6532	12	7	9	12	9	0	.	0	.	0	.	0	.	0	.	0	.	0	.	3	9	0	.	3
266	1	4	28	9	72	800	4250	6510	14	4	9	0	.	0	.	0	.	0	.	0	.	0	.	0	.	0	.	12	9	0	.	5
267	1	4	28	9	72	900	4252	6519	13	3	9	15	9	0	.	0	.	0	.	0	.	0	.	0	.	0	.	18	9	0	.	5
268	1	4	2	10	72	1100	4240	6515	14	12	9	0	.	0	.	0	.	0	.	0	.	0	.	0	.	0	.	22	9	0	.	1
269	1	4	2	10	72	1200	4245	6520	14	10	9	0	.	0	.	0	.	0	.	0	.	0	.	0	.	0	.	18	9	0	.	1
270	1	4	2	10	72	1300	4255	6518	14	8	9	0	.	0	.	0	.	0	.	0	.	0	.	0	.	0	.	10	9	0	.	1

Computer Table 2 (*continued*)

OBS	LS4	V4	DA4	MO4	YR4	TIME4	LAT4	LONG4	WT	NF	FDT	NS	SDT	NM	MDT	NSP	SPDT	NH	HDT	NB	BDT	NBO	BODT	NP	PDT	NK	KDT	NR	RDT	ND	DDT	NW
271	1	4	2	10	72	1400	4252	6505	14	10	9	0	.	0	.	0	.	0	.	0	.	0	.	0	.	0	.	8	9	0	.	1
272	1	4	2	10	72	1600	4258	6525	14	8	9	0	.	0	.	0	.	0	.	0	.	0	.	0	.	0	.	9	9	0	.	1
273	1	4	2	10	72	1730	4256	6514	14	3	9	2	9	0	.	0	.	0	.	0	.	0	.	0	.	0	.	4	9	0	.	1
274	1	4	3	10	72	1100	4302	6510	14	4	9	0	.	0	.	0	.	0	.	0	.	0	.	0	.	0	.	12	9	0	.	6
275	1	4	3	10	72	1200	4249	6510	13	5	9	2	9	0	.	0	.	0	.	0	.	0	.	0	.	0	.	14	9	0	.	6
276	1	4	3	10	72	1300	4252	6510	13	3	9	1	9	0	.	0	.	0	.	0	.	0	.	0	.	0	.	8	9	0	.	6
277	1	4	3	10	72	1430	4258	6515	13	8	9	0	.	0	.	0	.	0	.	0	.	0	.	0	.	0	.	20	9	0	.	6
278	1	4	4	10	72	1500	4258	6522	14	4	9	0	.	0	.	0	.	0	.	0	.	0	.	0	.	0	.	14	9	0	.	5
279	1	4	4	10	72	1600	4255	6515	14	2	9	0	.	0	.	0	.	0	.	0	.	0	.	0	.	0	.	18	9	0	.	5
280	1	4	4	10	72	1700	4251	6512	13	1	9	20	9	0	.	0	.	0	.	0	.	0	.	0	.	0	.	8	9	0	.	5
281	1	4	5	10	72	1400	4305	6510	14	3	9	0	.	0	.	0	.	0	.	0	.	0	.	0	.	0	.	7	9	0	.	4
282	1	4	5	10	72	1500	4255	6505	14	2	2	0	.	0	.	0	.	0	.	0	.	0	.	0	.	0	.	10	2	0	.	4
283	1	4	5	10	72	1530	4254	6508	14	4	9	3	9	0	.	0	.	0	.	0	.	0	.	0	.	0	.	8	9	0	.	4
284	1	4	5	10	72	1830	4247	6520	14	2	9	8	9	0	.	0	.	0	.	0	.	0	.	0	.	0	.	5	9	0	.	4
285	1	4	6	10	72	1400	4305	6505	14	8	9	0	.	0	.	0	.	0	.	0	.	0	.	0	.	0	.	25	9	0	.	4
286	1	4	6	10	72	1445	4257	6509	13	3	9	8	9	0	.	0	.	0	.	0	.	0	.	0	.	0	.	12	9	0	.	4
287	1	4	6	10	72	1600	4251	6510	14	15	9	3	9	0	.	0	.	0	.	0	.	0	.	0	.	0	.	8	9	0	.	4
288	1	4	6	10	72	1830	4255	6515	13	2	9	0	.	0	.	0	.	0	.	0	.	0	.	0	.	0	.	15	9	0	.	4
289	1	4	11	10	72	745	4300	6505	13	3	9	0	.	0	.	0	.	0	.	0	.	0	.	0	.	0	.	22	9	0	.	7
290	1	4	11	10	72	830	4257	6510	13	2	9	10	9	0	.	0	.	0	.	0	.	0	.	0	.	0	.	20	9	0	.	7
291	1	4	11	10	72	1800	4308	6507	14	3	9	0	.	0	.	0	.	0	.	0	.	0	.	0	.	0	.	18	9	0	.	7
292	1	4	12	10	72	1230	4305	6510	14	3	9	0	.	0	.	0	.	0	.	0	.	0	.	0	.	0	.	12	9	0	.	2
293	1	4	12	10	72	1315	4300	6510	14	4	9	1	9	0	.	0	.	0	.	0	.	0	.	0	.	0	.	20	9	0	.	2
294	1	4	12	10	72	1430	4257	6505	14	12	9	0	.	0	.	0	.	0	.	0	.	0	.	0	.	0	.	25	9	0	.	2
295	1	4	12	10	72	1500	4249	6507	14	8	9	0	.	0	.	0	.	0	.	0	.	0	.	0	.	0	.	10	9	0	.	2
296	1	4	12	10	72	1600	4255	6500	14	7	9	0	.	0	.	0	.	1	9	0	.	0	.	0	.	0	.	8	9	0	.	2
297	1	4	13	10	72	930	4305	6450	14	3	9	0	.	0	.	0	.	0	.	0	.	0	.	0	.	0	.	2	9	0	.	0
298	1	4	13	10	72	1030	4255	6450	14	12	9	0	.	0	.	0	.	0	.	0	.	0	.	0	.	0	.	5	9	0	.	0
299	1	4	13	10	72	1200	4245	6458	14	8	9	0	.	0	.	0	.	0	.	0	.	0	.	0	.	0	.	3	9	0	.	0
300	1	4	16	10	72	900	4300	6500	13	7	9	0	.	0	.	0	.	0	.	0	.	0	.	0	.	0	.	30	9	0	.	4
301	1	4	16	10	72	1000	4300	6507	13	9	9	0	.	0	.	0	.	0	.	0	.	0	.	0	.	0	.	25	9	0	.	4
302	1	4	16	10	72	1100	4300	6510	13	3	9	4	9	0	.	0	.	0	.	0	.	0	.	0	.	0	.	15	9	0	.	4
303	1	4	27	10	72	1200	4255	6516	11	65	9	0	.	0	.	0	.	12	9	6	9	0	.	0	.	0	.	4	9	0	.	2
304	1	4	27	10	72	1700	4300	6510	11	6	9	0	.	0	.	0	.	2	9	2	9	0	.	0	.	0	.	6	9	0	.	2
305	1	4	28	10	72	1000	4259	6504	10	10	9	0	.	0	.	0	.	4	9	0	.	0	.	0	.	0	.	3	9	0	.	3
306	1	4	28	10	72	1030	4257	6506	10	40	9	0	.	0	.	0	.	3	9	0	.	0	.	0	.	0	.	3	9	0	.	3
307	1	4	1	11	72	800	4323	6448	11	15	6	0	.	0	.	0	.	3	6	2	6	0	.	0	.	0	.	2	6	0	.	1
308	1	4	2	11	72	900	4321	6457	11	12	6	0	.	0	.	0	.	0	.	2	6	0	.	0	.	0	.	4	6	0	.	2
309	1	4	2	11	72	1000	4315	6512	11	28	6	0	.	0	.	0	.	0	.	3	6	0	.	0	.	0	.	2	6	0	.	2
310	1	4	7	11	72	1400	4240	6548	10	7	2	0	.	0	.	0	.	8	2	0	.	0	.	0	.	0	.	2	2	0	.	0
311	1	4	7	11	72	1500	4251	6533	10	8	2	0	.	0	.	0	.	6	2	0	.	0	.	0	.	0	.	3	2	0	.	0
312	1	4	12	11	72	1000	4253	6550	10	2	9	0	.	0	.	19	9	9	9	0	.	0	.	0	.	0	.	3	9	0	.	1
313	1	4	13	11	72	1700	4240	6510	10	12	9	0	.	0	.	0	.	17	9	0	.	0	.	0	.	0	.	3	9	0	.	0

Twentieth-Century Records of Right Whales (*Eubalaena glacialis*) in the Northwestern Atlantic Ocean

JAMES G. MEAD

Division of Mammals, National Museum of Natural History, Smithsonian Institution,
Washington, D.C. 20560, U.S.A.

ABSTRACT

I have been able to locate 1,408 records of right whales in the northwestern Atlantic and the Gulf of Mexico since the turn of the century. Of these, 1,326 represent published records, 12 are museum records and 70 are records accumulated by the Scientific Event Alert Network and the Marine Mammal Events Program of the Smithsonian Institution. There were 1,374 records of sightings, 20 strandings, 8 captures and 6 incidental catches in fishing gear. There are 296 records of two or more animals and 85 of those were records of a large whale and a substantially smaller whale which I have interpreted as an adult accompanied by a calf. There is a much higher incidence of adult/calf pairs reported from Florida (45 out of 79 records of two or more animals) suggesting that calving may take place primarily in the southern portion of their known range. There is an anecdotal report of a right whale giving birth in Florida waters. The records show pronounced geographic seasonality. From Virginia south they are mainly restricted to winter and early spring (November through April). Records from Maryland north through Massachusetts are randomly distributed throughout the year. Those north of Massachusetts are limited to the summer and fall (May through November). The length frequency distribution of stranded right whales shows three modal peaks. There is one at about 440 cm that represents newborn calves, one at about 1,100 cm that represents yearlings and one at about 1,700 cm that represents mature adults. The smallest calf was 407 cm long and the largest reliably measured adult was 1,650 cm.

INTRODUCTION

The right whale, once relatively abundant along the Atlantic coast of North America, has suffered at the hands of man until only a few hundred remain. This species formed the basis of an early shore-whaling fishery which had its peak in the latter part of the 17th century (Allen, 1916). By the beginning of the 18th century the fishery had begun to decline and was of almost negligible extent by 1750. The shore whaling tradition was kept alive along the shores of Long Island, New York until the early 20th century (Reeves and Mitchell, 1986). The last recorded catch by shore whalers was in 1918 at East Hampton, Long Island, New York (Edwards and Rattray, 1932, p. 161). The last capture by whalers in the western North Atlantic was in 1951 in Trinity Bay, Newfoundland (Sergeant, 1966). This species apparently has not recovered even though it has not been actively sought by whalers in the Atlantic in this century. This situation has resulted in records of sightings and strandings being our only historical key to the activities of this species during the current century. In this paper I have attempted to compile all records of right whales in the northwestern Atlantic since 1900. Because of the magnitude of the number of records produced by two projects, the Cetacean and Turtle Assessment Program (CETAP), which operated out of the University of Rhode Island (Winn, 1982) and the New England Aquarium's right whale project (Kraus and Prescott, 1983), I have not attempted to include them.

MATERIALS

The data consist of northwestern Atlantic records of right whales from 1900 to the present that have been extracted from the literature, museum records, reports that were presented by the Scientific Event Alert Network (SEAN) program of the Smithsonian Institution from October 1975 until it ceased recording biological events in August 1982 and the records of the Marine Mammal Events Program (MMEP) of the Smithsonian. The reports break down as follows: sightings – 464 literature reports (several literature reports do not specify how many individuals were involved in a particular sighting), 3 records from museum files, 41 SEAN records, 18 MMEP records; captures – 7 literature reports, 1 museum record; strandings – 11 literature reports, 8 museum records, 7 SEAN records, 2 MMEP records; incidental catches – 1 literature report, 4 SEAN records, 1 MMEP record. Details of these records are given in the appendices.

Captures are any record that involves deliberate taking by persons involved in whaling. Incidental catches are records that involve whales getting caught in fishing gear that was set for purposes other than whaling. Sightings are records of live whales that, as far as can be told, are going about their normal activities. Strandings involve whales that either run aground or drift ashore dead. Whales that have been harpooned by whalers, escaped and subsequently died are treated as captures. Whales that have been involved in collisions with vessels are treated as strandings because of the difficulty in ascertaining whether the whale was alive at the time of the collision or was dead and just drifted into the path of the vessel. Whales that were found drifting at sea with no apparent cause of death are treated as strandings even though they did not actually strand.

RESULTS

Spatial distribution

The overall distribution of right whale records (Table 1) may show mainly where the effort has been, not where the whales were. The high number of sightings in Nova Scotian waters (144) partly is the result of a summering population in the Bay of Fundy but mainly is the result of the consistent sighting effort of catcher vessels operating

Table 1.

Occurrences of right whales in the northwestern Atlantic since 1900. The numbers represent individual whales rather than individual events.

State or Province	Sightings	Captures	Strandings	Incidental catch
Quebec	6	1	–	–
Newfoundland	14	2	–	–
Nova Scotia	144	–	1	–
New Brunswick	2+	–	–	–
Maine	31	–	2	–
Massachusetts	795	–	4	3
Rhode Island	–	–	–	–
Connecticut	–	–	–	–
New York	28	3	4	–
New Jersey	7+	–	2	1
Delaware	1	–	–	–
Maryland	2	–	–	–
Virginia	4	–	–	–
North Carolina	70	1	–	1
South Carolina	6	–	2	–
Georgia	26+	–	2	–
Florida	233+	1	2	1
Gulf of Mexico				
Florida	2	–	–	–
Texas	–	–	1	–

off the south coast of Nova Scotia from the whaling station at Blandford. Maine (31 records) may represent a concentration of right whales. The number of sightings for Massachusetts (795) is almost entirely the result of Schevill, Moore and Watkins' (1981) efforts from 1955 to 1980. The high number of sightings for New York (28) represent multiple sightings of what could have been as few as two animals in 1974 and 1975. North Carolina (69), Georgia (17+) and Florida (228+) may represent real concentrations of right whales.

Temporal distribution

Plotting right whale occurrences by month (Table 2) shows that the furthest north records (Canada) have

Table 2.

Records of right whales (strandings, sightings, captures and incidental catches) plotted by month and location

Location	Jan	Feb	Mar	Apr	May	Jun	Jul	Aug	Sep	Oct	Nov	Dec
Canada												
Newfoundland	–	–	–	–	1	–	1	1	2	–	–	–
Nova Scotia	–	–	–	–	1	2	13	8	7	3	–	–
Nova Scotia												
(Bay of Fundy)	–	–	–	–	–	–	1	3	–	–	–	–
(Gulf of St Lawrence)	–	–	–	–	–	–	–	–	1	–	–	–
(Atlantic)	–	–	–	–	1	2	13	7	4	2	–	–
Quebec	–	–	–	–	–	1	–	–	2	1	–	–
Maine	–	–	–	–	2	1	5	2	3	–	3	–
New Hampshire	–	–	–	–	–	–	–	–	–	–	1	–
Massachusetts	6	3	16	121	71	5	2	2	1	2	–	–
New York	–	2	4	1	–	1	–	2	2	1	–	2
New Jersey	–	1	–	1	1	1	3	1	–	–	–	1
Maryland/Delaware	–	–	–	–	2	–	–	–	–	–	1	–
Virginia	–	–	2	–	–	–	–	–	–	–	1	–
North Carolina	5	6	8	5	–	4	–	–	–	–	–	3
South Carolina	2	–	–	1	2	–	–	1	–	–	1	1
Georgia	4	5	7	–	–	–	–	–	–	1	2	3
Florida (Atlantic)	45	34	57	7	–	–	–	–	–	–	1	6
Gulf of Mexico												
Florida	–	–	1	–	–	–	–	–	–	–	–	–
Texas	1	–	–	–	–	–	–	–	–	–	–	–

occurred only in the summer months (May–October). The same also holds for northern New England (Maine–New Hampshire). Massachusetts has records for all months except November and December. The states that border the New York Bight (New York and New Jersey) have records for all months of the year except January. The southeastern states (North Carolina–Florida) have records in all months except the summer (July–October), with the exception of a single August sighting for South Carolina. Florida has the most striking seasonality with records only in the winter and early spring (November–April).

I am inclined to interpret this temporal distribution as representing a migratory population that wintered off the coast of the southeastern United States and summered north and east of Cape Cod. However, this does not account for the records from New York Bight or the records from Massachusetts. I therefore hypothesize that the New York Bight and Cape Cod happen to be so attractive to right whales that a portion of the population stays there year round.

Distribution of calf sightings

Another aspect for which one can consider using these data is the presence of calves as an indication of recent (within a few months) parturition, although several simplifying assumptions have to be made. The first, and most plausible, is that when an observer records that there was a calf present it really was a whale that was of a size that it would be considered 'young of the year' and not just a juvenile. I suspect that any animal that is less than half the length of an adult was classified a calf which would include animals up to about 8 or 9 m. Very little information is available on the growth of right whale calves. Omura, Ohsumi, Nemoto, Nasu and Kasuya (1969, p. 41) give an estimated length at birth of < 6 m, length at six months of 10 m and length at 1.5 years of 12 m. If their reasoning is correct then animals < 10 m are less than six months old and thereby it would be safe to classify them as calves. However it must be remembered that their data refer to the North Pacific, where the animals are generally considered larger than in the North Atlantic.

Calves are usually sighted with an adult. This gives a reasonable basis on which an observer can estimate the length of the calf relative to the adult, although this is seldom stated explicitly in the results of the work. There is a tendency to refer to these sightings as 'cow and calf pairs', but without additional behavioral information on the adult, I have eliminated any suppositions as to its sex and relationship to the calf and have treated these as 'adult and calf' sightings.

One can assume that there were calves present that were not seen or recorded by the observer. It is often difficult to judge a whale's length and calves that are not seen with an adult for size comparison may not be counted as calves. This means that the reported percentage of sightings of calves is less than the actual percentage of calves in those areas. This bias is presumably distributed randomly throughout the sample.

The frequency of adult and calf sightings is markedly greater for Florida than for any other area. There are $1\frac{1}{3}$ times as many adult/calf sightings as there are sightings of two or more animals in Florida. This ratio drops off to 1 in Georgia, the next highest state.

Table 3.

Sightings of right whales in the northwestern Atlantic broken down by number of individuals and whether a calf was present. Listed by locality. Categories are exclusive. Combined records of a number of sightings could not be plotted and so they were left out. The series of right whale sightings around Long Island, New York in 1974 and 1975 was also left out because it is suspected that those sightings were due to the activities of one or two whales that were seen consistently around inlets.

Location	Single	Multiple	Adult and calf	Calf only
Canada				
Newfoundland		2	1	–
Quebec	1	3	–	–
Nova Scotia				
(Bay of Fundy)	–	4	1	–
(Atlantic)	6	22	–	–
New Brunswick	–	1	–	–
Maine	7	7	–	–
New Hampshire	1	–	–	–
Massachusetts	81	116	26	–
New York	4	1	1	–
New Jersey	3	–	–	–
Maryland/Delaware	3	–	–	–
Virginia	2	1	–	–
North Carolina	12	13	4	–
South Carolina	3	1	2	–
Georgia	12	5	4	–
Florida	55	33	46	2
Gulf of Mexico				
Florida	–	1	–	–

Table 4.

Size distribution of stranded right whales along the northwestern coast of the Atlantic. * = size was an estimate.

Length (cm)	Date	State	Length (cm)	Date	State
407	1976 Jan 12	S. Carolina	1,100*	1954 Oct	Nova Scotia
439	1970 Jan 26	Florida	1,100*	1976 Nov 5	Maine
464	1981 Dec 30	Georgia	1,100*	1979 Mar 5	New York
457	1982 Feb 20	Georgia	1,200*	1971	New York
600*	1972 Jan 30	Texas	1,550	1979 Dec 10	Florida
760	1976 Apr 15	Massachusetts	1,800*	1900	S. Carolina

In spite of the small sample and the weakness of the assumptions, one still is struck by the preponderance of sightings of calves in Florida. It may well be that the waters off that state are a calving or nursery area. This adds credibility to Layne's (1965, p. 136) report from a lifeguard who claimed to have seen a right whale come within 200 ft (60 m) of shore and give birth near Vero Beach, Florida in 1961.

Size distribution of stranded animals

There are four records of strandings of small calves (Table 4). The smallest of these is 407 cm. The rounded average of their lengths is about 440 cm. These animals stranded in South Carolina, Georgia and Florida in the months of December through February. Again this is a small sample but it is consistent with a calving period in mid-winter and a calving ground off the southeastern United States. The mean length (442 cm) of the stranded calves is slightly less than that usually accepted as the length at birth for right whales (4.5–6 m, Omura et al. 1969). It also must be borne in mind that stranded animals may represent an abnormal portion of the population.

There is a mode in the length distribution of strandings at about 11 m. This represents individuals that are about one year old and that are presumably just going through the process of weaning. It may be that this period of stress in the animals' life history contributes to death at this length.

There are only two records of stranded adults (1,550; 1,800 cm; mean 1,675 cm); I believe the length of the larger is an estimate and could be a bit high. The largest well documented length of a northwestern Atlantic right whale was a 1,650 cm female that was captured in 1907.

SUMMARY

After inequalities in sighting and reporting effort have been taken into account, right whales seem to have a summertime concentration in the Bay of Fundy and adjacent waters and a broad wintertime concentration in the southern part of their range. There is a marked concentration of calves in Florida and adjacent waters, leading one to postulate that there may be a calving area nearby. The youngest recorded calf was 407 cm long and the remainder of the length data for calves suggest that the North Atlantic calves might be slightly shorter than the North Pacific calves. There are insufficient data to warrant a comparison of adult size with any other right whale population.

REFERENCES

Allen, G. M. 1916. The whalebone whales of New England. *Mem. Boston. Soc. Nat. Hist.* 8(2): 105–322, pls. 8–16.

Andrews, R. C. 1908. Notes upon the external and internal anatomy of *Balaena glacialis* Bonn. *Bull. Am. Mus. Nat. Hist.* 24(10): 171–82, 6 figures.

Andrews, R. C. 1909. Further notes on *Eubalaena glacialis* (Bonn.). *Bull. Am. Mus. Nat. Hist.* 26(21): 273–5, 5 pls.

Andrews, R. C. 1929. *Ends of the Earth.* National Travel Club, G. Putnam's Sons, New York, 355 pp.

Anonymous, 1976. Rare right whales sighted. *South Carolina Wildlife*, July–August 1976: 53.

Anonymous, 1977. Rare whale photographed near Beaufort. *South Carolina Wildlife*, March–April 1977: 47.

Arnold, P. W. and Gaskin, D. E. 1972. Sight records of right whales (*Eubalaena glacialis*) and finback whales (*Balaenoptera physalus*) from the lower Bay of Fundy. *J. Fish. Res. Bd Can.* 29: 1,477–8.

Beamish, P. 1981. Rare sighting of a right whale. *Ceta-Research* 2: 2.

Burghard, A. 1935. Whaling in Florida waters. *Florida Conservator* 1(10): 4–5, 12.

Caldwell, D. K. and Caldwell, M. C. 1971. Sounds produced by two rare cetaceans stranded in Florida. *Cetology* 4: 6 pp.

Caldwell, D. K. and Caldwell, M. C. 1974. Marine mammals from the southeastern United States coast: Cape Hatteras to Cape Canaveral. pp. 704–22 *In: A Socio-Economic Environmental Baseline Summary for the South Atlantic Region between Cape Hatteras, North Carolina and Cape Canaveral, Florida*. Volume 3. Virginia Inst. Mar. Sci., Gloucester Point, Virginia.

Connor, P. F. 1971. The mammals of Long Island, New York. *Bull. NY St. Mus.* 416: v+78 pp.

Corrick, G. W. 1977. Monster of the inlet. *Florida Sportsman*, September 1977, p. 92.

Edwards, E. J. and Rattray, J. E. 1932. *Whale Off. The Story of American Shore Whaling.* Frederick A. Stokes Co., NY (reprinted 1956, Coward-McCann Inc., NY) 285 pp.

Golley, F. B. 1966. *South Carolina Mammals.* Charleston Museum, Charleston, S.C. xiv+181 pp.

Kraus, S. D. and Prescott, J. H. 1983. A summary of 1982 research on the North Atlantic right whale *Eubalaena glacialis* with notes on seasonal distribution and abundance and significant resightings of individuals. Rept. No. NA-81-FA-C-00030, Natl. Mar. Fish. Serv., Woods Hole.

Layne, J. N. 1965. Observations on marine mammals in Florida waters. *Bull. Florida St. Mus.* 9(4): 131–81.

Mitchell, E. D. 1974. Canada, progress report on whale research, May 1972 to May 1973. *Rep. int. Whal. Commn* 24: 196–213.

Mitchell, E. D. and Reeves, R. R. 1983. Catch history, abundance and present status of Northwest Atlantic humpback whales. *Rep. int. Whal. Commn (special issue 5)*: 153–212.

Moore, J. C. 1953. Distribution of marine mammals to Florida waters. *Am. Midl. Nat.* 49(1): 117–58.

Moore, J. C. and Clark, E. 1963. Discovery of right whales in the Gulf of Mexico. *Science* 141(3577): 269.

Neave, D. J. and Wright, B. S. 1968. Seasonal records of the harbor porpoise (*Phocoena phocoena*) and other cetacea in the Bay of Fundy. *J. Mammal.* 49(2): 259–64.

Norton, A. H. 1930. Mammals of Portland, Maine and vicinity. *Proc. Portland Soc. Nat. Hist.* 4(1): 1–151, 1 map.

Omura, H., Ohsumi, S., Nemoto, T., Nasu, K. and Kasuya, T. 1969. Black right whales in the North Pacific. *Sci. Rep. Whales Res. Inst., Tokyo* 21: 1–78, 18 pls.

Payne, R. S. and McVay, S. 1971. Songs of humpback whales. *Science* 173: 587–97.

Reeves, R. R. 1975. The right whale. *The Conservationist* 30(1): 32–3, 45.

Reeves, R. R. 1976. New Jersey's great whales. *N.J. Audobon* 2(1): 7–14.

Reeves, R. R., Mead, J. G. and Katona, S. 1978. The right whale, *Eubalaena glacialis*, in the western North Atlantic. *Rep. int. Whal. Commn* 28: 303–12.

Reeves, R. R. and Mitchell, E. 1986. The Long Island, New York, right whale fishery: 1650–1924. (Published in this volume.)

Schmidly, D. J., Martin, C. O. and Collins, G. F. 1972. First occurrence of a black right whale (*Balaena glacialis*) along the Texas coast. *Southwest. Nat.* 17(2): 214–15.

Schevill, W. E. 1968. Sight records of *Phocoena phocoena* and of cetaceans in general. *J. Mammal.* 49(4): 794–5.

Schevill, W. E., Moore, K. E. and Watkins, W. A. 1981. Right whale, *Eubalaena glacialis*, sightings in Cape Cod waters. Tech. Rep. Woods Hole Oceanogr. Instn WHOI–81-50, 16 pp.

Sears, R. 1979. An occurrence of right whales (*Eubalaena glacialis*) on the north shore of the Gulf of St. Lawrence. *Nat. Can.* 106: 567–8.

Sergeant, D. E. 1966. Populations of large whale species in the western North Atlantic with special reference to the fin whale. Fish. Res. Bd. Canada, Arctic Biol. Sta. Circ. No. 9. 13 pp. 9 tables, 9 figs.

Sergeant, D. E., Mansfield, A. W. and Beck, B. 1970. Inshore records of cetacea for eastern Canada, 1949–68. *J. Fish. Res. Bd Can.* 27: 1,903–15.

Slijper, E. J., van Utrecht, W. L. and Naaktgeboren, C. 1964. Remarks on the distribution and migration of whales based on observations from Netherlands ships. *Bijdr. Dierkd.* 34: 1–93.

Stick, D. 1958. *The Outer Banks of North Carolina* 1584–1958. Univ. No. Caro. Press, Chapel Hill, NC, xii+352 pp.

Sutcliffe, W. H. Jr and Brodie, P. F. 1977. Whale distributions in Nova Scotia waters. *Tech. Rep. Fish. Mar. Serv. (Can.)*, No. 722, vi+83 pp.

Watkins, W. A. and Schevill, W. E. 1972. Sound source location by arrival-times on a non-rigid three-dimensional hydrophone array. *Deep-Sea Research* 19: 691–706.

Winn, H. E. 1982. A characterization of the marine mammals and turtles in the mid- and north Atlantic areas of the US Outer Continental Shelf. Final Report, Contract number AA551-CT8-48, United States Bureau of Land Management. (10)+450+(126) pp.

Winn, H. E. 1984. Development of a right whale sighting network in the southeastern US. Report no. MMC-82/05 for the US Marine Mammal Commission, National Technical Information Service PB84-240548, v+12 pp.

Appendix 1

PUBLISHED RECORDS OF RIGHT WHALES IN THE NORTHWESTERN ATLANTIC SINCE 1900, ARRANGED CHRONOLOGICALLY

Date	Locality	Type of incident	Source	Remarks
1900 May 4	Myrtle Beach, SC	Stranding	Golley (1966:135)	Vertebra in the Charleston Museum, sixty foot (1,800cm).
1907 Feb 22	Amagansett, NY	Capture	Andrews 1908:17	[1]Two right whales. 1,650cm female (AMNH 42752), 1,230cm calf (BM(NH)) (Andrews, 1929:18)
1908 Dec 10	Amagansett, NY	Capture	Andrews,1909:273	848cm calf.
1909	Cape Lookout, NC	Capture	Stick,1958:194	Last one taken at Cape Lookout.
1909 Jan 15	Provincetown, MA	Incidental catch	Allen,1916:140	34ft 9inch female (1,060cm) entangled in a fish-trap.
1910	Provincetown, MA	Sighting	Allen (1916:140)	Spring of 1910.
1911 Apr	Amagansett, NY	Sighting	Edwards and Rattray,1932:158	Unsuccessful capture attempt. One whale.
1912	Sept-Iles, Quebec	Capture	Mitchell and Reeves,1983:171	140 barrel whale.
1913 May 24	Muskeget Island, MA	Sighting	Allen,1916:140	Two whales.
1918	Napateague, NY	Capture	Edwards and Rattray,1932:161	Summer of 1918.
1919	West Southport, ME	Stranding	Norton,1930:88	Sheepscot Bay at Jones Island, Summer of 1919.
1935 Mar 25	Pompano, FL	Capture	Burghard,1935	Off Hillsborough lighthouse. Moore (1953:122) commented on length. My estimate is 8m.
1950 Mar	Flagler Beach, FL	Sighting	Moore,1953:122	Two adults and a half grown calf.
1950 Mar 6	Daytona Beach, FL	Sighting	Moore,1953:122	An adult and calf.
1951 Sep	Trinity Bay, NFLD	Capture	Sergeant,1966:10	International Whaling Statistics (Number 29, page 30).
1954 May	Off Newfoundland	Sighting	Slijper et al.,1964:37	Twelve right whales.
1954 Oct	Pugwash, NS	Stranding	Sergeant,1966:10	11–12m. Sergeant, Mansfield and Beck, 1970:1905.
1959 Jul	Dildo Arm, NFLD	Sighting	Sergeant,1966:10	Probable right whale.
1960 Jun 8	Shinnecock, NY	Sighting	Connor,1971:48	
1963 Mar 10	Sarasota, FL	Sighting	Moore and Clark,1963	[2]Two right whales, lengths estimated at 12 and 17m.
1965	East Hampton, NY	Stranding	Connor,1971:48	Summer of 1965. Skull in E. Hampton Town Marine Museum.
1965 May	Off Blandford, NS	Sighting	Sergeant,1966:10	
1965 May 13	Wellfleet, MA	Stranding?	Schevill et al.,1981:12	Whale 'dying' 43 miles east of Wellfleet.
1966 Aug	Bay of Fundy, NS	Sighting	Neave and Wright,1968:261	15 right whales sighted from ferries connecting Yarmouth, NS and Bar Harbour, ME.
1970 Jan 26	Neptune Beach, FL	Stranding	Caldwell and Caldwell,1971	439cm female.
1970 Apr 13	Cape Cod Bay, MA	Sighting	Schevill et al.,1981:13	More than 70 individuals in three groups between Race Point and Manomet, Massachusetts.
1970 Apr 13	Bermuda	Sighting	Payne and McVay,1971:596	Pair of right whales 25 miles southwest of Bermuda.
1970 May	Cape Cod Bay, MA	Sighting	Watkins and Schevill,1972:702	'About 20' right whales.
1971 Aug	Passamaquoddy Bay, NB	Sighting	Arnold and Gaskin,1972:1,477	Several right whales. 22nd and 31st of August.
1971	Atlantic Beach, NY	Stranding	Reeves,1976:13	[3]Summer or fall of 1971.
1972 Jan 30	Freeport, TX	Stranding	Schmidly, Martin and Collins,(1972)	[4]Anterior half of whale.
1972 Mar 18	Savannah, GA	Sighting	Caldwell and Caldwell,1974	Two right whales off Savannah.
1976 May	North Edisto R., SC	Sighting	Anon,1976	11m adult and 8.5m calf.
1976 Sep 13	Moisie Bay, Quebec	Sighting	Sears,1979	3–4 whales.
1976 Nov 19	Trenchard's Inlet, SC	Sighting	Anon,1977	2 whales, estimated 35 feet long.
1976 Dec 24	St. Augustine Inlet, FL	Sighting	Corrick,1977	40–50 feet long.
1981 Aug 31	Newmans Cove, NFLD	Sighting	Beamish,1981	

[1] This appears to be the largest northwest Atlantic specimen with a well documented total length.
[2] First record of this species in the Gulf of Mexico.
[3] By comparison with figures of people in photograph, I would estimate it was more than 40 feet (12m) long.
[4] They estimated the total length of the whale at 35–40 feet (11–12m). In comparison to other stranded specimens I estimated that the total length was about 6m (Reeves *et al.*, 1978: 303).

Appendix 1A. Multiple published reports

Layne (1965, p. 134) published several records of right whale sightings during the 1950s and 60s. These were principally derived from the files of Marineland in St Augustine, Florida and represent sightings along the northeast coast of that state. They are given in Table a.

Table a.

Date	n	Locality	Date	n	Locality
1953 01 07	A+C	Flagler Beach	1959 01 20	A	St Augustine
1954 02 09	A+C	Summer Haven	1962 02 22	A?	S Pt Vedra Be
1957 03 15	30'C	St Augustine	1962 01 30	A	Flagler Beach
1957 03 15	2 A	Crescent Beach	1962 02 01	A+C	St Augustine
1957 03 25	2	St Augustine	1962 03 13	A+C	Canova Beach
Records of whales that appeared to be right whales					
1962 03 –	1 or 2	Flagler Beach	1963 01 23	1	Vero Beach
1963 01 10	30–40'	Daytona Beach	1963 02 05	1	Jupiter Inlet

Layne (1965, p. 136) also devotes much verbiage to the possibility of right whales breeding in Florida waters but offers no conclusive proof.

Mitchell (1974) reports tagging of right whales in Nova Scotian waters. Two were tagged on the research cruise of the MV *William S* in July–October 1966, 4 were tagged by the gunner on the whaling catcher MV *Chester* in June–November 1968 and 2 were tagged by the gunner on the whaling catcher MV *Thorarinn* in May–November 1971.

In the summer of 1974 there were various reports of a right whale along the shores of the New York Bight from Manasquan, New Jersey to the middle of Long Island, New York. Reeves (1975) hypothesised that these sightings were the result of the activities of a single animal. I was able to get some relatively poor quality 16 mm motion picture film from the air off Moriches Inlet, New York on 20 August 1974. Length estimates of the animal centered around 35 feet (11 m). Late in the summer of 1975 right whale reports again began to come in from Long Island. I was finally able to get good photographs of a sighting off Fire Island, New York on 15 August 1975. After comparing callosity patterns, this appeared to be the same individual that I had filmed from the air on 20 August 1974. Sightings of a single small right whale along the New York Bight for 1974 and 1975 are given in Table b. In 1974 I only have indications that there was one animal involved but in 1975 I have photographs of two individuals.

Table b.

Date	Locality	Date	Locality
1974 05	Raritan Bay, NJ	1974 09 15	Shinnecock In., NY
1974 07	Manasquan, NJ	1974 09 mid	Moriches Inlet, NY
1974 08 2nd wk	Long Beach, NY	1974 09 mid	Smith Point, NY
1974 08 18–20	Moriches In., NY	1974 09 22–3	Fire Island, NY
1974 08 22	Shinnecock In., NY	1974 09 30	Shinnecock In., NY
1974 08 23	Shinnecock In., NY	1974 10 1	Gilgo Beach, NY
1974 08 27	East Hampton, NY	1974 10 14	Cedar Beach, NY
1974 08 27	Shinnecock In., NY	1974 10 17	Tobay Beach, NY
1974 08 30	East Quogue, NY	1974 12	Georgica Pond, NY
1974 08 30	Shinnecock In., NY	1975 02	Mecox In., NY
1974 09 01	Shinnecock In., NY	1975 08 15	Fire Island, NY
1974 09 03	Shinnecock In., NY	1975 09 05	Rockaway, NY

Sutcliffe and Brodie (1977) reported on sightings that were made by whaling crews operating out of Blandford, Nova Scotia during the years 1966 to 1972. The data on right whales are given in Table c.

Table c.

Date	n	N	W	Date	n	N	W
1967 06 27	1	43°40'	62 51'	1969 07 04	4	43°17'	63 17'
1967 06 30	1	43°02'	65 04'	1969 07 06	7	43°20'	63 10'
1967 07 14	10	42°44'	63 34'	1969 07 07	6	43°18'	63 12'
1967 08 08	8	43°25'	63 01'	1969 07 08	4	43°02'	63 12'
1967 08 09	6	43°14'	63 00'	1969 07 21	2	42°57'	62 07'
1967 08 22	4	43°50'	61 54'	1969 07 21	4	43°04'	62 17'
1967 08 23	4	43°54'	62 10'	1969 07 22	6	43°07'	62 17'
1967 08 24	2	43°30'	62 08'	1969 07 24	8	43°50'	64 57'
1968 09 22	1	43°02'	65 31'	1969 07 28	10	43°09'	62 45'
1968 09 24	1	42°50'	65 36'	1969 07 29	6	43°02'	62 45'
1968 09 29	4	43°06'	65 10'	1969 07 31	2	42°55'	62 50'
1968 10 04	8	42°48'	65 27'	1969 08 24	1	43°03'	64 57'
1968 10 25	2	43°20'	65 00'	1969 09 07	1	42°47'	63 20'
1969 07 03	4	43°09'	63 22'				

Reeves, Mead and Katona (1978) presented data on a number of sightings from New England and the Maritime provinces of Canada for the years 1973–77. These are summarized in Table d. Sears (1979) reported 3–4 adult right whales sighted off Moisie Bay, Quebec, during the 13–16 September 1976.

Schevill, Moore and Watkins (1981) give a total of 758 individual right whales seen in 149 days between 1955 and 1980. They present tabularized data giving date, location, number of animals seen, presence of calves and behavioral notes for all sightings. There were 75 sightings of single animals, 115 sightings of multiple individuals and 26 sightings of adults and calves for a total of 216 sightings.

Table d.

Date	n	Locality	Date	n	Locality
1976 09 13	3–4	Q–Matamek	1976 07 05	1	Ma–Mt Desert Rock
1973 09 13	8	NS–Cape Sable	1977 07 06	A+C	Ma–Mt Desert Rock
1973 09 14	3	NS–Cape Sable	1977 08 15	2	Ma–Mt Desert Rock
1976 09 17	A+C	NS–Cape St. Mary	1976 09 24	1	Ma–Narragaugus B.
1976 08 05	A+C	NB–Grand Manan Is	1976 07 28	4	Ma–Platts Bank
1976 06 01	2	Ma–Bay of Fundy	1976 11 13	1	NH–Old Scantum Ledge
1976 09 09	1–2	Ma–Burnt Island			
1975 05 01	1	Ma–Jeffrey's Ledge	1975 05 08	9	Mass–Cape Ann
1975 11 09	2	Ma–Jeffrey's Ledge	1976 04 15	1	Mass–Cape Ann
1976 07 01	3	Ma–Jeffrey's Ledge	1976 04 30	1	Mass–Cape Ann
1976 08 20	7	Ma–Jeffrey's Ledge	1977 05 04	1	Mass–George's Bank
1976 05 09	1	Ma–Matinicus Rock	1976 05 05	1	Mass–George's Bank
1973 07 12	1	Ma–Mt Desert Rock	1975 04 29	1	Mass–Gloucester

Winn (1984, Table 1) published a series of records of right whale sightings from Florida to North Carolina. These were largely derived from the files of David and Melba Caldwell and Marineland of Florida in St Augustine. These are summarised in Table e.

[Table e is overleaf]

Table e.

Date	n	Locality	Date	n	Locality	Date	n	Locality
Florida								
1950 03 07	A+C	Marineland	1974 01 22	A+C	Ormond Beach	1982 01 25	A	Crescent Beach
1962 02 03	A+C	Flagler Beach	1974 02 02	2	Fernandina Beach	1982 02 10	A	Flagler Beach
1962 02 22	A+C	Marineland	1974 02 26	2	Marineland	1982 02 15	A	Flagler Beach
1962 03 19	1+	Flagler Beach	1974 03 12	A+C	Crescent Beach	1982 02 16	A	Ormond Beach
1963 01 24	1	Vero Beach	1974 11 –	A+C	Matanzas Inlet	1982 02 17	A	St Augustine Beach
1965 01 15	2A	Marineland	1974 12 –	1 or 2	Matanzas Inlet	1982 02 18	A	St Augustine Beach
1966 03 13	A+C	Marineland	1976 01 11	A	Marineland	1982 02 18	A+C	Ponce Inlet
1966 03 14	A	Flagler Beach	1976 01 13	A+C	Summer Haven	1982 02 20	A+C	St Lucie
1966 03 20	A	St Augustine North Beach	1976 01 13	A+C	St Augustine	1982 02 23	A+C	St Augustine Inlet
1966 03 21	2A	St Augustine Beach	1976 01 17	A	Flagler Beach			(5 miles N. of)
1966 03 21	2A	St Augustine North Beach	1976 01 21	A+C	Jacksonville Beach	1982 02 23	A	Melbourne
1966 04 04	A	St Augustine Beach	1976 01 24	A	Daytona Beach	1982 03 04	A+C	Matanzas Inlet
1967 01 25	A	Marineland	1976 02 06	A	Flagler Beach	1982 03 12	A+C	Ponte Vedra
1966 02 23	A	Crescent Beach	1978 02 28	A+C	Ormond Beach	1982 03 14	A	New Smyrna Inlet
1968 03 30	A+C	Daytona Beach	1978 03 13	A	Marineland	1982 04 –	A	Merritt Island
1969 02 12	A+C?	Jacksonville Beach	1978 03 15	A+C	Flagler Beach	1982 12 21	A+C	Ormond Beach
1970 01 14	A+C	Jupiter Inlet	1979 03 18	A	Ormond Beach	1983 01 04	A+C	Jacksonville Beach
1970 01 26	Calf	Jacksonville Beach	1979 02 08	A	Daytona Beach	1983 01 02	A	Amelia Island
1970 03 20	2	Marineland	1979 02 11	A	St Augustine Beach	1983 01 –	A	Vilano Beach
1970 03 30	A+C	Daytona Beach	1979 02 12	A+C	Palm Coast	1983 01 –	A	Fernandina Beach
1971 03 04	2	Flagler Beach	1979 02 12	A	Ormond Beach	1983 01 29	A+C	Melbourne Beach
1971 03 05	2	Flagler Beach	1979 02 14	A+C	Crescent Beach	1983 01 30	A+C	Titusville
1971 03 09	2	Marineland	1979 02 20	A+C	Marineland	1983 02 25	A+C	Ormond Beach
1971 03 11	2	Ponte Vedra	1980 02 12	A	Crescent Beach	1983 03 02	A	Marineland
1971 03 17	2	Marineland	1980 03 11	A+C	Marineland	1983 03 03	2A	Marineland
1972 01 10	2	South Ponte Vedra	1981 02 25	A+C	Ponte Vedra	1983 03 04	A+C	Marineland
1972 03 02	2	Marineland	1981 04 01	A+C	Sebastian Inlet	1983 02 25	A+C	Ormond Beach
1972 03 04	2	Flagler Beach	1981 12 12	A	St Augustine	1983 03 02	A	Marineland
1973 03 14	A+C	Daytona Beach	1981 12 24	A	Ormond Beach	1983 03 03	A+C	Marineland
1973 03 28	2	Marineland	1982 01 07	A	St Augustine Beach	1983 03 04	A+C	Marineland
1974 01 11	2	Flagler Beach	1982 01 08	A	Jacksonville Beach	1983 03 04	A+C	St Augustine Inlet
1974 01 12	2	Marineland	1982 01 20	A	Flagler/Volusia co. line	1983 03 15	A+C?	Ormond Beach
1974 01 12	2	Summer Haven	1982 01 20	A	St Augustine Beach	1983 03 18	A+C?	Vilano Beach
1974 01 21	2	Flagler Beach	1982 01 25	A	St Augustine Inlet	1983 03 23	A+C?	Neptune Beach
Florida – possible right whales								
1957 03 25	1	Ponte Vedra	1973 04 12	2	Ponte Vedra	1974 03 01	2	Ponte Vedra
1966 01 27	2A+2C	Marineland	1974 01 17	A	Vilano Beach	1974 03 01	2	Vilano Beach
1970 03 03	A+C	Titusville	1974 01 19	A	Vilano Beach	1974 03 09	A	Jacksonville Beach
1970 04 29	2	Ponte Vedra	1974 01 20	A	Vilano Beach	1977 03 02	A	Flagler Beach
1971 03 02	2	Ormond Beach	1974 01 22	A+C	Vilano Beach	1977 03 02	A	West Palm Beach
1973 04 02	2	Flagler Beach	1974 02 28	2	Vilano Beach			
Georgia								
1977 03 02	A+C	Savannah	1983 01 –	2A	Cumberland Island	1982 12 –	A	St Simons Island
South Carolina								
1981 12 –	A	Charleston Harbor	1983 04 01	A+C	Cape Romaine	1983 01 –	2A	Cumberland Island
North Carolina								
1979 06 10	3A	35°54'N, 75°38'W	1982 04 13	A	34°42'N, 76°40'W	1983 03 09	2A	Cape Lookout Shoals
1979 06 10	3A	36°48'N, 75°46'W	1983 02 21	5–19A	Masonborough Inlet	1983 03 20	A	Hatteras Inlet
1980 03 12	3A	36°01'N, 75°42'W	1983 02 21	A	Wrightsville Beach	1983 03 29	A	Cape Lookout Light
1980 03 17	10A	35°12'N, 75°42'W	1983 02 22	A	Bogue Inlet Pier			(5 miles N. of)
1981 06 10	3A	34°41'N, 77°20'W	1983 02 23	A+C	Masonborough Inlet	1983 04 13	A	Beaufort Inlet
1982 03 22	2A	34°41'N, 77°20'W						
Virginia						**Virginia – possible right whale**		
1979 03 29	A	36 45'N, 74 48'W	1979 11 14	2A	37 02'N, 75 35'W	1979 03 20	A	37 27'N, 75 15'W

Appendix 2

UNPUBLISHED REPORTS, ARRANGED CHRONOLOGICALLY

Those reports with SEAN in the sources column represent records that were reported to the Scientific Event Alert Network and presented in its monthly bulletin. Those with an MME number represent records that have been reported to the Marine Mammal Events Program at the Smithsonian Institution. USNM = United States National Museum, AMNH = American Museum of Natural History, MCZ = Museum of Comparative Zoology. In Appendix 2a, SE = serial numbers of the Southeast Regional Stranding Network (SRSN) University of Miami.

Table (Appendix 2)

Date	Locality	Type of incident	Source	Remarks
1937 Sep	Cape Race, NFLD	Capture	USNM files	1,130cm female.
1950	Gilgo Beach, NY	Stranding	AMNH 169829	Bulla.
1961 Jun	Hummock Pond, MA	Stranding	MCZ files	Early June.
1970 Jun	Cape Hatteras, NC	Sighting	Lyons, pers comm.	One whale.
1974 Jan 12	Edingsville Beach, SC	Stranding	USNM 500860	407cm male.
1975 May 11	Monomoy Is, MA	Stranding	USNM 504257	1,030cm male.
1975 Jun 17	Great Island, MA	Stranding	Same individual as above	
1976 Jan 29	Melbourne, FL	Sighting	SEAN 1034	Adult and calf.
1976 Apr 15	Wellfleet, MA	Stranding	USNM 504343, SEAN 1082	760cm male.
1976 May 12	Ocean City, MD	Sighting	SEAN 1100	9m.
1976 May 17	Rehoboth Beach, DE	Sighting	SEAN 1101	Same individual as SEAN 1100?
1976 Jun 20	New Jersey coast	Sighting	SEAN 1121	1 or more whales.
1976 Jul 1	Long Branch, NJ	Incidental catch	SEAN 1132	9m, entangled in lobster pot lines.
1976 Jul 20	Manasquan Inlet, NJ	Sighting	SEAN 1133	9m.
1976 Aug 21	Ship Island, NJ	Sighting	SEAN 1154	Same individual as SEAN 1133?
1976 Aug 25	Wellfleet, MA	Incidental catch	SEAN 1156	11m est. entangled in netting.
1976 Sep 16	Trinity Ledge, NS	Sighting	SEAN 1172	Adult and calf.
1976 Sep 24	Narraguagus Bay, ME	Sighting	SEAN 1173	One whale.
1976 Sep 27	Lanesville, MA	Sighting	SEAN 1174	6m+.
1976 Oct 3	Provincetown, MA	Sighting	SEAN 1196	At least two whales.
1976 Nov 5	Portland, ME	Stranding	SEAN 1226	11m.
1976 Nov 6	Ocean City, MD	Sighting	SEAN 1211	6+m.
1976 Nov 13	Old Scantum, ME	Sighting	SEAN 1212	One whale.
1977 Mar 2	Jacksonville Beach, FL	Sighting	SEAN 2119	Adult and calf.
1977 Apr 7	Ocracoke Inlet, NC	Sighting	SEAN 2207	Adult and calf.
1977 Apr 29	Vilano Beach, FL	Sighting	SEAN 2208	Adult and calf.
1978 Apr 5	Cape Hatteras, NC	Sighting	SEAN 3136	15m.
1978 Jun 16	Sesuit Harbor, MA	Incidental catch	SEAN 3264	12m. Gill net.
1978 Dec 2	Barnegat Light, NJ	Sighting	SEAN 3484	2+ whales.
1979 Jan 9	Hatteras Island, NC	Sighting	SEAN 4004	12-13m.
1979 Jan 11	Lookout Shoals, NC	Sighting	SEAN 1886	Two whales.
1979 Feb	Outer Banks, NC	Sighting	SEAN 1887	Two whales.
1979 Feb 28	Jekyll Island, GA	Sighting	SEAN 4095	Adult and calf.
1979 Mar 5	Wainscott, NY	Stranding	USNM 504886, SEAN 4096	Estimated length 11m.
1979 Oct 11	Cape Sable, NS	Sighting	SEAN 4395	One whale.
1979 Dec 10	Atlantic Beach, FL	Stranding	SEAN 4441	1,550cm female.
1980 Dec	Atlantic Beach, NC	Sighting	SEAN 1890	One whale.
1980 Dec 6	Wrightsville Beach, NC	Sighting	SEAN 1888	11m.
1980 Dec 28	Cape Lookout, NC	Sighting	SEAN 1889	Adult and calf.
1981 Jan 15	Wrightsville Beach, NC	Sighting	SEAN 1891	Two whales.
1981 Jan 19	Fort Macon, NC	Sighting	SEAN 1892	Two whales.
1981 Jan 22	Cape Lookout, NC	Sighting	SEAN 1893	Two whales.
1981 Jun 20	Wolf Bay, Quebec	Sighting	USNM files	Sears, Williamson and Wenzel. 3 right whales.
1981 Oct 6	Sheldrake, Quebec	Sighting	USNM files	Sears, Williamson and Wenzel. 1 whale.
1981 Nov 21	North Cumberland Is, GA	Sighting	SEAN 6902	One whale.
1981 Nov 25	Sapelo Island, GA	Sighting	SEAN 6912	2-5 large whales.
1981 Dec 28	Sapelo live bottom bouy, GA	Sighting	SEAN 7131	One whale. 15m.
1981 Dec 30	Little St Simons Is, GA	Stranding	SEAN 6973	464cm male calf.
1982 Jan 21	Blackbeard Island, GA	Sighting	SEAN 7132	15m.
1982 Jan 25	Brevard, FL	Sighting	SEAN 7070	Adult and calf.
1982 Feb 2	Vero Beach, FL	Sighting	SEAN 7164	19m.
1982 Feb 18	Jupiter, FL	Sighting	SEAN 7130	Adult and calf.
1982 Feb 20	Ossabaw Is, GA	Stranding	SEAN 7133	457cm female calf.
1982 Feb 25	Cumberland Island, GA	Sighting	SEAN 7134	10m.
1982 Mar 3	Jupiter, FL	Incidental catch	SEAN 7165	11m gill net.
1982 Mar 7	Cape Lookout, NC	Sighting	SEAN 7169	Adult (11m) and calf (7m).
1982 Mar 14	Cumberland Island, GA	Sighting	SEAN 7166	Adult (18m) and calf (9m).
1982 Mar 22	Atlantic, NC	Sighting	SEAN 7169A	Adult and calf.
1982 Mar 2	S. Point State Pk, NY	Sighting	SEAN 7170	Two whales (16 and 13m).
1982 Apr 19	Cape May, NJ	Stranding	MME00496	Floating carcass.
1983 Jan 14	Lake Worth Inlet, FL	Sighting	MME00463	10m.
1983 Jan 25	Pompano Beach, FL	Sighting	MME00464	One whale.
1983 Jan 26	Satellite Beach, FL	Sighting	MME00150	9m.
1983 Feb 3	Is Beach State Pk, NJ	Stranding	MME00084	11m male.
1983 Mar 4	Shinnecock Inlet, NY	Sighting	MME00085	12m.
1983 Mar 6	Montauk, NY	Sighting	MME00084	One whale.
1983 Apr 5	Wrightsville Beach, NC	Incidental catch	MME00146	7.5m gill net.
1983 Aug 18	Charleston, SC	Sighting	MME00247	15m.
1983 Oct 1	Jekyll Island, GA	Sighting	MME00351	13.5m.
1984 Jan 8	Gray's Reef, GA	Sighting	MME00529	Large whale.
1984 Jan 18	Cape Canaveral, FL	Sighting	MME00579	12m.
1984 Feb 17	St. Simons Is, GA	Sighting	MME00575	One whale.
1984 Feb 19	Cumberland Is, GA	Sighting	MME00576	12m.
1984 Mar 5	St. Simons Is, GA	Sighting	MME00581	11m.
1984 Mar 6	Fernandina Beach, FL	Sighting	MME00580	Two adults and one calf.
1984 Mar 11	Cumberland Is, GA	Sighting	MME00582	2 whales.
1984 Mar 11	Ponte Vedra, FL	Sighting	MME00583	Adult and calf.
1984 Mar 23	Jekyll Island, GA	Sighting	MME00620	Adult and calf.
1984 Mar 26	Cumberland Is, GA	Sighting	MME00621	Two whales.
1984 Dec 1	Cape Lookout, NC	Sighting	MME00970	One whale.

Appendix 2A. Details of unpublished reports

1937. Sept. Capture. The files of the Division of Mammals, USNM, have a photograph of a 37 ft (1,130 cm) female right whale that was taken by the catcher boat *Morelos* 14 miles southeast of Cape Race, Newfoundland.

1950. Stranding. The collections of the American Museum in New York city have a left auditory bulla of a stranded right whale that was picked up at Gilgo Beach, Long Island in 1950. The museum records give A. S. Westerfeld as the collector but do not give an exact date, length or sex.

1961. Early June. Stranding. A right whale was reported stranded west of Hummock Pond, Nantucket Island, Massachusetts (*Nantucket Inquirer and Mirror*, 9 June 1961). No further details were given but a sample of the baleen was collected for the MCZ at Harvard University.

1970. June. Sighting. Jim Lyons, a resident of Buxton, North Carolina, told me (pers. comm. 22 January 1978) of seeing a large whale off Cape Hatteras in the Gulf Stream in June of 1970. He described the callosities and the pronounced arching of the mouth line that is typical of right whales. He was, however, unable to give an estimate of the total length of the whale.

1974. 12 Jan. Stranding. A 407 cm male was found in a state of advanced decomposition on Edingsville Beach, Edisto Island, South Carolina. It was not ascertained whether the calf was a still or live birth. At such a small size there exists the possibility that this represents an aborted near-term fetus. The skull was collected for the USNM and cataloged as 500860.

1975. 11 May. Stranding. The coast guard reported a dead whale adrift 5 km south-southeast of the south end of Monomoy Island, Massachusetts. They towed it ashore on that island and graciously took William Schevill, Joseph Geraci, myself and a crew from the New England Aquarium out to investigate it. It turned out to be a 1,030 cm male that was in an extremely advanced state of decomposition. The carcass was left on the island in hopes that it would stay there. A piece of baleen was collected for the USNM and was cataloged as 504257. This stranding was also mentioned in Schevill *et al.* (1981, p. 14).

1975. 17 June. Stranding. The Smithsonian received a call from Richard Whittaker (NMFS, New Bedford) that there was a report of a very large, very dead whale ashore on Great Island, near Yarmouth, Massachusetts. We went up to investigate and it turned out to be the same individual that had stranded on Monomoy Island the month before.

1976. 29 Jan. Sighting. The US Fish and Wildlife Service laboratory in Gainesville, Florida reported a sighting of a right whale that they estimated to be 50–60 ft long (15–18 m) and a calf which they estimated was one third the length of the adult (5–6 m). They were seen swimming north just outside the surf line. Reports of what were presumably the same individuals continued for about 1 week. The sightings occurred south of Melbourne, Florida. (SEAN 1034)

1976. 15 April. Stranding. The New England Aquarium received a call that a right whale was washed up at Duck Harbor, Wellfleet, Massachusetts. They dispatched a crew to investigate the following day. The whale turned out to be a 760 cm male in moderately fresh condition. There were no signs of external damage and no evidence of broken bones. This was almost certainly the same whale that was reported adrift off Race Point, Massachusetts on 14 April. Baleen and photographs were deposited in the USNM and cataloged as 504343. This stranding was mentioned in Schevill *et al.* (1981, p. 15).

1976. 12 May. Sighting. The Smithsonian received a call that a large whale was apparently dying in the surf at Ocean City, Maryland. We went out there and searched for the animal until dark with no luck. Just after dark we spotted the whale and could see enough of it in the moonlight to identify it as a right whale and estimate its length at about 30 ft (9 m). (SEAN 1100).

1976. 17 May. Sighting. A right whale was sighted off Rehoboth Beach, Delaware. No photographs were taken and no length estimate was made. It could well have been the same animal that was seen five days earlier off Ocean City, Maryland, about 30 miles to the south. (SEAN 1101)

1976. 20–24 June. Sighting. They were several reports received in the offices of SEAN at the Smithsonian concerning right whales along the New Jersey coast between Asbury Park and Ocean City. Some reports stated that the animal had a gash in its blubber on its back. Apparently this gash was large enough to cause the reporting sources to be concerned about whether that animal was in mortal danger. Some reports did not mention this gash and there exists the possibility that more than one whale was involved. (SEAN 1121)

1976. 1 July. Incidental catch. A right whale was reported entangled in lobster pot lines about one mile east of the fishing pier at Long Branch, New Jersey. Divers managed to free it from the lines and it swam off. The next day a right whale (presumably the same individual) was found entangled in the same type of gear about three miles east of Long Branch. Divers again freed the animal from the gear and it was not subsequently heard from. The estimated length was 9 m. (SEAN 1132)

1976. 20–22 July. Sighting. I received a letter from Frederick Ulmer notifying me that a whale had been sighted in the vicinity of Manasquan Inlet, New Jersey and appeared to be entangled in a ¾-inch rope. It was reported to be anywhere from 25 to 40 ft in length. He spoke with a coast guardsman who had seen the whale the evening before and had estimated its total length at 30 ft (9 m) and who felt the 'rope' could have been a long gash in the animal's side exposing the white blubber. This may have been the same whale that was seen along the New Jersey coast a month before. This animal was last seen on 22 July below Point Pleasant, New Jersey heading out to sea. (SEAN 1133)

1976. 21 Aug. Sighting. A report was received in the SEAN office that a right whale had been seen around Ship Island, New Jersey. This was an animal about 30 ft (9 m) long and had two fresh gashes in its side. The similarity of this to the previous New Jersey reports leads me to believe it might be the same individual. (SEAN 1154)

1976. 25 Aug. Incidental catch. A fishing boat reported seeing a right whale 30–40 ft long (11 m est.) with netting and lines entangled about its head in the vicinity of Buoy 8, Wellfleet, Massachusetts. Later in the same day a right whale was reportedly seen off Brewster and it was presumed to have been the same individual. On the 26th a search was made for it by the coast guard but it could not be found. (SEAN 1156)

1976. 16 Sept. Sighting. The Canadian Wildlife Service (Bedford Institute of Oceanography, Dartmouth, Nova Scotia) reported sighting an adult and a calf just north of Trinity Ledge, Bay of Fundy, Nova Scotia (44° 2′ N, 66° 19′ W). They estimated the length of the adult at 30 ft (9 m) and said that the calf was somewhat smaller. (SEAN 1172)

1976. 24 Sept. Sighting. A member of the Maine Coast Whale Sighting Network (MCWSN) organized by the College of the Atlantic reported sighting a right whale in Narraguagus Bay, Maine. No length was estimated. (SEAN 1173)

1976. 27 Sept. Sighting. Fishermen reported seeing a right whale whose length was in excess of 20 ft (6 m +) about 1 mile (1.6 km) off the coast of Lanesville (near Gloucester), Massachusetts. (SEAN 1174)

1976. 3 Oct. Sighting. The MCWSN reported at least two right whales that were seen in the harbor of Provincetown, Massachusetts. No length estimates were given. (SEAN 1196)

1976. 5 Nov. Stranding. A fisherman reported seeing a dead right whale drifting 32 km southeast of Portland, Maine. He estimated the length to be 35 ft (11 m) and said that the animal had cuts and slashes on its back. The fisherman notified MCWSN who in turn notified SEAN. (SEAN 1226)

1976. 6 Nov. Sighting. The police department at Ocean City, Maryland sighted a right whale which they estimated to be at least 20 ft long (6 m +). This whale was observed for two hours swimming 50 to 150 yards (m) off Ocean City. (SEAN 1211).

1976. 13 Nov. Sighting. MCWSN reported a sighting of a right whale off Old Scantum, Maine. No length was estimated. (SEAN 1212)

1977. 2 Mar. Sighting. SEAN received a report from the coast guard at Maryport, Florida of an adult right whale accompanied by a calf. The animals were sighted swimming about a half mile (900 m) offshore from Jacksonville Beach, Florida. The adult's length was estimated at 50–60 ft (15–18 m) and the calf 30 ft (9 m). Several sightings of what appear to be the same individuals were reported between West Palm Beach and Jacksonville Beach. (SEAN 2119)

1977. 7 April. Sighting. A National Park Service pilot sighted an adult and calf just off Ocracoke Inlet, North Carolina and reported it to me over the radio. I was able to verify that it was a right whale sighting by his description of the callosities and the lack of a dorsal fin. He estimated the adult to be 50 ft (15 m) long and the calf to be about ⅔ of that (10 m). (SEAN 2207)

1977. 29 April. Sighting. The coast guard at Maryport, Florida reported sighting an adult right whale accompanied by a calf. They were seen 1–1.5 km offshore from Vilano Beach, Florida. The length of the adult was estimated at 70 ft (23 m) and the calf at 30–35 ft (9–10.5 m). (SEAN 2208)

1978. 5 April. Sighting. While flying I observed a right whale approximately 3 miles (5 km) east of Cape Hatteras, North Carolina. I estimated its length at 15 m. (SEAN 3136)

1978. 16 June. Incidental catch. A right whale became entangled in a gill net 3 km north of Sesuit Harbor, Massachusetts. The animal's length was estimated at 12 m. An unsuccessful attempt was made to free the animal of the remains of the net. (SEAN 3264)

1978. 2 Dec. Sighting. Frederick Ulmer reported sightings of right whales 16 miles (26 km) due east of Barnegat Light on Long Beach Island, New Jersey. Due to the poor visibility he was not sure how many whales there were but two was the most he sighted together at one time. One whale was estimated to be 50 ft (15 m) long. The sighting of two animals involved an adult and a well grown calf. (SEAN 3484)

1979. 9 Jan. Sighting. I sighted a right whale from a plane about 100 m off Hatteras Island, North Carolina (35° 31′ N, 75° 28′ W). The length was estimated at 12–13 m. (SEAN 4004)

1979. 11 Feb. Sighting. William Rossiter (*in litt.* 11 February 1981) notified me of sighting a pair of right whales 1 n. mile (1.8 km) northwest of Knuckle Buoy, Lookout Shoals, North Carolina. One animal appeared smaller than the other but not small enough to be a calf. (SEAN 1886)

1979. Feb. Sighting. William Rossiter (*in litt.* 11 February 1981) reported that a pair of right whales approached RV *Dan Moore* along the Outer Banks of North Carolina somewhere between Corolla and Oregon Inlet. (SEAN 1887)

1979. 28 Feb. Sighting. Officials from the Georgia Office of Information and the Coastal Resources Division of the Georgia Department of Natural Resources filmed an adult accompanied by a calf 6 miles (9.5 km) east of Jekyll Island, Georgia. They estimated the length of the adult to be between 35 and 45 ft (12 m est) and the calf to be half the length of the adult (6 m est). (SEAN 4095)

1979. 5 March. Stranding. A right whale carcass washed ashore at Wainscott, Long Island, New York. It was relatively fresh but had the tailstock severed, presumably by a ships propellor. The total length of the carcass was 868 cm. Comparing various morphometrics of this animal to other right whales, I estimated the original total length at 11 m. The skull was collected from this animal and it now bears the USNM catalog number 504886.

1979. 11 Oct. Sighting. SEAN received a letter dated 12 October 1979 from Dr R. G. B. Brown of the Seabird Research Unit, Canadian Wildlife Service, Dartmouth, Nova Scotia. He described a sighting of a possible right whale 40 km southeast of Cape Sable, Nova Scotia (43° 9′ N, 65° 15′ W). No length estimate was given. (SEAN 4395)

1979. 10 Dec. Stranding. A 1,550 cm female right whale washed ashore at Atlantic Beach, Florida in a state of moderate decomposition. It was examined by Marineland of Florida staff and then towed out to sea by the coast guard. This is the first recorded stranding of an adult right whale since 1900. (SEAN 4441)

1980. Dec. Sighting. Patricia Smith, a commercial fish spotting pilot, observed a right whale about 300 m off Atlantic Beach, North Carolina. She saw it throughout the day in the course of several flights but could not remember the exact date. No size estimate was obtained. (SEAN 1890)

1980. 6 Dec. Sighting. The coast guard out of Wrightsville Beach, North Carolina reported sighting a single right whale which they estimated to be 35 ft (11 m) long. The sighting occurred 1 mile (1.6 km) off the sea buoy at Wrightsville Beach (34° 9′ N, 77° 49′ W). (SEAN 1888)

1980. 28 Dec. Sighting. A fisherman notified the SEAN office that he had seen an adult and a calf along Seaside, approximately 18 km north of Cape Lookout, North

Carolina for about 4 days. (SEAN 1889)

1981. 15 Jan. Sighting. Patricia Smith, a commercial fish spotting pilot, observed two right whales about ¼ mile (0.3 km) off Wrightsville Beach, North Carolina. No size estimate was obtained. (SEAN 1891)

1981. 19 Jan. Sighting. John Reimer, a fisherman, sighted two right whales off Fort Macon, North Carolina. No size estimate was obtained. (SEAN 1892)

1981. 22 Jan. Sighting. John Reimer sighted another pair of right whales by the Rock Jetty Buoy off Cape Lookout, North Carolina. (SEAN 1893)

1981. 20 June. Sighting. Richard Sears, Michael Williamson and Frederick Wenzel report a sighting of three right whales near Wolf Bay, Quebec (50° 13′ N, 60° 13.5′ W) in a typescript report entitled 'Right whale (*Eubalaena glacialis*) sightings in the Gulf of St Lawrence', prepared for the Mingan Island Cetacean Study in May 1983.

1981. 6 Oct. Sighting. Sears, Williamson and Wenzel (see account under 20 June 1981) reported a sighting of a right whale 16 km southwest of Sheldrake, Quebec.

1981. 21 Nov. Sighting. Charles Cowman of the Georgia Department of Natural Resources reported that the Coast Guard Auxillary had seen a right whale 10.5 km east of North Cumberland Island, Georgia. There was no estimate of the total length of the animal but according to the report received from the SRSN (Southeast Regional Stranding Network) aerial photographs were taken. (SE 0675, SEAN 6902)

1981. 25 Nov. Sighting. The SRSN received a report of a sighting of at least 2, possibly as many as 5, large whales estimated to average 13 m in total length. These were reported by a private vessel 9.7 km east of Sapelo Island, Georgia. There were no photographs taken so this sighting is only tentatively referred to right whales. (SE 0674, SEAN 6912)

1981. 28 Dec. Sighting. Charles Cowman of the Georgia Department of Natural Resources reported that a right whale had been seen resting on the surface in calm weather near the Sapelo live bottom buoy, Georgia, by the captain of a fishing vessel. The length was estimated at 15 m. (SE 0726, SEAN 7131)

1981. 30 Dec. Stranding. A 464 cm male calf was found freshly dead on the northeast tip of Little Saint Simons Island, Georgia. The skull of this specimen was acquired by the Savannah Science Museum. (SEAN 6973)

1982. 21 Jan. Sighting. Charles Cowman reported that a right whale had been seen resting on the surface by a fishing vessel offshore about 20 km from Blackbeard Island, Georgia. The length of this whale was estimated at 15 m. (SE 0727, SEAN 7132)

1982. 25 Jan. Sighting. Cape Canaveral National Seashore reported an adult and a calf within 200 m of the shore at Brevard, Florida. They estimated the length of the adult at 40–50 ft (12–15 m) and the calf at about a third that size (4–5 m). (SEAN 7070)

1982. 2 Feb. Sighting. The Indian River sheriff's office reported a right whale headed south off Vero Beach, Florida. The estimated length was 19 m. (SE 0756, SEAN 7164)

1982. 18 Feb. Sighting. The Florida Marine Patrol at Jupiter, reported an adult and calf that appeared to be stuck in shallow water about a mile (1.6 km) south of the Saint Lucie power plant just north of Jupiter. The patrol reported that the calf had a gash on its back but seemed to be in fair condition otherwise. They managed to get

out of the shallows and were last seen about ¾ of a mile (1.2 km) offshore headed south. There were no length estimates made. (SE 0736, SEAN 7130)

1982. 20 Feb. Stranding. A 457 cm female calf was found in a state of advanced decomposition on the beach 0.4 km south of Bradley Slough, Ossabaw Island, Georgia. Its remains were collected by the University of Georgia, Museum of Natural History. (SE 0742, SEAN 7133)

1982. 25 Feb. Sighting. The Georgia Department of Natural Resources reported that a right whale was sighted 5.6 km offshore of Cumberland Island 4 km south of St Andrews sea buoy, Georgia, by a research vessel. The estimated length of this animal was 30–35 ft (10 m). (SE 0741, SEAN 7134)

1982. 3 March. Incidental catch. A right whale became entangled in a gill net 0.5 miles (0.8 km) east of the Saint Lucie Power Plant just north of Jupiter, Florida. The animal was released unharmed and swam off. The total length was estimated to be 11 m. (SE 0753, SEAN 7165)

1982. 7 March. Sighting. Cliff Turner, a reporter for the Raleigh, North Carolina, *News and Observer* reported seeing an adult and a calf off Cape Lookout, North Carolina. He took photographs of this sighting which were published in the *News and Observer* on 14 March. He estimated the length of the adult at 35 ft (11 m) and the calf at 20–25 ft (7 m). (SEAN 7169)

1982. 14 March. Sighting. SEAN received a report that a local resident had seen an adult and a calf approximately 40 km east of the north end of Cumberland Island, Georgia. The lengths were estimated at 60 ft (18 m) and 30 ft (9 m). (SEAN 7166)

1982. 22 March. Sighting. John Gaskill, a local resident, reported sighting an adult and a calf off Atlantic, North Carolina. No length estimate was made. (SEAN 7169A)

1982. 24 March. Sighting. SEAN received a report that two right whales had been sighted just outside the surf at South Point State Park, Long Island, New York. The lengths were estimated at 16 and 13 m. (SEAN 7170)

1982. 19 April. Stranding. Terry Joyce reported a dead right whale floating at 38° 58′ 50″ N, 69° 17′ 25″ W on cruise 83 of the RV *Endeavor*. Photographs were taken and the identification was confirmed by CETAP. No length or sex data was obtained. (SE 1259, MME 00496)

1983. 14 Jan. Sighting. The Coast Guard station at Lake Worth, Florida reported the sighting of a right whale 3 miles north of Lake Worth Inlet. A description of the bonnet was given and the length was estimated at 10 m. (MME 00463)

1983. 25 Jan. Sighting. The Coast Guard reported an unconfirmed right whale off the Pompano Pier, Pompano Beach, Florida. No length was given. (SE 1260, MME 00464)

1983. 26 Jan. Sighting. Robert Winters reported a right whale, which he estimated at 30 ft (10 m), off Satellite Beach, Florida. (SE 1017, MME 00150)

1983. 3 Feb. Stranding. A carcass of a male right whale washed ashore at Island Beach State Park, New Jersey. The carcass was in relatively fresh condition but its tail had been severed. The total length of the carcass was 31 ft plus an estimated 6 ft for the missing piece, giving an estimated total length of 37 ft (11 m). (MME 00084)

1983. 4 March. Sighting. Samuel Sadove reported a right whale sighting in Shinnecock Inlet, Long Island. Length was estimated at 40 ft (12 m). (MME 00085)

1983. 6 March. Sighting. Samuel Sadove reported a sighting of a right whale at Montauk, Long Island, New York. No length estimate was made. (MME 00084A)

1983. 5 April. Incidental catch. Frank Schwartz reported a right whale entangled in a gillnet that had been set for sturgeon off Wrightsville Beach, NC. The whale apparently was released from the netting. The whale's length was estimated at 25 ft (7.5 m). (SE 1068, MME 00146)

1983. 18 Aug. Sighting. José Castro reported a right whale approximately 25 miles off Charleston, SC. The identification was confirmed by the v-shaped blow and by the lack of a dorsal fin. Length was estimated at 40–50 ft (15 m). (MME 00247)

1983. 1 Oct. Sighting. Elise Tucker and Charles Cowman reported a right whale 250 yds (250 m) west of the 'F' reef buoy off Jekyll Island, GA. The length was estimated at 45 ft (13.5 m). (SE 1263, MME 00351)

1984. 8 Jan. Sighting. Frank Lee, a pilot for Gray's Reef National Marine Sanctuary, reported spotting a right whale from the air 17 miles offshore from Gray's Reef, GA. No length estimate was given. (SE 1358, MME 00529)

1984. 18 Jan. Sighting. A ranger at the Canaveral National Seashore, Florida, reported a right whale that he estimated was 20 ft (6 m) long headed south about 100 yds (100 m) off the beach at the seashore. (SE 1359, MME 00579)

1984. 17 Feb. Sighting. James Hildebrandt reported a right whale 8.7 n. miles (16 km) off St Simon's Island, GA. The whale breached near his boat and he was able to observe the callosities. No length was given. (SE 1443, MME 00575)

1984. 19 Feb. Sighting. W. B. Gibbs observed a right whale 13 n. miles (21 km) off Cumberland Island, GA. He estimated the length at 40 ft (12 m). The animal reportedly had no dorsal fin but he was not able to see the callosities. (SE 1442, MME 00576)

1984. 5 March. Sighting. Walt Caldwell observed a right whale 11¾ miles (19 km) off St Simons Island, GA. He estimated the length to be 35 ft (11 m). (SE 1453, MME 00581)

1984. 6 March. Sighting. Frank Lee observed two adults and a calf heading north 3 miles (5 km) east of Fernandina Beach, Florida. (SE 1452, MME 00580)

1984. 11 March. Sighting. Two adult right whales, estimated to be 40 ft (12 m) long were observed from an aircraft 12 miles (19 km) off the south end of Cumberland Island, GA. One was reported to have a 10 to 12 ft (3–3.5 m) fresh wound on its back. (SE 1452, MME 00582)

1984. 11 March. Sighting. A report was received by the Florida Marine Patrol of an adult and a calf 1 mile (2 km) off Ponte Vedra, Florida. (SE 1455, MME 00583)

1984. 11 March. Sighting. Charles Cowman reported observing an adult and calf from the air, 1.5 miles (2.4 km) southeast of artificial reef 'F' off Jekyll Island, GA. Photographs were taken. (SE 1480, MME 00620)

1984. 26 March. Sighting. Howard Winn observed an adult and calf 5 miles (8 km) off the north end of Cumberland Island, GA. Photographs were taken. (SE 1481, MME 00621)

1984. 1 Dec. Sighting. Gail Cannon observed a right whale in Lookout Bight, Cape Lookout, NC. The animal had no dorsal fin and what could have been callosities. (SE 1733, MME 00970)

Twentieth-century Records of Right Whales (*Eubalaena glacialis*) in the Northeast Atlantic Ocean

S. G. BROWN

Sea Mammal Research Unit, Natural Environment Research Council, c/o British Antarctic Survey, Cambridge, England, CB3 0ET

ABSTRACT

Twentieth-century records of catches and sightings of right whales (*Eubalaena glacialis*) in the northeast Atlantic Ocean are reviewed. Catch figures are probably incomplete, but a total of between 134 and 137 right whales are recorded caught from whaling stations in Iceland, the Faroe Islands, West Norway, the Shetland Islands, the Hebrides and Ireland in the period from 1900 to 1937, the last caught in 1926. Approximately 85% were taken by stations in the British Isles between 1906 and 1923. In addition, four whales were caught in the Azores and Madeira, the last in 1967.

About 23 sightings of some 48 animals recorded as right whales were made during the years 1901 to 1980. Insufficient information is available for a confirmed identification in most cases but they include perhaps six definite sightings of eight animals, seen off Iceland, Spain, the Azores and Madeira.

There are apparently no certainly identified strandings of right whales on the coasts of Western Europe in the twentieth century. The sightings records suggest that there are at present very few right whales in the eastern North Atlantic Ocean. They may belong to a small breeding population which perhaps exists on the desert coast of west or northwest Africa. Alternatively they may be stragglers from the more numerous population in the western North Atlantic Ocean.

INTRODUCTION

There is a long history of whaling for the right whale (*Eubalaena glacialis*) in the northeast Atlantic Ocean (Harmer, 1928), with the Basque fishery for this species dating back at least to the eleventh century (Aguilar, 1981). The species was much reduced in numbers by whaling and in the early nineteenth century it was believed to be extinct. However, with the spread of modern whaling in European waters in the latter part of the century, it again appeared in the catches of shore stations. In the twentieth century, evidence of the occurrence of right whales in the northeast Atlantic Ocean is available in the catch records of whaling operations. In addition there are some scattered records of sightings, or possible sightings, of the species at sea. There are apparently no certainly identified strandings on Western European coasts during this century, although some were recorded in the nineteenth century and earlier.

CATCHES

Jonsgård (1977) compiled tables of catches of large whales, including right whales, in the North Atlantic Ocean by modern whaling operations between 1868 and 1975. These were based mainly on figures from the Bureau of International Whaling Statistics and from Risting (1922). More detailed information on catches, with revised catch figures in some cases, is available for whaling stations in the British Isles in Thompson (1928) and Brown (1976a), for the Faroe Islands in Degerbøl (1940), for Spain in Aguilar and Lens (1981) and Aguilar and Sanpera (1982), and for the Azores in Clarke (1954). Catches of large whales from 1975 to 1980 are available in *International Whaling Statistics* (IWS), nos. LXXIX–LXXXVIII. No right whales are included in the catches. Statistics for some of the early years, including the earlier years of the twentieth century at some whaling centres, contain large unspecified catches. In the northeast Atlantic this applies especially to the Faroe Islands (1900–09) and Iceland (1900–12).

Table 1

Twentieth century whaling in the northeast Atlantic Ocean and right whale catches (1900–1982). The numbers of whales listed as unspecified are only approximate because catch figures given by different sources do not agree

Years operating	Unspecified catches		Right whales caught
	Years	Number	
North Norway – 32 yrs 1900–04,1918–20,1948–71	None	None	None
Iceland – 56 yrs 1900–15,1935–39,1948–82	13 yrs (1900–12)	10,189	8 or 9
Faroe Islands – 57 yrs 1900–16,1920–30,1933–39, 1946–58,1962–66,1968, 1978–79,1981	12 yrs (1900–10,1915)	1,462	7 or 9
West Norway – 52 yrs 1912–13,1918–39, 1941–65, 1967–69	1 yr (1912)	30	1
Shetland Islands – 21 yrs 1903–14,1920,1922–29	5 yrs (1904,1906–08, 1924)	140/149	6
Hebrides – 20 yrs 1904–14,1920, 1923–28,1950–51	3 yrs (1905,1911,1924)	33/42	94
Ireland – 9 yrs 1908–14,1920,1922	None	None	18
Spain/Portugal (including pelagic whaling) – 10yrs 1921–29,1934	3 yrs (1927–29)	Not known	None
Spain – 46 yrs ca 1929–38,1947–82	17 yrs (1929–38,1947–48, 1952–56)	286+	None
Portugal – 8 yrs 1944–51	None	None	None
Azores – 83 yrs 1900–82	None	None	1 (Lost)
Madeira – 41 yrs 1941–81	None	None	3
Pelagic whaling in northern waters – 8 yrs 1929–34,1937,1970	None	None	None

Table 1 lists the whaling centres catching large whales (excluding minke whales) at different periods since 1900 in the northeast Atlantic Ocean. For each centre the number of years in operation is shown, years with

Table 2

Right whale catches in the northeast Atlantic Ocean, 1900–1982. NW = No Whaling. Azores–whaling throughout the period 1900–1937, right whales caught in 1914–1 (Lost). Madeira – No whaling before 1941, right whales caught in 1959–1, 1967–2. (See text for sources of catch statistics)

Year	Iceland	Faroe Is.	West Norway	Shetland Is.	Hebrides	Ireland	Total
1900	–	–	NW	NW	NW	NW	–
01	–	–	NW	NW	NW	NW	–
02	1	–	NW	NW	NW	NW	1
03	3	1	NW	–	NW	NW	4
04	2	–	NW	–	–	NW	2
05	–	–	NW	–	–	NW	–
06	–	–	NW	–	6	NW	6
07	–	1 or 2	NW	–	24	NW	25 or 26
08	–	–	NW	–	20	5	25
09	–	–	NW	–	21	5	26
1910	–	2 or 3	NW	4	5	8	19 or 20
11	1 or 2	–	NW	–	–	–	1 or 2
12	–	–	–	–	11	–	11
13	1	–	–	1	–	–	2
14	–	–	NW	1	4	–	5
15	–	1	NW	NW	NW	NW	1
16	NW	–	NW	NW	NW	NW	–
17	NW	NW	NW	NW	NW	NW	NW
18	NW	NW	–	NW	NW	NW	–
19	NW	NW	–	NW	NW	NW	–
1920	NW	–	–	–	1	–	1
21	NW	1	–	NW	NW	NW	1
22	NW	1	–	–	NW	–	1
23	NW	–	–	–	2	NW	2
24	NW	–	–	–	–	NW	–
25	NW	–	–	–	–	NW	–
26	NW	–	1	–	–	NW	1
27	NW	–	–	–	–	NW	–
28	NW	–	–	–	–	NW	–
29	NW	–	–	–	NW	NW	–
1930	NW	–	–	NW	NW	NW	–
31	NW	NW	–	NW	NW	NW	–
32	NW	NW	–	NW	NW	NW	–
33	NW	–	–	NW	NW	NW	–
34	NW	–	–	NW	NW	NW	–
35	–	–	–	NW	NW	NW	–
36	–	–	–	NW	NW	NW	–
37	–	–	–	NW	NW	NW	–
Total	8 or 9	7 or 9	1	6	94	18	134–137

unspecified catches are noted and the total recorded catch of right whales is given.

In Table 2 the recorded catches of right whales at the different whaling centres in each year from 1900 to 1937 are listed, together with catches in later years at Madeira. No right whales are recorded as caught elsewhere in the northeast Atlantic from 1937 to 1982. In 1929 Norway gave total protection to right whales from Norwegian whaling worldwide. In 1935 an International Convention for the Regulation of Whaling gave total protection to all species of right whales, except for hunting by aborigines, but this convention was not adhered to by all whaling countries. In 1937 a new International Agreement for the Regulation of Whaling gave the same protection to right whales, but again was not signed by all whaling countries. This agreement was superceded in 1946 by the International Convention for the Regulation of Whaling which remains in force for member nations of the International Whaling Commission. This convention gives total protection to all species of right whales except for catches by, or on behalf of, aboriginal peoples. In recent years right whale catches have been restricted to bowhead whales from the Bering Sea stock.

The sources for the catch figures in Table 2 for the different whaling centres are given below. Ruud (1937) attempted to collect complete catch data on the numbers of right whales caught since the start of modern whaling but he states that this proved to be impossible because the different sources of catch statistics do not agree, because of gaps in the early records, and of catches not specifically identified. Tønnessen and Johnsen (1982, p. 736) note that 'Statistics for the right whale catch are very unreliable'. They give figures for the world catch from 1904 to 1918 only, and for 'Northern Seas' (equivalent to the Shetland Islands, Hebrides, Ireland, Iceland and the Faroe Islands) the numbers are slightly less than those given in Table 2.

Iceland – catch 8 or 9 right whales

As noted above, the available catch statistics include large unspecified catches for the years 1900–1912. IWS II (1931 p. 7) tabulates catches from 1890 to 1909 and, referring to unspecified catches in those years, notes that 'Sperm-whales and nordcapers were only present in very scanty numbers'. Jonsgård (1977) gives catches in 1904 (2) and 1913 (1). Risting (1922) notes these catches and one whale in 1911; the 1913 animal appears in IWS.

Collett (1909) states that in the twenty years 1889–1908, Norwegian whalers captured about 80 right whales in the waters of Iceland, the Faroe Islands, the Shetlands and the Hebrides. He lists 88 whales caught in these waters, including five in Ireland in 1908. Twenty-four whales were caught between 1889 and 1898 (22 off Iceland and 2 off the Faroe Islands). Sixty-four whales were caught between 1902 and 1908. His figures for the Hebrides and Ireland agree with those from other sources, and he lists three whales for the Faroe Islands (see below), and Icelandic catches in 1902 (1), 1903 (3) and 1904 (2).

Tønnessen and Johnsen (1982, table 48) include two right whales taken in Iceland and the Faroes 1910–11, relating to catches in 1911. As noted above, Risting (1922) records one whale in 1911 and it may be that two were in fact taken since no catch is recorded for the Faroe Islands in 1911 (see below).

Ruud (1937) states that

from the whaling near Iceland and the Faroe Islands during the period 1889 to 1905 we only know the number of nordkapers for some of the years, and that altogether about 30 whales were caught during these years.

Collett's figures (1909) total 31 whales for Iceland and the Faroe Islands during this time. It is probable that a few more right whales were caught in Icelandic waters between 1889 and 1915 so that the eight or nine from 1900 to 1915 given in Table 2 is a minimum figure.

There is very little available information on the Icelandic catch. Collett (1909) notes that a 54 ft pregnant female with a foetus about 39 inches in length was taken in August 1903.

The Faroe Islands – catch 7 or 9 right whales

Jonsgård (1977) lists catches in 1910 (3 whales), 1922 (1) and 1924 (1). The 1910 and 1922 catches appear in IWS. Degerbøl (1940) gives details of single animals taken in 1903, 1907, 1915, 1921 and 1922, and of two in 1910 (he notes that three are recorded in IWS). Collett (1909) records one animal in 1903 and two in 1907. The single whale in 1924 (Jonsgård, 1977) has been omitted from Table 2 since it is not recorded in IWS nor in Degerbøl. The latter records three males (37, 41, 48 ft),* three females (38, 39, 55 ft) and one of unknown sex (50 ft),

* Degerbøl's lengths given in Danish feet have been converted to English feet.

caught in June (2), July (4) and August (1). Four animals were caught from 24 to 80 n. miles south or east-south-east of the southernmost island of Suderø, and one near the Shetland Islands. This last was a 55 ft lactating female.

Jonsgård (1977) records unspecified catches in every year from 1900 to 1912 and in 1915 and 1916. Degerbøl (1940) specifies some of these catches but 1,462 whales in the twelve years 1900 to 1910 and 1915 remain unspecified. Most of these were blue, fin and humpback whales according to Degerbøl, but it may be that a very small number of right whales is included.

West Norway – catch 1 right whale

Jonsgård (1977) and IWS record one whale caught in 1926. No further details are available. Thirty unspecified whales were taken in 1912; they were mostly fin and some sei whales according to IWS.

The Shetland Islands – catch 6 right whales

Jonsgård (1977) gives only the total British catches and IWS list total Scottish catches. Brown (1976a) compiled from various sources separate catch statistics for the Shetland Islands, the Hebrides and Ireland. Right whales were caught at the Shetland Islands in 1910 (4), 1913 (1) and 1914 (1), to the west, northwest and northeast of the islands. Three animals of unknown sex were caught in June 1910 and one in June 1914. One male was taken in July 1910 and one female in August 1913. Unspecified catches are recorded in five years totalling between 140 and 149 whales.

The Hebrides – catch 94 right whales

Right whales were caught by the whaling station at West Loch Tarbert, Harris (Outer Hebrides) in most years from 1906 to 1914. Thompson (1928) plots the catch positions for 60 of the whales taken between 1908 and 1914. Almost all were caught in a limited area to the west and southwest of the Outer Hebrides between 56° N and 59° N, and as far as 10° W. About 50 animals were caught on the continental shelf within the 100 fathoms contour. The catch positions of other species taken by the same station show that this distribution was not solely due to the range of operation of the catcher boats. Thompson (1928) combines statistics for the Shetland Islands and Hebrides, and of 69 whales caught in the years 1908–23 (35 males, 34 females) lengths ranged from 31 to 59 ft (mean 46 ft males, 49 ft females). He notes that the measurements were probably made over the curve of the body. Of the Hebridean catch of 64 whales (1908–23), 63 were taken in May (3), June (41) and July (19). Collett (1909) notes that the 30 whales taken in 1906 and 1907, were caught in June (12), July (17) and August (1). Unspecified catches in three years totalled between 33 and 42 whales.

Ireland – catch 18 right whales

In the first three years of operation (1908–10) 18 right whales were caught, 14 from one station and four from the second station when it opened in 1910. In 1908 and 1909 all 10 whales were caught in the first two weeks of June, and in 1910 six of the eight whales caught by the two stations were taken by 7 June. The whales were caught close to the coast (Fairley, 1981).

The Azores – catch 1 right whale (lost).

Jonsgård (1977), IWS and Clarke (1954, 1981) do not list any catches of right whales in the Azores during this century, although Clarke (1981) refers to seven landed between 1873 and 1888. FAO (1978, p. 58) states that 'an individual was reported in the Azores catch of 1969 or 1970', but there is no other reference to this capture and it may be an error. Allen, Compton-Bishop and Gordon (n.d.) record 'a right whale that was fastened by a whaleboat from Lages das Flores in 1914. It proved too difficult and dangerous to capture and was cut loose'.

Madeira – catch 3 right whales

Jonsgård (1977) lists one right whale in 1959 and IWS record this as a 50 ft female. It was caught in January (Anon, 1960). Maul and Sergeant (1977) draw attention to a 47 ft female and a calf caught on 27 February 1967 off the north coast of the island. The accompanying 'male' escaped.

Summary

A total of 138 or 141 right whales were recorded caught in the eastern North Atlantic between 1900 and 1982 (Table 2). Except for the three animals taken in 1959 and 1967 at Madeira, the last individual was caught in 1926 off West Norway. Of the total North Atlantic catch, 118 whales (approximately 85%) were taken by whaling stations in the British Isles in ten years of operations between 1906 and 1923; 94 whales (80% of these) were caught by the Hebridean station. Elsewhere, in Iceland and in the Faroe Islands less than 10 whales were taken, three in Madeira, and single animals off West Norway and the Azores.

As already noted, it is likely that the catch figures in Table 2 are incomplete and a few additional whales may have been taken, especially in Icelandic waters. For example, Millais (1906, pp. 230/1) refers to seven being caught on the coast of Iceland in 1903 but this figure does not apparently appear elsewhere.

Some right whales may also have been caught in the eastern North Atlantic by American whaling vessels in the early years of this century. Mitchell (1973) draws attention to such catches, pointing out that whalers outward bound to other whaling grounds in more distant seas were unlikely to ignore any right whale they may have encountered, even if very few were seen on each voyage through the North Atlantic. Hegarty (1959) lists 22 voyages by American whaling vessels between 1900 and 1911, bound for the 'Atlantic' (not including 'Hudson Bay') which returned with cargoes of whale oil as well as sperm oil. Eight of these voyages lasted less than 18 months, and it seems likely that they at least, were confined to the Atlantic Ocean. Without examination of the relevant logbooks it is not possible to say more, but one of the voyages listed, that of the Daisy of New Bedford (31 October 1911 to 29 June 1913), did include a period in the northeast Atlantic, including a visit to the Cape Verde Islands. No right whales were taken, at least on the second half of the voyage, and the 1,200 barrels of 'whale oil' obtained presumably consisted partly if not entirely of sea elephant oil from South Georgia (Murphy, 1947). Reeves and Mitchell (1986) do not include 20th century voyages in their detailed examination of

American pelagic catches. However, Reeves (pers. comm.) referring to Mitchell and Reeves (1983) notes that in the 29 logbooks relating to twentieth-century voyages of American whaling vessels in the Atlantic Ocean which they examined for records of humpback whales, there were no records of right whales being caught or even seen. Half of the voyages are listed as sperm whaling voyages but it is unlikely that any right whales seen would have gone unrecorded, even if there was no intention to lower the boats for them.

RECORDS OF SIGHTINGS

At present, schemes for recording sightings of large cetaceans in the northeast Atlantic Ocean operate in British waters (Evans, 1976, 1980), in French waters (Anon, 1980) and on the Icelandic whaling grounds (Brown, 1976b). Observations are also made on a less systematic basis from merchant ships and other vessels.

Earlier schemes involving mainly British and Dutch merchant shipping and some naval vessels operated during the period 1952–66. A few sightings of right whales are included among the records resulting from these various schemes and they are noted here, together with records of incidental observations from other sources.

On the Icelandic whaling grounds in the Denmark Strait no right whales have been sighted during the whaling season (June to September) since the scheme started in 1969. The present whaling grounds are south of the area off the northwest coast of Iceland where some of the right whales were formerly caught. However, if these animals migrated northwards through the Denmark Strait to this area, and if this movement were still continued by a number of whales, they are likely to have been seen crossing the present whaling grounds.

Three sightings records of right whales in Icelandic waters are known to my colleague J. Sigurjónsson who has very generously sent me full details of them (pers. comm.). He notes that the Icelandic name *Sléttbakur* can refer to both the right whale (*E. glacialis*) and the bowhead whale (*Balaena mysticetus*), but there is only one confirmed sighting of a bowhead whale off Iceland in the last hundred years; one seen in spring 1879 at the ice edge 40 n. miles off Dýrafjördur, NW Iceland (Saemundsson, 1939). In July 1935 or 1936 three large whales were seen by many observers two to three miles from land in good visibility in Skjálfandaflói, N. Iceland (approx. 66° 05′ N, 17° 30′ W). In contrast to other large whales frequenting the area, these animals did not have dorsal fins and they were unanimously identified as Sléttbakur.

The second record is of a large whale shot using a grenade harpoon by a minke whaling vessel in the late 1950s in Isafjardardjúp, NW Iceland (approx. 60° 10′ N, 23° 00′ W). The whale broke the harpoon rope and escaped towards the open sea. From an observer's description the animal was identified as most likely to be a right whale. This identification is perhaps less certain than the previous record.

In the past 30 years only one whale has been certainly identified as Sléttbakur. This was observed by whalers on two minke whaling vessels early in 1971 off Flateyjardalur, N. Iceland (approx. 66° 10′ N, 17° 50′W). It was seen repeatedly at close range and its size, lack of dorsal fin, and shape of head and jaws were noted.

Further north, my colleague I. Christensen told me (pers. comm.) of a whale identified as either a right whale

or a bowhead whale seen by minke whalers between Iceland and Jan Mayen Island in 1967 or 1968. There are several other records of whales, all believed to have been bowhead whales, seen by Norwegian whalers, or other observers, in northeast Atlantic Arctic waters since 1958. These are listed by Jonsgård (1981) and the localities of the nine live animals and two dead whales are plotted on a map in Jonsgård (1982). At least two of the sightings were made close to the ice edge, or in drift ice, and the northerly positions of other sightings suggest that these whales were bowhead rather than right whales. Three sightings are in lower latitudes but one of these, at approximately 71° 00′ N, 28° 51′ E in May 1980, was identified as a bowhead whale by the white area on the lower jaw which was clearly seen (Haug, 1980). The other two sightings at approximately 61° 05′ N, 42° 10′ W in August 1979 off southeast Greenland are identified in Anon. (1981) as bowhead whales but it is perhaps possible that they were right whales.

No sightings of right whales in the North Atlantic were reported in the scheme for recording observations of whales from ships run by the British National Institute of Oceanography between 1952 and 1956 (Brown, 1958). More recently there have been sightings of possible right whales in British waters from the bird observatory on Cape Clear Island, Co. Cork, Ireland. Evans (1980) refers to two probable sightings of single individuals in June 1964 and August 1970. Both refer to 'large, all black whales with no dorsal fin observed when surfacing'. Maul and Sergeant (1977) presumably also note the 1964 record, referred to in a letter from Dr W. R. P. Bourne to Sergeant, December 1976. He

described convincingly a sight record of a right whale which breached at Cape Clear I., St George's Channel, Ireland on ca. 18th June 1964. It showed short fins and an all-black colour.

These sightings and others are noted in the reports of the bird observatory, e.g. Sharrock (1967) who gives a table of the percentages and numbers of 'identified' cetaceans seen off the island in 1959–66. Of 2,427 animals, there were 44 (1.8%) unidentified large whales, five (0.2%) right and two (0.1%) fin whales (*Balaenoptera physalus*). He notes that 'Since most of the records lack documentation, there must be some doubt regarding their reliability, especially since the proportions of the various species do not agree with the literature'. Preston (1975) in the same reports also lists unidentified large whales including 'one on 18 August 1970 (D. Woodward) was probably a Biscayan right whale *Eubalaena glacialis*'. Sharrock (1973) in his account of cetaceans in the account of the natural history of the island, stresses the problems of specific identification of cetaceans at sea. He notes that large whales have been reported on over 70 occasions, nearly always single individuals. 'The identification problems with these are very great. They mostly pass well out to sea'. He notes one fin whale positively identified, and continues

large whales have at least twice been seen leaping completely clear of the water, rising almost vertically and then belly-flopping back into the sea. In one case the whale was about three miles offshore but the noise as it crashed down into the water could be heard by observers on the island. In the other case (June, 1967), the huge elongated flippers identifying it as a Humpback Whale *Megaptera novaeangliae* were seen.

He does not identify any sightings of right whales in this account.

Another right whale sighting in British waters is

reported by Evans (1981). During a whale and seabird cruise in the northeast Atlantic off the west coast of Ireland and Scotland along the edge of the continental shelf in July to October 1980, a probable right whale was seen in 57° 52′ N, 08° 07′ W between Harris and St Kilda. This is in the area where catches were made from the Harris whaling station.

In the northern Bay of Biscay area Mr L. A. Carter told me (pers. comm.) of a report from a merchant vessel of a sighting in the first half of June 1980 of two whales identified as right whales by 'callosities' seen on one of them. The distinctive shape of the head and the absence of a dorsal fin were apparently not mentioned.

Aguilar (1981) reports that the catcher boats from the Spanish stations on the Galicia coast, operating in the area from the north of Cape Finisterre south to the Spanish–Portuguese border, have never sighted right whales since they began whaling in 1952. In September 1977, however, outside the usual whaling grounds, one was sighted in approximately 43° N, 10° 30′ W. This is apparently the only sighting of the species in this area in this century.

An older record off the coast of the Basque Province of Guipuzcoa, brought to the attention of biologists very recently by Nores and Perez (1983), is of a right whale 12 metres in length. This was killed off the port of Orio on 14 May 1901 by some fishermen using dynamite. A published photograph of the animal confirms the identification.

Around the Azores, Allen et al. (n.d.) state that the right whale 'has been seen on extremely rare occasions in this century'. Clarke (1981) notes that the chief lookout at Capelinhas, Fayal, told him in 1949 that he had sighted only one right whale in ten years of watching from the cliffs. No further details are available. The male right whale seen off Madeira on 27 February 1967 which escaped when the accompanying female and calf were caught (Maul and Sergeant, 1977) should be noted again here.

A school of 22 right whales in the Cape Verde Islands is mentioned by Mörzer Bruyns (1971, p. 159). He gives no details but notes that it seems rather unlikely and in his opinion they might have been humpback whales. This record is probably that mentioned immediately below in the report of the Dutch sightings scheme.

The Dutch scheme which ran for three years from 1954 was reported on by Slijper, Van Utrecht and Naaktgeboren (1964). Referring to records of right whales resulting from the scheme they state

> There were 24 sightings in the Atlantic Ocean, referring to 59 animals, 5 of which were observed in the South Atlantic. In August a herd of 22 animals with a calf was observed between 10° N and 20° N near the Cape Verde Isles. The average number of animals in the herds observed in the Atlantic Ocean amounted to 1.60 (the herd of 22 not included)…Because of the double Blåst, the absence of a dorsal fin and other characteristics, Right Whales are comparatively easy to recognize. Consequently we may assume that the determination of these animals will be fairly reliable.

There were 23 sightings of 37 counted whales and the one sighting of the estimated 22 whales in the Atlantic. In the North Atlantic east of 40° W sightings are shown on the chart (Fig. 25) in each 10 degree square from 0 to 40° W between 40 and 50° N. There are also sightings in the two 10° squares between 10 and 20° W and 20 and 40° N; and the Cape Verde Islands sighting and one in the Mediterranean Sea. From the available information it is not possible to give the exact number of sightings or number of whales seen in the northeast Atlantic (east of 40° W) but it is approximately eight sightings of 30 animals. Without more details of the individual sightings it is difficult to evaluate these records from the Dutch scheme. Maul and Sergeant (1977) also refer to these sightings but note that they cannot be verified.

Summary

The total of all the sightings in the northeast Atlantic Ocean listed above, including the Dutch records, is approximately 23 sightings of some 48 whales, spread over a period from 1901 to 1980. The number of definite right whale sightings is likely to be less than this. Omitting the Dutch records, for which insufficient information is available, there are at most 14 sightings of 17 whales. Of these perhaps only six sightings of eight animals (two sightings – four whales – off Iceland, two records off Spain and the single animals off the Azores and Madeira) can be considered definite records.

STRANDINGS

There are apparently no certainly identified strandings of right whales on the coasts of Western Europe during the twentieth century although there are nineteenth century and earlier records.

Casinos and Vericad (1976) refer to three dead right whales on the Spanish Asturian coast in 1895, 1917 and 1961 recorded by Garcia-Dory (1974). A. Aguilar (pers. comm.) has discussed these records with C. Nores of Oviedo University, who has completed an account of cetaceans in the Bay of Biscay. He states that the 1895 stranding was a fin whale (*Balaenoptera physalus*) and the 1961 stranding a sperm whale (*Physeter macrocephalus*). The 1917 animal weighed nearly 20 tonnes but it is not now possible to determine its species (Nores and Perez, 1983).

There are also references to skeletal remains of three animals washed ashore in 1952 on the beach at Deva (Guipuzcoa, Spain) and now in the Museo Oceanografico in San Sebastian (Gómez de Llarena, 1952; Casinos and Vericad, 1976). Aguilar (1981) notes that they are believed to date from an earlier time (Gonzalez Echegaray, 1978). The same thing probably applies to some bones in the Museo Zoologico, University of Porto, which were found prior to 1930 by a fishing vessel working near the coast at Porto, Portugal (Teixeira, 1979).

Although not stranded, the animal mentioned by Tomilin (1967, p. 55) may also be included here:

> A Biscayan whale was last observed at the coasts of the Kola Peninsula in summer 1935; it was found dead on the surface of the sea and towed to Murmansk (local newspapers erroneously described it as 'Greenland whale').

DISCUSSION

It is believed that there were two populations of right whales in the North Atlantic Ocean with separate breeding areas on the eastern and western sides of the ocean in winter and which migrated northwards to more northern feeding grounds for the summer. Thompson (1928) refers to the eastern population being in southern waters (northwest African coast, Mediterranean, Bay of Biscay) in winter and early spring, and migrating

Table 3

Monthly distribution of right whale catches, 1900–1967

Whaling area	Total catch	Known monthly catch					
		Jan	Feb	May	June	July	Aug
Iceland	8 or 9	–	–	–	–	–	1
Faroe Islands	7 or 9	–	–	–	2	4	1
West Norway	1	–	–	–	–	–	–
Shetland Islands	6	–	–	–	4	1	1
Hebrides	94	–	–	3	53	36	1
Ireland	18	–	–	–	16	–	–
Azores	1	–	–	–	–	–	–
Madeira	3	1	2	–	–	–	–

northwards in late spring and early summer westwards of the British Isles to Norwegian and Icelandic waters for the summer. He notes that the autumn migration southwards was unknown and mentions the possibility that both eastern and western populations mingled in mid-Atlantic in early winter, perhaps in the latitude of the Azores.

The dates of capture of all the right whales listed in Tables 1 and 2 are not available in the literature. Those which are recorded are given by months for each whaling area in Table 3. Clarke (1981) gives the date of capture of three of the seven right whales taken at Flores and Pico in the Azores between 1873 and 1888. They were in January, March and April. He notes that these dates tend to support Thompson's conclusions on the movements of this species in the North Atlantic. Clarke also draws attention, however, to Maury's whale chart for 1852 which shows that American whaleships cruised for right whales on the Azores ground in summer, between May and August.

Of the six sightings considered as definite records in the present paper, one of two in Icelandic waters was in July but the other was 'early in 1971', which does not suggest a date in summer. The two Spanish records were in September and May, and the male was off Madeira in February. There is no date for the Azores sighting.

Taken together, these dates of catches and sightings tend to support the generally accepted picture of right whale migrations in the eastern North Atlantic Ocean. This involves animals in southern waters in winter and early spring migrating northwards to feeding grounds in colder northern waters for the summer and returning southwards again in the autumn. However, the small number of southern records and of the most northern records should be noted. In this connection it should also be remembered that the small number of sightings in southern waters may to some extent be a reflection of the fact that modern whaling in the region takes place in summer when right whales are believed to be in more northern waters.

Reeves (1982) has suggested that originally there may have been a number of geographically separate stocks in the North Atlantic Ocean, with little or no interchange. In considering the reasons which have prevented recovery of right whales in the North Atlantic in spite of almost half a century of protection, he suggests that one reason may be simply that there were very few whales left when whaling stopped. Some stocks (e.g. in the Bay of Biscay and off Iceland and Finmark) may have been exterminated.

The sightings records listed above certainly suggest that at present there are very few right whales in the eastern North Atlantic Ocean. Reeves (1982) has, however, pointed out that 'North Atlantic right whales are notoriously difficult to detect at times, and no one seems to be able to predict when or where concentrations of them will be encountered'. In this connection, Schevill and Moore's (1983) analysis of Townsend's unmapped North Atlantic right whale records from the logbooks of American whaleships is of considerable interest. They show that two vessels (the *Richmond* in November, February and March 1857/58, and the *A. J. Ross* in November 1877) caught or sighted at least 13 right whales in Cintra Bay (23° N latitude) on the west African coast in Mauritania. Schevill (pers. comm.) notes that this seems to have been a low-key fishery, but it appears to be in a previously unrecorded location, likely to have been a breeding area.

Reeves told me (pers. comm.) before the Workshop meeting that there were additional records for Cintra Bay, and Reeves and Mitchell (1986) give a detailed account of American whaling for right whales in this area in the period 1855 to 1880 during which at least 35 visits were made by American whaling vessels.

The atlas maps indicate that this is a desert coast with no coastal road and only a desert track passing some distance inland. The possibility that a few right whales might still occur in winter in this bay arises, and if this is so, they could account for at least some of the very few recent sightings, and the female and calf caught at Madeira in February 1967. If they do not occur here, then, unless right whales occur elsewhere on the desert coast of west and northwest Africa, it seems likely that no breeding stocks still exist in the eastern North Atlantic Ocean and that the recent occurrences are of stragglers from the more numerous population in the western North Atlantic. A systematic search of Cintra Bay and the adjacent coast could perhaps answer this question.

ACKNOWLEDGEMENTS

In compiling this review I am much indebted to several colleagues for their valuable assistance with information relating to published and unpublished records of right whales. A. Aguilar discussed the Spanish stranding records with me and drew my attention to Nores's work. He also confirmed the Spanish sightings. I. Christensen told me of the 1967/68 Norwegian minke whalers sighting. J. Sigurjónsson very generously gave me details of the unpublished Icelandic sightings. W. E. Schevill kindly sent me a copy of his paper with K. E. Moore before publication, and commented on the Cintra Bay records; R. R. Reeves also mentioned his additional records from this area and the result of his examination of the logbooks of twentieth century American whaleships in the Atlantic Ocean. L. A. Carter at the Workshop meeting gave me the merchant vessel record of the two whales in the Bay of Biscay area. C. Nores drew my attention to the newly reported Spanish record and sent me a copy of his paper in which it appears. Finally, two reviewers offered constructive comments on the original draft. I thank them all for their help.

REFERENCES

Aguilar, A. 1981. The Black right whale, *Eubalaena glacialis*, in the Cantabrian Sea. *Rep. int. Whal. Commn* 31: 457–9.

Aguilar, A. and Lens, S. 1981. Preliminary report on Spanish whaling acitivities. *Rep. int. Whal. Commn* 31: 639–43.

Aguilar, A. and Sanpera, C. 1982. Reanalysis of Spanish sperm, fin and sei whale catch data (1957–80). *Rep. int. Whal. Commn* 32: 465–70.

Allen, P., Compton-Bishop, Q. and Gordon, J. (n.d.) The report of Cambridge Azores Expedition 1979. 46 pp. (Unpublished manuscript.)

Anon. 1960. Catch statistics. The summer season 1959. *Norsk Hvalfangsttid.* 49(7): 327–8.

Anon. 1980. Regardez en naviguant. Connaître les espéces Marins. *Annales Soc. Sci. Nat. Charente-Maritime.* Supp. March 1980. 14 pp.

Anon. 1981. Norway. Progress report on cetacean research June 1979–May 1980. *Rep. int. Whal. Commn* 31: 209–10.

Brown, S. G. 1958. Whales observed in the Atlantic Ocean. *Mar. Obs. Lond.* 28: 142–6, 209–16.

Brown, S. G. 1976a. Modern whaling in Britain and the northeast Atlantic Ocean. *Mammal Rev.* 6(1), 25–36.

Brown, S. G. 1976b. Sightings of blue and humpback whales on the Icelandic whaling grounds 1969 to 1974. *Rep. int. Whal. Commn* 26: 297–9.

Casinos, A. and Vericad, J. R. 1976. The cetaceans of the Spanish coasts: a survey. *Mammalia* 40(2): 267–89.

Clarke, R. 1954. Open boat whaling in the Azores. The history and present methods of a relic industry. *Discovery Rep.* 26: 281–354.

Clarke, R. 1981. Whales and dolphins of the Azores and their exploitation. *Rep. int. Whal. Commn* 31: 607–15.

Collett, R. 1909. A few notes on the whale *Balaena glacialis* and its capture in recent years in the North Atlantic by Norwegian whalers. *Proc. Zool. Soc. Lond.* 1909: 91–8.

Degerbøl, M. 1940. Mammalia. pp.1–132. *In:* A. S. Jensen *et al.* (Eds) *Zoology of the Faroes.* Copenhagen.

Evans, P. G. H. 1976. An analysis of sightings of Cetacea in British waters. *Mammal Rev.* 6(1): 5–14.

Evans, P. G. H. 1980. Cetaceans in British waters. *Mammal Rev.* 10(1): 1–52.

Evans, P. G. H. 1981. Report of the NE Atlantic Summer 1980 Whale and Sea Bird Cruise. 40 pp. (Unpublished manuscript.)

FAO. 1978. Mammals in the Seas. Volume 1. Report of the FAO Advisory Committee on Marine Resources Research, Working party on Marine Mammals. *FAO Fish. Ser.* (5) Vol. 1: 275 pp.

Fairley, J. 1981. *Irish Whales and Whaling.* Blackstaff Press Limited. Belfast. xv+218 pp.

Garcia-Dory, M. A. 1974. Aves y mamiferos extinguidos en Asturias durante los ultimos cien años. *Asturnatura* 2: 105–7.

Gomez de Llarena, J. 1952. Restos de una ballena de Deva. *Munibe* 4: 220–3.

Gonzalez Echegaray, R. 1978. *Balleneros Cantabros.* Institucion Cultural de Cantabria, Santander. 290 pp.

Harmer, S. F. 1928. The history of whaling. *Proc. Linn. Soc. Lond.* Session 140: 51–95.

Haug, T. 1980. En grønlandshval observert på Tanasnaget (N 71° 00′, Ø 25° 51′) i mai 1980. *Fauna* 33: 158–9.

Hegarty, R. B. 1959. *Returns of whaling vessels sailing from American ports – 1876–1928.* The Old Dartmouth Historical Society and Whaling Museum, New Bedford. ii+58 pp.

International Whaling Statistics. The Committee for Whaling Statistics. Sandefjord.

Jonsgård, Å. 1977. Tables showing the catch of small whales (including minke whales) caught by Norwegians in the period 1938–75, and large whales caught in different North Atlantic waters in the period 1868–1975. *Rep. int. Whal. Commn* 27: 413–26.

Jonsgård, Å. 1981. Bowhead whales, *Balaena mysticetus*, observed in Arctic waters of the eastern North Atlantic after the Second World War. *Rep. int. Whal. Commn* 31: 511.

Jonsgård, Å. 1982. Bowhead (*Balaena mysticetus*) surveys in Arctic northeast Atlantic waters in 1980. *Rep. int. Whal. Commn* 32: 355–6.

Maul, G. E. and Sergeant, D. E. 1977. New cetacean records from Madeira. *Bocagiana*, no. 43. 8 pp.

Millais, J. G. 1906. *The Mammals of Great Britain and Ireland*, vol. 3. Longmans Green, London. xii, 384 pp.

Mitchell, E. D. 1973. The status of the world's whales. *Nature Canada* 2(4): 9–25.

Mitchell, E. and Reeves, R. R. 1983. Catch history, abundance, and present status of northwest Atlantic humpback whales. *Rep. int. Whal. Commn* (special issue 5): 153–212.

Mörzer Bruyns, W. F. J. 1971. *Field Guide of Whales and Dolphins.* Tor and Mees, Amsterdam. 258 pp.

Murphy, R. C. 1947. *Logbook for Grace. Whaling Brig Daisy, 1912–1913.* Macmillan, New York. xiv, 290 pp.

Nores, C. and Perez, M. C. 1983. Mamiferos marinos de la costa Asturiana: I. Relaciones de observaciones, capturas y embarrancamientos hasta 1982. *Bol. Cien. Nat. IDEA* 31: 17–48.

Preston, K. 1975. Mammals at Cape Clear Island in 1970–73. *Rep. Cape Clear Bird Observatory* No. 13 (1972–74): 34–7.

Reeves, R. 1982. What hope for North Atlantic right whales? *Oryx* XVI (3): 255–62.

Reeves, R. R. and Mitchell, E. 1986. American pelagic whaling for right whales in the North Atlantic. (Published in this volume.)

Risting, S. 1922. *Av Hvalfangstens Historie.* Cappelens, Kristiania. 631 pp.

Ruud, J. T. 1937. Nordkaperen. *Balaena glacialis* (Bonnaterre). *Norsk Hvalfangsttid.* 26(8): 270–8.

Saemundsson, B. 1939. *Mammalia, The Zoology of Iceland*, vol. 4, part 76. Copenhagen and Reykjavik.

Schevill, W. E. and Moore, K. E. 1983. Townsend's unmapped North Atlantic right whales (*Eubalaena glacialis*). *Breviora* 476, 8 pp.

Sharrock, J. T. R. 1967. Cetacea off Cape Clear Island. *Rep. Cape Clear Bird Observatory* 8 (1966): 42–4.

Sharrock, J. T. R. 1973. Dolphins, porpoises and whales, pp. 156–8. *In:* Sharrock J. T. R. (Ed.) *The Natural History of Cape Clear Island.* T. and A. D. Poyser, Berkhamsted. 208 pp.

Slijper, E. J., Van Utrecht, W. L. and Naaktgeboren, C. 1964. Remarks on the distribution and migration of whales, based on observations from Netherlands ships. *Bijdr. Dierkd.* 34: 3–93.

Teixeira, A. M. A. P. 1979. Marine mammals of the Portuguese coast. *Z. Säugetierkunde* 44(4): 221–8.

Thompson, D'A. W. 1928. On whales landed at the Scottish whaling stations during the years 1908–1914 and 1920–1927. *Rep. Fish. Bd Scot. Sci. Invest.* 1928, part 3: 40 pp.

Tomilin, A. G. 1967. *Cetacea. Mammals of the USSR and adjacent countries*, vol. 9. Israel Program for Scientific Translations. xxii, 717 pp. [Translation of the Russian volume originally published in 1957.]

Tønnessen, J. N. and Johnsen, A. O. 1982. *The History of Modern Whaling.* Hurst, London. xx+798 pp.

The Distributional Biology of the Right Whale (*Eubalaena glacialis*) in the Western North Atlantic

HOWARD E. WINN, CAROL A. PRICE AND PETER W. SORENSEN

Graduate School of Oceanography, University of Rhode Island, Kingston, Rhode Island 02881, USA

ABSTRACT

Right whale sighting data from Florida to Nova Scotia were analyzed for patterns of distribution, movements and relationships to certain environmental variables. The distribution of calves, surface feeding and social activities on the northern feeding grounds were also examined. A general pattern of distribution has emerged with calving occurring during the winter off Georgia and Florida. The winter distribution of social units other than cow-calf pairs is poorly known. In the spring, large numbers of right whales arrive in the Great South Channel (between Cape Cod and Georges Bank) where they feed for up to several months and in the Cape Cod–Massachusetts Bay area. In June they migrate across the Gulf of Maine to the Bay of Fundy and the southeastern Scotian Shelf, where they also feed for several months. In late October–November, they leave these areas, presumably migrating rapidly southward with no prolonged stops along the way. There are, however, scattered sightings in the study area that do not fit the general pattern.

Social behavior was not distributed differently with regard to water depth, bottom slope, nor surface temperature, and occurred throughout the northern feeding range. The whales are located generally in water with surface temperatures of 8 to 15 °C, over areas 100 to 200 m deep except in the shallower Cape Cod Bay and adjacent to steeply sloping bottom topography. Calves were observed closer to shore and in shallower areas with steeper sloping bottom topography than non-calf sightings. Surface feeding sightings occurred at shallower depths than non-feeding sightings and were generally uncommon except in Cape Cod Bay. Areas of concentrations of right whales were found in the Great South Channel, Cape Cod Bay, the Bay of Fundy, and the southeastern Scotian shelf.

It is hypothesized that the patchy distribution of the right whale is related to a similar patchiness of their principal prey, *Calanus finmarchicus*.

INTRODUCTION

Very few sightings of right whales were recorded in the western North Atlantic from 1913 until the late 1950s when Watkins and Schevill (1982) began seeing right whales in Cape Cod waters and at a time when Moore (1953) was reporting cows and cow-calves off Florida. Since then many sightings of right whales have been made from Newfoundland to Florida. The majority of these represent opportunistic observations in limited geographic areas. More extensive information was collected from 1978 to 1982 by the Cetacean and Turtle Assessment Program (CETAP), which conducted systematic aerial and shipboard surveys from the northern Gulf of Maine to Cape Hatteras, North Carolina, USA, (Winn, 1982a). Extensive data are now also available from the Bay of Fundy (Kraus and Prescott, 1981; 1982; 1983). Despite these research efforts, limited information is currently available on several aspects of right whale biology including seasonal distribution; migratory patterns; and habitat utilization for feeding, mating, and calving. Increased knowledge in these areas is necessary to develop management policies capable of protecting this endangered species.

In this study the CETAP right whale sighting data were combined with additional data collected by other research groups from the Bay of Fundy and Scotian Shelf to Florida. These data were analyzed to characterize right whale distribution and biology. Sightings were plotted to determine overall distribution, and then adjusted for effort to determine areas of concentration. Water temperature, depth and bottom topography (slope) were characterized for all sightings. Temporal patterns were also evaluated. Areas containing concentrations of right whales, calves, and where feeding behavior and social behavior were observed, were plotted, and their temperatures, depths and slopes characterized and statistically compared to both areas of general distribution and areas without sightings. Findings were evaluated within the context of prey distribution. The annual distributional cycle of the right whale is divided into a series of smaller units (phases) and is discussed in detail.

MATERIALS AND METHODS

Sightings of live right whales made from Cape Hatteras northward after 1965 and from Cape Hatteras to Florida after 1950 were collected from all known reliable sources. Only sightings judged to be probable or definite right whales and with positions accurate to within one minute of longitude and latitude were used. The following data bases were employed:

(1) The Cetacean and Turtle Assessment Program (CETAP; University of Rhode Island; H. E. Winn, Scientific Director). CETAP conducted surveys and collected data on cetacean distribution and abundance shoreward of the 1,000 fathom (1,829 m) isobath between Cape Hatteras and Nova Scotia from October 1978 through January 1982. Methodology and findings are described in the final report (Winn, 1982a). Four types of data were collected and used in this analysis.

    (a) Dedicated aerial surveys – random transect aerial surveys were conducted in defined blocks to calculate species abundance (see Scott and Gilbert, 1982). Several special surveys were designed to determine right whale abundance in areas of high concentrations (171 sightings; 472 individuals).

    (b) Platforms of opportunity (POP) surveys – trained observers were placed on board various ships and aircraft operating within the CETAP study area (52 sightings; 88 individuals).

    (c) Opportunistic – data reported to CETAP by reliable observers also working within the CETAP area (148 sightings; 227 individuals).

(d) Historical – miscellaneous data collected within the CETAP area prior to CETAP (1960–1978) and judged to be reliable, (138 sightings; 394 individuals).

(2) Data collected by the authors in 1982 and 1983 including:

(a) A 10-day cruise in May 1982 and another in May 1983 to the Great South Channel (between Cape Cod and Georges Bank) aboard the R/V *Regina Maris* (30 sightings; 51 individuals).

(b) Four single-day flights in May 1982 and another four in May 1983 aboard Coast Guard Offshore Law Patrol flights (22 sightings; 71 individuals).

(3) Data collected by Mitchell, Kozicki and Reeves (1986) from ship surveys and whaling operations conducted off the southeast coast of Nova Scotia (southeast Scotian Shelf) between 1966 and 1972 (313 sightings; 1,889 individuals).

(4) Data collected by Kraus and Prescott (1982) in the Bay of Fundy between August and October of 1981 using ship and aerial surveys (161 sightings; 310 individuals).

(5) Miscellaneous data collected between 1981–1983 and reported to H. E. Winn (see acknowledgements) (26 sightings; 57 individuals).

(6) Data summarized in Winn (1984) from Florida to Cape Hatteras (182 sightings; 249 individual sightings).

The data base comprised a grand total of 1,243 sightings of 3,808 animals. Because the data base necessarily contained many multiple sightings of individual whales, analyses were limited to patterns of distribution and movement. Also, because positions of survey tracks were only available for the dedicated aerial and POP data collected by CETAP, these data alone were used in effort analyses.

All sightings were plotted to determine overall distribution. To test the validity of this distribution, a separate analysis of sightings per unit effort was performed using the dedicated aerial and POP data collected by CETAP (south to Cape Hatteras only). The CETAP study area was divided into adjoining blocks 10 minutes of latitude by 10 minutes of longitude. For each block the total number of right whales sighted was then divided by total effort (km surveyed by airplane or ships but not including measurement of effective track width) and multiplied by 1,000 to produce a sighting index (S.I.) in units of right whales sighted per 1,000 km of track surveyed. This method is described in detail in Kenney and Winn (1986). Blocks were then classified into three categories according to the value of their sighting indices: low density $(10 \geqslant S.I. > 0)$; medium density $(100 \geqslant S.I. > 10)$ and high density $(S.I. > 100)$, and the positions plotted.

To evaluate patterns of migration the entire study area was divided into nine regions (Fig. 1) defined as:

Southeastern U.S.: Between 26° 00′ and 34° 00′ N From 65° 00′ W westward to land

Cape Hatteras: Between 34° 00′ and 37° 00′ N From 65° 00′ W westward to land

Mid-Atlantic: Between 37° 00′ and 40° 30′ N From 65° 00′ W westward to land

Long Island: Between 40° 30′ and 42° 30′ N From 70° 00′ W westward to land

Great South Channel: Between 40° 30′ and 42° 30′ N From 68° 00′ to 70° 00′ W

Massachusetts and Cape Cod Bays: Between 41° 42′ and 42° 30′ N From 70° 00′ W westward to land

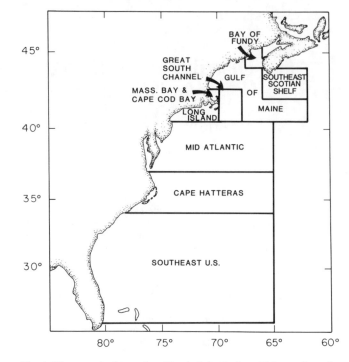

Fig. 1. The areas in the western North Atlantic for which a variety of analyses were made.

Bay of Fundy: Between 44° 00′ and 45° 12′ N From 66° 00′ to 67° 30′ W

Southeast Scotian Shelf: Between 42° 00′ and 44° 00′ N From 62° 00′ to 66° 00′ W

Gulf of Maine: Area bounded on the north by the Bay of Fundy and southeastern Scotian Shelf, and on the south by Massachusetts Bay and Great South Channel and mid-Atlantic areas, eastward to 62° W.

The total number of individuals seen in each of these regions for each month was plotted as a series of histograms.

The next step in the analysis was to look for significant relationships of right whale sighting distribution to various environmental factors. A large majority of the sightings in the data set also included water depth at the sighting position, and many included sea surface temperature as well. To look for potential relations to bottom topography, a large data set containing water depths digitized at two minute intervals was partitioned into adjoining 10-minute blocks (i.e. 25 depth values per complete block). Two measures of bottom topography were calculated for each 10-minute block. The first is Hui's contour index (Hui, 1979):

$$\frac{\text{maximum depth} - \text{minimum depth}}{\text{maximum depth}} \times 100$$

This measures the relative bottom slope in a block. The second index is simply the coefficient of variation of the depth values, which measures relative variability of the depth within a block. The mean of the depths within each block was also calculated.

Each sighting was classified according to the occurrence of three items: calves, feeding behavior, and social behavior. A calf was defined as any small individual seen in constant close proximity to an adult-sized animal, presumably the cow. Mitchell *et al.*'s (1986) data were excluded from this analysis because they were unsure whether their data source consistently reported this

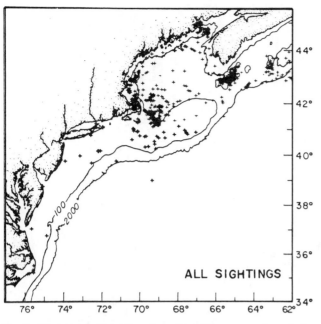

Fig. 2. All right whale sightings from Cape Hatteras northward, the CETAP study area. Depths in meters. Data bases 1 through 5.

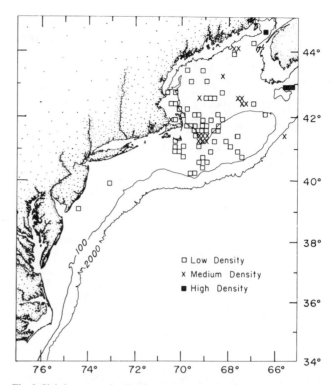

Fig. 3. Sightings per unit effort in 10 minute blocks for the CETAP study area. Depths in meters. Data bases 1a and 1b.

information. Observations of feeding were defined as those where individuals were seen with open mouths; this necessarily limited the observations to surface or very near-surface feeding only. Social behavior was defined to include any group (two or more whales) where interactions, including touching, rolling, and penis extrusion, took place. Mitchell *et al.*'s (1986) data were excluded from both feeding and social behavior comparisons, since their data did not include behavioral descriptions.

The water depth and surface temperature data for sightings with calves, with feeding, and with social behavior were compared respectively, to the data for all other sightings in a series of separate tests. The comparisons were done using the Wilcoxon Rank Sum test, a non-parametric one-way analysis of variance. Non-parametric statistics require no assumptions about distribution of the data. Wilcoxon Rank Sum tests for differences in mean depth. Hui's contour index, and coefficient of variation of depth values in 10-minute blocks were calculated for the following comparisons:
(a) Blocks with sightings vs. blocks without sightings.
(b) Blocks with 10 or more sightings vs. all other blocks.
(c) Blocks with calf sightings vs. all other blocks.
(d) Blocks with only calf sightings vs. blocks with only non-calf sightings.
(e) Blocks with feeding sightings vs. all other blocks.
(f) Blocks with only feeding sightings vs. blocks with only non-feeding sightings.
(g) Blocks with social behavior sightings vs. all other blocks.
(h) Blocks with only social behavior vs. blocks with only non-social behavior sightings.
The cutoff value for significance in all tests was defined as p = 0.10. These comparisons were limited to blocks north of 41° N latitude (feeding region), thereby including 95% of the sightings while eliminating a major source of variability, since activities to the south are presumably different (migration, calving, non-feeding).

Sightings made in the Great South Channel in March–July of 1979–1983 were plotted by year. The area was divided into four equal quadrants along north–south and east–west axes. The number of days in which either aerial or shipboard sampling was conducted in each quadrant was determined for each year as an estimate of effort. CETAP personnel were responsible for all of these sightings. Sightings made in the Bay of Fundy were also plotted using all available data, although 90% of these sightings were actually made by Kraus and Prescott (1982) in the summer of 1981. All sightings over the southeastern Scotian Shelf were plotted; 98% of these were actually from Mitchell *et al.* (1986) between 1966 and 1972. The median depths and temperatures at sightings within these three areas were calculated, and the depth and temperature data were tested for significant differences between areas. Values of Hui's index, coefficient of variation of depth, and mean depth for 10-minute blocks with right whale sightings within the three areas were also tested for significant differences between areas. These tests were done using the Kruskal-Wallis test, again a non-parametric analysis of variance, for data classified into three or more groups.

RESULTS

Sightings made in the area north of 41° N latitude which were used in the calf, feeding, and social behavior analyses are plotted in Fig. 2. Right whale sightings per unit effort in 10-minute blocks north of 41° N latitude are plotted in Fig. 3. These two plots showed similar patterns of distribution with the greatest concentrations occurring in the Great South Channel, Bay of Fundy and southeastern Scotian Shelf just beyond the 100 m depth contour. Another area with a number of sightings is in Massachusetts and Cape Cod Bays (Fig. 2), but when this is effort corrected (Fig. 3), it is not as concentrated as the

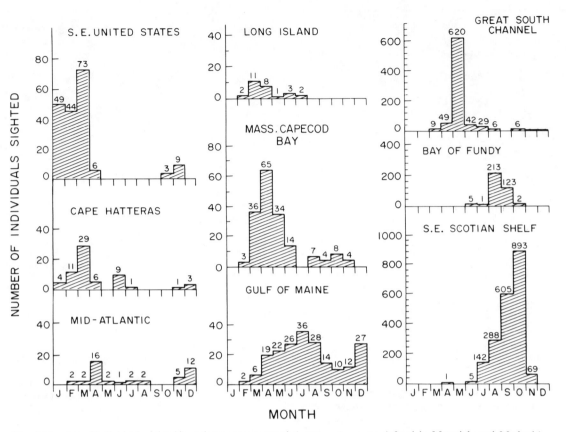

Fig. 4. Number of individuals sighted in each area versus month (areas and sources defined in Materials and Methods). Depth in meters. S.E. = southeast. Data bases 1 through 6.

above areas over a long period of time. Recent work by Charles Mayo (personal communication) may show that this area is a significant area of concentration.

In the southeastern United States most sightings occurred from January through March as was true at Cape Hatteras (Fig. 4). There were several fall sightings and a few in the summer at Cape Hatteras. There were sightings over many months in the mid-Atlantic with a peak in December and a peak in April one month after the Cape Hatteras March peak. Long Island sightings were from February to June with a minor peak in March and April. Generally, in the areas north of Cape Hatteras, there were few winter sightings (January–February). Further north, a large concentration occurred in the Great South Channel during April to early June. The May peak may represent a sampling bias since these sightings are not effort corrected. The concentration of right whales in the Great South Channel was only discovered in 1979 (Winn, Goodale, Hyman, Kenney, Price and Scott, 1981). Concentrations of right whales were present in Massachusetts and Cape Cod Bays from March through June. Sightings in the Gulf of Maine were made throughout the year peaking in July and again in December. Concentrations were observed in the Bay of Fundy from August through September, but only a few were seen in October despite the surveys conducted by Kraus and Prescott (1982) at this time. Sighting frequency increased over the southeastern Scotian Shelf from July through October dropping to a low level in November. Winter sightings were absent but there was a lack of any effort. About one third of all sightings analyzed in this study were reported from the Scotian Shelf.

The median sighting depth in the northern feeding range was 134 m, with a range of 5–4,095 m. Those depths shallower than 100 m were primarily from Cape Cod Bay and calf sightings. Three-quarters of all sightings occurred between 46 and 170 m. The median temperature at a sighting was 12.5 °C, with a range of 2.2°–21.8 °C. Three-quarters of all sightings had temperatures of 8.0–14.8 °C. Neither slope index (Hui's index and coefficient of variation of depth) for blocks with sightings (n = 215) was significantly different at p ≤ 0.10 from blocks without sightings (n = 842). The mean depth of blocks with sightings was significantly shallower (p = 0.038) than for blocks without sightings, however. Comparisons of slope indices and mean depth of those blocks with 10 or more sightings versus all other blocks showed no significant differences.

Calves were sighted 58 times, most of which were closer to shore than the non-calf sightings (Fig. 5). The median depth of these sightings was 77 m (range: 9–190 m) and the median temperature 7.7 °C (range 6.0–14.5 °C). Three-quarters of these sightings had depths of 16–152 m and temperatures of 6.0–12.5 °C. Calves were sighted at shallower depths (p = 0.002) than sightings without calves, although water temperature was not significantly different. There were 28 10-minute blocks with calf sightings, and these were over steeper slopes (Hui's index: p = 0.009; coefficient of variation: p = 0.024) than all other blocks north 41° N, although mean depths were not significantly different. There were five blocks containing only cow-calf sightings and 126 with only non-calf sightings. Only Hui's index was significantly different between these blocks (p = 0.073), those with calf sightings only having steeper slopes. No calves were seen

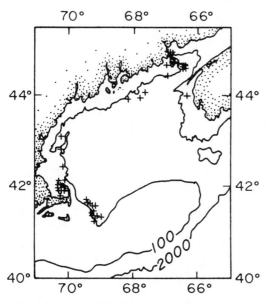

Fig. 5. Calf sightings in the CETAP study area. Depths in meters. Data bases 1, 2, 4 and 5.

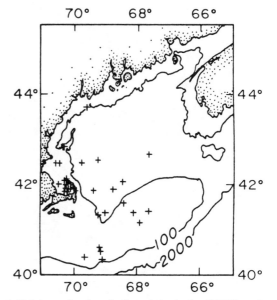

Fig. 6. Sightings of surface feeding whales in the CETAP study area. Depths in meters. Data bases 1, 2, 4 and 5.

over the southeast Scotian Shelf, but Kraus (pers. comm.) saw two in the summer of 1985. Calves were sighted in most months of the year on the northern feeding grounds exclusive of December and February. In the southeast, calves were sighted from December through April.

Surface feeding was observed 36 times. Most occurrences were in Massachusetts–Cape Cod Bay with scattered records in the Great South Channel and Gulf of Maine (Fig. 6). The median water depth for sightings of feeding was 48 m (range: 9–265 m); the median temperature at these sightings was 9.4 °C. Three-quarters of these sightings had depths of 9–123 m and temperatures of 6.5–12.5 °C. Water depth at sightings with feeding was significantly shallower (p < 0.001) than for all other sightings, but temperature was not significantly different. Twenty-four 10-minute blocks contained sightings of feeding behavior, and only average depth was significantly different (shallower, p = 0.025) from all other blocks north of 41° N. Eleven blocks contained only sightings with feeding behavior, and there were no significant differences in bottom topography or mean depth between these blocks and blocks with only non-feeding sightings (n = 131). Surface feeding was observed from March through October in the north.

Social behavior was seen 59 times. There was no discernible pattern to its distribution except that it occurred in all the areas of right whale concentrations (Fig. 7). Neither depth (median = 128 m; range = 18–338 m) nor temperature (median = 7.0 °C; range = 4.6–20.0 °C) differed from that of all other sightings. Three quarters of these sightings had depths of 41–151 m and temperatures of 5.0–13.0 °C. Twenty-five blocks contained sightings with social behavior, with no significant differences in either of the two slope indices or in mean depth from all other blocks north of 41 °N. Social behavior was observed March through December exclusive of June and September.

A total of 293 sightings was made in the Great South Channel area (Fig. 8). These sightings had a median depth of 146 m and median temperature 8.6 °C. There was considerable variability in sampling effort in this region; 1979 had a very high level of evenly distributed effort, 1980 and 1981 a moderate level with the northeast

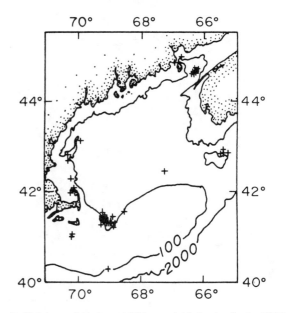

Fig. 7. Sightings of whales exhibiting social behavior in the CETAP study area. Depths in meters. Data bases 1, 2, 4 and 5.

quadrant not sampled in 1981, and both 1982 and 1983 had a low level of unevenly distributed effort (Table 1). The 1979 sightings were mostly in water deeper than 100 m, and some occurred at depths deeper than 200 m. There was no discernible pattern and the sightings were evenly distributed. By contrast, most sightings in 1980, 1981, 1982, and 1983 occurred in water slightly deeper than 100 m, and in well defined concentrations either along the western or southern edge of the channel. The specific locations of these concentrations varied with year, however.

One hundred and seventy-four sightings were made in the Bay of Fundy. Their median depth was 141 m. Too few temperatures (n = 2) were measured to provide a meaningful median. Two apparent areas of concentration were evident (see Kraus and Prescott, 1982): a major concentration on the northern edge of the central basin and in water slightly shallower than 200 m; and a smaller concentration to the northwest of the first, in water

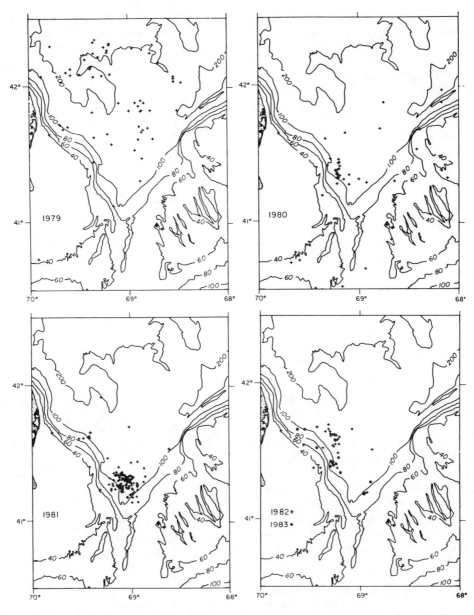

Fig. 8. Sightings in the Great South Channel between Cape Cod and Georges Bank for five years. Depths in meters. Data bases 1a, b, c, 2 and 5.

Table 1.

Sighting effort (expressed as days of aerial or shipboard surveys) in the Great South Channel between March and July, delineated by year and quadrant, with corresponding numbers of right whale sightings.

Year	Effort per quadrant				Total effort	No. of sightings
	NW	NE	SE	SW		
1979	60	27	31	62	180	61
1980	35	13	38	12	98	40
1981	20	0	16	26	62	131
1982	9	4	5	7	25	37
1983	5	5	8	8	26	18

slightly shallower than 100 m and much closer to shore (Fig. 9). About one-third of the sightings in the latter concentration were cows and calves.

Three hundred and eighteen sightings were made over the southeastern Scotian Shelf. Most sightings were concentrated in the area bordered by Browns and Emerald Banks and between the 100 m and 200 m depth contours (Fig. 10). Their median depth was 146 m, and median temperature was 13.5 °C.

Table 2 shows the results of comparisons between areas. Only mean depth of 10-minute blocks with right whale sightings was not significantly different at $p > 0.10$. Water depth was deepest for Scotian Shelf sightings and about the same for the other two areas, with the differences significant at $p = 0.08$. Surface temperature was much warmer for both the Scotian Shelf and Bay of Fundy (only 2 values), a highly significant ($p = 0.0001$) difference. Both indices of bottom slope/topography show highly significant differences, with slopes in the Bay of Fundy the steepest.

DISCUSSION

With the updated and more extensive data base we can now modify our original model of the annual distribution of the right whale in the western North Atlantic (Winn and Price, in Winn, 1982a). Also, we can compare our conclusions with the general patterns discussed in Reeves, Mead and Katona (1978) and in Katona, Steiner and

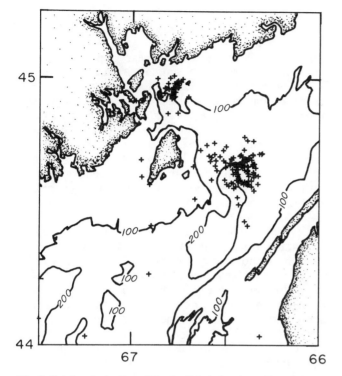

Fig. 9. Sightings in the Bay of Fundy. Depths in meters. Data bases 1a and 4.

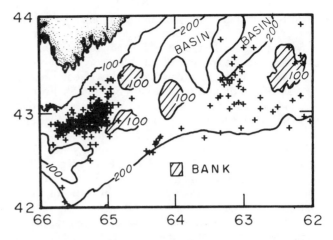

Fig. 10. Sightings over the Scotian Shelf to the south and east of the southern end of Nova Scotia. Depth in meters. Data bases 1a and 3.

Table 2.

Comparisons of environmental variables for right whale sightings, for 10-minute blocks with right whale sightings, among the three defined areas, showing average value for each area and the significance probability (p) from a Kruskal–Wallis test for differences between areas.

Variable	Great South Channel	Bay of Fundy	Scotian Shelf	p
Depth at sighting (n)	134.5m (293)	131.6m (174)	183.3m (318)	0.0836
Temperature (n)	9.04 C (152)	13.90 C (2)	13.69 C (269)	0.0001
Mean depth (n)	129.1m (64)	103.7m (18)	197.4m (71)	0.2395
Hui's index (n)	38.86 (64)	67.99 (18)	41.71 (71)	0.0001
C.V. of depth (n)	16.27 (64)	36.71 (18)	19.95 (71)	0.0008

Winn (1978). Although a clear general pattern is emerging there are significant unknowns in the system. The annual distribution can be separated into a series of distinct phases.

Phase 1 – During the winter, cows and calves are found along the Georgia–Florida coast in shallow water (Winn, 1984; Mead, 1986). So far the incomplete evidence suggests that this only accounts for 15 to 30 individuals per year (Winn, 1984 and unpublished data). There are a few winter sightings at Cape Hatteras. If there is a three-year calving period (Kraus, Prescott, Knowlton and Stone, 1986), then each year, for three years, different individuals would be involved. This leaves up to several hundred individuals unaccounted for. Whether or not some or most of these may be found further from shore in the southeast is unknown. Charles Mayo's recent

observations (pers. comm.) of winter individuals near Cape Cod and their historical presence around Long Island (Reeves and Mitchell, 1986) allows one to hypothesize that the remainder of the population is scattered along the whole coast of the eastern United States and is made up of non-cow-calf groups.

Phase 2 – During late winter and early spring, there is a strong northward component to the migration as stated in Reeves et al. (1978). The movement is presumed to be primarily northward passing Cape Hatteras, the Mid-Atlantic and Long Island. It has now been established that at least some of the Georgia–Florida wintering individuals move northward through the Great South Channel to the Bay of Fundy and southeastern Scotian Shelf in the summer (Kraus, Moore, Price, Crone, Watkins, Winn and Prescott, 1986). If some individuals stay all winter around Cape Cod then the above movements apply to only a portion of the population. Some individuals move along the shore (Reeves et al., 1978), and these may be primarily pregnant females and cows with calves. Others must migrate northward over deeper water, perhaps coming up in the Gulf Stream which would be energetically efficient. Our sightings near the 200 m counter in early March 1980 lend credence to this suggestion.

Phase 3 – During March to May (peak in April) most sightings were made in the Cape Cod–Massachusetts Bay area (see also Reeves et al., 1978) and the Great South Channel (peak in May), where feeding takes place. Calves have been seen in both areas. Some calving may occur here (Watkins and Schevill, 1982). What interrelationships exist between the two areas is unknown. Allen (1916) showed that right whales were common off Cape Cod in April and May, with only sporadic sightings at other times. It is hypothesized that most of the population occupies these two areas during this time. The maximum residence time for the Great South Channel so far detected was 24 days (Price and Winn, unpublished data). Whether or not most of the population moves through the Great South Channel is unknown. Some right whales are also beginning to be seen in the Gulf of Maine during this period.

Phase 4 – During June and July, individuals move across the Gulf of Maine, without any long pauses to migration, to the Bay of Fundy and southeast Scotian Shelf. Identified individuals are known to move from the

Great South Channel to the summering areas in the far northern Gulf of Maine thus having to cross the Gulf. Movement across the Gulf by some individuals probably also occurs in the spring and some few stay in the Gulf.

Phase 5 – Most individuals occur in two feeding areas, the Bay of Fundy and southeastern Scotian Shelf, from July to October. The connection between these two areas is poorly understood, but a few identified individuals have been seen in both areas (Kraus *et al.*, 1986).

Phase 6 – From October through January, the right whales leave the Nova Scotian–Bay of Fundy region. The whales do not pause in migration for any protracted time, but appear to be moving steadily southward. For those that go past Cape Cod, the migrants move offshore, and some presumably continue southward. A segment of the population may migrate along the eastern side of Georges Bank. Then some individuals appear around Cape Hatteras and move onto the continental shelf off the southeastern states, thus completing the annual cycle. Allen (1916) stated that a decrease of sightings off Cape Cod during December indicated a movement to the south. Since southward migrations have not been observed, they may take place offshore (Caldwell and Caldwell, 1974). Best (1970) suggested that southern right whales, when migrating northward from the Antarctic, travel offshore and move much faster than in the reverse migration as is the apparent case in the western North Atlantic. Similar data are presented by Katona *et al.* (1978) and Reeves *et al.* (1978).

Generally, the model as presented agrees with the historical sightings and catches, which indicate that right whales all over the world shift latitudinally during the year (Townsend, 1935). They feed in colder regions in the summer, and then calve in warm temperate water in the winter (Tomilin, 1957). The movement of western Pacific right whales seems to be similar to the pattern suggested here for the western North Atlantic (Omura, 1958; Omura, Ohsumi, Nemoto, Nasu, and Kasuya, 1969; Klumov, 1962) Based on sightings and catch data from the shore net fishery, right whales were found off southern and western Japan from December to March. They then appeared in cold nutrient rich waters off northern Japan in April and May (similar to the Great South Channel) with a movement northward into cold near-polar waters in the summer. Sightings were fewer in the fall. Two pregnant female right whales were caught in the eastern Pacific with half-grown fetuses, suggesting that the calves would have been born in the winter. The winter habitat of the eastern Pacific right whale was considered to be off Oregon and perhaps northern and Baja California with some possibly going to Hawaii (Gilmore, 1956; Herman, Baker, Forestall and Antinoja, 1980; Rice and Fiscus, 1968). The latter group would be similar to observing some whales near Bermuda in the north Atlantic during the winter and probably only represent strays.

There are very few recent sightings outside the area considered in the model. A couple of records exist for the Gulf of Mexico (Moore and Clark, 1963; Schmidley, Martin and Collins, 1972). Payne and McVay (1971) saw two individuals in 1970 near Bermuda. A sighting was recorded both for the Gulf of St. Lawrence during 1976 (Sears, 1979) and Newfoundland in 1981 (J. Lien, pers. comm.). Three other Canadian sightings are listed in Reeves *et al.* (1978). The evidence to date suggests that only a few individuals move beyond the area from Nova Scotia to Florida.

The various phases of activity represent central tendencies. Early arrivals and late arrivals are always present. However, they seem to represent exceptional individuals. The few sightings near Cape Cod in the winter may represent a few animals arriving early (phase 2) or a few leaving late in the southerly movement (phase 6), or they may indeed stay there all winter as suggested in the literature (e.g. Reeves *et al.*, 1978). There seems to be a scarcity of sightings in the north from mid-January through February. This could be due to the difficulty of observation in the winter. However, the CETAP surveys indicate no great numbers or concentrations present in mid-winter. The majority of historical and recent observations suggest a movement to the south in the winter.

The use of historical data to interpret current distribution has certain inherent difficulties. The proposed prime movement of most of the present day right whales between Nova Scotia and the southeastern U.S., with a stopover of many of the individuals in the Great South Channel on the northward migration, does not totally agree with the historical data (see summary in Reeves *et al.*, 1978). Right whales once were distributed more or less continuously northward to Greenland with large winter concentrations from Cape Cod southward (e.g. Long Island, Delaware Bay). It seems reasonable to suggest that today mostly what remains is the southerly remnant of the once much larger and more widely distributed western North Atlantic right whale population. The more northerly segment of this inhabited the now partially empty winter habitats of Delaware Bay northward to Cape Cod. The lack of any recent sightings in Delaware Bay may support this contention.

Evidence for calving is so far restricted to the period January to April. If the gestation period is 11 to 12 months as generally believed, then successful mating occurs only during this same period. However, many observers (Kraus and Prescott, 1982; Winn, 1982a) describe mating behaviors at other times of the year. It is likely that activities often interpreted as mating are for other purposes such as socialization. Fertilization could be controlled in some manner, for instance, by seasonal ovulation or seasonal maturation of sperm.

Right whale cows and calves are found on the shoreward edge of the population's distribution, thus in shallower water over steeper bottom slopes. The west side of the Great South Channel, Massachusetts Bay and the Bay of Fundy appear to represent nursery grounds which may offer more shelter and/or isolation from the vigorous social encounters which commonly occur within the main concentrations of animals. Interestingly, within our data set no calves have been observed in the open waters of the Scotian Shelf (although Kraus saw two calves there in the summer of 1985, personal communication).

Sightings of social behavior were not differently distributed to all other sightings. This concurs with observations that social behavior is a common facet of right whale life (Kraus and Prescott, 1982; Winn, 1982b).

In the north, right whales do most of their feeding beneath the surface (Watkins and Schevill, 1979, 1982; Kraus and Prescott, 1982; Winn, 1982a). The small number of feeding incidents (all at or near the surface) analyzed in this study (5.6% of all sightings, excluding Mitchell *et al.*, 1986 and those south of Cape Hatteras) supports this conclusion since more time must be spent feeding in order to meet their energetic requirements.

Like most cetacean species, the distribution and ecology of right whales is probably determined by distribution of prey (Gaskin, 1982). In the three areas of concentration, right whales distribute themselves in 100 to 150 m of water depth usually near but not necessarily over steep bottom slopes. Preliminary studies suggest that, at least in the Great South Channel, this is a zone of complex physical and biological processes with fronts, upwelling, and very high concentrations of *Calanus finmarchicus* (Winn, 1982b; Scott, Kenney, Owen, Hyman, and Winn, 1985). Bigelow (1926) mentioned the existence of extremely high summer densities of *C. finmarchicus* in the area where the right whale concentrates off the southeastern Scotian Shelf, and at a time of low whale density in the Cape Cod region. Cape Cod and Massachusetts Bays, where right whales occur in the spring, have depths generally less than 60 m. Surface feeding on slicks commonly occurs here but generally not in the other areas. The whale's 'selection' of these areas may be based on particular sets of physical conditions resulting in the development of high density patches of their preferred copepod prey. A model of right whale energetics concludes that, in order to meet its metabolic needs, concentrations of prey must be two to three orders of magnitude higher than those recorded by average water column samples (Kenney, Hyman, Owen, Scott and Winn, 1986). Thus it is hypothesized that dense patches of *C. finmarchicus* established by special oceanographic conditions and/or their own behavior control the geographic distribution of right whales on the western North Atlantic feeding grounds. Whether or not euphausiids and other plankton play an important role is unknown.

ACKNOWLEDGEMENTS

The preparation of this paper was made possible by funding through the Minerals Management Service, US Department of the Interior, contract number 14-12-0001-30090. This report has been reviewed by the Minerals Management Service and approved for publication. Approval does not signify that the contents necessarily reflect the views and policies of the Service, nor does mention of trade names or commercial products constitute endorsement or recommendation for use. The CETAP study was also funded by MMS, contract number AA551-CT8-48. We would like to collectively acknowledge the many individuals who contributed to the success of the CETAP study. We are also grateful to E. D. Mitchell, J. H. Prescott, S. D. Kraus, S. N. Mercer, J. P. Ross, G. LeBaron, W. T. Rummage, S. S. Sadove, W. A. Watkins, K. E. Moore, C. A. Mayo, W. Rossiter, P. M. Payne and J. G. Mead, who allowed us to use their sighting information. The United States Coast Guard graciously allowed us to use their platforms for sampling and the National Marine Fisheries Service assisted in developing the data base used for depth analyses. J. R. Green, NMFS, Narragansett advised us on the distribution of zooplankton. G. B. Epstein developed the computer algorithm to measure track line surveyed per block, R. A. Medved and R. D. Kenney provided statistical advice, and M. Nigrelli typed the manuscript. Elizabeth Scott helped with the figures. R. D. Kenney reviewed the manuscript.

REFERENCES

Allen, G. M. 1916. The whalebone whales of New England. *Mem. Boston Soc. nat. Hist.* 8: 107–322.

Best, P. B. 1970. Exploitation and recovery of right whales (*Eubalaena australis*) off the Cape Province. *Investl Rep., Div. Sea Fish S. Afr.* 80: 1–20.

Bigelow, H. B. 1926. Plankton of the offshore waters of the Gulf of Maine. *Bull. U.S. Bur. Fish.* 40(II): 1–509.

Caldwell, D. K. and Caldwell, M. C. 1974. Marine mammals from the southeastern United States coast: Cape Hatteras to Cape Canaveral. pp. 704–772. *In: A Summary for the South Atlantic Region Between Cape Hatteras, North Carolina and Cape Canaveral, Florida.* Virginia Institute of Marine Science, Gloucester Point, VA.

Gaskin, D. E. 1982. *The Ecology of Whales and Dolphins.* Heinemann, London. i–xii + 459 pp.

Gilmore, R. 1956. Rare right whale visits California. *Pacif. Discov.* 9(4): 20–5.

Herman, L. M., Baker, C. S., Forestall, P. H., and Antinoj, R. C. 1980. Right whale *Balaena glacialis* sightings near Hawaii: a clue to the wintering grounds? *Mar. Ecol. Progr. Ser.* 2: 271–5.

Hui, C. A. 1979. Undersea topography and distribution of dolphins of the genus *Delphinus* in the southern California Bight. *J. Mammal.* 60: 521–7.

Katona, S., Steiner, W. and Winn, H. 1978. Marine mammals. pp. XIV-1-165. *In:* Center for Natural Areas. *A Summary of Environmental Information: Continental Shelf. Bay of Fundy to Cape Hatteras,* Vol. 1, Book 2. Bureau of Land Management, Washington, DC. AA550-CT6-45.

Kenney, R. D., Hyman, M. A. M., Owen, R. E, Scott, G. P. and Winn, H. E. 1986. Estimation of prey densities required by western North Atlantic right whales. *Mar. Mamm. Sci.* 2(1): 1–13.

Kenney, R. D. and Winn, H. E. 1986. Cetacean high-use habitats of the northeast United States continental shelf. *Fish. Bull., U.S.* 84(2): 345–57.

Klumov, S. K. 1962. Gladklye (yaponsklye) Kity Tikhogo Okeana *Trudy Inst. Okeanol.* 58: 202–97.

Kraus, S. D., Moore, K. E., Price, C. A., Crone, M. J., Watkins, W. A., Winn, H. E. and Prescott, J. H. 1986. The use of photographs to identify North Atlantic right whales (*Eubalaena glacialis*). (Published in this volume).

Kraus, S. D. and Prescott, J. H. 1981. Distribution, abundance, and notes on the large cetaceans of the Bay of Fundy, summer and fall 1980. Report in fulfillment of Natl. Mar. Fish. Serv. contract NA-80-FA-00048.

Kraus, S. and Prescott, J. H. 1982. The North Atlantic right whales (*Eubalaena glacialis*) in the Bay of Fundy, 1981, with notes on distribution, abundance, biology, and behavior. Final report to U.S. D.C., Nat. Mar. Fish. Serv., Contract No. NA-81-FA-C-00030, and to World Wildlife Fund.-US, Washington.

Kraus, S. D. and Prescott, J. H. 1983. A summary of 1982 research on the North Atlantic right whale, *Eubalaena glacialis*, with notes on seasonal distribution and abundance and significant resightings of individuals. Report in fulfillment of Natl. Mar. Fish. Serv., Contract No. NA-81-FA-C-00030 and World Wildlf. Fund.

Kraus, S. D., Prescott, J. H., Knowlton, A. R. and Stone, G. S. 1986. Migration and calving of western North Atlantic right whales *Eubalaena glacialis*). (Published in this volume).

Mead, J. G. 1986. Twentieth century records of right whales (*Eubalaena glacialis*) in the northwestern Atlantic Ocean. (Published in this volume).

Mitchell, E., Kozicki, V. M. and Reeves, R. R. 1986. Sightings of right whales, *Eubalaena glacialis*, on the Scotian Shelf, 1966–1972. (Published in this volume).

Moore, J. C. 1953. Distribution of marine mammals to Florida waters. *Amer. Midl. Nat.* 49(1): 117–58.

Moore, J. C. and Clark, E. 1963. Discovery of right whales in the Gulf of Mexico. *Science* 141(3577): 269.

Omura, H. 1958. North Pacific right whale. *Sci. Rep. Whales Res. Inst., Tokyo* 13: 1–52.

Omura, H., Ohsumi, S., Nemoto, T., Nasu, K. and Kasuya, T. 1969. Black right whales in the North Pacific. *Sci. Rep. Whales Res. Inst., Tokyo* 21: 1–78.

Payne, R. S. and McVay, S. 1971. Songs of humpback whales. *Science* 173(3997): 585–97.

Reeves, R., Mead, J. and Katona, S. 1978. The right whale, *Eubalaena glacialis*, in the western North Atlantic. *Rep. int. Whal. Commn* 28: 303–12.

Reeves, R. and Mitchell, E. 1986. The Long Island (New York) right whale fishery: 1650–1924. (Published in this volume).

Rice, D. W. and Fiscus, C. H. 1968. Right whales in the southeastern North Pacific. *Norsk Hvalfangst – Tid.* 57(5): 105–7.

Scott, G. P. and Gilbert, J. R. 1982. Problems and progress in the US BLM-sponsored CETAP surveys. *Rep. int. Whal. Commn* 32: 587–600.

Scott, G. P., Kenney, R. D., Owen, R. E., Hyman, M. A. M. and Winn, H. E. 1985. Biological and physical oceanographic correlatives to cetacean density distribution in the Great South Channel. Paper C.M. 1985/N:6/Ref. L presented to the Int. Council for the Expl. of the Sea, Oct. 1985. (unpublished). 36 pp.

Schmidley, D. J., Martin, C. O. and Collins, G. F. 1972. First occurrence of a black right whale (*Balaena glacialis*) along the Texas coast. *Sthwest. Nat.* 17(2): 214–5.

Sears, R. 1979. An occurrence of right whales (*Eubalaena glacialis*) on the north shore of the Gulf of St. Lawrence. *Nat. canad.* 106: 567–8.

Tomilin, A. G. 1957. *Zveri SSSR i prilezhashchikh stran. Zveri vostochnoi Evropy i sevornoi Azii. IX. Kitoobraznye.* Akad. Nauk. Moscow 756 pp. (Translated in 1967 as *Mammals of the USSR and adjacent countries. Vol. IX. Cetacea.* Israel Program for Scientific translations. xxii+717 pp.

Townsend, C. H. 1935. The distribution of certain whales as shown by logbook records of American whaleships. *Zoologica N.Y.* 19: 1–50.

Watkins, W. A. and Schevill, W. E. 1979. Aerial observation of feeding behavior in four baleen whales: *Eubalaena glacialis, Balaenoptera borealis, Megaptera novaeangliae,* and *Balaenoptera physalus. J. Mammal.* 60: 155–63.

Watkins, W. A. and Schevill, W. E. 1982. Observations of right whales *Eubalaena glacialis,* in Cape Cod waters. *Fish. Bull., U.S.* 80: 875–80.

Winn, H. E. 1982a. A Characterization of Marine Mammals and Turtles in the Mid- and North-Atlantic Areas of the US Outer Continental Shelf, Final Report. Bureau of Land Management, Washington, DC. 538 pp. (Natl. Tech. Inform. Service, Springfield, VA 22161, Ref. No. PB83215855).

Winn, H. E. 1982b. Abundance and distribution of cetaceans in the Great South Channel area in relation to physical and biological variables. Appendix C, pp. 1–61. *In*: A Characterization of Marine Mammals and Turtles in the Mid- and North-Atlantic Areas of the US Outer Continental Shelf, Final Report. Bureau of Land Management, Washington, DC. (Natl. Tech. Inform. Service, Springfield, VA 22161, Ref. No. PB83215855).

Winn, H. E. 1984. Development of a right whale sighting network in the southeastern US Report no. MMC-82/05. US Marine Mammal Commission, Washington, DC. 16 pp. (Natl. Tech. Inform. Service, Springfield, VA 22161, Ref. no. PB84240548).

Winn, H. E., D. R. Goodale, M. A. M. Hyman, R. D. Kenney, C. A. Price, G. P. Scott. 1981. Right whale sightings and the right whale minimum count. pp. VI-1-37. *In*: A Characterization of Marine Mammals and Turtles in the Mid- and North-Atlantic Areas of the US Outer Continental Shelf, Annual Report for 1979. Bureau of Land Management, Washington, DC. (Natl. Tech. Inform. Service, Springfield, VA 22161, Ref. No. PB81243289).

Migration and Calving of Right Whales (*Eubalaena glacialis*) in the Western North Atlantic

SCOTT D. KRAUS, JOHN H. PRESCOTT, AMY R. KNOWLTON AND GREGORY S. STONE.

Harold E. Edgerton Research Laboratory, New England Aquarium, Boston, Massachusetts, USA

ABSTRACT

Over 200 right whales (*Eubalaena glacialis*) have been photographically identified between March and November in the Gulf of Maine from 1980 to 1985. Aerial surveys over the coastal waters of the southeastern USA in February and March of 1984 and 1985 yielded sightings and photographs of 25 right whales, including seven newborn calves and one juvenile. This indicates that the region is a significant calving ground for these whales in the western North Atlantic. Twenty-one of the 25 right whales sighted along the southeastern US coast are individuals that have been previously identified in the Gulf of Maine. Long-term sighting data indicate that right whale cows reproduce every 2 to 5 years ($\overline{X} = 3.12$, SD = 0.6, n = 17) and segregate themselves from the rest of the population to give birth and nurse their young. These findings suggest that right whales inhabiting US and Canadian waters of the western North Atlantic comprise a single inter-breeding stock, and confirm a long-distance seasonal migration by this population.

INTRODUCTION

The right whale (*Eubalaena glacialis*) is one of the most endangered whale species in the world today. In the North Atlantic continuous and extensive hunting from the late 900s to the early 1900s severely diminished the populations and, as a result, cetologists have had few opportunities to study the species. Current population estimates for the Western North Atlantic range from 100 to 640 with a generally accepted average of 200 individuals (CETAP, 1982; IWC, 1986). Recent studies on these right whales include research on distribution and abundance (CETAP, 1982; Kraus, Prescott, Turnbull and Reeves, 1982; Watkins and Schevill, 1982; Winn, 1984); acoustics (Watkins and Schevill, 1976); and behavior (Watkins and Schevill, 1976; 1979), but major gaps still exist in our understanding of their migration, reproductive biology, behavior, and habitat use.

North Atlantic right whales are found seasonally at several locations in the Gulf of Maine. Each spring, from early April to the end of May, multiple sightings of large aggregations of right whales (10–30 individuals) are made within Cape Cod Bay, Massachusetts, near the eastern tip of Cape Cod, and in the Great South Channel which separates Georges Bank and the Nantucket shoals (41°00 N 69°00 W, approximately 100 km southeast of Cape Cod) (Watkins and Schevill, 1982; Winn, Scott and Kenney, 1985). In June and July, individuals, pairs and small groups (3–5 individuals) of right whales are sighted along the New England coast and offshore. Each year, toward the end of July, aggregations of whales numbering between 25 and 75 individuals appear in the lower Bay of Fundy between Maine, New Brunswick, and Nova Scotia (Kraus *et al.*, 1982), and in a 10 km² region 40 km south of the southern tip of Nova Scotia on the Nova Scotian shelf (Sutcliffe and Brodie, 1977; CETAP, 1982; Mitchell, Kozicki and Reeves, 1986). Right whales have been sighted yearly at these two locations from August through November.

Between November and the beginning of April, the distribution of the North Atlantic right whale population remains unknown. Aerial surveys for marine mammals conducted from 1979 to 1982 by the University of Rhode Island from Maine to Cape Hatteras, North Carolina,

between the coast and the edge of the continental shelf, yielded few winter sightings of right whales (CETAP, 1982). Although sporadic sightings have been reported in the winter months along the US east coast from Massachusetts to Florida (Schevill, Moore and Watkins, 1981; Moore and Clark, 1963; Schmidly, Martin and Collins, 1972; Winn, 1984), no large aggregations equivalent to those seen in wintering South Atlantic right whales, *E. australis* (Best, 1981; Payne, 1986) have been reported.

Since 1980, we have studied the summer and autumn distribution, abundance, behavior and movements of *E. glacialis* in the Gulf of Maine. During the winters of 1984 and 1985, we also conducted aerial surveys over the coastal waters of the southeastern US. Utilizing high resolution photography, individual right whales were identified by the unique patterns and topography of their callosities in conjunction with characteristic pigmentation and scars (Payne, Brazier, Dorsey, Perkins, Rowntree and Titus, 1983; Kraus, Moore, Price, Crone, Watkins, Winn and Prescott, 1986). Analysis of over 16,000 photographs taken in our surveys and those of collaborating organizations (see Acknowledgements) has resulted in a catalog of 207 clearly identifiable individual animals. Based on these recent winter surveys and established photographic identification techniques, we report here the first confirmation of a long-distance seasonal migration by North Atlantic right whales and present data suggesting that right whales inhabiting US and Canadian waters of the western North Atlantic comprise a single stock.

METHODS

Since 1980, aerial and shipboard surveys have been used to study North Atlantic right whales in the Gulf of Maine and along the southeastern US coast (Table 1; Figs 1 and 2). Aerial surveys in all areas employed standard transect methods to estimate distribution and abundance (Scott and Gilbert, 1982; Burnham, Anderson and Laake, 1980; Kraus *et al.*, 1982) and photographs were taken of callosity patterns, scars, and natural markings to identify individual whales (Payne *et al.*, 1983; Kraus *et al.*, 1986).

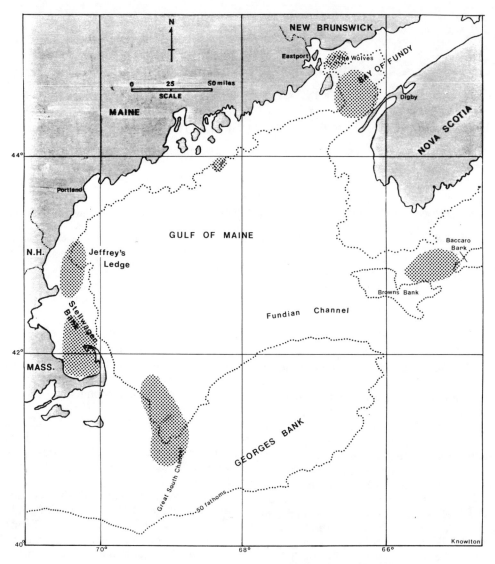

Fig. 1. Right whale survey areas in the Gulf of Maine: 1980–1985.

Table 1.

Survey effort (no. of days) for right whales by area and platform type: 1980–85.

	Bay of Fundy (1980–1985)	Nova Scotian shelf (1981–1985)	Southeastern US (1984–1985)
Shipboard	210	12	1
Aerial	25	5	9

Shipboard surveys consisted of systematically placed parallel transects at two to five nautical mile intervals across areas shown by aerial surveys to be highly used by right whales. Both aerial and shipboard transects were interrupted to photograph and count all right whales seen within one mile of the vessel. Transects were resumed at the point of departure after photoidentification procedures were completed. Loran C was used for navigation and to determine sighting locations. Observers on both aerial and shipboard surveys were experienced in field identification and photography, and written data records were supplemented with hand-held tape recorders and video recorders.

A variety of 35 mm cameras with 200 to 300 mm telephoto lenses, using primarily *Ektachrome 400* and *Kodachrome 64* color transparency film, were utilized to photograph right whales. For shipboard photo-identification, the vessel was slowly maneuvered around a whale until both left and right sides of its head and callosity patterns, and any supplementary identifying features, were photographed. During aerial surveys, the aircraft circled while observers attempted to obtain clear vertical views of the rostral callosity patterns. In subsequent analysis, all photographs were collated with the recorded information to provide the date, time, location and associations of each sighting and individual.

All photographically identified right whales were cataloged and coded according to identifying features, such as callosities, marks and scars. Composite drawings that include all identifying features were created for each whale, and these formed the basis of a catalog of individual right whales. To identify a newly photographed whale, the best available photographs of the callosity patterns and any other useful features were compared with all similar-looking right whales within the composite catalog. Computerization and coding of the identifying features speeded the comparison process, but the final identifications and 'match' confirmations were done by eye from good photographs representing all sightings of a whale. Details of the methods used to make 'matches' of individuals are described in Kraus, *et al.* (1986). Data

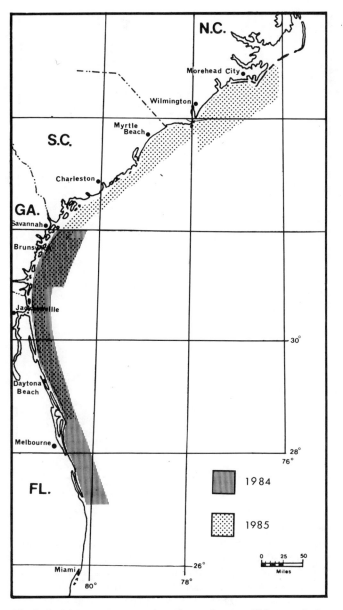

Fig. 2. Aerial survey coverage along the southeastern U.S. coast during the winters of 1984 and 1985.

Table 2.

Long distance resightings of right whales in the western North Atlantic. Key: BOF = Bay of Fundy; CCB = Cape Cod Bay; MB = Massachusetts Bay; GSC = Great South Channel; SS = Nova Scotian shelf (Browns Bank); JL = Jeffrey's Ledge (New Hampshire); GA = Georgia; NC = North Carolina; FL = Florida.

Whale no.	Sex	Month	Year	North	South	Comments
1. 1001	F	Oct	1978	JL		w/1012 (adult)
		Feb	1979		GA	w/calf 1006 (newborn)
		May	1983	CCB		w/calf 1301 (1st yr)
		Aug	1983	JL		"
		Aug–Oct	1983	BOF		"
						Transit from JL to BOF in 6 days.
2. 1027	F	Sep	1980	BOF		
		Jul	1982	SS		
		Sep–Oct	1982	BOF		
		Sep	1983	BOF		
		Mar	1984		GA	w/1401 (adult)
3. 1135	F	Aug–Sep	1981	BOF		w/calf 1163 (1st yr)
		Aug–Oct	1982	BOF		w/calf 1163 (2nd yr)
		Feb	1984		FL	w/calf 1406 (newborn)
		Aug–Sep	1984	BOF		w/calf 1406 (1st yr)
4. 1142	F	Aug–Sep	1981	BOF		w/calf 1123 (1st yr)
		Feb	1984		GA	w/calf 1411 (newborn)
		Aug–Sep	1984	BOF		w/calf 1411 (1st yr)
5. 1153		Aug	1980	BOF		
		Aug	1981	BOF		
		Jul–Oct	1982	BOF		
		Apr	1983	CCB		
		Jul	1983	BOF		
		Feb	1984		FL	w/1321 (adult)
		Apr	1984	CCB		
6. 1171	F	Oct	1981	BOF		w/calf 1170 (1st yr)
		Feb	1984		GA	w/calf 1405 (newborn)
		Aug–Sep	1984	BOF		w/calf 1405 (1st yr)
7. 1217		Aug–Sep	1982	BOF		(1/2 fluke)
		Feb	1984		FL	w/2225 (adult)
		Aug	1984	SS		
8. 1264	F	Mar	1982		NC	w/calf 1265 (1st yr)
		Sep	1982	CCB		
		Apr	1985	CCB		w/calf 1502 (1st yr)
9. 2225		Jul	1982	SS		
		Feb	1984		FL	w/1217 (adult)
10. 1401		Mar	1984		GA	w/1027 (adult)
		Aug	1984	SS		
11. 1321		Sep	1983	SS		
		Feb	1984		FL	w/1153 (4 yrs old)
12. 1407	F	Feb	1984		GA	w/calf 1408 (newborn)
		Aug–Sep	1984	BOF		w/calf 1408 (1st yr)
13. 1201	F	May	1982	GSC		w/calf (1st yr)
		Aug	1983	SS		
		Sep	1984	BOF		
		Feb	1985		FL	w/calf 1508 (newborn)
		Sep	1985	SS		w/calf 1508 (1st yr)
14. 1266	F	Jul	1982	MB		w/calf 1267 (1st yr)
		Feb	1985		GA	
		Aug–Sep	1985	BOF		w/calf 1507 (1st yr)
15. 1013	F	Jul	1980	BOF		w/calf (1st yr)
		Apr	1983	CCB		
		Feb	1985		GA	w/calf (newborn)
16. 1422	M	Aug	1984	SS		
		Feb	1985		NC	(Alone)
17. 1424		Aug	1984	SS		
		Feb	1985		GA	(Alone)
18. 1501	F	Mar	1984	CCB		
		Feb	1985		GA	w/calf (newborn)

used in these analyses are primarily from New England Aquarium surveys, but include photographs contributed by other institutions and individuals (see Acknowledgements).

RESULTS

Southeastern U.S.

In February and March of 1984, 15 right whales were sighted, including four cows with newborn calves estimated to be between 4.25 m and 5.5 m in length, and one juvenile estimated to be approximately 10 m long. The ten adult whales sighted during these surveys have all been identified with photographic confirmation as whales that have been observed in the Gulf of Maine (Table 2). All four of the cows with their newborn calves (females No. 1135, No. 1142, No. 1171, and No. 1407) sighted in February 1984 off Georgia and Florida were observed in the Bay of Fundy in August and September of 1984. Two of the remaining six adult whales sighted in February 1984 off the Georgia/Florida coast were

resighted in the North Atlantic on the Nova Scotian shelf (No. 1217 and No. 1401) (Table 3 and Fig. 3).

The aerial surveys conducted during February 1985 along the southeastern US coast resulted in sightings of 10 right whales, including 3 cows with calves (Females No. 1013, No. 1201 and No. 1266). Six of the seven adults were whales that had been photographically identified from the Gulf of Maine. A summary of these resightings is given in Table 2 and Fig. 4. The cumulative distribution

Table 3.

Right whale calving (from total 33 cows) in the western North Atlantic, 1979–1985. Key: 1 = sighted with 1st-yr calf; 2 = sighted with 2nd-yr calf; 0 = sighted without calf. Fourteen cows displayed 3-year intervals (numbers: 1014, 1126, 1135, 1142, 1145, 1157, 1160, 1171, 1201, 1222, 1240, 1248, 1266). One cow displayed a 2-year interval (no. 1318), one a 4-year interval (no. 1001) and one a 5-year interval (no. 1013). Total number of calves since 1979 = 50.

Cow no.	1979	1980	1981	1982	1983	1984	1985
1001	1(79)				1	0	
1012					1	0	
1013		1			0		1
1014		1		1			
1025		1			0		
1118			0			1	
1127			1			1	
1135			1	2		1	
1140			0	1			
1142			1			1	0
1145			1		0	1	
1157			1			1	
1160			1		0	1	0
1168			0	0		1	
1171			1			1	
1201				1	0	0	1
1222	0(79)			1			1
1240				1			1
1242				1			
1246				1			
1248				1			1
1264				1			1
1266				1			1
1268				1			
1303					0	1	
1310					1		
1312					1		
1314					1		
1316					1		
1318					1		1
1407						1	
1412						1	
1501							1
Total calves	1	3	7	10	8	12	9

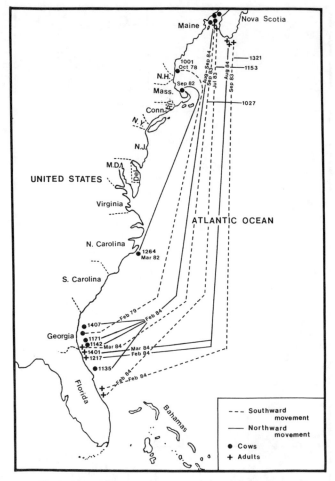

Fig. 3. Long-distance resightings of right whales: 1978–1984.

pattern of cows with newborn calves appears significant. Of the seven such cows sighted by these winter surveys in 1984 and 1985, six of them have been observed within 15 miles of shore between Amelia Island, Florida, and Brunswick, Georgia (Fig. 5).

Photographs contributed by colleagues provide additional data that support this seasonal pattern of movement and calving. A cow (No. 1001) first observed and photographed off the coast of New Hampshire in October 1978 with another adult female (No. 1012), was re-photographed off the coast of Georgia in February 1979 with a newborn calf. The calf appears to have been nursing in photographs taken by the Georgia Department of Natural Resources in 1979. This female was observed several times in 1983 with a new calf, first in Cape Cod Bay, then near Jeffrey's Ledge off New Hampshire, and by mid-summer in the Bay of Fundy. In addition, we have confirmed that a cow with a calf (No. 1264 and No. 1265) photographed off Cape Lookout, North Carolina, in March of 1982, were observed in Cape Cod Bay in September 1982.

Neonates have stranded on the Georgia and Florida coasts during the months of January and February (Caldwell and Caldwell, 1971), and analysis of photographs taken of the cows with calves during these surveys show the calves range in size from 15 to 19 ft (4.7 to 5.8 m). The small calf size indicates all sightings were newly born right whales, and the variation in sizes suggests that the North Atlantic right whale calving

season extends over several months or that there is great size variation at birth. These data indicate that some females calve off the southeastern US Atlantic coast from late December to March and migrate north to the Gulf of Maine by mid-summer (Figs. 3 and 4).

Twenty-nine of the 33 cows with calves identified in the Gulf of Maine since 1980 have occurred in the Bay of Fundy during the summer and fall. Ten of these cow/calf pairs represent resightings of females with calves observed previously in the spring in the southern Gulf of Maine. This suggests that most cows bring their calves to the Bay of Fundy in the summer and fall during the calves' first year. Only two cows with calves have been identified in 110 right whale sightings in the Nova Scotian Shelf region during this six-year research program. This suggests segregation by nursing cows in the Bay of Fundy during the summer and fall within the Western North Atlantic population. Sightings for *E. australis* from wintering grounds in the Southern Hemisphere indicate a similar segregation (Best, 1981; Tabor and Thomas, 1983).

Calving intervals and rates

Of the 33 identified cows observed with calves since 1979, seventeen were identified as whales that gave birth to at least two calves. Calving intervals ranged from 2 to 5 years, with a mean birth interval of 3.12 yrs (SD = 0.6, n = 17) (Table 3). If cows on longer calving intervals are less likely to be photographed than those on shorter intervals, the 3.12 mean interval may be artificially low,

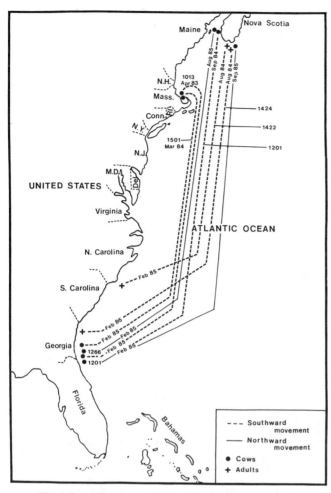

Fig. 4. Long-distance resightings of right whales: 1985 data.

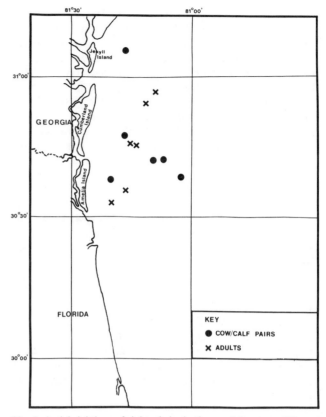

Fig. 5. Aerial sightings of right whales in the coastal waters of Georgia and Florida in the winters of 1984 and 1985.

but these data agree with reports on South Atlantic right whales (Payne, 1986) and one previous record from the North Atlantic (Watkins and Schevill, 1982).

In one instance we observed a calf (No. 1163) that stayed with its mother (No. 1135) through two summer/fall seasons (Table 2). Because of this sighting, our designation of 'calf' is not based exclusively upon a single year association with an adult, but also includes size data. Our designations are as follows: neonates range from 4.25 m to 5.5 m; first-year, summer calves, 5 to 7.5 meters in length, and the approximate size of two known second-year whales was 8.5 to 9.75 m.

All seven cow/calf sightings from the winters of 1984 and 1985 were concentrated in the coastal waters off southern Georgia and northeastern Florida. These sightings corroborate previous anecdotal reports (Reeves, Mead and Katona, 1978; Winn, 1984; Mead, 1986), and establish that the region is a calving ground for North Atlantic right whales. We recognize that sightings of seven calves and one pregnant cow (No. 1266) made by us in the winters of 1984 and 1985 do not represent all births of the year for a minimum estimated population of 200 whales, since an additional 12 cow/calf pairs were observed in the Gulf of Maine during 1984 and 1985. Our winter surveys may have missed additional whales, or another calving ground may exist elsewhere.

Since 1981, the minimum number of calves produced each year in this population has ranged from 7 to 12, with a mean of 9.2 (SD = 1.9). It is likely that cow/calf pairs occur seasonally elsewhere and remain unreported to us.

If we accept a population estimate of 200, 9 calves per year represent a reproductive rate of slightly over 4%. However, excluding calves, over 20% of the 1984 and 10% of the 1985 right whale sightings were whales new to the Aquarium's catalog of right whales. This indicates the population is larger than earlier estimates have suggested, but it also means that the reproductive rate may be lower than 4%. Since Best (1981) and Whitehead, Payne and Payne (1986) have reported population growth rates around 7% for two different populations of South Atlantic right whales (*E. australis*), this low reproductive rate raises questions about the completeness of current samples, or the health of the North Atlantic population.

DISCUSSION

The data indicate that some female right whales migrate nearly 1,800 miles from a northern summering ground to the southeastern US Atlantic coast during the winter months for calving and initial rearing of their young. However, the question of the location of wintering grounds for the rest of the population remains an enigma. A long-distance migration for this population has been established, but the migration routes and timing are still unknown. The two years of data on cow and calf distribution off the southeast US coast suggest that the area is a primary calving ground, although the numbers of whales indicate that it may not be the only one.

The extensive sighting effort throughout the Gulf of Maine suggests that most calves born to this population will be identified with their mothers within their first year, and that annual calf counts should provide reasonable indications of this population's reproductive health. For example, assuming a three-year calving interval, the Western North Atlantic right whale population apparently produced three more calves in 1984 than did the same 'year class' of cows in 1981 (Table 3). However, the Bay of Fundy data reveal that all three cows that had calves in 1980 returned in 1983, but two were without calves (Table 3). These 1980 Bay of Fundy cows have not been observed anywhere else other than in the Bay on the three-year cycle, and it is possible that the 1983 sightings are indicative of calf mortality, reproductive failure, or a longer calving interval. Since the photographic data collection effort has varied from year to year in each area, it may not be appropriate to compare the total number of cow/calf pairs seen annually throughout the Gulf of Maine to identify trends. Nevertheless, the differences in reproductive rates and success between different year classes (e.g. 1980/1983 and 1981/1984) indicate that accurate analysis of reproduction and population trends may be possible through the monitoring of each year class over two or more reproductive cycles.

The 'nearshore' tendency of right whale cows with young throughout their range suggests potential conflicts with fishing activities, shipping, and coastal development. To determine the effects of human activities upon the survival and recovery of this endangered species will require research to further define the winter distribution, the specific migration routes, and long-term reproductive patterns of the Western North Atlantic right whale population.

ACKNOWLEDGEMENTS

We are grateful to Martie Crone, Jane Harrison, Wendy Van Dyke, Susan Carver, Kathy Hazard, Laurel Code, Jean Bassett, Moira Brown, and Brian Hoover, for their dedicated work on this program.

Dr. Charles Mayo, Carol Danton, and Carole Carlson of Center for Coastal Studies, Dr. Steven Katona, Steve Mullane, Ann Rivers, and Harriet Corbett of Allied Whale at College of the Atlantic, Scott Marion of Seafarers Expeditions, Bobby Bowman of Maine Whalewatch, Scott Mercer of New England Whalewatch, Mason Weinrich of the Gloucester Fisherman's Museum, Dr. Perran Ross of the Ocean Research and Education Society, Dr. William Watkins and Karen Moore of Woods Hole Oceanographic Institution, Dr. Howard Winn and Carol Price of the University of Rhode Island, and Carl Haycock, have all made significant contributions to the Aquarium's research program on right whales.

Work in southern portions of the range was made possible by the volunteer efforts of a group of Delta Airline pilots: Dave Mattingly, Jon Hanson, Robert Harrison, Greg Sherman, Taylor Spangler, George Terwilliger, Mal Harper, and Wynn Baker. We thank the Georgia Department of Natural Resources, particularly Duane Harris, Chuck Cowman, Susan Shipman, Richard Daigle, Susan Solomon, Nancy Sanchez, and Gib Johnson for their assistance.

Support was provided by the National Marine Fisheries Service Northeast Center, U.S. Department of Commerce, World Wildlife Fund-U.S., Earthwatch/Center for Field Research, the US Marine Mammal Commission, and the Raytheon Corporation.

We thank Cecile Cusson and Eleanor Jensen for typing the several versions of this paper.

REFERENCES

Best, P. B. 1981. The status of right whales (*Eubalaena glacialis*) off South Africa, 1969–1979. *Investl. Rep. Sea Fish. Inst., S. Afr.* 123: 1–44.

Burnham, K. P., Anderson, D. R. and Laake, J. L. 1980. Estimation of density from line transect sampling of biological populations. *Wild. Monog.* 72, 202 pp.

Caldwell, D. K. and Caldwell, M. C. 1971. Sounds produced by two rare cetaceans stranded in Florida. *Cetology*, 4: 1–6.

CETAP. 1982. A characterization of marine mammals and turtles in the mid- and north Atlantic areas of the U.S. outer continental shelf. Final Report of the Cetacean and Turtle Assessment Program to the U.S. Dept. of Interior under Contract AA551–CT8-48. H. E. Winn, Scientific Director.

International Whaling Commission. 1986. Report of the Workshop on the Status of Right Whales. (Published in this volume).

Kraus, S. D., Prescott, J. H., Turnbull, P. V. and Reeves, R. R. 1982. Preliminary notes on the occurrence of the north Atlantic right whale, *Eubalaena glacialis*, in the Bay of Fundy. *Rep. int. Whal. Comm* 32: 407–11.

Kraus, S. D., Moore, K. E., Price, C. E., Crone, M. J., Watkins, W. A., Winn, H. E. and Prescott, J. H. 1986. The use of photographs to identify individual North Atlantic right whales (*Eubalaena glacialis*). (Published in this volume)

Mead, J. 1986. Twentieth century records of right whales (*Eubalaena glacialis*) in the northwestern Atlantic Ocean. Published in this volume).

Mitchell, E. D., Kozicki, V. M. and Reeves, R. R. 1986. Sightings of right whales, *Eubalaena glacialis*, on the Scotian Shelf, 1966–1972. (Published in this volume).

Moore, J. C. and Clark, E. 1963. Discovery of right whales in the Gulf of Mexico. *Science* 141 (3,577): 269.

Payne, R. 1986. Long term behavioral studies of the southern right whale (*Eubalaena australis*). (Published in this volume).

Payne, R., Brazier, O., Dorsey, E. M., Perkins, J. S., Rowntree, V. J., Titus, A. 1983. External features in Southern Right Whales (*Eubalaena australis*) and their use in identifying individuals. Pp. 371–445 *In*: R. Payne (ed.), *Communication and Behavior of Whales*, AAAS Selected Symposium 76, Westview Press, Boulder, Co.

Reeves, R. R., Mead, J. G. and Katona, S. K. 1978. The right whale, *Eubalaena glacialis*, in the western North Atlantic. *Rep. int. Whal. Commn* 28: 303–12.

Schevill, W. E., Moore, K. E. and Watkins, W. A. 1981. Right whale, *Eubalaena glacialis*, sightings in Cape Cod waters. *WHOI Tech. Rept. WHOI-81-50*; 1–16.

Schmidly, D. J., Martin, C. O. and Colins, G. F. 1972. First occurrence of a black right whale (*Balaena glacialis*) along the Texas coast. *Southwest. Nat.* 17(2): 214–15.

Scott, G. P. and Gilbert, J. R. 1982. Problems and progress in the U.S. BLM-sponsored CeTAP surveys. *Rep. int. Whal. Commn* 32: 587–600.

Sutcliffe, W. H., Jr. and Brodie, P. F. 1977. Whale distributions in Nova Scotia waters. *Tech. Rep. Fish. Mar. Serv. (Can.)* 722: vi+1–83.

Tabor, S. and Thomas, P. 1983. Calf development and mother-calf spatial relationships in southern right whales. *Animal Behav.* 30(4): 1,072–83.

Watkins, W. A. and Schevill, W. E. 1976. Rigth whale feeding and baleen rattle. *J. Mammal.* 57(1): 58–66.

Watkins, W. A. and Schevill, W. E. 1979. Aerial observations of feeding behavior in four baleen whales: *Eubalaena glacialis, Balaenoptera borealis, Megaptera novaeangliae*, and *Balaenoptera physalus. J. Mammal.* 60(1): 155–63.

Watkins, W. A. and Schevill, W. E. 1982. Observations of right whales, *Eubalaena glacialis*, in Cape Cod waters. *Fish. Bull., U.S.* 80(4): 875–80.

Whitehead, H., Payne, R. and Payne, M. 1986. Population estimate for the right whales of Peninsula Valdes, Argentina, 1971–1976. (Published in this volume.)

Winn, H. E. 1984. Development of a right whale sighting network in the southeastern U.S. *NTIS Publication No. PB84 240548*, 12 pp.

Winn, H. E., Scott, E. A. and Kenney, R. D. 1985. Aerial surveys for right whales in the Great South Channel, Spring 1984. *NTIS Publ. No. PB85-207926*. 14 pp.

The Use of Photographs to Identify Individual North Atlantic Right Whales (*Eubalaena glacialis*)

SCOTT. D. KRAUS[1], KAREN E. MOORE[2], CAROL A. PRICE[3], MARTIE J. CRONE[1],
WILLIAM A. WATKINS[2], HOWARD E. WINN[3] AND JOHN H. PRESCOTT[1]

[1]*New England Aquarium, Central Wharf, Boston, MA 02110*
[2]*Woods Hole Oceanographic Institution, Woods Hole, MA 02543*
[3]*University of Rhode Island, Narrangansett, RI 02882*

ABSTRACT

Photographic techniques for identifying individual North Atlantic right whales (*Eubalaena glacialis*) were investigated. The effects of differences between aerial and shipboard photography were indicated and related to cataloging and matching methods. Photographs of known female right whales were compared, using the collections of Woods Hole Oceanographic Institution (photos from 1956–1983), University of Rhode Island (1973–1984), New England Aquarium (1973–1985), and Center for Coastal Studies (1979–1984). Matches of photographs of individual right whale cows provided information on distribution and minimum calving intervals. The stability of individually identifiable features over time was analyzed in the New England Aquarium's collection, demonstrating that some features such as callosity outline could change, while others, such as ventral white patches and lip crenations, appeared stable over at least the five years compared. Suggestions were made for collecting, analyzing and interpreting future right whale photographs.

INTRODUCTION

The use of photographs of naturally occurring features to identify cetaceans individually has been increasing during the last 10 years. Natural marks have proven useful in assessing distribution, migrations, abundance, and other basic biological and behavioral information in humpback whales, *Megaptera novaeangliae* (Katona, Harcourt, Perkins and Kraus, 1980; Katona and Whitehead, 1981), killer whales, *Orcinus orca* (Chandler, Goebel and Balcomb, 1977), gray whales, *Eschrictius robustus* (Hatler and Darling, 1974), and minke whales (Dorsey, 1983). Callosity patterns of both southern (*E. australis*) and northern (*E. glacialis*) right whales have been used to identify individuals (Payne, 1972; Payne, Brazier, Dorsey, Perkins, Rowntree and Titus, 1983; Watkins and Schevill, 1979; Watkins and Moore, 1983; Kraus, Prescott, Turnbull and Reeves, 1982; Price and Winn, 1981).

The photographic identification procedures for North Atlantic right whales represent a moderate departure from the identification techniques described by Payne *et al.* (1983) for *E. australis*. North Atlantic right whale investigators have had to develop methods to accommodate three special problems: (1) In *E. australis*, callosity patterns of most of the population are 'discontinuous', having areas of smooth epidermis between discrete patches of cornified epidermis, called callosities, along the rostrum (Payne *et al.*, 1983). In *E. glacialis*, however, nearly one half of the photographed population has callosities that are 'continuous' from the anterior tip of the rostrum to the blowholes, which display fewer variations useful for individual identification (Figs 1 and 2). (2) Identification photographs were taken by several contributors from a variety of platforms and in different formats. (3) Changes were found in the appearance of some individuals' callosity patterns and other identification features. This report details these photo-identification procedures for North Atlantic right whales, presents the results of an analysis of the stability of identifying features, and summarizes the results of 'matching' sessions using photographs from collections

at the New England Aquarium (NEA), University of Rhode Island (URI), Woods Hole Oceanographic Institution (WHOI), and the Provincetown Center for Coastal Studies (CCS).

METHODS

Photographs of right whales have been collected in the western North Atlantic since the 1950s from aircraft and ships. Most of the early photographs were obtained by WHOI researchers during the course of other cetacean work near Cape Cod. Recent fieldwork by URI (1978–1985), NEA (1980–1985), and the CCS (1982–1985), has resulted in additional collections of right whale photographs. Using the basic terminology described by Payne *et al.* (1983), each institution sorted its collection by individual whale, based on the shape, position, and surface topography of callosities and other identifying features. These separate collections were then organized so that individual whales with similar callosity patterns were grouped together.

To 'match' different sightings of the same whale, composite drawings and photographs of the callosity patterns of individual right whales were compared to other individuals with a similar appearance. Whales that looked alike in the first sorting were examined for callosity similarities, as well as for supplementary features, including scars, natural pigmentation patterns, crenations along the lower lips, and morphometric ratios. A 'match' between different sightings was considered positive when the callosity pattern in addition to one or more of the above features could be matched independently by at least three experienced researchers. Exceptions to this requirement of matching several features included whales which had unusual callosity patterns and/or scars, birthmarks, or deformities that were so clearly photographed that a match could be based on only one feature.

The process of matching right whale photographs and identifying individuals was very slow, and required cautious review of numerous photographs of each whale.

Fig. 1. Example of 'continuous' callosity pattern

Fig. 2. Example of 'discontinuous' callosity pattern

The three-dimensionality of callosity patterns accentuated problems associated with orientation angle, glare, cyamid covering, and water distortion. Photographs often include breaking water or foam at or near identifying features, distorting or obscuring certain features, such as callosities along the upper edge of the lower lips. Also, changes occurred in the cyamid coverage and in the shape of the callosity tissue itself (see section on Stability of Identifying Features).

Photographs of some whales with 'continuous' callosities proved to be particularly difficult to work with, due to the reduced amount of information available in their patterns. Although some 'continuous' whales had distinctive callosity patterns with several 'peninsulas' present on each side, many did not, and were difficult to identify without clear photos of other features such as scars or lip crenations. Further, movements of cyamids on the periphery of 'continuous' callosities sometimes changed the apparent pattern configuration, making re-identifications based on callosity patterns alone difficult over long periods of time.

In May, 1985, right whale researchers from NEA, URI, and WHOI met to compare composite drawings and photographs from each collection. Photographs from CCS were also made available. This collaboration ensured that all available data were examined, since each institution has worked in different regions and at different times. Known females (accompanied by newborn calves or positively sexed by photos of the genital area) were chosen for this comparison as a convenient subset for testing individual identification methods, and because they represented an identifiable group within each collection. Focussing on cows also provided the opportunity to estimate the rate of calf production for the population and for individual females.

In addition to this cooperative effort, the New England Aquarium right whale photograph collection was analyzed to examine long-term stability of identifying features in 10 adult males, 11 whales first observed as calves, and 17 known females, all of which were double marked (e.g. callosity patterns and a distinctive scar) and catalogued by photographs from two or more years.

Callosity patterns and surface topography, natural marks, scars, lower lip crenations, and ventral white patches were examined for changes. Changes were categorized as none (N = no detectable differences), slight (S = slight detectable differences, but not enough to prevent an identification or match, i.e. minor changes in callosity or scar tissue that did not alter the overall pattern), and large (L = significant differences that might inhibit reidentification of that feature on the whale, e.g. callosity tissue patterns or scars altered to the point where preliminary examination would miss matching the individual whale). These results are given in Tables, 5, 6, and 7.

Age was determined in this collection by photo-documentation of calves through their first years of growth, and sex was determined only by photographs of the genital area (in males and females) or by long-term repeated association with a first-year calf (in females).

RESULTS

Photo-identification and matching

Each research group organized its photographs of right whale cows, and began to assess and organize photographs of other identified individuals. The number of whales identified in each collection is given by area (Table 1), and by year (Table 2). Appendix 1 defines each area. The total number of the right whales in each collection (Individual Totals, Table 1) is actually lower than the Table 1 and 2 row totals because many whales were resighted in several places or at different times. Also, the numbers of right whales in the population cannot be derived by adding institution counts, since considerable overlap has been demonstrated between the collections. It is important to note that each collection included known cows that were not identified in the other photo collections.

Comparisons of cows between the photograph collections at WHOI (n = 16), NEA (n = 36) and URI (n = 14), revealed 13 positive matches between at least two collections. A summary is given in Table 3.

An analysis of callosity pattern types in sexed North Atlantic right whales suggests that there are differences between the sexes within the population, perhaps analogous to Payne and Dorsey's (1983) findings on *E. australis*. At least 69% of the known right whale females have discontinuous callosity patterns (81% of the WHOI collection; 69% in the NEA collection; 93% in the URI collection). Females are significantly more likely to be discontinuous than continuous (Table 4). It is possible that the high rate of intercollection matches of cows may not be representative of future comparisons among other parts of the population having a higher proportion of continuous callosity patterns.

Within each collection, a number of matches had already been made (Price and Winn, 1981; Watkins and Schevill, 1982; Kraus, Prescott and Stone, 1984). However, as Table 3 shows, comparisons between all institutions' photoidentification collections yielded significant additional data on individual movement, birthing intervals, and seasonal distribution. A cow seen with a calf in Cape Cod Bay in 1970 was photographed twelve years later, in 1982, apparently without a calf, on the Southeast Scotian shelf. A cow with a calf in 1974 in Cape

Table 1.

Occurrence of photographically identified right whales by Area (see Appendix 1) through 1984. SS = Southeast Scotian shelf, BF = Bay of Fundy, GM = Gulf of Maine, MB = Massachusetts Bay, GSC = Great South Channel, LI = Long Island, MA = Mid-Atlantic, CH = Cape Hatteras, SE = Southeastern US.

Collection	Area									Total
	SS	BF	GM	MB	GSC	LI	MA	CH	SE	
NEA	61	111	26	41	15	–	–	1	23	207
WHOI	–	–	–	67	1	1	–	–	–	69
URI	16	12	15	7	71	2	7	–	6	103
CCS	–	–	–	33	–	–	–	–	–	33

Table 2.

Sightings of right whales photographically identified by year and collection. Some of the individuals catalogued by NEA came from photographs submitted by CCS and other institutions.

	Year																		
	56	59	60	61	70	72	73	74	75	76	77	78	79	80	81	82	83	84
WHOI	2	2	3	2	1	1	4	14	4	1	8	8	5	1	3	3	7	–
NEA	–	–	–	–	–	–	1	–	2	2	2	4	5	22	108	155	97	126
URI	–	–	–	–	–	–	1	–	1	2	1	3	10	48	42	10	4	17
CCS	–	–	–	–	–	–	–	–	–	–	–	–	–	3	3	2	4	23	24

Table 3.

Photographic matches of right whale cows or known females, giving locations and presence of calves. (1) = with 1st year calf, (2) = with 2nd year calf, (0) = no calf present.

Institutional whale number	Pre-1980	1980	1981	1982	1983	1984	1985
NEA 2201				SS(0)			
WHOI 13/IV/70	MB(70)(1)						
NEA 1025		BF(1)			BF(0)		
URI 8016		GSC(1)					
NEA 1501							SE(1)
URI 8001		GSC(1)					
NEA 1171			BF(1)			SE(1),BF(1)	
URI 9008			BF(1)				
NEA 1201				SS(0)	SS(0)		SE(1)
URI 9034	GSC(79)(0)	SS(0)		GSC(1)	GSC(0)		
WHOI 25/V/82				GSC(1)			
NEA 1310				BF(1)			
URI 9168				GSC(1)			
NEA 1268				SE(1)			
URI 7005		GSC(0)	GSC(0)	SE(1)			
NEA 1014		MB(1),BF(1)			MB(1),BF(1)		
URI 9043		MB(1),BF(1)					
WHOI 11/IV/77	MB(77)(1)						
NEA 2203				SS(0)	SS(0)		
URI 9145	MB(78)(0)		GSC(1)				
NEA 1135			BF(1)	BF(2)		SE(1),BF(1)	
URI 7004			SE			SE(1)	
WHOI 29/IV/74; 12/VI/81	MB(74)(1)		MB(1)				
NEA 1222				BF(1)			
URI 7006		GSC(0)	GSC(0)	SE(1),MB(1)			
WHOI 1+2/V/79	MB(79)(0)						
NEA 1150			BF(0)	SS(0)	MB(0)		
WHOI 20/VI/79; 23/IV/81	MB(79)(0)		MB(0)				
URI 9001	MB(75)(0)	BF(1)					
WHOI 8/V/75	MB(75)(0)						

Table 4.

Incidence of callosity pattern type for known females tested against the frequency of pattern occurrence in each institution's total photographic collection minus all known females. Expected frequencies were derived separately from the total population minus the females in each data set.

	Continuous	Discontinuous	n
NEA data			
Females	13	42	55
Total (n) – Females	67	75	142*
$\chi^2 = 12.3276$, df = 1, p < 0.001			
URI data			
Females	1	13	14
Total (n) – Females	30	59	89
$\chi^2 = 4.9770$, df = 1, 0.05 p < 0.025			
WHOI data			
Females	3	13	16
Total (n) – Females	29	8	37
$\chi^2 = 27.000$, df = 1, p < 0.001			

* 10 whales that appeared to change pattern types or were ambiguously categorized have been excluded from this analysis.

Cod Bay was re-photographed with a calf in 1981 in both Cape Cod Bay and the Bay of Fundy. Between the 1981 sightings in Cape Cod Bay and the Bay of Fundy, this cow acquired a large wound on the rostrum. In 1982 she was photographed again in the Bay of Fundy with her two-year old calf (born in 1981). In 1984 she was photographed in February off Florida with a newborn calf, and in September with her calf in the Bay of Fundy. A cow photographed in 1977 in Cape Cod Bay was photographed in 1980 in Cape Cod Bay and in the Bay of Fundy, and again in 1983 in Cape Cod Bay, off Mt. Desert Rock, and in the Bay of Fundy. Each of these years she was accompanied by a new calf.

Our concern about the compatibility of shipboard and aerial photographic collections has been alleviated by the number of matches (10 out of 13) that involved photographs from both platforms. The principal difficulty with shipboard photographs was the low angle view of the callosity, which often obscured the overall pattern. The major problems with aerial photographs were resolution and magnification: significant callosity details, small scars, and markings were frequently obscured or were too small in poorer quality photographs. However, there were solutions to these problems. Carefully drawn composites of each right whale's identifying features proved essential in comparisons. Shipboard photographs of both sides of a right whale's head from several angles allowed definition of the callosity pattern. Photographs from shipboard also provided good resolution and the opportunity to photograph supplementary features, such as small pigmentation irregularities and scars on the whales' side, back, or flukes. For aerial photography, longer lenses (*ca* 300 mm) in conjunction with the newer high-speed films have continued to improve photographic quality.

Stability of identifying features over time

In the NEA collection, callosity patterns in 80% of the known adult male right whales appeared to be unchanged over 1- to 4-year periods (Table 7). In contrast, most (90%) right whales first photographed as calves displayed at least minor changes in callosity patterns during the first few years (Table 5). Nearly two-thirds (64%) of the cows

Table 5.

Changes in the identifying features of right whale calves. Key: B = Bonnet, I = Islands, Li = Lips, C = Coaming, PB = Post blowwhole, H = Head, Bo = Body, T = Tail, LC = Lip crenations, WV = White ventrum; L = large changes, S = slight changes, N = no change, X = not seen in more than one year, / = identification feature absent, + = increase in callosity height, – = decrease in callosity height.

NEA no.	Years sighted	Configuration/Topography B	I	Li	C	PB	Vertical growth B	I	Li	C	PB	Scars H	Bo	T	Misc. LC	WV
1006	79,82	L	L	L	L	S	+	+	+	+	+	/	X	X	X	N
1032	80,82,83	S	S	L	S	S	N	+	–	+	+	/	X	X	N	X
1128	81,83	X	X	X	X	X	X	X	X	X	X	X	X	X	X	N
1134	81–84 incl	S	S	N	N	N	N	N	N	N	N	/	N	N	N	X
1153	80–84 incl	L	S	/	N	S	N	N	/	N	+	/	/	N	N	X
1161	81,82,83	S	S	N	N	S	N	+	N	–	+	/	/	X	N	N
1163	81,82,83	N	L	/	N	N	N	N	/	N	N	L	/	/	N	X
1170	81–84 incl	S	/	N	S	S	N	/	N	N	N	/	N	/	N	N
1241	82,84	L	S	L	S	S	–	N	–	–	N	/	X	X	N	N
1245	81,83	S	L	S	S	S	N	+	–	+	N	/	N	S	X	X
1308	83,84	S	/	S	S	S	–	/	–	N	N	/	/	/	X	X
Totals	X	1	1	1	1	1	1	1	1	1	1	1	5	4	4	7
	N	1	0	3	4	2	6	4	3	5	6	0	3	2	7	4
	S	6	5	2	5	8						0	0	1	0	0
	L	3	3	3	1	0						1	0	0	0	0
	+						1	4	1	3	4					
	–						3	0	4	2	0					
	/	0	2	2	0	0	0	2	2	0	0	9	4	3	0	0

Table 6.

Changes in the identifying features of female right whales over time. Key as for Table 5.

NEA no.	Years sighted	Configuration/Topography B	I	Li	C	PB	Vertical growth B	I	Li	C	PB	Scars H	Bo	T	Misc. LC	WV
1001	78,79,83	N	S	/	N	N	N	N	/	N	N	N	X	X	N	X
1005	76,84	S	N	L	S	X	N	N	–	N	X	/	X	X	X	X
1012	78,83	L	/	L	N	N	N	/	+	N	N	N	N	X	N	X
1013	80,83	S	S	/	N	X	X	X	X	X	X	X	N	X	N	X
1014	80,83	S	/	/	N	S	N	/	N	N	N	N	S,N	X	N	X
1025	80,82,83	X	X	/	N	X	X	X	X	X	X	N	X	X	X	X
1127	81,84	S	/	S	N	N	–	/	N	N	N	X	/	X	N	N
1135	81,82,84	S	/	L	N	N	+	/	–	N	N	S,N	X	N	N	N
1140	81,82	S	S	N	S	N	N	N	N	N	N	/	/	X	N	X
1142	81,84	N	/	N	N	N	N	/	N	N	N	/	/	N	N	N
1145	81,83,84	N	S	S	S	N	N	N	N	N	N	/	/	X	N	X
1157	81,84	S	/	S	N	S	–	/	N	N	N	N	/	X	N	X
1160	81,84	N	N	/	N	N	N	N	/	N	N	N	X	N	N	X
1171	81,84	N	N	N	N	N	N	N	N	N	N	N	/	N	N	X
1201	82,83,84	X	X	X	N	X	X	X	X	X	X	/	N	X	X	X
1222	79,82	X	N	/	N	X	N	N	/	N	N	N	X	X	X	X
1303	79,83,84	S	S	/	N	N	N	N	/	N	N	N	/	N	N	X
Totals	X	3	2	1	0	5	3	3	3	3	4	2	4	12	5	14
	N	5	4	3	14	10	11	8	6	14	13	10	5	5	12	3
	S	8	5	3	3	2						1	1	0	0	0
	L	1	0	3	0	0						0	0	0	0	0
	+						1	0	1	0	0					
	–						2	0	2	0	0					
	/	0	6	7	0	0	0	6	5	0	0	5	8	0	0	0

that were analyzed displayed minor changes over as much as nine years in the appearance of the 'bonnet', or anterior portion of the callosity, but most showed high stability in the 'coaming' (anterior to the blowholes) and post-blowhole callosities (Table 6). From this sample of cows, males, and calves (n = 38), 35 scars on head, body, and tail areas of 22 whales were examined for change over periods up to nine years. Of these, 5 (14%) appeared to

Fig. 3. Callosity patterns have been known to change from discontinuous to apparently continuous and vice versa (see text)

diminish in visibility, but in the remainder there was no evidence of change. Within these 38 whales, eight had ventral white patches that were photographed over at least two years without showing any change. Of 27 whales with appropriate photo-documentation in at least two years, all displayed consistently stable patterns of crenations along the lower lips up to five years, although allometric growth was noted in young whales.

Within the New England Aquarium's collection of photographically identified right whales (n = 207), 6 whales have changed from discontinuous to apparently continuous callosity patterns, and 2 have gone from continuous to discontinuous (Fig. 3). Of these 8 showing such changes, 3 were first photographed as calves in the Bay of Fundy. Some callosity patterns apparently did not stabilize before the whales were at least one year old, in contrast to the apparent absence of age-related changes in southern right whales (Payne et al., 1983). In the remaining five whales for which major callosity pattern changes appeared to have occurred, some of these may have been due to significant alterations in the distribution of cyamid covering. In all these cases, reidentifications were possible only through the use of supplementary identifying features.

Table 7.

Changes in the identifying features of male right whales over time. Key as for Table 5.

		Callosities													
NEA no.	Years sighted	Configuration/ Topography					Vertical growth					Scars			Misc.	
		B	I	Li	C	PB	B	I	Li	C	PB	H	Bo	T	LC	WV
1103	81,82	L	/	/	S	X	+	/	/	N	N	N	/	X	X	X
1112	80–84 incl	S	/	S	N	N	N	/	N	N	N	X	/	X	N	X
1136	81,82,84	N	N	/	S	N	N	N	/	N	N	X	/	X	N	X
1144	81,82,84	N	/	N	N	N	N	/	N	N	N	N	N	N	N	X
1147	81,83	L	/	S	S	X	N	/	N	N	N	N	X	X	N	X
1154	81,84	N	/	N	N	N	N	/	N	N	N	X	/	N	X	X
1167	81,82	S	/	N	S	X	N	/	N	N	N	/	/	X	N	X
1203	81,84	S	S	X	N	N	N	N	X	N	N	N	/	X	N	X
1218	81,82,83	N	N	/	N	N	N	N	/	N	N	N	N	N	N	N
1226	81,84	N	/	/	N	N	N	/	/	N	N	/	/	S	N	X
Totals	X	0	0	1	0	3	0	0	1	0	0	3	1	6	2	9
	N	5	2	3	6	7	9	3	5	10	10	5	2	3	8	1
	S	3	1	2	4	0						0	0	1	0	0
	L	2	0	0	0	0						0	0	0	0	0
	+						1	0	0	0	0					
	−						0	0	0	0	0					
	/	0	7	4	0	0	0	7	4	0	0	2	7	0	0	0

Two species of whale lice (*Cyamus ovalis* and *C. gracilis*) have been found on North Atlantic right whale callosites in large numbers (Rowntree, pers. comm.), and have been observed to change the apparent outline of callosity patterns by occupying and/or vacating the smooth skin along the sides of rostral callosities. Therefore, the large variations in apparent patterns of some callosities may have been due to cyamid movements between the coaming and bonnet or rostral islands. Callosity tissue without cyamids in adult North Atlantic right whales can appear black or grey, so the detection of low topography callosity tissue in the absence of cyamids may be difficult. In calves, callosities were often white or light grey, and cyamid infestations were generally heavy through the first year, often covering the smooth skin of the rostrum as well as the callosity tissue, thus obscuring the underlying patterns.

A few other significant changes in identifying features have been noted. One cow, NEA No. 1135, had clearly visible lower lip callosities (not cyamids) in 1981, but these had nearly disappeared by 1984. Three whales (NEA's 1124, 1153, and 1241) were first photographed with several rostral callosity islands, but subsequent photographs showed that one or more of these islands had become joined to the bonnet or the coaming callosity, probably by cyamids. A calf from 1981 (NEA 1163) acquired a large (est. 2×5 cm) white scar on the right side of the rostrum by the spring of 1982, but by 1983, the scar had disappeared, leaving only a dark grey patch.

In all of these situations, matches were possible because of clear photographs which included features other than callosities. It appeared that all identifying features except for the patterns of lower lip crenations and ventral white patches could change to some degree in some whales. The changes occurred slowly and in a small number of whales, and it was possible, therefore, to identify and track the changes in photographs over several years. There may be rare cases in which the same individual might not be recognized using callosity photographs taken several years apart. However, the photographic data indicated that identifiable features on *E. glacialis* were not likely to all change simultaneously, so that 'double marking' of whales by photographing callosity patterns and at least one other distinctive identifier ensured reliable resightings.

DISCUSSION

In this study of photographic identification in the North Atlantic right whale, discontinuous callosity patterns were easier to use than continuous patterns. Positive identification of a whale with a continuous callosity pattern usually required multiple photographs with good resolution and a well photographed secondary feature (scar, white patch, etc.). New scars, such as those from killer whales or fishing gear, could alter previous identifying features, requiring that field workers be cognizant of all possible features in addition to callosity patterns that are useful in identifying individual right whales. These features include scars on the chin, tail stock, and flukes, crenations along the lower lips, white pigmentation patterns along the margins of the blowholes, on the belly, chin, and back, as well as a variety of scratches or spots that in some cases are remarkably stable.

Photographs of callosity patterns provide a good organizational basis for cataloging North Atlantic right whales; however, the use of additional marks whenever possible provides certainty in the identifications, particularly for whales with 'continuous' callosites. The feasibility of using resightings based on natural markings to answer significant biological questions about this genus has already been well demonstrated (Payne *et al.*, 1983). The WHOI/NEA match of a right whale cow over 12 years demonstrates the long-term utility of the technique for *E. glacialis*, and the inter-institutional matching results (Table 3) show that monitoring individuals over several years and in a variety of places is feasible. These data also suggest that detailed information on calving intervals and gross annual reproductive rates could be obtained from a more comprehensive photographic effort. Careful use of individual photographic identifications over time could also yield estimates of minimum population sizes, age at first reproduction, any sex and age segregation by season and/or habitat, age and/or sex specific behaviors, habitat use, individual growth rates, and information on mortality rates and causes. Long-term photographic monitoring of these parameters may be useful for monitoring population trends.

ACKNOWLEDGEMENTS

This work was made possible by contracts from the Marine Mammal Commission, Washington, D.C., and the Habitat Protection Branch of the National Marine Fisheries Service, Gloucester, Ma. The Center for Coastal Studies (Provincetown, Ma.) kindly contributed photographs to this analysis. The collection of photographs by each institution was made possible through support from the Minerals Management Service, World Wildlife Fund-U.S., The Oceanic Biology Program of the Office of Naval Research (U.S.), the National Marine Fisheries Service, and the Marine Mammal Commission. Helpful comments along the way have been made by R. Payne, S. K. Katona, G. Stone, V. J. Rowntree, W. E. Schevill, E. Dorsey, F. Fairfield, and others. Thanks to Cecile Cusson, Eleanor Jensen and Laurel Code for typing this report, and to Jane Harrison for computerizing the Aquarium's catalog data. This is Contribution No. 6073 from the Woods Hole Oceanographic Institution.

REFERENCES

Chandler, R., Goebel, C. and Balcomb, K. 1977. Who is that killer whale? A new key to whalewatching. *Pacific Search* 11(7): 25–35.

Dorsey, E. M. 1983. Exclusive adjoining ranges in individually identified minke whales (*Balaenoptera acutorostrata*) in Washington state. *Can. J. Zool.* 61: 174–81.

Hatler, D. F. and Darling, J. D. 1974. Recent observations of the grey whale in British Columbia. *Can. Field-Naturalist* 88: 449–59.

Katona, S. K., Harcourt, P., Perkins, J. and Kraus, S. 1980. *Humpback whales in the Western North Atlantic Ocean: A fluke catalog of individuals identified by means of fluke photographs.* 2nd edition. College of the Atlantic, Bar Harbor, Me. 169 pp.

Katona, S. K. and Whitehead, H. P. 1981. Identifying humpback whales using their natural markings. *Polar Record* 20(128): 439–44.

Kraus, S. D., Prescott, J. H. and Stone, G. 1984. Right whales in the northern Gulf of Maine. *Whalewatcher* 17(4): 18–21.

Kraus, S. D., Prescott, J. H., Turnbull, P. V., and Reeves, R. R. 1982. Preliminary notes on the occurrence of the North Atlantic right whale, *Eubalaena glacialis*, in the Bay of Fundy. *Rep. int. Whal. Commn* 32: 407–11.

Payne, R. 1972. Swimming with Patagonia's right whales. *Nat. Geogr.* 142: 576–87.

Payne, R. and Dorsey, E. M. 1983. Sexual dimorphism and aggressive use of callosities in right whales (*Eubalaena australis*). pp. 295–329, *In*: Payne, R. (ed.), *Communication and Behavior of Whales*. AAAS Selected Symposia Series 76. Westview Press, Boulder, CO. 643 pp.

Payne, R., Brazier, O., Dorsey, E. M., Perkins, J. S., Rowntree, V. J.. and Titus, A. 1983. External features in southern right whales (*Eubalaena australis*) and their use in identifying individuals. pp. 371–445 *In*: R. Payne (ed.), *Communication and Behavior of Whales*, AAAS Selected Symposium 76, Westview Press, Boulder, CO. 643 pp.

Price, C. A. and Winn, H. E. 1981. Development of methodology for identifying individual right whales, *Eubalaena glacialis*, based on

bonnet patterns and other markings, with a report on preliminary results. Appendix A in the 1980 CeTAP Annual Report to the Bureau of Land Management, NTIS PB-83-149905, 28pp.

Watkins, W. A. and Moore, K. E. 1983. Three right whales (*Eubalaena glacialis*) alternating at the surface. *J. Mammal*. 64: 506–8.

Watkins, W. A. and Schevill, W. E. 1979. Aerial observations of feeding behavior in four baleen whales, *Eubalaena glacialis*, *Balaenoptera borealis*, *Megaptera novaeangliae*, and *Balaenoptera physalus*. *J. Mammal*. 60: 155–63.

Watkins, W. A. and Schevill, W. E. 1982. Right whales, *Eubalaena glacialis*, in Cape Cod waters. *Fish Bull., U.S.* 80: 875–80.

Appendix 1

AREAS REFERRED TO IN THIS STUDY

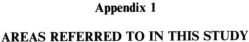

Cow and calf (*E. glacialis*), Peninsula Valdes, Argentina (Photo courtesy R. Payne)

Southern Right Whales: Status off Australia from Twentieth-Century 'Incidental' Sightings and Aerial Survey

J. L. BANNISTER

The Western Australian Museum, Perth, Western Australia

ABSTRACT

Information to 1982 obtained by questionnaire from sources in each Australian State (mainly newspaper accounts, incidental sightings by the interested public, biologists and fisheries officers) has resulted in 128 'incidental' records, of 272 right whales, this century.

Before 1960 there were very few sightings recorded, with only 11 records, of 15 animals. Since 1970, and particularly since 1975, there has been a marked increase, but mainly from two States (Victoria and Western Australia) which account for 71% of records since 1970. While reporting effort cannot be quantified, but has presumably increased recently, these data cannot give unequivocal evidence of an increase in the population, although it seems likely that such an increase has occurred.

In a series of spotting flights off southern Western Australia since 1976, once a month from July/August to October/November, 229 right whales have been seen, with up to 73 in one year (1980); 41 were recorded in 1982. Most animals have been in singles or pairs (mostly cows and calves), but up to 15 adults have been recorded from one locality at one time. Some of the large groups must contain males. Some parts of the coast are frequented more than others. For those months when animals are most often seen (August and September) there may have been an overall increase since 1976. Continuation of such programmes should provide quantifiable evidence of population trends.

INTRODUCTION

Chittleborough (1956), in drawing attention to the sighting of a cow and calf right whale near Albany in 1955, remarked on the lack of published Australian sightings of the species to that time this century. Other authors have remarked likewise (e.g. Aitken, 1971, p. 95: 'since no authenticated sighting of this whale [has been] made in South Australia during the first half of the present century, the species was presumed to have vanished from the waters around the state'). Happily, like Chittleborough, he was able to report the sighting of a cow and calf, this time from Port Lincoln, South Australia in 1968. Indeed, ten years later, he and Ling (Ling and Aitken, 1981) were able to write 'they are again to be seen around our south coast and at the entrances to the two gulfs, often in spring time...'.

While published records are scarce, there is no doubt that in many sheltered bays around the southern coast of Australia right whales are now being reported more frequently than before, particularly in late winter and spring. This account summarises such 'incidental' records available to the author, and compares results with information obtained from recent aerial surveys for this species off Western Australia.

'INCIDENTAL' RECORDS

Data available

In attempting to document right whale sighting records this century, the author circulated a one-page questionnaire (see Appendix A) to 13 colleagues in Australia (biologists, museum and fisheries officers, private individuals) whom he believed might either possess or have access to (or have contacts who might have) information on right whale sightings. The response was very generous. Including contacts followed up, 16 persons eventually responded to requests for information.

The questionnaire referred specifically to right whales, and the author has relied on the judgement of those responding to include only those whales they believe can be identified as such. For example, no 'possibles' but all 'probables' have been included; the latter are only a very small proportion of the total. Wherever feasible, for example for newspaper reports, photographs or other independent evidence have been taken into account.

Trends

Numbers

Plots of the number of records in each year for each State and for Australia as a whole, are given in Fig.1. A 'record' has been taken as any discrete sighting of a whale or group, made in one place at one time, which is not, from its size, location, or lapse of time since a previous observation, in the opinion of the observer or the author's informant (and/or occasionally the author) likely to have been the same whale or whales as seen on a previous (and usually fairly recent) occasion.

Comments on the information available for each State are given below.

(*a*) *New South Wales.* With two very early records, both 'probably right whales', of animals taken off Eden, NSW (1904, 1906) and another taken there apparently in 1918, plus a stranding record for 1932, this State has by far the widest time span of records, although overall the number (13, representing only 19 individuals) is relatively low. The few recent records have all occurred since 1960, with one each year since 1978.

(*b*) *Tasmania.* With no records until 1959, none from then until 1973, and few since, the number of records is disappointingly small, particularly given the importance of right whales there early last century. Dakin (1963) refers to an 1804 report, where because of so many whales in the River Derwent 'it was dangerous for the boat to go up the river unless you kept to the shore'. By contrast only 11 records are available this century, representing 15 animals.

(*c*) *Victoria.* There is one record from 1942 (Wakefield, 1967), another from 1947, and then one or more from

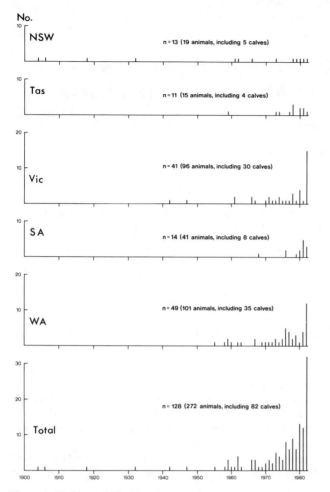

Figure 1. Number of "incidental" records in each year since 1900, Australian coast.

with one or more each year since then. As in the case of Victoria, the 1982 results (12 records of 29 animals) are considerably higher than those for previous years. With an active whale-watching scheme instituted in 1981, coupled with some locally heightened interest from the aerial survey programme since 1976, it is perhaps not surprising that this State's records are higher in number than elsewhere (49, representing 101 animals).

The overall picture off Australian coasts this century is thus of a scarcity of right whale records at least up to about 1960. Up to and including that year, only 12 records (17 animals) have been reported during this project. Plots of the data by 5-year groups (Table 1) show a distinct increase from 1965, with a steeper increase after 1975 (Fig. 2). The plot for 'animals' shows the same pattern as for 'sightings' but with a steeper increase. Given that a single animal would be less likely to be noticed than a group, the early records may be more of an underestimate of the number present, but this would be offset if the number in a group was itself underestimated, which is likely.

Distribution

The records for which specific locality data are available extend from just north of Sydney (i.e. about 34° S) on the east coast, to Geraldton (about 29° S) in the west (Fig. 3). These are close to the limits of coastal distribution indicated in Townsend's Indo-Pacific right whale chart in which he plots the positions of American whaling vessels,

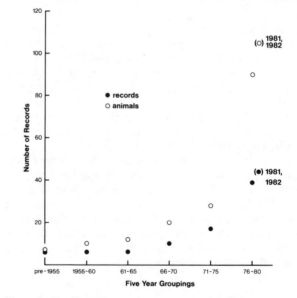

Figure 2. "Incidental" records, and number of animals reported, by 5-year groups, Australian coast.

each year since 1970. The indication is of a resurgence of the species, even without the much-publicised recent 'return' of animals to the Warrnambool area south-west of Melbourne, where in 1982 'by early August there was a herd of eight adults and seven calves in the area' (Anon., 1982), the first animal being reported late in May, the last in October. The numbers of records available (41, of 96 animals) is second highest of all the States; the 1982 figure (15 records, 41 animals) is highest for any State in any year.

(d) *South Australia.* Again, given the early significance of right whaling in this State's economy, the overall number of records this century is disappointingly low although several multiple groupings have been reported; the 14 records available represent 41 individuals.

(e) *Western Australia.* Following Chittleborough's 1955 sighting, there were intermittent records until 1969,

Table 1

Number of "incidental" records (I), Number of animals (N) and Number of calves (C) included,
before 1955 and by 5-year periods since then, Australian coast.

State	Pre 1955 I	N	C	1955–60 I	N	C	1961–65 I	N	C	1966–70 I	N	C	1971–75 I	N	C	1976–80 I	N	C	1981,1982 I	N	C	Total I	N	C
New South Wales	4	5	1	–	–	–	2	4	1	1	1	–	1	2	1	3	5	2	2	2	–	13	19	5
Tasmania	–	–	–	1	1	–	–	–	–	–	–	–	2	3	1	6	9	3	2	2	–	11	15	4
Victoria	2	2	–	–	–	–	2	4	2	4	10	3	7	12	4	10	23	5	16	45	16	41	96	30
South Australia	–	–	–	–	–	–	–	–	–	1	2	1	–	–	–	5	18	1	8	21	6	14	41	8
Western Australia	–	–	–	5	9	4	2	4	1	4	7	3	7	11	3	15	35	11	16	35	13	49	101	35
Total	6	7	1	6	10	4	6	12	4	10	20	7	17	28	9	39	90	22	44	105	35	128	272	82

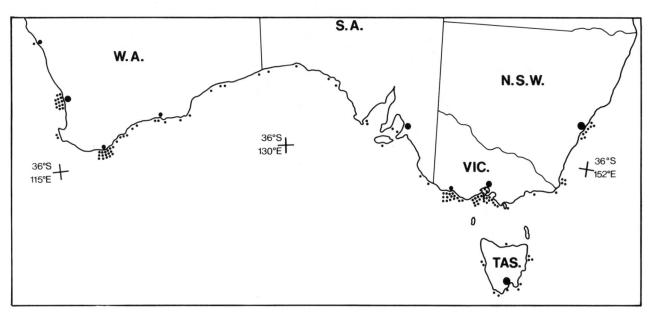

Figure 3. Locations of "incidental" records obtained, Australian coast, 1904–1982.

obtained from available logbooks, on days when one or more were taken (Townsend, 1935). Townsend's most northerly east coast location is just south of Sydney; on the west coast it is just north of Perth, at about 31° S.

This is in some contrast to the information plotted by Maury (1851) where right whales are indicated as occurring off the northwest coast (15–20° S) in the southern winter and well off the central east coast (25–30°S) in the southern autumn. There is no obvious reason why Maury's information should be different in this respect from Townsend's; the time span of his data (late 1840s) fits within Townsend's. Other distributional anomalies occur in Maury data sets, e.g. a lack of sperm whales north of 40° N in the North Pacific in his 1851 charts (Maury, 1852) even though the species obviously occurs there, and he records right whale sightings there (see Bannister and Mitchell, 1980).

Fig. 3 indicates that many of the records come from places frequented by persons likely to report sightings such as interested amateurs, weekend yachtsmen and local newspaper reporters; records from more remote areas are relatively few. This points to the difficulty of assessing rates of change in population numbers from such information, particularly when public interest in whales has increased considerably as it has in the past few years (see also 'Conclusions', below).

Timing of occurrence

Plots of available dated records by month (Fig. 4) show that overall most have occurred in a three-month period from mid winter to early spring (July to September), with a peak in August and a range covering a nine-month period from April to December. Among the State records, those from Tasmania span the whole range, but sparsely, with none recorded in June. In Victorian records the peak occurs slightly earlier (July) than in the other States. Western Australia lacks records for April, May and December; New South Wales has none in April, May, June or December and South Australia has none in April, July, November or December.

Although numbers are very small there is a hint of movement of animals from the south, for example from

Tasmania to Victoria or New South Wales, through the early part of the season. This was once a strongly held view, as reported both by Dakin (1963) and Aitken (1971). The latter (p. 96) quotes an 1842 report in which right whales are said to approach Tasmania from about the beginning of April, then move north towards Portland Bay (western Victoria) before continuing to move westwards towards the Great Australian Bight. That report also comments on the additional arrival of animals along the whole southern coast direct from the south, which seems to fit present observations along the Western Australian coast. Then, 'At Cape Lewin [sic] the great body of whales seems to strike off Southward, for in October and November they are again working towards the south-east, by keeping two or three hundred miles from the land...' That fits with Townsend's plots which show a well-defined September catching ground close to the WA south coast (between Esperance and Bremer Bay), while plots from October to January appear further west and south, and back towards Tasmania; there are then a few February plots approaching that area from the west, south of the Bight.

Townsend's plots south of the Bight also fit well with recent sightings data; between 23 December 1981 and 17 January 1982, 75 right whales were seen by Japanese scouting vessels south of Western Australia between 40° and 50° S (Ohsumi and Kasamatsu, 1986).

The high proportion of females with calves in sightings of right whales close to such coasts is a well-remarked feature of the species; of the 272 animals represented in the records obtained in this project, 82 (30%) were calves. In Fig. 4, where overall the most common months for calves are shown to be August and September, there is a suggestion that animals without calves may occur earlier in the season, which would not be surprising if females give birth some time after their arrival on the coast.

AERIAL SURVEY RESULTS

Since 1976 a series of flights has been undertaken between Cape Leeuwin (34° 22′ S, 115° 08′ E) eastwards to Cape Arid (34° 01′ S, 123° 09′ E), along some 450 nautical miles

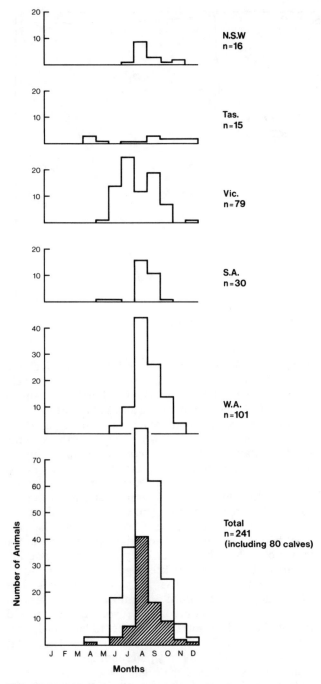

Figure 4. Monthly frequency of "incidental" dated records (individual animals) for each State and total (latter including records with calves).

Table 2

Southern right whale aerial surveys, S.W. coast of Western Australia, summarised numbers of animals recorded 1976–82. Total number of animals recorded was 229, including 50 calves. Figures in brackets equal number of calves included.
[1] In two flights.   [2] Flights occurred on the turn of the month; taken as an "August" figure.

	1976	1977	1978	1979	1980	1981	1982
Jul	–	2(1)	–	–	14(3)	–	–
Aug	3(1)	–	11(5)	9(2)	25(6)	40(1)[2]	20(7)
Sept	–	19(4)[1]	23(6)	6	29(3)	–	21(9)
Oct	Nil	–	Nil	Nil	5(1)	Nil	Nil
Nov	–	Nil	Nil	2(1)	–	Nil	Nil
Dec	–	Nil	–	–	Nil	Nil	–
Total	3(1)	21(5)	34(11)	17(3)	73(13)	40(1)	41(16)

July or August each year to November or December. Summaries of results for each year are given in Table 2, which shows that while sightings have been made in all months except December, most animals have been seen in August and September. Indeed, in 1982 whales were only seen in those months. Between 1976 and 1982 the number seen per flight in those two months has been: [3], [9.5], 17, 7.5, 27, [40] and 20 respectively. Bracketed figures are for one month only.

Despite the wide range in numbers and lack of consistency in the time series the overall trend seems to have been upward over the past few years. A logarithmic regression fitted to the data shows a significant increase at the 5%, but not the 1% level ($y = 3.669e^{0.325x}$).

From colour photographs taken to show head callosity patterns some 93 individuals have been identified since 1979. From these one of three adults in a bay some 60 miles east of Esperance on 30 August 1982 was identified as one of two adults seen some 20 miles nearer Esperance $3\frac{1}{2}$ weeks earlier. This is the first record from the aerial survey work of any animal spending any time on the coast, although local observers have recorded that individuals may be present for more than eight weeks. Although some preliminary sorting of photographs has been carried out, it is not yet possible to say conclusively whether any of those so far recognised individually are animals returning to the coast from an earlier year. Rather few have any individual marks or distinctive colour patterns to corroborate the information from callosities. Of those photographed, five adults were 'grey' or 'white', with various degrees of dark speckling; one other was distinctively speckled with white on its dark body. Two small calves were 'light coloured' or 'greyish'; another had two large white patches on its back.

Some generalisations based on 1976–81 data have been presented elsewhere (Bannister, 1985). They are updated below by inclusion of 1982 records.

(1) Right whales occur most frequently in August and September. Few are recorded after September.

(2) Most observations (73% of the 229 individuals seen) have been of single animals or pairs; of the latter (149 animals) 68% were females with calves. Of the remainder, there were 3 groups of 3 animals, 3 of 5, 1 of 9, 1 of 10 and 1 of 15. None of the groups of three or more included calves, although 1 pair and 1 threesome were recorded as each including a 'yearling'.

(3) There are yearly fluctuations in the proportions of calves observed. The latter account for up to 45% of the

(approx. 800 km) of the southern Western Australian coast.

Flights have followed the coastline, in a highwing aircraft (Cessna 172) at approximately 1,500 ft and 100 knots. The plane is flown virtually along the beachline, with pilot and observer looking downwards and seawards. Wherever possible flights take place in 'good' weather conditions, i.e. winds less than 15 knots, calm to low swell, and good visibility. All sightings are circled to establish group size. The same pilot has flown each year, accompanied by an observer. Since 1980 the same observer (an experienced photographer) has almost invariably been available. A regular photographic record was introduced in that year and circling time has probably increased slightly.

Flights have generally been made once a month from

number seen in one month (August 1978). The relatively high proportion of such sightings is in line with the generally held view that southern right whales approach coasts in late winter to give birth, suggesting that many of the adult animals observed are females. But from observations of extended penises and of mating behaviour on a least one occasion (September 1980), and of animated behaviour amongst a large group (when, in September 1981, individuals were seen chasing each other, breaching, lying close together) males must also be present, possibly in relatively large numbers at times.

(4) Most cow and calf pairs have been recorded in August and September, with a few in July. Most pairs of adults have been seen in September, with some in August. The three largest groupings were all recorded in September. There is therefore a suggestion that calving may be taking place rather earlier than mating, assuming that some of the adult pairs and larger groupings include males.

(5) Some parts of the coast are frequented more often than others. Individuals are regularly seen near Flinders Bay (Augusta) (34° 19′ S, 115° 09′ E), in the Bremer Bay–Point Ann–Hopetoun area (34° 24′ S, 119° 26′ E–33° 57′ S, 120° 07′ E), and just east of Esperance (33° 52′ S, 121° 54′ E). These are also the places where cows and calves are most often seen, suggesting that they represent regular calving grounds. As shown above, the Bremer Bay–Esperance area features prominently as a 'September' whaling ground for this species in Townsend's right whale chart (Townsend, 1935).

CONCLUSIONS

From the well-marked increase in Australian 'incidental' records of right whale sightings in recent years, particularly since 1975, one would like to be able to conclude unequivocally that this species is now increasing, possibly at a rapid rate, in this part of its former range. Unfortunately, without some measure of the effort involved in making the records it is difficult to give a true measure of their significance. No doubt in the 1950s and 1960s the appearance of a large whale very close to the coast, to a layman's eyes often about to strand, would have caused considerable interest among those fortunate enough to witness the event; such records might well be reported, often finding their way into the press; indeed, many of those referred to here from those years originated from that source.

With the great expansion of public interest in whales and the environment generally from the early 1970s there is now probably a greater chance of a right whale's approach to the coast being witnessed and reported, except in very remote areas. Such interest must also increase the chance of duplicate or multiple sightings of the same whale or group of whales, particularly if the whales move along the coast. Nevertheless, it seems unlikely that the whole of the increase observed in the 'incidental' records cited in this project is due to greater reporting effort, although the effect may have been greater in Victoria in 1982 and Western Australia from

1981. On that basis, a real increase in numbers must have occurred recently. The absolute extent of such an increase can, however, only be gauged accurately from regular standardised observations, from programmes of aerial survey and the like. Hopefully such programmes will continue and even intensify, so that the true rate of this species' likely recovery off the Australian coast can be monitored effectively.

ACKNOWLEDGEMENTS

This report is based almost entirely on information provided to the author by others. Grateful acknowledgement is given to those who so promptly replied to his questionnaire and to others who subsequently responded to requests for information, as follows: M. M. Bryden, G. Cerini, P. Congreve, R. G. Chittleborough, W. H. Dawbin, J. M. Dixon, E. R. Guiler, I. Kirkegaard, J. K. Ling, H. Marsh, T. McManus, K. McNamara, B. Munday, D. J. Needham and R. M. Warneke. Thanks are also due to J. Bell, D. Hembree, V. Milne, R. Smith and C. B. Tassell who have been involved closely with the aerial survey work off the Western Australian coast since 1976; to V. Milne also for her enthusiasm in organising the south coast whale watching scheme, and to those many others who have reported records of this species and other cetaceans to Museums, Fisheries Departments and other bodies over the years. The 1976–78 aerial surveys were financed from the Department of Primary Industry Fisheries Development Trust Fund; since then they have been undertaken under contract to, and funded by, the Australian National Parks and Wildlife Service. J. M. Breiwick and G. P. Kirkwood provided statistical advice.

REFERENCES

Aitken, P. F. 1971. Whales from the coast of South Australia. *Trans. R. Soc. S. Aust.* 95 (2): 95–103.

Anon. 1982. *Southern Right Whale.* Fisheries and Wildlife Division, Victoria.

Bannister, J. L. 1985. Southern right (*Eubalaena australis*) and humpback (*Megaptera novaeangliae*) whales off Western Australia: some recent aerial survey work. *In*: Ling, J. and Bryden, M. M. (eds), *Studies of Sea Mammals in South Latitudes.* South Australian Museum, Adelaide.

Bannister, J. L. and Mitchell, E. D. 1980. North Pacific sperm whale stock identity: distributional evidence from Maury and Townsend Charts. *Rep. int. Whal. Commn.* (special issue 2): 219–30.

Chittleborough, R. G. 1956. Southern right whale in Australian waters. *J. Mammal.* 37(3): 456–7.

Dakin, W. J. 1963. *Whalemen Adventurers.* Sirius Books, Sydney.

Ling, J. K. and Aitken, P. F. 1981. Marine Mammals in South Australia. *In*: *S.A. Year Book*, 1981. Australian Bureau of Statistics, Adelaide.

Maury, M. F. 1851. *Whale Chart (Preliminary Sketch).* Series F. Miscellaneous, no. 8514. U.S. Hydrographic Office, Washington.

Maury, M. F. 1852. *Whale Chart of the World* [The Wind and Current Charts], Series F., U.S. Hydrographic Office, Washington.

Ohsumi, S. and Kasamatsu, F. 1986. Recent off-shore distribution of the southern right whale in summer. (Published in this volume)

Townsend, C. H. 1935. The distribution of certain whales as shown by logbook records of American whaleships. *Zoologica*, N.Y. 19(1): 1–50.

Wakefield, N. A. 1967. Whales and dolphins recorded for Victoria. *Victorian Nat.* 84: 273–81.

Appendix A

QUESTIONNAIRE CIRCULATED IN MARCH 1982

1. Chittleborough (J. Mammal. 37: 456), reporting a cow and calf off Albany in 1955, could find no previously published reference to 20th Century Right Whale records near the Australian coast. Do you have any evidence that Right whales might have occurred in Australian waters between 1900 and 1955?

                                                                                    Yes/No

If Yes, please give details or references:-

2. Do you have evidence of Right Whales near the Australian Coast since 1955?

                                                                                    Yes/No

If Yes, are the data a) Published/Unpublished
                      b) In your possession?

If published, are the records: in newspapers/the "grey literature"/scientific publications?

If the data are in your possession, would you be prepared to: send me copies, if necessary at my expense/allow me to examine them if I were to visit you?

If the data are not in your possession, whom should I contact?

3. If the answer to Question 2 is Yes, are the data for: one year/several years/most years, since 1955? or since any subsequent year?

Do they indicate: mainly single animals/cows and calves/larger groupings?

4. Can you suggest anyone I should contact, other than those listed in 2 above or in my letter, who may have information on Southern Right Whales?

Records of the Southern Right Whale, *Eubalaena australis* (Desmoulins, 1822) from Chile Between 1976 and 1982

ANELIO AGUAYO L.

Laboratorio de Vertebrados, Facultad de Ciencias, UNAM Ap. postal 70–572, 04510 Mexico, D.F., Mexico

AND DANIEL TORRES N.

Subdireccion Cientifica, Instituto Antártico Chileno, Luis Thayer Ojeda 814, Correo 9, Santiago, Chile

ABSTRACT

Five new sighting records of southern right whales from Chile between 1976 and 1982 are reported. These sightings support the view of Clarke (1965) that right whales never completely disappeared from Chilean waters.

INTRODUCTION

The right whale, *Eubalaena australis*, was exploited off central and southern Chile, particularly off Concepcion, Aruco, Valdivia and Chiloé. Captures in the South Pacific began after 1790 and the Chilean fishery had begun to decline by the mid 19th century although sporadic catches were made up to 1968; 13 were taken since 1952 (Clarke, 1965; Aguayo, 1974).

Recent published sightings are confined to a sighting of a cow and calf near Playa Grande, Cartagena (33° 32′ S) on 27 August 1964 (Clarke, 1965) and two animals marked with Discovery marks (nos 23572 and 23580) near Chiloe Island (41° 58′ S) in October 1966 (Aguayo, 1974).

No sightings of right whales were reported by Gilmore (1971) during a cruise from Valparaíso to San Félix and San Ambrosio Islands to the coast at Chañaral (north of Coquimbo) and south to Talcahuano, from 23 June to 6 July 1970.

This paper presents data on five new right whale sightings off Chile between 1976 and 1982 (Fig. 1).

SIGHTINGS

(1) *October 1976, Constitucion* (and see Torres, 1977)

A right whale which was seen near the coast at Constitucion (35° 26′ S) was filmed and reported on television news on 20 October 1976. The film clearly showed the bonnet, double blows and absence of a dorsal fin. The whale had remained near Constitucion for 45 hours and in the vicinity for almost three days. On 21 October, DTN went to Constitucion but was unable to locate the animal which according to fishermen had left moving northwards. No subsequent sightings of the animal were reported.

(2) *October 1979, Golfo de Penas*

On 1 October 1979, W. Church saw a single right whale in the Golfo de Penas at 47° 10′ S, from the R/V *Hero*; the animal blew three times then sounded (P. J. Lenie, pers. comm. to R. N. P. Goodall and A. R. Galeazzi, 1980).

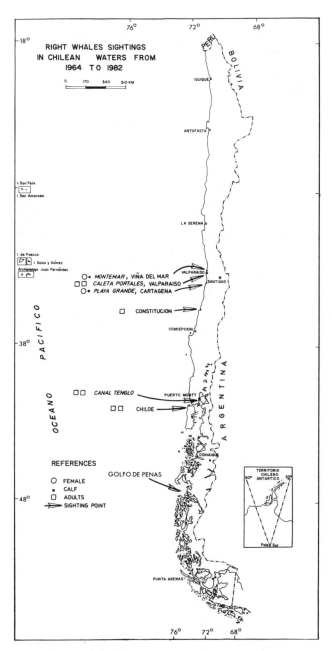

Fig. 1. Right whale sightings in Chilean waters, 1964 to 1982.

(3) *October 1980*, Renaca and Cochoa

On 24 October 1980, two whales were seen moving slowly northwards near the shore at Reñaca, Montemar (32° 59′ S) and then Cochoa, Viña del Mar. Photographs published in the Valparaíso newspaper *El Mercurio* (25 October 1980) clearly identified these as an adult and calf. Species identification was based on the lack of a dorsal fin, the blow, the bonnet of the adult and the shape of the flukes.

(4) *January 1981, Canal Tenglo*

On 15 January 1981, Mr C. Cochifas saw and filmed two adult right whales in Canal Tenglo (41° 29′ S) from the yacht *Skorpios*. The animals swam slowly, close to the shore for about half an hour before heading out to sea. D.T.N. saw the film and species identification was based on the large head and bonnet, blow, lack of a dorsal fin, body colour and broad flippers.

(5) *September 1982, Caleta Portales*

On 15 September 1982 from 1500 to 1700 hours two right whales were seen by many people near Caleta Portales, Valparaíso Bay (33° 00′ S) and a television film report made. From the report, DTN identified the animals as right whales based on the bonnet and callosities, blows, absence of dorsal fin and body colour; the animals were apparently swimming slowly northwards, 150–200 m from the coast. No subsequent sightings of these animals were reported.

DISCUSSION AND CONCLUSION

As discussed in IWC (1986), sightings of right whales in various parts of the Southern Hemisphere have been increasing in recent years (e.g. Australia − Bannister, 1986; Argentina – Whitehead, Payne and Payne 1986; Mermoz, 1980; New Zealand – Cawthorn, 1983; southern South America and the Antarctic Peninsula – Goodall and Galeazzi, 1986; South Africa – Best, 1981; Brazil – Castello and Pinedo, 1979).

The sightings reported in this paper support the view of Clarke (1965) that although considerably reduced in numbers, right whales never completely disappeared from Chilean waters.

ACKNOWLEDGMENTS

The authors give their thanks to Mr Alipio Vera, journalist of Television Nacional in 1976, who kindly showed the film to one of us. Thanks are also extended to Mr Constantino Cochifas, owner of the yacht *Skorpios*, who kindly lent us the video-tape from which we learned about right whales filmed by himself. Especial thanks are given to our colleagues R. N. P. Goodall and A. R. Galeazzi from Argentina, who kindly gave us the data of the sighting at Golfo de Penas. The Instituto Antartico Chileno provided the equipment to project the video-tape and facilities to obtain some slides and photos. R. Clarke, P. B. Best and R. L. Brownell Jr and G. P. Donovan read the paper and made comments.

REFERENCES

Aguayo L., A. 1974. Baleen whales off continental Chile, pp. 209–17. *In*: W. E. Schevill (ed.) *The Whale Problem: a Status Report*. Harvard University Press, Cambridge, Mass. 419 pp.

Bannister, J. L. 1986. Southern right whales: status off Australia from twentieth-century 'incidental' sightings and aerial survey. (Published in this volume).

Best, P. B. 1981. The status of right whales (*Eubalaena australis*) off South Africa, 1969–1979. *Investl. Rep. Sea Fish. Inst. S. Afr.* 123: 1–44.

Castello, H. P. and Pinedo, M. C. 1979. Southern right whales (*Eubalaena australis*) along the southern Brazilian coast. *J. Mammal.* 60(2): 429–30.

Cawthorn, M. W. 1986. Current status of right whales off New Zealand—20th century sightings and trends. Paper SC/35/RW10 presented to the IWC Workshop on the Status of Right Whales, Boston, June 1983 (unpublished). 4pp. + 1 table + 1 fig.

Clarke, R. 1965. Southern right whales on the coast of Chile. *Norsk Hvalfangsttid.* 54(6): 121–8.

Gilmore, R. M. 1971. Observations on marine animals and birds off the coast of southern and central Chile, early winter 1970. *Antarct. J., U.S.* 6: 10–11.

Goodall, R. N. P. and Galeazzi, A. R. 1986. Recent sightings and strandings of southern right whales off subAntarctic South America and the Antarctic Peninsula. (Published in this volume).

International Whaling Commission. 1986. Report of the Workshop on the Status of Right Whales. (Published in this volume).

Mermoz, J. F. 1980. Preliminary report on the southern right whale in the southwestern Atlantic. *Rep. int. Whal. Commn* 30: 183–6.

Torres, N. D. 1977. Explotación y conservacion de mamiferos marinos en la Antartica. pp. 186–225. *In*: F. Orrego V. y A. Salinas A. (eds) *El Desarrollo de la Antartica*. Inst. Est. Intern. Univ. de Chile e Inst. Pat. Editorial Universitaria, Santiago, Chile. 373 pp.

Whitehead, H., Payne, R. and Payne, M. 1986. Population estimate for the right whales off Peninsula Valdes, Argentina, 1971–1976. (Published in this volume).

Long Term Behavioral Studies of the Southern Right Whale (*Eubalaena australis*)

ROGER PAYNE

World Wildlife Fund-US, 191 Weston Road, Lincoln, Massachusetts, 01773, USA

ABSTRACT

Since 1970, southern right whales have been studied on their winter/spring aggregation areas in protected waters near the coast of Peninsula Valdes, Argentina. These areas have been repeatedly surveyed from the air and from shore and over 580 individuals have been identified from aerial photographs of natural markings on their heads. Many individuals return to the area each year, but mature females tend to be seen only in years when they give birth (usually every third year). Seventy-four of the known females have had two or more calves, with a mean calving interval of 3.7 ± 1.25 years (n = 89 calving intervals). The age of first calving for two females was seven years. Mothers with young calves are usually positioned along the coast in water about 5 m deep. Right whales are found at Peninsula Valdes in three separate areas: one predominantly occupied by mothers and calves, a second predominantly occupied by males and mature females in non-calf years, and a third occupied by all categories of whales including subadults and mating groups.

INTRODUCTION

Right whales (genus *Eubalaena*) occupy two broad bands of ocean encircling the world between 20 and 60° latitude in Northern and Southern Hemispheres. The number of species in the genus is unresolved, but most authors consider there to be two species, *Eubalaena glacialis* in the Northern Hemisphere and *Eubalaena australis* in the Southern Hemisphere. This paper concerns the southern right whale which we have studied since 1970 during the Southern Hemisphere winter and spring in the waters surrounding Peninsula Valdes, Argentina (42.5 °S, 64°W).

Most major recent advances in behavioral studies of free-ranging populations of large mammals seem to have come from research in which two conditions were fulfilled: first, it was possible to recognize individuals, and second, it was possible to extend the study over several years.

We looked for a practical way to identify individual right whales and soon discovered that an excellent natural marker existed in the pattern of callosities – patches of raised, thickened epidermis on their heads (see Fig. 1). Some of the callosities are exposed every time a whale surfaces to blow. The number, position and shape is unique to each whale, and although minor changes occur with time, the overall pattern remains identifiable from birth and almost certainly throughout the life of the whale (Payne, Brazier, Dorsey, Perkins, Rowntree and Titus, 1983).

To make a long-term study at Peninsula Valdes feasible, we built a permanent field station in the southeast corner of Golfo San Jose overlooking an area frequented by right whales in winter and spring. This has been occupied since 1972 and data have been collected from this area every year since 1970, mostly between August and mid-November.

METHODS AND MATERIALS

Frequent air flights were made throughout the season in order for us to take photographs of the heads of right whales to identify individuals, mostly using a CESSNA 182, single engine, high wing aircraft. Our usual practice was to search for whales along the coast, flying at 200 m or less. When whales were sighted we would drop down to between 150 m and 65 m and circle them until we had taken a series of photographs which we felt was sufficient to identify the whales. We also made observations from cliffs, boats and occasionally from underwater (for a complete description of survey techniques see Payne *et al.* 1983). The study is in its sixteenth year (1985) and we plan to continue it indefinitely. Most data reported here were taken during the first 12 field seasons. Our most complete data were collected in 1973. The data base is extensive and includes, for example, over 40,000 still photographs.

Fig. 1. Aerial photograph of a southern right whale showing atypical callosity pattern.

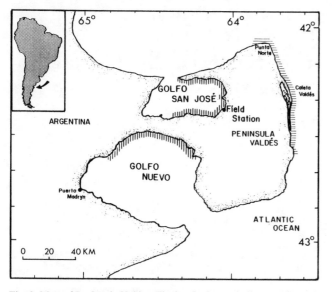

Fig. 2. Map of Peninsula Valdes. The hatched areas indicate regions of concentrations of right whales. (Taken from AAAS Selected Symposium Series Volume 76, *Communication and Behavior of Whales*, R. Payne (ed.) copyright 1983 by the American Association for the Advancement of Science)

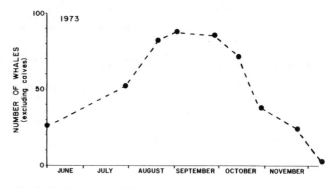

Fig. 3. Build-up and decline of right whales at Peninsula Valdes during 1973. Dots indicate the number of whales (excluding calves) identified, observed and extrapolated in each of nine flights along the coastline.

Over 580 individuals have been identified and we have been able to determine the sex of many of them from anatomical and/or behavioral evidence (for a description of techniques used in sexing right whales see Payne and Dorsey, 1983).

The coastline of Peninsula Valdes is 495 km long (see Fig. 2). We repeatedly surveyed the coast, dividing it into five sections: Golfo San Jose, the Northern Outer Coast, the Eastern Outer Coast, the Southern Outer Coast, and Golfo Nuevo. Of these, three (Golfo San Jose, the Eastern Outer Coast and Golfo Nuevo) were 'aggregation areas' (areas where whales were frequently encountered). Within these aggregation areas were 'regions of concentration', stretches of coast along which right whales regularly congregated. A few flights across the two large bays and many observations from shore led us to the conclusion that the great majority of the right whales wintering at Peninsula Valdes are concentrated near the coast.

We had to develop several new techniques in order to study these whales. We sought to measure length of the whales at the surface to provide a clue to age. To do this we developed several techniques based on aerial photographs. For example, we took aerial photographs of whales next to a boat which was carrying a white disc one m. in diameter. In the resulting photographs of disc and whale, the longest apparent diameter of the disc can be used as a ruler with which to measure the whale. We also measured whales by noting the ratio of head length to body length, which we found to be an age-dependent variable, and by using whales of known length as rulers with which to measure whales of unknown length lying parallel to them. In these ways, we could distinguish subadults from adults, and in a few cases, even calculate growth rates of free-swimming right whales. Details of these techniques are given in Whitehead and Payne (1981).

When whales can be seen from shore, it is possible to track their movements with useful accuracy out to a distance of five or more kilometers by means of a surveyor's theodolite. The distance at which whales can be followed depends on the height of the observation

platform. Bearings to the whale are taken in the vertical and horizontal plane. The vertical bearing is used to compute the distance to the whale. That distance applied along the horizontal bearing gives the map position of the whale. This technique has since been used successfully by a number of researchers (see Würsig and Würsig, 1979 and Tyack, 1981).

RESULTS

The whales are present at Peninsula Valdes only during the winter and spring seasons, during which their normal food is in low abundance and they probably get little or nothing to eat. Data from 1973 (in which we had the broadest coverage) illustrates how the population at Valdes builds and declines within the year. Fig. 3 shows the number of whales seen in each of nine flights. (There were ten flights, but those for 22 and 24 November have been combined into a single flight since they covered different areas.) Three curves are shown giving the number of whales (excluding calves) identified, observed and 'extrapolated'. The last category merely corrects the three flights that covered only two of the three aggregation areas by adding a value for the missing area which was midway between the totals observed there during flights immediately before and after the missing date. The extrapolated curve is probably our best estimate of the lower limit to the number of whales actually present (lower because we undoubtedly failed to see whales that were present but out of sight underwater when the plane was overhead). Fig. 3 shows that the population builds slowly, remains at a high value for about eight weeks, and then declines more rapidly than it built up, suggesting that at the end of the long winter of semi-starvation the whales depart relatively rapidly for their summer feeding grounds.

Structure of the herds at Peninsula Valdes

The term 'herd' has many usages. It is used here to describe a very local grouping: all whales seen in and near a single aggregation area at Peninsula Valdes, e.g., the Golfo San Jose herd or the Eastern Outer Coast herd. The whales in a given region move together as a loosely knit group while staying roughly clustered about a focal group. Local land forms, like headlands and bays, delineate the different herds. In all three aggregation areas, the herd was usually found in the same general

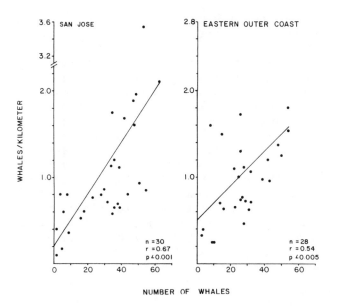

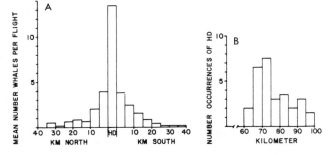

Fig. 5. Spatial distribution of the Golfo San Jose herd. A. The mean distribution of whales observed around the densest five km segment of coast (HD). B. The variation in location of the densest segment (HD) of the herd.

Fig. 4. The correlation between the number of whales observed and their density, in Golfo San Jose and along the Eastern Outer Coast. n = the number of flights with sufficient coverage to see the entire herd. In both areas there is a significant positive correlation.

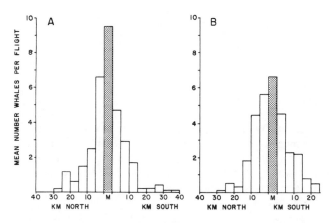

Fig. 6. The distribution of the herd around its mean position (M): Golfo San Jose vs the Eastern Outer Coast.

area. The herd in Golfo Nuevo was much smaller than the others during most of our study and usually more spread out. Our usual experience was to fly for many kilometers of coastline without seeing whales and then to come upon a lone individual or pair. This signalled a buildup in the next 10–30 km to a central group of whales, usually more than 10. Having passed the densest concentration, the numbers fell off in much the same way that they had increased. We considered that we had reached the end of a herd, or at least sampled it adequately, once we had flown 10 km or more beyond the last whale sighted without seeing another whale.

We have made 6 complete surveys along the entire coast of Golfo San Jose and 19 surveys along the entire Eastern Outer Coast. In 23 of these 25 complete surveys, the herd was clustered together regardless of where we found it.

The overall mean herd width for all of Peninsula Valdes was about 37 km. The mean herd width for females with calves was 22 km. Females with calves were often located near the center of the herd, although it appears to be all females, and not just those lactating, that are the focus of the herd.

In both Golfo San Jose and the Eastern Outer Coast, there is a significant positive correlation between numbers of whales and density (Fig. 4), i.e. the whales do not spread out over a longer stretch of coast to maintain the same density as their numbers increase, which they might do if they were maintaining territories and which they could easily do because the available coastline is much longer than the width of the herd. Instead, they apparently incorporate additions to their group by crowding more tightly into a relatively small area. (We have found no evidence for territoriality in this species.)

In order to study the distribution of the herds in space, we counted the number of whales seen in every consecutive 5 km segment of coastline. We plotted the mean herd shape for Golfo San Jose by taking the distribution plots for each flight and sliding them so as to line up the 5 km strip with the greatest number of whales. We then calculated the mean number of whales

seen in each of the 5 km segments flanking the densest segment. The result (Figure 5A) is a sharp, symmetrical curve representing the mean shape of the herd in Golfo San Jose.

The herd does not stay fixed in space but moves back and forth along sections of the coast 30–40 km in length, apparently with no relation to such natural features as water temperature or food abundance. It therefore appears that at this season at least, whales are attracted to each other. Fig. 5B shows that the herd kept mostly to one end of a 40 km stretch of coast along the perimeter of Golfo San Jose.

In Fig. 6 we compare the shape of the herd at Golfo San Jose with the herd shape along the Eastern Outer Coast by the same means outlined above for Golfo San Jose. The Golfo San Jose herd tends to have a higher density of whales at the center than the Eastern Outer Coast herd and also tends to spread out a little further to the south of its mean position.

Depth Preference

To look at depth preferences, we used a surveyor's theodolite from three prominent cliff lookouts to locate the positions of all whales within the study area. We made censuses on 18 calm days in 1973 and 1974 and calculated 857 whale positions. The positions were mapped on a detailed chart of the bay, and the depths were corrected for the tide height at the time the whale was observed. In Fig. 7 the number of whales is plotted for each half meter interval of depth. The striking preference for shallow water, and particularly for a depth of 5 m, is apparent.

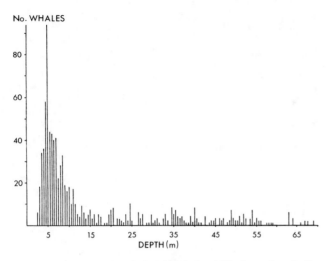

Fig. 7. Depth preference of all right whales visible from shore in the southeast corner of Golfo San Jose.

For these reasons it appeared as though staying within or following the 5 m contour was a convenient way for right whales to encounter each other. We feel that different age/sex categories may gain different advantages from shallow water, but that the majority of individuals could benefit from using the 'whale road' as a means of meeting each other. Unlike rorquals, whose low, loud voices can travel in deep ocean for hundreds of kilometers under some circumstances before being lost in background noise (Payne and Webb, 1971), the right whale vocalizations are at significantly higher frequencies and are made in shallow water. Thus they do not appear to be well suited to long range communication. As a result, it seems likely that right whales need to have a meeting place, and the 'whale road' both within and between aggregation areas (particularly along sections of relatively unfrequented coast hundreds of kilometers long) may provide a region for rendezvous.

This preference was not an artifact of decrease in sightability with increase in depth. The three different lookouts from which we worked were at each end and in the middle of a long strip of coast. When working from either of the two end cliff lookouts we were noting whales 8–10 km away which were right in close to the shore at or near the other end of the strip of coast. From these end lookouts, all of the whales seen in deep water were closer to us than the most distant nearshore whales along the coast. In order to be sure that the result was not simply a consequence of the distribution of average water depths in our study area, we calculated the distribution of mean depths (Fig. 8). By comparing Figs 7 and 8, it is apparent that the whales are selecting specific depths. These results suggest that there may be important selective pressures on right whales for remaining in 5 m of water at Peninsula Valdes.

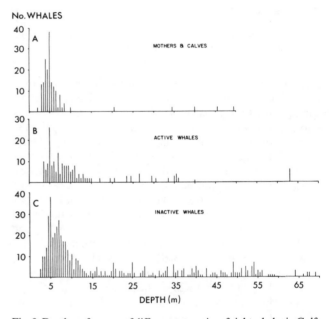

Fig. 9. Depth preferences of different categories of right whales in Golfo San Jose.

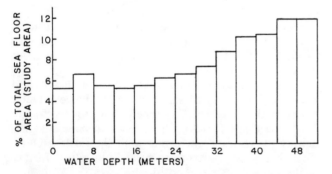

Fig. 8. Distribution of water depths during an average tidal cycle within the south east corner of Golfo San Jose. This is the same area for which the depth preferences of whales are given in Fig. 7 and 9.

The strong preference of right whales for a depth of 5 m caused us to start referring to the 5 m depth contour as the 'whale road'. Whales usually swam along this contour and carried out social interactions (sometimes lasting for hours) with the other individuals they encountered. Their trips kept to this contour even when a shortcut through deeper water would have brought them to their day's final destination much more quickly.

During most cliff surveys there was a second observer watching through a telescope to determine for each whale or group of whales the type of behavior. This behavior was put into one of five categories: active groups (obviously moving or white water present), breaching, lobtailing, flippering, and inactive animals (not moving). Our division into age/sex categories was limited to two groups, females with calves and all other whales. The results are given in Fig. 9, which again presents the number of whales by depth. They show that females with calves, Fig. 9A, are almost never seen in water over 10 m deep and that most activity, Fig. 9B, takes place within water less than 15 m deep. Most of the activity observed was group activity and the great majority of groups whose behavior could be determined were obviously involved in mating behavior (see below). Fig. 9 shows that most whales which were found in water deeper than 15 m were inactive. Because of the local restrictions on flying over water in single engine planes, we know very little about these deep water individuals.

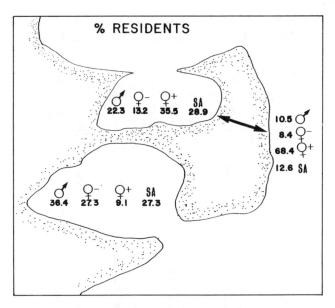

Fig. 10. Proportion of known age/sex categories in all identified residents for each area. ♂ = known males, ♀+ = known females with calves, ♀- = known females without calves, SA = subadults.

Table 1. Residence times (days) by age/sex category in the three aggregation areas at Peninsula Valdes. The flight dates and effort are the same in Golfo San Jose and along the Eastern Outer Coast, but different in Golfo Nuevo. Therefore direct comparisons are possible only between Golfo San Jose and the Eastern Outer Coast

	Males	Females in non–calf years	Females in calf years	Subadults	All known age/sex categories	
Golfo San Jose						
x̄	29.5	28.1	38.1	35.8	34.0	
sd	16.17	15.68	20.39	23.38	20.28	Balanced flights
n	27	16	43	35	121	
Eastern Outer Coast						
x̄	36.8	42.3	48.3	30.3	44.3	
sd	37.59	18.95	24.90	22.26	26.16	
n	10	8	65	12	95	
Golfo Nuevo						
x̄	37.0	24.0	27.0	70.0	41.6	
sd	34.80	9.85	–	5.20	27.63	Principal flights
n	4	3	1	3	11	

Different uses of the aggregation areas

One of the most unexpected results that we found at Peninsula Valdes was that the three aggregation areas (Golfo Nuevo, Golfo San Jose, and the Eastern Outer Coast) have different functions. We have been studying the usage of the three different areas ever since 1971 when we first noticed that the three areas had different ratios of females with calves to mating groups. A possible separation of mating and calving areas has also been observed by Best (1981). The three aggregation areas are occupied for different lengths of time by different proportions of the various age/sex categories.

To explore these differences, we calculated the proportion of the known age/sex categories in all identified 'residents' in each area, that is, whales seen two or more times in that area in one year. Fig. 10 presents the results. The age/sex categories that were used were: known males, females with calves, females without calves and subadults. Because males are considerably harder to sex than females, we do not know the absolute sex ratios at Peninsula Valdes and these figures can only be used for comparisons between areas.

The area in which the proportion of females with calves is the greatest among identified residents is the Eastern Outer Coast, suggesting that this is principally a calf rearing area. We have seen eight unaccompanied females along that coast which were accompanied by calves later in the same year, so we suspect it is also a calving region.

The area in which the proportion of males to other known categories is largest is Golfo Nuevo. Golfo Nuevo also has a high percentage of females without calves, suggesting that it is principally a mating area. In the last four years, however, females with calves have been seen in increasing numbers in this area. We seem to be witnessing the founding of a calving/nursery area within a mating area.

Golfo San Jose appears to contain good samples of all categories, including the largest ratio, as well as the largest number, of subadults. Golfo San Jose and Golfo Nuevo appear to be important areas in which subadults can undergo their development. The former is also a major mating area, as indicated by the high ratios of males and females without calves and by the high incidence of mating activity observed there during census flights. We have therefore classified it as a 'general' area.

An examination of the mean periods of residency for differing age/sex categories in the different aggregation areas (Table 1) shows that females with calves have the longest residency times, both in Golfo San Jose and along the Eastern Outer Coast.

Also with respect to area use, we investigated the question of which area individual adult females prefer in their calving and non-calving years. The Eastern Outer Coast was found to be the preferred location in calving years and Golfo San Jose in non-calf years. It thus appears that individual females are switching from one area to another depending on whether they have a calf that year, which again supports the view that different areas at Peninsula Valdes have different functions.

Age at sexual maturity

Matthews (1938), working from dissected animals, noted that a male southern right whale of 13.5 m length and two females of 15.2 and 14.4 m were sexually mature. Collett (1909) showed that North Atlantic right whale females were sexually mature at 13 m. According to the growth curve for southern right whales of Whitehead and Payne (1981), these lengths correspond to ages between 3 and 5.7 years. This suggests that sexual maturity occurs quite early in life. We have not yet completed the analysis of all our data taken from 1980 onwards. However, a preliminary look at some of the females with calves from those years reveals two females first identified in their calf year which were seen with calves of their own 7 years later. If, as some believe, gestation is about 10–12 months (see review in Lockyer, 1984), these individuals were sexually mature at the latest by the age of 6 years. For North Pacific right whales Klumov (1962) gives lengths at sexual maturity of 14–14.5 m for females and 14–15 m for males, while Omura, Ohsumi, Nemoto, Nasu and Kasuya (1969) conclude that males reach sexual maturity at 14.5–15.5 m and females at 15–16 m. Although these data seem to support our belief that the onset of sexual maturity is at a greater length than indicated by Collett (1909) and Matthews (1938), this may not necessarily be true since North Pacific right whales apparently attain a greater size (17–21 m Klumov '1962') than Southern Hemisphere right whales.

Calving interval and questions of conception

By keeping track of the years in which we saw recognizable females with and without calves, we were able to determine the calving interval. The data for each female who had more than one calf are shown in Fig. 11 by year. Each year has been graded from A to D. This grade is a measure of the extent of analyzed aerial surveys for that year. A failure to see a given individual in the years with low grades (1974, 1978 and 1979) means less than a failure to see her in years with an A grade.

We found calving intervals from 2 to 7 years. The six year intervals have been pooled with the three year intervals in Fig. 11 and it is clear that the most common interval is three years. The observed mean calving interval was $3.7 \pm$ SD 1.25 years (n = 89 observed calving intervals). This mean may however be subject to biases in both directions. Cases of early calf mortality as well as our failure to observe a calf that was born in a year with poor coverage (e.g. 1974) would produce upward biases on the mean (for example we have probably included several 6-year intervals where there actually were twice that number of 3-year intervals). On the other hand, since our data cover only nine years, there is a downward bias against multiple observations of long calving intervals.

There appear to be three different groups of adult females using the calving areas, such that it takes at least three years for a complete cycle of occupancy (still longer when females on longer calving intervals are taken into account). We call the three female groups 'year-classes'. The sizes of the three year-classes appear to be different. Fig. 11 shows that there were 13 females calving in a 3-year cycle in the year-class first seen in 1971 (the 'class of 1971') while 17 such females were seen in the class of 1972, and 23 in the class of 1973 (plus 4 new recruits which first joined this class in 1976). In the nine years presented in Fig. 11, the class of 1973 was always larger than the other two year-classes of females.

There really is not adequate evidence from which to deduce the length of the gestation period of right whales. In spite of this, as noted earlier, it is usually considered to last about one year – an assumption whose best support may simply be that most other mysticetes seem to have one-year gestation periods. If there is no delay in fertilization or fetal growth, and if gestation indeed lasts about one year, we would expect most females to appear at Valdes the year prior to giving birth if that is where they are impregnated. There can be no question that mating is taking place at Valdes; one of the commonest group behaviors we see during the winter/ spring is mating (including numerous direct observations of intromission). However there is some question whether the observed mating results in the observed calves. Only 18 out of 91 females (19.8%) were seen at Valdes one year before their first calf (by first calf we mean the first calf seen by us). This statement includes females for which the year prior to the first calf was an A-grade survey year. It also includes females seen with only one calf and not included in Fig. 11. After the first calf, however, the tendency of females to return to Valdes one year prior to giving birth decreases dramatically. With females that have had more than one calf (those in Fig. 11), we could have seen 44 returns in A-grade survey years prior to the second or third calf but we saw only 3 (6.8%). If we combine the return rates for first calves and for

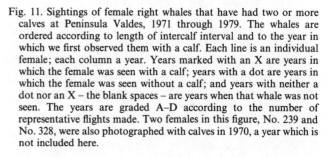

Fig. 11. Sightings of female right whales that have had two or more calves at Peninsula Valdes, 1971 through 1979. The whales are ordered according to length of intercalf interval and to the year in which we first observed them with a calf. Each line is an individual female; each column a year. Years marked with an X are years in which the female was seen with a calf; years with a dot are years in which the female was seen without a calf; and years with neither a dot nor an X – the blank spaces – are years when that whale was not seen. The years are graded A–D according to the number of representative flights made. Two females in this figure, No. 239 and No. 328, were also photographed with calves in 1970, a year which is not included here.

subsequent calves, out of 135 possible returns one year before calving, females were observed at Valdes in only 21 cases (15.6%). Does this mean that almost 84% of conceptions are taking place outside of Valdes?

I see several possible alternative explanations to the above: (1) the gestation period may be up to two years (since we have one female who calved on a two-year interval, two years must be the upper limit); (2) delayed fertilization or implantation may occur as it does in several other mammals; or (3) during the year before calving, females may return only briefly to mate and thus could be missed in our aerial surveys. I favor the last alternative but have no firm evidence for it. The timing and location of conception in these right whales is an enigma that awaits explanation.

SUMMARY

(1) Southern right whales migrate annually to the coast of Peninsula Valdes, Argentina. They begin to appear in the area in May and June. Their numbers build to a peak in late September, then decline more rapidly than they built up so that only a few right whales remain in the area by early December.

(2) At Peninsula Valdes, right whales concentrate in three separate areas. The composition of groups within these areas varies – one area being predominantly mothers with calves, a second predominantly males and females without calves and a third composed of all categories of whales, including subadults and mating groups.

(3) Right whales at Peninsula Valdes show a preference for water 5 m deep, a preference exhibited particularly strongly by mothers with calves.

(4) Two females identified in their calf year have been seen with calves of their own at seven years of age. If gestation is about one year then the age of sexual maturity for these two animals was no more than six years.

(5) In females which calved more than once at Peninsula Valdes, calving intervals ranged from 2 to 7 years with a 3-year interval being by far the most common.

ACKNOWLEDGEMENTS

We gratefully acknowledge the help of many friends during all phases of research described herein. The following made especially large contributions: D. and J. Bartlett, J. Bird, A. and P. Brayton, O. Brazier, R. Brownell, H. Callejas, R. Chariff, K. Chu, N. Cisson, C. and J. Clark, W. Conway, L. Cowperthwaite, R. Christensen, W. Curtsinger, P. DeNormandie, E. Dorsey, B. French, C. and J. Gould, N. Griffis, I. Guinee, G. and P. Harris, J. Heyman, I. Karnovsky, L. Leland-Strutsaker, C. Nicklin, K. Payne, M. Payne, J. Perkins, V. Rowntree, M. Smith, S. Taber, A. Titus, P. Thomas, C. Walcott, H. Whitehead, B. and M. Würsig and several anonymous reviewers. V. Rowntree helped with many aspects of this paper, including the writing and editing and the preparation of figures.

In Argentina we received invaluable assistance both from institutions and from individuals. Our deepest thanks go to the Bernadino Rivadavia Museum of Natural Sciences, especially J. M. Gallardo; to the Chubut Department of Tourism, especially to A. Torrejon and J. Pepitone; to the Department of National Parks, in particular F. LaRiviere and A. Tarak; and to the Fundacion Alfredo Fortabat, particularly Senora A. LaCroze de Fortabat. We are grateful to the Government of Chubut and the Argentine Navy for making planes available. The Aero Club of Trelew made possible the regular flights from which the majority of data reported here were gathered. F. Erize, E. Fero, P. and S. Ferrero, C. Garcia, D. Giolosa, J. Gomes, J. Korschenewski, S. Larreburo, M. and M. Larriviere, J. Llavallol, J. C. and D. Lopez, N. Monocchio, J. Munos, J. Olazabol, S. Ortega, T. and M. Ortiz-Basualdo, J. diPascuali, J. and M. Perez Macchi, A. and A. Pereyra-Iraola, M. Reynal, M. Sanchez-Elia, Teniente Seisdedos, A. Sosa, A. and A. Torrejon, and Teniente Viossay have given help in many and varied ways and we extend our gratitude for their contributions.

This research was supported by grants and contracts from the Marine Mammal Commission (Contract No. MM6ACO17), the Fundacion Alfredo Fortabat, the National Geographic Society, the New York Zoological Society, the People's Trust for Endangered Species and the World Wildlife Fund-US.

REFERENCES

Best, P. B. 1981. The status of right whales (*Eubalaena glacialis*) off South Africa, 1969–1979 *Investl Rep. Div. Sea Fish. S. Afr.* 123: 1–44.

Collett, R. 1909. A few notes on the whale *Balaena glacialis* and its capture in recent years in the North Atlantic by Norwegian whalers. *Proc. Zool. Soc. Lond.* 7: 91–7.

Klumov, S. K. 1962. The right whales in the Pacific Ocean. *Trudy Inst. Okeanog.* 58: 202–97 [In Russian, privately translated].

Lockyer, C. 1984. Review of baleen whale (Mysticeti) reproduction and implications for management. *Rep. int. Whal. Commn* (special issue 6): 27–50.

Matthews, L. H. 1938. Notes on the southern right whale, *Eubalaena australis*. *Discovery Rep.* 17: 169–82.

Omura, H., Ohsumi, S., Nemoto, T., Nasu, K. and Kasuya, T. 1969. Black right whales in the North Pacific. *Sci. Rep. Whales Res. Inst. Tokyo* 21: 1–78.

Payne, R., Brazier, O., Dorsey, E. M., Perkins, J. S., Rowntree, V. J., and Titus, A. 1983. External features in southern right whales (*Eubalaena australis*) and their use in identifying individuals. pp. 371–445. *In*: R. Payne (ed.), *Communication and Behavior of Whales*. AAAS Selected Symposium 76, Westview Press, Boulder, Colorado. 643pp.

Payne, R. and Dorsey, E. M. 1983. Sexual dimorphism and aggressive use of callosities in right whales (*Eubalaena australis*). pp. 295–329. *In* R. Payne (ed.), *Communication and Behavior of Whales*. AAAS Selected Symposium 76, Westview Press, Boulder, Colorado. 643pp.

Payne, R. and Webb, D. 1971. Orientation by means of long range acoustic signaling in baleen whales. *Ann. N.Y. Acad. Sci.* 188: 110–42.

Tyack, P. 1981. Interactions between singing Hawaiian humpback whales and conspecifics nearby. *Behav. Ecol. Sociobiol.* 8: 105–16.

Whitehead, H. and Payne, R. 1981. New techniques for measuring whales from the air. *U.S. Dept. Commer.* NTIS PB81–161143, 36pp.

Würsig, B. and Würsig, M. 1979. Behavior and ecology of the bottlenose dolphin, *Tursiops truncatus*, in the South Atlantic. *Fish. Bull.*, U.S. 77: 399–412.

Population Estimate for the Right Whales off Peninsula Valdes, Argentina, 1971–1976

HAL WHITEHEAD

Newfoundland Institute for Cold Ocean Science, Memorial University of Newfoundland,
St John's, Newfoundland, Canada A1B 3 X1.
(Current Address: Biology Department, Dalhousie University, Halifax, Nova Scotia, Canada B3H 4J1.)

ROGER PAYNE

World Wildlife Fund – U.S., 1601 Connecticut Ave NW, Washington, D.C., USA 20009.

AND

MICHAEL PAYNE

Manomet Bird Observatory, Manomet, Mass., USA 02345.

ABSTRACT

Identifications of right whales from photographs of their callosity patterns were used to make mark-recapture estimates of the population wintering off Peninsula Valdes, Argentina. Between 1971 and 1976 there were an estimated 450–600 individuals coming to Valdes, of which 120–220 were known females. The population is estimated to have been increasing at 6.8% per year (95% CL 0.0–13.6%). For the total population, the estimates may be biased to the low side because of a tendency for some individual whales to be more frequently photographed than others.

INTRODUCTION

Over the past 12 years the right whales (*Eubalaena australis*) which winter off Peninsula Valdes, Argentina (42.5° S, 64° W) have been the subjects of an extended study (Payne, 1972; 1976). One of the techniques developed during this research has been the individual identification of living right whales from photographs of their callosities (Payne, Brazier, Dorsey, Perkins, Rowntree and Titus, 1983). These callosities, which have proved to remain sufficiently constant for reliable identifications over periods of years, are a useful tool for the study of right whale behaviour and population biology (Payne *et al.*, 1983).

Photographic identifications of humpback whales (*Megaptera novaeangliae*) from fluke photographs have been used to make population estimates for the humpback whales in the northwest Atlantic, by the application of mark-recapture methods (e.g. Whitehead, 1982).

In this paper we present a mark-recapture analysis of the identifications of the right whales off Peninsula Valdes.

METHODS

The right whales occupying the waters near Peninsula Valdes were identified from photographs of their callosity patterns taken from a fixed-wing aircraft between June and December each year from 1970 to 1977. Each flight, or group of flights, was planned to cover all the major areas of whale distribution off Peninsula Valdes, and identifying photographs were taken in each area. A total of 52 airflights was made, 44 between September and November. The number of right whales at Peninsula Valdes builds up slowly from May until mid-August, and then stays fairly constant until early October, after which it drops suddenly (Payne, 1986). A detailed description of the flights, equipment used, and identification techniques is given by Payne *et al.* (1983).

First-year right whale calves, although often identifiable, were not considered for this analysis. Females could often be distinguished from the consistent presence of a calf, or, occasionally, from behavioural characteristics (Payne and Dorsey, 1983). Because of the consistency with which calves were seen close to their mothers, and the rate at which mother-calf pairs were resighted (Payne and Dorsey, 1983), it seems likely that a large proportion of the calf-bearing females present at Peninsula Valdes in the years 1971–1977 are included in the category of known females. However there are also immature females included, especially during the earlier part of the study.

The numbers of whales (calves excepted) and known females identified during each year are given in Tables 1

Table 1

Mark recapture estimates for all whales (except calves). N = number of whales photographically identified in each year. M = whales photographed in a given year and a previous year. Z = whales photographed in a previous year and a later year, but not in the given year. R = whales photographed in a given year and a later year. P = population estimate by Seber-Jolly method. SE = estimated standard error of population estimate.

Year	N	M	Z	R	P	SE
1970	9	0	0	9		
1971	177	3	6	154	583.8	285.6
1972	182	75	85	139	452.1	35.8
1973	196	120	104	126	460.2	28.8
1974	85	63	167	51	460.5	46.4
1975	140	99	119	52	593.1	66.0
1976	121	88	83	31	566.5	85.6
1977	180	114	0	0		

Table 2.

Mark-recapture estimates for known females (except calves). Notation as in Table 1.

Year	N	M	Z	R	P	SE
1970	2	0	0	2		
1971	60	1	1	59	121.0	85.6
1972	54	24	36	50	141.5	17.7
1973	65	41	45	56	147.8	12.2
1974	23	21	80	17	141.5	18.2
1975	50	44	53	18	217.3	37.8
1976	45	42	29	9	200.4	53.5
1977	42	38	0	0		

and 2. As can be seen, most animals were photographed in two or more years.

All the airflights within a year constituted a sampling period. For any year an individual was considered marked if one or more clear photographs of its callosity pattern were taken.

For the total population (except calves), and for the population of known females, mark-recapture analyses were carried out using the Seber-Jolly method (Jolly, 1965; Seber, 1965). This computes estimates of the size of the population being studied at each sampling period, together with immigration/birth numbers, and emigration/death rates, and their estimated standard errors, assuming (assumptions from Seber (1973) rephrased):

(1) Each living animal in the population, whether previously photographed or not, had the same probability of being photographed in each year.

(2) At any time, mortality/emigration rates were the same for each previously photographed living animal in the population.

(3) No animals lost their identifying marks.

(4) No animals left the population to later return.

(5) There was no substantial immigration/birth or emigration/death within a sampling period.

Little mortality would be expected over three months for animals which live tens of years, and in twelve years of study only two adult right whale corpses have been found at Peninsula Valdes. As calves were not considered part of the population, birth within a sampling period can be ignored. Thus, defining an animal as being within the population from the time that it first came to Peninsula Valdes until the time it last left, assumptions 4 and 5 are reasonably valid. Payne *et al.* (1983) have shown that assumption 3 is tenable, and, given the low rates of annual natural mortality in baleen whales, and protected status of the Peninsula Valdes right whales, any failures in assumption 2 would not be expected to much influence population estimates.

In order to check assumption 1 and the underlying validity of the model, we performed the two tests suggested by Seber (1973) which seemed most likely to detect any shortcomings that there might be in the data. The two data sets (for known females and the whole population, excluding calves) were tested for the validity of the underlying model using the method of Leslie, Chitty and Chitty (1953), as described by Seber (1973, pp. 224–5). There were no significant differences between the estimated numbers of identified animals in the population, from calculations using the entire data set, and just the previously photographed animals. There were also no significant differences between the actual number of animals photographed for the first time in any

season, and the estimated numbers from calculations using just the identified population.

The two data sets were also subjected to Leslie's (1958) test for equal catchability as described by Seber (1973, pp. 161, 226–8). The whales photographed over five or more years were grouped by their first and last sighting years. These groups were then combined to produce sets each containing more than 20 animals (Seber, 1973), and the actual and expected numbers photographed once, twice, etc. in the intermediate years were calculated and compared. For the females there was no significant indication that some whales were more likely to be photographed than others ($\chi^2 = 65.16$, with 61 d.f., $P > 0.25$). However for the total population (excluding calves) there was significantly greater variance in the number of intermediate seasons in which animals were photographed than would be expected were all animals present equally likely to be photographed in any season ($\chi^2 = 216.9$, with 167 d.f., $P = 0.02$). Thus there were some animals in the population which were more likely to be photographed than others. This will tend to have depressed the estimates of the total population.

In order to test whether the non-calf population size changed significantly between 1971 and 1976, regression lines were fitted to the population estimates, weighted by the inverses of their estimated variances. This was done in two ways:

(1) Linear regression. This assumed that the population changed by a constant number each year.

(2) Logarithmic regression. This assumed that the population changed by a constant proportion each year.

RESULTS

Tables 1 and 2 give the estimated population sizes, with their estimated standard errors, and the data needed to compute the estimates, for all whales (excluding calves) and the known females, during the sampling years. The method does not give estimates for the first and last years – 1970 and 1977. The point estimates of female population size ranged from about 120–220 for the females, and 450–600 for the entire population (excluding calves). However these latter estimates may have been biased to the low side because of the failure of assumption 1 mentioned above.

The estimates of emigration/death rates, and immigration/birth numbers have considerable variance, as is usual in Jolly-Seber analyses (e.g. the example in Jolly (1965)), and are not presented here.

The results of the regressions for examining changes in the whole population (excluding calves), and for the females are given in Table 3. Both populations appear to have been increasing, but the increases are only significant at $P < 0.10$. The estimated intrinsic rate of increase of the population is 6.8% per annum (95% CL

Table 3.

Results of weighted regressions of population estimates on year. Levels at which the increases (linear regression) and rates of increase (logarithmic regression) are significantly different from zero are marked.

	Linear regression Increase per year		Logarithmic regression Rate of increase per year	
All whales	30.0 animals	($P < 0.1$)	0.068	($P < 0.1$)
Known females	12.7 animals	($P < 0.2$)	0.104	($P < 0.1$)

0.0–13.6%). However these estimates should be treated cautiously as the population estimates from which they are derived are probably underestimates.

DISCUSSION

The finding that some whales were more photographable than others agrees with a behavioural analysis by one of us (R.P.) of these and other data collected on the right whales off Peninsula Valdes. The implication is that the area was more of a 'home' to some whales than others. A portion of the whales tended to be present most years and/or to stay in residence for a long time, thus increasing their probability of being photographed, whereas others appeared only rarely and/or for short periods. Our estimates can be considered to be principally representing the 'core' population, but with a reasonable representation of the more 'transient' members. (Excluding those animals photographed during only one season from the analysis reduced the population estimates by 20–35%).

As can be seen by comparing the rates of return in Tables 1 and 2, the females were more prone to be photographed repeatedly at Peninsula Valdes. (However the difference between the rates of return of known females and other whales was not the only reason for the differential rate at which whales were photographed – with the known females excluded there was still a significantly different rate at which individual whales were photographed.) There appear to have been proportionally fewer 'transient' females, although this may have been due to the fact that animals photographed only a very few times will have been less likely to be positively recognized as females. The known females in our population estimates are principally sexually mature animals, with a few immatures, especially in the earlier years. Payne (1986) found that female right whales tended not to appear at Peninsula Valdes in the years between calvings (which usually happened every three years). However this did not appear as a detrimental factor for the population estimates of known females, according to the tests that we performed. The greater availability of females to photographers in the years when they visit Peninsula Valdes seems to outweigh these periodic effects, leading to an overall greater catchability of females.

The estimated intrinsic rate of increase of the population of 6.8% per annum is in close agreement with the estimated rate of increase of the population of right whales off South Africa of 7% (Best, 1981). The South African and Argentinian right whales are apparently from distinct stocks (Payne et al., 1983). Our calculated rates of increase should be treated cautiously given the uncertainty in the underlying estimates.

We believe that we have produced useful estimates of the number of right whales off Peninsula Valdes in the early 1970s, the numbers of mature females, and the rate of increase of the population. The accuracy and relevance of these estimates will be increased when identifications from subsequent years are processed.

ACKNOWLEDGEMENTS

We thank Hugo Callejas, Christopher Clark, James Gould, Katherine Payne, Peter Thomas and Bernd Würsig for their help in obtaining the photographs. Oliver Brazier, Eleanor Dorsey, Judith Perkins and Victoria Rowntree made most of the identifications, and Kevin Chu helped with the manscript. Teresa Oritz Basulado, Carlos Garcia, Juan Olazabol, Santiago Ortega, and many other friends in Argentina provided invaluable help in expediting our research. The Museo Argentino de Ciencias Naturales 'Bernardino Rivadavia' and the Direccion Provincial de Turismo for the Province of Chubut, coordinated our research through the kind offices of Dr Jose Maria Gallardo and Antonio Torrejon. The field work was founded by the National Geographic and New York Zoological Societies and laboratory analyses by the New York Zoological Society, Marine Mammal Commission and the People's Trust for Endangered Species. We also thank R. L. Brownell Jr. and two anonymous referees for their constructive comments. This is Newfoundland Institute for Cold Ocean Science Contribution Number 21.

REFERENCES

Best, P. 1981. The status of right whales (*Eubalaena glacialis*) off South Africa, 1969–1979. *Investl. Rep. Div. Sea Fish. Inst. S. Afr.* 80: 1–44.

Jolly, G. M. 1965. Explicit estimates from capture-recapture data with both death and immigration – stochastic model. *Biometrika* 52: 225–47.

Leslie, P. H. 1958. Statistical appendix. *J. Animal Ecol.* 27: 84–6.

Leslie, P. H., Chitty, D. and Chitty, H. 1953. The estimation of population parameters from data obtained by means of the capture-recapture method. III: An example of the practical applications of the method. *Biometrika* 40: 137–69.

Payne, R. S. 1972. Swimming with Patagonia's right whales. *Nat. Geog.* 142: 576–87.

Payne, R. 1976. At home with right whales. *Nat. Geog.* 149: 322–41.

Payne, R., Brazier, O., Dorsey, E., Perkins, J., Rowntree, V. and Titus, A. 1983. External features in southern right whales (*Eubalaena australis*) and their use in identifying individuals. pp. 371–445. *In*: R. Payne (ed.) *Communication and Behavior of Whales.* AAAS Selected Symposia Series 76. Westview Press, Boulder, Colorado. 643 pp.

Payne, R. and Dorsey, E. M. 1983. Sexual dimorphism and aggressive use of callosities in right whales (*Eubalaena australis*). pp. 295–329. *In*: R. Payne (ed.) *Communication and Behavior of Whales.* AAAS Selected Symposia Series 76. Westview Press, Boulder, Colorado. 643 pp.

Payne, R. 1986. Long term behavioral studies of the southern right whale, (*Eubalaena australis*). (Published in this volume.)

Seber, G. A. F. 1965. A note on the multiple-recapture census. *Biometrika* 52: 249–59.

Seber, G. A. F. 1973. *The Estimation of Animal Abundance and Related Parameters.* Hafner Press, New York. i–xii + 506 pp.

Whitehead, H. 1982. Populations of humpback whales in the northwest Atlantic. *Rep. int. Whal. Commn* 32: 345–53.

Recent Sightings and Strandings of Southern Right Whales off Subantarctic South America and the Antarctic Peninsula

RAE NATALIE PROSSER GOODALL AND ALEJANDRO R. GALEAZZI

Centro Austral de Investigaciones Científicas, 9410 Ushuaia, Tierra del Fuego, Argentina

ABSTRACT

Thirty sightings and five strandings of southern right whales are reported. Opportunistic sightings occurred off Patagonia (thirteen), Tierra del Fuego (six), South Georgia (four) and the South American sector of the Antarctic (seven). Sightings were of one or two animals except for a group of 14 off Puerto Deseado. Whales were seen in the Antarctic during the southern summer (December to March), at the South Orkneys in fall (April), at South Georgia and Tierra del Fuego mostly in fall (April–May) but also in February, July and October, and the Patagonian sightings were from May to October, where animals are known to congregate during winter and spring. A single right whale was seen accompanying a humpback whale. Only five known strandings of this species have been recorded on Tierra del Fuego since 1968, in spite of intensive stranding surveys in the area.

INTRODUCTION

The southern right whale *Eubalaena australis* was the object of extensive exploitation throughout the nineteenth and early twentieth centuries on both coasts of South America, which took it to the edge of extinction (Aguayo, 1974). Although protected since 1935, it is still considered one of the least abundant whales. For this reason, even few and scattered sightings of this species, such as those presented here, are worth reporting.

METHODS AND MATERIALS

Since 1976, a continuous cetacean investigation program has been carried out in Tierra del Fuego. Although the main emphasis of this program has been on strandings and incidental captures of the smaller cetaceans, sighting forms were devised and distributed to officers of ships which navigate the waters of southern South America and the Antarctic Peninsula. The forms were also used for opportunistic sightings from shore. In no case was there a specific right whale observation program.

Compared with the Northern Hemisphere, the whole of the Southern Ocean has little maritime traffic. Both coasts of Patagonia are traversed by occasional cargo ships, fishing boats, oil tankers and, during the summer, tourist ships, but cetacean observations aboard these vessels are usually lost to science. Even fewer ships cross the Drake Passage to the Antarctic Peninsula. These include some eight to ten tourist ship crossings per year, as well as Argentine, Chilean, British, American and other scientific expeditions. One of the most regular, in crossings from Tierra del Fuego to the peninsula, has been the U.S. research vessel *Hero*, which operated in the area from 1968 until 1984; ten or more crossings have been made per year (Fig. 1) and its officers have been most consistent in returning sighting forms.

Sightings were used only when descriptions were specific enough to be able to determine the species.

RESULTS

During the first six years of our program, over 1,000 sighting forms were returned, encompassing 22 species.

During the period 1973–1985 (including the R/V *Hero* log of 1973–1977), only 30 sightings of the southern right whale were returned.

Sighting

Sighting localities are plotted in Fig. 1. For convenience, we will discuss them by latitude.

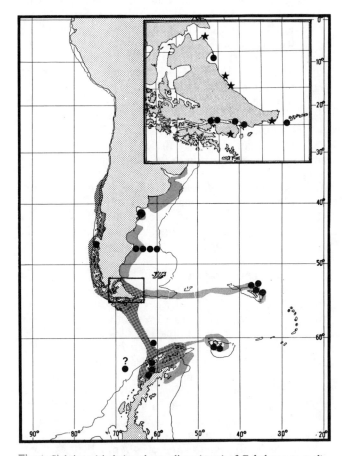

Fig. 1. Sightings (circles) and strandings (stars) of *Eubalaena australis* presented in this paper. The large circle represents known breeding grounds at Península Valdés. The cruise track of the R/V *Hero* off southern South America from 1968–1984 is shown: dark hatching, numerous expeditions; lighter shading, less numerous cruises.

40°–50° S. Northern Patagonia. Eight sightings were made in the waters of Península Valdés by the R/V *Hero* during the months July, September, October and December. Since this is a well known breeding area for southern right whales (Payne, 1976), and is discussed in other papers, we will not further mention these sightings.

Four sightings were made in 1984 and 1985 at Puerto Deseado, south of Valdés (Table 1). In three cases the lone animal came 2–3 kms within the estuary, in front of the town, and stayed several hours. The 14 whales seen in 1985 headed south after leaving the river.

On the west coast of South America, one new sighting was reported in the Golfo de Penas at 47° 10′ S (and see Aguayo and Torres, 1986). This single animal, which blew three times, then sounded and disappeared, was the only one ever observed on the Chilean side of the continent by the *Hero*, which has, in the last 10 years, made a number of geological surveys in the Chilean channels and trips to and from Tierra del Fuego to the dry dock at Talcahuano (P. J. Lenie, pers. comm. 1980).

Aguayo (1974) reported 119 captures for this coast between 1929 and 1970; these and his own observations were all north of this area. Clarke (1965) showed that Townsend's (1935) capture records from 1785 to 1913 concentrated between 30° to 50° S on this coast, and felt that captures further south were hindered by bad weather and dangerous shores. These also hinder present day observations.

50°–60° S. Southern Patagonia and Tierra del Fuego. We received four sightings from South Georgia and six from Tierra del Fuego (Table 1). The South Georgian sightings were on the north side of the island (few ships go to the southern side) and two of them mentioned krill and/or debris in the water. The two sightings from the *John Biscoe*, within two days of each other, may have been of the same animals.

Four of the sightings in Fuegian waters were within the Beagle Channel, one 5 km SW of Isla de los Estados and one just inside Bahía San Sebastián, off the tip of the Península Páramo. Each of these sightings involved one animal, no two occurring in the same year.

South of 60° S. Antarctica. Although generally considered a species that remains north of the convergence, seven sightings were reported south of 60° S. Four were from the Antarctic Peninsula, one from north of the South Shetlands, and two from Signy Island in the South Orkneys.

No sightings of this species had been made during the many trips of the R/V *Hero* through the Peninsula waters during November to April between 1973 and 1980. Their first sighting, in March, 1980, was of a 'really big, old animal' swimming in an area full of krill. Two whales were sighted by officers of the *John Biscoe* just south of 60° S, north of the South Shetlands, in January 1980, and one animal, without precise locality, was seen by R. Straneck from the *World Discoverer* in December 1977. In January 1984, one animal was seen from the *Hero*, swimming in circles and surface feeding with clearly visible open mouth.

The whale off Signy Island on 4 April 1980 was seen by most of the crew of the British base there. The two whales seen on 11 April 1982 showed more of the head and tail and photographs were taken from a tower (J. C. Ellis-Evans, pers. comm.).

Table 1.

Sightings of *Eubalaena australis*, arranged by latitude and geographic area (AP = Antarctic Peninsula). Sightings near Peninsula Valdes are not included.

Key. Platform: He = *Hero*, sh = shore, CS = *C. Somellera*, sp = ship, IO = *Islas Orcadas*, JB = *J. Biscoe*, WD = *World Discoverer*. Observers: WC = W. Church, M. Day = M. O. Day, NG = N. Goodall, RB = R. Boekelhide, OV = O. Vasquez, ML = M. Lawrence, AG = A. Galeazzi, AL = A. Lichter, TT = T. Targett, JP = J. Polkinghorn, SN = S. Norris, JE = J. Ellis-Evans, RS = R. Straneck, KJ = K. Jordan, CM = C. Mays, PL = P. Lenie.

Date	Time	Locality	Position °S	°W	No.	Platform (observer)
45–50 S, Patagonia						
01.10.79	0935	Golfo de Penas, Chile	47°10′	75°20′	1	He (WC)
–.08.84	–	Rio Deseado	47°30′	65°58′	1	sh (MD)
15.10.84	–	Rio Deseado	47°30′	65°58′	1	sh (MD)
04.05.85	1200	Rio Deseado	47°30′	65°58′	1	sh (MD)
13.05.85	1400	Off Rio Deseado	47°30′	65°50′	14	sh (MD)
50–60 S, Tierra del Fuego						
02.05.76	1100	Bahia de Ushuaia	54°48′	68°19′	1	sh (NG)
15.02.77	1830	Peninsula Paramo	53°10′	68°15′	1	sh (RB)
23.09.79	1311	Isla Hakenyeshka, Canal Beagle	54°55′	67°07′	1	CS (OV)
07.05.82	1545	Estancia Moat, Canal Beagle	54°57′	66°47′	1	sh (ML)
18.07.83	1559	Bahia de Ushuaia	54°48′	68°19′	1	sh (AG+NG)
02.84	–	5km SW Isla de los Estados	54°55′	63°50′	1	sp (AL)
South Georgia						
05.75	–	Right Whale Bay			1	IO (TT)
06.04.77	1620	N of Cape Saunders	54°04′	36°37′	2	He (JP)
11.04.80	am	N of South Georgia	53°50′	36°30′	2–3	JB (DB)
13.04.80	1135	N of South Georgia	53°50′	36°18′	1	JB (SN)
South of 60 S, Antarctica						
04.04.80	–	Factory Cove, Signy I	60°40′	45°36′	1	sh (JE)
11.04.82	–	Borge Bay, Signy I	60°42′	45°36′	2	sh (JE)
20.12.77	1730	Antarctic Peninsula	–		1	WD (RS)
31.01.80	am	Drake Passage	60°12′	61°05′	2	JB (RW)
12.03.80	1930	Crocker Passage, AP	63°57′	61°41′	1	He (KJ)
10.02.83	0800	Leige Island, AP	63°58′	61°42′	2	He (CM)
07.01.84	0700	Cape Murray N, AP	64°17′	61°38′	1	He (PL)

Number of animals

Three of the sightings at Puerto Deseado were of single animals, but one was of at least 14.

The Tierra del Fuego observations were of single animals, while two of the South Georgia sightings contained two or three animals. In the Antarctic there were four observations of one whale and three of two whales. On this very limited evidence, we can conclude that south of 50° S, the whales were not seen in large groups. No calves were mentioned by any of the observers.

Months of observations

In Fig. 2, our sightings are analyzed by latitude and by month. Between 40° and 50° S, whales are usually found in the area of Península Valdés from July to December. The sightings at Puerto Deseado, well south of Valdés, occurred in May, August and October. The single Chilean sighting, at nearly 50° S, occurred in October.

Those in Tierra del Fuego and South Georgia were from late (southern) summer to winter, mostly in April and May. Both the winter sightings were in the Beagle Channel.

The Antarctic Peninsula sightings were in summer, from December to March, while the South Orkneys sightings were in April (fall).

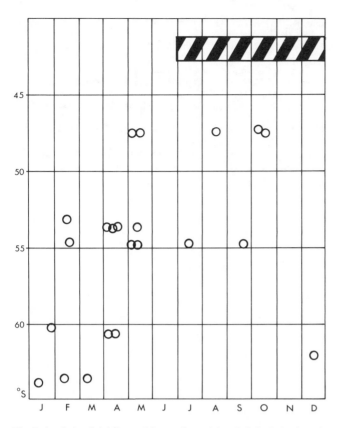

Fig. 2. Analysis of sightings of the southern right whale by latitude and by month. The bar at the top represents the normal stay of the whales at Península Valdés.

Table 2.
Known strandings of the Southern right whale in the study area.
*Ref = Barrett (1970).

Field no.	Date found	Locality	Proof/Reference
–	– Dec 1968	Bahia Winhond, Isla Navarino	Photograph*
RNP 127	18 Dec 1975	Rio Chico north, Isla Grande T.F.	Cervicals (broken skull on beach)
RNP 692	14 May 1978	Punta Maria north, Isla Grande T.F.	Cervicals (broken skull on beach)
RNP 912	10 Nov 1981	Bahia Valentin, Isla Grande T.F.	Photograph (worn skull on beach)
RNP 1153	14 Nov 1984	Cabo Espiritu Santo, Isla Grande T.F.	Baleen (skeleton on beach)

Punta María on the NE coast on 14 May 1978, and another weathered specimen was found at the Río Chico (RNP 127) on 18 December 1975. Photographs were made of a large, beach worn cranium (RNP 912) found at Bahía Valentín at the SE tip of the island on 10 November 1981. A southern right whale stranded north of Cabo Espíritu Santo in Chilean Tierra del Fuego in March or April 1984; its baleen washed southward into Argentina and was collected (RNP 1153) on 14 November 1984 (Fig. 1, Table 2).

A weathered right whale skull found at Bahía Windhond on the south side of Isla Navarino by the K. S. Norris team aboard the R/V *Hero* in 1968 is shown by Barrett (1970). Sielfeld (1983) mentioned no specimen of this species in the collection at IPPA (Instituto de la Patagonia, Punta Arenas, Chile).

Interspecific relations

At the Península Valdés breeding grounds, southern right whales have been observed at various times associating with other marine mammals. Payne (1974), during his study in this area, watched sea lions and porpoises playing with these whales and described particular 'games'. Interactions between killer whales (*Orcinus orca*) and southern right whales at Valdés have been interpreted as predatory attacks (Cummings, Fish, Thompson and Jehl, 1971), but there is also evidence of the whales co-existing with the killer whales (J. C. López, pers. comm.). Ellis (1980) reported dusky dolphins (*Lagenorhynchus obscurus*) and bottlenose dolphins (*Tursiops* sp.) swimming with right whales at Valdés.

In 1977 at South Georgia, J. Polkinghorn (chief mate of R/V *Hero*) observed a southern right whale swimming with a humpback whale (*Megaptera novaeangliae*), 'travelling together, staying together through all maneuvers for approximately half an hour...'. In the Antarctic in March, 1980, a southern right whale was seen feeding in an area full of krill, soon after a sighting of a humpback whale.

STRANDINGS

Although our stranding program has been concentrated on the smaller cetaceans, weathered remains of many large whales can be found on the beaches of Tierra del Fuego. Some right whale specimens (auditory bones or cervical vertebrae) were collected and photographs were taken of skulls left on the beach.

Skulls, various bones and a very weathered set of cervical vertebrae (RNP 692) were found 4 km north of

DISCUSSION AND CONCLUSIONS

From the small amount of material presented here, few conclusions can be drawn. The sightings presented are wholly opportunistic and no attempt has been made to correlate them with the total number of expeditions through the area or the number of observation hours.

Nevertheless, compared to the sightings of other species received, it would seem that the southern right whale is still rare off the southern tip of South America. This can be borne out by other surveys. For example, during the 1981–82 two-month minke whale assessment cruise by the IWC, only two sightings, involving only two whales, were made of right whales in Antarctic Area II (0° to 60° W). Both were in the western sector, near the Antarctic Peninsula (Hembree, 1982).

ACKNOWLEDGEMENTS

The work in Tierra del Fuego has been backed by grants from the Committee for Research and Exploration of the National Geographic Society and the Centro Austral de Investigaciones Cientifícas (CADIC). The U.S. National Science Foundation sponsored an expedition aboard the R/V *Hero*, during which the whale skull was found at Bahía Valentín. We thank all those who gave information, especially Capt. P. J. Lenie and the crew of the *Hero*, S. Norris of the *John Biscoe*, and J. C. Ellis-Evans of British Antarctic Survey. A. Pivorunas kindly identified the photograph of the cranium at Bahía Valentín. P. B. Best, R. L. Brownell Jr. and R. Bastida reviewed the manuscript.

REFERENCES

Aguayo L., A. 1974. Baleen whales off continental Chile. pp. 209–17 *In*: W. E. Schevill (ed.) *The Whale Problem: a status report.* Harvard University Press, Cambridge, Mass. 419 pp.

Aguayo L., A. and Torres N., D. 1986. Records of the southern right whale, *Eubalaena australis* (Desmoulins, 1822) from Chile between 1976 and 1982. (Published in this volume.)

Barrett, R. 1970. In Darwin's footsteps. *Pacif. Discov.* 6: 16–22.

Clarke, R. 1965. Southern right whales off the coast of Chile. *Norsk Hvalfangsttid.* 54:121–8.

Cummings, W. C., Fish, J. F., Thompson, P. O. and Jehl, J. R. Jr. 1971. Bioacoustics of marine mammals off Argentina: R/V *Hero* Cruise 71–3. *Antarct. J. US* 6: 266–8.

Ellis, R. 1980. Argentina's Valdés Peninsula. *Americas* (Sept. 1980): 1, 113–21.

Hembree, D. 1982. Report of the IWC/IDCR minke whale assessment cruise in Area II (60° W–0°). Paper SC/34/Mil2 presented to the IWC Scientific Committee, June 1982 (unpublished).

Payne, R. 1974. A playground for whales, but for how long? *Anim. Kingd.* (Apr. 1974): 7–12.

Payne, R. 1976. At home with the right whales. *Nat. Geogr. Mag.* 149(3): 322–39.

Sielfeld. K. W. 1983. *Mamíferos Marinos de Chile.* Ediciones de la Universidad de Chile. 199 pp.

Townsend, C. H. 1935. The distribution of certain whales as shown by logbook records of American whaleships. *Zoologica NY* 19: 1–50.

Recent Off-shore Distribution of the Southern Right Whale in Summer

SEIJI OHSUMI

Far Seas Fisheries Research Laboratory, 5-7-1 Orido, Shimizu 424, Japan

AND FUJIO KASAMATSU

Japan Whaling Association, 2–4 Kasumigaseki 3 chome, Chiyodya-ku, Tokyo 100, Japan

ABSTRACT

The off-shore distribution of southern right whales in summer is examined using sightings data collected by Japanese research vessels during the years 1965/66–1981/82. Most of the southern right whales seen were distributed in mid-latitudinal waters, between the Sub-tropical and the Antarctic Convergences in summer, although some whales penetrated into the waters south of the Antarctic Convergence. The highest density of right whales was found in the waters south of Western Australia; no right whales were found in the area between 155–85°W. In most areas right whales migrate furthest south in January. The possibility of the existence of six stocks of southern right whale is proposed from the density distributions. A special sightings cruise was conducted in the waters south of Western Australia in 1981/82, and school sizes, body length composition, sightings efficiency, etc., studied and compared with those from coastal waters at a different time of year. The whaling grounds of the open-boat whaling age did not cover the total range of the right whale even in summer, when they were limited to the northern parts of the range. The distribution of the right whale in recent years is somewhat different from that in the past, possibly due to the different population levels. An increase in density is evident from sightings in off-shore waters south of Western Australia.

Natural markings were photographed of three right whales from Antarctic Areas I and II.

INTRODUCTION

The historical distribution of southern right whales can be estimated from logbook data from 18th and 19th century open-boat whaling (e.g. Townsend, 1935). Over-exploitation by first open-boat and then modern whaling had already greatly depleted the populations of this species by the time the first international convention for the regulation of whaling gave protection to them in 1935. About a half century has passed since the worldwide ban on catching right whales, although some animals were caught during these years (Best, 1981), and the current status of these stocks is thus of particular interest.

Sighting surveys are the only way to monitor protected whale stocks. Many papers have been published on southern right whale sightings e.g. from South Africa (Best, 1970; 1981), Australia (Anon., 1980), New Zealand (Gaskin, 1964; 1968), Chile (Clarke, 1965; Aguayo, 1974), Argentina (Gilmore, 1969; Payne, 1972; Mermoz, 1980). However, these have all been limited to coastal regions although logbook records reveal that the Southern right whale was distributed widely in off-shore waters (Townsend, 1935).

In 1966 the Japanese Government established a collection system for whale sightings data from Japanese scouting boats which belonged to fleets operating in the North Pacific and the Southern Hemisphere (Ohsumi and Yamamura, 1982), and many papers have reported on these data (e.g. Masaki, 1977). In 1976 the Government began to provide large amounts of money to charter catcher boats for sightings and marking to be carried out independently from North Pacific and Southern Hemisphere whaling operations, in order to maintain sightings effort in spite of the decline in pelagic whaling. Some of the chartered boats have been offered

for the IWC/IDCR minke whale population assessment cruises in the Southern Hemisphere which have taken place each season since 1978/79 (e.g. Best and Ohsumi, 1980). In the summer of 1981/82, a chartered boat carried out a right whale survey recommended by the IWC Scientific Committee in the waters south of Western Australia.

This paper examines the recent offshore distribution of the right whale in the Southern Hemisphere using sightings data which had been accumulated up to the 1981/82 season, and compares this with the historical distribution. A detailed analysis of the 1981/82 cruise off Western Australia is also presented as well as an examination of the density trends described from the data collected over the last 13 years.

The junior author participated in the IWC/IDCR minke whale assessment cruises in Areas II and I in the 1981/82 and 1982/83 seasons, respectively, and had chances to photograph natural markings on three right whales. These are discussed in Appendix 1.

MATERIALS AND METHODS

The analysis of the recent distribution pattern of right whales uses sightings data collected from Japanese scouting boats (including those participating in the IWC/IDCR cruises) from 1965/66 to 1981/82. The mode of operation of these vessels, the data format and the data handling were described in detail by Ohsumi and Yamamura (1982). The computed tables used in this paper are:

Table 1. Distance steamed by month, by 5° square.

Table 4. Number of whales sighted per 10,000 n. miles steamed by species, month and 5° square.

The density distribution is represented as the number of whales sighted per 10,000 n. miles of research distance and an index of abundance (IA) was calculated for each 5° square (Table 7) as follows:

$$IA = n\,S/L$$

where n is the number of whales sighted, S is the area (n. miles²) and L is the navigation distance for each 5° square.

Data for waters south of 10°S were used, and the months covered were from October to April.

For the examination of right whale sightings in the waters south of Western Australia, the following data were collected and used: (a) school size; (b) estimated body length; (c) angle and radial distance of sighting from boat; (d) surface water temperature; (e) searching distance; (f) catchers day's worked (CDW) and number of right whales found per effort by operating catcher boats from 1969/70 to 1977/78.

Photographs of natural markings are discussed in Appendix 1.

RESEARCH AREAS AND DISTRIBUTION OF SIGHTINGS EFFORT

Fig. 1 shows the research areas covered by Japanese scouting boats during the years 1965/66–1981/82. Table 1 shows the sighting effort as the distance steamed by area (see below). Table 2 shows the distribution of sightings effort by 5° latitudinal zone. Although most of the Southern Hemisphere was covered (except north of 35°S

in the South Atlantic and the middle of the South Pacific) research effort was not distributed evenly in each 5° square, with relatively large amounts of effort being put into the mid-latitudinal waters of the western South Atlantic, Indian Ocean and western South Pacific.

Although the effort was not distributed evenly and was small in waters north of 30°S and south of 65°S, a relatively large amount of effort was put into those zones which included the summer whaling grounds for right whales in the Southern Hemisphere (Townsend, 1935). The total research distance was 2,418,756 n. miles: 93.6% of the total effort was put in the zones 30–65°S.

Sightings were conducted from October to April although 98.3% of the effort was carried out from November to March. There was no effort expended between 70–30 °W in March. There was no effort between 130–30°W or south of 45°S in October. Effort was low between 35–45°S in October, an area where right whales used to occur. Effort was also low between 10–35°S in January, but this is not so important as most right whales would have been distributed south of 35°S in this month.

AREAL DISTRIBUTION OF THE RIGHT WHALE

Fig. 2 shows the density distribution of the southern right whale for all research months combined. Right whales were sighted from 25–35°S to 60–65°S, but most were seen between 30–55°S. None was found between 145°

Table 1.

Sighting distance (nautical miles in searching mode) of Japanese scouting boats in the Southern Hemisphere during years 1965/66–1981–82.

Areas	October	November	December	January	February	March	April	Total
30 E–90 E	1,051	92,128	114,231	246,094	260,991	125,931	733	841,159
90 E–150 E	9,115	188,626	250,000	141,375	12,715	23,280	4,620	629,731
150 E–130 W	23,973	89,894	168,896	107,199	83,840	57,220	1,233	532,255
130 W–70 W	–	11,123	12,505	8,098	16,179	5,307	–	53,212
70 W–30 W	–	7,069	57,777	47,748	9,151	–	–	121,745
30 W–30 E	160	33,148	44,936	47,557	93,608	21,245	–	240,654
Total	34,299	421,988	648,345	598,071	476,484	232,983	6,586	2,418,756

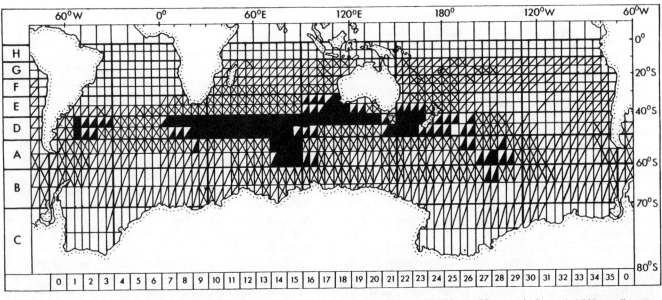

Fig. 1. Research areas for Japanese scouting boats in the Southern Hemisphere, 1965/66 to 1981/82. □: Not searched, ◲: 1–1,000 n. miles, ⊠: 1,001–5,000 n. miles, ◪: 5,001–10,000 n. miles, ■: 10,000 + n. miles.

Table 2.

Sighting distance of Japanese scouting boats in 5° latitudinal zones of the Southern Hemisphere during years
1965/66–1981/82.

Latitude (°S)	October	November	December	January	February	March	April	Total
10–15	7,499	14,256	1,434	–	542	3,887	–	27,618
15–20	5,029	12,457	1,377	–	2,333	4,043	–	25,239
20–25	6,561	9,704	1,812	–	2,969	3,505	–	24,551
25–30	5,439	13,483	5,361	–	5,598	5,103	–	34,984
30–35	7,941	62,966	9,799	834	7,127	9,196	–	97,863
35–40	1,537	100,951	68,933	7,130	5,255	10,152	–	193,958
40–45	293	133,215	413,015	252,407	111,110	46,184	2,215	958,439
45–50	–	23,976	79,228	122,037	157,806	82,490	2,606	468,143
50–55	–	14,675	27,978	86,411	67,402	40,267	494	237,227
55–60	–	13,223	19,668	73,087	52,097	25,248	1,271	184,594
60–65	–	21,027	17,039	36,787	45,973	2,908	–	123,734
65–70	–	2,055	2,701	18,779	15,551	–	–	39,086
70–75	–	–	–	599	2,721	–	–	3,320
Total	34,299	421,988	648,345	598,071	476,484	232,983	6,586	2,418,756

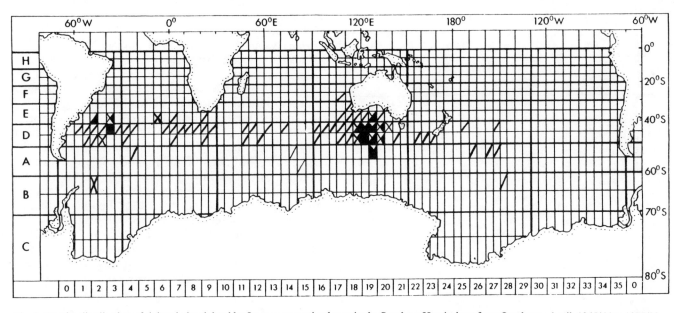

Fig. 2. Density distribution of right whales sighted by Japanese scouting boats in the Southern Hemisphere from October to April, 1965/66 to 1981/82. Each symbol represents numbers of right whales sighted per 10,000 n. miles steamed by the scouting boats. ▨: 1–10, ▨: 11−20, ▨: 21–30, ▨: 31–50, ▨: 51–75, ■: 76+.

and 85°W, although some effort was put into this area. Right whales were not evenly distributed even in those waters where they were sighted; the largest concentration, to the south of Western Australia, will be discussed later. A second concentration was observed to the southeast of South America. Although it is not possible to identify different stocks solely from the density distribution shown in Fig. 2, the review (given below) of the distribution patterns shown in Figs 2, 3 and 4, appears to reveal six stocks with the following boundaries: 30°E, 90°E, 150°E, 130°W, 70°W and 30°W.

Tables 3A–3F show the latitudinal IA distributions for these Areas. The highest IA values were generally in the 40°–45°S zone apart from between 150–130°W where the highest value was in the 50°–55°S zone. However, it should be noted that the level of effort in each zone was not equal for each Area.

The IA value in an Area represents its relative population size and so the largest populations are in areas 90–150°E and 70–30°W; the smallest is in the area 130°–70°W where right whales were seldom seen.

Fig. 3 shows the distribution of right whales in

January. The pattern is not very different from that in Fig. 2, other than that the northern boundary was 40°S in January, whereas some right whales were sighted north of 40°S in Fig. 2.

Fig. 3 also shows the positions of the sub-tropical and Antarctic convergences. Most of the animals sighted in January were found in the waters between them, although some were seen south of the Antarctic Convergence. The latitudinal position of the Antarctic Convergence differs by ocean, being further south in the South Pacific than in the Indian and South Atlantic Oceans. If right whale distribution is related to this convergence one might expect them to have been found further south in the South Pacific but this was not the case (Fig. 3).

MONTHLY DISTRIBUTION OF THE RIGHT WHALE

The traditional pattern of baleen whale migration suggests that right whales should alternate between winter breeding grounds in lower latitudinal waters and summer feeding grounds in the higher latitudes.

Table 3.

Indices of abundance of right whales sighted by Japanese scouting boats, 1965/66–1981/82.

Latitude (°S)	Oct	Nov	Dec	Jan	Feb	Mar	Apr	Total
A. 30°E–90°E								
25–30	0	0	0	–	0	0	–	0
30–35	0	0	0	0	0	0	–	0
35–40	–	0	0	0	0	0	–	0
40–45	–	65	46	76	27	0	0	47
45–50	–	0	0	94	0	70	0	28
50–55	–	0	0	0	11	0	–	4
55–60	–	0	0	0	5	17	–	5
60–65	–	0	0	0	0	0	–	0
Total	0	65	46	170	43	87	0	84
B. 90°E–150°E								
25–30	0	63	0	–	–	0	–	52
30–35	0	12	0	–	0	0	–	8
35–40	0	531	90	0	0	0	–	359
40–45	–	2,101	1,076	1,989	6,458	0	0	1,551
45–50	–	0	434	1,994	0	0	0	1,076
50–55	–	0	0	606	0	0	0	410
55–60	–	0	0	0	0	0	0	0
60–65	–	0	0	0	0	0	0	0
Total	0	2,707	1,510	4,589	6,458	0	0	3,456
C. 150°E–130°W								
25–30	0	0	0	–	0	0	–	0
30–35	0	0	0	–	0	0	–	0
35–40	0	0	0	0	0	0	–	0
40–45	0	38	36	0	0	23	0	43
45–50	–	0	9	221	0	0	0	51
50–55	–	0	0	97	88	0	0	79
55–60	–	0	0	0	0	0	0	0
60–65	–	0	0	0	0	0	–	0
Total	0	38	36	318	88	23	0	173
D. 130°W–70°W								
25–30	–	0	0	–	–	–	–	0
30–35	–	0	0	–	–	–	–	0
35–40	–	0	0	–	–	–	–	0
40–45	–	0	0	0	–	0	–	0
45–50	–	183	0	0	0	0	–	50
50–55	–	0	0	0	0	0	–	0
55–60	–	0	0	0	0	0	–	0
60–65	–	0	0	0	9	0	–	6
Total	–	183	0	0	9	0	–	56
E. 70°W–30°W								
25–30	–	–	–	–	–	–	–	–
30–35	–	–	–	–	–	–	–	–
35–40	–	–	468	0	–	–	–	468
40–45	–	550	707	793	0	–	–	671
45–50	–	0	65	160	0	0	–	137
50–55	–	0	0	0	0	0	–	0
55–60	–	–	0	0	0	–	–	0
60–65	–	–	0	64	0	–	–	20
65–70	–	–	0	0	0	–	–	0
Total	–	550	1,240	1,017	0	0	–	1,294
F. 30°W–30°E								
25–30	–	–	–	–	–	–	–	–
30–35	–	0	0	–	0	–	–	0
35–40	0	192	147	0	0	–	–	173
40–45	–	74	463	131	210	0	–	250
45–50	–	0	0	157	100	0	–	100
50–55	–	0	0	48	0	0	–	0
55–60	–	0	0	–	0	–	–	0
60–65	–	–	0	0	0	–	–	0
65–70	–	–	–	0	0	–	–	0
Total	0	266	610	336	310	0	–	523
G. Total areas								
20–25	0	0	0	–	0	0	–	0
25–30	0	63	0	–	0	0	–	52
30–35	0	12	0	0	0	0	–	8
35–40	0	723	705	0	0	0	–	1,000
40–45	0	2,828	2,328	2,989	6,695	23	0	2,562
45–50	–	183	508	2,626	100	70	0	1,442
50–55	–	0	0	751	99	0	0	521
55–60	–	0	0	0	5	17	0	5
60–65	–	0	0	64	9	0	–	26
65–70	–	0	0	0	0	–	–	0
70–75	–	–	0	0	0	–	–	0
Total	0	3,809	3,541	6,430	6,908	110	0	5,616

Table 3G shows the latitudinal IA distribution by month. No right whales were seen in October, probably due to the low level of effort and the fact that it was spent mainly to the north of 35°S where right whales are not so abundant. By November, it appears that many right whales have reached mid-latitudinal waters since they were found between 25–50°S with a mode between 40°–45°S. In December right whales were observed in a relatively narrow latitudinal zone between 35°S and 50°S, again with a mode between 40°–45°S. Some whales were found as far south as 60–65°S in January, and none was found north of 40°S (although there was little effort in that area). The IA values for the zones 45–50°S and 40–45°S were similar. The latitudinal range of the distribution in February was the same as in January, but the mode was further north. The southernmost whales sighted in March were at 55–60°S, with a range from 40–60°S. No animals were sighted in April, but, as for October, this is probably a reflection of the low level of effort (see Tables 1 and 2).

The IA values for January (6,430) and February (6,908) were similar, and higher than the November (3,809) and December (3,541) values, suggesting that a large proportion of animals may have been in the lower latitudinal waters which were not surveyed in the latter months. This may also be true for March.

The monthly latitudinal distribution pattern appears to differ by area. A clear southerly migration from November to January is seen for the area between 90° and 150°E. Although no clear pattern is apparent from January to March in this area, it seems likely that the whales are found in the most southerly waters in January, and begin to move northward in February. Similar patterns were observed in the areas 150°E–130°W and 30°W–30°E. However, for the area 30–90°E, the whales appeared to move to higher latitudinal waters (55–60°S) in February and March suggesting that the migration and distribution pattern in this area may be different from the other areas.

RIGHT WHALE SIGHTINGS IN THE WATERS SOUTH OF WESTERN AUSTRALIA

The IWC Scientific Committee had recommended in 1981 that sighting vessels in transit to and from the Antarctic should undertake systematic surveys between 40–50°S and 117–130°E, an area where concentrations of right whales are believed to occur from November to February (IWC, 1982). The Japanese Government accepted this recommendation, and a special sightings cruise was conducted by a chartered ex-catcher boat, *Kyomaru No. 27* on its way to the Antarctic in the 1981/82 season.

The vessel arrived in the recommended area on 25 December 1981, and sightings were carried out in these waters between 38–46°S and 115–137°E moving westward with a zigzag track until 17 January 1982. The total sightings distance in the research area was 2,271 n. miles, and 75 right, 2 fin, 4 sei, 30 sperm and 3 ziphiid whales were seen. The right whales were not widely distributed, all being observed between 41–44°S 116–124°E and in waters with a surface temperature of 11.5–12.5 °C. Most (85%, 65 animals) were found in the small area 42–43°S, 118–119°E. Only three of the 35 right whale schools sighted had clear swimming directions: one lone whale was seen moving to the southwest, and

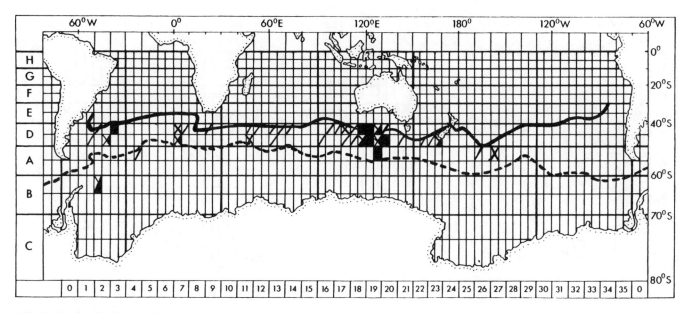

Fig. 3. Density distribution of right whales sighted by Japanese scouting boats in the Southern Hemisphere in January, 1965/66 to 1981/82, and the relationship with the positions of the sub-tropical (solid line) and Antarctic (broken line) convergences. Density symbols as in Fig. 2.

a single animal and a pair were seen moving to the south. This suggests that the research area was a feeding ground and that some right whales moved further south during the research period.

Table 4a shows the frequency distribution of school sizes of right whales sighted during the 1981/82 cruise. Single whales comprised 49% of all schools, and the largest school size was 8 whales with a mean of 2.14 whales. Table 4b shows the frequency distribution of estimated body lengths (n = 75) for the same cruise. The smallest whale was 34 ft and the largest 50 ft with a mode at 42 ft. No calves were found in the research area. This is very different from the situation reported for the same species in coastal areas. According to Best (1981), for the coastal waters off South Africa, 37.9% of all right whale schools were adults with calves. However, the frequency distribution of school sizes for unaccompanied whales off South Africa was similar to that in the present study: 49.4% single whales and a maximum school size of eight.

There are three possible explanations for this:

(i) that adults with calves were found in waters other than the present research area in summer;

(ii) that weaning finishes before the arrival of the animals at the research area;

(iii) that identification of suckling calves is difficult from a vessel.

In this connection, Japanese scouting records from 1965/66 reveal 6 cow/calf pairs between 40–50°S and 110–130°E between November and January. Despite the small numbers, this does show that the identification of cow/calf pairs is not impossible from research vessels. Although the largest recorded body length of a Southern Hemisphere right whale is 60 ft, the largest estimated length during this cruise was 50 ft. This may be either a true reflection of the size distribution or a result of the fact that current whalers have no experience in catching right whales, and thus may find it difficult to estimate the body length of swimming right whales by eye. Further research is needed to determine whether or not there is segregation of large whales and/or cow/calf pairs in summer.

Although angle and distances from the vessel to the

Table 4a.

School sizes of right whales observed. The mean school size is 2·14 (SD 1.66)

School size	Number of schools	Percent	School size	Number of schools	Percent
1	17	48.6	6	2	5.7
2	9	25.7	8	1	2.9
3	4	11.4			
4	2	5.7	Total	35	100.0

Table 4b.

Estimated body size distribution of right whales sighted. The mean body length was 41.17 (SD 1.86)

Length (ft)	No.	%	Length (ft)	No.	%
34	1	1.3	43	5	6.7
36	1	1.3	44	1	1.3
38	2	2.7	45	1	1.3
40	20	26.7	50	1	1.3
41	18	24.0			
42	25	33.3	Total	75	100.0

Table 4c.

Right angle distances in each case when right whale schools were sighted.

Date	Angle (°)	Distance (n. miles)	Right angle distance (n. miles)	Number of whales and schools sighted (whales/schools)
3 Jan	L 15	1.5	0.39	1/1
13 Jan	L 20	2.0	0.68	1/1
	R 45	1.0	0.71	1/1
	L 10	3.0	0.52	44/12
	–	–	–	4/2
	–	–	–	3/3
	L 20	3.0	1.03	3/1
	L 30	4.5	2.25	2/2
	L 40	2.0	1.29	1/1
	L 40	3.0	1.93	1/1
	L 20	3.0	1.03	6/4
	R 10	2.0	0.35	1/1
14 Jan	R 40	4.0	2.57	1/1
	R 25	2.5	1.06	1/1
	L 05	3.0	0.26	2/1
	R 30	4.0	2.00	2/1
15 Jan	–	–	–	1/1

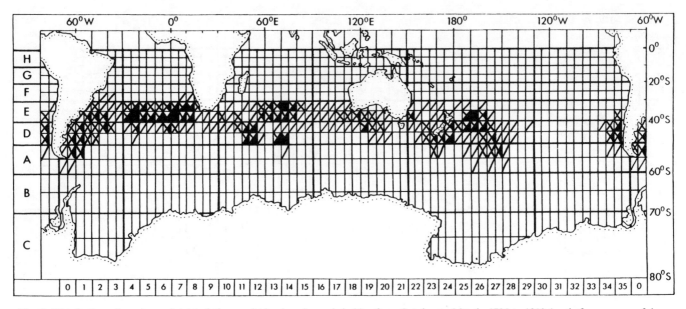

Fig. 4. Distribution of numbers of right whales caught by American whaleships from October to March, 1785 to 1913 (made from a map of days when one or more whales were caught in 5 × 5° square). ▨: 1–10, ▨: 11–25, ▨: 26–50, ◪: 51–75, ■: 76–100, ■: 101+.

sighting were measured and recorded on 14 occasions during the cruise, there are insufficient data to calculate a reliable population estimate. The mean sightings angles were 22° to port (range 5–40°) and 30° to starboard (range 10–45°). The mean radial distance was 2.75 n. miles (SD 0.995).

COMPARISON OF RECENT AND HISTORIC DISTRIBUTION PATTERNS

Townsend (1935) plotted monthly catch positions of right whales taken by American open-boat whaling vessels between 1785–1913. From these we counted the number of days when one or more whales were caught by 5° square between October and March although it was difficult to accurately count them for the more dense areas. Fig. 4 shows the relative numbers of right whales caught thus counted. Right whales were caught to the south of 25° by open-boat whaling, a similar northern limit to that recorded in recent years. Most whales were caught to the north of 55°S, except to the south of South America, where some right whales were caught between 55–60°S. The recent southern margin thus appears to lie further south than in the past. However, we do not think this reflects a true change in right whale distribution. The open-boat whaling grounds were limited to the waters north of 50°S even for the sperm whale (except in some coastal waters). As sea conditions are usually bad in waters around the Antarctic Convergence, it seems more likely that this was the limiting factor for open-boat whaling operations in the south. In support of this, some numbers of right whales were caught by modern whaling in the waters around South Georgia (Matthews, 1938), to the south of the Antarctic Convergence; no right whales had been caught there by open-boat whaling (Townsend, 1935). It thus appears that some right whales have always moved to the south of 50°S despite the scarcity of catch records.

No right whales were caught in the area between 130°W and 90°W in the period of open-boat whaling (Fig. 4). Fig. 2 reveals a similar feature in recent sightings data. The fact that some sperm whales were caught in

these waters in the open-boat whaling age (Townsend, 1935), and that catcher and sightings boats operated in these waters in recent years, show that this is not merely a reflection of little effort. Thus it appears that the southern right whale has never been distributed throughout all middle latitudinal waters of the Southern Hemisphere. This distribution pattern has been maintained from the age of open-boat whaling to recent years, at least in off-shore waters in summer.

Fig. 4 shows the classes of total number of days when one or more right whales was caught in each 5° square, but they do not always represent the density distribution of the whales, because they are not presented as the number of whales per unit of whaling effort. However, it can be assumed that more whales were caught from areas where more whales were distributed, so that the figure gives some indication as to where right whales were densely distributed in the open-boat whaling age. It is clear that they were not distributed evenly, with 'dense' areas being observed in the regions of 45–80°E, 115–125°E, 170°E–150°W, 85–75°W, 65–40°W and 30°W–15°E. The separation of the six Areas used in this paper was based on this in conjunction with Figs 2 and 3. Although similar patterns emerge in Figs 2 and 4, the relative density levels are different. For example, large numbers of right whales were caught in the past in the area between 30°W and 30°E, where the density is now low. This may mean that the population in this area was greatly reduced, although it is maintaining a low level. By contrast, although catches in the waters south of Western Australia were also among the largest in the past, the effect of these on the stock does not appear to have been so great when compared with other whaling grounds, as it is in this region that right whales appear currently to be most abundant.

A comparison of Figs 2 and 4 suggests that the population in the area between 70–30°W has recovered to some extent, while the populations in the other three areas remain at low levels. It can thus be concluded that the apparent differences in distribution patterns between past and recent times are not the result of a change in the environment of the right whale or in migration patterns.

Indeed a comparison of the distribution between these two periods shows that distribution in fact has remained quite similar, despite the great change in population levels.

TRENDS IN POPULATION DENSITY IN THE WATERS SOUTH OF WESTERN AUSTRALIA

Recently, increases in population density of Southern Hemisphere right whales have been reported from several regions. Best (1970, 1981) reports that the sightings from aerial surveys off the South Africa coast show a positive trend. Whitehead, Payne and Payne (1986) report an increase in the waters off Argentina. Bannister (1986) reports a positive trend for right whales off Australia, and Cawthorn (1983) reports a similar trend for right whales off New Zealand and Auckland Island. However, all of these sightings have been carried out in the coastal waters of each region.

Table 5 summarises the results from Japanese systematic whale sightings in the waters south of Western Australia (40–50°S, 110–130°E) from December to February for the seasons 1971/72–1981/82 in the case of scouting boats and 1969/70–1977/78 in the case of operating catcher boats. Both independent sources of data show an increasing trend in density. Although the trend was not statistically significant in the case of the operating boats, it was significant at the 5% level in the case of the scouting boats, with an annual rate of increase of 3.5% (95% C.L. 0.9%; 6.1%).

COMPARISON OF DISTRIBUTION PATTERN WITH THAT OF SEI WHALES

Mitchell (1975) and Kawamura (1978) have pointed out that the distributions of sei and right whales seem to be sympatric throughout the summer months. Fig. 5 shows the density distribution of sei whales sighted by Japanese scouting boats in the Southern Hemisphere in the same months and years as the right whales sightings. Although their density is considerably greater than that of right whales, the distribution patterns of the two species are

Table 5.

Searching distance, L (in nautical miles), and number of right whales sighted, n, by Japanese scouting and operating catcher boats in the area between 40–50° S, 110–130° E from 1969/70 to 1981/82 (December–February). CDW = catcher days worked. The zero value for 1978/79 has been excluded from the trend analysis.

	Scouting boats			Catcher boats		
	L	n	n/L	CDW	n	n/CDW
1969/70	–	–	–	163	32	0.196
1970/71	–	–	–	171	2	0.012
1971/72	23,925	68	0.0028	315	84	0.267
1972/73	18,427	52	0.0028	416	249	0.599
1973/74	17,955	85	0.0047	228	424	1.860
1974/75	12,884	53	0.0041	165	141	0.855
1975/76	6,405	45	0.0070	96	122	1.271
1976/77	7,551	13	0.0017	74	31	0.419
1977/78	11,649	72	0.0062	137	117	0.854
1978/79	548	0	0.0000	–	–	–
1979/80	–	–	–	–	–	–
1980/81	–	–	–	–	–	–
1981/82	1,736	75	0.0432	–	–	–

similar. However, the southern margin of the sei whale distribution is further south and it is also found in the area between 140–85°W where right whales were seldom or never sighted or caught. In addition, the distribution of 'dense' areas is somewhat different between the two species.

Given their similar distributions it is possible that interspecific competition for food and space as discussed by Mitchell (1975) and Kawamura (1978) exists, so that a change in the population size of one species might affect that of the other, as noted by Best (1982).

DISCUSSION

The sightings data have shown that the right whale is distributed widely in the mid-latitudinal off-shore waters as well as along the coasts of the Southern Hemisphere in recent years. Although the recent relative density patterns in off-shore waters are not identical with those in the past, the summer distribution is similar to the old open-boat whaling grounds. Mermoz (1980) reported

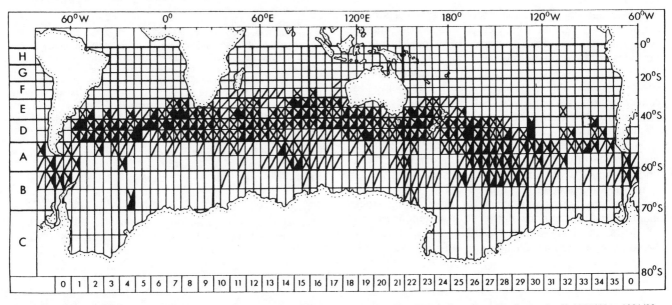

Fig. 5. Density distribution of sei whales sighted by Japanese scouting boats in the Southern Hemisphere from October to April, 1965/66 to 1981/82. Each symbol represents the number of sei whales sighted per 10,000 n. miles steamed by the scouting boats. ▨: 1–50, ▨: 51–100, ▨: 101–250, ▨: 251–500, ▨: 501–750, ■: 751+.

that right whales appear to return to the places they frequented in the early days of whaling, although significant changes in local movements have been observed along the southeast American coast. The present study has also indicated that the open-boat whaling grounds did not cover the total summer range of the right whale, in that some right whales are found in waters south of the Antarctic Convergence, which were not covered by open-boat whaling vessels.

Best (1970) examined the seasonality of the right whales off South Africa by using the catch positions of open-boat whalers, and found that the right whales were caught furthest south (between 45–50°S) in the waters between 30°W and 80°E in February to April. In this study, right whales were sighted furthest south between 55–60°S in February and March (30–90°E), although January was the month when right whales were sighted furthest south (between 60–65°S) in all areas combined. One of the reasons for the differences in this result and that of Best is the difference already noted between the old whaling grounds and the total range of the animal. It is possible that the February to April period might in fact be part of the northward migration of the right whale. On the other hand it may be that the migration pattern is different by area, and in particular that it is later in the area between 30–90°E, Cawthorn (1978) reported that the Campbell Island stock moved north in spring and summer. Gaskin (1968) proposed that the timing of right whale movements may have changed in recent years, but this is not apparent for the open seas in the data presented here.

The apparent recovery of southern right whale populations has already been noted from several coastal regions of the Southern Hemisphere including off Western Australia (Bannister, 1986). The present study has shown, for the off-shore waters south of Western Australia, an increasing trend in right whale population density from sightings data. As the right whales in this area can be regarded as belonging to the same stock as those in the coastal waters of Western Australia, these two independent studies indicating an increasing trend in the population suggest that the observed increase in this stock is real.

Whale sighting by Japanese scouting boats has been conducted in the months October to April (mainly November to March). The present paper therefore provides information on only the summer distribution of the southern right whale. According to Townsend (1935), southern right whales were only caught in winter in coastal waters, with no records from off-shore waters. Although sightings have been carried out in the Southern Hemisphere in winter in recent years, the coverage has been limited to coastal waters. A knowledge of the winter distribution of the right whale is important for our understanding of the breeding of this species, as winter is its breeding season (Best, 1982). Knowledge of the breeding grounds is important for determining stock identity, and the methods of protection and management of the species will differ depending on whether the breeding grounds are coastal or in off-shore waters. If

they are in coastal waters, the protection of the right whale will become increasingly difficult with the social development of these coastal regions. If there are some breeding areas in off-shore waters, protection is easier to establish. Systematic sightings in off-shore waters in winter are needed for a better knowledge of right whale populations.

REFERENCES

Aguayo L., A. 1974. Baleen whales off continental Chile, pp. 209–17. *In*: W. E. Schevill (ed) *The Whale Problem: a status report*. Harvard Univ. Press. 419 pp.

Anon. 1980. Australia: progress report on cetacean research 1978–79. *Rep. int. Whal. Commn* 30: 143–4.

Bannister, J. L. 1986. Southern right whales: status off Australia from twentieth-century 'incidental' sightings and aerial surveys. (Published in this volume).

Best, P. B. 1970. Exploitation and recovery of right whales (*Eubalaena australis*) off the Cape Province. *Investl Rep. Div. Sea Fish. S. Afr.* 80: 20pp.

Best, P. B. 1981. The status of right whales (Eubalaena glacialis) off South Africa, 1969–1979. *Investl Rep. Sea Fish. Inst. S. Afr.* 123: 44pp.

Best, P. B. and Ohsumi, S. 1980. International Whaling Commission/International Decade of Cetacean Research (IWC-/IDCR) southern minke whale assessment cruise, 1978–79. *Polar Rec.*, 20 (124): 52–7.

Cawthorn, M. W. 1978. Whale research in New Zealand. *Rep. int. Whal. Commn* 28: 109–12.

Cawthorn, M. W. 1983. Current status off New Zealand – 20th century sightings and trends. Paper SC/35/RW10 submitted to the IWC Workshop on the Status of Right Whales, June 1983 (unpublished) 6pp.

Clarke, R. 1965. Southern right whales on the coast of Chile. *Norsk Hvalfangsttid* 54 (6): 121–8.

Gaskin, D. E. 1964. Return of southern right whale (*Eubalaena australis* Desm.) to New Zealand waters, 1963. *Tuatara* 12: 115–8.

Gaskin, D. E. 1968. The New Zealand cetacea. *Fish. Res. Bull.* (*N.Z.*) 1: 1–92.

Gilmore, R. M. 1969. Populations, distribution and behaviour of whales in the western South Pacific: cruise 69–3 of R/V *Hero. Antact. J. U.S.* 4(6): 307–8.

International Whaling Commission 1982. Report of the Scientific Committee, *Rep. int. Whal. Commn* 32: 43–67.

Kawamura, A. 1978. An interim consideration on a possible interspecific relation in southern baleen whales from the viewpoint of their food habits. *Rep. int. Whal. Commn* 28: 411–20.

Masaki, Y. 1977. Japanese pelagic whaling and whale sightings in the Antarctic, 1975–76. *Rep. int. Whal. Commn* 27: 148–55.

Matthews, L. H. 1983. Notes on the southern right whale, *Eubalaena australis. Discovery Rep.* 17: 169–82.

Mermoz, J. F. 1980. Preliminary report on the southern right whale in the southwestern Atlantic. *Rep. int. Whal. Commn.* 30: 183–6.

Mitchell, E. 1975. Trophic relationships and competition for food in northwest Atlantic whales. *Proc. Canad. Soc. Zool.* 1974: 123–33.

Ohsumi, S. and Yamamura, K. 1982. A review of the Japanese whale sightings system. *Rep. int. Whal. Commn* 32: 581–6.

Omura, H., Ohsumi, S., Nemoto, T., Nasu, K. and Kasuya, T. 1969. Black right whales in the North Pacific. *Sci. Rep. Whales. Res. Inst* Tokyo, 21: 1–78.

Payne, R. 1972. *Report from Patagonia: the right whales*. New York Zool. Soc.: 4pp.

Payne, R. 1976. At home with right whales. *Nat. Geogr. Mag.* 149(3): 322–39.

Townsend, C. H. 1935. The distribution of certain whales as shown by logbooks of American whaleships. *Zoologica*, N. Y. 19(1): 1–50.

Whitehead, H., Payne, R. and Payne, M. 1986. Populations estimate for the right whales off Peninsula Valdes, Argentina, 1971–76. (Published in this volume).

Appendix

NATURAL MARKING OF RIGHT WHALES

As part of the IWC/IDCR Southern Hemisphere minke whale assessment cruises, the international researchers who participated were requested to take as many photographs of natural markings of right whales and humpback whales as possible to identify individuals. Photo-identification is particularly useful for protected whales, and has been used for the right whale in some regions of the Southern Hemisphere. The junior author participated in the cruises and had the opportunity to observe and photograph three right whales in Antarctic Areas I and II in the 1981/2 and 1982/3 seasons (Appendix Table 1).

Whale C was the southernmost right whale observed in the present study. Whale A provided evidence that the right whale can swim in waters colder than 0° C. Although feeding was not observed, right whales could possibly eat krill (*Euphausia superba*) in the Antarctic. judging by the numerous patches of krill seen around Whale A.

Callosites on the head are one of the characteristics of the right whales, and the pattern of these is considered to have individual variation, and is being used as the major natural marking feature (Payne, 1972). Several photographs were taken of the three right whales in the Antarctic, as shown in Plate 1A, B and C. The natural markings of Whales A and C were successfully photographed, but no good photographs were obtained of Whale B. The callosities of this individual were seen to be white, possibly caused by the infestation of the callosities with large amounts of whale lice. Light gray body colour patches were distributed on both sides of the middle part of the body in Whale C. Although there is individual variation in body colour patches of the right whale (Omura *et al.*, 1969), these patches are not suitable as a character for natural marking, as the body colour patch is usually on the belly and seldom exposed for photography. It was recognized that taking photographs for natural marking studies using callosities was actually more difficult from vessels than from aircraft or from land. Photographs of both sides of the head will be useful for natural marking, as the arrangement of the callosities is not symmetrical.

Plate I. Right whales photographed in the Antarctic. Top: whale A. Middle: whale B. Bottom: whale C.

The present cases may be the first instances of natural marking of southern right whales in off-shore waters. If these whales are found and the individuals identified in lower latitudinal waters, valuable ecological information will be obtained.

Appendix Table 1.

Details of sightings of right whales in Areas I and II

	Whale A	Whale B	Whale C
Date	1 January 1982	1 January 1983	2 January 1983
Position	60°52'S, 47°48'W	62°34'S, 61°42'W	63°16'S, 62°45'W
Est. length	45 feet	50 feet	45 feet
Surface temp.	− 0.4°C	0.8°C	0.4°C
Comments	In region with many krill patches, 350m from large iceberg.	Swimming near surface 1/2 ml from large iceberg when seen & moved to it on approach of vessel.	Stationary & resting with head under small iceberg (5+ minutes). On closing swam slowly & milled around iceberg.

Flensing whales in open waters, probably in the 17th century [Reproduced from Sañez Reguart, A. (1791) *Diccionario Histórico de los Artes de la Pesca Nacional* (Madrid): 330–453]

Archaeological Evidence of the 16th Century Basque Right Whale Fishery in Labrador

STEPHEN L. CUMBAA

Zooarchaeological Identification Centre, National Museum of Natural Sciences, National Museums Canada, Ottawa, Ontario K1A 0M8, Canada

ABSTRACT

Bones found at Red Bay, Labrador during the excavation of a Basque whaling station and associated shipwreck have confirmed Basque hunting of both right, *Eubalaena glacialis*, and bowhead, *Balaena mysticetus*, whales in the Strait of Belle Isle in the last half of the 16th century.

Identification of the two species has thus far been based primarily on the basis of differences in the scapula, humerus and maxilla. The stratigraphic context of the bones indicates contemporaneity of the two species, with roughly equal numbers of each having been taken. There is little evidence of exploitation of calves.

The apparent presence of significant numbers of bowheads may have ramifications for estimates of numbers of right whales killed in Newfoundland and Labrador waters in the 16th century, as most estimates from historical sources have assumed catches of right whales only. Further, the established presence of both species in the Strait of Belle Isle helps confirm aspects of their distributional history which were unclear.

INTRODUCTION

Field crews from Parks Canada's Marine Archaeology Section and from the Department of Anthropology at Memorial University, St. John's, Newfoundland, have been involved in a multi-disciplinary investigation of a 16th century Spanish Basque whaling station and associated shipwreck since their discovery at Red Bay, Labrador in 1977 and 1978 (Tuck and Grenier, 1981). Research on a related topic in Basque archives in Spain by historian Selma Barkham for the Public Archives of Canada led to the discoveries. This paper focusses on whale remains from the site (Fig. 1) which I have been studying since the first full season of excavation in 1979. Through the 1982 season, approximately 1,500 whale bones from both terrestrial and underwater deposits have been examined in some detail.

Research by Barkham indicates that the whaling station at Red Bay operated on a more or less annual basis from at least the 1530s to perhaps the first decade of the 17th century (Barkham, 1984). In peak years, as many as 20 Basque ships made Red Bay their base during the season, which usually ran from June through November. Ships occasionally over-wintered, although apparently not on purpose. Red Bay was one of the most important whaling stations of the several that were in operation along the Strait of Belle Isle. The wreck being investigated by Parks Canada, only 30 meters offshore from a tryworks complex on Saddle Island in the

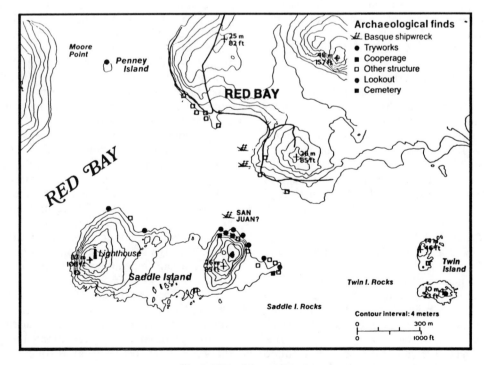

Fig. 1. Map of the study area

harbour, is thought to be that of the *San Juan,* which sank in a storm in 1565 while being loaded with barrels of whale oil for the return trip to Spain.

IDENTIFICATION

Limb bones found in anatomical position amid the wreckage of the ship, as well as a number of partial skulls on a nearby beach, were examined on site by E. D. Mitchell in 1979. Mitchell identified them as probable *E. glacialis* (pers. comm.). Since that time, more than a dozen other such 'articulated' flippers (units including the humerus, radius, ulna, carpals, metacarpals and phalanges) have been found in strata in and around the wreck, as well as many isolated limb elements, vertebrae, skull fragments, and occasional ribs and scapulae. These bones have been excavated, collected, and catalogued within Parks Canada's provenience system based on a grid overlying the site. The bones discussed here were found in stratigraphic contexts indicating deposition during the period of Basque occupation. Relatively few whale bones, and none of those discussed in this paper, have come from excavations on Saddle Island. Surveys of whale bone presence and distribution have been made on a number of transects across the harbour floor, as well as on shore for several miles in either direction along the coast.

I have examined the bones discussed here on site and later with access to museum comparative collections, within the limits of portability. Identification has been as specific as possible. Some of the more diagnostic skull elements, the mandibles, the major limb bones, scapulae, cervical vertebrae, and baleen, have been identified to family, and where possible, to species level. The rest of the vertebrae, the ribs, and the metacarpals and phalanges have not yet been examined in detail. All but two of the bones examined in detail to date and identified to at least family level are balaenid.

I have been able to examine osteological characteristics of both *E. glacialis* and *B. mysticetus* through examination of a small comparative skeletal series. Specimens of *E. glacialis* examined include complete skeletons from the Museum of Comparative Zoology, Harvard University; the United States National Museum, Washington D.C. (2); the American Museum of Natural History, New York; the New England Aquarium, Boston; the British Museum (Natural History), London; and the Santander Museum, Spain (from photographs). Fewer *B. mysticetus* skeletons have been examined, partly reflecting their scarcity in museum collections. Those examined include specimens at the British Museum (Natural History), London; the United States National Museum, Washington D.C. (skull only); and the National Museum of Natural Sciences, Ottawa (skull only). Examination of comparative material has been supplemented by published works, such as Eschricht and Reinhardt (1866); Van Beneden and Gervais (1880); Turner (1913); Omura, Ohsumi, Nemoto, Nasu and Kasuya (1969); and Nishiwaki and Kasuya (1970).

The osteological papers on the two species are usually descriptive and rarely comparative, but some useful distinctions have been pointed out. While reserving judgment on some of the described differences, I feel safe in giving a specific identification of *B. mysticetus* to strips of baleen over 10 feet in length which have been found adjacent to Basque structures on Saddle Island (J. A.

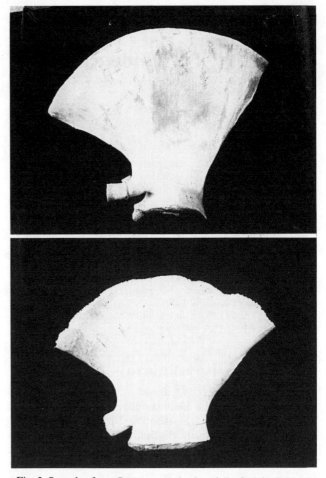

Fig. 2. Scapulae from *B. mysticetus* (top) and *E. glacialis* (bottom)

Tuck, pers. comm.), and to two of the three scapulae found to date, which display well-developed coracoid and acromion processes (Fig. 2). The coracoid process is lacking or weakly developed in *E. glacialis* (Eschricht and Reinhardt, 1866; Turner, 1913).

The humerus is potentially the most useful element for separating the species found at Red Bay and for giving some idea of the relative proportions of right and bowhead whales taken. This large paired element, frequently found whole in the underwater excavations along the shore of the island where flensing operations must have taken place, differs between the species. The humerus of *B. mysticetus* is generally more elongate with a straighter shaft, whereas that of *E. glacialis* is proportionately wider, with a deeply curved postero-dorsal shaft margin, viewed laterally (Fig. 3). Turner (1913) mentioned no differences in this element, and Eschricht and Reinhardt's (1866) figured specimen '...is covered with abnormal osseous protuberances, by which it is very much deformed.' Certainly more *B. mysticetus* skeletons need to be examined to confirm this difference, which thus far seems relatively clear cut. Of the humeri found through the 1982 season, which represent at least 17 individuals, nine appear to be from *B. mysticetus* and eight from *E. glacialis.*

Another potentially useful distinction is in the maxilla. On the lateral surface, the large nutrient foraminae are more numerous in *B. mysticetus*, occurring from a point below the nasal region well along the postero-ventro margin. Other osteological distinctions between the species, both published and not, are of limited utility due

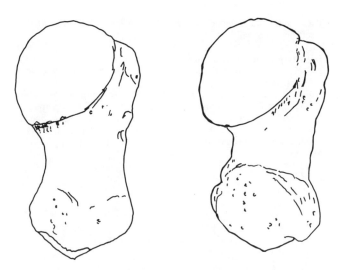

Fig. 3. Left humerus of *B. mysticetus* (left) and *E. glacialis* (right)

to the particular composition of the Red Bay sample, which is heavily biased toward limb elements and caudal vertebrae.

DISCUSSION

The appearance of remains of significant numbers of *B. mysticetus* (albeit in a small sample) in this 16th century whaling station site may have ramifications for estimates of numbers of right whales killed by Basque whalers in Newfoundland and Labrador waters, because most estimates have assumed one species was taken and are based on numbers extrapolated from cargos of oil. From the apparent evidence at Red Bay, half the whales killed were *B. mysticetus*, and as *B. mysticetus* produces significantly more oil and baleen than *E. glacialis*, the estimates of numbers of right whales killed could be much reduced on this basis.

The presence of both *B. mysticetus* and *E. glacialis* in the Strait of Belle Isle in the last half of the 16th century is interesting as well from a distributional standpoint. As Lamb (1982) and others have pointed out, the mid-16th century was the 'Little Ice Age,' a period of 150 years or more characterized by great variations in temperature, but in general, the coldest regime at anytime since the last major ice age ended 10,000 years ago. Lamb (1982) notes that in the second half of the 16th century, Greenland was already cut off by the spreading of Arctic ice, and that by the 1580s Denmark Strait was in several summers blocked entirely by pack-ice. Elsewhere sea temperatures became up to 5 °C colder than is usual today, and many glaciers advanced significantly. Even the summers, especially in the 1570s, were 'outstandingly cold' (Lamb, 1982). Surely conditions such as this would favour increased use by *B. mysticetus* of what had probably been marginal range; as Reeves, Mitchell, Mansfield and McLaughlin (1983) and others have said, some variability in the distribution of *B. mysticetus* may be expected from year to year as ice conditions change.

The assumption by Reeves *et al.* (1983) of the 'distinct possibility' that the early Basque whalers and later the Yankee pelagic whalers caught *B. mysticetus* early and late in their whaling seasons in or near the Strait of Belle Isle seems borne out by climatic possibilities, documentary, and now archaeological evidence.

However, the same conditions that may have fostered a range 'extension' of *B. mysticetus* may have worked against *E. glacialis*, probably already near the northern end of its range in the Strait of Belle Isle. Reeves, Mead and Katona (1978), in their discussion of right whales in the western North Atlantic, also point out the possible overlap in ranges of the two species, but assume summer catches have been *E. glacialis*. Significantly colder summers in some years may have forced the Basques farther south to hunt *E. glacialis*, if colder temperatures and ice were avoided by this species.

On balance, it seems possible that the Basque whalers, arriving at stations along the Strait of Belle Isle in June, may have hunted the straggling remnants of the bowhead population heading north. More likely, from late June or early July to mid-October they probably hunted *E. glacialis*, and from about November until they left in early December the Basques must have hunted bowheads. A 16th century Basque document recently translated refers quite clearly to the 'second season' which extended the hunt right to freeze-up (R. Grenier, pers. comm.). No doubt the timing as well as the 'mix' of the catch varied somewhat with conditions from year to year.

The question of species aside, it seems from the evidence at Red Bay that there was little if any catch of calves. Of the 17 individual whales documented so far from the underwater excavation sample, no more than one individual appears to have been in the 0–1 year group (less than 8–9 meters in length), although there is quite a range in the size of the animals present. The greatest number seem to have been fully adult, as indicated by size, fusion of vertebral and limb epiphyses, and other osteological indicators such as excess bone growth of the type normally associated with aged individuals. One or two bones of what may be a fetal whale (species undetermined) in the deposits around the shipwreck may attest to the killing of a mature female.

Excavations at Red Bay as well as related historical research on Basque whaling will continue through at least 1985 and possibly 1986. The benefit of this research, an increased bone sample size, and the opportunity to visit other comparative collections and to compare osteological notes with other researchers should prove increasingly valuable in the study of this early right and bowhead whale fishery and its effect on the North Atlantic population.

All whale bone recovered from the excavations except excessively worn elements or very small fragments has been saved, and hopefully will be deposited in one or more museums. The matter is under discussion between the federal and provincial governments, and it is likely that some of the bones will go to the Newfoundland Provincial Museum, St. John's; some to the National Museum of Natural Sciences, National Museums Canada, Ottawa; and some will remain in Red Bay at an interpretation centre.

REFERENCES

Barkham, S. H. 1984. The Basque whaling establishments in Labrador 1536–1632 – A summary. *Arctic* 37: 515–19.

Eschricht, D. F. and Reinhardt, J. 1866. On the Greenland right-whale (*Balaena mysticetus*, Linn.), with especial reference to its geographical distribution and migrations in times past and present, and to its external and internal characteristics, pp. 1–150. *In:* W. H. Flower, (ed.) *Recent Memoirs on the Cetacea*. The Ray Society, London (Transl. from Danish publ. of 1861).

Lamb, H. H. 1982. *Climate, History and the Modern World*. Methuen, London and New York, 378 pp.

Nishiwaki, M. and Kasuya, T. 1970. A Greenland right whale caught at Osaka Bay. *Sci. Rep. Whales Res. Inst., Tokyo* 22: 45–62.

Omura, H., Ohsumi, S., Nemoto, T., Nasu, K. and Kasuya, T. 1969. Black right whales in the North Pacific. *Sci. Rep. Whales Res. Inst., Tokyo* 21: 1–78.

Reeves, R. R., Mead, J. G. and Katona, S. 1978. The right whale, *Eubalaena glacialis*, in the western North Atlantic. *Rep. int. Whal. Commn* 28: 303–12.

Reeves, R., Mitchell, E., Mansfield, A. and McLaughlin, M. 1983. Distribution and migration of the bowhead whale, *Balaena mysticetus*, in the eastern North American Arctic. *Arctic* 36(1): 5–64.

Tuck, J. A. and Grenier, R. 1981. A 16th-century Basque whaling station in Labrador. *Sci. Am.* 245(5): 180–90.

Turner, W. 1913. The right whale of the North Atlantic, *Balaena biscayensis*: its skeleton described and compared with that of the Greenland right whale, *Balaena mysticetus*. *Trans. R. Soc. Edinburgh* 48, Part 4 (No. 33): 889–922.

Van Beneden, P.-J. and Gervais, P. 1880. Osteographie des cetaces vivants et fossiles, comprenant la description et l'iconographie du squellette et du systeme dentaire de ces animaux; ainsi que des documents relatifs a leur histoire naturelle. A. Bertrand, Libraire-editeur, Libraire de la Societe de Geographie, Paris. 634 pp. +Atlas.

A Review of Old Basque Whaling and its Effect on the Right Whales (*Eubalaena glacialis*) of the North Atlantic

ALEX AGUILAR

Department of Zoology (Vertebrates), Faculty of Biology, University of Barcelona, Barcelona 08028, Spain

ABSTRACT

The available information from ancient Basque whaling is reviewed. The operations have been divided into three episodes according to the areas of exploitation.

In the local fishery of the Bay of Biscay, *Eubalaena glacialis* was the main target species, although *Physeter macrocephalus* and other species might also have been harvested at least occasionally. Whaling seems to have appeared first in the French Basque country in the 11th century and later it spread gradually to the remaining areas but this should not be related to a reduction of stocks. A peak in the overall operations was probably reached around the 16th and 17th centuries but thereafter a decline in the fishery is evident. The catch rate per season was probably not very high but other factors such as the preference of the whalers for the calves would have had detrimental effects on the stock. The total removals are impossible to estimate but the present population in the Bay of Biscay must be negligible, since only a few records of this species have occurred during this century.

Whaling in Newfoundland began during the 1530s and reached its maximum success at the end of the 16th century. *Eubalaena glacialis* probably represented the bulk of the catches, although *Balaena mysticetus* was also taken, especially from 1610, when the Basques moved further to the north due to the scarcity of whales on the initial whaling grounds. The average catch per boat is estimated at 12 whales or thereabouts and thus, the total harvest per season ranged from 300 to 500 whales. This means that about 25,000 to 40,000 whales might have been killed from 1530 to 1610, when the stock showed signs of depletion. Basque whaling on the Canadian grounds continued until the end of the 17th century.

Little information is available for whaling operations in the northeastern North Atlantic, since most of the capital invested came from outside the Basque whaling community, and often they only acted as harpooners or sailors. Purely Spanish expeditions were only occasionally carried out, and they took place from the 15th to the middle of the 18th century. The target species in Ireland, Norway and Iceland was probably *E. glacialis*, but in North Greenland and Spitzbergen it was *B. mysticetus*.

At the beginning of the 18th century, Spanish whaling operations, both in local and northern grounds, were in clear decline. Several companies, some of them with the support of the Crown, were created in order to carry on whaling in the northern seas, the Canary Islands and South America. However, all the enterprises failed and, in 1797, the last overseas Spanish whaler was back in port.

INTRODUCTION

In recent years, extensive reviews of historical sources and data for the different regions of the Bay of Biscay involved in old whaling have been carried out, and a fairly high proportion of the information about this subject is easily available and intelligible. Fischer (1871) in Southern France, Ciriquiain (1979) in the Basque country, Gonzalez Echegaray (1978) in Santander, Castañon (1964) in Asturias and Meijide (1971) in Galicia compiled part of the still-existing information about the local whale fishery, and Barkham (1979) has gone deeper into the Newfoundland operations. However the passage of time, the rather high incidence of warfare against neighbouring nations and Spanish internal struggles, all contributed towards gaps and uncertainties in the already reduced written material from these operations, and much information is still stored in the hundreds of manuscripts existing in Spanish libraries, to which access is difficult.

MATERIALS AND METHODS

In the present paper, I have used the above mentioned reviews and many other papers, together with original manuscripts preserved in the following archives:

Archivo Histórico Nacional (Madrid): AHN
Archivo Histórico Provincial (Santander): AHPS
Archivo de los Protocolos de Guipúzcoa (Oñate): APG
Biblioteca Real Academia de la Historia (Madrid): BRAH
Colección Vargas Ponce, Museo Naval (Madrid): VP
Museo Naval, Ministerio de Marina (Madrid): MN

RESULTS

Essentially, the inhabitants of the coastal areas of the Bay of Biscay were involved in three theatres of whaling: the local fishery off the coasts of their countries, the Newfoundland and Labrador expeditions, and the whaling in the northeastern European grounds (Greenland, Iceland, Norway and Spitzbergen). In Table 1, the most important features of these stages have been put together for an easier comparison.

The bulk of old whaling was carried out by Basques although often with crew or capital from other areas (AHPS 1587; AHPS 1554; AHPS 1596) and, when mentioning them, I will usually refer both to the Spanish and the French Basques.

Local whaling off the coasts of Northern Spain and Southern France

Responsibility for ancient Spanish local whaling has been traditionally apportioned to the Basques but although this was true in the overseas expeditions, it should in fairness be shared, in the local operations, among all the countries or regions whose coasts fringe the Bay of Biscay, from Southern France to the Cape Finisterre.

Along this coastline, up to 47 ports are known to have sustained whaling settlements at some time. Both culturally and administratively, five different regions can be distinguished (French Basque country, Spanish Basque country, Santander, Asturias and Galicia), and it is worth keeping them in mind when examining the trends of the fishery (Fig. 1).

Table 1.

Main features of whaling operations in the different whaling grounds and areas. For references see text.

Whaling ground	First document certifying Basque whaling	First signs of decline	Last whale caught[1]	Target species	Other possible target species
French Basque Country	1059	ca. 1500	1567	N. Atlantic right whale	Sperm and gray whale?
Spanish Basque Country	1150	ca. 1600	1893	N. Atlantic right whale	Sperm and gray whale?
Santander	1190	ca. 1650	1720	N. Atlantic right whale	Sperm and gray whale?
Asturias	1232	ca. 1650	1722	N. Atlantic right whale	Sperm and gray whale?
Galicia	1371	ca. 1650	1720	N. Atlantic right whale	Sperm and gray whale?
English Channel	XIV cent.?	?	XVI cent.?	N. Atlantic right whale	Sperm and gray whale?
Newfoundland	1530	ca. 1610	1713	N. Atlantic right whale	Bowhead whale
Greenland	1613	ca. 1650?	ca. 1750	N. Atlantic right and bowhead	–
Spitzbergen	XVI cent.?	ca. 1650?	ca. 1750	Bowhead whale	–
Iceland	1412	ca. 1650?	ca. 1750	N. Atlantic right whale	Bowhead whale

[1] Or last document certifying commercial Basque whaling.

In the Basque country, whaling was carried out as a cooperative enterprise among all the fishermen of the town, who launched small rowing boats every time a whale was spotted and in which they approached and eventually killed the cetacean. Spotting of cetaceans was the task of full time watchmen located on suitable look-out towers and, consequently, the whaling ground was limited to only several miles around the port. In the remaining areas, the pattern of operation was basically the same although small vessels which allowed the whalers to chase the whale in open waters were occasionally used, mainly in Galicia. Castañón (1964), Gonzalez Echegaray (1978) and Ciriquiain (1979) have described such operations and may be consulted if further detail is desired.

The actual origin of whaling in the area has been extensively discussed over the years and for simplicity I will assume here that the fishery started just when the first extant document giving notice of it appeared. Thus, the beginning may be fixed in the year 1059 (Lefèbvre, 1933) when a regulatory measure was taken in order to concentrate whale meat in the market of Bayonne. Whaling in the remaining areas began a little later, and considerably later in Galicia, from which we have no documentation until the end of the 14th century.

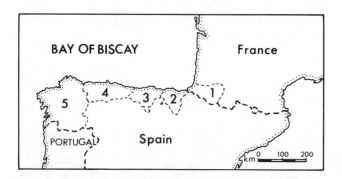

Fig. 1. Whaling settlements and areas in the coastal operations of the Bay of Biscay. (1): *French Basque country:* Biarritz, St. Jean de Luz, Irún. (2): *Spanish Basque country:* Bermeo, Lequeitio, Ondarroa, Motrico, Zumaya, Guetaria, Zarauz, Orio, San Sebastián, Pasajes, Fuenterrabía, Deva. (3): *Santander:* San Vincente de la Barquera-Uriambre, Comillas, Suances, Santander, Santoña, Laredo, Castro Urdiales. (4): *Asturias:* Llanes, Ribadesella, Lastres, Tazones, Gijón, Candás, Luanco, Avilés, Cudillero, Cadavedo, Luarca, Puerto de Vega, Tapia, Figueras, Antrellusa. (5): *Galicia:* Camariñas, Lage, Corme, Malpica, Cayón, Cedeira, Foz-Nois, San Ciprián, Ribadeo, Burela.

Without doubt, the most important target species of the local Spanish whalers was the North Atlantic right whale, *Eubalaena glacialis*, which was chased when approaching the coast on its winter migration. Nevertheless, although most contemporary pictures and skeletal remains from the catches proved to be of this species, other species such as the sperm whale, *Physeter macrocephalus*, are known to have been caught, and the possibility that other cetaceans were occasionally killed has been discussed elsewhere (Graells, 1889; Aguilar, 1981). Furthermore, the discovery of subfossil remains from gray whales, *Eschrichtius robustus*, in the North Sea, some of them being only about fifteen hundred years old, puts forward the possibility that this species was also hunted by the ancient whalers (Deinse and Junge, 1937; De Smet, 1981). However, most evidence indicates that the North Atlantic right whale dominated the catch, at least at the time of heaviest exploitation.

The whaling season in Northern Spain and Southern France lasted from October–November to February–March, with a probable peak around January (AHPS 1607; 1640; VP 1685; Molina, 1549). Besides the Bay of Biscay whaling, catches and sightings of *E. glacialis* at various times are known to have occurred occasionally in several other localities of the eastern temperate North Atlantic. Fischer (1881), Teixeira (1979), Clarke (1981) and Brown (1986) reported them from the Cape Verde Islands, Azores, Madeira and continental Portugal, and Gasco (1878) and Jouan (1891) described the appearance of two North Atlantic right whales in the Mediterranean, one in Italy and another in Algiers. These last reports refer to encounters which took place in winter and at the beginning of spring, which, together with the October-March season in the Bay of Biscay and the essentially summer season in the Hebrides, Faroes and Iceland (Collett, 1909; Schevill and Moore, 1983), support a typical north–south migration rather than the Gulf Stream-linked movement suggested by Thompson (1918).

Many authors have considered that the Basques first heavily reduced the whales in their area and then, impelled by the scarcity of catches in their grounds, moved to the adjacent provinces (Gonzalez Echegaray, 1978; Ciriquiain, 1979). Nevertheless, this assertion has to be carefully considered, since evidence of whaling appears gradually along the coast with a difference of only a few decades from one region to the next. Thus, the first document regulating the whale fishery in the French Basque country dates from 1059 (Lefèbvre,

1933), in the Spanish Basque country from 1150 (Soraluce, 1878), in Santander from 1190 (Gonzalez Echegaray, 1978) and in Asturias from 1232 (Graells, 1889).

This small but gradual shift in the appearance of documentation suggests not a reduction of the stock but a successive transfer of whaling experience and techniques. In addition, the fishery was then in its infancy and was to continue in the region for about 250 years more, all of which seems to indicate that the stock was quite healthy at this time.

In order to estimate the evolution of whaling operations in the different areas, I have used the number of extant manuscripts or written references from each settlement over the years as an index of activity. This estimator must be viewed cautiously since the relative abundance of documents does not necessarily imply a proportional intensity of whaling (*i.e.* it is reasonable to expect a higher proportion of written material in the later centuries than in the former ones, both because of better preservation and a more extended use of writing). Nevertheless, this is the only raw material available to me, and I have assumed that the existing bias would operate similarly for every region in a given period of time. A close selection of the material has been necessary and thus, the number of references considerably reduced. For example, quite often papers gave information about trade or tax regulations on whale fat or oil but it was not clear whether they referred to the local or the overseas operations. The sifted material comprises 224 references which I have put together in groups for every 50 years. The result of this exercise is represented in Fig. 2.

It is worth noting here that, although the timing of the beginning of the activity appears only slightly different from one area to the next (with the sole exception of Galicia), subsequent patterns seem to differ clearly between the different areas.

In the French Basque country, where whaling first seemed to occur, it never attained the primary importance that was achieved in the Spanish settlements. The number of towns devoted to this industry was only a few and the number of whales taken was probably small. Documentation is not abundant, possibly due to the antiquity of the fishery, which probably reached its maximum success around the 13th century and declined later. Although cetaceans were opportunistically killed from time to time, the last documents denoting strict commercial whaling in the area were produced around the middle of the 16th century (Darracq, 1859; Fischer, 1881). The reasons which impelled the French Basques to give up whaling are uncertain but it cannot be a depletion of the stock, since the Spanish – as we will see – went on whaling several centuries more in the adjacent waters.

The Spanish Basque country is where whaling operations were most successfully carried on. The fishery may have begun around the 12th century and lasted until the 19th century, although only a few whales were harvested then (Aguilar, 1981). Written evidence shows a peak around the second half of the 16th century with a subsequent decline. This coincides with the general expansion of the Basque fisheries (mainly for cod and whales) to Galicia, Newfoundland and the northern seas. To what extent such expansion was due to the lack of catches in their local grounds is unknown because the Basques traditionally carried out expeditions to remote places, even when their own localities were not unfruitful.

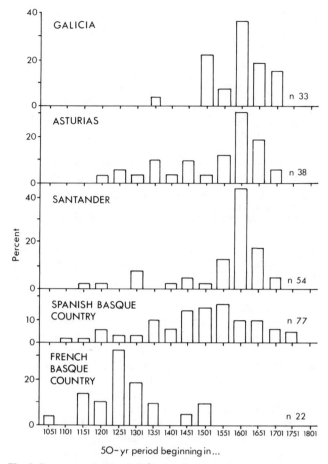

Fig. 2. Percentage distribution of selected written references regarding whaling operations, from the different areas in the Bay of Biscay over time. See comments in the text. Material from: Aguirre (1952); Canga Argüelles (1841); Casariego (1959); Castañón (1964); Cavanilles (1858); Ciriquiain (1979); Duguy (1972); Fernández Duro (1881); Fischer (1881); Gonzalez Echegaray (1978); Graells (1870); Guiard (1913); Lence Santar (1950); Markham (1881); Meijide (1971); Rabot (1928); Rey (1912); Soraluce (1878); Terán (1949); Tobío (1927); Yturbide (1918), and from the archives: A.H.N., V.P. and A.H.P.S.

Nores (1981) suggested that, since local whaling took place in winter and the northern variety in summer, the whalers would move from one place to the other and that would result in economic gain. However, this was not certainly the case, since the vessels of the northern expeditions were back in their port of origin in December or even January and sailed again in April of the following year (Barkham, 1979), thus leaving little time for local whaling, which began as early as October. In addition the operations in the areas were different and, for example, large galleons would be useless in the local operations in the Bay of Biscay. Finally, the private capital invested in the northern expeditions was independent of the cooperatively developed operations of the Basque country (Barkham, 1981).

Some catch statistics from three whaling settlements from the 16th to the 18th century are known (Aguilar, 1981) and they show a decline over the years (Fig. 3). However, it is impossible to determine what the catch rates were in preceding years. One of the series (that of Lequeitio) begins in the year 1517, when it seems that whaling had attained its greatest significance and the number of whales taken was roughly two for every three years. According to Madoz (1811), 55 whales were caught off Zarauz from 1637 to 1801, which gives a catch rate

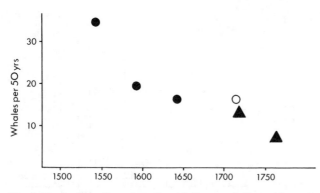

Fig. 3. Catch results from three Spanish Basque whaling settlements, expressed as number of whales taken per 50 years period. For references, see text. ● Zarauz, ▲ Lequeitio, ○ Guetaria.

of one whale for every three years. Fernandez Duro (1881) speaks of 4 to 10 whales in one year but it is not clear if he refers to the catch of the most successful seasons or to an average over many seasons.

It has been repeatedly said (Gonzalez Echegaray, 1978; Ciriquiain, 1979) that these catch levels must be very low in comparison with those of the preceding centuries but no evidence at all substantiates this assertion. In fact, we completely lack serial catch records prior to the 16th century and thus, no conclusion can be drawn. Nevertheless, it is feasible that the given catch is fairly representative of what the operations were like before the decline, which clearly started in the 17th century. It should be kept in mind that whales were killed essentially on an opportunistic basis (they had to approach the shore close enough to be spotted with the naked eye) and that, with the exception of the watchmen in the lookout towers, no other people were receiving a salary while there were no catches (VP 1685). Thus the economic investment was small and the profits from one single whale were enormous, since their value was very high in those days (Tuck and Grenier, 1982).

In this way, a catch rate per port of around one whale for every one or two years seems reasonable and might keep the fishery profitable. A more difficult question, however, is to estimate the size of the catch along the whole coast in a given year. Up to now, 47 whaling settlements have been identified in the Bay of Biscay but this does not mean that all of them worked at the same period of time. It is well known, for example, that some towns only hunted whales for a short period but the lack of detailed information on this precludes determination of the total catch number. Furthermore, it is also certain that small galleons whaled – especially in Galicia – without a land settlement, and no details at all exist of such operations (Ciriquiain, 1979).

From this it seems that the total catch per year would not much exceed some dozens, possibly reaching one hundred or thereabouts. It is not my intention here to arrive at a value but to suggest that the catches were not of the order of hundreds or thousands per year as has often been reported.

Whether such a catch rate was enough to severely reduce the stock is unclear, but two factors must be considered. Firstly, whaling was carried out from many other points in the North Atlantic, and E. glacialis was the primary target in most of them. The stock identity of

this species in the North Atlantic is unknown (Reeves, Mead and Katona, 1978) and either a large extended population was harvested from many areas or a small discrete stock inhabited the Bay of Biscay and was therefore more susceptible to being over-exploited.

Secondly, the catching method of the Basques was particularly harmful for population maintenance, since the chase was mostly directed at calves, which were more easily taken and which the whalers knew would result in the mother coming to its aid so that she too could be killed. Consequently, the harpooner who first hit the calf had a proportionately higher share in the profits (Ciriquiain, 1979). This practice was also used by Spanish whalers in South America (Sañez Reguart, 1971) and in the California gray whale fishery with serious results for the populations (Harmer, 1928), and its effects would be emphasised because cow/calf pairs of E. glacialis show a preference for inshore waters (Kraus, Prescott, Turnbull and Reeves, 1982). According to the available catch statistics from Guetaria and Lequeitio (Aguilar, 1981), from a total of 86 whales killed, up to 22% were calves. Of course, the slaughter of such a high proportion of calves and in particular the associated adult females, would have detrimental consequences for this species which may have a lower birth rate than other baleen whales (Lockyer, 1984).

As Fig. 2 suggests, the industry probably began to decline in the Spanish Basque country as early as the end of the 16th century. Thereafter, an increase in whaling operations seems to have occurred in the neighbouring waters of Santander, Asturias and Galicia in which a clear rise in documentation occurs in the first half of the 17th century. Basques played an important role in these operations and seasonally hired the land factories, especially in Galicia (AHPS 1592; 1609; Meijide, 1971). It seem probable that by this period the local population of E. glacialis was already severely affected and the change of whaling grounds produced a temporary increase in the catch. Moreover, this also coincides with the Newfoundland whaling decline, and it is likely that some of the unemployed material and crews was divided between this and the northeastern operations.

French vessels also tried to whale in these waters but they were soon faced with strict regulations which prevented them from catching cetaceans or selling their products in Spanish towns (MN 1531; 1619; VP 1531, among others).

However this revival was short-lived and a general decline runs through the latter half of the 17th century. Many experienced whalers chose, despite the restrictions endorsed by the Spanish Crown, to crew in boats flying an alien flag, and it is likely that this strengthened the local whaling decline (VP 1690, 1717). The war gave the 'coup de grâce' to the activity, and whaling ceased in all areas around the 1720s (Fernandez Duro, 1881; Meijide, 1971; Nores, 1981) except in the Spanish Basque country, where it barely survived. In the 19th century only four whales (Rios Rial, 1890; Soraluce, 1878; Cabrera, 1914) were caught and, since then, only a few sightings of E. glacialis in the Bay of Biscay area have occurred (Slijper, van Utrecht and Naaktgeboren, 1964; Aguilar, 1981), which denotes the negligible size of the eastern North Atlantic population (if it still exists).

The Newfoundland and Labrador expeditions

It is difficult to know in which year the Basques first arrived in North American waters. Van Beneden (1878) gave priority of the re-discovery of Newfoundland to the Basques in the year 1372, which seems to be rather dubious, although substantiated by several existing documents. Other sources indicate that the Basques were present there at the end of the 15th century (Teran, 1949). However, this opinion has been widely debated and full-scale fishing operations certainly did not begin in the Newfoundland area at least until the 1530s (Fernandez Duro, 1881; Ciriquiain, 1979). From this decade onwards, the yearly trips of whaling vessels from the northern Spanish ports rapidly increased and were maintained for a considerable period, although the Royal recognition of a stable fishery in Newfoundland arrived somewhat later (VP 1557).

Barkham (1979) and Tuck and Grenier (1982) have given good descriptions of how whaling operations were carried out in the Canadian grounds. They seem to have been somewhat different from those in the Spanish coastal fishery. Nevertheless, some basic features of the catch would be similar and it seems likely that calves, for example, would have been the primary target of the harpooners, although Cumbaa (1986) found few juvenile bones in the area.

According to the contemporary maps available, the whale fishery was mainly located in the Strait of Belle Isle, where the Basques arrived every spring in large galleons. Flensing of the whale, extraction of its baleen plates and trying out of oil was done on land and the vessels only served as floating stores for keeping whaling materials and the produce of the catch. For this reason, galleons remained anchored in the harbour, and spotting of whales was directly conducted from the small launches, which also carried out the catch (Barkham, 1977b; 1979).

Therefore the target species would have to be those with a coastal distribution, capable of being taken by the available technology. Two species, the North Atlantic right and the bowhead whale, would fit these conditions well, and extensive discussion about which was the main species has occurred. Since the different populations of both species in the North Atlantic had already been depleted by the beginning of this century, it is impossible to ascertain the former ranges of distribution of the unexploited stocks and, furthermore, the relatively late clarification of the taxonomy of balaenids confuses interpretation of most of the papers about this subject produced during the last century. It is interesting to point out that several researchers (Eschricht and Reinhardt, 1866; Fischer, 1871; Allen, 1908) were aware of the fact that two different species had been distinguished by the Basque whalers fishing in the Canadian grounds. One had shorter baleen plates and the other had longer ones, which almost certainly corresponded to *E. glacialis* and *B. mysticetus*.

The pagophilic habits of the bowhead whale and the well known presence of the North Atlantic right whale in the neighbouring Bay of Fundy and Nova Scotia waters (Reeves *et al.*, 1978; Kraus *et al.*, 1982) have led, however, to the general assumption that only this latter whale inhabited the Labrador and Newfoundland area when the Basques established their industries. Nevertheless, some bone remains discovered in an ancient whaling settlement in the Strait of Belle Isle were classified as belonging both to bowhead and North Atlantic right whales (Cumbaa, 1986). This finding suggests that the ranges of both species probably overlapped in the ancient whaling grounds and were consequently available to the Basques. This is a still unresolved question but the descriptions of shape and size of the baleen plates seem to indicate that *E. glacialis* predominated within the catches (Eschricht and Reinhardt, 1866).

The whaling season usually lasted from June to November or December (Teran, 1949) which agrees well with the migration pattern of the North Atlantic right whale in the area (Kraus *et al.*, 1982).

Unfortunately, no catch records from the Newfoundland operations are available and it is difficult to evaluate the number of whales caught by this fishery. Some estimates can be made, however, from the number of galleons involved, and their hypothetical hold capacities.

Thus, the usual yield from a single whale was between 70 and 140 barrels of fat (Martinez de Isasti, 1625). Each barrel weighed about 250 kg and contained 180 l of oil, and their size and capacity were rigorously controlled in order to avoid fraud (Ciriquiain, 1979). Allen (1908) gathered contemporary information about the right whales of "Greenland" (Spitzbergen), and estimated the oil production per whale as 80 to 100 hogsheads. Taking into account that such a measure is the equivalent of 140 l, the total yield is quite similar to that given by Martinez de Isasti.

A number of contemporary documents show that whaling galleons usually had a tonnage of between 200 and 700 tons and enough capacity for 600 to 1,500 Spanish barrels (VP 1643; Barkham, 1977b, 1979; Ciriquiain, 1979, among others). Taking as an average value a yield per whale of 85 barrels and a capacity per vessel of 1,000 barrels, the mean catch per boat per season would be around 12 whales, without considering the unknown number of struck but lost whales.

Another estimate has been made possible through a manuscript (VP 1584) which detailed the produce from a whaling season of one small galleon, which carried back to Spain 2,700 baleen plates, a figure which would correspond to 10 right whales.

These catch numbers may seem very low, but we must bear in mind two points. Firstly, flensing, boiling and storing operations of the produce from one whale might mean many days of work for such non-mechanised primitive whalers, and occupy all the crew of the expedition, even those usually in charge of the small launches used for hunting whales. Secondly, a fair portion of the time had to be spent building and repairing the houses and stores, the barrels and all the whaling material which, according to Tuck and Grenier (1982) was made, at least in part, in Newfoundland. Furthermore, Novo Colson (1880) says that a whaling expedition to the Greenland coast in 1611 'packed their vessel with more than 12 whales', and it seems that such catch results were so good that they impelled further trips to the same area in the following years. Another reference says that the boats 'were carrying oil corresponding to seven whales' (Ciriquiain, 1979).

The number of boats travelling to Newfoundland varied from year to year, being influenced not only by the economic means of the ship owners, but also by the military necessities of the Spanish Crown, which often confiscated vessels or forced sailors to sign on according to its needs (VP 1642; 1645; Meijide, 1971; among others). However, a figure between 20 and 30 whaling galleons working every season in Newfoundland seems fairly accurate (VP 1643; Eschricht and Reinhardt, 1866; Barkham, 1977b; Ciriquiain, 1979). This number would refer both to the Spanish and French Basques, since it seems that they worked cooperatively when pursuing whales on these grounds. During the 16th century, French vessels were usually of a considerably lower tonnage than those from Spain, and most were not fit for whaling and had to engage in cod fishing (Barkham, 1979). The few French galleons, moreover, had to winter in the shelter of the much better provided Spanish harbours and thus, they are already included in the shipping accounts (Soraluce, 1878). Thome Cano (1611) said that there were more than 200 vessels whaling in Newfoundland and such a figure has been repeatedly cited by several later authors although it was an evident exaggeration.

From the above, annual catches of mainly right whales in the Canadian grounds were probably of the order of 300 to 500 individuals per season, without considering struck but lost whales.

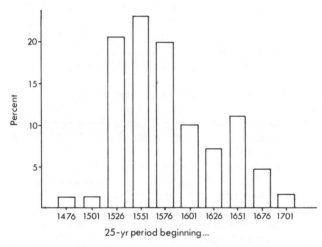

Fig. 4. Percentage distribution of selected written references regarding whaling operations in Newfoundland and Labrador. See comments in the text. Material from: Barkham (1977b, 1979); Castañón (1964); Ciriquiain (1979); Gonzalez Echegaray (1978); Graells (1870); Guiard (1913) and Terán (1949), and from the archives: A.P.G., A.H.P.S. and V.P.

A similar approach (Fig. 4) to that used for Spanish coastal whaling shows that numbers of selected documents decreased sharply after 1601, having been spread fairly uniformly for the previous 80 years. A decline in the fishery was evident, and was referred to in many of the later documents along with requests for help from the Crown to reduce the economic losses (VP 1639; 1643; among others).

Barkham (1979) suggested the decade of 1620 as the possible date when Basque whaling ceased in the Canadian grounds but it certainly went on for many years more although with lesser intensity. There is evidence, for example, that in 1681 twelve whaling galleons were still travelling to Newfoundland from the port of Pasajes alone (VP 1681b) and many documents speak of a continuing industry (VP 1657; 1658; 1681a, b; among others).

The reasons for such a decline have been the subject of much speculation but the confiscations and high level of taxes imposed by the Spanish authorities have been considered as being the main reason for it (Barkham, 1981). Thus, documents asking for a relaxation of the laws for the galleons and the companies involved in the Newfoundland, Norway, Greenland and Spitzbergen fisheries are abundant (VP 1642; 1645; among others).

Nevertheless, several sources indicate that this was not the only reason in the case of Newfoundland and that, already in 1609, 1612 and 1613, references exist which show that whales began to be scarce in the area and the whalers had to go northwards to new grounds (VP UD1, UD2; Castañón, 1964). Probably the Basques had to move from their former settlements in the Belle Isle Strait to the Gulf of St. Lawrence, where they would find an unfished local stock of E. glacialis or, perhaps, the southern limits of the unexploited bowhead whale population, as has been stated above.

In those times, whaling in the area was carried out solely by the Basques and thus an approximate cumulative catch for the period 1530 to 1610 would be between 25,000 to 40,000 whales including an unknown proportion of bowhead whales. This, in addition to the fact that density dependence mechanisms would probably have operated over at least part of such a long period, means that no conclusions with respect to initial population size can be easily drawn.

It is currently impossible to ascertain catch levels after 1610, because many factors combine to veil the question. Firstly, the increasing problems of Basque ship owners, secondly the decrease of whale availability in the traditional whaling grounds, and thirdly the transformation of the almost purely Basque operation into an international fishery with a variety of interests and keen competition.

The same reasons progressively impelled the Basques to try their hand in other whaling grounds but it seems that the real end was in 1697, when they were prevented from continuing the fishery (VP 1728; 1748a) while the Treaty of Utrecht in 1713 finally expelled them from Newfoundland and the Gulf of St. Lawrence (Ciriquiain, 1979). Royal threats similar to those in the local Spanish fishery were made to the Basques joining foreign whaling vessels for Newfoundland (VP 1690; 1729; 1731; among others) but they were in vain and, although attempts to start whaling again in North American waters were made by several individuals and institutions, they were unsuccessful and the already dying industry had to centre on the northeastern grounds (VP 1620; 1697; 1698; among others).

Basque whaling in the Northeastern Atlantic

From very early times, the Basques carried out several different types of fisheries – whaling among them – in the waters of Southern Ireland and the English Channel. Seasonal trips took place at least from the 14th century (Teran, 1949) and especially during the 16th century when these waters were very familiar to the sailors due to the commercial routes with Flanders.

Later on, operations moved further north and, according to Guiard (1913) and Vaucaire (1941), Basque whalers arrived in Iceland as early as 1412. From the end of the 16th century, the presence of Spanish whalers off the coast of Norway and Spitzbergen was also documented and, in 1613, they arrived off the northern-most coast of Greenland (Fernandez Duro, 1881; VP 1613; Ciriquiain, 1979). According to Harmer (1928),

Fig. 5. Old whaling in the Bay of Biscay. From a picture in the coat of arms of Lequeitio (Graells, 1870).

bowhead whaling in the neighbourhood of Spitzbergen, Jan Mayen and the east coast of Greenland began in 1611; the Basques were thus involved in it from the outset.

Nevertheless, contrary to the Newfoundland fishery of the 16th and 17th centuries, Spanish participation in the eastern North Atlantic whaling was negligible. Normans, Flemings, Danes and Norwegians probably caried out whaling in their home waters (De Smet, 1981) and ships flying the Spanish colours were only a fraction of those in the whaling grounds of Spitzbergen and Greenland (Fischer, 1881; Harmer, 1928).

Documents substantiating a Basque whale fishery in the northern seas appear from time to time throughout the 17th and 18th centuries (Gonzalez Echegaray, 1978; Ciriquiain, 1979), especially when difficulties of access to the Canadian grounds became greater. But the Basque maritime economy had been severely damaged by the Crown's policy of ship embargoes and levies of men (Barkham, 1977b) and the experienced north Spanish whalers had joined the crews of many foreign whaling expeditions. Restrictive regulations forbidding such contracts had been produced by the Spanish authorities in the past, both for the local and the Newfoundland fishery, but they took on special relevance when applied to the northeastern operations, including threatening the law-breakers with death (VP 1614b, 1615).

Thus, whaling in this part of the Atlantic, although often carried on by Basque crews, had an international character usually dominated by British, Dutch and Danish capital. Written material from these activities is

therefore scarce in the Spanish archives and many uncertainties exist about the operational patterns of the Spanish participation in this fishery, which lasted at least from the beginning of the 17th until the middle of the 18th century (VP 1614a).

Several findings of bones in old whaling settlements and some modern captures support the idea that *E. glacialis* also represented the bulk of the captures in Iceland and Norway (Guldberg, 1884; Buchet, 1895; Collett, 1909) although it would have been replaced in the northernmost grounds, especially in northern Greenland and Spitzbergen, by *B. mysticetus* (Eschricht and Reinhardt, 1866). The possibility exists that the gray whale was also caught in the former period of exploitation.

The Spanish registered boats involved in this fishery were of a smaller tonnage than those taking part in the Newfoundland expeditions and the catch per boat was somewhat lower, since the vessels used had reduced capacity due to their smaller overall length and because try works for rendering blubber were installed on board, in order to avoid the payment of taxes imposed by the sovereigns of northern lands (Rabot, 1928).

Under such conditions, the number of whales taken during each trip seems to have been about seven (Ciriquiain, 1979). Scoresby (1820) detailed the catch results of several expeditions to Spitzbergen, and he gives more successful results (between 7 and 44 whales per boat), but he refers to vessels of other nationalities, working in the later 18th and 19th centuries, which were larger ships with a different pattern of operation.

The number of vessels employed fluctuated greatly depending on the state of the fickle relations of the Spanish Crown with the rest of Europe. Probably no more than 30 to 40 boats sailed from Spain to the northern seas each year and, according to Vaucaire (1941) only 24 of 355 whaling vessels operating in these waters in 1721 were Basque.

The overall northern whale fisheries began to decline as early as the second half of the 17th century, and whaling companies slowly moved to the Pacific and southern seas (Harmer, 1928). Several attempts to restore Spanish whaling were carried out, but they were unsuccessful and such activity soon vanished.

Spanish whaling in the 18th century

At the beginning of the 18th century, prospects for Spanish whalers were very poor. Local whaling in the Bay of Biscay had already collapsed, the northern grounds were inaccessible because of political disputes, and the various attempts to reactivate such a fishery in the preceding century had failed (VP 1620; 1697; 1698, among others). In addition, it seems that the occasional whaling expeditions to other grounds such as the Brazil coast were unsuccessful and, therefore, no longer attempted (AHPS 1602).

The Basque maritime economy had been seriously weakened, and it was only with substantial financial support by the Crown that an attempt to create a whaling company was undertaken. In 1728 the so-called 'Real Compañía Mercantil de Ballenas de San Sebastian' was established but, although the support of the Crown was strengthened again in 1734 (VP 1751), it seems that whaling was never really begun, and different opinions exist about the fate of its vessels (AHN 1781a, b, c; Gonzalez Echegaray, 1978).

Another enterprise was later created, which sent a boat to the northern grounds in 1753, but the profits were poor and political reasons forced them to give up the activity the following year (AHN 1781a, b, c; Sañez Reguart, 1791).

From 1778 to 1799 several attempts to set up a whaling industry in the Canary Islands were carried out (Gonzalez Echegaray, 1978) but, again, the effort was unsuccessful and just a few whales were caught with a high economic outlay. The target species of this fishery is unknown but since several reports mention whales of 60 feet in length, it is likely that they were fin or sperm whales.

Several surveys made by Sañez Reguart with respect to the abundance of whales and the possibilities of a reintroduction of whaling in Spain (MN 1789a, b), convinced the Crown that it should participate again in a new enterprise, the 'Real Compañía Marítima' which was created in 1789 and which carried out its first campaign at the end of the same year. For eight seasons, several vessels of this company harvested sea lions and whales – probably southern right whales – in South American waters, having its main base at the mouth of La Plata river. A full description of how, where and when this fishery operated, is given by Sañez Reguart (1791) who personally headed the Company. Despite high investment and official support, the expeditions finally became too expensive, whales too difficult to pursue and whaling had to cease.

ACKNOWLEDGEMENTS

Thanks are given to M. Olmos and C. Sanpera for their assistance. Partial support for this research has been provided by the Fisheries Subsecretariat of Spain.

REFERENCES

Aguilar, A. 1981. The black right whale, *Eubalaena glacialis*, in the Cantabrian Sea. *Rep. int. Whal. Commn* 31: 457–459.

Aguirre, L. de 1952. España vuelve por sus fueros balleneros. *Inf. Com. Española, Rev.* 1–2: 336–342.

Allen, J. A. 1908. The North Atlantic right whale and its near allies. *Bull. Amer. Mus. Nat. Hist.* 24 (18): 277–329.

Archivo Historico Nacional. 1781a. Estado, Mansc. by Sañez Reguart, Leg. 3012.

Archivo Histórico Nacional. 1781b. Estado, Mansc. by Sañez Reguart, Leg. 3124.

Archivo Histórico Nacional. 1781c. Estado, Mansc. by Sañez Reguart, Leg. 3218.

Archivo Histórico Provincial Santander. 1554. Sec. Protocolos de Castro, Leg. 1706, fol. 211.

Archivo Histórico Provincial Santander. 1587. Sec. Protocolos de Castro, Leg. 1697, fol. 69.

Archivo Histórico Provincial Santander. 1592. Sec. Protocolos de Castro, Leg. 1700, fol. 20.

Archivo Histórico Provincial Santander. 1596. Sec. Protocolos de Castro, Leg. 1700, fol. 41.

Archivo Histórico Provincial Santander. 1602. Sec. Protocolos de Castro, Leg. 1702, fol. 81–2.

Archivo Histórico Provincial Santander. 1607. Sec. Protocolos de Castro, Leg. 1704, fol. 85–6.

Archivo Histórico Provincial Santander. 1609. Sec. Protocolos de Castro, Leg. 1705, fol. 49.

Archivo Histórico Provincial Santander. 1640. Sec. Protocolos de Castro, Leg. 1730, fol. 117.

Archivo Protocolos Guipúzcoa. 1616. Partido San Sebastián, Doc. 463. fol. 59.

Barkham, S. H. 1977a. First will and testament on the Labrador coast. *Geog. Mag.* 49 (9): 574–581.

Barkham, S. H. 1977b. Guipuzcoan shipping in 1571, with particular reference to the decline of the transatlantic fishing industry. *Anglo-American Contr. to Basque Studies: Essays in Honour of Jon Bilbao*, Reno: 73–81.

Barkham, S. H. 1979. Los balleneros vascos en Canadá, entre Cartier y Champlain (siglo XVI). *Bol. R. Soc. Bascongada Amigos del País* 35 (1–2): 3–24.

Barkham, S. H. 1981. Burgos insurance for Basque ships: maritime policies from Spain, 1547–1592. *Archivaria* 11: 87–109.

Beneden, P. J. van. 1878. Un mot sur la pêche de la baleine et les premiéres expeditions arctiques. In Graells (1889).

Brown, S. G. 1986. Twentieth century records of right whales (*Eubalaena glacialis*) in the northeast Atlantic Ocean. (Published in this volume).

Buchet, G. 1895. De la baleine des Basques dans les eaux islandaises et de l'aspect des grands cétacés a la mer. *Mém. Soc. Zool. France* 8: 229–231.

Cabrera, A. 1914. Fauna Ibérica, Mamíferos. *Mus. Nac. Cienc. Nat.*, Madrid, 441 pp.

Canga Argüelles, F. 1841. *La Pesca de la ballena en las costas de Asturias y sus inmediatas.* Bib. R. Acad. Hist. Madrid, mansc. E-143: 137–141.

Casariego, J. E. 1959. La antigua caza de la ballena. *Nautilus* 162: 222–228.

Castañón, L. 1964. Notas sobre la pesca de la ballena en relación con Asturias. *Bol. Inst. Est. Asturianos*: 1–26.

Cavanilles, A. 1858. *Lequeitio en 1857.* Madrid. Chpt. 8: 93–103.

Ciriquiain, M. 1979. *Los Vascos en la pesca de la ballena.* Ed. Vascas Argitaletxea, San Sebastián, 354 pp.

Clarke, R. 1981. Whales and dolphins of the Azores and their exploitation. *Rep. int. Whal. Commn.* 31: 607–615.

Collett, R. 1909. A few notes on the whale *Balaena glacialis* and its capture in recent years in the North Atlantic by Norwegian whalers. *Proc. Zool. Soc. Lond.* 7: 91–98.

Cornide, J. de. 1785. *Descripción circunstanciada de la costa de Galicia, noticia de la pesca que se hace en sus puertos y de los barcos y aparejos de sus matriculados.* Bib. R. Acad. Hist. Madrid, mansc. E-103: 189–216.

Cumbaa, S. L. 1986. Archaeological evidence of the 16th century Basque right whale fishery at Red Bay, Labrador. (Published in this volume)

Darracq, V. 1859. Réponse aux diverses questions posées par M. Eschricht de Copenhague, relatives à l'ancienne pêche de la baleine dans le Golfe de Gascogne, ainsi qu'à la présence des marsouins dans ce même Golfe. *Act. Soc. Linn. Bordeaux* 22: 432–434.

De Smet, W. M. A. 1981. Evidence of whaling in the North Sea and English Channel during the Middle Ages. *FAO Fish. Ser.* 5 (3): 301–309.

Deinse, A. B. van and Junge, G. C. A. 1937. Recent and older finds of the California gray whale in the Atlantic. *Temminckia* 2: 161–188.

Duguy, R. 1972. Quelques remarques sur les cétacés du Golfe de Gascogne. 97ème Congrés National des Societés Savantes, Nantes, 8 pp.

Eschricht, D. F. and Reinhardt, J. 1866. On the Greenland right-whale (*Balaena mysticetus*). pp. 121–50 In: W. H. Flower (ed.) *Recent Memoirs on the Cetacea*, The Ray Society, London, 312 pp. + 5 pls.

Fernández Duro, C. 1881. *Disquisiciones Naúticas.* Vol. 4. Madrid.

Fischer, M. P. 1871. Documents pour servir a l'histoire de la baleine des Basques (*Balaena biscayensis*). *Ann. Sci. Nat.* 5e. Sér. 15 (3): 1–20.

Fischer, M. P. 1881. Cétacés du Sud-ouest de la France. *Actes Soc. Linn. Bordeaux*: 5–220.

Gasco, F. 1878. In torno alla balena presa in Taranto nel Febbraio 1877. *Atti. Roy. Accad. Sci., Napoli* 7 (16): 1–47.

González Echegaray, R. 1978. *Balleneros Cántabros.* Institución Cultural de Cantabria, Santander, 290 pp.

Graells, M. P. 1870. *Exploración científica de las costas del departamento marítimo del Ferrol*, Madrid: 275–294.

Graells, M. P. 1889. Las ballenas en nuestras costas oceánicas. *Mem. Real Acad. Cien. Exact. Fis. Nat. Madrid* 13 (3): 115 pp.

Guiard, T. 1913. *Historia del Consulado y Casa de Contratación de la villa de Bilbao.* Facs. La Gran Enciclopedia Vasca, 1972, vol. 1.

Guldberg, G. A. 1884. Sur la présence, aux temps anciens et modernes, de la Baleine de Biscaye (ou Nordcaper) sur les côtes de Norwege. *Bull. Acad. Roy. Belgique*, ser. 3, 7 (4): 374–402.

Harmer, S. F. 1928. The history of Whaling. *Proc. Linn. Soc., Lond.* Session 140: 51–95.

Jouan, H. 1891. Aparition des cétacés sur les côtes de France. *Bull. Soc. Linn. Normandie* 5: 137–165.

Kraus, S. D., Prescott, J. H., Turnbull, P. V. and Reeves, R. R. 1982. Preliminary notes on the occurrence of the North Atlantic right whale, *Eubalaena glacialis*, in the Bay of Fundy. *Rep. int. Whal. Commn* 32: 407–411.

Lefèbvre, T. 1933. *Les modes de vie dans les Pyrenées atlantiques orientales.* Paris, In Terán (1949).

Lence Santar, E. 1950. La pesca de las ballenas en la costa de la antigua provincia de Mondoñedo. *Bol. Comis. Prov. Monum. Hist. Art. Lugo* 4: 100–104.

Lockyer, C. 1984. Review of baleen whale (Mysticeti) reproduction and implications for management. *Rep. int. Whal. Commn* (special issue 6): 27–50.

Madoz, P. 1811. *Diccionario geográfico-estadístico-histórico de España y sus posesiones de ultramar* vol. 16: art. Zarauz.

Markham, C. R. 1881. On the whale-fishery of the Basque provinces of Spain. *Proc. Zool. Soc. Lond.* 63: 969–976.

Martínez de Isasti, Lope de. 1625. *Compendio Historial de Guipuzcoa.* Facs. La Gran Enciclopedia Vasca, 1972.

Meijide, A. 1971. Economía marítima de la Galicia Cantábrica en el siglo XVIII. *Universidad de Valladolid, Estudios y Documentos* 32: 245 pp.

Molina, F. 1549. *Descripción de Galicia.* 3rd. part, included in the document by Cornide (1785).

Museo Naval. 1531. Col. Fernández Duro, Mansc. MS 2106, Doc. 3, fol. 7–8.

Museo Naval. 1619. Patentes, Mansc. 2321, Doc. 29, fol. 55.

Museo Naval. 1789a. Compañía, Mansc. 1817, Doc. 1–4, fol. 2–42.

Museo Naval. 1789b. Miscelánea, Mansc. 1446, Doc. 34, fol. 310–324.

Norés, C. 1981. Las ballenas en las costas asturianas. Paper presented at *Primeras Jornadas Ibéricas sobre Mamíferos Marinos*, Santiago de Compostela, 5pp.

Novo Colsón, P. 1880. *Historia de las Exploraciones Articas.* Madrid, 115 pp.

Rabot, C. 1928. La pêche de la baleine par les basques. *La Nature*, Paris, 404–408.

Reeves, R. R., Mead, J. G. and Katona, S. 1978. The right whale, *Eubalaena glacialis*, in the Western North Atlantic. *Rep. int. Whal. Commn* 28: 303–312.

Rey, A. A. 1912. La pesca de las ballenas en las costas gallegas. *Bol. R. Acad. Gallega* 7 (62): 33–36.

Rios Rial, C. 1890. *La ballena euskara (Balena euskariensis).* San Sebastián, 99 pp.

Sañez Reguart, A. 1791. *Diccionario histórico de los artes de la pesca nacional*, Madrid 3: 330–453.

Schevill, W. E. and Moore, K. E. 1983. Townsend's unmapped North Atlantic right whales (*Eubalaena glacialis*). *Breviora* 476: 1–8.

Scoresby, W. 1820. *An account of the Arctic regions, with a history and description of the northern whale fishery.* Edinburgh 2 vols., Facs. rep., 1969.

Slijper, E. J., Van Utrecht, W. L. and Naaktgeboren, C. 1964. Remarks on the distribution and migration of whales, based on observations from Netherlands ships. *Bijdr. tot Dierk.* 34: 3–93.

Soraluce, N. de. 1878. *Memoria acerca del orígen y curso de las pescas y pesquerías de ballenas y bacalaos así que sobre el descrubrimiento de los bancos e isla de Terranova.* Vitoria, 52 pp.

Teixeira, A. M. A. P. 1979. Marine mammals of the Portuguese coast. *Z. säugetierk.* 44: 221–238.

Terán, M. de. 1949. La *Balaena biscayensis* y los balleneros españoles del mar Cantábrico. *Est. Geog. (C.S.I.C.)* 37: 639–668.

Thomé Cano. 1611. *Arte para fabricar, fortificar y aparejar naos de guerra y merchante.* Sevilla. In González Echegaray (1979).

Thompson, D. W. 1918. On whales landed at the Scottish whaling stations, especially during the years 1908–14. Part 1 The Nordcaper. *Scot. Nat.*: 197–208.

Tobio, L. 1927. Aportazón o estudo da historia da pesca da balea nas costas de Galiza. *Arch. Semin. Est. Gallegos* 1: 89–93.

Tuck, J. A. and Grenier, R. 1982. Establecimiento ballenero vasco del siglo XVI en el Labrador. *Inv. Cien.* 64: 82–91.

Vaucaire, M. 1941. *Histoire de la pêche à la baleine.* Paris, 178 pp.

Vargas Ponce. Unknown date, 1. Vol. 4, Doc. 86, fol. 239–240.

Vargas Ponce. Unknown date, 2. Vol. 4, Doc. 57, fol. 152.

Vargas Ponce. 1531. Vol. 3, Doc. 1, fol. 2–4.

Vargas Ponce. 1557. Vol. 3, Doc. 6, fol. 10–12.

Vargas Ponce. 1584. Vol. 3, Doc. 10, fol. 22–26.

Vargas Ponce. 1613. Vol. 3, Doc. 41, fol. 82.

Vargas Ponce. 1614a. Vol. 3, Doc. 45, fol. 85–90.

Vargas Ponce. 1614b Vol. 3,, Doc. 48, fol. 94.

Vargas Ponce. 1615. Vol. 3, Doc. 49, fol. 95.

Vargas Ponce. 1620. Vol. 3, Doc. 56, fol. 193.

Vargas Ponce. 1639. Vol. 3, Doc. 69, fol. 128.

Vargas Ponce. 1642. Vol. 3, Doc. 71, fol. 130–133.

Vargas Ponce. 1643. Vol. 3, Doc. 72, fol. 134–138.

Vargas Ponce. 1645. Vol. 3, Doc. 74, fol. 141–144.

Vargas Ponce. 1657. Vol. 3, Doc. 79, fol. 157–158 and 160.

Vargas Ponce. 1658. Vol. 3, Doc. 77, fol. 149.

Vargas Ponce. 1681a. Vol. 3, Doc. 90, fol. 186.

Vargas Ponce. 1681b. Vol. 3, Doc. 91, fol. 187–189.

Vargas Ponce. 1685. Vol. 3, Doc. 92, fol. 190–194.

Vargas Ponce. 1690. Vol. 3, Doc. 93, fol. 195–197.

Vargas Ponce. 1697. Vol. 3, Doc. 97, fol. 204.

Vargas Ponce. 1698. Vol. 3, Doc. 100, fol. 207–210.

Vargas Ponce. 1717. Vol. 4, Doc. 138, fol. 392.

Vargas Ponce. 1720. Vol. 3, Doc. 105, fol. 219–222.

Vargas Ponce. 1728. Vol. 3, Doc. 109, fol. 231.

Vargas Ponce. 1729. Vol. 3, Doc. 112, fol. 236–240.

Vargas Ponce. 1731. Vol. 3, Doc. 187, fol. 240–249.

Vargas Ponce. 1748a. Vol. 3, Doc. 117, fol. 249–250.

Vargas Ponce. 1748b. Vol. 3, Doc. 116, fol. 246–247.

Vargas Ponce. 1751. Vol. 3, Doc. 118, fol. 251–252.

Vargas Ponce. 1781. Vol. 3, Doc. 121, fol. 263–268.

Yturbide, P. 1918. La pêche des baleines au Pays Basque du XII au XVIII siécle. *Soc. Bayonnaise d'Etudes Régionales, Bull. Supplém.* 3.

The Long Island, New York, Right Whale Fishery: 1650–1924

RANDALL R. REEVES AND EDWARD MITCHELL

Arctic Biological Station, Ste-Anne-de-Bellevue, Province of Québec, Canada H9X 3R4

ABSTRACT

The Long Island right whale fishery began in about 1650, and the last documented striking of a right whale by local shore whalers was in 1924. Centered at the east end of the island's south shore, the fishery apparently was active continuously between 1650 and 1924, with a probable peak between approximately 1670 and 1725. The highest documented one-year catch during this peak period was estimated from oil production to be 111 whales taken in 1707. We documented a total of about 400 right whales caught off Long Island before 1820, but believe this greatly under-represents the actual catch. Data for years after 1820 are more complete. Peaks in catch and activity (and documented catches) for the last century of the fishery appear to have occurred in 1840–54 (an estimated 56 whales killed) and 1885–89 (an estimated 20 whales killed).

The seasonal Long Island fishery, which usually began in November and ended in April or early May, was mainly for right whales. Principal whaling communities were Southampton, Bridgehampton, East Hampton, Wainscott and Amagansett. Open boats, hand harpoons, and hand lances were used until the late nineteenth century, when shoulder guns and bomb lances (darting guns) were introduced on a limited scale.

Mean oil yield used for converting production statistics is estimated as 36 barrels. A high proportion of the landed catch consisted of females (many of them 'dry-skins') and calves.

Analysis of catch statistics is confounded by several factors. First, documentation is incomplete and our search for data has not been exhaustive. Second, documented catches for most of the period covered by this study were made by shore whalers who only chased whales that were first sighted from land, but catches during the 1840–54 peak include a high proportion of whales caught by vessels cruising alongshore. Thus, effort levels between periods are difficult to compare. Finally, the Long Island fishery was but one of several that exploited right whales in the western North Atlantic before and after 1650. A quantitative assessment of early population size cannot be made until catch histories have been reconstructed for at least some of these other fisheries that exploited the same stock.

INTRODUCTION

An assessment of the North Atlantic right whale's (*Eubalaena glacialis*) present status requires not only a reliable estimate of current population size but also an estimate of 'initial' population size. We have reconstructed catch histories and made conservative estimates of 'initial' size for some other North Atlantic mysticete populations using cumulative catch (Mitchell and Reeves, 1981; 1983). The extensive, protracted nature of right whale exploitation makes the task of fully reconstructing the catch history of this species in the western North Atlantic laborious. As Starbuck (1878, pp.1–2n) pointed out, much of the documentary material required for an exhaustive treatment has been destroyed or lost. For some areas and periods, no records were ever kept. Therefore, even though the scope of this paper is restricted to a comparatively small geographic region, we regard it as a preliminary and incomplete account.

Several knowledgeable authors have reviewed aspects of the New England and Long Island right whale fisheries (e.g. Dudley, 1725; Macy, 1835; Clark, 1887; True, 1904; Allen, 1908; Allen, 1916; Edwards and Rattray, 1932, 1956). Some of these authors also mention shore-based whale fisheries along the US east coast south of Long Island and pelagic whale fisheries to the north and east of New England, especially in the Gulf of St Lawrence and Strait of Belle Isle and on or near certain offshore banks. These fisheries certainly involved right whales, but documentation for them is fragmentary and sporadic. We have recently studied the American pelagic fishery for right whales in the North Atlantic (Reeves and Mitchell, 1986).

Attempts have been made to estimate current population size in the western North Atlantic by direct census in portions of the species' range (Winn, Goodale,

Hyman, Kenney, Price and Scott, 1981; Winn, 1982; Kraus, Prescott, Turnbull and Reeves, 1982), and a review of sightings and strandings has been used to describe limits of present-day range and seasonal distribution (Reeves, Mead and Katona, 1978). It is usually assumed that the total number of right whales is lower now than it was in the early colonial period (but see Schevill, Watkins and Moore, 1986). Although right whales still occur over a large proportion of their known former range, they appear to be rare or absent in some areas of past abundance such as Delaware Bay (Cope, 1865; True, 1904; pp. 24–6; Lipton, 1975, p. 4), the New York Bight (Roueche, 1949; Ulmer, 1961; Connor, 1971; Reeves, 1976) and the Gulf of St Lawrence/Strait of Belle Isle region (True, 1904; Wakeham, Bernard and Riendeau, 1913, p. 223).

It is likely that 'the first organized prosecution of the whale fishery in America [other than by aborigines and Basques] was made along the shores of Long Island' (Starbuck, 1924, p. 350). Also, the last known capture of a right whale off the east coast of the United States, except for a calf killed by a sportfisherman off Pompano, Florida, in 1935 (Moore, 1953), was made in 1918 by the last of the Long Island shore whalers (Edwards and Rattray, 1956, p. 9). We selected the Long Island shore fishery as the subject of this preliminary study because of its continuous, long-term and relatively well-documented character. We hoped that trends in this fishery might serve as an index of stock abundance or aid in estimation of early abundance.

MATERIALS AND METHODS

Available published sources were read and indexed for information on right whales killed off Long Island (Fig. 1). The *Whalemen's Shipping List and Merchants' Transcript* (*WSL*; 1843–1914) was scanned (but not

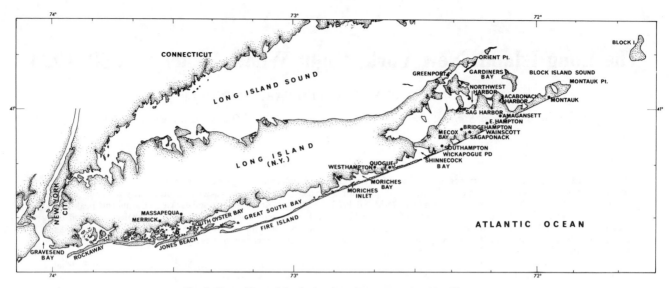

Fig. 1. Map of Long Island, showing place names mentioned in text.

exhaustively read) for North Atlantic right whale and humpback whale (*Megaptera novaeangliae*) data (Mitchell and Reeves, 1983; Reeves and Mitchell, 1986). The partially first-hand account by Edwards and Rattray (1932; 1956), Rattray's (1953) genealogy of East Hampton families and Palmer's (1959) Ph.D. thesis on the history of Long Island whaling gave us leads to relevant primary sources. Starbuck (1878), Allen (1882; 1908), True (1904), and Allen (1916) had searched early literature and some Long Island and Nantucket newspapers and we re-examined many of their sources.

Reeves spent one week on Long Island and in New York City visiting libraries and historical societies to study manuscript materials, published town records and early newspapers including the *New York Times*, *East Hampton Star*, *Glen Cove Gazette*, *Sag Harbor Corrector*, *Sea-Side Times*, *Long Island Farmer*, *Nantucket Inquirer* and *Frothingham's Long-Island Herald*. (Abbreviations for these periodicals, and references to others cited in Table 1, appear in the References section, below.) The bulk of this work was done at the Long Island Collection of the East Hampton Free Library (EHFL), at the library of the Long Island Historical Society (LIHS) in Brooklyn, and at the Nantucket Atheneum Library (NAL) in Nantucket. Most available published material, except newspapers, was adequately covered in our search, but the possibility still exists that important manuscript sources will be found. We are certain that further sampling of local contemporary newspapers is warranted.

A compilation was made of kills, attempted kills and other whaling activity between 1644 and 1924 (Table 1*). A histogram of total estimated fishing mortality for the period 1820–1924, by quinquennia, is given as Fig. 2.

It sometimes was impossible to conclude whether two or more records referred to the same event. We attempted to verify species identifications by reference to descriptive comments, oil yield, and length or weight of baleen; but for many records none of this information was available. Some of our decisions about species identification had to be subjective, but for reasons outlined below under 'Catch Composition', we believe most whales listed in our table were in fact right whales.

* This appears at the end of the paper.

NUMBER of RIGHT WHALES KILLED

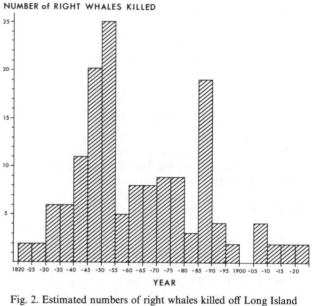

Fig. 2. Estimated numbers of right whales killed off Long Island 1820–1925, by quinquennia.

Oil production statistics were converted to an estimate of whales landed using 36 barrels per whale as an average yield (see 'Oil and Baleen Yields' section). In addition to whales that were killed outright but could not be retrieved, we assumed whales that escaped spouting blood were moribund. Some proportion of the others that escaped after being struck died, even if they were not reported to be spouting blood.

RESULTS

Origins of the fishery

Whaling was a prominent part of early colonial life on eastern Long Island. Even the schoolmaster's salary was paid during the 1670s 'in whale oil, bone [baleen], and sundries' (Rattray, 1953, p. 78). 'Boat whaling was considered of such consequence, that every man of sufficient ability was obliged to take his turn in watching for whales' (Thompson, 1918a, vol. 2, p. 100). The town records for East Hampton and Southampton in particular contain frequent early references to whales and whaling

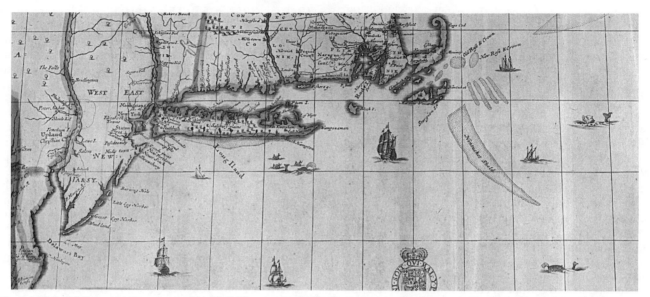

Fig. 3. Detail of 17th century map engraved by W. J. Binneman, published by R. Morden, London, probably between 1670 and 1680. Three boats, presumably launched from shore, are shown chasing a whale off Southampton. (Courtesy of F. B. Lothrop Collection, Peabody Museum of Salem.)

(Gardiner, Baker and Osborne, 1887; Hedges, Pelletreau and Foster, 1874).

The earliest indication that settlers intended to establish a whale fishery on Long Island is the Southampton town ordinance, dated 1644, setting forth rules for disposing of drift whales (Hedges *et al.*, 1874, pp. 31–2; Adams, 1918, pp. 228–9). Some authors (e.g. Howell, 1880; Rattray, 1933, p.17) have interpreted this order to mean that whaling had begun. However, Adams (1918, p. 229) regarded it as no more than an indication that the people took advantage of 'such whales as were by hard luck and the kindness of Providence cast up on the beach'. Exactly when the colonists began the active pursuit of living whales is unclear. However, in January 1650 'the first private whaling company in America' was licensed at Southampton 'to kill whales upon the South sea [i.e. along the south coast of Long Island]' (Hedges *et al.*, 1874, p. 70; Adams, 1918, pp. 229–30). In Table 1 we have listed various published comments concerning whaling activity on Long Island between 1644 and the end of the seventeenth century.

In the inhabitants' view, it took about twenty years to 'bring it [the whale fishery] to any perfection', but by *ca* 1670 the enterprise was well established and apparently profitable (Adams, 1918, p. 231). 'Upon the south side of Long Island, in the winter, lie store of whales and grampuses, *which* the inhabitants begin with small boats to make a trade catching, to their no small *benefit*' (Denton, 1670, quoted in Hubbard, 1815, p. 673). Through the rest of the seventeenth century, whaling continued to be 'an increasing and prosperous enterprise' (Hedges, 1897, p. 66). It was considered second in importance only to agriculture. Fourteen companies of 12 men each are known to have been active at Southampton alone by 1687, with tryworks at Sagaponack, Mecox, Wickapogue, Southampton, Shinnecock Point, Quogue and Ketchaponack (Howell, 1887, pp. 180–1; see Fig. 1 for place names mentioned in text). Adams (1918, pp. 228, 236 facing) reproduced an early sketch of colonial whaling on Long Island; it is dated 'about 1690' (see Fig. 3). In 1690 the trying-out of whales on shore was prohibited 'on account of its offensiveness' (Thompson, 1918a, vol. 2, p. 184).

F. T. Siebert of Old Town, Maine (*in litt.*, 12 June 1985) described for us an account book in his possession which was kept by a Long Island trader during 1686–90. Most of the transactions recorded in the book were made with local Indians and white settlers on south central Long Island. Among the articles traded were rum, shot, powder, cloth, mittens, stockings, tobacco, cider, apples, corn and barrels of whale oil. For example, on 25 April 1688 an exchange was made with Richard Smith for '16 barrels of wal oyl at 30 won shili and 6 pone a barel'.

The town clerk at East Hampton kept records of 'all important agreements – particularly those made with the Indians for killing of whales' (Thompson, 1918a, vol. 2, p. 100). Unfortunately, it appears that no one kept records of whales killed or oil produced during some years. In 1688 the Duke of York tried to determine how many whales had been taken on Long Island during the previous six years, so that he could assess 'his share' (Starbuck, 1878, p. 15). His agent advised him that 'there has been no record kept'. Thus, detailed information on the catch was sometimes concealed from contemporary claimants and, in turn, from whaling historians.

It has proven impossible to determine catch levels for much of the first half-century of Long Island shore whaling (1650–99). There are, however, data for a few years that give some idea of how extensive the activity had become. In 1669, 12–13 whales were taken before the end of March and at least two more were struck but lost (Starbuck, 1878, p. 11). In 1687, Southampton reportedly had 2,148 barrels on hand, 'probably the catch of one season'; East Hampton reported 1,456 barrels on hand as of 15 April 1687 (Howell, 1887, pp. 180–1). Assuming 36 barrels per whale as mean yield , a landed catch of 100 whales was made at the east end this year. In December 1688 the Long Island whalers were said to have had 'pretty good luck', with three large whales taken along the west end and five or six small ones along the east end (Nicholson, 1688, quoted in Starbuck, 1878, p. 15). A statement of July 1699 indicates that 12–13 whales had again been taken at the east end of the island (Anon., 1882, p. 29). At least one whaling company of 24 men was active at East Hampton at the turn of the century (Rattray, 1953, p. 96).

From these data, it appears that catches of eight to 100 whales were made in some years between 1650 and 1699. We estimate the average catch to have been in the order of 25–30 whales per year.

Other seventeenth-century whaling

Two other groups of whalers, in addition to the English settlers, may have caught whales along the coast of Long Island during the seventeenth century. The Dutch West India Company certainly took an interest in whaling near New York City. At least one whale was captured there in March or April 1656 (Starbuck, 1878, p. 11; de Jong, 1978, p. 276). However, most Dutch whaling activity apparently was south of New York, especially in Delaware Bay (True, 1904, pp. 24–6; Lipton, 1975, pp. 3–4; de Jong, 1978, pp. 274–6).

A whaling tradition may have existed among the Montauk and Shinnecock Indians who inhabited the island long before European colonization, but we know of no documentary evidence that they did more than to take advantage of drift whales that came ashore in fresh condition. They roasted the 'fynnes and tayles', offering them to their gods in religious festivals; the 'other parte' of the meat was consumed as a delicacy (Rattray, 1953, p. 175). The 'fynnes and tayles' of drift whales were sometimes legally assigned to the Indians even after white settlement had become well established (Adams, 1918, p. 228). The Indians' whaling equipment allegedly consisted of dugout canoes, 'crude' stone-tipped harpoons, lines of 'Indian hemp' or deerskin thong, and wooden drogues (defined by Ashley [1926, p. 129] as 'a square block of wood fastened to a whaleline and used to check the whale') (Rattray, 1953, p. 64; Palmer, 1959, p. 2; also see Lipton, 1975, p. 11).

According to Rattray (1953, p. 31), the Long Island Indians 'introduced' white settlers to the whale fishery. At first, the colonists did hire all-Indian crews to whale on their behalf (Palmer, 1959, pp. 83 et seq.). For example, in 1668 a crew of six Indians was hired at three shillings a day apiece, 'craft and tackling furnished' (Rattray, 1953, pp. 64, 562; also see Thompson, 1918a, vol. 2, pp. 117–18). In November 1672 it was ordered that:

> Whosoever Shall Hire an Indyan to go a Whaling shall not give him for his Hire above one Trucking Cloath Coat for each Whale, hee and his Company Shall Kill or half the Blubber, without the Whale Bone under a Penalty therein exprest (Fernow, 1883, p. 675).

Presumably, as entrepreneurs became more directly involved in the chasing and killing, the Indian harpooners adopted the Yankee technique of fastening the boat to the whale with the harpoon and line.

The issue of whether or not North American east coast aborigines hunted whales at sea before they had come into contact with Europeans (Dow, 1925, p. 7 and references) remains moot (Little, 1981).

Early eighteenth century whaling

A 'great exodus' from East Hampton to Cape May (New Jersey) occurred ca 1690–1710, apparently in part because whaling 'was very good at the time around Cape May' (Rattray, 1953, p. 65; see Watson, 1855; Lipton, 1975, pp. 4 et seq.). During the early eighteenth century the Long Islanders outfitted small sloops with white and Indian crews, to make expeditions lasting two or three weeks

(Rattray, 1953, p. 66). They cruised 'close inshore along this coast', and whales were brought into Sag Harbor for processing. Eventually, these small sloops 'ranged the ocean at a considerable distance from the coast', but at least until after the War of Independence, which ended in 1783, they continued to bring caught whales to shore for trying out (Thompson, 1918a, vol. 2, p. 177).

Between 1696 and 1718 problems arose due to the British governor's attempts to license whalers and collect a duty on whales caught (Popple, 1713; Mulford in O'Callaghan, 1855, pp. 474–5; O'Callaghan, 1855, pp. 365–8, 518, 503, 498; Adams, 1918, pp. 231–2; Gabriel, 1960, pp.117–18; Rattray, 1933; 1953, p. 129). Previously (from at least 1664), the Crown had claimed a share of the products from drift whales (defined by Mulford as whales 'thrown on shoar') but exempted from any duty whales 'killed at sea by persons who went on that design'. The colonists continued 'chearfully, and with success, to carry on the [whale] fishing trade'. In 1696 the new Governor (Lord Cornbury, now Earl of Clarendon) declared all whales, whether drift or captured, to be 'Royal Fish'. Whaling licenses were required, and a duty of $\frac{1}{14}$ part of the 'Oyle and Bone when cut up' was imposed. Whale products were to be exported only through New York. Mulford, in his petition to the Board of Trade, claimed that the imposition of a duty on whales successfully pursued at sea had made some whalers 'wholly discouraged from fishing' and that the trade in oil and bone 'sensibly declined thereupon'. In his view, England's taxation policy had 'almost intirely destroy'd' the trade in whale products on Long Island.

Governor Hunter (in O'Callaghan, 1855, pp. 498–9) denied these allegations, arguing 'if ye Whale fishing be decay'd it is not for want of numbers of fishers for it is evident they encrease yearly'. He insisted that the wounding and unsuccessful pursuit of some whales had made the rest more difficult to catch. As for a decline in trade, Hunter claimed that the colonists simply had begun shipping their oil and bone clandestinely to Boston instead of New York, thus giving the appearance of a decline where in fact there was none.

At or immediately after the turn of the eighteenth century there may have been a peak in Long Island shore whaling. 'Trayn oil' was a major export to England and the West Indies (Cornbury, 1708, p. 57). The stations in Nassau County (western Long Island) enjoyed 'a brief boom period' at this time (Schmitt, 1972, p. 11). Whaling 'companies' were active at Mecox and Shinnecock (Rattray, 1953, p. 96), and a house was to be built at Montauk in 1704 'for the purpose of whaling' (Rattray, 1953, p. 66). Lord Cornbury (1708, p. 59) reported to the Board of Trade:

> The quantity of Train Oyl made in Long Island is uncertain, some years they have much more fish [sic] than others, for example last year [1707] they made four thousand Barrils of Oyl, and this last Season [1708] they have not made above Six hundred.

Using 36 barrels per whale as average yield, this suggests a landed catch of 111 whales in 1707 and 17 in 1708. When 'but four whales' were taken on Long Island in 1722, a newspaper reported that a 'deficiency of whales is intimated' and 'but little oil is expected from thence' (Watson, 1855, p. 428). Substantial catches are documented for only a few other years in the first half of the eighteenth century: ca 27 whales in 1711 (Anon., 1882, p. 29; Howell, 1887, p. 181; Edwards and Rattray, 1956,

p. 275; Schmitt, 1972, p. 8, 12); 40 in 1721 (Anon., 1882, p. 29); and 11 in 1732/3 (Pelletreau, 1732/33).

An estimate of 20–30 whales taken per year may be reasonable for the period 1700–25; whereas, for the second quarter of the century the average annual catch was probably lower.

1750–1849

By the middle of the eighteenth century, whaling from shore had become less profitable and we have found few catch records for the second half of that century (Table 1). The incentive for making long-distance voyages seems to have increased during this time. In 1760 the sloops *Goodluck*, *Dolphin* and *Success* cruised far offshore in latitude 36° N, between Bermuda and Nantucket Shoals (Thompson, 1839, p. 221; 1918a, vol. 2, p. 177; Adams, 1918, p. 233; Stackpole, 1953, p. 72). A small whaling schooner, the *Eagle*, cruised along the south shore of Long Island in 1784. None of these vessels was equipped with tryworks on board and thus needed to return to shore with the blubber intact. Aboard-ship tryworks may have been used by American whalers as early as the 1740s, certainly by the 1760s (Kugler, 1980, pp. 4–5n). It was not until 1784 that a Long Island whaler went to sea prepared for pelagic processing; this was the *Hope*. Her voyage was a failure, producing only 30 barrels of oil (Cook, 1858).

We are not able to confirm that these early voyages were aimed at right whales rather than sperm whales (*Physeter macrocephalus*). Presumably, the vessels did encounter sperm whales on or *en route* to the grounds. However, a Sag Harbor resident wrote in 1858 that the small sloops sailing from that port between 1760 and 1775 cruised 'in about the latitude of 36 or 37 degrees North, and would generally succeed in taking one or more right whales' (Cook, 1858). His sources for this statement apparently were 'the aged men' of the community. Without examining logbooks of these vessels (the existence of which we have been unable to establish), we cannot be certain about the species caught. However, it would be reasonable to assume that these whalers, like the eighteenth-century Nantucket whalers, were interested in catching either sperm whales or right whales, or both.

Between 1775, when the American War of Independence began, and 1815, when the War of 1812 with Great Britain ended, shore whaling activities on Long Island were interrupted in some degree (Cook, 1858; Thompson, 1918a, vol. 2, pp. 177, 185: Palmer, 1959). We have little information on shore whaling after 1750 and before the 1820s, but there is no doubt that it continued (Table 1). In 1815 'the Hamptons settled down to the successful prosecution of whaling' once again (Rattray, 1953, p. 162). Hubbard (1815, p. 668) referred to the 'notable kind of dexterity' at whaling displayed by the inhabitants of the east end, and the 'beneficial' trade in whale products resulting from their winter fishery. Pelagic whaling drew more and more of the shore whalers on long voyages, and many Hampton men pursued careers in what local people called 'blue-water whaling'. At Southampton 'nearly every other man...is a Whaling captain, and most of those who are not have been a few voyages at sea' (*SHE* 10[43]: 22 April 1869). During periods on shore, these men often participated in whale hunts.

During 1822–23, some whaling by sloops and smacks from New London, Sag Harbor and Providence took place off Sandy Hook (New Jersey). We assume, judging by the season, that they were hunting right whales. Four smacks sailed for Long Island in mid-March 1822 and took at least three whales, one producing 50 barrels, and struck but lost a fourth – all before the end of April (*NI* 2[18]: 2 May 1822). 'We understand a similar enterprise last summer [1821] was very successful' (*NI* 2[13]: 28 March 1822). The whales were said to be abundant a short distance from shore. In mid-February 1823 the sloops *Ocean* of Sag Harbor and *Hampton* of Providence were reportedly chasing 12 whales about 10 miles off Sandy Hook (*NI* 3[10]: 4 March 1823).

We were able to document somewhat less than one whale taken per year on Long Island during the 1820s and 1830s (Table 1; Fig. 2), but we cannot judge whether this represents the actual magnitude of the fishery or merely the incompleteness of our data. Thompson (1839, p. 221) claimed that 'some [whales] are taken by boats...almost every year' at East Hampton and Southampton. There appears to have been either an increase in whaling effort or a higher catch per unit of effort during the 1840s. DeKay (1842, p. 125) wrote: 'Along the southern coast of Long Island, whaleboats are still kept in readiness; and upon the appearance of a whale, the people in the vicinity quickly assemble, and soon are in pursuit of the animal'. Cook (1858) saw five recently captured whales on the Southampton beach some time between 1840 and 1845, and seven were 'lying on the shore at one time' between Southampton and East Hampton in 1847 (Halsey, 1935, p. 107). We were able to document a kill of about 30 whales during the 1840s, an apparent three-fold increase over the catches in each of the previous two decades.

1850–1924

Although the California gold rush at mid-century and the American Civil War during the 1860s may have reduced the availability of whalemen or disrupted their activities, shore whaling continued after 1850. It was reported in 1853 that the Long Island whaling companies had acquired new 'copper-fastened boats' and were 'as well, or better fitted for whaling than they have ever been before' (*WSL* 11[3]: 22 March 1853). Approximately two kills by the shore whalers per year have been documented for the 1850s (Table 1; Fig. 2).

In addition, whaling vessels from Cape Cod, Nantucket and Greenport visited the south coast of Long Island in pursuit of right whales (*WSL* 11[8]: 26 April 1853). The *Union* of Provincetown cruised there for seven weeks in 1853 without success and the *Hamilton* of Nantucket took a 25-barrel right whale off Southampton on 21 April 1853. The *Hamilton* was one of 'three fine schooners' fitted out in 1852 to take advantage of the 'recent close approach of whales to the island [of Nantucket]' (*SHC*: 19 June 1852). Her first cruise apparently began 12 June 1852 (*SHC*: 26 June 1852). Starbuck's (1878, pp. 498–9, 508–9, 518–19) tables do not list the *Hamilton* for 1852 but show a return of 101 barrels of whale oil for five short voyages by the *Hamilton* between 8 April 1853 and 15 September 1853. During three months of cruising in late spring and early summer 1854, the *Hamilton* secured 136 barrels of whale oil. We suspect her catch consisted primarily of humpbacks and right whales.

Two Greenport schooners, the *Armida* and *Amulet* (but not the *Corwin* as stated by Allen, 1916, p. 136), cruised along the south shore of Long Island during February–

April 1853 (*WSL* 11[8]: 26 April 1853). At least three whales were brought back to Greenport for trying out by the *Armida* (*SHC* 31[93]: 20 April 1853). Whaling activity was so intensive during the right whale season that on 11 April 1853 there were 10–15 boats seen chasing, with the two Greenport schooners in sight, off Southampton at the same time (*SHC* 31[91]: 13 April 1853).

During the rest of the nineteenth century, effort appears to have remained relatively stable, although there is no evidence that the aforementioned schooners continued to visit Long Island after the 1850s. The shore whalers took 'a few' whales each winter/spring season through the 1880s (Cook, 1858; Howell, 1887, p. 181; Brisbane, 1885; Table 1), but by *ca* 1890 the documented mean annual catch had declined to less than one whale.

> The whale fisheries formerly furnished subsistance for most of the inhabitants there [on the eastern end of Long Island], and on the decay of that industry they turned their attention to the menhaden [*Brevoortia tyrannus*] and other fisheries (Mather, 1887, p. 344).

We have accounted for only five catches, plus five strikes, at least four of which probably resulted in a kill, by the Long Island whalers after 1900. During the early twentieth century, right whales were taken only 'now and then' off Long Island (*NYT* 56 [17928]: 24 February 1907). Right whales were still sighted occasionally, but no effort at catching them was made after 1924.

The incentive for shore whaling on Long Island was destroyed partly by the lack of demand for baleen. A local newspaper article in 1922 (*EHS* 37[10]: 20 January 1922) indicated that only two concerns willing to handle whalebone remained on the east coast (*contra NYT* 69[22779]: 12 June 1918). 'The driving horse is fast disappearing and with him has gone the demand for whalebone whips'. Also, 'the ladies have decided that they no longer need whalebone stays in corsets and dresses'. Not long before, whalebone supposedly had sold for $11 per pound; now the rate was $0.50 per pound. Although the quote of $11 per pound may have been somewhat exaggerated (Tower, 1907, p. 128, indicated a peak average annual price before 1906 of $5.80 per pound in 1904; Edwards and Rattray, 1956, p. 274, gave $4.50 in 1907 as the peak price of Long Island whalebone), the bottom clearly had fallen out of the market by 1922. The introduction of spring steel in 1907 destroyed the market for bowhead (*Balaena mysticetus*) baleen, causing the price to drop from $5.00 per pound to less than $0.50 per pound in three years (Bockstoce, 1977, p. 52). A million pounds of whalebone were said to be in storage in San Francisco in 1922. The only remaining New York market was for export to France, where the baleen was 'ground up and mixed in order to make artificial things' (*EHS* 37[10]: 20 January 1922).

The price of whale oil had fallen to a 'very low' level by 1907 (Edwards and Rattray, 1956, p. 274). According to Tower (1907, p. 128, table 5), annual average whale oil prices peaked at $1.45 per US gallon in 1865 and had declined to $0.31 per US gallon by 1905. By the time the price of baleen collapsed, whale oil was not valuable enough to make shore whaling worthwhile.

Seasonality and geographic scope of the fishery

The season for whaling on Long Island was strictly proscribed. A serious watch began to be kept in mid-October or November, and there was little activity after April or early May (Cornbury, 1708, pp. 59–60; Adams, 1918, p. 230; our newspaper sample). The main season could best be described as December through April, of 'the cold season' (*NYT* 43 [13323]: 6 May 1894), although right whales 'appeared occasionally at all seasons of the year' (DeKay, 1842, p. 125). Allen (1916, p. 142) considered April to be the peak month for the right whale's appearance off Long Island.

Fishery activity seems to have been determined by availability of whales rather than by social, economic or other factors. For a time even the school term was geared to accommodate the whaling season. The East Hampton schoolmaster's contract in 1675 provided that school be in session 'untill the last of December next and then to break off by reson of the Whale Designe untill the first of Aprill next ensueing' (Rattray, 1953, p. 78). Two whales were taken in June 1872 – 'a notable occurrence, as, almost invariably, whales make their appearance off the coast of Long Island in cold weather' (*NYT* 35 [10742]: 5 February 1886). When a large right whale appeared in 1896 off Amagansett during August – 'nobody would expect a whale along then' – the whalers managed to assemble a crew and chase it (Edwards and Rattray, 1956, p. 61). There are several other records of catches or attempted kills during summer (Table 1).

The whalers considered most of the whales to be on migration as they passed Long Island. 'If they found feed they would stay around a few days; if not, they would continue on' (Edwards and Rattray, 1956, pp. 18–9). Newspaper accounts indicate that whales were seldom seen in a given area for more than several days at a time, and groups of more than three animals were encountered only exceptionally. The appearance of a 'school' of nine within 25 km of shore in January 1885 was explained by the presence along the coast of 'immense quantities' of whale food – 'a minute insect' (*NYT* 34 [10415]: 20 January 1885).

Shore whaling occurred mainly at the east end of Long Island, along the south shore. Occasionally whales were taken in Gardiners Bay (Edwards and Rattray, 1956, p. 251) and near Sag Harbor (Thompson, 1918a, vol. 2, p. 176). Observations inside Long Island Sound were considered unusual (Table 1).

The whales 'do not apparently strike in shore near enough to be seen from the beach more than about thirty-five miles westward from Montauk', i.e. off Shinnecock Bay (Ayres, 1886). From *ca* 1845 to 1886 there were 'whaling stations' at Southampton, Bridgehampton, East Hampton and Amagansett. These sites, along with Wainscott, were clearly the most active during the nineteenth and early twentieth centuries, with Amagansett generally regarded as the 'whaling headquarters of Long Island' (*NYT* 43[13323]: 6 May 1894). It was at Amagansett that 'the whales come nearest to the land; they are sighted first within a few miles of Amagansett' (*Harper's Weekly* 41[2103]: 1897). In earlier years (seventeenth and early eighteenth centuries) there were tryworks at Quogue (Edwards and Rattray, 1956, p. 201) and 'whaling stations' as far west as Jones Beach opposite Merrick and Massapequa, Oyster Bay South, and Rockaway (Schmitt, 1972, p. 4). According to Bailey (1954), 'practically every portion of the south shore from Jamaica to Montauk Point' had a whaling station. One whaling captain reported in 1886 that whales were sometimes seen off Fire Island and Great South Bay (*NYT* 36[11022]: 29 December 1886). As vessels began to

Fig. 4. 'Whaling off Long Island' by W. P. Bodfish. From an article in *Harper's Weekly*, 31 January 1885. (Courtesy of F. B. Lothrop Collection, Peabody Museum of Salem.)

search for whales farther from shore toward the end of the eighteenth century, an area 'a few degrees to the southward and eastward of Montauk Point' became a popular cruising ground (Cook, 1858). We assume right whales were the principal target here as well as alongshore.

Whaling technology

Non-aboriginal shore whaling on Long Island was a conservative enterprise, its methods changing very little between the seventeenth and twentieth centuries. The standard whaleboat was 28 ft long, with oak ribs and cedar planking (Roueche, 1949; Edwards and Rattray, 1956, pp. 55–63; and see Ansel, 1978, pp. 124–5). A crew consisted of six men. The boat header steered the boat to within striking distance of the whale, after which the harpooner struck the animal with one, and if possible a second, harpoon. Once the boat was fast to the whale, the harpooner took over the steering oar and tended the line. The harpoon line was coiled in a tub at midship, then wrapped round a loggerhead in the stern. Lancing was done by the boat header.

The darting gun or bomb lance was not introduced to the fishery until the late nineteenth century (*NYT* 43 [13323]: 6 May 1894). At Amagansett at least, it was never popular (Edwards and Rattray, 1956, pp. 56, 97). The whale killed off Amagansett in 1918 was 'the only one we ever chased under power' (*ibid.*, pp. 161–2). On this occasion, a steamer was used to carry the whaleboats within rowing range. (A right whale was, however, taken in March 1882 between Amagansett and East Hampton by boats lowered from the steamer *Fanny Sprague* – *NYT* 31 [9529]: 23 March 1882.)

All whales in the Long Island right whale fishery were tried out on shore (*NYT* 43 [13323]: 6 May 1894; Figs. 4, 5). Also, most of the whales were sighted from shore before being chased (e.g. *NYT* 35 [10742]: 5 February 1886).

Species composition of the catch

Edwards was quoted as saying (*in* Roueche, 1949): 'The only whale we ever hunted was the right whale.' This statement seems generally consistent with other accounts

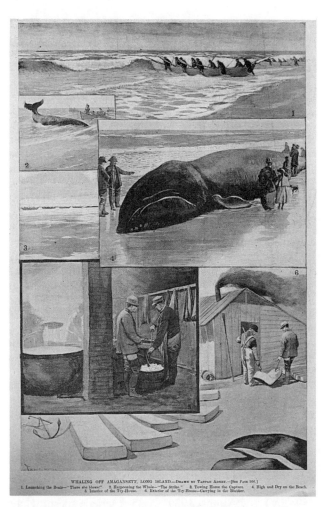

WHALING OFF AMAGANSETT, LONG ISLAND.—Drawn by Tappan Adney.—[See Page 566.]
1. Launching the Boats—"There she blows."   2. Harpooning the Whale—"The Strike."   3. Towing Home the Capture.   4. High and Dry on the Beach.
3. Interior of the Try-House.   6. Exterior of the Try-House—Carrying in the Blubber.

Fig. 5. 'Whaling off Amagansett' by Tappan Adney, from *Harper's Weekly* 41 (2103), 1897. 1. Launching the boats. 2. Harpooning the whale. 3. Towing the whale to shore. 4. High and dry on the beach. 5. Interior of the try-house. 6. Exterior of the try-house – carrying in the blubber. (Courtesy of F. B. Lothrop Collection, Peabody Museum of Salem.)

of the Long Island fishery, in which whalebone (baleen) was considered an important product and in which open-boat, hand-harpoon/lance techniques prevailed. Nineteenth-century newspaper accounts occasionally specify which species of whale was involved; from these it is clear that 'whales' hunted from shore on Long Island were right whales (e.g. *NYT* 43 [13323]: 6 May 1894). Infrequently other species were chased or taken.

Although Edwards himself never tried to catch the fast-swimming finbacks (*Balaenoptera physalus*) that were common along the coast (e.g. *NYT* 57 [18437]: 17 July 1908), his father once fastened to one 'just to see what it was like' (Edwards and Rattray, 1956, pp. 115–16). A Montauk fishing party took a small finback in 1929 and in August 1936 one was shot with an 'elephant gun' and a 'swordfish harpoon' (*EHS*: 6 August 1936). A 'finback' was taken off East Hampton in November 1858 and produced 15 barrels of oil (*NI* 39[94]: 30 November 1858). The Southampton whalers chased 'several fin-back whales' unsuccessfully on 23 January 1860 (*SHC* 38[36]: 28 January 1860) and the East Hampton whalers chased a few in early December 1874 (*SHE* 16[23]: 17 December 1874) and again in early May 1875 (*SHE* 16[44]: 13 May 1875). A 'black fin-back' whale, reportedly 30–40 ft long, was brought ashore in New York harbor in July 1887, but the circumstances surrounding its 'capture' suggest that it died from some other cause than whaling (*NYT* 36[11186]: 8 July 1887).

In early May 1860 the whalers at Southampton chased not only three right whales but a finback and 2–3 'sulphurbottoms' (*WSL* 18[10]: 15 May 1860). The sulphurbottoms (blue whales, *Balaenoptera musculus*) were considered 'a very "limber" fish' and had 'to be approached with extreme caution.' A 'sulphur-bottom' that 'came ashore' at Sagaponack was said to have been 'the only one of its kind ever seen here' (Edwards and Rattray, 1956, p. 114). A photograph of this whale (Edwards and Rattray, 1956, p. 114 facing), however, does not confirm that it was a blue whale, only that it was probably a blue whale or a fin whale.

Humpbacks, which could be captured with nineteenth-century techniques and offered enough oil to be valued by some Yankee whalers (Mitchell and Reeves, 1983), were rarely reported as being seen on the Long Island whaling grounds. A small humpback was taken at Southampton on 12 June 1852 (*SHC*: 16 June 1852) and several were chased along with the right whales on 30 April 1866 off Amagansett (*SHE* 7[44]: 3 May 1866). A humpback was shot with a 'whale-gun' off Amagansett in 1913, but it escaped when the line parted (Edwards and Rattray, 1956, pp. 116–17).

Sperm whales were probably rarely seen from the beach. A 16-ft calf was discovered 'fast on the sand' off East Hampton on 19 March 1891 (*EHS* 6[14]: 20 March 1891). At the time, it was said that this 'variety…[of whale] has not been …seen off this shore in a number of years.' A large sperm whale was caught in Fishers Island Sound in December 1894 and this was considered an unprecedented event (*NYT* 44 [13511]: 11 December 1894; *NYS*: 7 August 1939). A 35-ft female sperm whale stranded at Great South Beach opposite Bellport on 28 February 1918 (*sic*) (*NYT* 69 [22632]: 11 January 1918).

We conclude that nearly all the whales killed off Long Island were right whales. Balaenopterids were struck only casually; while some may have drifted ashore after dying of wounds, most of those that were struck probably were not landed. As Allen (1916, p. 132) argued,

> it may usually be assumed that when 'whales' are mentioned in the old accounts as seen and pursued, the Right Whale is the species intended. Especially is this the case, since Finbacks or Humpbacks are usually so designated.

Oil and baleen yields

Best (1970) used an average yield of 600 lb of baleen per whale to convert production statistics to number of right whales secured in the right whale fishery off South Africa. For the Long Island fishery, available data refer much more often to barrels of oil than to pounds of baleen and thus we sought an average yield of oil rather than of baleen. In 1675 a New York court declared 'The Oyl Cask or Barrels are to Containe 31 gallons and a halfe' (Edwards and Rattray, 1956, pp. 274–5). We assume, therefore, that barrels (bbls) used by Long Island whalers normally contained $31\frac{1}{2}$ US gallons.

Dudley (1725, p. 257) summarized yields expected from right whales of different age-classes taken off New England. A 'year old' calf, called a 'short-head', could produce 50 bbls, but its mother, at this stage called a 'dry-skin', was not likely to produce more than 30 bbls. A 'two-years old' whale, called a 'stunt', would give 24–28 bbls. Whales more than two years old, called 'scull

[school]-fish', could produce 150 bbls of oil and 6- to 7-ft-long baleen weighing 1000 lb.

Cornbury's (1708, p. 60) Long Island estimates differed somewhat from Dudley's New England estimates: 50 bbls for 'yearlings' and 50–60 for 'stunts', with the largest individuals producing 110 bbls of oil and 1200 lb of baleen. The whalers' classification of age-groups, while based on observed differences in size and associations between individuals, was made without a scientific basis.

Lipton (1975, p. 26), based on her examination of manuscript material on shore whaling in New Jersey, gave 20 to 90 bbls as the range in production from right whales killed there. One traveler to Long Beach Island commented in 1823 that a whaler there 'has taken some whales of ninety barrels of oil'. Clearly whales yielding 90 or more barrels were exceptional in the New York Bight.

General statements by commentators like Dudley and Cornbury can be compared to the catch by one Long Island whaling company during 1707 (Smith, n.d.; Thompson, 1918a, Vol. 2, p. 336):

Jan. 16 – one 'suct whale', 28 bbls;
24 – one 'yearling', 27 bbls;
Feb.   4 – one 'stunt', 12 bbls;
22 – one 'yearling', 36 bbls;
24 – one 'Schoule whale', 35 bbls;
Mar. 13 – one 'small Yearling', 30 bbls;
17 – two 'yearling', 14 and 27 bbls.

Although these data may not be representative, they suggest that the yields given by both Dudley and Cornbury are maxima for each class of whale. The mean yield for the eight whales listed above is *ca* 26 bbls.

Palmer (1959, p. 11) used 40 bbls, 'an average figure', as a conversion factor for Long Island right whales. The 76 whales whose oil yields are given individually in Table 1 averaged about 36 bbls. We assume that if there is a bias in this sample, it comes from a tendency to report the yields of unusually large whales more regularly than those of small or medium-sized whales. For example, the yield of the 75-bbl whale killed in January 1885 is mentioned in various accounts, while those of the three other whales taken at this time are not given (see Table 1). Also, in many instances the yield reported is only the whalers' optimistic estimate, made prior to trying out. They sometimes got less oil than the whale's body size had led them to expect. Thus, even 36 bbls is more likely a high estimate than a low estimate of average yield for right whales caught off Long Island. In converting oil production statistics, we used 36 bbls per whale to make what we consider conservative estimates of whales landed.

Using nineteenth-century trying out methods in the South Atlantic fishery, Yankee pelagic whalers expected a 'full grown' male right whale to produce 40–60 bbls of oil and an adult female to produce 60–80 bbls, with an overall average of 69 bbls (Clark, 1887, p. 16). The largest yields from North Atlantic right whales mentioned by Allen (1916, p. 171, and see contained references) range from 100 to 130 bbls. Although True (1884) reported 130 bbls as the (maximum?) yield of North Pacific right whales, Bodfish (1936, p. 95) referred to a North Pacific specimen that yielded 325 bbls. It must be borne in mind that many of the right whales caught off Long Island were calves, juveniles or lactating females. The last of these – adult females accompanied by sucklings – frequently proved to be 'dry-skins', yielding less oil than even their own calves. For example, a large female taken on 15 March 1869 was expected to produce 40 bbls (*SHE* 10[38]: 18 March 1869). However, she proved to be a 'dry-skin' and produced 'only a little over 13' bbls when tried out (*SHE* 10[44]: 29 April 1869).

The whales taken off Long Island in late winter and spring were believed to be on their northward migration. Some other mysticetes are known to fast more or less completely while wintering at low latitudes. If this were true of the right whales passing Long Island, it could mean their lipid reserves were seasonally reduced. Rice and Wolman (1971, p. 35) demonstrated that southward migrating gray whales (*Eschrichtius robustus*) have mean yields of oil and other products two and one-half or three times those of northward migrating gray whales. Thompson's (1918b) sample of 67 right whales killed off Scotland, mainly in June and July, exhibited a bimodality in girth-to-body length ratios, suggesting dramatic seasonal changes in condition, possibly correlated with a more or less rigid migration schedule and life history. We consider it reasonable to suppose that right whales killed during the winter/spring season off Long Island had lower oil yields than those killed at different times of year on certain other grounds in the North Atlantic (see Reeves and Mitchell, 1986).

An interesting by-product of the hunt was jawbones. The mandibles were 'always cleaned off and used to form an arch over some gateway' (*NYT* 43[13323]: 6 May 1894).

Hunting loss

We have insufficient information on which to base an estimate of the loss rate in the Long Island fishery. A loss rate factor of 1.85 (total number killed ÷ number secured) such as was used to estimate total fishing mortality in the American pelagic humpback fishery in the West Indies (Mitchell and Reeves, 1983) is probably too high because right whales more often float after being killed and generally are easier to capture than humpbacks. Starbuck (1878, p. 661 n) and others (*WSL* 36[14]: 21 May 1878) used a loss rate of 20% for right whales (which they attributed to Scammon, 1874) to estimate whales killed in addition to whales secured by American pelagic whalers. Scammon's (1874, p. 251) estimate of loss rate was based on his experience in the North Pacific, and it is not clear that he was referring to balaenids rather than to mysticetes in general. Mitchell (1977 MS) used a loss rate factor of 1.18 for pelagic bowhead fisheries, and Bannister, Taylor and Sutherland (1981) used 1.20–1.61 for the Yankee pelagic sperm whale fishery in the South Pacific. The appropriate figure for Long Island is probably closer to these estimates than to 1.85.

Dead right whales do not invariably float (Allen, 1916, p. 171). A North Pacific whaling captain wrote that whales sink more often on some grounds than on others and that 'right whales sink more than bowheads' (Winegar, 1860; *contra* Brown, 1887, p. 270). He reported that in a season on the Kodiak Ground 28 right whales were killed, of which 11 sank. The ship *Braganza*'s crew secured 29 right whales and killed but lost five more due to sinking during two seasons (1841–42) on the Northwest Coast Ground (*Braganza*, 1840–44, MS). Brown (1887, p. 270) stated that 'It is not unusual for the right whale to sink when killed.' He added that whales which sink in very deep water 'may never come to the surface.' Of 15

right whales killed in Edwards' presence off Long Island, three went 'straight to the bottom'; the rest floated (Edwards and Rattray, 1956, p. 66). The extraordinary effort made by the Long Island whalers to retrieve the carcass of a sunken whale is illustrated in the following (*NYT* 43[13323]: 6 May 1894):

> When the whale sinks, the crew make the line attached to their harpoon fast in the bow of their boat, and then all hands climb aft. This raises the boat's bow out of the water, causing the whale's body to ascend. The men then jump forward and take in the slack in the line, and when it is taut, hurry aft again. This operation is repeated until they get the whale to the surface, when all the boats fasten to it and the return journey is begun.

A whale taken off East Hampton in early March sank 11 km from shore in 20 fathoms: 'The whale's body is buoyed and two boats' crews alternate in watching it' (*NYT* 36[11078]: 4 March 1887).

Whales that sank after being killed off Long Island were not necessarily lost, even when the line parted or the iron drew. Attempts to raise a sunken whale off Amagansett in about 1884 were unsuccessful, but the carcass drifted ashore and was salvaged three days later (Edwards and Rattray, 1956, p. 62).

The frequency with which whales were struck but lost in the Long Island fishery was substantial. In *ca* 1716 Governor Hunter (*in* O'Callaghan, 1855, p. 498) complained about 'the frequent wounding of whales, which not being catched freight away the rest'. A newspaper account of 1875 (*GCG* 18[46]: 20 March 1875) stated that if a whale

> darts off with the boat in tow at such rate as to swamp it, their only resource is to attach a buoy to the line, cut it and let him go. This is frequently done.

Dudley (1725, p. 263), in describing the New England right whale fishery, stated:

> The whale is sometimes killed with a single Stroke, and yet at other Times she will hold the Whale-men in Play, near half a Day together, with their Lances, and sometimes they will get away after they have been lanced and spouted blood, with Irons in them, and Drugs [=drogues; see above] fastened to them....

Edwards took part in about 30 'chases' off Long Island, of which 15 were 'successful' (Roueche, 1949). If whales were struck and lost on even half the unsuccessful chases, the loss rate would be one-third. Assuming full mortality of struck whales, the loss rate factor would be 1·5.

An important aspect of the Long Island fishery was the vigilance that seems to have existed both on- and offshore during the whaling season. An agreement between the whaling companies at Southampton and East Hampton in 1667 called for a generous reward to any person finding 'any dead Whalls upon the shore that eyther Company should have killed' (Gardiner *et al.*, 1887, pp. 271–2). The finder of a carcass at sea was required to notify the company responsible for killing the whale and received half the profits 'for their paynes.' If a 'wounded' whale was encountered and killed, the company securing the carcass was required to return any irons found in it to the owners. Thus, even when whales were killed or wounded but not immediately secured, there was a reasonable prospect of their being recovered later. Mention is made in the newspaper account quoted above (*GCG* 18[46]: 20 March 1875) of a whale harpooned off the Hamptons during winter 1873/4, which swam 20 miles before dying. It was found floating and was towed to the beach by a schooner. A right whale killed off Amagansett on 15

January 1885 sank 'and drifted twenty miles down the coast, and was finally washed ashore off Shinnecock Point' on 17 January (*NYS*: 22 January 1885). Various other newspaper accounts attest to the fact that a portion of struck or killed but lost whales were eventually recovered on the beach or while floating at sea.

In his study of whaling for gray whales in the eastern North Pacific, Henderson (1972, p. 260) concluded that 'losses of mortally wounded whales appear to have been fewer among along-shore whalers in vessels than among shore whalers'. This difference, while of considerable interest, cannot, without further study, be assumed by analogy for the Long Island right whale fishery.

DISCUSSION AND CONCLUSIONS

There is clearly a wealth of material documenting the Long Island right whale fishery. A preliminary search, mainly of published sources, allowed us to account for at least 139–142 whales killed, including those found on shore, killed and lost, or lost spouting blood, between 1650 and 1699: 252 between 1700 and 1749; 63 between 1750 and 1849; and somewhat less than 100 between 1850 and 1924 (Table 1). We believe the peak in whales caught occurred between 1670 and 1725. After this time, whaling continued, but was less rewarding, through 1924. A directed search for additional data on catches off Long Island prior to 1820 would be very time-consuming and probably would yield a fairly low return per unit of effort.

Newspapers read by whalemen were printed as early as the 1820s at such places as New York, Sag Harbor, Greenport, New London and Nantucket, and later at Southampton and East Hampton. They appear to constitute the best single source of precise catch records. Because our search of relevant newspapers for this study was only partial due to time constraints, we feel an extended search would amply repay the effort and expense by augmenting our record of catches between 1820 and 1924.

The lack of adequate documentation of catches for series of years prior to 1820 means that trends in population size (i.e. whale availability) cannot be reliably postulated. For years after 1820, the apparent peak in catch during 1840–54 (Fig. 2) is at least partly attributable to the activities of vessel whalers cruising along the coast of Long Island. Analysis is thus confounded for this period both by incomplete and probably uneven documentation and by inconsistency of whaling effort. If effort after 1854 is assumed to have been stable, then the documented kill of about 20 whales from 1885 to 1889 may indicate a somewhat increased availability of whales during this quinquennium. At least five right whales were taken during the second half of January 1885 and Southampton's 'oldest resident' could not remember 'when so large a school of whales has been sighted off Long Island' (*Harper's Weekly*, 31 January 1885). The low catches (less than one whale per year) after 1890 may be taken to mean that right whales had become rare off Long Island, particularly in view of the increasing value of whalebone through the early 1900s.

It is impossible to make a useful estimate of absolute pre-exploitation population size from our data alone. This stock of whales may have been exploited by Indians before European colonization of eastern North America. The Basques hunted balaenids, many of them undoubtedly *Eubalaena glacialis*, near Newfoundland and in the Gulf of St Lawrence as early as the 1530s (Aguilar, 1986). Therefore, the whale population may not have been in an unexploited state when the Long Island fishery began in about 1650. After that date and until the early twentieth century, the stock was exploited contemporaneously in shore fisheries based at North and South Carolina, New Jersey, Long Island, Connecticut, Rhode Island, Massachusetts and Maine, as well as in the American (and other?) pelagic whale fishery. Only after catch histories have been reconstructed for these other fisheries can an estimate of pre-exploitation population size for the entire stock be attempted.

Fig. 6. Young male right whale washed ashore at Wainscott, Long Island, on 5 March 1979. Its tail had been severed, apparently by a ship's propeller. (Photo by S. Sadore, courtesy of Okeanos Ocean Research Foundation.)

Fig. 7. Head of animal from Fig. 6. (Photo credit as Fig. 6.)

RECOMMENDATIONS

(1) Further searches of contemporary newspapers should be made to document more completely the activities of Long Island shore whalers from 1820 to 1924, with emphasis on establishing total catches and loss rates. Such searches should include newspapers from metropolitan New York, Connecticut and Nantucket as well as Long Island.

(2) A search should be made for logbooks or journals of vessels (e.g. *Union* of Provincetown, 1853; *Hamilton* of Nantucket, 1852–53; *Armida* and *Amulet* of Greenport, 1853; and others) which cruised along the coast of Long Island for right whales. Special effort should be made to assess whether the loss rates experienced by these whalers were different from those experienced by the shore whalers.

(3) Additional reconstructions of catch histories for other areas on the US east coast, even if superficial, should be made to permit comparisons among the peak periods and sizes of kills with those for the Southeast US Coast Ground (1876–82 [19] – Reeves and Mitchell, 1986) and the Long Island fishery (1840–54 [56]; 1885–89 [20]).

(4) The above-documented seasonal occurrence (mainly December–April) of the right whale off eastern Long Island should be used as a basis for intensive field surveys to determine whether a remnant of the population fished by the shore whalers continues to migrate along this coast today (Figs. 6 and 7).

(5) Since the Dutch were major early colonizers of New York, it would be interesting and useful to explore further any Dutch (and Basque?) involvement in technology transfer, shore whaling, or even offshore whaling in the New York Bight. It is possible that such activities contributed to the origin and nature of Long Island shore whaling. C. de Jong (pers. comm.) has pointed out that the archives of the Dutch West India Company are in the Algemeen Rijksarchief, The Hague.

ACKNOWLEDGMENTS

We thank the Okeanos Ocean Research Foundation in Hampton Bays, N.Y., for financial support. G. Ferrand, G. Horonwitsch and A. Hallé assisted with the figures, R. Olsen aided in searching sources at the NAL and A. Evely verified the references. L. Ingalls and S. Sadove provided some of the illustrations. Useful comments on the manuscript were received from E. A. Little, J. G. Mead and C. de Jong.

REFERENCES

Adams, J. T. 1918. *History of the Town of Southampton (east of Canoe Place)*. Hampton Press, Bridgehampton, L. I. Frontis+i–xx+map +424 pp.

Aguilar, A. 1986. A review of old Basque whaling and its effect on the right whales (*Eubalaena glacialis*) of the North Atlantic. (Published in this volume.)

Allen, G. M. 1916. The whalebone whales of New England. *Mem. Boston Soc. Nat. Hist.* 8(2): 107–322+pls. 8–16.

Allen, J. A. 1882. Preliminary list of works and papers relating to the mammalian orders of Cete and Sirenia. Author's ed. Washington, Department of the Interior, U.S. Geological Survey. Extracted from the *Bulletin* of the Survey, 6(3): 399–562.

Allen, J. A. 1908. The North Atlantic right whale and its near allies. *Bull. Am. Mus. Nat. Hist.* 24(18): 277–329+pls. 19–24.

Andrews, R. C. 1908. Notes upon the external and internal anatomy of *Balaena glacialis* Bonn. *Bull. Am. Mus. Nat. Hist.* 24(10): 171–82.

Andrews, R. C. 1909. Further notes on *Eubalaena glacialis* (Bonn.). *Bull. Am. Mus. Nat. Hist.* 26(21): 273–5+pls 46–50.

Anonymous. Ms. 1794–95. [Accounts for cutting up whale at Montauk. Boats *Democrat* and *Equality*.] East Hampton Free Library, [Call letters KN 108]. Four handwritten pages.

Anonymous. 1882. *History of Suffolk County, New York, with illustrations, portraits, & sketches of prominent families and individuals*. W. W. Munsell & Co., 36 Vesey Street, New York. Frontis+488 pp. [town histories paginated separately]+pls+ folding map.

Ansel, W. D. 1978. *The Whaleboat. A Study of Design, Construction and use from 1850 to 1970*. Mystic Seaport Museum, Inc., Mystic, Conn., [i]–[vi]+147 pp. [some folding].

Ashley, C. W. 1926. *The Yankee Whaler*. Houghton Mifflin Co., The Riverside Press, Cambridge, Boston and New York. Frontis+xix +379 pp.

Ayres, W. O. 1886. The Atlantic right whale. *Sci. Am.* 55(8): 117.

Bailey, P. 1959. *Long Island Whalers*. [Published privately], Amityville, N.Y. 36 pp.

Bannister, J. L., Taylor, S. and Sutherland, H. 1981. Logbook records of 19th century American Sperm whaling: A report on the 12 month project, 1978–79. *Rep. int. Whal. Commn* 31: 821–33.

Barnum, P. T. 1873. *Struggles and Triumphs; or, Forty Years' Recollections of P. T. Barnum*. Author's edition. Warren, Johnson & Co., Buffalo, N.Y. [i]–[viii]+[13]–772, 837–847 pp.+[i–ii]+33 unnumb. pls.

Beneden, P.-J. Van. 1885. Sur l'apparition d'une petite gamme de vraies baleines sur les côtes des Etats-unis d'Amérique. *Bull. Acad. R. Belg.* Sêr. 3, 9: 212–14.

Best, P. B. 1970. Exploitation and recovery of right whales *Eubalaena australis* off the Cape Province. *Investl Rep. Div. Sea Fish. S Afr.* 80: [i–iv]+1–20.

Bockstoce, J. R. 1977. *Steam Whaling in the Western Arctic*. With contributions by William A. Baker and Charles F. Batchelder. New Bedford Whaling Museum, Old Dartmouth Historical Society, New Bedford, Massachusetts. 127 pp.

Bodfish, H. H. 1936. *Chasing the Bowhead*. [Recorded for him by J. C. Allen.] Harvard University Press, Cambridge. [x]+281 pp.+frontis +8 unnumb. pls.

Braganza. 1840–44 MS. [Journal kept by Ichabod Norton on the ship *Braganza* of New Bedford, Charles Waterman, Master. 1 Dec. 1840–29 May 1844.] Dukes County Historical Society, Edgartown, Massachusetts.

Brisbane, A. 1885. Whaling off Long Island. *Harper's Young People. An Illustrated Weekly*, 6(276) : 226–7.

Clark, A. H. 1887. 1. History and present condition of the fishery, pp. 3–218 of Part xv. The whale fishery. *In*: Goode, G. B. (Ed.) *The Fisheries and Fishery Industries of the United States. Section V. History and Methods of the Fisheries*. In two volumes, with an atlas of two hundred and fifty-five plates. Vol II. Government Printing Office, Washington. xx+881 pp.

Connor, P. F. 1971. The mammals of Long Island. *N.Y. St. Mus. Sci. Serv. Bull.* 416: v+1–78.

Cook, L. D. 1912–13 [1858]. History of the early settlement of the town of Southampton and village of Sag Harbor. *Sag Harbor Express*. [Weekly articles running from 5 Dec. 1912 to 13 Mar. 1913.] ['This history is taken from an address delivered before the Sag Harbor Lyceum and Institute by Luther D. Cook, Chairman of the Geographical and Historical Committee on the evening of Monday, April 19, 1858...']

Cope, E. D. 1865. Note on a species of whale occurring on the coasts of the United States. *Proc. Acad. Nat. Sci. Phila.* 17: 168–9.

Cornbury, Lord. 1855 [1708]. Lord Cornbury to the Board of Trade. pp. 55–61, vol. 5. *In*: E. B. O'Callaghan (Ed) [cited below].

DeKay, J. E. 1842. Zoology of New-York, or the New York Fauna; comprising detailed descriptions of all the animals hitherto observed within the State of New-York, with brief notices of those occasionally found near its borders, and accompanied by appropriate illustrations. Albany: Printed by W. & A. White & J. Visscher. Part 1. Mammalia, [In 5 Vols.]. Vol. 1. [xvi] + 146 pp. + pls. 1–33 of *Natural History of New York*. D. Appleton & Co and Wiley and Putnam, New York; Gould, Kendall & Lincoln, Boston; Thurlow Weed, Albany. [In 5 Parts, 26 Volumes in 30.]

Dow, G. F. 1925. *Whale Ships and Whaling. A pictorial History of Whaling during Three Centuries. With an Account of the Whale Fishery in Colonial New England.* Marine Research Society Publication 10, Salem, Massachusetts. [xii] + 446 pp.

Dudley, P. 1725. An essay upon the natural history of whales, with a particular account of the ambergris found in the *Sperma Ceti* whale. In a letter to the publisher, from the Honourable *Paul Dudley*, Esq; F.R.S. *Phil. Trans.* 33(387): 256–69.

East Hampton Star (EHS), East Hampton, L. I., New York. [December 1885 to present.]

Edwards, E. J. and Rattray, J. E. 1932. '*Whale Off!*'. *The Story of American Shore Whaling.* Frederick A. Stokes Company, New York. xvi + 285 pp. + frontis + 17 pls.

Edwards, E. J. and Rattray, J. E. 1956. '*Whale Off!*' *The Story of American Shore Whaling.* Coward-McCann, Inc., New York. Frontis + xxiv + 285 pp. + 15 pls.

Edwards, T. M. 1929. Reminiscences of old East Hampton by the sea. As given by one of her native townsmen. pp. i–ix + 1–300 typescript. [On file at:] East Hampton Free Library, East Hampton, N.Y.

Fernow, B. 1883. *Documents Relating to the History of the Early Colonial Settlements Principally on Long Island, with a Map of its Western Part, made in 1666.* Weed, Parsons and Company, Albany, N.Y. Folding map + xxxiii + 800 pp.

Frothingham's Long-Island Herald, vol. I, no. 1 (10 May 1791) – vol. VI, no. 317 (17 Dec. 1798).

Gabriel, R. H. 1960. *The Evolution of Long Island. A Story of Land and Sea.* Ira J. Friedman, Port Washington, Long Island, N.Y. Frontis [folding map] + 194 pp.

Gardiner, J. T., Baker, J. and Osborne, J. S. 1887. *Records of the Town of East-Hampton, Long Island, Suffolk Co., N.Y., with other Ancient Documents of Historic Value.* [In 5 Vols.: Vol. 1, 1696 to 1679–80; Vol. 2, 1679–80 to 1701–2; Vol. 3, 1701 to 1734; Vol. 4, 1734 to 1849; Vol. 5, 1850 to 1900.]

Glen Cove Gazette (GCG), Glen Cove, L. I., New York. [May 1857 to 1891.]

Halsey, W. D. 1935. *Sketches from Local History.* Bridgehampton, Suffolk County, New York, 189 pp. + 11 2-page maps.

Hedges, H. P. 1897. *A History of the Town of East-Hampton, N.Y., including an Address Delivered at the Celebration of the Bi-centennial Anniversary of its Settlement in 1849.* Introductions to the four printed volumes of its records, with other historic material, an appendix and genealogical notes. J. H. Hunt, Printer, Sag-Harbor. Frontis + [v] + 344 pp. + [i], Errata + 1–10, Index.

Hedges, H. P., Pelletreau, W. S. and Foster, E. H. 1874. *The First Book of Records of the Town of Southampton with other Ancient Documents of Historic Value, including all the Writings in the Town Clerk's Office from 1639 to 1660.* Transcribed with notes and an introduction by Wm. S. Pelletreau, and compiled by the undersigned Committee, chosen at Town Meeting, April 1st, 1873, and published at the expense of the town, by its authority. John H. Hunt, Sag-Harbor, N.Y. Frontis + v + [2nd] frontis + xi + [i], errata + 177pp.

Henderson, D. A. 1972. *Men & Whales at Scammon's Lagoon.* Dawson's Book Shop, Los Angeles, California. 313 pp. + [i] + 4 maps.

Holder, J. B. 1886. The Atlantic right whale. *Sci. Am.* 54 (20 February): 117.

Howell, G. R. 1880. Whaling on Long Island in early times. Sag Harbor: *The Express*, Suffolk County, N.Y., 16 September.

Howell, G. R. 1887. *The Early History of Southampton, L.I., New York, with genealogies.* Revised, corrected and enlarged. 2nd ed. Weed, Parsons and Company, Albany. 473 pp.

Hubbard, W. 1815. *A General History of New England, from the Discovery to MDCLXXX.* Published by the Massachusetts Historical Society. Cambridge…Hilliard & Metcalf. vi + 676 pp.

Jong, C. de. 1978. *Geschiedenis van de oude Nederlandse Walvisvaart, Deel Twee, Bloei en Achteruitgang 1642-1872.* Gedrukt te Johannesburg. Frontis + xii + 536 pp.

Kraus, S., Prescott, J. H., Turnbull, P. and Reeves, R. R. 1982. Preliminary notes on the occurrence of the North Atlantic right whale, *Eubalaena glacialis*, in the Bay of Fundy. *Rep. int. Whal. Commn* 32: 407–11.

Kugler, R. C. 1980. The whale oil trade 1750–1775. New Bedford, Mass. *Old Dartmouth Historical Sketch* 79: [1]–[24] + 4 unnumb. pls.

Little, E. A. 1981. The Indian contribution to along-shore whaling at Nantucket. Nantucket, MA 02554, Nantucket Historical Association, *Nantucket Algonquian Studies* 8: 1–85 (processed).

Lipton, B. 1975. Whaling days in New Jersey. *Newark Mus. Quart.* 26(2 & 3): 1–72 + map [inside back cover].

Long Island Farmer (LIF), Jamaica, L. I., New York. [4 Jan. 1821 to 31 Dec. 1920.]

Long Island Herald (LIH). Sag Harbor, L. I., New York [10 May 1791 to 17 Dec. 1798.]

Macy, O. 1835 *The History of Nantucket; being a Compendious Account of the First Settlement of the Island by the English, Together with the Rise and Progress of the Whale Fishery; and other Historical Facts Relative to said Island and its Inhabitants.* Hilliard, Gray, and Co., Boston. Frontis [map] + xii + 300 pp. + 1–8 [advertisements] + 1 pl.

Mather, F. 1887. New York and its fisheries. Part VI, pp. 341–77. In: G. B. Goode (ed.) *The Fisheries and Fishery Industries of the United States.* Section II. A geographical review of the fisheries industries and fishing communities for the year 1880. US Comm. Fish and Fisheries. Government Printing Office, Washington. ix + 787 pp.

Mitchell, E. 1977. MS. Initial population size of bowhead whale (*Balaena mysticetus*) stocks: cumulative catch estimates. Paper SC/29/Doc. 33, presented to the IWC Scientific Committee June 1977 (unpublished). 1–113 pp. + figures 1–5 + tables 1–13 [typescript].

Mitchell, E. and Reeves, R. R. 1981. Catch history and cumulative catch estimates of initial population size of cetaceans in the Eastern Canadian Arctic. *Rep. int. Whal. Commn* 31: 645–82.

Mitchell, E. and Reeves, R. R. 1983. Catch history, abundance, and present status of Northwest Atlantic humpback whales. *Rep. int. Whal. Commn* (special issue 5): 153–212.

Moore, J. C. 1953. Distribution of marine mammals to Florida waters. *Am. Midl. Nat..* 49(1): 117–58.

Nantucket Inquirer (NI). Nantucket, Massachusetts [23 June 1821 to 1865; became the *Inquirer and Mirror* (NIM), 1865 to present.]

New York Sun (NYS), New York City, New York. [13 April 1833 to 28 Sept.1840.]

New York Times (NYT). New York City, New York. [18 Sept. 1851 to present.]

O'Callaghan, E. B. [Ed.] 1855. *Documents Relative to the Colonial History of the State Of New York; procured in Holland, England and France, by John Romeyn Brodhead, Esq., Agent, under and by virtue of an act of the legislature entitled 'An Act to appoint an Agent to procure and transcribe Documents in Europe relative to the Colonial History of the State,' passed May 2, 1839.* [In 14 volumes, 1853–83.] Albany: Weed, Parsons and Company Printers. Vol. V. Transcripts Of Documents in the Queen's State Paper Office; in the Office of the Privy Council; in the British Museum; and in the Library of the Archbishop of Canterbury at Lambeth, in London. London Documents: XVII–XXIV. 1707–33. xix + 985 pp.

Odell, M. O. 1952. Shore whalers of Wainscott. *Long Island Forum* 15(2): 27, 35–7.

Palmer, W. R. 1959 [1981]. The whaling port of Sag Harbor. Ph.D. thesis, Faculty of Political Science, Columbia University, 1959. Publ. by University Microfilms International, Ann Arbor, Michigan, USA; London, England, [vi] + v + 327 pp.

Pelletreau, F. 1732/3. [Personal letter to Mr E. Delenscey of Southampton describing the whale fishery.] [On file at:] The East Hampton Free Library, East Hampton, L.I., New York.

Popple, W. 1713 [1855]. Secretary Popple to Attorney-General Northey. p. 368, vol. 5. In: E. B. O'Callaghan, (Ed.) [Cited above.]

Rattray, J. E. 1933. Long Island's off-shore whaling. pp. 17–22, In: *Colonial History of Long Island. A Collection of Papers Read at the Thirty-third Annual Conference of the New York State Historical Society held at Southampton, October 6, 7, and 8, 1932.* The Star Press, East Hampton, Long Island, New York.

Rattray, J.E. 1953. *East Hampton History including Genealogies of Early Families.* East Hampton, Long Island, New York. [xviii] + 619 pp. + 32 pls.

Reeves, R. R. 1976. New Jersey's great whales. Occasional Paper No. 122, *N.J. Audubon* 2(1): 7–14.

Reeves, R. R., Mead, J. G. and Katona, S. 1978. The right whale, *Eubalaena glacialis*, in the western North Atlantic. *Rep. int. Whal. Commn* 28: 303–12.

Reeves, R. R. and Mitchell, E. 1986. American pelagic whaling for right whales in the North Atlantic. (Published in this volume..

Reutershan, P. V. 1927. Agent Reutershan writes prize fish story in Herald-Tribune contest. *Long Island Railroad Inf. Bull.* 5(1): 28–9.

Révoil, B. H. 1863. *Pêches dans l'Amérique du nord.* L. Hachette et Cie, Paris. 320 pp.

Rice, D. W. and Wolman, A. A. 1971. The life history and ecology of the gray whale (*Eschrichtius robustus*). *Am. Soc. Mamm. Spec. Publ.* No. 3: viii+1–142.

Roueché, B. 1949. Shore whaler. *New Yorker*, 24 Sept., pp. 37–40, 42–8.

Sag Harbor Corrector (SHC), Sag Harbor, L.I., New York. [3 Aug. 1822 to 30 Dec. 1911.]

Sag Harbor Express (SHE), Sag Harbor, L.I., New York. [14 July 1859 to 10 April 1921.]

Scammon, C. M. 1874. *The Marine Mammals of the North-western coast of North America, Described and Illustrated; Together with an Account of the American Whale-Fishery.* J. H. Carmany & Co., San Francisco. 320+v pp.+pls. 1–27.

Schevill, W. E., Watkins, W. A. and Moore, K. E. 1986. Status of *Eubalaena glacialis* off Cape Cod. (Published in this volume.)

Schmitt, F. P. 1972. *Whale Watch. The Story of Shore Whaling off Nassau County, New York.* Whaling Museum Society, Inc., Cold Spring Harbor, L. I., New York. 15 pp. [Originally published in the *Nassau County Historical Society Journal* 31 (1–2), 1971.]

Sea-Side Times (SST), Southampton, New York. [10 Dec. 1891 to 1920.]

Smith, W. T. n.d. Memmerrandom [*sic*]. [A 1 p. typed copy of entries for 'the pig-skin book', dated 1706/7–1707/8 begun by Col. Wm (T.) Smith 1697.] [On File at:] The East Hampton Free Library, East Hampton, L.I., New York.

Stackpole, E. A. 1953. *The Sea-Hunters. The New England Whalemen during Two Centuries 1635–1835.* J. B. Lippincott Company, Philadelphia, New York, 510 pp.+16 pls.

Starbuck, A. 1878. *History of the American Whale Fishery from its Earliest Inception to the year 1876. Rep. U.S. Comm. Fish.* (4) 1875–76, Appendix A, 768 pp.+pls. 1–6.

Starbuck, A. 1924. *The History of Nantucket. County, Island and Town including Genealogies of First Settlers.* C. E. Goodspeed & Co., Boston. 871 pp.+4 folding maps.

Thompson, B. F. 1839. *History of Long Island: Containing an Account of the Discovery and Settlement; with other Important and Interesting Matters to the Present Time.* E. French, New York. 536 pp.+2 pls.

Thompson, B. F. 1918a. *History of Long Island from its Discovery and Settlement to the Present Time.* The third edition revised and greatly enlarged with additions and a biography of the author by Charles J. Werner, member of the Long Island Historical Society. [In 3 volumes]. Robert H. Dodd, New York. Vol. 1, Frontis+[x]+xi–l +538 pp.+folding map; vol. 2, frontis+649 pp.; vol. 3, 2 frontis +677 pp.

Thompson, D. W. 1918b. On whales landed at the Scottish whaling stations, especially during the years 1908–1914. Part 1. The Nordcaper. *Scot. Nat.* 81: 197–208.

Tower, W. S. 1907. *A History of the American Whale Fishery.* Publications of the University of Pennsylvania, Philadelphia. Series in Political Economy and Public Law, No. 20 x+145 pp.

True, F. W. 1884 *Catalogue of the Aquatic Mammals Exhibited by the United States National Museum.* Great International Fisheries Exhibition, London, 1883. Government Printing Office, Washington. 22 pp.+[i] Errata.

True, F. W. 1885. Report of a trip to Long Island in search of skeletons of the right whale, *Balaena cisarctica. Bull. US Fish Comm.* 5: 131–2.

True, F. W. 1904. The whalebone whales of the western North Atlantic compared with those occurring in European waters with some observations on the species of the North Pacific. *Smithson. Contr. Knowl.* 33: xii+viii+332 pp.+pls. 1–50.

Ulmer, F. A., Jr. 1961. New Jersey's whales and dolphins. New Jersey Audubon Society, *N.J. Nature News* 16(3): 80–93.

Wakeham, W., Bernard, C. A. and Riendeau, J. 1913. Appendix No. 6. Quebec. *Forty-Sixth Annual Report of the Department of Marine and Fisheries 1912–13. Fisheries.* Printed by order of Parliament. C. H. Parmelee, Printer to the King's Most Excellent Majesty, Ottawa. pp. 221–53.

Watson, J. F. 1855. *Annals of Philadelphia and Pennsylvania, in the Olden Time; Being a Collection of Memoirs, Anecdotes, and Incidents of the City and its Inhabitants, and of the Earliest Settlements of the Island Part of Pennsylvania, from the Days of the Founders. Intended to Preserve the Recollections of Olden Time, and to Exhibit Society in its Changes of Manners and Customs, and the City and Country in their Local Changes and Improvements. Embellished with engravings, by T. H. Mumford.* In 2 vols. Parry and McMillan, Successors to A. Hart (late Carey and Hart). Vol. 1, vii+591 pp.; vol. 2, xvi+609 pp.+22 unnumb. pls.

Whalemen's Shipping List, and Merchants' Transcript (WSL). New Bedford, Mass. [Vol. 1, no. 1 (17 March 1843) to Vol. 72, no. 52 (29 December 1914).]

Winegar, S. P. 1860. Cruise of the whaleship Julian. *Whalemen's Shipping List, and Merchants' Transcript*, 18(33), 23 October.

Winn, H. E. 1982. A characterization of marine mammals and turtles in the Mid- and North Atlantic areas of the U.S. Outer Continental Shelf. Final Report of the Cetacean and Turtle Assessment Program, University of Rhode Island, Graduate School of Oceanography, Kingston, Rhode Island 02881. Prepared for: U.S. Department of the Interior, Bureau of Land Management, Washington, DC 20240, Under Contract AA551 – CT8-48. p. [i–x]+[1] – 450+Special Topics [45 additional papers, variously paginated]+2 transparencies [contained in back cover pocket].

Winn, H. E., Goodale, D. R., Hyman, M. A. M., Kenney, R. D., Price, C. A. and Scott, G. P. 1981. Right whale sightings and the right whale minimum count. pp. 49–51. In: *A Characterization of Marine Mammals and Turtles in the Mid- and North-Atlantic Areas of the U.S. Outer Continental Shelf.* Executive Summary for 1979 Cetacean and Turtle Assessment Program, University of Rhode Island, Sponsored by the Bureau of Land Management under contract AA551-CT8-48, pp. 1–75 (mimeo).

Table 1.

Catch data and evidence of activity in the Long Island whale fishery, 1644–1926. Whales are assumed to be right whales, unless otherwise noted. Locality abbreviations are: SH = Southampton, EH = East Hampton, NY = New York, LI = Long Island, NW = Northwest, MK = Montauk, BH = Bridgehampton, CT = Connecticut, BI = Block Island. See Fig. 1 for localities of these. Newspaper abbreviations are: LIH = Long Island Herald, SHC = Sag Harbor Corrector, NI = Nantucket Inquirer, WSL = Whalemen's Shipping List, SHE = Sag Harbor Express, GCG = Glen Cove Gazette, NYT = New York Times, EHS = East Hampton Star, NYS = New York Sun, SST = Sea-Side Times.

YEAR	CATCH	LOCALITY	REMARKS	SOURCES
1644		SH	"Whaling list" - evidence of activity?	Rattray, 1953, p. 219.
1644		SH	Whaling "established".	Allen, 1908, p. 314.
1644			"First organized whaling company in America"; 44 men agreed "to take care of the valuable right whales off the beach on Eastern Long Island".	Rattray, 1953, p. 368.
1651		EH	Whaling "established".	Allen, 1908, p. 314.
1651		EH	6 Sept. Men "ordered to be called out by succession to look out for whale".	Starbuck, 1924, p. 351.
1652		EH	Whaling industry "flourishing".	Edwards and Rattray, 1956, p. 178.
1653	1	EH		Starbuck, 1878, p. 10; Edwards and Rattray, 1956, p. 232.
1656	1	NY waters	Prior to 4 April.	Starbuck, 1878, p. 11
1657	1 (+?)	EH	F. Davis actively whaling.	Rattray, 1953, p. 262.

Table 1 (*continued*)

YEAR	CATCH	LOCALITY	REMARKS	SOURCES
1662/3		EH	Town divided into 3 districts "for the cutting-in of the whales".	Rattray, 1953, p. 512.
1666		EH	J. Loper came here "for the whaling".	Rattray, 1953, p. 438.
1666/73		EH	J. Miller and R. Garrison had rights to Accabonac Harbor for whaling.	Rattray, 1953, p. 448.
1667		EH, SH	An agreement made among shore whaling companies of EH and SH.	Rattray, 1953, p. 490.
1668		EH	Suit concerning whaling agreement.	Hedges, 1897, p. 52.
1668		EH	J. Schellinger and J. Loper hired an Indian crew to whale, from 1 Nov. to 1 April.	Rattray, 1953, p. 64; Thompson, 1918a, Vol. 2, p. 117-8.
1668		NW	Harbor exporting whale oil and "bone".	Rattray, 1953, p. 96
1668/69		EH	A. Miller required to make "whale-oil casks for town use" in return for land.	Rattray, 1953, p. 449.
1668/72		SH	Permission to issue gunpowder etc. to Indians for whaling.	Fernow, 1883, p. 608-9, 645-6, 664.
1669	12-13 at least 2 s/l	Eastern LI	Before end of March.	Starbuck, 1878, p. 11.
1669		EH, SH	Companies from the two towns agreed on disposition of drift whales "killed by ye other".	Thompson, 1918a, Vol. 2, p. 118.
1670/71		Huntington	Petition for buying land on the south shore "for ye Convenience of the Whale-Fishing".	Fernow, 1883, p. 648.
1672		LI	Whaling subjected to legal regulation, "having endeavoured it [whale-fishing] above these twenty yeares".	Starbuck, 1878; Allen, 1908, p. 314.
1672		Oyster Bay	Three "Drift Whales cast upon the Beach".	Fernow, 1883, p. 665.
1672		EH	Suit concerning ownership of blubber.	Hedges, 1897, p. 52
1673		Seatalcott, Brookhaven	Whaling active.	Fernow, 1883, p. 678.
1674	At least one	EH	A "parsell of Whale bone" at issue. March.	Gardiner et al., 1887, p. 376.
1675		EH, SH	13 Indians whaling on behalf of J. Schellinger and J. Loper; Schellinger and Co. "had already been employing Indian crews for eight or nine years".	Rattray, 1953, p. 438, 534; Edwards and Rattray, 1956, p. 197; Fernow, 1883, p. 707-9.
1675	Some	EH	11 English settlers hired two Indian crews to whale, promising them "halfe ye blubber & halfe ye whale bone". Apparently at least seven "loads of whale" carted.	Rattray, 1953, p. 64; Edwards and Rattray, 1956, p. 197-8; Gardiner et al., 1887, p. 408, 375-6.
1676		LI	Unchechaug Indians given "liberty to whale & fish upon their owne Acct".	Fernow, 1883, p. 720.
1678/80		LI	Shore-based whale hunt described.	Schmitt, 1972, p. 4
1678		EH	P. Leek and others engaged Indians to go whaling for them in two boats.	Rattray, 1953, p. 425.
1678	Some	SH	Winter transaction made involving much whale oil and baleen.	Starbuck, 1878, p. 14-5; also see Fernow, 1883, p. 735.
1679		LI	Whale oil worth one pound ten shillings per barrel.	Gabriel, 1960, p. 65.
1680/1		EH	J. Stratton, Sr. & Jr., hired two Indians to kill whales for them.	Rattray, 1953, p. 562.
1680/1		Seatalcutt	Oil transaction recorded.	Fernow, 1883, p. 762.
1683/8	Some			Starbuck, 1878, p. 15.
1685		EH	J. Miller and J. Dayton "made an agreement with the Indians for whaling".	Rattray, 1953, p. 449.
1687		East End	Whale oil being exported to NY and Connecticut.	Rattray, 1953, p. 123.
1687	(60)	SH	14 whaling companies active; tryworks at Sagaponack, Mecox, Wickapogue, Southampton, Schinnecock Pt., Quogue, and Ketchaponack; 2,148 bbls of whale oil landed.	Howell, 1880; 1887, p. 180-1; 1898.
1687	(40)	EH	1,456 bbls as of 15 April.	Howell, 1887, p. 180-1.
1688	3 large 5-6 small	Graves End, Easte End	Baleen 3 ft+. December.	Starbuck, 1878, p. 15.
1692		EH, SH	A [whaling] "company" moved to Cape May, N.J.	Rattray, 1953, p. 352.
1698		EH	J. Miller moved to Cohansey on Delaware Bay for whaling.	Rattray, 1953, p. 448.
1699		MK	"Lord John" Gardiner employing Indian crews to whale for him.	Rattray, 1953, p. 66.
1699	12-13	East End	July.	Anon., 1882, p. 29.

Table 1 (*continued*)

YEAR	CATCH	LOCALITY	REMARKS	SOURCES
1700	1	LI	March.	Edwards and Rattray, 1956, p. 216-7.
1700/40	1	EH	D. Miller and his sons and slaves "took a whale and sold enough oil to buy a 40-acre farm".	Rattray, 1953, p. 450.
Ca. 1702	13	BH to EH	Seen "on the shore ... between the two places".	Hedges, 1897, p. 11.
1704	(6)	EH	At least 233 bbls oil and 1,620 lbs baleen shipped to England.	S. Mulford's diary, examined at EHFL.
1705	(1)	EH	Consignment of 200-300 lbs "whalebone".	S. Mulford's diary, examined at EHFL.
1706	(1+)	EH	Reference to 60 bbls "oyle at Long Island to pay at forty shillings a barrell at Boston".	S. Mulford's diary, examined at EHFL.
1707	(111)	All LI	"They made four thousand barrils of Oyl".	Cornbury, 1855, p. 59.
1707	8	St. George's Manor	16 Jan.-17 March; 209 bbls.	Smith, n.d.; Thompson, 1918a, Vol. 2, p. 336.
1708	(17 or less)	All LI	"They have not made above six hundred [Barrils]."	Cornbury, 1855, p. 59.
1711	(At least 7)	EH, SH	Total 252 bbls on hand as of 18 April, but "greater part" of season's catch probably already exported by that date.	Howell, 1880; 1887, p. 181.
1711	(5)	Western LI	112 [bbls] oil and 1,300 [lb] bone taken at Mereck Beach; 81 [bbls] and 900 [lb] bone at Rockaway Beach.	Schmitt, 1972, p. 8, 12.
1711	4	MK		Anon., 1882, p. 29.
1711	8	SH		Anon., 1882, p. 29.
1711	2	EH	48 bbls and 36 barrels. Oil carted to Northwest and shipped to England. April.	Edwards and Rattray, 1956, p. 275.
1711	2	Moriches		Anon., 1882, p. 29.
1711	3	Brookhaven	One a calf.	Anon., 1882, p. 29.
1711	2	Islip		Anon., 1882, p. 29.
1711		?	"Drift", 20 bbls.	Anon., 1882, p. 29.
1719	1 struck	EH	24 Feb. Four men drowned after their boat was "staved" by a harpooned whale.	Hedges, 1897, p. 11.
1721	40	LI		Anon., 1882, p. 29.
1722	4	LI	"A deficiency of whales is intimated ... there are but four whales killed on LI."	Watson, 1855, p. 428; Anon., 1882, p. 29.
1732/ 33	3 large 8 small	EH, SH	Winter. Six secured, expected to make 220 bbls oil and 1,500 lb large "whalebone"; 5 "still afloat" would add 150 bbls and 1,000 lb large "whalebone".	Pelletreau, 1732/3.
1741	4	LI	Whales "reported as being more abundant [than in 1722]".	Anon., 1882, p. 29.
1753		EH	Three men drowned while whaling.	Rattray, 1953, p. 211.
1760-1775		Sag	"Several small sloops ... ranged the ocean at a considerable distance from the coast"; whales still were towed ashore for trying out; sloops Goodluck, Success, and Dolphin cruised in lat 36°N in 1760, between Bermuda and Nantucket Shoals.	Thompson, 1839, p. 221; 1918, Vol. 2, p. 177; Stackpole, 1953, p. 27.
1792	12 "very stout"	Off so. side LI	Before 12 April, "this spring".	LIH 1(47): 12 IV 1792.
1794	2	MK, SH	"Demorest" and "Equality". December.	Palmer, 1959, p. 55-6; Edwards and Rattray, 1956, p. 245; Anon., 1794/5 MS.
1822	2	LI	One produced 50 bbls.	Allen, 1916, p. 134; LIH 2(65): 28 III 1822.
1826	1, 1 s/l	WA	Mid-May. 40 bbls ("it being a Calf"). 3 chased but only one caught.	SHC 5(1): 29 IV 1826; Allen, 1916, p. 126, 135.
1826	1	WH	100 bbls. "Calf".	SHC 5(1): 29 IV 1826; Allen, 1916, p. 135.
1829		LI Sound	Large right whale seen opposite New Haven.	SHC 8(33): 12 XII 1829.
1830	1	BH	"Calf." 23 Feb. 10-12 bbls.	SHC 8(44): 27 II 1830.
1830	1	SH	12 March. 35-40 bbls.	SHC 8(46): 13 III 1830.
1832	1	So. shore, east. LI	16 Jan. 20-25 bbls. "Calf".	SHC 10(39): 21 I 1832.
1832	1	BH	30 Dec. 40 bbls.	SHC 11(38): 5 I 1833.
1833	1	SH	1st wk of March. 40 bbls.	SHC 11(46): 9 III 1833.
1834	1	SH	20 May. 50 bbls. "Calf".	SHC 13(5): 24 V 1834.

Table 1 (*continued*)

YEAR	CATCH	LOCALITY	REMARKS	SOURCES
1835		EH	A 40 ft whale "drifted on shore ... without any mark of a wound upon it, from man or other enemy".	SHC 14(3): 9 V 1835.
1837	3	AM		Newspaper clipping examined at EHFL.
1838	1	EH	20 Dec. 30 bbls.	Edwards and Rattray, 1956, p. 259-60; SHC 17(66): 22 XII 1838; Hedges, 1897, p. 178-9.
1839	1	AM	11 March. 30 bbls.	SHC 17(88): 13 III 1839.
1839	1	SH	31 July. 40 ft, 40 bbls.	SHC 18(25): 3 VIII 1839.
1840	1	SH	7 May. 30-40 bbls.	SHC 19(1): 9 V 1840.
1840	1	AM	Ca. 1 May. "40-barrel".	Allen, 1916, p. 135; SHC 18(102): 29 IV 1840.
1840	2	Between Stonington, CT, and MK	27 and 60 bbls.	Allen, 1916, p. 135.
1840/45	5	SH	One season. 15-35 bbls each.	Cook, 1858.
1841	2	EH, AM	One on 28 July. Whale seen in Gardiners Bay, June 1.	Edwards and Rattray, 1956, p. 260; Hedges, 1897, p. 234.
1846	1			Ayres, 1886.
1846		Jones Beach	Large whale stranded. Identity unclear.	
1847	4 "good-sized"	Sag	April 13-14.	Thompson, 1918a, Vol. 2, p. 176.
1847	1	AM	22 Jan.	Hedges, 1897, p. 235.
1847	1	WA	25 March.	Hedges, 1897, p. 235.
1847	6	EH, BH, SH	13-14 April. "A great show of whales off the coast, such as has not been known for many years."	Hedges, 1897, p. 235; Halsey, 1935, p. 107.
1847	1	EH	15 April.	Halsey, 1935, p. 107.
1847	1	EH	19 April. "Seven whales lying on the shore at one time."	Halsey, 1935, p. 107.
1848	1 killed but lost	SH	Several seen. One killed 20 Jan., "but his captors were obliged to cut from him, night coming on".	SHC : 22 I 1848, 2 II 1848; Allen, 1916, p. 136; NI 28(8): 28 I 1848.
1848	1	AM	2 March.	Hedges, 1897, p. 235.
1848	2	Eastern LI	Ca. mid-April. "Several others were fastened to but the irons drew."	Allen, 1916, p. 136; Edwards and Rattray, 1956, p. 260; NI 28(33): 17 IV 1848.
1848	1	Eastern LI	March. Taken by 500-ton whaling vessel Jackson, which went out of NY Harbor after learning of sighting. Products valued at $3,000.	Révoil, 1863.
1851	2	SH	March. One 44 ft, 30 bbls (March 1); the other 25 bbls.	Allen, 1916, p. 136; NI 31(30): 10 III 1851; 31(35): 2 III 1851.
1851	1	SH	1 March. Ca. 40 bbls.	SHC : 5 III 1851.
1851	1	SH	10 March. 25 bbls.	SHC : 12 III 1851.
1851	1	BH	11 Nov. 30 bbls.	SHC : 12 XI 1851.
1851		SH	Whale chased, no strike.	SHC : 12 XI 1851.
1852	5	SH	May. 40 bbls (1); 70 bbls (2 combined).	Allen, 1916, p. 136; SHC 29 V 1852.
1852	1, 1 killed/ lost	SH	28 April. 50 bbls.	SHC : 1 V 1852.
1852	1	SH	40 bbls. 7 May.	SHC : 12 V 1852.
1852	1 s/1	WA	"Drawed."	SHC : 12 V 1852.
1853	3	LI	15 April and earlier. By schooner Armida of Greenport. 41, 70-80, and 65 bbls.	WSL 11(5): 5 IV 1853; 11(8): 26 IV 1853; SHC 31(88): 2 IV 1853; 20 IV 1853; Allen, 1916, p. 136; Starbuck, 1878, p. 512-513; NI 33(50): 29 IV 1853; 33(43): 13 IV 1853.
1853	1	SH	11 April. 25 bbls.	SHC 31(91): 13 IV 1853.
1853	1	SH	21 April. Ca. 25 bbls. By schooner Hamilton of Nantucket.	WSL 11(8): 26 IV 1853.

Table 1 (*continued*)

YEAR	CATCH	LOCALITY	REMARKS	SOURCES
1853	1 s/1	AM	19 March.	WSL 11(3): 22 III 1853; Allen, 1916, p. 136; SHC 31(88): 2 IV 1853; NI 33(43): 13 IV 1853.
1853	1	EH	26 March. Ca. 30-40 bbls. First of season for shore whalers.	SHC 31(87): 30 III 1853; NI 33(39): 1 IV 1853.
1853	1	SH-MK	Mid-April. 50 ft, 45 bbls.	WSL 11(3): 22 III 1853; 11(7): 19 IV 1853; Allen, 1916, p. 136; NI 33(45): 18 IV 1853.
1853		60 mi. so. of Block Island	11 April. Seen floating.	WSL 11(7): 19 IV 1853.
1854	1 s/1	SH	29 April. Spouting blood, "mortally wounded". "30 barrel."	WSL 12(10): 9 V 1854; Allen, 1916, p. 127, 137; NI 34(55): 10 V 1854.
1855(ca)		WH	A "young black whale" was "thrown upon the beach"; 12 ft long; purchased from fishermen by P.T. Barnum and exhibited in NY. The stranding called "a thing never heard of before in this vicinity".	Barnum, 1873, p. 413-4.
1855	1	SH	16 April. Ca. 30 bbls.	Allen, 1916, p. 137; NI 35(49): 25 IV 1855.
1858		MK	Late February. Several chased by schooner Black Diamond.	WSL 15(51): 2 III 1858.
1858	1	SH	27 February. 40 bbls. (30 bbls acc. to Cook.)	WSL 15(52): 9 III 1858; Allen, 1916, p. 137; Anon., 1882, p. 29; Cook, 1858; NI 30(123): 5 III 1858.
1858	1	EH	Late November. Ca. 30 bbls.	WSL 15(52): 9 III 1858; Allen, 1916, p. 137; NI 39(94): 30 XI 1858.
1859	2 killed	Gardiners Bay	23 Oct. A "school" chased by crew of smack Andrew Jackson, 50 bbl whale killed by shot from bomb gun, sank. Apparently a calf also killed. "It is not often that whales make their appearance inside of Montauk."	SHE 1(16): 27 X 1859; newspaper clipping examined at EHFL.
1859		AM	Chasing. Nov. 15.	SHE 1(19): 17 XI.
1859		BH	Large whale "came ashore"; "had probably been dead two or three weeks". Nov. 19.	SHE 1(20): 24 XI 1859.
1860		SH	Three large right whales chased in early May - "evidently 'old settlers', being exceedingly cunning and shy".	WSL 18(10): 15 V 1860.
1860		So. LI	The past 2 wks. Several whales chased.	SHE 1(43): 3 V 1860.
1860	1	SH	Jan. 24. 30-40 bbls. Chasing again 26 Jan.	SHE 1(29): 26 I 1860; SHC 38(36): 28 I 1860.
1860		BI	Ca. 1 June. Found floating. More than 30-40 bbls.	WSL 18(13): 5 VI 1860; NI 40(41): 29 V 1860.
1861		AM	Unsuccessful chase. May 1.	SHE 2(43): 2 V 1861.
1862		BH	Unsuccessful chase. Jan. 11.	SHE 3 : 16 I 1862.
1862	1	BH	May 12.	SHE 3(45): 15 V 1862.
1864	1	EH		Edwards and Rattray, 1956, p. xxii, 260.
1864	1	AM	27 Jan. Two seen, one killed but sank. Recovered at BH 29 Jan. 60 bbls.	SHE 5(31): 4 II 1864; Hedges, 1897, p. 236.
1864	1, 2 s/1	SH	10 May. 3 chased, struck. One 30 bbl secured, two escaped "with the irons fast in them".	SHE 5(45): 12 V 1864.
1864	1	Bellport	Found dead. "... probably one of those struck off Southampton about a week since."	SHE 5(46): 19 V 1864.
1864	1, 1 s/1	EH	26 Nov. Two "shot". One killed but sank. Fate of other not known.	SHE 6(22): 1 XII 1864.
1865	1	Quogue	Found "drifted ashore". "... probably one which was struck off Wainscott" ca. 28 Jan.-2 Feb.	SHE 6(32): 9 II 1865.
1866	1 s/1	AM	First wk Jan. "... irons drawed."	SHE 7(28): 11 I 1866.
1866		AM	30 April. Several right and humpback whales chased. No strikes.	SHE 7(44): 3 V 1866.
1866		Gardiners Bay	18 June. Whale seen. "Boats were soon got ready, but before they started the whale disappeared."	SHE 7(51): 21 VI 1866.
1867		South side	10 Jan. "Quite a number" chased by crews from AM and WA.	SHE 8(29): 17 I 1867.
1868	1 s/1	BH	Last wk Febr. Line cut.	SHE 9(36): 5 III 1868.

Table 1 (*continued*)

YEAR	CATCH	LOCALITY	REMARKS	SOURCES
1868		AM	First wk Dec. Whales chased.	SHE 10(24): 10 XII 1868.
1869		AM	4 May, chasing whales.	SHE 10(45): 6 V 1869.
1869			3-4 March. Whales chased.	SHE 10(37): 11 III 1869.
1869	2	AM	24 May. One boat "stove". 40-50 bbls total.	SHE 10(48): 27 V 1869; Edwards, 1929; Edwards and Rattray, 1956, p. 22-3.
1869	1	AM	15 March. Female, "dryskin", 25-35 bbls.	SHE 10(38): 18 III 1869; 10(40): 1 IV 1869.
1869	1	AM	18 March. Calf, 20 bbls.	SHE 10(39): 25 III 1869.
1869	1	AM	25 March. 20 bbls.	SHE 10(40): 1 IV 1869.
1869	1	SH	15 April. Initially considered a 30 bbl whale but produced only 13 bbls.	SHE 10(43): 22 IV 1869; 10(44): 29 IV 1869.
1870	1	AM	7 Jan. Expected yield 25 bbls, actual yield 33 bbls.	SHE 11(27): 13 I 1870; 11(28): 20 I 1870.
1870		SH	Whales seen, "none were taken".	SHE 12(13): 6 X 1870.
1870		Quogue	"School" of 25 whales - "the genuine black skins" - seen, 20 Nov.	SHE 12(21): 1 XII 1870.
1871		AM	11-12 Dec. Whale chased.	SHE 13(23): 14 XII 1871.
1872	5	AM	Two in June. The catch of 5 said to have been "the greatest catch within a quarter of a century."	NYT 35 (10742): 5 II 1886.
1873	1	AM	Killed after being stranded.	Edwards, 1929.
1874		BH	Winter. Whale "drifted ashore dead".	Edwards and Rattray, 1956, p. 262.
1874	1	SH	13 Apr. Struck, "swam twenty miles before he died. He was recovered and towed back to the beach by a schooner". 8 ft 3 in. baleen. "It is very seldom that so large a whale is killed in these waters." Baleen "bunched and ready for shipment" weighted 920 lbs. "Dry skin", 18 bbls.	GCG 18(46): 20 III 1875; SHE 15(40): 16 IV 1874; 15(41): 23 IV 1874; 15(42): 30 IV 1874; Rattray, 1933, p. 22.
1874	1	Rockaway Beach	Young "Black Whale" stranded 16 July. Killed with "pocket knife" with 5-in blade in 1 hr. Blubber 13 in thick. 14-ft whale, 6 ft "between the eyes"; 18 ft max. girth; weighed whole, 2160 lbs; made 5 bbls oil; exhibited at Fulton St., NY; first capture of its kind in this area for 30 yrs; whale believed to be ca 6 mos old.	SHC 53(8): 25 VII 1874.
1875	1	AM	13 March. 20-30 bbls.	GCG 18(46): 20 III 1875.
1875	1 (+?)	Sag	27 Feb. By J. Edwards. (A LI specimen thought to have been taken this year was in the AMNH; Allen, 1908, p. 320.)	WSL 33(3): 9 III 1875.
1875	1	AM	29 Feb. Expected to produce 25 bbls, but made 32 bbls.	SHE 16(34): 4 III 1875; 16(36): 18 III 1875.
1875		AM	Chasing whales 20 Nov.	SHE 17(20): 25 XI 1875.
1876	1	SH	Small, 20-35 bbls. Ca. 13 Jan. Another whale made a "narrow" escape.	SHE 17(28): 20 I 1876.
1876	2	AM	Cow and calf. 5 May. Expected 25 bbls apiece, 1,000 lbs baleen from mother.	SHE 17(44): 11 V 1876.
1877	1	AM	"The largest whale ever killed by Amagansett men."	NYT 35(10742): 5 II 1886
1878	1	AM	1 Oct. 40 ft. "The whalebone alone paid for the trouble, and every man got two barrels of whale oil."	SHC 57(22): 26 X 1878.
1879	1	EH	28 ft, killed with shotgun in bay of Promised Land. 5 bbls. "Never before or since has a whale been killed in the bays bordering East Hampton."	EHS 45(43): 29 VIII 1930.
1880		AM	Last wk. April, chasing.	SHE 31(34): 4 III 1880.
1882		SH, AM	Two whaling "stations" active.	Edwards and Rattray, 1956, p. 260.
1882	1	AM, EH	22 March. 70 bbls expected. Exhibited in New York City.	NYT 31(9529): 23 III 1882; 31(9530): 24 III 1882; 31(9531): 25 III 1882
1884		LI	End of March. Large cow and calf chased.	WSL 42(7): 25 III 1884; Allen, 1916, p. 129-30.
Ca 1884	1	AM	One killed, sunk, recovered on third day.	Edwards and Rattray, 1956, p. 62.
Ca 1884	1	AM	"Good-sized", ca. 50 ft.	Edwards and Rattray, 1956, p. viii, 34-6.

Table 1 (*continued*)

YEAR	CATCH	LOCALITY	REMARKS	SOURCES
1885	6	EH, AM, SH	Group of 9 chased. One produced 75 bbls, 8 ft bone - "the largest ever taken off the coast of Long Island in the memory of the present generation" (WSL). One taken 19 Jan. at SH (the third taken since 15 Jan.) est. 40 ft long, 70 bbls. The three taken 20 Jan. were "two cows and a calf" (NYT). One killed Jan. 15 sank and drifted ashore at Shinnecock on Jan. 17.	WSL 42(51): 27 I 1885; 42(52): 3 II 1885; Holder, 1886; Van Beneden, 1885; True, 1885; Brisbane, 1885; NYS 22 I 1885; Harper's Weekly: 31 I 1885; newspaper clipping examined at EHFL; NYT 34(10415): 20 I 1885; 34(10416): 21 I 1885.
1885	1	BH	Two boats. 14 Jan. 55 ft whale, 40 bbls. Cut up at Mecox.	GCG 28(39): 24 I 1885.
1885	2	AM	12 Dec. Both females, 60 and 45 ft, 25 and 45 bbls respectively, 1,000 lbs baleen total. Three whaleboats active.	EHS 1(1): 26 XII 1885; WSL 43(46): 22 XII 1885; Edwards and Rattray, 1956, p. 51-54; Holder, 1886; NYT 35(10742): 5 II 1886.
1886	1	AM	Before 5 Feb.	Holder, 1886; NYT 35(10742): 5 II 1886
1886		AM	Large whale chased ca 15 Dec. Another seen later in the month.	NYT 36(11022): 29 XII 1886
1887	2; 1 s/l	AM	2-3 March. Large "cow" taken; $1,200 worth of oil and bone. A second whale taken this season or next with a "shouldergun" and hand lance. One struck/lost, "hurt so badly he would die"; two whaling "gangs" active, total of 5 boats.	True, 1904, p. 63; Edwards Edwards and Rattray, 1956, p. 65-8, 73-81; EHS 47(17): 26 II 1932; NYT 36(11078): 4 III 1887
1887/8	1	AM	45 ft.	Edwards and Rattray, 1956, p. 82-3.
1887	1 small	WA	April. Bomb lance used. Whale "with short bone but very fat"; it brought $1,500 in all.	Edwards and Rattray, 1956, p. 155; Odell, 1952.
1887-ca. 1900	1; 1 s/l	WA	One taken in Nov. Line had to be cut for second whale.	Edwards and Rattray, 1956, p. 155-7; Odell, 1952.
1888	2	AM	11 January. Male taken (p. 84-9); one of 2 large whales chased. March. Male (50 ft) taken (p. 97-8).	Edwards and Rattray, 1956; WSL 45(50): 17 I 1888. True, 1904, p. 246 NYT 37(11348): 13 I 1888.
1888		AM	Unsuccessful chase; no strike.	EHS 3(10): 25 II 1888.
1889		AM	Two whales seen, no chase, 20 Feb.	EHS: 23 II 1889.
1890	1	AM		Edwards and Rattray, 1956, photo opposite p. 68.
1890		AM	One large whale seen 21 Oct., no chase.	EHS: 25 X 1890.
1890's	1	AM	Winter.	Edwards and Rattray, 1956, p. 104-7.
1891/3	0	AM		Edwards and Rattray, 1956, p. 99.
1893	1	SH	Dec. 27. 75 ft (sic) male.	NYT 43(13213): 28 XII 1893.
1894	1	AM, EH	April. First whale taken here in 4 years. Large, one of 2 that were chased.	Roueche, 1949; Edwards and Rattray, 1956, p. 102-3; NYT 43(13299):8 IV 1894.
1894	[1]	Middle Island	Floated ashore dead, late April or early May. Believed to have been "companion of the one captured off Amagansett about two weeks ago."	NYT 43(13323): 6 V 1894.
1895		EH, AM	Right whale chased; no strike.	EHS 10(45): 18 X 1895
1896		Quogue, AM	Large whale chased during 2nd week of Jan.	NYT 45(13854): 15 I 1896.
1896	1 s/l	AM	August. Iron drew.	Edwards and Rattray, 1956, p. 61-2.
1897	1	AM, SH	20 Feb. 9 boats chased a "school" of at least 3 whales. Bomb lance used. Young 40 ft male, 30 bbls, 600-700 lbs baleen.	SST 16(7): 25 II 1897; NYT 46(14199): 21 II 1897; Harper's Weekly 41(2103): 1897.
1897		SH, AM	Two whales chased. Mid-Feb.	SST 16(7): 25 II 1897.
1897	1	AM	15 March. 50 ft.	Andrews, 1908; NYT 46(14219): 16 III 1897; Harper's Weekly 41(2103): 1897
1898		SH	9 March. Three boats chased a whale; no strike.	SST 17(10): 10 III 1898.
1906		AM	Mid-Nov. Chasing.	SHC: 17 XI 1906.

Table 1 (*continued*)

YEAR	CATCH	LOCALITY	REMARKS	SOURCES
1907	1; 1 s/1	AM	22 Feb. Female, ca 54 ft. First sighted 1 mi offshore. Shoulder gun used. Baleen 7 ft 2 in; 2,000 gals oil. Four whaleboats active, one from EH and 3 from AM. Another large individual bombed but escaped when line was cut, "spouting red" and "mortally wounded". "Biggest whale ever brought up on the Long Island shore" (NYT).	NYT 56(17927): 23 II 1907; Anon., 1907; Andrews, 1908; Roueche, 1949; Edwards and Rattray, 1956, p. 132 et seq.; Reutershan, 1927; newspaper clipping examined at EHFL; EHS 22(13): 1 III 1907.
1907	1	WA	22 Feb. Baleen 3 ft. Whale 40 ft 3 in, female; described as a "calf" (NYT).	NYT 56(17928): 24 II 1907; EHS 22(13): 1 III 1907; NYT 56(17929): 25 II 1907; Anon., 1907; Andrews, 1908; Odell, 1952.
1907		AM	23 Feb. Three more whales seen - "a fine bull" and 2 "smaller ones".	NYT 56(17929): 25 II 1907.
1907			LI whalebone price at its peak: $4.50/lb. Price of oil very low.	Edwards and Rattray, 1956, p. 274.
1908	1	AM	10 Dec. Carcass lost in storm. Female 8.48 m, 15-20 bbls, "good fat right whale".	Andrews, 1909; Allen, 1916, p. 120; newspaper clipping, EHFL.
1909		Long Beach	20 July. Small (18 ft) black whale stranded in surf, killed for oil.	NYT 58(18806): 21 VII 1909.
1910	1	EH, AM	Large.	NYT 69(22632): 11 I 1918.
1911		EH	13 April. Three boats chased; no strike.	EHS 26(19): 14 IV 1911.
1911	1 s/1	AM	8 April. Large. Escaped with harpoon and 6 fathoms of line. As it was struck a "stream of blood spurted up"; whalers believed "the creature received its death blow". Whale had been in vicinity for 3 wks., chased on 4 occasions.	EHS 26(19): 14 IV 1911; Edwards and Rattray, 1956, p. 158-60; NYT 60(19433): 9 IV 1911.
1912		Arverne	19 May. Humpback stranded alive, killed by local residents.	NYT 61(19840): 20 V 1912.
1913		EH, AM	Feb. Chasing. Humpback struck, bomb lance failed to explode, line parted.	Newspaper clipping examined at EHFL.
1913		Long Beach	22 July. A large whale chased by several boats.	NYT 62(20269): 23 VII 1913.
1914		Long Beach	February. A large whale, species unspecified, stranded.	NYT 69(22632): 11 I 1918.
1918		EH, SH	"Some [whales] are still occasionally captured."	Thompson, 1918a, Vol. 2, p. 184.
1918		SH	Early January. Whale seen but not chased.	NYT 69(22632): 11 I 1918.
1918	1; 1 s/1	AM	9 August. Young whale "exceptionally fat", expected to produce 25-30 bbls. Only 30 gals of oil recovered, none sold. Darting gun used. Last whale landed by the LI shore whalers. Struck but lost whale was "spouting blood".	EHS 33(39): 16 VIII 1918; Roueche, 1949; Edwards and Rattray, 1956, p. 9, 161-5.
1919			Two large whales chased, no strike.	EHS 34(36): 25 VII 1919.
1920		SH	Whale sighted first wk of Jan., not chased.	EHS 35(8): 9 I 1920.
1921		AM, SH, EH	20-25 Dec. Unsuccessful chase. Large whale seen "just inside the outer bar, and about a quarter or a half mile offshore at SH. Large whale and calf seen within 200 ft. of shore on 24-25 Dec.	EHS 37(6): 23 XII 1921; NYT 71(23342): 21 XII 1921; (23343): 22 XII 1921; (23344): 23 XII 1921; (23345): 24 XII 1921; (23346): 25 XII 1921; (23347): 26 XII 1921.
1921		Staten Island	A "young whale" (18 ft.) stranded alive and was killed on 24 June. Its "bone and oil" expected to be worth $1500.	NYT 70(23163): 25 VI 1921.
1922	1 s/1	BH, SH	Three crews chased 50 ft whale, 7 Jan. Fastened. "The bomb ... failed to take effect and the whale being only slightly injured gave them an exciting hour or two." Line cut after one-hour tow. According to NYT, whale was "mortally injured", expected to be "washed ashore in a few days".	EHS 37(9): 13 I 1922; Rattray, 1933, p. 22; NYT 71(23360): 8 I 1922.
1922		SH	Whale seen ca 3 mi offshore, 13 October.	NYT 72(23639): 14 X 1922.
1923		EH	Whale seen 18 Dec., not chased.	EHS 39(6): 21 XII 1923.
1924		EH	Female and calf seen "feeding" for two days near Egypt beach, no chase.	EHS 39(12): 1 II 1924.
1924	1 s/1	EH	1 Feb. 40 ft whale struck with bomb lance. "The bomb exploded giving the whale an awful wound and scare"; escaped "spouting blood". Only incentive said to be "the sporting one". Whale was accompanied by a calf.	EHS 39(13): 8 II 1924; NYT 73(24,120): 7 II 1924.
1926		AM	60 ft. female and 25 ft. calf sighted, late June. Not chased.	EHS 41(33): 25 VI 1926.
1926		AM	Large [right] whale seen May 4, not chased.	Edwards and Rattray,

American Pelagic Whaling for Right Whales in the North Atlantic

RANDALL R. REEVES AND EDWARD MITCHELL

Arctic Biological Station, 555 St Pierre Boulevard, Ste-Anne-de-Bellevue, P. Québec H9X 3R4, Canada

ABSTRACT

A sample of eighteenth- and nineteenth-century whaling logbooks and journals in American east-coast collections was examined for information on sightings and catches of North Atlantic right whales, *Eubalaena glacialis*. Three major nineteenth-century North Atlantic grounds were identified: the Cape Farewell Ground, the Southeast US Coast Ground, and the Cintra Bay Ground.

The Cape Farewell Ground, centered at about 60–62° N, 33–35° W, approximately 400–500 km east of Greenland, was visited during summer months (June–September). We accounted for a minimum of 12 vessel-seasons on this ground, covering the period 1868–98. An estimate of total fishing mortality from 1868 to 1897 is 25 right whales.

The Southeast US Coast Ground, consisting of coastal waters between North Carolina and northern Florida, was mainly a winter and early spring right whaling ground (January–March). Seven vessels are known to have cruised there for right whales between 1875 and 1882, accounting for at least 17 vessel-seasons of effort. Including a few catches by shore whalers, at least 25–30 right whales were killed on the Southeast US Coast Ground from 1876 to 1882.

The Cintra Bay Ground, another winter and early spring right whaling ground (November–April), consisted mainly of Bahía de Cintra (23° N, 16° 15′ W), Bahía de Gorrei (22° 50′ N, 16° 20′ W) and nearshore waters along the northwest African coast north and south of these two bays, or generally the southwest coast of the former Spanish Sahara. At least 44 vists to this ground were made by Yankee whaling vessels between 1855 and 1880, mainly from 1855–56 to 1857–58. During this 3-year period approximately 82 right whales were killed on this ground.

A possible 'Iceland Ground' for right whales was centered at 63°–67° N, 11°–16° W; the cruising season there was April to August. Right whales were occasionally encountered by the nineteenth-century American pelagic whalers elsewhere in the North Atlantic, particularly on the Commodore Morris Ground in summer. During the second half of the eighteenth century, the Nantucket and Dartmouth whalers cruised for right whales east of the Grand Bank, in the Strait of Belle Isle and north along the Labrador coast. There is some uncertainty about whether early-season catches at the higher latitudes were of right whales or bowheads, *Balaena mysticetus*.

Estimates of hunting loss in the pelagic right whale fishery resulted in loss rate factors of 1.25–1.57. Mean oil yield on the three major North Atlantic grounds combined was 58–59 barrels (bbls) per whale. At least 20–30% of the whales struck on these grounds were mothers or calves.

The hypothesis that there are at least two stocks of right whales in the North Atlantic, one migrating along the east coast of North America and the other migrating along the coast between northwest Africa and northern Europe, is supported by the available evidence.

Of the three main nineteenth-century whaling grounds, only the Southeast US Coast Ground is known to be used by right whales today. Field surveys of the Cape Farewell Ground and the Cintra Bay Ground are recommended.

INTRODUCTION

The value of historical research in framing and answering questions essential to the wise management of whale stocks has been demonstrated (e.g. see documents in Tillman and Donovan, eds., 1983). Although there is an extensive body of literature on American, or 'Yankee', nineteenth-century pelagic whaling (e.g., Starbuck, 1878; 1964; Tower, 1907; Clark, 1887a; Stackpole, 1953; 1972; Hohman, 1928; Townsend, 1935), few attempts have been made to quantify catches in this fishery by species, and to use these catches to assess trends in whale population abundance (Best, 1970; Henderson, 1972; Bannister, Taylor and Sutherland, 1981; Bockstoce and Botkin, 1983; Mitchell and Reeves, 1983).

Of all the species that have been hunted commercially in the North Atlantic Ocean, the right whale (*Eubalaena glacialis*) was exploited and depleted the earliest and possibly the most seriously. In fact, most authorities agree that by about 1750 it was 'commercially extinct' (Allen, 1908; and see Allen, 1916). Thus, any attempt to reconstruct the history of the right whale's exploitation in the North Atlantic is certain to be frustrated by the shortage of documentation and by the antiquity and relative inaccessibility of what documentation there is.

The fisheries involved in the North Atlantic right whale's exploitation spanned nearly a millenium and were geographically diverse. Spanish Basques pursued right whales from shore, beginning in the eleventh century or earlier (Markham, 1881; Aguilar, 1981), and subsequently from ships as well. Their activities spread across the North Atlantic to Labrador and Newfoundland before 1600 and north to Spitsbergen afterward (Barkham, 1977; 1984). There was probably an early fishery for right whales along the north coast of Norway (Guldberg, 1884a, b; Van Beneden, 1886); Fraser (1970) suggested that the gray whale (*Eschrichtius robustus*) also may have been involved. Early American colonists established an intensive shore fishery directed principally at right whales that lasted from the mid-seventeenth century to the early twentieth century (Dudley, 1725; True, 1904; Allen, 1908; 1916; Edwards and Rattray, 1932, 1956; Reeves and Mitchell, 1986). Modern Norwegian whalers caught small numbers of right whales from shore stations in Scotland (Haldane, 1908; Thompson, 1918; 1928), Ireland (Fairley, 1981) and elsewhere in the Northeast Atlantic (Collett, 1909).

Recent assessments of whale stocks in the North Atlantic have not been encouraging with respect to recovery of the right whale population. Mitchell (1974a) referred to a 'moderate recovery' at the north end of a presumed migration route along the east coast of North America, but concluded:

Estimates based upon sightings and strip census data indicate a population numbered only in the tens of individuals in the region off eastern Canada in summer months.

Analysis of sightings reported on the Scotian Shelf by the Canadian whaling industry between 1966 and 1972 showed no consistent trends but did verify that at least 70 right whales used this area in summer and fall (Mitchell, Kozicki and Reeves, 1986). Kraus and Prescott (1982MS) reported 61 different right whales photodocumented in the Bay of Fundy in summer 1981, and at least 20 right whales were seen in a single day in July 1981 in the Browns Bank region. A research team from the University of Rhode Island counted 46 right whales on Browns Bank during an overflight in August 1980 (Winn, 1982). At least 85 individuals have been identified from aerial photographs and 67 from shipboard photographs on the continental shelf between Cape Hatteras and Cape Sable (Winn, 1982). The peak average abundance estimate for this area, based on extensive aerial census data, was 380 ± 688 whales in spring (Winn, 1982). There are no population estimates for the northeast Atlantic.

The present study is part of a reconstruction of the history of right whale exploitation in the western North Atlantic. We approached this work on a regional basis, beginning with the relatively well-documented Long Island shore fishery (Reeves and Mitchell, 1986). Some information on the fisheries in the Gulf of St Lawrence/Strait of Belle Isle/Labrador region has been presented previously (Mitchell and Reeves, 1983; Reeves and Mitchell, 1982MS) but this segment deserves a more comprehensive study. In the present paper, the American pelagic fishery for right whales throughout the North Atlantic is examined. This leaves the large, protracted shore fisheries in New England and between New Jersey and Florida yet to be addressed in detail. Substantial progress in documenting these fisheries was made ancillary to this and previous work, but our studies are not yet completed.

The quantitative results of this study have been disappointing because they have not led to a useful estimate of absolute population abundance for any area or period. Of course, before such estimates can be attempted, we need the data from all the fisheries involved in the exploitation of the stock or stocks with which we are concerned, and for this we must await the completion of at least the further studies mentioned above. However, the present study has had unanticipated rewards. For example, the elucidation of several grounds in the North Atlantic where right whales were hunted during the nineteenth (and late eighteenth) century should help to focus future field survey efforts. It also enables us to frame and evaluate hypotheses concerning stock relationships of right whales in the North Atlantic.

MATERIALS AND METHODS

Our approach to this work was similar to that used in a previous study of North Atlantic humpback (*Megaptera novaeangliae*) whaling (Mitchell and Reeves, 1983). We searched the published literature, including the *Whalemen's Shipping List and Merchants' Transcript* (*WSL*), published weekly in New Bedford from 1843 to 1914, and several other local newspapers, most fruitfully the *Inquirer and Mirror* of Nantucket (*NIM*), 1821–present. In addition, searches of archival documents were made at seven institutions: the Peter Foulger Museum (PFM) in Nantucket; the Nantucket Atheneum Library (NAL) in Nantucket; the Melville Whaling Room, New Bedford Free Public Library (NBFPL), New Bedford; the Old

Dartmouth Historical Society (ODHS), New Bedford Whaling Museum, New Bedford; the Dukes County Historical Society (DCHS), Gale Huntington Library of History, Edgartown, Massachusetts; the G. W. Blunt White Library (BWL), Mystic Seaport Museum, Mystic, Connecticut; and the Kendall Whaling Museum (KWM), Sharon, Massachusetts. The humpback project (mentioned above) involved the selection and reading of a sample of whaling logbooks and journals from two major collections: the ODHS and the Nicholson Collection, Providence Public Library (PPL), Providence, Rhode Island (see Mitchell and Reeves, 1983, Table 8). Many of the documents in these collections which we would have selected according to the sampling procedures outlined below, were read and indexed for both humpback and right whale information during the humpback study. Thus, we considered additional sampling from these two collections a low priority for this project. The PPL was not revisited, but a small sample of PPL manuscripts was examined or re-examined for this study.

Logbook/journal sampling procedures

We selected a non-random sample of logbooks and journals with the intention of identifying and reading as many manuscripts as possible that contained evidence of right whaling in the North Atlantic. Our search and selection procedures were based on the following rationale.

(1) Because the North Atlantic right whale fishery peaked early, probably before 1800, we examined all available documents covering eighteenth-century voyages, of which few are available outside the NAL (Fonda, 1969; Table 1*).

(2) Because Provincetown vessels usually cruised in the North Atlantic, and because the sample of such voyages is very small in all collections, we read all available Provincetown documents (see Mitchell and Reeves, 1983).

(3) We examined all the documents we could find which Townsend (1935; see Schevill and Moore [1983] and the section below called 'Comments on Townsend's [1935] Sample') identified as having reported captures of North Atlantic right whales.

(4) Knowing that the Southeast US Coast, Cape Farewell and Cintra Bay grounds were areas where some nineteenth-century right whaling took place (Clark, 1887a, b; Mitchell and Reeves, 1983, Table 8; Schevill and Moore, 1983), we checked subject indexes to collections, compiled by the holding institutions, for voyages that visited areas on or near these grounds as well as other areas of interest. Key place names such as Brunswick (Georgia), Fernandina (Florida), Port Royal (South Carolina), Newfoundland, Greenland, Cape Farewell, Iceland and Cintra Bay, were used.

(5) Names of vessels seen or 'spoken' on the grounds were frequently entered in logbooks or journals (Fig. 1). We used such entries in manuscripts that we examined to identify promising voyages made by other vessels. Even if a manuscript covering one of these voyages could not be found, we used data from Starbuck (1878), Hegarty (1959), Wood (n.d., MS), and other sources to make inferences about the nature and size of right whale catches made on them (Tables 2, 3, 4). In some instances, two or three vessels 'mated' on the grounds; thus, a

* All Tables appear after the References section.

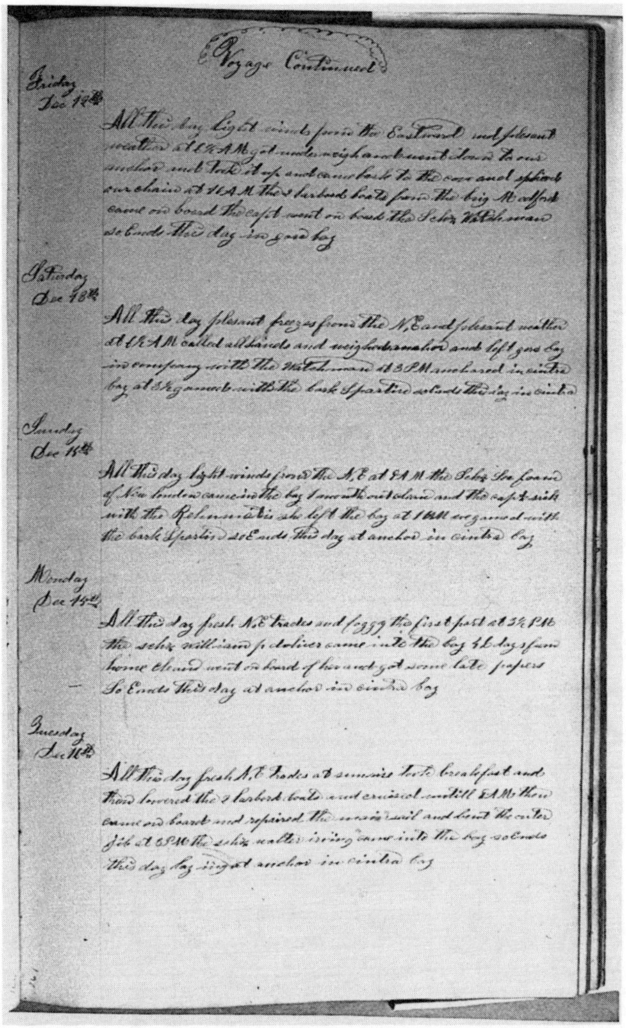

Figure 1: Page from a journal kept on the voyage of the *E. Nickerson* (1856–57, Ms.), 12–16 December 1856, on the Cintra Bay Ground. On 12 December the brig *Medford* and schooner *Watchman* were with the *Nickerson* in Bahia de Gorrei. In subsequent days, the bark *Spartan*, the schooner *Sea Foam* (probably actually the *Sea Witch*), the schooner *William P. Dolliver*, and the schooner *Walter Irving* joined them on this ground. (Courtesy Kendall Whaling Museum).

considerable amount of information about one vessel's activities could sometimes be found in an extant logbook or journal kept aboard another vessel.

(6) While searching for documents of voyages to the North Atlantic right whaling grounds, we examined a few which contained legible, detailed records of seasons spent whaling on right whale grounds outside the North Atlantic. This small sample was used as an independent check on our assumptions concerning the magnitude of hunting loss in the North Atlantic fishery (Table 5).

Whaling abstracts

Three sets of whaling abstracts proved especially useful for this study. The Dennis Wood Abstracts (Wood, n.d., MS), indexed by vessel name, contain intelligence concerning the whereabouts, dates and whale products on board for more than 3,500 Yankee whaling voyages.

The BWL at Mystic has two sets of abstracts which appear to have been written by the same hand and which have at least partially duplicate coverage (Anon., [voyages 1833–1910] n.d., MS a; Anon, [voyages 1832–1905] n.d., MS b). Useful comments on where and when right whales could be found in the North Atlantic are included in both these sets of abstracts.

Mystic's inventory of maritime logbooks and journals

An inventory of maritime logbooks and journals available in some institutional collections was begun some years ago at the BWL in Mystic. The BWL staff call it their 'Union List of Logbooks and Journals'; it consists of many cards, indexed by vessel name. In the absence of a comprehensive list such as the one begun by Stuart Sherman of Brown University, Providence, Rhode Island (Tillman and Donovan, eds., 1983, 'Introduction'), Mystic's inventory can facilitate searches for manuscripts. We used it to check the availability of documents covering voyages by vessels which we knew or had reason to suspect had made voyages at some time in their career to one of the North Atlantic right whaling grounds.

Scope of study

With the exception of the few high-quality documents examined for data on hunting loss in right whale fisheries outside the North Atlantic (Table 5), we confined our search to the American, sailing-vessel, pelagic whale fishery throughout the North Atlantic. Many other fisheries exploited the same stock or stocks of right whales before, during and after the period covered by this study (*ca* 1750–1900; see 'Introduction').

At least occasionally, vessels from non-US ports, especially Portuguese vessels based at the Azores and Cape Verdes (Clarke, 1954, p. 295), participated in the nineteenth-century pelagic sailing-vessel fishery. For example, the brig *Gazelle* of Fayal (Azores) reportedly took a large right whale (105 bbls oil, 950 lb bone), possibly on the northwest coast of Africa in early 1889 (*WSL* 47[7]: 19 March 1889); and the Portuguese brig *Water Witch* mated with the *Richmond* (1857–60, MS) to hunt right whales in Bahía de Cintra during winter 1857–58 (Table 4). Starbuck (1878) and Hegarty (1959) did not list the *Gazelle* or the *Water Witch*. The activities of such vessels will generally be overlooked in a study like ours which relies almost entirely on logbooks and journals of voyages originating in New England ports.

RESULTS

Three areas were identified in this study as the principal nineteenth-century North Atlantic right whaling grounds. We have named these the Cape Farewell Ground, the Southeast US Coast Ground, and the Cintra Bay Ground. The Cape Farewell Ground was a summer ground, and the other two were winter grounds. In separate accounts below, we discuss the nature and amount of documented whaling effort on each of these grounds. In addition, we describe what we know about a possible 'Iceland Ground', and summarize some observations and catches of right whales made outside the three main grounds. A few vessels also cruised for right whales in the New York Bight during the 1820s and 1850s, but their activities are discussed elsewhere (Reeves and Mitchell, 1986).

224

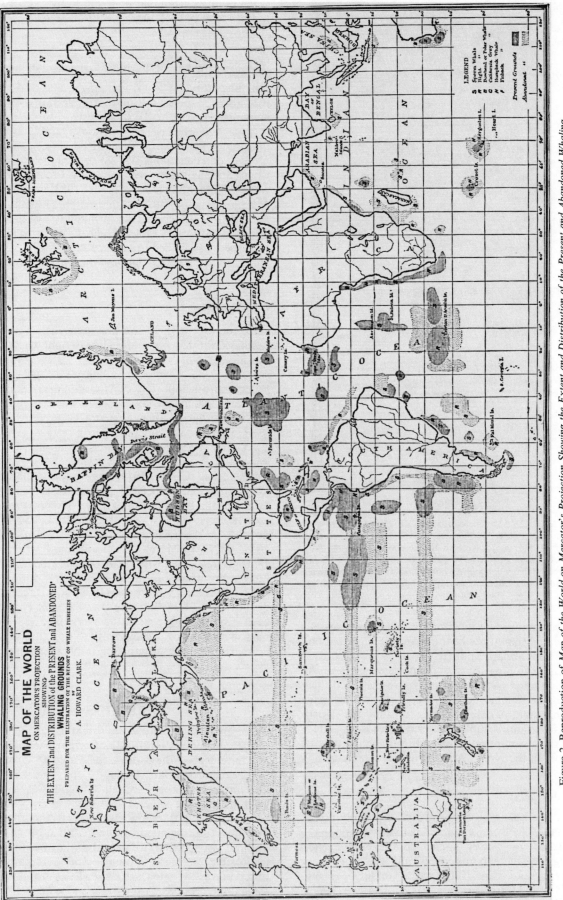

Figure 2. Reproduction of *Map of the World on Mercator's Projection Showing the Extent and Distribution of the Present and Abandoned Whaling Grounds* prepared for the illustration of the report on whale fisheries by A. Howard Clark (1887b, plate 183).

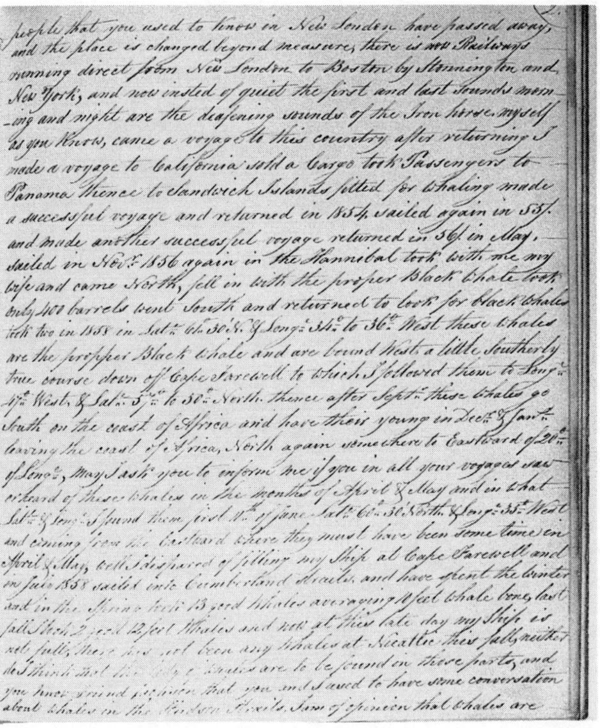

Figure 3: Second page of a letter to William Jackson from Christopher Chapel, dated 16 October 1859, found at the back of the logbook of the *Violet* (1853, Ms) of Hull, ms. no. 200. (Courtesy Kendall Whaling Museum.)

I. Cape Farewell Ground

Eschricht and Reinhardt (1866, p. 5) indicated that bowheads (*Balaena mysticetus*) were rarely encountered along the west coast of Greenland south of 65° N, although they knew of a few young individuals being seen between 61° N and 62° N, one of which was seen 23 July – 'at a season most extraordinary'. Of particular interest, however, is a whale taken at Holsteinsborg (66° 56′ N), 23 March 1782, which had 5-foot whalebone, produced only about 640–768 gallons of oil and yet was judged to be an old individual (Eschricht and Reinhardt, 1866, pp. 19–20). It was the second of its kind to have been caught at Holsteinsborg during 70 years of whaling and the Greenlanders called it an *Osterboygds Hval*, or 'east coast whale'. Eschricht and Reinhardt evidently believed this whale was *Eubalaena*, and by inference it can be assumed that the Greenlanders recognized it as a species found near the east coast of Greenland, perhaps in Denmark Strait.

Right whales, listed explicitly as 'Noordkapers', were caught occasionally during the 1770s by Dutch pelagic whalers whose main quarry was the bowhead in Davis Strait and the Greenland Sea (e.g. Van Sante, 1770, pp. 197, 205, 222, 227, 252; also see de Jong, 1983, p. 91). The right whales included in the Dutch 'Arctic' catch were certainly from a North Atlantic population, possibly from the stock found on the Cape Farewell Ground in summer. French pelagic bowhead whalers who visited Spitsbergen and Davis Strait from 1817 to 1837 may also have taken a few right whales, but the French statistics for this period do not distinguish between the two species (DuPasquier, 1982, pp. 17–18). The *Sarde* whales (right whales) taken by French Basques during the seventeenth century were caught mainly in Iceland waters (Du Pasquier, 1984).

(i) *Extent of the grounds*

Most charts of the nineteenth-century whaling grounds do not show a Cape Farewell Ground for right whales. For the vicinity of Cape Farewell, Clark (1887b; Fig. 2) showed only the eastern extremity of a bowhead whaling ground, continuous across lower Davis Strait and into Hudson Strait, although he (Clark, 1887a, p. 15) mentioned that right whales were taken 'during the summer months off the southern end of Greenland'. We found two charts showing the Cape Farewell Ground as an area of right whale concentration. One appears in the generally uncritical work by Mörzer Bruyns (1971, chart 6); the basis for his outline of a right whale migration between Newfoundland and Denmark Strait is not known. The other was prepared by a sub-committee of the IWC Scientific Committee in 1974 (IWC, 1976); their fig. 11 indicates possible right whale concentrations in Denmark Strait and off North Cape, Norway. The basis for this chart was not rigorous, being an agreement among participants in the meeting that the distributions as sketched were realistic approximations based on sightings and kill records, not all of which were published. The approximate distributions were not based on plots of records, *per se*.

The Cape Farewell Ground was well known to at least some members of the New England whaling community during the second half of the nineteenth-century. Various forms of intelligence provide clues to the location of the ground and to the period of heaviest exploitation of it.

An interesting account is given in a letter from Captain Christopher B. Chapel to Captain William Jackson, dated 16 October 1859 (*Violet*, 1853, MS; Fig. 3). While summarizing a recent part of his whaling career, Chapel mentions that he sailed 'North' in November 1856 in the *Hannibal*, 'fell in with the proper Black Whale', and returned with 'only' 400 bbls of oil. In the next sentence he claims to have 'returned to look for black whales', taking two of them in 1858 at 61° 3′ N, 34–36° W. He stresses that these were 'the propper Black Whale and are bound West a little Southerly true course down off Cape Farewell....' Chapel 'followed' this body of whales to 50–57° N, 47° W;

thence after Sept[r] these whales go South on the coast of Africa and have their young in Dec[r] & Jan.[y] leaving the coast of Africa, north again somewhere to Eastward of 20 ° of Long[e].

Chapel found these whales first on 11 June at 60° 30′ N, 35° W, 'coming from the Eastward where they must have been some time in April & May'. Chapel's letter was written from Cumberland Sound, where he had gone in July 1858, having 'dispared of filling my ship at Cape Farewell'.

Starbuck (1878, pp. 544–5) indicated that the *Hannibal* sailed from New London on 6 November 1856 bound for the 'Pacific Ocean', returning on 23 November 1859 with 1,880 bbls of whale oil and 24,600 lbs of baleen on board, having sent home 356 bbls and 6,500 lbs during the 3-yr cruise. However, Decker (1973, pp. 150–1) gave the *Hannibal*'s destination as 'Cumberland St'. Wood (n.d. MS, vol.—, p. 550) gave 'N. Pacific' as the destination for this cruise but indicated that the *Hannibal* went instead to the Azores and Spitzbergen before arriving at Cumberland Sound. The itinerary appears to have been highly irregular. The vessel called at Port Praya on 24 December and landed 30 bbls of sperm oil at Fayal on 18 March 1857. She was next 'spoken' at 65° 10′ N,

6° 10′ W, on an unspecified date, 'cruising'. On 29 September she was back to Fayal 'fm Spitzbergen 450 Wh 4000 Bone'. She sailed again on 15 October 'to cruise'. By 12 August 1858 the *Hannibal* had finally reached Cumberland Sound.

P. Goldring (*in litt.*, 14 March 1985), who has studied New London whaling in the northern North Atlantic, notes that the *Hannibal*'s voyage did fit the pattern of voyages sponsored by Perkins and Smith, which often involved experimental whaling in high latitudes. The *Hannibal*'s consort for part of this voyage, the *Daniel Webster*, also cleared for the North Pacific, but not until June 1858. Her home port was New Bedford, but her captain, Dexter Bellows, was a New Londoner. It would be interesting to know when and where the two vessels met before reaching Cumberland Sound.

New London voyages 'for Greenland' began in May 1864 (schooner *Leader*) and May 1865 (schooner *Erie*); both vessels went to Cumberland Sound, where they apparently overwintered (Wood, N.D., MS, vol. IV, pp. 315, 343). In an abstract of the schooner *Petrel*'s voyage of 1866, it is noted (Anon., n.d., MS b, p. 71; also see Anon., n.d., MS a, p. 14):

Greenland.		Right whale Ground
Lat.		Long.
60.00 N		33.00 W.
to		to
62.00 N		35.00 W.

At the end of his journal of the 1878 voyage by the *A. J. Ross* (1878–79, MS) to Hudson Bay, James A. Sinclair made the following notes:

Lat & Long of Whales seen on the East Coast
of Greenland
Sch[r] Abbie Bradford
60.11 N 34–48 W
59–00 18 to 60–00 N 39 to 41 W
Sch[r] Astoria
June 13, 14, 15 / 56–10 N 42.7 W
July 30–31 Aug 1. 2. 3.
　59.5518 38–52 W
Aug 4. 5. 6. 7. 8th
　59.56 N – 40–15 W.

Sinclair did not specify that these were right whales. It is reasonable to suppose that they were, however, since the *Ross* had been on a right whaling cruise to the Cape Farewell Ground the previous year (*John A. Ross*, 1877–78, MS), and in 1878–79 Sinclair's main quarry was the bowhead. Moreover, Ferguson's (1938, pp. 8–12) journal of the 1878–79 voyage of the *Abbie Bradford* indicates that 'right whales' were hunted on the Cape Farewell Ground in June 1878, probably at the positions given by Sinclair (above). Ferguson's (1938, p. 35) account of a 'gam' with the *A. J. Ross* in Roes Welcome Sound on 31 July 1878 suggests that the *Abbot Lawrence* may have taken a right whale that summer at the Cape Farewell Ground or elsewhere *en route* to Hudson Bay. Captain David Gray, a Peterhead whaleman, told Southwell (1904, p. 85) that he knew of instances when right whales had been seen "in about the latitude of Cape Farewell."

(ii) *Period, season and effort*

In addition to the above data, we have the information contained in manuscripts covering nine more voyages to this whaling ground (Table 2). The voyages span the period 1868–98, which we assume to be the period when the popularity of this ground reached a peak. Reference

Figure 4: First page of William Poole's journal kept aboard the *Bartholomew Gosnold* in 1881 (1881–3, Ms.), indicating that after looking for whales at 39° 30′–42° N, 57° 30′–63° W, and finding only 'Finbacks', she "left for Right-whaling of[f] Cape Farewell". (Courtesy Kendall Whaling Museum.)

is made in the manuscripts to 'Greenland Right-whaling' (*Canton*, 1895–96, MS a) and 'Right-Whaling of[f] Cape Farewell' (*Bartholomew Gosnold*, 1881–83, MS; Fig. 4). The earliest arrival on the Cape Farewell Ground was about 5 June; the latest departure, in early September. Catches were made between 12 June and 24 August. Of the vessels visiting this ground, six were barks, two were brigs, one was a schooner and one was a ship, with sizes ranging from 115 to 441 tons. All but one of the vessels that we know visited this ground were from New Bedford; the *Hannibal* was from New London. At least four vessels made repeat visits – *Hannibal* (1856, 1858), *Abbie Bradford* (1878, 1884), *A. R. Tucker* (1880, 1895, 1897), and *Canton* (1895, 1897).

(iii) *Itineraries*

In its review of the whale fishery for 1878, the *WSL* (36[48]: 14 January 1879; and see Clark, 1887a) noted: 'A number of whalers are wintering in Hudson's Bay and Cumberland Inlet, several of which cruised off Greenland for Right whales during the Summer, but without success'. Several vessels in our logbook/journal sample (e.g. Table 2, entry nos 7 and 9) included visits to the Cape Farewell Ground in itineraries aimed principally at reaching the Hudson Bay bowhead grounds. The *Abbie Bradford* sailed in May 1878, reached a 'good whaling ground off some islands on the east coast of Greenland' in five weeks, and encountered right whales there on 11 June. That these whales were *Eubalaena* rather than *Balaena* cannot be proven by reference to Ferguson's (1938, p. 8) comments, but we strongly suspect they were. Although only one whale was captured, Ferguson believed the vessel was 'into the middle of quite a school of whales, for they could be heard spouting in different directions all around us any time during the night'. After a brief call at Iceland, the *Abbie Bradford* proceeded on 26 June directly round Cape Farewell and to Hudson Strait 'looking for whales all the while, but without success' (Ferguson, 1938, p. 12). Voyages by the *Abbie Bradford* (1884–85, MS) and the *Canton* (1895–96, MS a, b) were marked by singularly uneventful cruises on the Cape Farewell Ground. Both sailed in May and arrived on the Cape Farewell Ground in mid-June. Neither vessel's crew sighted a right whale there, although they saw finner whales (*Balaenoptera* spp.) and 'plenty Feed' (*Canton*, 1895–96, MS b). Both vessels departed the vicinity of Cape Farewell and headed for Resolution Island, at the entrance of Hudson Strait, in early July.

One of the more interesting itineraries was that of the bark *Palmetto* (1886, MS). She sailed 24 June for 'Hudson Bay' (Hegarty, 1959, p. 19). By 17 July, however, the *Palmetto* was at 61° 14′ N, 36° 12′ W, i.e. on the Cape Farewell Ground. Right whales were first sighted 20 July and by 9 August the crew had taken their fifth right whale alongside. This catch was evidently judged large enough to take home, and after a brief port call at Fayal (Azores) in early October, the bark arrived back at New Bedford 6 November. This short (*ca* $4\frac{1}{2}$ months) voyage is the only one we discovered in which right whaling on the Cape Farewell Ground proved to be the only profitable activity. Although Hegarty (1959, p. 19) listed no products for this voyage, we know 150 bbls of oil were recovered from the first two whales taken and that all or most of the whalebone was 'stowed away' and later scraped, washed and bundled (*Palmetto*, 1886, MS). It is possible that the cargo was sold at Fayal, which might explain why the returns for New Bedford showed no catch. The *Palmetto* sailed again slightly more than three weeks after her arrival at New Bedford, this time with a different captain and with the 'Atlantic' given as a destination (Hegarty, 1959, p. 19). Her returns from this voyage, which lasted more than three years, included 1,840 bbls of sperm oil, 160 of whale oil and no whalebone.

Another interesting itinerary was that of the brig *A. J. Ross* in 1877–78 (*John A. Ross*, 1877–78, MS). Tilton (1928, p. 24) reported that the vessel was 'fitting out for a Greenland voyage' when he shipped aboard as a spare boatsteerer. The brig sailed directly to the Cape Farewell Ground, where four right whales were taken during August (Table 2). Tilton (1928, p. 25) described the experience as follows: 'There wasn't any ice but the weather was the dirtiest I had ever seen. We found whales, so tame that we couldn't help getting them....' For three weeks the fog was too thick for sighting whales. Thus:

Not being able to find our way into any Greenland port or bay, the old man [captain] got mad and started for the coast of Africa, after 'right' whales (Tilton, 1928, p. 26).

The *A. J. Ross* visited the Canary Islands, then anchored in Bahía de Cintra for three weeks, during which time no whales were sighted. After a port-call at the Cape Verde Islands, they went to Bermuda, 'the Old Man planning to write home to the owners for provisions and to refit and go back to Greenland' (Tilton, 1928, p. 29). However, orders came for the vessel to return to New Bedford, where it arrived in early April 1878.

In his study of Hudson Bay whaling, Ross (1974) used three different approaches to estimate the nineteenth-century kill of bowheads in the bay. Two of these used returns of oil and whalebone listed by Starbuck (1878) and Hegarty (1959) for Hudson Bay voyages. The catch of right whales by some Hudson Bay-bound vessels, documented above, means that some of the products listed for these voyages were not from bowheads. Ross's third method, in which the average catch by a sample of voyages (documented by logbooks or journals) is attributed by extrapolation to all voyages bound to Hudson Bay, runs the risk of including voyages such as that of the *Palmetto* (1886, MS), mentioned above. Ross neither listed the logbooks and journals he consulted, nor did he provide details on how Starbuck's statements of destination were 'corrected' to avoid inclusion of non-Hudson Bay voyages in the extrapolation.

The itinerary of the *Hannibal* in 1856–59 apparently involved at least two excursions to the Cape Farewell Ground as well as two or three winters in Cumberland Sound (see above). An examination of this vessel's logbook (if it exists) would be of great interest.

II. Southeast US Coast Ground

Earll (1887b, p. 518; also see Clark, 1887a, p. 49) described the discovery of this ground as follows.

Formerly, and for a number of years, a portion of the New Bradford and Provincetown whaling fleet, while cruising on the 'Bahama Grounds' during the fall and winter, made a practice of running into Fernandina, Fla., to ship their cargoes of oil and bone instead of taking the time to carry them home. While in this vicinity they frequently sighted whales and occasionally succeeded in taking some of them. The yellow fever at Fernandina several years ago caused some of the vessels to change their landing place to Brunswick. In the winter of 1875–'76 the schooner Golden Eagle,[1] after landing her cargo, remained in this region to cruise for whales, making Brunswick her headquarters for over two months. During this time she secured one whale. The next year two vessels came to cruise in the same locality and met with fair success. Others followed, and in the winter of 1879–'80 five whalers made Brunswick their headquarters while cruising along the shore, and up to March 1 they had taken five whales, yielding 226 barrels of oil and 2,750 pounds of bone, all of which was shipped to the Massachusetts whaling ports.

(i) Extent of the grounds

The winter right whaling ground 'discovered' by the *Golden City* in 1875–76 appears to have been centered close along the coasts of South Carolina and Georgia, where right whales were considered 'more plenty...than they have been for many years' (Earll, 1887b, p. 514; also see Manigault *in* Holder, 1883, p. 104; Manigault, 1885). The whale taken in 1875–76 was actually caught off Fernandina Light (*Golden City*, 1876, MS). We have seen a reference to the 'Fernandina Ground' (*NIM* 57[35]: 24

---

[1] We have sought, without success, evidence of a New England schooner called *Golden Eagle* (see Hegarty, 1959; 1964; Starbuck, 1878). However, the clipper ship *Golden Eagle* sailed from Boston to San Francisco in December 1852 (Shoemaker, 1937, p. 29) and from Honolulu to New Bedford in 1859 (Anon., 1859). In the latter instance, she carried a cargo of whale oil and whalebone from the North Pacific fleet. The bark *Black Eagle* of Sag Harbor (and later New Bedford) was whaling in the Arctic between 1851 and 1872, and she was sold to Beverly in 1873 'for freighting' (Starbuck, 1878, p. 625). We are confident that Earll did not mistakenly call the *Black Eagle* the *Golden Eagle*. All circumstantial evidence points to the schooner *Golden City* of New Bedford as being the vessel Earll had in mind when referring to the schooner *Golden Eagle*. The *Golden City*'s first whaling voyage, after being bought from Boston, was to the Atlantic Ocean in 1875–76, and she returned to New Bedford with a cargo of 440 bbls of sperm oil and 40 bbls of whale oil (Starbuck, 1878, pp. 650–1). The whale oil was from a right whale taken on 25 February 1876 off Fernandina (*Golden City*, 1875–76, MS).

February 1877) but assume from the context that this was an offshore sperm whaling ground, not the coastal right whaling ground discussed here. Although right whales were hunted by shore-based crews in boats along the coast of North Carolina from the late seventeenth century until the early twentieth century (Brimley, 1894; True, 1904; Stick, 1958; Muse, 1961), only two large vessels are known to have cruised there during winter, using Beaufort as their headquarters (Earll, 1887a, p. 490). These unrewarding attempts took place in 1874–75 (the *Daniel Webster*) and 1878–79 (the *Seychelle*).[2] A plan for the Southampton (N.Y.) sloop *Speedwell* to hunt whales along the Outer Banks was set in motion in 1666–67, but we know nothing of the outcome (Palmer, 1959, pp. 12–14).

Evidently some whalemen believed there was a bay in the vicinity of Port Royal harbor 'sought by them [right whales] during the month of March – the breeding season' (*WSL* 37[6]: 25 March 1879). The whaling ground between Brunswick and Port Royal was said to be 'on a bar only about 4 miles from the shore' (Clark, 1887a, p. 49).

(ii) *Period, season and effort*

In a statement generally corroborating that of Earll (1887b) quoted above, Clark (1887a, p. 49) indicated that most vessels involved in this fishery were small, ranging from 53 to 117 tons. The seven vessels (all schooners) which we know participated in the right whale fishery on this ground averaged about 86 tons (range: 54 to 112 tons; Table 3). Two hailed from Edgartown, the rest from New Bedford. The period of documented exploitation by pelagic whalers was from 1875 to 1882, although we might infer from Earll's (1887b) statement (above) that some whaling activity had occurred in the vicinity of Fernandina several years before 1875, and there is evidence of at least one more catch off South Carolina in 1884 (Allen, 1916, p. 130).

Right whales apparently were not observed on the Southeast US Coast Ground before the end of January or after early March. Clark (1887a, p. 49) noted that the vessels cruised there during 'the winter and early spring months'.

There were at least 17 vessel-seasons for which we have documentation (Table 3). Repeat visits to the Southeast US Coast Ground were made by the *Golden City* (6), *Charles W. Morse* (3), *E. B. Conwell* (2), *Emma Jane* (2), and *Lottie E. Cook* (2). We believe our accounting is incomplete. Earll (1887b) referred to five vessels on the grounds in 'the winter of 1879–'80'; and Clark (1887a) referred to four vessels on the grounds 'in 1879'; but both authors gave the same production figures 'up to March 1'. Earll's version is more consistent with our evidence (Table 3). Although we cannot confirm it, we suspect the *Ellen Rizpah* of Provincetown may have taken right whales on this ground in 1878. She made a short (7

month) voyage from 4 February to 7 September that year and returned with 170 bbls of whale oil and 1,900 lbs of whalebone (Hegarty, 1959, p. 7). We also have indirect evidence that the *Surprise* may have cruised there during February 1881 (*NIM* 61[36]: 5 March 1881), although Hegarty (1959, p. 10) listed no oil or bone for this voyage.

(iii) *Itineraries*

The *Golden City* (1878–80, MS) anchored at Brunswick on 30 January 1879 after a season of sperm whaling on the Charleston Ground and on that day lowered her boats to chase a right whale. She continued 'cruising for right whales' along the coast of Georgia until mid-March, when she returned to the Charleston Ground and resumed sperm whaling. Two years later on 19 January 1881, the *Golden City* (1880–81, MS) was back at anchor off Brunswick, having followed an itinerary in 1880–81 similar to that of 1878–79. However on 14 February, in the midst of her right whaling season, a telegram arrived at Brunswick 'with orders to go Sperm Whaling'. After another autumn of sperm whaling on the Charleston Ground in 1881, the *Golden City* (1881–82, MS) arrived at Port Royal on 11 January 1882. Upon leaving Port Royal on 21 January she cruised along the Georgia coast, taking a small (25-bbl) right whale off Brunswick on 26 February. The *Golden City* sailed from Brunswick that year on 6 March, bound for the West Indies sperm whaling.

The schooner *E. H. Hatfield* (1880–82, MS) of Edgartown followed a slightly different itinerary. She visited the Bahamas in December 1880 and cruised for sperm whales on the Southern Ground until February. After being anchored for about ten days (5–16 February) at Morehead City, N.C., the *Hatfield* 'steered down the coast to the southward looking for Right Whales'. Working in company with the schooner *Emma Jane* of Edgartown, the *Hatfield* remained on the right whaling ground until 17 May, when she finally weighed anchor at Fort Macon, Ga., and headed for Bermuda. She had cruised 'outside the bar' but within several miles of shore until well into April, calling periodically at Macon and Fort Caswell. She took on crew at Wilmington, N.C., on 1 May. The fact that only one whale – a 'finback' – was sighted by the *Hatfield*'s crew during the entire period 5 February–17 May might, at least in part, explain this vessel's failure to return to the Southeast US Coast Ground the next year. The *Hatfield* went sperm whaling on the Charleston and Western grounds the following year, but she attempted humpbacking at the Cape Verde Islands during the winter of 1881–82 instead of right whaling off the US coast.

The *Charles W. Morse* of New Bedford apparently made an extraordinary catch of right whales along the coast of Georgia in 1880. Without examining her logbook for this season, we can only speculate about her activities by inference. On 23 February she was reported off Brunswick and had 'previously taken a right whale in company with schooner E. B. Conwell, which made 35 to 40 bbls' (*WSL* 38[4]: 9 March 1880). Later, the *Morse* was reported at sea, no date, four months out, with 265 bbls of sperm oil, 110 whale and 1,200 lb of bone (baleen) (*WSL* 38[4]: 9 March 1880). She was again reported 'at sea' on 17 March, 'having taken one whale making 30 bbls since last report – 265 bbls. sperm, 250 do. whale oil and 2,500 lb. bone, all told' (*WSL* 38[7]: 30 March 1880). A cargo transshipped from Fernandina by

[2] According to Earll (1887a, p. 490) the *Daniel Webster* was a 241.5 ton vessel with a Provincetown crew. Neither Starbuck (1878) nor Hegarty (1959; 1964) mentioned a vessel by this name as having sailed in 1875, although the 327-ton bark *Daniel Webster* of New Bedford is known to have sailed on a 3½-year voyage to the Atlantic in 1877 (Hegarty, 1959, p. 5). This bark saw a schooner out of Boston called 'Daniel Webster', off Flores on 30 August 1877 (*Daniel Webster*, 1877–78, MS). The 210-ton 2-masted schooner *Daniel Webster* was built in Charlestown in 1853 (*fide* R. Webb, pers. comm., 14 May 1984, from Boston Ship Register). No vessel called *Seychelle* is listed by either Starbuck or Hegarty.

the *Morse* on the *Western Texas* arrived in New York on 13 April (*WSL* 38[10]: 20 April 1880). It included 310 bbls of whale oil and 2,900 lb of bone. Assuming these were the products of right whales caught off Georgia, it is probably safe to conclude that the *Morse* killed and secured a minimum of four right whales that season.

III. Cintra Bay Ground

This appears to have been the most frequented cruising ground for right whales in the North Atlantic during the nineteenth century. Many vessels visited the nearby Canary and Cape Verde islands and the opportunity to catch right whales along the coast of Africa during winter was both appealing and convenient.

(i) *Extent of the grounds*

The whaling ground which we call the Cintra Bay Ground has not been named or recognized by most whaling historians. Clark (1887a, p. 16) mentioned the Cintra Bay Ground and identified it on his chart of the whaling grounds (Clark, 1887b). Clark (1887a, p. 16) described the ground as 'along the west coast of Africa, in latitude 15° north, and in Center Bay, about latitude 23° north'. Judging by statements from our sample of logbooks and journals, it consisted mainly of Bahía de Cintra (23° N, 16° 15′ W), Bahía de Gorrei (22° 50′ N, 16° 20′ W) and coastal waters from approximately 10 miles north of Puntilla de las Raimas (the north end of Bahía de Cintra) to 20 miles south of Bahía de Gorrei. The most southern capture mentioned in our manuscript sample was made about 20 miles north of Cabo Barbas (*Walter Irving*, 1856–57, MS; Table 4, entry no. 20). The American whalemen called the bays Cintra, Centra, Center or Senter, and Gora, Gore or Goree. We found no evidence, published or unpublished, to support Clark's (1887a, p. 16) reference to the catching of right whales at 15° N on the west coast of Africa. His illustration of this ground (Clark, 1887b) shows it to be mainly south of Bahía de Cintra (Fig. 2). Bahía de Cintra and Bahía de Gorrei are on the southwest coast of the former Spanish Sahara.

(ii) *Period, season and effort*

We were able to identify 44 voyages that included the Cintra Bay Ground in their itineraries (Table 4), although for some of these (e.g. entry nos 11, 12, 21, 23, 24) there is no particular reason to believe a serious attempt was made to cruise there for right whales. The voyages span the period 1855 to 1880; however, the vast majority of the voyages (84%) took place between 1855 and 1858.

The season for whaling on the Cintra Bay Ground was prolonged in comparison to that for the other North Atlantic winter ground, the Southeast US Coast Ground. Vessels arrived on the grounds as early as 14 November and departed as late as 26 April (Table 4). Unlike the Southeast US Coast Ground, the Cintra Bay Ground was not in the immediate vicinity of a major port which might attract vessels for reasons unrelated to the prospect of finding whales (e.g. securing crews, taking on provisions, trans-shipping oil and bone). Right whales were sighted there as early as 20 November and as late as 18 or 19 April; thus, the season spanned close to five months. The distribution of known catches was as follows: November (1), December (4), January (7), February (13), March (5) and April (3). Of the eight records mentioned for the coasts of France, Spain and the

Mediterranean by Jouan (1890, as cited *in* Allen, 1908, p. 303), one was in early November, one in late December, three in January and two in February (the Algiers record of January 1888 having been wrongly assigned by Jouan to February or March – see Pouchet and Beauregard, 1888).

Clark (1887a, p. 16) claimed that only 'a few small vessels have cruised with indifferent success for right whales' on this ground. Except for the three consecutive winters from 1855–56 to 1857–58 when the whaling effort included at least 37 vessel-seasons, our data are consistent with the impression that both effort and results on this ground were 'indifferent'. However, not all the vessels that cruised here were 'small'. Tonnages ranged from 92 to 451 tons ($\bar{x} = 178$, $n = 33$). Of the 34 vessels we know visited this ground, 15 were schooners (44%), 12 barks (35%), 6 brigs (18%) and one a ship (3%). Most of them hailed from Provincetown (35%), New Bedford (21%), Orleans (12%) or New London (9%).

(iii) *Itineraries*

Our knowledge of itineraries involving a hunt for right whales on the Cintra Bay Ground comes mainly from manuscripts covering seven voyages (Table 4, entry nos 1, 3, 13, 20, 29, 40, 41).

Among the most legible and well documented is that of the *E. Nickerson* (1856–57, MS) of Provincetown. She sailed 22 August 1856 and headed directly for the Azores, then to the southward, blackfishing and sperm whaling in the eastern North Atlantic until mid-November. On 12 November the *Nickerson* stopped at Grand Canary Island to get wood. Then on 17 November the vessel reached Cape Barberus (Cabo Barbas) and began working up the west coast of Africa. She was anchored in Gora Bay (Bahía de Gorrei) on 20 November, when the first 'wright whales' – a cow and calf – were sighted. A routine was established which typified the whaling on this ground (Fig. 5). The vessel was anchored in or near one of the two whaling bays, cruising off and on between them. Boats generally would be lowered in the morning to search for whales until dusk. Carcasses were towed to the vessel for trying-out on board. Whaling crews frequently went in boats to catch fish ('mullet' – *Mugil* sp.?) near shore, but they only rarely ventured onto the land – 'in the wildes of Africa' as one whaling captain's wife described it in her journal (*Ohio*, 1875–78, MS.). Many times two or three vessels 'mated', their crews working together to catch whales. A carcass would be towed to the nearest vessel for processing, and later the products (oil and whalebone) would be exchanged, as appropriate. Such matings are responsible for the fractions of whales listed in our Tables 3 and 4.

During early February the *Nickerson* extended her search south along the coast to 20 miles below Bahía de Gorrei, but returned to Bahía de Cintra on the 20th, where she remained until 2 March. Having seen no whales (except some killer whales, *Orcinus orca*) since 14 February, when a small female right whale was taken south of Bahía de Gorrei, the *Nickerson* 'weighed anchor in cintra by for the Cape de verds' on 2 March. At the Cape Verde Islands she joined several other vessels chasing humpbacks. The humpbacking season ended by mid-April and the *Nickerson* returned to the sperm whaling grounds further north. After a successful season of sperm whaling, she arrived home on 3 August 1857; the entire voyage lasted somewhat less than a year.

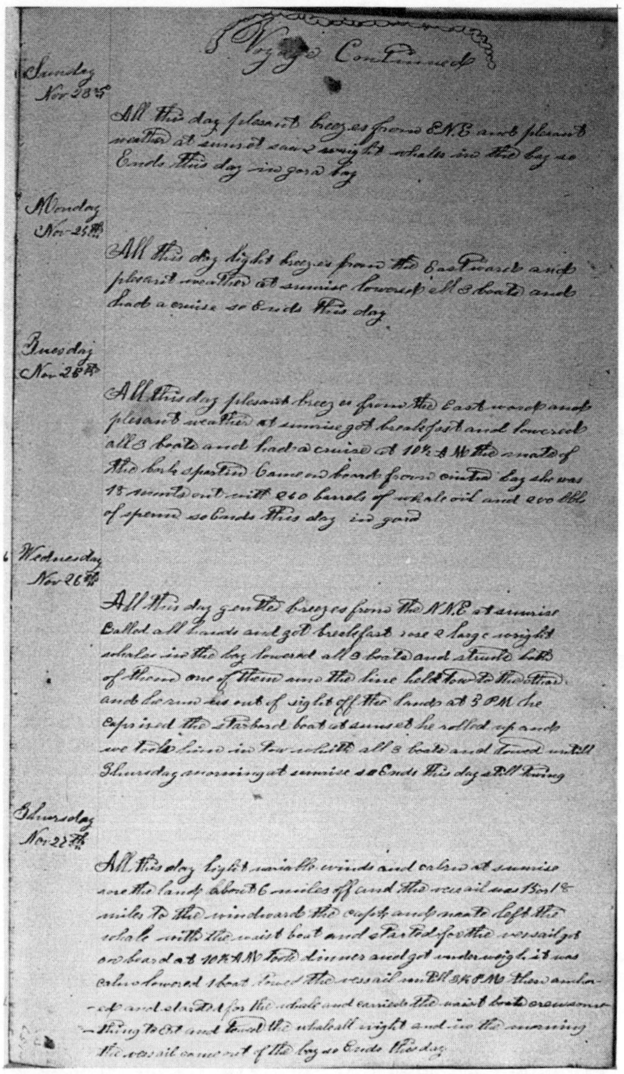
Voyage Continued

Sunday Nov 23rd
All this day pleasant breezes from E.N.E and pleasant weather at sunset saw 2 wright whales in the bay so Ends this day in good bay

Monday Nov 24th
All this day light breezes from the Eastward and pleasant weather at sunrise lowered all 3 boats and had a cruise so Ends this day

Tuesday Nov 25th
All this day pleasant breezes from the Eastward and pleasant weather at sunrise got breakfast and lowered all 3 boats and had a cruise at 10½ A.M the mate of the bark Spartan came on board from cintra bay she was 18 months out with 260 barrels of whale oil and 200 bbls of sperm so Ends this day in good

Wednesday Nov 26th
All this day gentle breezes from the N.N.E at sunrise called all hands and got breakfast saw 2 large wright whales in the bay lowered all 3 boats and struck both of them one of them ran the line held tow to the other and he run us out of sight off the lands at 3 PM he capsized the starboard boat at sunset he rolled up and we took him in tow with all 3 boats and towed until Thursday morning at sunrise so Ends this day still towing

Thursday Nov 27th
All this day light variable winds and calm at sunrise saw the land about 6 miles off and the vessel was 15 or 18 miles to the windward the capt and mate left the whale with the waist boat and started for the vessel got on board at 10½ A.M took dinner and got underweigh it was calm lowered 1 boat towed the vessel until 3½ P.M then anchored and started for the whale and carried the waist boat crew something to eat and towed the whale all night and in the morning the vessel came out of the bay so Ends this day

Figure 5: Page from *E. Nickerson* (1856–57, Ms.), 23–27 November 1856, on the Cintra Bay Ground. "Wright whales" were seen on 23 and 26 November; two were struck on the 26th. With some difficulty, one of the two was finally taken. (Courtesy Kendall Whaling Museum.)

Shortly after the *Nickerson*'s return to Provincetown, the bark *Richmond* (1857–60, MS) sailed directly from New Bedford to the Cintra Bay Ground, arriving 30 November 1857. She promptly began whaling in company with the bark *Huntress* and the Portuguese brig *Water Witch*. Four other vessels were reported to be at anchor and whaling about 7 miles south of Bahía de Cintra. After sharing a whale with the mated vessels, the *Richmond* sailed 6 December for the Canary Islands to replace a lost anchor. By 8 January she was back in Bahía de Cintra with her 'boats off cruising for whales'. From then until mid-April the crew was fully occupied in hunting right whales. On 7 March they saw one at the 'head of the bay [Cintra]' and chased it 'out to the reef'. A 'great number of killers' were seen on 17 March and again on 31 March. On 6 April the *Richmond's* crew 'Saw & chased killers' on the right whaling grounds. Finally, on 15 April she left the Cintra Bay Ground. *En route* to the Canaries, several blackfish (*Globicephala* sp.) were taken, and the boats were lowered for sperm whales. After securing provisions at the Canaries, the vessel went north to the Azores, sperm whaling. By late October 1858 she had worked her way south past the Equator, and in early December she was hunting humpbacks, right whales and sperm whales in the South Atlantic. The *Richmond* did not return to the North Atlantic until late February 1860, when she headed directly for New Bedford. She arrived in New Bedford on 24 March after a cruise of nearly 2½ years, having spent one successful winter season on the Cintra Bay Ground.

The bark *Ohio* (1875–78 MS) of New Bedford sailed in early July 1875, heading directly for the Azores. After cruising for sperm whales on the Western Islands Ground, she departed Fayal on 12 January 1876 for the Cintra Bay Ground, where she anchored on 24 January. The visit proved short – and disastrous. A boat (with crew) was lost under mysterious circumstances and no whales were seen. On 5 February the vessel went 'to Sea bound to Bravo to get some more men'. After picking up more men at the Azores, the bark cruised off the islands through May. Subsequently, she visited the Commodore Morris and Western grounds before heading south to the Cape Verde Islands in November. The *Ohio* did not return to the Cintra Bay Ground. Rather, she spent the remainder of this 3+-year voyage cruising in the South Atlantic and on various sperm whaling grounds in the North Atlantic.

The brief visit to the Cintra Bay Ground by the brig *A. J. Ross* (*John A. Ross*. 1877–1878, MS; Tilton, 1928) is recounted in Section I (iii), above.

IV. 'Iceland Ground'

Our only new information on this ground is from the notation in Anon. (n.d., MS b, p. 69; also see Anon., n.d. a, p. 13):

> Iceland Grounds. Right Whales
> April to August Lat 63 to 67 N Long 11 to 16 W.

This cryptic notation appears on the same page with memoranda concerning cruises by the *Young Phoenix*, *Cape Horn Pigeon* (1867), *Henry Taber*, *Ohio* (1872–3) and *Pioneer*. It is unclear where the writer got his information. Presumably, however, the whalers considered this ground to be centered close inshore along the east coast of Iceland. This same general area may have been where Basques hunted right whales (*Sarde*) during the seventeenth century (Du Pasquier, 1984).

Saemundsson (1939, p. 32) reported the right whale as 'very rare' at Iceland during the twentieth century, but he considered it to have been 'very frequent' there until the early eighteenth century. The capture of six specimens by Norwegian whalers off the island's northwest coast [in 1890], and 10 more there in 1891, 'showed that there was still a small stock' in Icelandic waters at that time (catches were: 1889 [1], 1890 [6], 1891 [10], thus 17 total — Guldberg, 1891, p. 11; and see Guldberg, 1893, pp. 7–8). According to Buchet (1895) the total for 1890–91 was 19 right whales. One was seen but not caught in 1892 (Buchet, 1895). A few more details on these catches, made by modern catcher-boats (see Tønnessen and Johnsen, 1982, p. 78), were given by Collett (1909), who mentioned a total of 28 right whales taken off Iceland between 1889 and 1908. 'Several' of the ten taken in 1891 were caught 'about 50 miles to the west of that island [Iceland]', i.e. in Denmark Strait. The rest for which a locality is stated were taken to the east or southeast of the island. Most of the biological data presented by Collett referred to specimens caught at the Hebrides rather than off Iceland. However, he did mention: (1) a 13.1 m female taken in April 1889 'to the east of Iceland', (2) a 13.1 m female and a 14.4 m male taken in 1891, (3) a 14 m female taken in 1897, and (4) a 16.4 m, pregnant female taken in August 1903. Buchet (1895) stated that of 14 right whales taken by Captain Berg off Iceland during 1890–91, about the same number were males as females; no fetuses were found. A right whale was taken off Iceland in 1922 (Hjort and Ruud, 1929, p. 72).

We have not yet found any definite evidence of right whale catches near Iceland or on this 'Iceland Ground' by the nineteenth-century American whalers, although we suspect a directed search would reveal some. Thomas Welcome Roys apparently struck at least one right whale while experimenting with explosive harpoons off Iceland in 1859 (Schmitt, de Jong and Winter, 1980, p. 75), and he reported that 'the right whales have been killed there until only a few is left' (ibid., p. 112). The brig Edward (1817) of Nantucket cleared for a 'Voyage Intended from Nantucket to Iceland' in May 1817. However, this vessel appears only to have done some desultory whaling on the Cape Farewell Ground, taking blackfish at 55° 09′ N, 32° 35′ W on 8 June and at 59° 30′ N, 30° 12′ W on 14 June, then proceeding to the west coast of Iceland (63° 49′ N, 27° W on 17 June) before heading southeast to the Azores and eventually to the Cape Verde Islands. 'Finbacks' were seen, but right whales are not mentioned in the journal we examined.

V. Observations outside the principal right whale grounds

Judging by the manuscripts and published accounts we examined, right whale distribution in the North Atlantic was very concentrated during the nineteenth century, much as it seems to be today. Rarely did the American whalers encounter right whales on or *en route* to grounds other than those designated explicitly as right whale grounds.

(i) Western Ground

An article in the New Bedford *Morning Mercury* in 1907 (Anon., 1907) stated that Captain Daniel McKenzie of New Bedford, in an unspecified year, caught a right whale while cruising (presumably for sperm whales) on the Western Ground in the bark *Platina*:

This is a strange happening, for in all the many years that the whalemen have been cruising this well known ground, it was the first time that a right whale was ever known to be captured there.

On 20 June 1881, four days after the *Bartholomew Gosnold* (1881–83, MS) left Cape Farewell 'Bound for the Western Ground', it was reported: 'Saw a great many Sulphur Bottoms [*Balaenoptera musculus*] and some Right Whale feed'. One other possible record of a right whale being taken on 'the whaling grounds to the westward of the Azores' comes from an account by Capt. John Cook of Provincetown (*New York Times* 38 [11751]: 28 April 1889). He reported taking a 'large bone whale' there while hunting for sperm whales in an unspecified year; the whale yielded 108 barrels of oil[3]. Townsend (1935, p. 12) considered the Western Ground to be centered at 31° N, 50° W, 'in the great mid-ocean Sargasso region', nearer Bermuda than Madeira. Ashley (1926, p. 146) gave the limits of this ground as 28–36° N, 21–24° W, i.e. much closer to Madeira than to Bermuda.

(ii) Commodore Morris Ground

Although we do not consider the Commodore Morris Ground a major nineteenth-century right whale ground, right whales were observed on it occasionally. Townsend (1935, p. 12) described this ground as the 'farthest north of the sperm whaling areas', centered at 47–51° N, 20–25° W; he considered its moderate sea temperatures to be due to the North Atlantic Drift of the Gulf Stream. Ashley (1926, p. 145) gave its location as 50–52° N, 21–24° W, noting that it was also called the Camilla Ground.

The bark *Daniel Webster* (1877–79, MS) cruised for sperm whales on the Commodore Morris Ground during May 1877, then visited the Cape Farewell Ground in June for right whales. The vessel returned to the Commodore Morris Ground for sperm whales, reporting frequent sightings there of blue whales (*B. musculus*), fin whales (*B. physalus*) and humpbacks as well as sperm whales throughout July and the first half of August. The following year, while back 'Cruising on the Morris Ground', a group of three right whales was encountered and chased at 49° 23′ N, 23° 17′ W, 8 May, and another whale, 'what we called a Right Whale', was seen in the same area on 23 May. One member of the group of three was killed and lost – 'call her (a cow the others being bulls) 100 bbls'. The barks *Reindeer*, *Commodore Morris* and *Ohio* were also whaling in the vicinity of these encounters, so their logbooks may contain additional details about right whale observations (e.g. the whale seen 23 May 'had probably been gallied by Com. Morris'). In fact, a journal kept by the captain's wife covering an earlier voyage of the *Ohio* (1875–78, MS) mentions that on 2 July 1876 (or two years before the *Daniel Webster*'s reports of right whales), two of the *Ohio*'s boats were lowered, without success, for 'a Right Whale' at 49° 25′ N, 22° 22′ W, squarely on the Commodore Morris Ground. The *Ohio* had been to the Cintra Bay Ground during January and February of the same year (see Table 4, entry no. 40; and Section III (iii) above), but this whale was 'the first one of that kind we have seen'.

(iii) Newfoundland Banks

Townsend (1935, p. 12) referred to the 'Newfoundland Banks' as an area where some nineteenth-century sperm whaling took place, but 'these grounds were fished mainly toward the end of the Eighteenth Century'. Ashley (1926, p. 145) referred to the Grand Banks Ground. While *en route* to the Cape Farewell Ground, the *Canton* (1897–98, MS) chased two right whales on 30 May 1897 at 46° 37′ N, 43° 19′ W. This encounter seems to have been incidental, as the vessel was apparently under full sail and not cruising for whales at the time. Thus, there is no reason to believe from this evidence that the area was considered a right whale ground by the nineteenth-century American

---

[3] The following statement is in "The Report of Cambridge Azores Expedition 1979" (by Q. M. Compton-Bishop, J. C. D. Gordon, P. Le G. Allen, and N. Rotton; p. 10):

One record we came across was of a right whale that was fastened by a whaleboat from Lages das Flores [Azores] in 1914. It proved too difficult and dangerous to capture and was cut loose.

Clarke (R., "Whales and Dolphins of the Azores and their Exploitation", *Rep. int. Whal. Commn* 31: 607–615, 1981) listed seven captures of right whales at the Azores between 1873 and 1888. All took place during January-April. Clarke also referred to a sighting made near Fayal, probably during the 1940s.

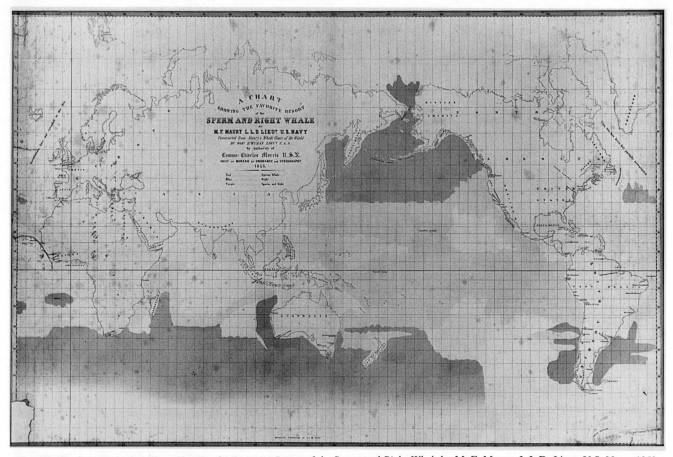

Figure 6: Reproduction of *A Chart Showing the Favourite Resort of the Sperm and Right Whale* by M. F. Maury, L.L.D. Lieut. U.S. Navy, 1853.

whalers. It is, however, significant to note that the position of the encounter (just southeast of Flemish Cap, in water more than 2,000 m deep) is in the general vicinity of the grounds where eighteenth-century Nantucket whalers occasionally took right whales during summer. The records in Table 1 show a summer distribution of right whales during the 1750s and 1760s along the eastern edge of the Grand Bank (also see Maury, 1835, pp. 38, 54; Starbuck, 1964, p. 23; 1924, pp. 357, 359). Also, Maury's (1853) whale chart shows a right whale ground several degrees south and east of this area (Figs 6 and 7) and Clark (1887a, pp. 15–16) claimed that right whales 'were formerly taken in great numbers...east-ward of the Newfoundland fishing-banks'. Slijper, van Utrecht and Naaktgeboren (1964, fig. 25, table 5) indicated sightings in or near these areas.[4]

Although we have not examined the original, Arvy's (1980, p. 635) reproduction of Robert de Vaugondy's 1749 chart showing the distribution of cetaceans off the south coast of Newfoundland deserves critical comment. Arvy's legend and key for the chart suggest there was an area just *west* of the Grand Bank where 'baleines' (balaenids, judging by the context) were found, and an area farther south and west where 'marsouin-bélugas' (*Delphinapterus leucas*) were found. We consider the beluga concentration spurious (see Reeves and Katona,

1980; Reeves and Mitchell, 1984), but the balaenid concentration is interesting. It might be interpreted as a route connecting the right whale grounds on the Scotian Shelf (Mitchell *et al.*, 1986) with those to the east of the Grand Bank (see above).

(iv) *Lower Davis Strait, Labrador Coast, Strait of Belle Isle and Gulf of St. Lawrence*

Ashley (1926, pp. 145–6) referred to Davis Straits, Labrador, and Straits of Belle Isle whaling grounds. To these should be added the Gulf of St. Lawrence (e.g. Starbuck, 1878). The data in Table 1 demonstrate that balaenids (*Eubalaena* and/or *Balaena*) were hunted by the Nantucket and Dartmouth whalers during the eighteenth century in lower Davis Strait, along the Labrador coast and in the Gulf of St. Lawrence and Strait of Belle Isle (also see returns mentioned by Starbuck, 1878). The latitude and timing of the observations mentioned in entry nos 9, 33, 34, and 35 (Table 1) – from 51° N to 62° N and from 27 May to 20 August – are consistent with the whales having been of either species. On 21 June 1753 the sloop *Greyhound* took a whale with 8 ft 3 in bone near 60° N in Davis Strait amongst heavy ice (see Stackpole, 1953, pp. 43–4). This was probably a bowhead. The 'south-west fishing' ground of the British Arctic whalers in the nineteenth century was centered at 61–62° N and 60–64° W (Reeves, Mitchell, Mansfield and McLauchlin, 1983). Their season on this ground often lasted through June, but whales, presumably bowheads, could still be caught in the ice-fields along the Labrador coast as late as July. We have no reason to believe the large mysticetes caught regularly in this phase of the

---

[4] Identifications are unconfirmed. Also, there is a discrepancy between the position indicated in the text and table (Slijper *et al.*, 1964, p. 37, table 5) for a May 1954 sighting – 12 individuals at 40–50° N, 50–60° W – and that indicated in the chart (*ibid.*, fig. 25) – two dots in the 40–50° N, 40–50° W square and one in the 30–40° N, 50–60° W square, but none in the 40–50° N, 50–60° W block.

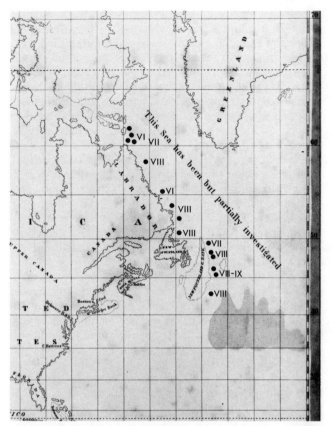

Figure 7: Portion of *A Chart Showing the Favourite Resort of the Sperm and Right Whale* by M. F. Maury, L.L.D. Lieut. U.S. Navy, 1853. The right whale distribution illustrated by Maury is uncoded for effort and date of occurrence, and it does not reflect the limited data plotted for the North Atlantic right whale in his 1852 et seq. *Whale Chart of the World.* The positions plotted with months of occurrence in Roman numerals are 18th century records from our Table 1, plotted hereon as a test of the Maury distribution. The dots clearly do not coincide with the Maury distribution. We have no idea what the Maury distribution represents, other than that he coloured it "Right Whale". Did someone mark it the wrong colour, and could it refer to "Sperm Whale" instead?

Arctic fishery were anything other than bowheads (cf. Eschricht and Reinhardt, 1866). However, Clark's (1887a, p. 15) statement that right whales were taken during summer 'to a limited extent in the lower part of Davis Strait, near Resolution Island' tends to support the view that at least some of the whales taken by the eighteenth-century whalers in these relatively high latitudes may have been right whales.

We also remain uncertain about the identity of the whales seen and chased by the sloop *Reliance* in the Strait of Belle Isle, northward along the Labrador coast and at the mouth of Hudson Strait (Table 1, entry nos 33–35). The schooner *Council* of Provincetown sailed in September 1847 'for the Strt^e of Belleisle to Winter Among the Ice to take right whales' (Wood, n.d., MS). She was reported at Bradore on 17 July 1848 with only 24 bbls of blackfish oil on board and refitting to sail for the Western Islands (Azores). The *Council* made another, shorter cruise to 'Straits Belleisle' in 1850, sailing 23 May and returning 18 September with 50 barrels of blackfish oil (Wood, n.d., MS). It is unlikely that right whales would be encountered in the ice conditions implied for the *Reliance* and *Council* (in winter of 1847–48) voyages mentioned here. On the other hand, the whales seen and chased by the *Reliance* from late June to late August,

especially those at 58° N and further south, including the Strait of Belle Isle (Table 1, entry nos 33–35), were more likely right whales than bowheads. Similarly, the timing of the *Council's* 1850 cruise to the Strait of Belle Isle implies that she was hopeful of catching right whales, not bowheads, during the season of open water. In 1768 the sloop *Tryall* of Dartmouth sailed 25 April for 'straits of Belle Isle'; she was in the company of 50–60 other ships in Canso Harbor on 29 April (Starbuck, 1878, p. 50n). Her first whale was taken on 22 July. She returned to Dartmouth on 5 November. The *SS Learned*, a 116-ton schooner from Sag Harbor, sailed for 'Straits of Belleisle' on 24 June 1856 and returned 8 April 1858 with 30 bbls of whale oil and 100 lbs of whalebone (Finckenor, 1975, p. 69). The brig *Samuel Cook* of Provincetown sailed for 'Labrador' on 8 May 1855 and returned on 13 September 1855 with 80 bbls of whale oil (Wood, n.d., MS, vol. III, p. 654). This same vessel was lost the following summer on Green Island, 'Coast of Labrador', in a gale. Two whales, one of them producing 120 bbls of oil and 2,000 lbs of whalebone (thus probably a bowhead), were taken by the *Ansel Gibbs* in mid to late May 1871 'somewhere off the Coast of Labrador' (Wales, 1871 MS). On 21 October 1865 the schooner *S.B. Howes* of New London sailed for 'Coast of Labrador' but returned 'clean' (with no cargo) on 3 June 1866, having been 'frozen up on the Labrador coast several months' (Wood, n.d., MS, vol. IV, p. 319). Clark (1887b) indicated a right whaling ground off the southeast coast of Labrador, near the mouth of the Strait of Belle Isle.

Elsewhere, we have discussed the identity of the 'Grand Bay whale' or 'River St. Lawrence whale', probably the bowhead, which was hunted by early Basque and American whalemen in the Strait of Belle Isle (Grand Bay) and Gulf of St. Lawrence (Reeves and Mitchell, 1982 MS; and see Eschricht and Reinhardt, 1866; True, 1904; Allen, 1908; Tuck and Grenier, 1981; Du Pasquier, 1984). The new evidence presented here indicates that at least some American whaling in the Strait of Belle Isle involved attempts at overwintering or arrival on the grounds early in the spring while ice was still present. Although there is no definite evidence that bowheads winter as far south as the Strait of Belle Isle today (Reeves *et al.*, 1983), the balaenids seen by the *Reliance* during late May in the 'very thick' ice of Bradore Bay may have been overwintering bowheads beginning a northward migration.

We also examined several eighteenth-century French manuscripts in the Archives nationales du Québec. From these, it is clear that 'la Baleine de grande baye' was relatively common as far up the St Lawrence as the area from Manicouagan to Sept-Iles (Anon., 1736 MS), and that the French whalers saw an advantage in wintering along the North Shore so that whaling could proceed very late and early in the season (D'Aragorry, 1735MS; Beauharnois and Hocquart, 1736MS). The French whalers evidently struck many 'gibarts', or finner whales (*Balaenoptera* spp.), with a high loss rate, but clearly preferred balaenids.

(v) *Other areas*

Clark's (1887a, pp. 15–16) claim that whalers found right whales during winter months 'on the Hatteras Ground, in the Gulf of Mexico, and in the Caribbean Sea' was questioned by Allen (1908, p. 313n):

No authority was given for the statement that 'whalers find them...in the Gulf of Mexico, and the Caribbean Sea,' and in the face of explicit statements that it [the right whale] is not found there, its occurrence in these waters seems highly doubtful.

In the course of our search, we handled numerous manuscripts covering cruises to the Hatteras Ground, the Gulf of Mexico, and the Caribbean region; but we found no evidence in the logbook/journal samples examined for this study and for our previous humpback study (Mitchell and Reeves, 1983) to support any part of Clark's contention quoted by Allen. There is recent sighting and stranding evidence of right whales entering the Gulf of Mexico (Moore and Clark, 1963; Schmidly, Martin and Collins, 1972), however, so there may have been some justification for the right whaling ground indicated there on Clark's (1887b) chart of the whaling grounds. Three nineteenth-century records of 'whales' in or near Galveston Harbor, Texas, give no indication of the species involved (*New York Times*, 11 July 1875).

There has also been a relatively recent sighting near Bermuda (Payne and McVay, 1971), another area for which we found no definite evidence of right whale encounters with the American pelagic whalers, but for which one chart of whale distribution (IWC, 1976) shows a possible concentration of right whales. In an earlier essay on whaling at Bermuda, we discussed the nature of available evidence concerning target species in the fishery there (Mitchell and Reeves, 1983). Our conclusion was that humpbacks were the principal targets, but we consider the question of whether or not right whales were involved during the early years to be still unresolved.

Schevill and Moore (1983) found no records of right whales being sighted by the American pelagic whalers 'near the New England or Canadian coasts'; nor did we (except for the Labrador coast – Table 1). A possible sighting was made by the *John R. Manta* on 30 August 1911, just south of Nantucket at 36° 52′ N, 63° 44′ W (R. J. Stangroom, *in litt.*, 26 January 1983; based on his study of manuscripts in the Kendall Whaling Museum). The whale was described as a 'bone whale'.

VI. Hunting loss

Although right whales are reputed to be among the easiest whales to capture with harpoon-line-open boat whaling methods, their pursuit from small vessels involved many risks and uncertainties. Boats were occasionally capsized by wounded whales, towing lines often parted or became fouled and killed whales sometimes sank. It has been estimated that 20% of all 'right whales' (probably with no distinction being made between bowhead and right whales) killed by the American pelagic whalers were lost (Starbuck, 1878; *WSL* 36[14]: 21 May 1878). The manuscripts examined for this study indicate that all pre-modern right whaling involved hunting losses. We quantified loss rates to facilitate estimations of total fishing mortality from statistics on secured catch. A loss rate factor (LRF) was calculated by dividing the estimated total number of whales killed by the number secured.

Our eighteenth-century sample, although small, indicates that approximately as many right whales were struck but lost as were captured on the grounds east of the Grand Bank (Table 1). This could also be said of the Strait of Belle Isle and southern Davis Strait, but we cannot be certain of whether the balaenids being hunted on these grounds were bowhead or right whales.

For the nineteenth-century grounds, the available sample is not large. Our records for the Cape Farewell Ground (Table 2) indicate 13 whales captured, six killed but lost and one struck but lost. One of the secured whales was a calf which was discarded because it lacked sufficient baleen. We were not certain in several cases that all strikes were noted in the logbooks and journals, but a rate of at least one whale killed and lost for every two captured is implied by these few data. Therefore, the LRF for the Cape Farewell Ground would be 1.5.

The data available for the Southeast US Coast Ground (Table 3) include 18 secured whales, only four of which are mentioned in logbooks or journals that we read. The only record of hunting loss is that of a calf 'which had sunk' (*WSL* 40[4]: 7 March 1882), and this record was not found in our manuscript sample. We doubt that every other whale struck on this ground was secured, but we have no basis for calculating a LRF.

For the Cintra Bay Ground, we have definite evidence of 38 whales secured, one killed but lost and five struck but lost (Table 4). One calf was killed and secured but 'let go'. It can be assumed that our record of catches and losses is incomplete for those vessels whose logbooks or journals were not read. Of the seven 'read' vessels, right whales were taken or struck on only four of the voyages (entry nos 3, 13, 20, 29). On these four voyages, $19\frac{2}{3}$ whales were secured, $\frac{1}{3}$ of a whale was killed but lost and four were struck but lost. There is reason to believe the numbers killed but lost and the numbers struck but lost are under-reported even in this 'read' sample. However, assuming 100% mortality of struck whales and rounding the $19\frac{2}{3}$ to 20 and the $\frac{1}{3}$ to 1, we can estimate the ratio as 20 secured: 5 killed but lost, implying a LRF of 1.25. This is substantially less than the LRF for the Cape Farewell Ground and may be explained, in part, by differences in environmental conditions and whaling procedures on the two grounds (see the respective discussions of itineraries, above). The fact that the *Walter Irving* (1855–56, MS) managed to secure two whales that had been killed and lost (due to sinking) two days earlier suggests that the less exposed and more stationary nature of whaling in Bahía de Cintra may have improved the chances of eventually securing whales that had been struck or killed but lost there (cf. whaling for gray whales in Scammon's Lagoon, Henderson, 1972, p. 260*n*). In addition the density of whalers was usually higher (judging by our small sample) on the Cintra Bay Ground than on the Cape Farewell Ground (compare in Tables 2 and 4, the column headed 'Vessels Seen or Spoken...'), making it more likely that a whale struck or killed but lost would be resighted and secured.

In North Atlantic areas outside the principal grounds, there seems to have been a relatively high loss rate, although our sample is too small to support any firm conclusion. The *Daniel Webster* (1877–79 MS) struck three right whales at 49° 23′ N, 23° 17′ W (see Section V(ii) above). One was killed but abandoned due to rough weather; the 'iron drew' from one; and the 'line parted' from the third.

A small sample of voyages outside the North Atlantic was read to estimate losses experienced on grounds where right whales were still relatively common during the nineteenth century (Table 5). The sample was selected on the basis of a subjective judgement concerning the legibility and level of detail found in a given logbook or journal. Because of its small size and our uncertainty

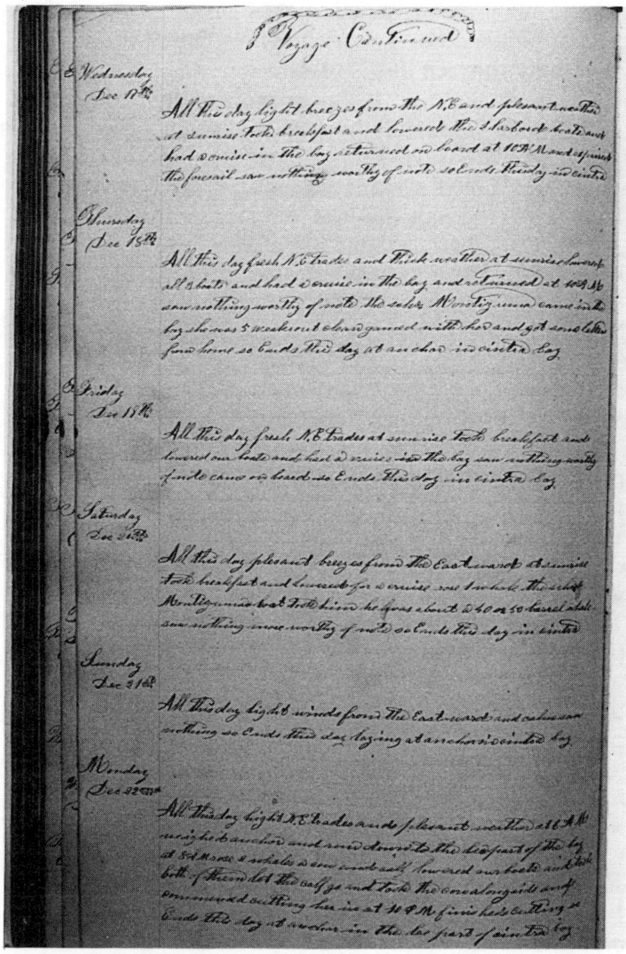

Figure 8: Page from *E. Nickerson* (1856–57, Ms.), 17–22 December 1856, on the Cintra Bay Ground. On 22 December "rose 2 whales a cow and calf lowered our boats and took both of them let the calf go and took the cow alongside and commence cutting her in." (Courtesy Kendal Whaling Museum.)

about how representative it is, we consider this sample to provide nothing more than a crude, preliminary estimate. However, it is interesting that the LRF derived from the combined data for this small sample of 15 vessel-seasons is 1.69, somewhat higher than that for the Cape Farewell Ground.

Wray and Martin (1983, p. 227) mentioned 74 right whales 'killed by vessels under examination' in their sample of Indian Ocean whaling manuscripts, but their appendix lists only 64. Of the 64, three were described as having been 'lost' and four as having 'sunk' (two more were called 'stinkers'). This suggests that at least seven of 64 whales killed outright (*ca* 11%) were not secured, indicating a LRF of more than 1.1.

VII. Selectivity, catch composition and yield

The high value of whalebone in comparison to whale oil toward the end of the nineteenth century clearly influenced decisions by the Yankee whalers in the Western Arctic concerning whether or not to chase and attempt to catch a given bowhead (Bodfish, 1936). We found no evidence that the North Atlantic pelagic whalers hunted selectively for a given size or sex of right whale. However, the *Canton* (1897–98, MS) killed and secured a calf on the Cape Farewell Ground, then cut loose from it after discovering that it 'did not have any

bone'. Also, the *E. Nickerson* (1856–57, MS), after killing a cow and calf on the Cintra Bay Ground, 'let the calf go' (Fig. 8).

Of 20 whales struck on the Cape Farewell Ground, we know at least six (30%) were mothers or calves. Oil yields varied from 20 to about 100 bbls ($\bar{x} = ca$ 67, $n = 9$). Of 19 whales struck on the Southeast US Coast Ground, at least four (21%) were mothers or calves. Oil yields ranged between 25 and 80–90 bbls ($\bar{x} = ca$ 53, $n = 10$). Of 44 whales struck on the Cintra Bay Ground, at least 12 (27%) were mothers or calves. Oil yields of 6.5 to 85 bbls were reported ($\bar{x} = ca$ 54, $n = 10$). Our records for Cintra Bay include a whale whose 'blubber being young [did] not yield oil' (*Richmond*, 1857–60, MS) and a 'small cow' which produced only 32 bbls (*E. Nickerson*, 1856–57, MS).

Thus, on each of the three main grounds for which we have nineteenth-century evidence, mothers and calves comprised at least 20–30% of the total whales known to have been struck. Because details are lacking for age and sex of many of the whales struck, we suspect this is a low estimate.

If we combine all the caught whales in our sample for which oil production is stated (Tables 2, 3 and 4), the mean yield per right whale is 58–59 bbls ($n = 29$). Individual yields ranged from 6.5 to about 100 bbls. In their sample of right whales taken in the Indian Ocean, Wray and Martin (1983) found yields of 20 to 80 bbls ($\bar{x} = 59$, $n = 11$).

VIII. Catches and kills

Estimated total fishing mortality for the three principal nineteenth-century North Atlantic right whaling grounds is summarized in Table 6. Although in a few instances we have included some known kills by shore-based whalers, most of this mortality was the result of activities of American pelagic whalers.

At least 19 right whales were killed on the Cape Farewell Ground between 1868 and 1897 (Table 2). In addition, we can infer from indirect evidence that three whales were taken (and two more killed but lost; LRF of 1.5) by vessels seen or spoken on the grounds (Table 2, entry nos 4, 10, 11). Assuming the one whale known to have been struck-but-lost (Table 2, entry no. 8) died of its wounds, our estimate of total fishing mortality for the stated period on this ground is 25 right whales. Since two whales were taken by the *Hannibal* in 1858, and possibly others a year or two earlier (letter from Chapel to Jackson, *Violet*, 1853, MS), it is reasonable to suspect that additional right whales were killed on the Cape Farewell Ground during the decade preceding 1868.

For the Southeast US Coast Ground, we have direct evidence of 19 right whales killed by the pelagic whalers from 1876 to 1882, and there is indirect evidence to conclude that at least several more were taken (see Section II above). In January 1880 'a large one [right whale] was cast ashore on Sullivan's Island [South Carolina] which had already been stripped of its baleen and blubber' (and thus may have been one of the six listed for that year in Table 3); and in the same month a right whale was taken by shore-based crews at Charleston, South Carolina (Manigault *in* Holder, 1883; Manigault, 1885; *New York Times*, 11 January 1880; Fig. 9). Shore whalers near Beaufort, North Carolina, caught five [right] whales in early 1879 and one in 1880 (Earll, 1887a, p. 490). Thus, we estimate total fishing mortality for this

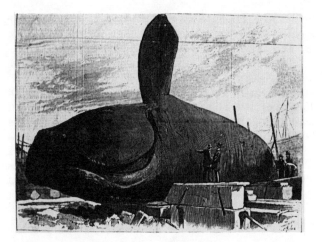

Figure 9: "Whale captured in the harbor of Charleston, South Carolina". From an article in *Harpers Weekly*, 31 January 1880, pp. 77–8. (Courtesy F. B. Lothrop Collection, Peabody Museum of Salem.)

ground during 1876–82 as at least 25–30 right whales. Catches made in subsequent years on the Southeast US Coast Ground include a near-term pregnant female taken near Port Royal in February 1884 (Manigault, 1885); a female and juvenile taken off Cape Lookout, North Carolina, on 20 March 1894 (True, 1904, p. 246); and another female taken off Cape Lookout on 15 February 1898 (True, 1904, p. 246). Brimley (1946) mentioned a specimen taken near Beaufort in 1875.

We have documented a minimum kill on the Cintra Bay Ground of 38 right whales between winter 1855–56 and winter 1857–58 (Table 4). We are confident that there were more kills, judging by whale oil and whalebone returns and itineraries of vessels known to have visited the Cintra Bay Ground but whose logbooks or journals were not examined. Using a mean yield of 60 bbls to convert whale oil production statistics, we estimate an additional 33 whales secured (based on 2,000 barrels of whale oil, Table 4). Correcting this number for hunting loss (LRF = 1.25) gives an estimate of 41 whales killed. If 3 of the 5 whales known to have been struck but lost are considered moribund and added to the total killed, we can estimate that about 92 right whales were killed on the Cintra Bay Ground during the 3-year period 1855–56 to 1857–58. The only other nineteenth-century kill on this ground of which we are aware was made in 1880 (*WSL* 38[5]: 16 March 1880; Table 4, entry nos 43, 44).

The 105 bbl right whale taken by the brig *Gazelle* of Fayal in 1889 (*WSL* 47[7]: 19 March 1889) may have been on or near the Cintra Bay Ground. However, the only information we have on it is that the *Gazelle* called at St Lucia, Cape Verde Islands, on 9 February, having taken the whale, we assume, not long before.

IX. Comments on Townsend's (1935) sample

Townsend (1935) made a well-known effort to describe the Yankee whaling grounds and whale distribution on the basis of information found in logbooks and journals, but he did not bother plotting the positions of the 'few' bowheads and right whales recorded as having been caught in the North Atlantic. As Schevill and Moore (1983) have demonstrated, even the few North Atlantic right whale records (35 in number) in Townsend's file would have been useful to later researchers if he had plotted them on his charts. Like Schevill and Moore, we

found some inconsistencies between the right whale catches tabulated by Townsend and what we found upon examining thirteen of his fifteen sources.

Although both our examination and that by Schevill and Moore (1983) of the logbook of the *Emma Jane* (1879–80, MS) revealed no confirmation that a right whale was taken on this vessel's 1879–81 voyage (per Townsend, 1935), it is clear from statements in the *WSL* (37[49]: 20 January 1880; 38[3]: 2 March 1880; 38[18]: 15 June 1880) that a right whale was in fact caught by the *Emma Jane* in company with the schooner *Surprise* of New Bedford on 15 February 1880 near Brunswick (Anon., n.d., MS b, p. 128; Townsend and Watson, n.d., MS). The *Emma Jane* was again off Fort Macon and Morehead City during February–April 1881, searching for right whales in company with the schooner *E. H. Hatfield* of New Bedford (*WSL* 39[9]: 12 April 1881; 39[12]: 3 May 1881; *E. H. Hatfield*, 1880–82, MS). The ODHS logbook of the *Emma Jane*'s 1879–81 voyage ends with the 1 January 1880 entry; at this time the vessel was at 29° 14' N, 77° 43' W. Thus, it appears that Townsend had access to a more complete document than was available to us and that the right whale capture was made later in the voyage than the period covered in the extant manuscript (see Schevill and Moore, 1983, postscript).

Townsend (1935) also attributed the capture of one right whale to the sloop *Greyhound* in 1753. Schevill and Moore (1983) were unable to locate a document for this voyage, but we found one in the Nantucket Atheneum collection as part of Peleg Folger's journal (see Fonda, 1969; Table 1, entry no. 9). The whale, definitely a balaenid, was taken 21 June amongst heavy ice in southern Davis Strait near 60–61° N (*Greyhound*, 1753, MS). Its baleen was 8 ft 3 in long, but the whale produced only 68 bbls of oil – ' the blubber not being so fat as we hop'd for'. Folger described it as 'a very Large Deep whale'. We believe this was a bowhead and that Townsend understandably but mistakenly scored it as a right whale. Incidentally, the *Greyhound*'s boats struck but lost two more 'right whales' (probably bowheads) and heard on 13 July about the capture of another (bowhead?) by Jonathan Coffin, apparently also in southern Davis Strait, which had 7-ft bone and produced 179 bbls of oil.

One anomaly found in the Townsend and Watson (n.d., MS) worksheets is the listing of six right whales taken by the ship *Eliza Adams* in October 1867 at approximately 7° 10' N, 19° 44' W. Townsend's (1935) published table of catches indicates a total catch for the *Eliza Adams*' 1867–70 voyage of 48 sperm whales and 16 *southern* right whales (7 from the Pacific, 9 from the Atlantic). The totals listed on the worksheets include 9 right whales from the South Atlantic, 12 right whales from the South Pacific, and 37 sperm whales. It seems very likely that the six 'right whales' attributed to the North Atlantic on the worksheets were in fact sperm whales. However, this can only be determined with certainty by reference to a logbook or journal.

DISCUSSION AND CONCLUSIONS

Perceptions of nineteenth and early twentieth century naturalists about right whales

There was a pervasive belief among nineteenth-century naturalists that the right whale was very close to extinction in the North Atlantic. Upon learning that a right whale had been taken off South Carolina in 1880, Van Beneden (1880) remarked that 'l'espèce est presque complètement exterminée'. Later he (Van Beneden, 1885) admitted to knowing of only three right whale captures in the North Atlantic 'depuis un quart de siècle' - all on the European side. Guldberg (1884b) stated: 'From the eighteenth century we hear no more about the catching of the North Cape whale [*E. glacialis*] in European waters'; and, to his knowledge, this whale was not hunted off eastern North America from the beginning of the nineteenth century until the late 1870s or early 1880s. Gray (1870) believed right whales on the European side of the North Atlantic were 'as completely exterminated...as wild boars, wolves, beavers, bustards, and other animals are in great Britain', but he knew they were still caught 'more or less frequently' along the American coast.

Harmer (1928) claimed that the hunt for the right whale had ended on the European side in about 1700 and on the American side in about 1800.

> It had become excessively rare, and for many years it was believed to be extinct. About 1850 the Biscay whale [*E. glacialis*] began to re-appear, with an occasional stranding on the Atlantic Islands or the north coast of Spain, and by 1880 it had become the object of a moderate whaling industry off the Eastern United States.

These authorities evidently were not well acquainted with the activities of the American pelagic and shore whalers during the nineteenth century. Not only were right whales caught consistently on a small scale off Long Island from the 1820s through the early 1900s (Reeves and Mitchell, 1986), but pelagic whalers continued to catch small numbers of right whales on various North Atlantic grounds between 1855 and 1898. Van Beneden's (1885) and Gray's (1870) ignorance of captures made on the Cintra Bay Ground between 1855 and 1858, when at least 38 right whales were taken there, indicates a lack of communication to British and European scientists of information concerning Yankee whaling in the eastern North Atlantic. Even Allen (1908), who was well aware of the catches by shore whalers off Long Island and North Carolina, seems to have been unacquainted with many of the activities of the American pelagic whalers.

Recent or current status of right whales on the principal nineteenth-century grounds

1. Cape Farewell Ground

The observation of 'in all probability two bowhead whales' by Norwegian whalers off southeast Greenland (at *ca* 61° 05′ N, 42° 10′ W), 2 August 1979 (Jonsgård, 1981), was made very close to the Cape Farewell Ground. The statement

> Neither the observer nor the whalers had seen bowhead whales before, and the identification of the species may be doubted although for several reasons it does not seem likely that bowhead whales have been confused with black right whales (Nordkaper) (Anon., 1981)

certainly leaves open the possibility that the whales were *Eubalaena*. As we have pointed out elsewhere (Reeves *et al.*, 1983), the argument that these were bowhead 'stragglers' from Davis Strait (Jonsgård, 1981) is weakened by the historic absence of this species along the west coast of Greenland south of 65° N, especially during summer (Eschricht and Reinhardt, 1866, p.5). The absence of additional evidence that right whales

continue to use the Cape Farewell Ground in summer may be due to a lack of observational effort there. It is useful to compare our description of the limits of this whaling ground (Section I(i), above) with the limits of the present-day Icelandic whaling grounds. Postwar Icelandic whaling for large whales has been restricted to activities based at Hvalfjördur on the southwest coast, where a whaling station was established in 1948 (Jonsson, 1965). There is no overlap between the Hvalfjördur whaling grounds (as shown by Jonsson, 1965; Rørvik *et al.*, 1976) and the Cape Farewell Ground (as described in Section I(i), above); the latter is well to the south and west of the former (see our Fig. 10). The lack of sightings by the Icelandic whalers cannot therefore be taken as evidence that right whales no longer inhabit the Cape Farewell Ground.

Some whaling for minke whales (*Balaenoptera acutorostrata*) is done by vessels based along the coasts of Iceland (Sigurjónsson, 1982), and this activity might provide coverage of at least portions of the historic eastern 'Iceland Ground' (Section IV above).

2. Southeast US Coast Ground

Right whales still occur on the Southeast US Coast Ground (Moore, 1953; Layne, 1965; Reeves, Mead and Katona, 1978). It is especially interesting that many of the records for the last 25 years refer to areas well south of Fernandina. This may reflect a relatively high level of observational effort along the northeast coast of Florida, in comparison to the coasts of Georgia, South Carolina and North Carolina; or it may reflect the failure of American pelagic whalers to hunt in nearshore waters south of Fernandina (during the period for which we sampled their logbooks and journals) and the survival of a southern 'remnant' population.

Farther north along the US coast, off east Long Island where right whales were hunted between 1650 and 1924, there is little evidence of a consistent nearshore migration in the present day (Reeves, 1975; 1976; Reeves *et al.*, 1978). While the low level of observational effort at the appropriate season (December–April) may partly explain the low number of sightings, the lack of more sightings in this area by Winn (1982) is nevertheless puzzling.

3. Cintra Bay Ground

The Cintra Bay Ground remains relatively unexplored by modern cetologists. Duguy (1975) estimated that 'about twenty' species of cetacean are known from coastal waters of northwest Africa between Rio de Oro and Senegal. His list, however, does not include the right whale. Duguy cited an upwelling area near Nouadhibou (Port-Etienne) as being responsible for locally high productivity and in turn for the diversity of cetacean species found there. Nouadhibou is about 120 miles south of Bahía de Gorrei.

Although the species identifications are suspect for all sightings reported by Slijper *et al.* (1964), their fig. 25 indicates several right whale encounters near the Cintra Bay Ground. Of special interest are the clump of sightings in the 10–20° N, 20–30° W square and the report of 22 right whales near the Cape Verde Islands in August. The latter sighting has been described as 'highly suspect' because late summer seems an unlikely time for right whales to be in these low latitudes (Reeves *et al.*, 1978; also see Mörzer Bruyns, 1971, pp. 159–60). Except for the kills of right whales at Madeira in 1959 (IWS, 1961, p. 26) and

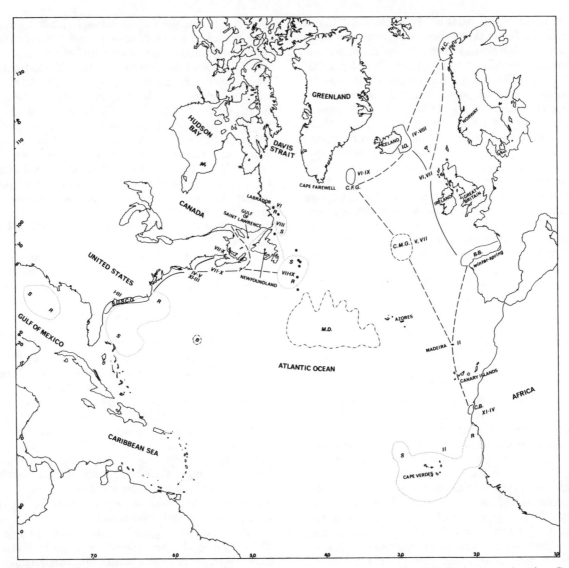

Figure 10: Portion of the North Atlantic Ocean and Arctic Sea (base map sheet 19; Serial Atlas of the Marine Environment, American Geographical Society, New York, 1962). Known or suspected whaling grounds for the North Atlantic right whale are plotted from published sources; plots, abbreviations, and data are as follows:

Outlines used for demarcating whaling grounds:
solid lines equal verified grounds; dashed lines equal possible whaling grounds: dash-dot-dash-dot lines equal Maury's (1853) right whale distribution; dotted lines equal Clark's (1887b) Sperm/Right whaling grounds ("S,R" as Clark placed them).

Inferred migration routes:
solid line equals well-documented routes; dashed line equal migration routes inferred on the basis of contiguity and continuity of occurrences; dotted line equals possible migration routes.

Abbreviations for whaling grounds:
IG equals "Iceland Ground", CFG equals Cape Farewell Ground, NC equals North Cape, BB equals Bay of Biscay, CB equals Cintra Bay Ground, CMG equals Commodore Morris Ground, SUSCG equals Southeast United States Coast Ground, B equals Bermuda, MD equals Maury distribution, [S/R] equals Clark's grounds as he mapped them. Roman numerals represent months of occurrence. Dots east of Newfoundland-Labrador represent eighteenth century kills (see Table 1).

1967 (Maul and Sergeant, 1977) and the inference that these may have been animals migrating to or from the Cintra Bay Ground, we have no other evidence that this ground has been occupied by right whales during the twentieth century[5].

Speculations on migration and stock identity

(1) Previous literature relevant to North Atlantic right whale distribution

Because right whales were severely depleted in the North Atlantic by the mid-eighteenth century, most of the

[5] Aguilar's (1981) reference to a right whale sighting at 43° N, 10° 30′ W in September 1977 also may be relevant here.

literature on their distribution and movements is retrospective. It consists mainly of summary statements based on anecdotal evidence and of attempts to chart the whaling grounds. Several of the whale charts discussed below are reproduced in Reeves and Mitchell (1983).

(a) Charts kept by private enterprise. Whalers kept their own charts with plots of whale distribution, kills, and likely new grounds. For example, when Captain Thomas Welcome Roys discovered the bowhead grounds north of Bering Strait and returned with a spectacular catch, he was free with his information (e.g. Anon., 1849; 1854). Within a year or two, E. and G. W. Blunt, a company in New York that printed blank books used by whaling masters as logs and journals, had printed a

'Polar Chart of Behring Sea and Strait', 1849, that was in use for just this purpose (cf. Johnson, 1982, item 52; and see item 53 for a chart with whale sighting data entered similarly). In general, the charts were jealously guarded and considered to be private (and company) commercial intelligence. Few of the charts survive in institutional collections and few historians have mentioned or used them.

(b) *Compilations of whale charts sponsored by US government agencies.* Wilkes (1845) was the first person, to our knowledge, to attempt to chart the world distribution of whales. He surveyed many of the sperm whale grounds and discussed their distribution in detail, but he mentioned right whale distribution only casually. The usefulness of his chart showing ocean currents and whaling grounds is diminished because it confounds the two species; we consider it to show mainly (or solely) sperm whale distribution.

Maury (1851; 1852; 1853; see Bannister and Mitchell, 1980, for a discussion and full citations to these charts) produced three sets of whale charts which were based on records from whaling logbooks and journals. The 1851 chart summarizes world distribution by species, of sperm and right whales, but omits data for the North Atlantic. His 1852 charts present quantitative information on searching effort and whale observations by species (sperm and right only) and include some coverage of the North Atlantic. Maury's 1853 chart is nonquantitative, possibly a summary, with color-coded shading used to show sperm whale and right whale distributions (Fig. 6). The only indication of right whales in the North Atlantic is a large shaded area in mid-ocean, at about 35–43° N, 30–49° W (Fig. 7). These coordinates are close to those given for the Western Ground (see above). The season when whales occupy this area is not indicated.

The engraved, folded world map 'Sea Drift and Whales, on which the movements of the sea, as indicated by the Thermometer are shewn' (Maury, 1856, pl. 9 – see Bannister and Mitchell [1980] for full citation and Reeves and Mitchell [1983] for a reproduction) includes a dashed line indicating the 'Equat'l limits of Right Whale ground' in the North Atlantic. The line begins in Cabot Strait, the southeast entrance of the Gulf of St Lawrence, and extends in a curve to the Iberian Peninsula, near the entrance to the Mediterranean Sea. It passes through Madeira. The implication is that right whales were hunted mainly to the north of this line, i.e. north of about 40–45° N in the west and ca 33° N in the east.

The Maury charts are among the most important works of their kind, but unfortunately many aspects of their preparation and publication remain confusing and unexplained. For example, one copy of the 1851 sheet with a color overlay exists in the Library of Congress (reproduced by Whipple, 1979). It includes several areas in the North Pacific and Southern Hemisphere, apparently right whale grounds, that are shaded blue, but with no key to what the blue shading means.

We examined (on microfilm at the ODHS) a sample of documents in the Maury Abstract Log Collection, National Archives and Records Service, Washington, D.C. These abstracts of logbooks were prepared on Maury's behalf by agents in various ports, such as New Bedford, Nantucket and New London. In particular, we selected abstracts of whaling voyages whose itineraries included the North Atlantic. To do this, we consulted a copy of the 'Descriptive List of Log Book Extracts' at the ODHS, which includes name of ship, type, master, port of origin, destination, dates and volume number for several thousand voyages. A small proportion, probably less than 10%, of these voyages were whaling voyages. Many of the abstracts note only that 'whales' were sighted or killed, giving no information about which species was involved. Also, the agents who compiled the abstracts apparently were instructed not to record the data on North Atlantic segments of voyages. Thus, the first entry of a given abstract often refers to the last position of the vessel before it crossed the equator into the Southern Hemisphere. In approximately 40 abstracts examined, we found no mention of right whales in the North Atlantic.

The third major US government initiative to map the whaling grounds was carried out by Clark (1887a, b). His chart (Fig. 2) is interesting, useful and indicative as a guide to the whaling grounds, but apparently lacks the rigor of a quantitative data base such as that used by Maury. Clark presumably was advised by knowledgeable individuals from the New England whaling industry, but we do not know how many informants there were and whether his study involved the actual plotting of kills and sightings from primary sources.

(c) *Compilations of whale charts by historians.* The well-known work by Townsend and Watson (n.d., MS; Townsend, 1935) is mentioned above. Because they were prepared from information in whaling logbooks and journals, we consider Townsend's charts, along with those of Maury, to be the most authoritative.

(d) *Compilations of whale charts and commentaries by scientists.* Van Beneden's (1868; Van Beneden and Gervais, 1880, text-plate, following p. 630) chart of world balaenid distribution portrays right whales as occurring in a continuous, diagonal band across the North Atlantic (Fig. 11). This chart reflects Van Beneden's belief that the North Atlantic right whale was closely associated with the Gulf Stream and that there was one stock in the North Atlantic. He in fact proposed 'Baleine du *Gulf-stream*' as an appropriate name for the species (Van Beneden, 1886, p. 20). Van Beneden did not, to our knowledge, use primary materials in constructing his scheme for right whale distribution. Two color-coded charts by Guérin (1874) purporting to show the 'Aires de Circulation des Cétacés' also suggest an affinity for the Gulf Stream and a continuous trans-Atlantic distribution. One (Fig. 12) shows balaenid distribution by species; the other (Fig. 13), overall balaenid distribution as distinct from world sperm whale distribution.

Gray (1870) strongly opposed van Beneden's 'theory of whales inhabiting bands across the different oceans'. He remained unwilling to accept the distinctions between the bowhead and the North Atlantic right whale and preferred to view the right whales seen in temperate waters as wanderers from the Arctic. Gray (1868) noted that a few sightings of right whales had been made 'in the midchannel between Morocco and North America', but he dismissed these animals as strays.

The perceived problem of how many species of right whale inhabit the North Atlantic was finally resolved in the late nineteenth century (see True, 1904, for a critical literature review). True (1904), even though working with a very small sample, was able to comment on (and by so doing, to emphasize) variations in pigmentation in European, Icelandic and North American specimens.

J. A. Allen's (1908) review of the species resulted in a

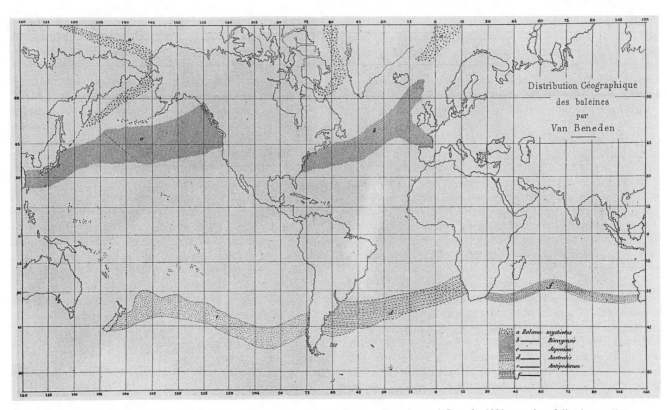

Figure 11: World distribution of balaenids as sketched by van Beneden (van Beneden and Gervais, 1880, textplate following p. 630).

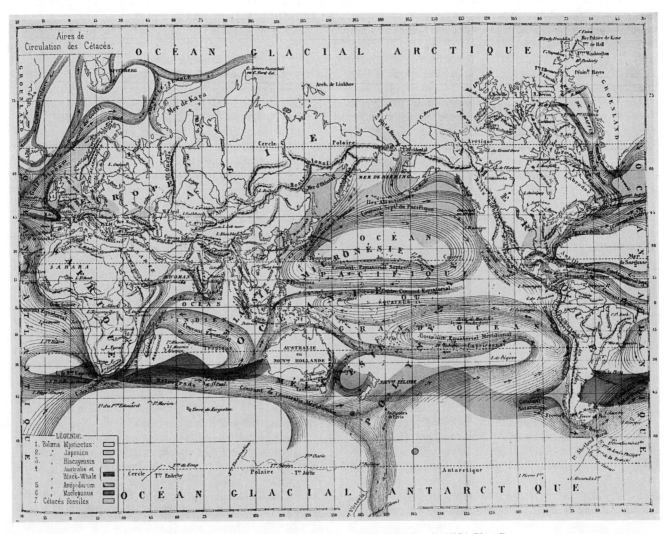

Figure 12: World balaenid distribution as mapped by Guerin (1874, Plate I).

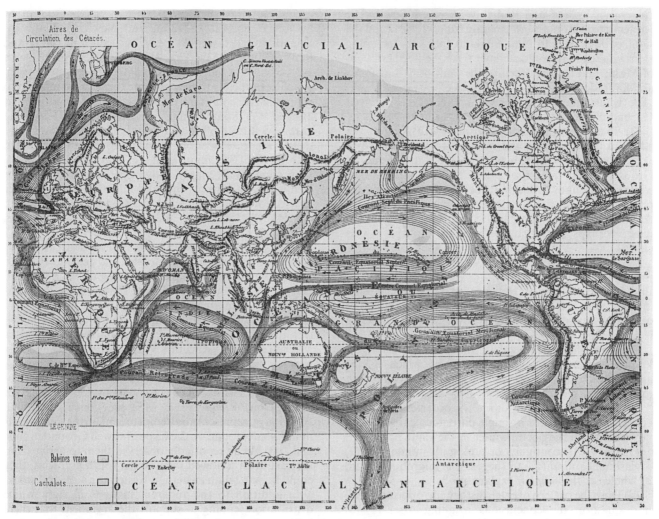

Figure 13: World distribution of balaenids (all species combined) and sperm whales, as mapped by Guerin (1874, Plate II).

clear and generally accurate summary of the North Atlantic right whale's distribution:

> from the coast of Florida and the Bermudas on the western side to the entrance to Davis Strait, the southern and southwestern coast of Greenland, and the waters about Iceland; and on the eastern side from the coast of Spain and (casually at least) the Mediterranean Sea northward to the seas between Norway and Spitzbergen; in other words, approximately that part of the North Atlantic between the January isotherms of 10° and 50° Fahrenheit, it occupying the northern part of the area in summer, and the southern part in winter.

Allen considered as valid True's (1904) important conclusion that there is no basis for regarding the right whales on the American and European sides of the North Atlantic as belonging to separate species. He did not, however, address directly the question of stock separation.

G. M. Allen's (1942, p. 502) discussion of the North Atlantic right whale's distribution implied that there were eastern and western stocks, and he speculated that whales of the western stock summered off southern Greenland and Iceland.

Mitchell (1974b) recognized two stock units, one on the eastern and one on the western side of the North Atlantic. Schevill and Moore (1983) queried:

> Did the relative abundance that we report for Denmark Strait a hundred years ago hint that right whales from both sides of the North Atlantic summered together, indicating one general population for this ocean? Or might there have been two stocks, with Cintra Bay

perhaps being in the winter range of the nordkapers of the Barents Sea?

Although radio tagging and tracking, as recommended by Schevill and Moore, would help to resolve the issue of stock identity, it is useful, for the present, to consider the hypotheses of one, two or three stocks in the light of our findings reported above.

2. Hypotheses regarding stock identity

Our hypotheses for discussion are the following.

(1) There is (or at least was) a single stock of right whales in the North Atlantic, with a coastal distribution in the southern portions of its range and offshore extensions (east and south of the Grand Bank, Cape Farewell Ground, 'Iceland Ground') in the north. The mixing of whales from the American and European sides would probably occur, according to this construct, mainly in summer at relatively high latitudes, perhaps in southern Denmark Strait as suggested by Schevill and Moore (1983).

(2) There are two stocks in the North Atlantic, an eastern and a western stock. The wintering grounds for the eastern stock would lie between the northwest coast of Africa and the Bay of Biscay (note the records for November through March in the Bay of Biscay and Mediterranean Sea summarized by Allen, 1908); the summering grounds, from the British Isles to North Cape

(Norway), Iceland and probably Denmark Strait. The western stock would winter mainly from Florida (and the Gulf of Mexico?) to New England (possibly including Bermuda?) and it would summer from the northern Gulf of Maine and Scotian Shelf to the Gulf of St Lawrence and Labrador coast and offshore east of the Grand Bank. (The whales hunted in summer on the Cape Farewell Ground might possibly be attributed to this stock).

(3) There are three stocks in the North Atlantic. In addition to the eastern and western stocks proposed in (2) above, the whales inhabiting the Cape Farewell Ground would comprise a third, central stock. The wintering grounds for such a stock would be difficult to pinpoint, but they might be looked for near Bermuda, the Azores or in mid-ocean well away from any island or land mass, perhaps in the shaded area on Maury's (1853) chart.

3. Evaluation

In the absence of any other evidence on right whale stock identity, we have used distributional data and records of catches to evaluate the above hypotheses. Our reasoning is as follows.

(1) Are there predictable, latitudinally arranged, known concentrations of right whales which fit the assumption that these animals make north-south migrations?

(2) Given (1), do times of known occurrence in these concentration areas fit a simple chronological schedule, i.e., summer in the north, winter in the south?

(3) Does (1) – contiguity or proximity – unite with (2) – seasonal continuity – to suggest one migrating stream of whales as the *simplest* explanation?

(4) Does the pattern of catch history corroborate or call into question the conclusions resulting from (1)–(3) above?

There appear to be real hiatuses in distribution between known wintering areas (the Cintra Bay Ground to the Bay of Biscay on the east, the Southeast US Coast Ground to New England on the west) which are not simply misperceptions due to a lack of observational effort. The Basque and later American whalers searched widely and intensively in the North Atlantic for concentrations of right whales and sperm whales. Many were combination whalers, taking both sperm whales and right whales (as well as humpbacks and blackfish) concurrently. Their experience provided detailed knowledge of sperm whale grounds (e.g., Townsend, 1935; Gilmore, 1959, fig. 1). The lack of similar information on right whales can be taken, in part, as evidence that they were absent or rare on (or on routes connecting) the major sperm whaling grounds. Slijper *et al.* (1964) plotted some records that might be taken to suggest movement by right whales across the North Atlantic, but the dates and details of most of their records were not presented, and we cannot rely on the identifications made in these instances by untrained observers.[3] Thus, during the winter and early spring season when reproductive activities of right whales are thought to reach a peak (Tomilin, 1957; Klumov, 1962; Best, 1970; but see Collett, 1909; Payne, 1984; Kraus, Prescott, Turnbull and Reeves, 1982), the geographic separation between the eastern and western stocks would very likely be complete.

During summer, however, right whales are widely distributed in the North Atlantic. Although part of the western stock remains in waters of the continental shelf and slope (Bay of Fundy, Scotian Shelf, Gulf of St Lawrence, coastal Labrador and Newfoundland), the animals found historically east and south of the Grand Bank (Maury, 1953; Clark, 1887a; Table 1) constitute an exception. Are they a component of the western stock which periodically moves offshore, perhaps in relation to reproductive condition, in a manner similar to that implied for South Atlantic right whales (*Eubalaena australis*) studied off Patagonia (see Payne, 1984)? Or are they a separate offshore population, closely associated with the Gulf Stream in winter (cf. Van Beneden's [1886] suggestion) and simply moving northward to richer feeding grounds in summer and fall? Could the Basques have followed the right whale westward across the North Atlantic by discovering and exploiting these 'offshore' whales after depleting the coastal eastern stock?

The summer distribution of the eastern stock is between the northern British Isles and Iceland (Collett, 1909; Thompson, 1918), and possibly as far north and east as North Cape (Guldberg, 1884a, b) or the Kola Peninsula (Tomilin, 1957).

The Cape Farewell Ground is clearly a problem, but it is possible that whales reported on the Commodore Morris Ground (see Section V(ii) above) in May and July were *en route* to (or from) the Cape Farewell Ground, following an offshore route far out of the reach of shore-based whalers. The comments by Chapel (in letter to Jackson, *Violet*, 1853, MS; see above), although speculative, represent an attempt to explain the movements of the whales found on the Cape Farewell Ground in June and July. As he reportedly observed them to arrive from the east, then followed them to the south and west, they could be part of an eastern, a western or a central stock.

In addition to the apparent hiatuses in right whale distribution tending to support the argument that there is more than one stock, the pattern of exploitation provides another line of evidence favoring a multiple-stock hypothesis. On a broad scale, the westward expansion of Spanish Basque whaling across the North Atlantic from Europe to Newfoundland (Aguilar, 1981) might be regarded as evidence that, as the whale population on the east side of the ocean was depleted, the more plentiful population on the west side attracted the whalemen to the shores of the New World. On a finer scale, the catch records summarized in Table 6 also show an interesting, nonsynchronous pattern.

During the 1850s there was an intensive episode of whaling on the Cintra Bay Ground, and the local population appears to have been depleted by the late 1850s (Table 4). A short, intensive episode of whaling also took place on the Southeast US Coast Ground from 1875 to 1882 (Table 3). As in the case of the Cintra Bay Ground, right whales were probably locally common at the beginning and locally depleted at the end of this period (else why would the episode have ended as it apparently did?). In contrast to the Cintra Bay and Southeast US Coast grounds, the Cape Farewell Ground was visited by the Yankee whalers over a period of 40 years (1858–98; Table 2), during which time catches were reasonably consistent (Table 6; Schevill and Moore, 1983).

The available record of nineteenth-century exploitation, incomplete though it is, suggests a degree of independence between eastern and western North Atlantic populations. Whales from the two sides may have mixed in Denmark Strait, but any supply to this area from the Cintra Bay Ground would have been greatly reduced by about 1860, shortly after right whaling began on the Cape Farewell Ground. Superficially, the partial overlap in timing of the peak exploitation periods on the Southeast US Coast Ground and the Cape Farewell Ground suggests that the same stock of whales was involved. Such an interpretation contradicts our conclusion from the distributional data alone (Fig. 10) that the Cape Farewell Ground is a summering area for whales from the Cintra Bay Ground, but it leaves open the possibility that the Cape Farewell whales belong to neither a western nor an eastern coastal stock, but rather to a central stock associated with the Gulf Stream, the Mid-Atlantic Ridge, or some other mid-ocean oceanographic or bathymetric feature.

RECOMMENDATIONS

(1) An extended search of manuscript material, designed to select documents with a high likelihood of containing information on right whaling on the Cape Farewell and Cintra Bay grounds in particular, is desirable. Not only would it refine further our understanding of where and when to look for concentrations of right whales in these areas, but it would improve the prospects of eventually making a useful estimate of early population size. A review of the non-English language literature by a Scandinavian researcher probably would produce a more detailed picture of historic right whale distribution on the Cape Farewell Ground and near Iceland and North Cape.

(2) Efforts should be made, possibly in conjunction with Icelandic or Norwegian whaling, sighting or tagging cruises, to survey the Cape Farewell Ground and the historic eastern 'Iceland Ground' for right whales, using the positions and times of occurrence indicated above as a basis for cruise scheduling. If possible, visual or radio-tagging of right whales should be attempted, as well as intensive photography of callosity patterns and distinctive pigmentation on any animals observed. Consideration should be given to requesting the help of the Icelandic minke whalers in documenting sightings (if any) of right whales seen on or near the old 'Iceland Ground'.

(3) An expedition to Bahía de Cintra and Bahía de Gorrei during the period November to March is warranted for the following reasons:

(a) This area was, as recently as the 1850s and possibly the 1870s, an assembly area for northeast Atlantic right whales, including mothers and calves. Thus, it may have been a mating, calving or nursing area.

(b) Although the Yankee whalers appear to have depleted the stock and abandoned the ground by about 1880, no whaling or whale research has been done in Cintra Bay, to our knowledge, since that time. Thus, it is possible that a remnant of the population survives, having been overlooked for the last century. Widespread interest in the colony of Mediterranean monk seals (Monachus monachus) at Cap Blanc, Mauritania (Maigret, Trotignon and Duguy, 1976; Trotignon, 1979), is added incentive for an expedition to the region. The advice of experienced monk seal researchers should be sought concerning logistics, the need for permits to visit or work in these waters and existing or potential means of communicating with local fishermen and others who may have information on right whales.

(c) If right whales still use the Cintra Bay Ground, measures to ensure their conservation and to promote their recovery should be initiated. This ground may well be the eastern North Atlantic equivalent of the Peninsula Valdés area of Patagonia in the western South Atlantic (Payne, 1972; 1976).

(d) The relationship of Cintra Bay right whales to populations elsewhere can be tested through radio-tagging or photoidentification and resight studies.

(4) An initiative should be made to investigate sighting, stranding and capture records of whalemen and others at Madeira in order to determine whether more right whales have been seen (or killed) there during the twentieth century than the few mentioned by Maul and Sergeant (1977).

(5) The Southeast US Coast Ground is still used by right whales (see Reeves et al., 1978; Kraus, Prescott, Knowlton and Stone, 1986). Since more than 170 individual North Atlantic right whales have now been photodocumented and catalogued, mainly off the North American coast from Cape Cod north (Kraus, pers. comm.), an intensive effort to photograph right whales on the Southeast US Coast Ground is desirable. Comparison of callosity patterns on animals sighted in winter and summer should help to elucidate stock affinities and migratory behaviour.

(6) A careful examination of historical materials and artifacts in and from Bermuda should be made to determine in what degree (if any) right whales were hunted there, ancillary to what we believe was mainly a humpback fishery (Mitchell and Reeves, 1983). Also, recent efforts to observe and photograph humpbacks at Bermuda should be evaluated to determine: (1) whether right whales have been encountered more than once (see Payne and McVay, 1971) and (2) whether there has been coverage at appropriate seasons and in specific areas where right whales might be expected to occur in this region.

(7) Pigmentation patterns on right whales may prove useful in differentiating stocks (True, 1904; Thompson, 1918), in a manner similar to that used for humpback whales and being developed for killer whales (Evans and Yablokov, 1978) and sperm whales (Veinger, 1969; 1974; 1980). An obvious problem is the lack of a large sample of photographs showing the lateral and ventral sides of specimens. However, we believe the existing sample, including published and available unpublished photographs of carcasses, combined with collections of photographs of living specimens from South Africa, Argentina, eastern North America and elsewhere, is adequate to evaluate whether there are differences between geographically separate populations, and then to begin testing hypotheses concerning stock identity. Callosity patterns may also provide evidence of stock discreteness (Best, 1970), as might parasite faunas.

ACKNOWLEDGEMENTS

The museum directors, curators, and librarians of the following institutions are acknowledged for their co-operation: Peter Foulger Museum, Nantucket Atheneum Library, Dukes County Historical Society, New Bedford Free Public Library, Old Dartmouth Historical Society, G. W. Blunt White Library (Mystic Seaport Maritime Museum), Providence Public Library, and Kendall Whaling Museum. A. Evely verified some of the references; A. Hallé helped prepare the figures. R. Olsen assisted in the reading of some logbooks and journals. J. Bird, V. Rowntree, S. Kraus, and R. Kugler gave us useful advice. Partial financial support for this project came from the International Whaling Commission.

For critical comments and constructive suggestions concerning the manuscript we thank R. L. Webb, Kendall Whaling Museum; P. Goldring, Parks Canada, Ottawa; and R. Kugler, New Bedford Whaling Museum.

UNPUBLISHED ARCHIVAL REFERENCES

Abbreviations are: KWM, Kendall Whaling Museum; ODHS, Old Dartmouth Historical Society; PPL, Providence Public Library: NBFPL, New Bedford Free Public Library; NA, Nantucket Atheneum; DCHS, Dukes County Historical Society; PFM, Peter Foulger Museum; BWL, G. W. Blunt White Library.

Abbie Bradford. Logbook of the schooner *Abbie Bradford* of New Bedford, Gilbert B. Borden, Master. 22 May 1884–29 Sept. 1885. [KWM]

A. J. Ross, Journal kept by James A. Sinclair on the brig *A. J. Ross*, James A. Sinclair, Master. 15 May 1878 – wrecked in Hudson Bay 24 Sept. 1878. Sinclair returned home on brig *Abbot Lawrence* of New Bedford, 1 Sept. 1879. [Private Collection]

Anonymous. No date, Ms.a. Compilation of abstracts of whaling voyages, 1833–1910. Author unknown. Misc. vol. 51, 50 p. MS [BWL]

Anonymous. No date, Ms.b. Abstracts of whaling voyages, 1832–1905. Coll. 58, vol. 5, pp. 51–222 [of a journal book]. [BWL]

Anonymous. 1736. [Mémoire du Directeur du Domaine sur la pêche de la baleine dans le fleuve Saint-Laurent, entreprise par le Sr D'Arragorry.] 20 Sept. 1736, Québec. Microfilm at Archives nationales du Québec. Correspondance générale. M. de Beauharnois, Gouverneur Général M. Hocquart, Intendant. Colonies. CIIA, vol. 65, fo. 72, 17½ pp.

Ansel Gibbs. [Logbook of] the bark *Ansel Gibbs*, E. B. Fisher, Master. 3 June 1868–4 Sept. 1869. [ODHS]

A. R. Tucker, Journal kept on the bark *A. R. Tucker* of New Bedford, Asa Grinnell, Master. 20 Sept. 1866–26 April 1867. [PPL]

A. R. Tucker, Logbook of the bark *A. R. Tucker* of New Bedford, Henry Gifford, Master. 13 April 1880–24 May 1883. [NBFPL]

Bartholomew Gosnold. Journal kept by William H. Poole, on the bark *Bartholomew Gosnold* of Nantucket, William H. Poole, Master. 23 Apr. 1881–21 Feb. 1883. [KWM]

Beauharnois, de, and Hocquart. 1736. [Pêche a la baleine dans le fleuve Saint-Laurent par le Sr. D'Arragorry, et au loup-marin sur la côte du Labrador par le Sr de Lafontaine.] 8 Oct. 1736, Québec. Microfilm at Archives nationales du Québec. Correspondance générale. M. de Beauharnois, Gouverneur Général. M. Hocquart, Intendant. Colonies. CIIA, vol. 65, fo. 68, 4½pp.

Braganza. Journal kept by Ichabod Norton on the ship *Braganza* of New Bedford, Charles Waterman, Master. 1 Dec. 1840–29 May 1844. [DCHS]

Bristol. Journal kept by Peter Folger on the sloop *Bristol* of Nantucket, William Folger, Master. 4 July–25 Sept. 1759. [NA]

Bristol. Journal kept by Peter Folger on the sloop *Bristol* of Nantucket, William Folger, Master. 10 July–2 Sept. 1760 [NA]

Canton (a). Journal kept by Geo. F. Allen on the bark *Canton* of New Bedford, W. H. Poole, Master. 1 May 1895–7 Oct. 1896. [KWM]

Canton (b). Logbook of the bark *Canton* of New Bedford, W. H. Poole, Master. 30 May 1895–7 Oct. 1896. [KWM]

Canton. [Logbook of] the bark *Canton* of New Bedford, Charles W. Fisher, Master. 8 May 1897–11 Sept. 1898. [NBFPL]

Cicero. Journal kept on the ship *Cicero* of New Bedford, Owen Hillman, Jr., Master. 26 July 1835–Sept. 1836. [DCHS]

Daniel Webster. Journal kept by Gilbert Borden on the bark *Daniel Webster* of New Bedford, Gilbert Borden, Master. 17 April 1877–21 Sept. 1879. [PPL]

D'Arragorry, S., Ms. 1735 [Le Sr Simon D'Arragorry rend compte de sa pêche a la baleine dans le Saint-Laurent.] 28 Oct. 1735, Québec. Microfilm at Archives nationales du Québec. Correspondance générale M. Hocquart, Intendant. Colonies. CIIA, Vol. 64, Fo. 168–169.

Diamond. Journal kept by Thomas Kempton on the sloop *Diamond* of Nantucket. ——— Aiken, Master. 6 July–18 Oct. 1765. [PFM]

Dolphin. Journal kept by George Gardner on the sloop *Dolphin* of Nantucket, Richard Gardner, Master. 5 July–11 Oct. 1763. [NA]

Dolphin. Journal kept by Benjamin Paddack on the sloop *Dolphin* of Nantucket, Benjamin Paddack, Master. 23 Feb.–5 Oct. 1790. [NA]

Edward. Journal kept on the brig *Edward* of Nantucket, ——— Paddack, Master. 15 May–29 Dec. 1817. [PFM]

E. H. Hatfield, Logbook of the schooner *E. H. Hatfield* of Edgartown, William Kirkconnell, Master. 30 Nov. 1880–19 Aug. 1882. [PPL]

Emma Jane. Logbook of the schooner *Emma Jane* of Edgartown, Cornelius M. Marchant, Master. 30 Sept. 1879–1 Jan. 1880. [ODHS]

Endeavor. Journal kept by Peter Folger on the sloop *Endeavor* of Nantucket, Peter Folger, Master. 30 June–8 Aug. 1761. [NA]

Endeavor. Journal kept by Peter Folger on the sloop *Endeavor* of Nantucket, Peter Folger, Master. 7 July–23 Sept. 1762. [NA]

E. Nickerson, Journal by an unknown keeper on the schooner *E. Nickerson* of Provincetown, R. Freeman, Master. 22 Aug. 1856–3 Aug. 1857. [KWM]

Enterprise. Journal kept by Peleg Folger on the sloop *Enterprise* of Nantucket, Benjamin Gardner, Master. 13 March–4 Apr. 1760. [NA]

Enterprise. Journal kept by Peleg Folger on the sloop *Enterprise* of Nantucket, Benjamin Gardner, Master. No date, but sometime between April and July 1760 (Fonda, 1969, p. 25). [NA]

Enterprise. Journal kept by Peleg Folger on the sloop *Enterprise* of Nantucket, Benjamin Gardner, Master. 1 July–29 Aug. 1760. [NA]

Francis. Journal kept by Peter Folger on the sloop *Francis* of Nantucket, Benjamin Barnard, Master. 28 June–21 Sept. 1758. [NA]

George Porter. Journal kept on the ship *George Porter* of New Bedford, Ephraim Poole, Master. 26 July 1835–1 May 1836. [DCHS]

Golden City. Logbook of the schooner *Golden City* of New Bedford, Henry Clay, Master. 9 Dec. 1875–29 Sept. 1876. [PPL]

Golden City. Logbook of the schooner *Golden City* of New Bedford, W. A. Martin, Master. 28 Nov. 1878–18 March 1880. [ODHS]

Golden City. Logbook of the schooner *Golden City* of New Bedford — Avery, Master. 2 June 1880–22 Aug. 1881. [ODHS]

Golden City. Logbook of the schooner *Golden City* of New Bedford — Frates, Master. 13 Oct. 1881–18 Sept. 1882. [ODHS]

Grampus. Journal kept by Peleg Folger on the sloop *Grampus* of Nantucket, Benjamin Barnard [?], Master. 1–15 May 1751. [NA]

Grampus. Journal kept by Peleg Folger on the sloop *Grampus* of Nantucket, Benjamin Barnard [?], Master. 18 May–18 June 1751. [NA]

Grampus. Journal kept by Peter Folger on the sloop *Grampus* of Nantucket, Benjamin Barnard [?], Master. 23 June 1751. [NA]

Grampus. Journal kept by Peleg Folger on the sloop *Grampus* of Nantucket, Benjamin Barnard [?], Master. 2 July–20 July 1751. [NA]

Greyhound. Journal kept by Peleg Folger on the sloop *Greyhound* of Nantucket, Richard Pinkham, Master. 17 March–10 Apr. 1753 [NA]

Greyhound. Journal kept by Peleg Folger on the sloop *Greyhound* of Nantucket, Richard Pinkham, Master. 7 May–24 Sept. 1753. [NA]

Hunter. Journal kept by Asa Tobey on the ship *Hunter* of New Bedford, Asa S. Tobey, Master. 25 Oct. 1863–10 Aug. 1864. [PPL]

India. Journal kept on the ship *India* of New Bedford, Richard Flanders, Master. 25 Aug. 1858–3 Nov. 1861. [DCHS]

John and Edward. Journal kept on the ship *John and Edward* of New Bedford, F. C. Smith, Master. 8 Jan. 1855–10 Dec. 1858. [DCHS]

John A. Ross. [Logbook of] the brig *John A. Ross* of New Bedford, J. N. Hyatt, Master. 17 July 1877–10 Apr. 1878. [ODHS]

Jolly Nancy. Journal kept on the sloop *Jolly Nancy* of Nantucket, Daniel Folger, Master. 14 June 1759. [NA]

Jolly Nancy. Journal kept on the sloop *Jolly Nancy* of Nantucket, Daniel Folger, Master. 4–25 July 1759. [NA]

Jolly Nancy. Journal kept on the sloop *Jolly Nancy* of Nantucket, Daniel Folger, Master. 18 Aug.–16 Sept. 1759. [NA]

Lark. Journal kept by Obed Fitch on the schooner *Lark* of Nantucket, Solomon Coffin, Master. 24 Nov. 1784–26 May 1785. [NA]

Mary. Journal kept by Peleg Folger on the sloop *Mary* of Nantucket, Richard Pinkham, Master. 16 March–12 Apr. 1752. [NA]

Mary. Journal kept by Peleg Folger on the sloop *Mary* of Nantucket, Richard Pinkham, Master. 15 Apr.–26 May 1752. [NA]

Mary. Logbook of the ship *Mary* of Edgartown, Henry Pease, Master. 1 Dec. 1844–9 Oct. 1847. [DCHS]

N. D. Chase, [Logbook of] the bark *N. D. Chase* of Beverly, Hussey, Master. 15 Oct. 1855–1 May 1856. [ODHS]

Ohio. Diary kept by Sallie G. Smith on the bark *Ohio* of New Bedford, Fred H. Smith, Master. 6 July 1875–17 Oct. 1878. [BWL]

Olive. Journal kept by George Gardner on the sloop *Olive* of Nantucket, Paul Pinkham, Master. 11 July–10 Oct. 1764. [NA]

Olive. Journal kept by George Gardner on the sloop *Olive* of Nantucket, Paul Pinkham, Master. 9 July–5 Oct. 1765. [NA]

Palmetto. [Logbook of] the bark *Palmetto* of New Bedford, J. W. Buddington, Master. 24 June–6 Nov. 1886. [ODHS]

Phebe. Journal kept by Peleg Folger on the sloop *Phebe* of Nantucket, Christopher Baxter, Master. 9 March–28 Apr. 1754. [NA]

Phebe. Journal kept by Peleg Folger on the sloop *Phebe* of Nantucket, Christopher Baxter, Master. 6–30 May 1754. [NA]

Phebe. Journal kept by Peleg Folger on the sloop *Phebe* of Nantucket, Christopher Baxter, Master. 11 July–12 Sept. 1754. [NA]

Phebe. Journal kept by Peleg Folger on the sloop *Phebe* of Nantucket, Christopher Baxter, Master. 20 Apr.–23 May 1757. [NA]

Phebe. Journal kept by Peleg Folger on the sloop *Phebe* of Nantucket, Christopher Baxter, Master. 28 May–23 June 1757. [NA]

Phebe. Journal kept by Peleg Folger on the sloop *Phebe* of Nantucket, Christopher Baxter, Master. 10 Aug. 1757. [NA]

Phebe. Journal kept by Peleg Folger on the sloop *Phebe* of Nantucket, Christopher Baxter, Master. 22 Aug.–13 Sept. 1757. [NA]

Reliance. Journal kept by John Howland on the sloop *Reliance* of Dartmouth, John Howland, Master, 14 Apr.–15 Oct. 1768. [NBFPL]

Reliance. Journal kept by John Howland on the sloop *Reliance* of Dartmouth, John Howland, Master. 22 Apr.–10 July, 1769. [NBFPL]

Reliance. Journal kept by John Howland on the sloop *Reliance* of Dartmouth, John Howland, Master. 27 Apr.–14 Aug. 1771. [NBFPL]

Richmond. Logbook of the bark *Richmond* of New Bedford, Edward B. Hussey, Master. 1 Oct. 1857–24 March 1860. [ODHS]

Seaflower. Journal kept by Peleg Folger on the sloop *Seaflower* of Nantucket, Christopher Coffin, Master. 3 June–26 Aug. 1752. [NA]

Sea Ranger. Journal kept by William H. Tilton on the bark *Sea Ranger* of New Bedford, J. N. Holmes, Master. 4 June 1879–14 Oct. 1881. [PPL]

Silver Cloud. Journal kept by Hiram Borden on the bark *Silver Cloud* of New Bedford, Frederick Coggeshall, Master. 12 Nov. 1856–7 Jan. 1860. [KWM]

Triton. Journal kept on the ship *Triton* of Portsmouth, – Flanders, Master. 28 Sept. 1834–26 Feb. 1835. [DCHS]

Tropic Bird. Journal kept by John A. Beebe on the bark *Tropic Bird* of New Bedford, William B. Stanton, Master. 19 Apr. 1851–28 Sept. 1853. [PFM]

Union. Journal kept by Peter Folger on the sloop *Union* of Nantucket, Master unknown. 9 July–4 Sept. 1757. [Vessel name is from Fonda, 1969, p. 24.] [NA]

Violet. Logbook of the brig *Violet* of Hull, William Jackson, Master. 31 Jan.–18 Oct. 1853. [KWM]

Wales, G. 1871 Ms. [An account of the voyage of the *Ansel Gibbs*, 1871.] [NBFPL – not seen by authors; except (p. 7) supplied by P. Goldring, *in litt.*, 14 March 1985.]

Walter Irving. Logbook of the schooner *Walter Irving* of Provincetown, Lysander N. Paine, Master. 9 Nov. 1855–16 Sept. 1856. [PPL]

Walter Irving. Logbook of the Schooner *Walter Irving* of Provincetown, Hiram Holmes, Master. 18 Nov. 1856–7 Oct. 1857. [PPL]

Wood, D. No date. Abstracts of whaling voyages [1835–75]. 5 vols. [NBFPL]

PUBLISHED AND UNPUBLISHED REFERENCES

Aguilar, A. 1981. The black right whale, *Eubalaena glacialis*, in the Cantabrian Sea. *Rep. int. Whal. Commn* 31: 457–9.

Allen, G. M. 1916. The whalebone whales of New England. *Mem. Boston Soc. Nat. Hist.* 8(2): 107–322 + pls. 8–16.

Allen, J. A. 1908. The North Atlantic right whale and its near allies. *Bull. Am. Mus. Nat. Hist.* 24(18): 277–329 + pls. 19–24.

Allen, G. M. 1942. *Extinct and Vanishing Mammals of the Western Hemisphere with the Marine Species of all the Oceans.* Special Publication No. 11, Cooper Square Publishers, New York, i–xvi + 620 pp. + frontis.

Anonymous. 1849. Arctic Ocean. Yankee whaling enterprise. *Nautical Magazine and Naval Chronicle, for 1849.* [A Journal of papers on Subjects connected with Maritime Affairs]: 694–5.

Anonymous. 1854. New whaling grounds. *Nautical Magazine and Naval Chronicle, for 1854.* [A Journal of Papers on Subjects connected with Maritime Affairs.]: 544–5.

Anonymous. 1859. [Arrivals – The clipper ship *Golden Eagle*.] [From *N. B. Mercury*.] Mystic, Conn., Mystic Seaport Museum, Inc., G. W. Blunt White Library. [Newspaper Clipping File] Collection 58. [Source not indicated.]

Anonymous. 1907. Whaling in the olden days. New Bedford, *The Morning Mercury*, August 7, 1907. Mystic Conn., Mystic Seaport Museum Inc., G. W. Blunt White Library. [Newspaper Clipping File] VFM 904.

Anonymous. 1981. Norway Progress Report on Cetacean Research June 1979–May 1980. *Rep. int. Whal. Commn* 31: 209–10.

Arvy, L. 1980. Les cétacés du Canada: la baleine à tête d'arc (*Balaena mysticetus*) et le marsouin blanc (*Delphinapterus leucas*) au temps de Charlevoix et de Maurepas. *Ann. Soc. Sci. nat. Charente-Maritime* 6(7): 633–45.

Ashley, C. W. 1926. *The Yankee Whaler.* Houghton Mifflin, Boston and New York; Riverside Press, Cambridge. Frontis + [i]–xxiv + 379 pp.

Bannister, J. and Mitchell, E. 1980. North Pacific sperm whale stock identity: distributional evidence from Maury and Townsend charts. *Rep. int. Whal. Commn* (special issue 2): 219–30.

Bannister, J. L., Taylor, S. and Sutherland, H. 1981. Logbook records of 19th century American sperm whaling: A report on the 12 month project, 1978–79. *Rep. int. Whal. Commn* 31: 821–33.

Barkham, S. H. 1977. Guipuzcoan shipping in 1571 with particular reference to the decline of the transatlantic fishing industry. Desert Research Institute (Univ. Nevada, Reno), *Publ. Soc. Sci.* 13: 73–81.

Barkham, S. H. 1984. The Basque whaling establishments in Labrador 1536–1632 – a summary. *Arctic* 37: 515–19.

Beneden, P.-J. van. 1868. Les baleines et leur distribution géographique. *Bull. Acad. R. Belg.* Sér. 2, 25: 9–21 + fold. map.

Beneden, P.-J. van. 1880. [Baleine échouée le 7 janvier 1880 sur les côtes de Charleston, État de la Caroline du Sud.] *Bull. Acad. R. Belg.* Sér. 2, 49: 313–15.

Beneden, P.-J. van. 1885. Sur l'apparition d'une petite gamme de vraies baleines sur les côtes des États-Unis d'Amérique. *Bull. Acad. R. Belg.* Sér. 3, 9: 212–14.

Beneden, P.-J. van. 1886. Histoire naturelle de la baleine des Basques (*Balaena biscayensis*). *Mém. couronnés et autres mém. Acad. R. Belg.* 38: 1–44.

Beneden, P.-J. van and Gervais, P. 1880. *Ostéographie des Cétacés Vivants et Fossiles, Comprenant la Description et l'Iconographie des Squelette et du Systéme Dentaire de ces Animaux; ainsi que des Documents Relatifs à leur Histoire Naturelle.* A. Bertrand Paris: [i–iv] + i–viii + 634 pp. (text) and pls. 1–64 (some folding) + 21bis, 23bis (fold.) 27bis (fold.), (Atlas).

Best, P. B. 1970. Exploitation and recovery of right whales *Eubalaena australis* off the Cape Province. *Investl Rep. Div. Sea Fish. S. Afr.* 80: [i–iv] + 1–20.

Bockstoce, J. R. and Botkin, D. B. 1983. The historical status and reduction of the Western Arctic bowhead whale (*Balaena mysticetus*) population by the pelagic whaling industry, 1848–1914. *Rep. int. Whal. Commn* (special issue 5): 107–41.

Bodfish, H. H. 1936. *Chasing the Bowhead.* [Recorded for him by J. C. Allen.] Harvard University Press, Cambridge, [x] + 281 pp. + frontis + 8 unnumb. pls.

Brimley, C. S. 1946. The mammals of North Carolina. Installment No. 18. Elon College, North Carolina, Carolina Biological Supply Co., *Carolina Tips* 9: 6–7.

Brimley, H. H. 1894. Whale fishing in North Carolina. *Bull. N. C. Dep. Agric.* 14(7): 4–8. [n.v.]

Buchet, G. 1895. De la baleine des Basques dans les eaux islandaises et de l'aspect des grands cétacés à la mer. *Mém. Soc. Zool. France* VIII (1895) 229–31 + pls VI–VIII.

Clark, A. H. 1887a. 1. History and present condition of the fishery. pp. 3–218 of Part XV. The whale fishery. *In:* G. B. Goode, (ed.), *The Fisheries and Fishery Industries of the United States.* Section V. History and methods of the fisheries. In two volumes, with an atlas of two hundred and fifty-five plates. Vol. II. Government Printing Office, Washington, i–xx + 881 pp.

Clark, A. H. 1887b. Plates 183–210. [To accompany text above, Clark, A. H. 1887a]. *In:* G. B. Goode, (ed), *The Fisheries and Fishery Industries of the United States.* Section V. History and methods of the fisheries. In two volumes, with an atlas of two hundred and fifty-five plates. Plates. Government Printing Office, Washington, pls. 1–255.

Clarke, R. 1954. Open boat whaling in the Azores. The history and present methods of a relic industry. *Discovery Rep.* 26: 281–354 + folding table + pls. 13–18.

Collett, R. 1909. A few notes on the whale *Balaena glacialis* and its capture in recent years in the North Atlantic by Norwegian whalers. *Proc. Zool. Soc. Lond.* 1909: 91–8 + pls. 25–27.

Decker, R. O. 1973. *Whaling industry of New London.* Liberty Cap Books, York, Pennsylvania. 202 pp.

Dudley, P. 1725. An Essay upon the Natural History of Whales, with a particular Account of the Ambergris found in the *Sperma Ceti* Whale. In a letter to the publisher, from the Honourable *Paul Dudley*, Esq; F.R.S. *Phil. Trans.* 33(387): 256–69.

Duguy, R. 1975. Contribution à l'étude des mammifères marins de la côte Nord-Ouest Afrique. *Rev. Trav. Inst. Pêch. marit.* 39(3): 321–32.

Du Pasquier, J. T. 1984. The whalers of Honfleur in the seventeenth century. *Arctic* 37: 533–38.

Du Pasquier, T. 1982. *Lew Baleiniers Français au XIXe Siècle (1814–1868).* Terre et Mer, 4 Seigneurs, Grenoble. 256 pp.

Earll, R. E. 1887a. North Carolina and its fisheries. Part XII, pp. 475–97 *In:* G. B. Goode, (ed), *The Fisheries and Fishery Industries of the United States.* Section II. A geographical review of the fisheries industries and fishing communities for the year 1880. Washington, Government Printing Office, [i]–ix + [2]–787 pp.

Earll, R. E. 1887b. The fisheries of South Carolina and Georgia. Part XIII, pp. 499–518 In: G. B. Goode, (ed), *The Fisheries and Fishery Industries of the United States*. Section II. A geographical review of the fisheries industries and fishing communities for the year 1880. Washington, Government Printing Office, [i]–ix+[2]–787 pp.

Edwards, E. J. and Rattray, J. E. 1932. '*Whale Off!' The Story of American Shore Whaling*. Frederick A. Stokes Company, New York, i–xvi+285 pp.+frontis+17 pls.

Edwards, E. J. and Rattray, J. E. 1956. '*Whale Off!' The Story of American Shore Whaling*. Coward-McCann, Inc., New York. frontis+i–xxiv+285 pp.+15 pls.

Eschricht, D. F. and Reinhardt, J. 1866. On the Greenland Right-Whale. (*Balaena mysticetus*, Linn.), with especial reference to its geographical distribution and migrations in times past and present, and to its external and internal characteristics. pp. 1–150 In: W. H. Flower, (ed.), *Recent Memoirs on the Cetacea by Professors Eschricht, Reinhardt and Lilljeborg*. Published for the Ray Society by Robert Hardwicke, 192, Piccadilly, London, i–xii+312 pp.+6 pls.

Evans, W. E., and Yablokov, A. V. 1978. Intraspecific variation of the color pattern of the killer whale (*Orcinus orca*). pp. 102–15. In: V. E. Sokolov and A. V. Yablokov (eds) *Advances in studies of cetaceans and pinnipeds*, 'Nauka', Moscow, (In Russian with English summary). [*n.v.*]

Fairley, J. 1981. *Irish Whales and Whaling*. Blackstaff Press, Belfast, [i–viii]+218 pp.

Ferguson, R. 1938. *Arctic Harpooner. A Voyage on the Schooner Abbie Bradford 1878–1879*. Edited by L. D. Stair, illustr. by P. Quinn. Univ. of Pennsylvania Press, Philadelphia, x+216 pp.

Finckenor, G. A. 1975. *Whales and Whaling. Port of Sag Harbor, New York*. William Ewers, Sag Harbor, N.Y. 159 pp.

Fonda, D. C. Jr. 1969. *Eighteenth Century Nantucket Whaling*. As Compiled from the Original Logs and Journals of The Nantucket Atheneum and The Nantucket Whaling Museum. Privately Printed for the Author, Nantucket, 30 pp.

Fraser, F. C. 1970. An early 17th century record of the Californian grey whale in Icelandic waters. *Invest. Cetacea* 2: 13–20.

Gilmore, R. M. 1959. On the mass strandings of sperm whales. *Pac. Nat.* 1(10): 9–16.

Gray, J. E. 1868. On the geographical distribution of the *Balaenidae* or right whales. *Ann. and Mag. of Nat. Hist.*, vol. I, 4th ser., no. IV: 242–7.

Gray, J. E. 1870. Observations on the whales described in the 'Ostéographie des Cétacés' of MM. Van Beneden and Gervais. *Ann. Mag. nat. Hist.* Ser. 4, 33: 193–204.

Guérin, R. 1874. *Études Zoologiques et Paléontologiques sur la Famille des Cétacés*. Typographie Georges Chamerot, Paris, 145 pp.+Errata pls. I–III (fold. maps).

Guldberg, G.-A. 1884a. Sur la présence, aux temps anciens et modernes, de la Baleine de Biscaye (ou Nordcaper) sur les Côtes de Norwège. *Bull. Acad. R. Belg.* Sér. 3, 7: 374–402.

Guldberg, G. A. 1884b. The North Cape whale. *Nature* 30: 148–9.

Guldberg, G. 1891. Bidrag til noiere kundskab om Atlanterhavets rethval (*Eubalaena biscayensis*, Eschricht). *Christiania Videnskabs-Selskabs Forhandlinger for 1891* 8: 3–14.

Guldberg, G. 1893. Zur Kenntnis des Nordkapers. (*Eubalaena biscayensis* Eschr.). *Zool. Jahrb. (Syst. Ökol. Geogr. Tiere)* 7: 1–22+pls. 1–2.

Haldane, R. C. 1908. Whaling in Scotland for 1907. *Ann. Scot. Nat. Hist.* 66: 65–72.

Harmer, S. F. 1928. The history of whaling. *Proc. Linn. Soc. Lond.* Session 140: 51–95.

Hegarty, R. B. 1959. *Returns of Whaling Vessels Sailing from American Ports. A Continuation of Alexander Starbuck's 'History of the American Whale Fishery' 1876–1928*. The Old Dartmouth Historical Society, and Whaling Museum, New Bedford, Massachusetts, 4 unnumbered+58 pp.

Hegarty, R. B. 1964. *Addendum to 'Starbuck' and 'Whaling Masters'*. New Bedford Customs District. Reynolds Printing, Inc. New Bedford, Mass. 110 pp.

Henderson, D. A. 1972. *Men and Whales at Scammon's Lagoon*. Dawson's Book Shop, Los Angeles, 313 pp.+4 maps.

Hjort, J. and Ruud J. T. 1929. Whaling and fishing in the North Atlantic. *In*: Whales and Plankton in the North Atlantic. A contribution to the work of the Whaling Committee and of the North Eastern Area Committee. *Rapp. P.-V. Réun. CIEM* 56: 1–123.

Hohman, E. P. 1928. *The American Whaleman. A Study of Life and Labor in the Whaling Industry*. Longmans, Green and Co., New York, i–xiv 355 pp.+21 pls.

Holder, J. B. 1883. Article VI.—The Atlantic Right Whales: A Contribution, embracing an Examination of (1.) The exterior characters and osteology of a cisarctic Right Whale—male. (2.) The exterior characters of a cisarctic Right Whale—female. (3.) The osteology of a cisarctic Right Whale—sex not known. To which is added a concise résumé of historical mention relating to the present and allied species. *Bull. Am. Mus. Nat. Hist.* 1(4): 99–137+pls. 10–13.

The Inquirer [NI]. Nantucket, Mass. (23 June 1821 to 1 April 1865).

The Inquirer and Mirror [NIM]. Nantucket, Mass. 1 April 1865 to present).

International Whaling Commission 1976. International Decade of Cetacean Research. Research Proposals for the North Atlantic. *Rep. int. Whal. Commn* 26: 142–79.

International Whaling Statistics. Edited by The Committee for Whaling Statistics. (Det Norske Hvalrads Statistiske Publikasjoner.) Grondahl and Son. Oslo. Nr. 1 (1930) to Nr. 90 (1982).

Johnson, B. 1982. *The Barbara Johnson Whaling Collection: Part II. New York Galleries, September 24 and 25, 1982*. New York, Sotheby Parke Bernet Inc., [i–vi]+[1–137]+[i–v] pp. [Exhibition and Auction Catalogue.]

Jong, C. de. 1983. The hunt of the Greenland whale: a short history and statistical sources. *Rep. int. Whal. Commn* (special issue 5): 83–106.

Jonsgård, Å. 1981. Bowhead whales, *Balaena mysticetus*, observed in Arctic waters of the eastern North Atlantic after the Second World War. *Rep. int. Whal. Commn* 31: 511.

Jónsson, J. 1965. Whales and whaling in Icelandic Waters. *Norsk Hvalfangsttid*. 54(11): 245–53.

Klumov, S. K. 1962. Gladkie (Yaponskie) kity Tikhogo Okeana. *Tr. Inst. Okeanol.* 58: 202–97. [In Russian with English Summary, p. 297, The right whales in the Pacific Ocean; translated in 1962 as 'The right whales in the Pacific Ocean *Eubalaena sieboldi*. 73 pp. typescript+ copies from original pls. and tables.]

Kraus, S. D. and Prescott, J. H. 1982MS. The North Atlantic right whale (*Eubalaena glacialis*) in the Bay of Fundy, 1981, with notes on distribution, abundance, biology and behavior. Final Report to US Dept. Commerce, National Marine Fisheries Service in fulfillment of Contract NA-81-FA-C-00030, and to the World Wildlife Fund–US., Washington, DC., p. [i–vi]+1–105+[i] Errata typescript.

Kraus, S., Prescott, J. H., Knowlton, A. R. and Stone, G. S. 1986. Migration and calving of right whales (*Eubalaena glacialis*) in the western North Atlantic. (Published in this volume.)

Kraus, S., Prescott, J. H. Turnbull, P. and Reeves, R. R. 1982. Preliminary notes on the occurrence of the North Atlantic right whale, *Eubalaena glacialis*, in the Bay of Fundy. *Rep. int. whal. Commn* 32: 407–11.

Layne, J. N. 1965. Observations on marine mammals in Florida waters. *Fla. State Mus. Bull. Biol. Sci.* 9(4): 131–81.

Macy, O. 1885. *The History of Natucket; being a Compendious Account of the First Settlement of the Island by the English, together with the Rise and Progress of the Whale Fishery; and other Historical Facts Relative to said Island and its inhabitants*. Hilliard, Gray, and Co., Boston. Frontis [map]+xii+300pp.+1–8 [Advertisements]+1 pl.

Maigret, J., Trotignon, J. and Duguy, R. 1976. Le phoque moine, *Monachus monachus* Hermann 1779, sur les côtes méridionales du Sahara. *Mammalia* 40: 413–22.

Manigault, G. E. 1885. The black whale captured in Charleston Harbor January, 1880. *Proc Elliott Soc* Sept., 1885, p. 98–104.

Markham, C. R. 1881. On the whale-fishery of the Basque provinces of Spain. *Proc. Zool. Soc. Lond.* 1881: 969–76.

Maul, G. E., and Sergeant, D. E. 1977. New cetacean records from Madeira. *Bocagiana* 43: 1–8.

Maury, M. F. 1853. *A Chart Showing the Favourite Resort of the Sperm and Right Whale by M. F. Maury, LLD Lieut. US Navy*. Constructed from Maury's Whale Chart of the World, by Robt. H. Wyman, Lieut. USN by Authority of Commo: Charles Morris USN Chief of Bureau of Ordnance and Hydrography. Washington, 1 sheet.

Mitchell, E. 1974a. Present status of Northwest Atlantic fin and other whale stocks. pp. 108–69 In: W. E. Schevill (ed.) *The Whale Problem: a status report*. Harvard University Press, Cambridge, i–x+419 pp.+pls. 1–7.

Mitchell, E. D. 1974b. Endangered whales in waters off Canada, pp. 162–4 In: D. Stewart (ed.), *Canadian Endangered Species*, Gage Publishing Limited, Toronto.

Mitchell, E., Kozicki, V. M. and Reeves, R. R. 1986. Sightings of right wales, *Eubalaena glacialis*, on the Scotian Shelf, 1966–1972. (Published in this volume.)

Mitchell, E. and Reeves, R. R. 1983. Catch history, abundance, and present status of Northwest Atlantic humpback whales. *Rep. int. Whal. Commn* (special issue 5): 153–212.

Moore, J. C. 1953. Distribution of marine mammals to Florida waters. *Am. Midl. Nat.* 49(1): 117–58.

Moore, J. C. and Clark. E. 1963. Discovery of right whales in the Gulf of Mexico. *Science* 141(3577): 269.

Mörzer Bruyns, W. F. J. 1971. *Field Guide of Whales and Dolphins.* C. A. Mees, Amsterdam. 258 pp.

Muse, A. 1961. *Grandpa Was A Whaler. A Story of Carteret Chadwicks.* Owen G. Dunn Co., New Bern, N. C. [i]−v+126 pp.+1 fold. pl.

Palmer, W. R. 1959 [1981]. The whaling port of Sag Harbor. Ph.D. thesis, Faculty of Political Science, Columbia University, 1959. Publ. by University Microfilms International, Ann Arbor, Michigan, USA; London, England. [vi]+v+327 pp.

Payne, R. 1972. Swimming with Patagonia's right whales. *National Geographic* 142: 576–87.

Payne, R. 1976. At home with right whales. *Nat. Geogr.* 149(3): 322–39.

Payne, R. 1984. Reproductive rates and breeding area occupancy in the southern right whale, *Eubalaena australis. Rep. int. Whal. Commn* (special issue 6): 482.

Payne, R. and McVay, S. 1971. Songs of humpback whales. *Science* 173(3997): 585–97.

Pouchet, G. and Beauregard, A. 1888. Sur la présence de deux Baleines franches dans les eaux d'Alger. 2 pp. separate, printed by Gauthier-Villars et fils, Imprimeurs-Libraires des comptes rendus des séances de l'académie des sciences, Paris.

Reeves, R. 1975. The right whale. *Conservationist* 30(1): 32–3, 45.

Reeves, R. 1976. New Jersey's great whales. Occasional Paper No. 122, *N. J. Audubon* 2(1): [7]–14.

Reeves, R. R. and Katona, S. K. 1980. Extralimital records of white whales (*Delphinapterus leucas*) in eastern North American waters. *Can. Field-Nat.* 94: 239–47.

Reeves, R. R., Mead, J. G. and Katona, S. 1978. The right whale, *Eubalaena glacialis*, in the Western North Atlantic. *Rep. int. Whal. Commn* 28: 303–12.

Reeves, R. R. and Mitchell, E. 1982 MS. The cetacean fauna of the River and Gulf of St Lawrence. Submitted to Parks Canada, Ottawa, in partial fulfillment of Contract No. OSD81–00170, 129 pp.+Tables 1–3 typescript.

Reeves, R. R. and Mitchell, E. 1983. Yankee whaling for right whales in the North Atlantic Ocean. *Whalewatcher, Journal of the American Cetacean Society.* 17 (4): 3–8.

Reeves, R. R. and Mitchell, E. 1984. Catch history and initial population of white whales (*Delphinapterus leucas*) in the River and Gulf of St Lawrence, eastern Canada. *Nat. Can. (Rev. Ecol. Syst.)* 111: 63–121.

Reeves, R. and Mitchell, E. 1986. The Long Island, New York, right whale fishery: 1650–1924. (Published in this volume.)

Reeves, R., Mitchell, E., Mansfield, A. and McLaughlin, M. 1983. Distribution and migration of the bowhead whale, *Balaena mysticetus*, in the eastern North American Arctic. *Arctic* 36: 5–64.

Rørvik, C. J., Jónsson, J., Mathisen, O. A. and Jonsgård, Å. 1976. Fin whales, *Balaenoptera physalus* (L.), off the west coast of Iceland. Distribution, segregation by length and exploitation. *Rit Fisk.* 5(5): 1–30.

Ross, W. G. 1974. Distribution, migration, and depletion of bowhead whales in Hudson Bay, 1860–1915. *Arctic Alpine Res.* 6(1): 85–98.

Saemundsson, B. 1939. Mammalia. pp. 1–38 *In: The Zoology of Iceland.* Ejnar Munksgaard Copenhagen and Reykjavik, Vol. 4, Pt. 76.

Sante, G. Van. 1770. Alphabethische Naam-Lyst…gevaaren. Te Haarlem, Gedrukt by Johannes Enschede, Stads-Drukker. [i–ii] (Blank)+*Frontis*+[i–xii] (t.p.+Dedication+List of names) + i–xlviii + 1–16 + [i–iv] + 17–40 + [i–viii] + 41–50 + [i–iv] + 51–56 + [i–iv] + 57–62 + [i–iv] + 63–72 + [i–iv] + 73–114 + [i–xii] + 115–126 + [i–iv] + 127–142 + [i–ii] + 143–162 + [i–iv] + 163–170 + [i–ii] + 171–174 + [i–ii] + 175–178 + [i–iv] + 179–186 + [i–ii] + 187–190 + [i–ii]+191–218+[i–ii]+219–222+[i–ii]+223–246+[i–iv]+247–264 + [i–iv] + 265–274 + [i–ii] + 275–276 + [i–iv] + 277–278 + [i–ii] + 279–280 + [i] 'Drukfouten'. Brit. Lib. copy, shelf no. 10460. df. 9.

Schevill, W. E. and Moore, K. E. 1983. Townsend's unmapped North Atlantic right whales (*Eubalaena glacialis*). *Breviora* 476: 1–8.

Schmidly, D. J., Martin, C. O. and Collins, G. F. 1972. First occurrence of a black right whale (*Balaena glacialis*) along the Texas coast. *Southwest. Nat.* 17(2): 214–15.

Schmitt, F. P., de Jong, C. and Winter, F. H. 1980. *Thomas Welcome Roys, America's pioneer of modern whaling.* Univ. of Virginia Press, Charlottesville, for the Mariners Museum, Newport News, Virginia. *Frontis*+xiv+253 pp.

Shoemaker, E. [ed.] 1937. *Ships Logs and Captains' Diaries of Old Cape Cod.* Hyannis, Massachusetts, Cape Cod Chamber of Commerce, 36 pp.

Sigurjónsson, J. 1982. Icelandic minke whaling 1914–1980. *Rep. int. Whal. Commn* 32: 287–95.

Slijper, E. J., Van Utrecht, W. L. and Naaktgeboren, C. 1964. Remarks on the distribution and migration of whales, based on observations from Netherlands ships. *Bijdr. Dierkd.* 34: 3–93.

Southwell, T. 1904. On the whale fishery from Scotland, with some account of the changes in that industry and of the species hunted. *Ann Scottish Nat. Hist* 50: 77–89+pl. IV+table.

Stackpole, E. A. 1953. *The Sea-Hunters. The New England Whalemen during Two Centuries 1635–1835.* J. B. Lippincott Company, Philadelphia, New York. 510 pp. +16 pls.

Stackpole, E. A. 1972. *Whales and Destiny. The Rivalry between America, France and Britain for control of the Southern Whale Fishery, 1785–1825.* The University of Massachusetts Press, i–xiv+427 pp.

Starbuck, A. 1878. History of the American Whale Fishery from its earliest inception to the year 1876. *Rep. U.S. Comm. Fish* (4) 1875–76, Appendix A, 768 pp.+pls. 1–6.

Starbuck, A. 1924. *The History of Nantucket. County, Island and Town including Genealogies of First Settlers.* C. E. Goodspeed & Co., Boston, 871 pp.+4 folding maps.

Starbuck, A. 1964. *History of the American Whale Fishery from its Earliest Inception on the Year 1876.* Argosy-Antiquarian Ltd, New York. 2 Vols: Vol. 1, [i–viii]+i–x+1–407+1 pl.; Vol. 2, [i–v]+408–779.

Stick, D. 1958. *The Outer Banks of North Carolina 1584–1958* University of North Carolina Press: Chapel Hill, NC. 352 pp.

Thompson, D. W. 1918. On whales landed at the Scottish whaling stations, especially during the years 1908–1914—Part I. The Nordcaper. *Scot. Nat.* 81: 197–208.

Thompson, D. W. 1928. On whales landed at the Scottish whaling stations during the years 1908–1914 and 1920–1927. *Fishery Board for Scotland, Scientific Investigations*, 1928, No. III, 40 pp.

Tillman, M. F. and Donovan, G. P. [Eds.] 1983. Historical Whaling Records, including the Proceedings of the International Workshop on Historical Whaling Records, Sharon, Massachusetts, September 12–16, 1977. *Rep. int. Whal. Commn* (special issue 5): 1–269.

Tilton, G. F. 1928. '*Cap'n George Fred' Himself.* Doubleday, Doran and Company, Inc., New York, [i]–[xviii]+295 pp.+frontis.+17 unnumb. pls.

Tomilin, A. G. 1957. *Zveri i SSSR prilezhashchikh stran.* Tom 9, Kitoobraznye. Izdatel'stvo Akademii Nauk SSSR, Moskva. 756 pp.+pls. 1–12. [Translated in 1967 as *Mammals of the USSR and Adjacent Countries.* Vol. 9, *Cetacea* by the Israel Program for Scientific Translations, Jerusalem. i–xxii+717 pp.]

Tønnessen, J. N. and Johnsen, A. O. 1982. *The History of Modern Whaling.* Translated from the Norwegian by R. I. Christophersen. C. Hurst & Company, London, [&] Australian National University Press, Canberra. [i]–xx+798 pp.

Tower, W. S. 1907. *A History of the American Whale Fishery.* Publications of the University of Pennsylvania, Philadelphia. Series in Political Economy and Public Law, No. 20. i–x+145 pp.

Townsend, C. H. 1935. The distribution of certain whales as shown by logbook records of American whaleships. *Zoologica* 19(1): 1–50+pls. 1–4 [Maps].

Townsend, C. H. and Watson, A. C. MS. No date. [Records of kills by vessel, date, position, species and number from logbooks of whaleships.] Incomplete typescript, vessels A–J, in archives of New York Zoological Society.

Trotignon, J. 1979. Le phoque moine (*Monachus monachus*) en Mauritanie: données récentes. pp. 133–9 *In*: K. Ronald and R. Duguy (eds), *The Mediterranean monk seal. Proceedings of the First International Conference, Rhodes, Greece, 2–5 May 1978.* United Nations Environment Programme Tech. Ser., Vol. 1, Pergamon Press, Oxford. [i]–viii+183 pp.

True, F. W. 1904. The whalebone whales of the western North Atlantic compared with those occurring in European waters with some observations on the species of the North Pacific. City of Washington, Published by the Smithsonian Institution, *Smithson. Contrib. Knowl.* 33: i–xii+i–viii+1–332 pp.+pls. 1–50.

Tuck, J. A. and Grenier, R. 1981. A 16th-Century Basque whaling station in Labrador. *Sci. Am.* 245(5): 180–184, 186–184, 186–188, 190.

Veinger, G. M. 1969. What the colour of sperm whales tells us. *Piroda* 4: 71–3. [In Russian]

Veinger, G. M. 1974. Determination of population structure of sperm whales on the basis of colour analysis, pp. 153–64. *In: Issledovaniya po Biologii Ryb i Promyslovoi Ojeanografii, Iss. 5*, Vladivostok. (In Russian.)

Veinger, G. N. 1980. Intraspecies structural data of sperm whales in the North Pacific. *Rep. int. Whal. Commn* (special issue 2): 103–5.

Whalemen's Shipping List, and Merchants' Transcript. New Bedford,

Mass. Vol. 1, no. 1 (17 March 1843) to Vol. 72, no. 52 (29 December 1914).

Whipple, A. B. C. 1979. *The Whalers*. The Seafarers, Time-Life Books, Alexandria, Virginia, 176 pp.

Wilkes, C. 1945. *Narrative of the United States Exploring Expedition. During the years 1838, 1839, 1840, 1842*. Lea and Blanchard, Philadelphia. In Five Volumes, Vol. 4, p. [i–ii]+i–xiv+1–539+3 maps.

Winn, H. E. 1982. A characterization of marine mammals and turtles in the Mid- and North Atlantic areas of the US Outer Continental

Shelf. Final Report of the Cetacean and Turtle Assessment Program, University of Rhode Island, Graduate School of Oceanography, Kingston, Rhode Island 02881. Prepared for: US Department of the Interior, Bureau of Land Management, Washington, DC 20240, Under Contract AA551 – CT8–48. p. [i–x]+[1]–450+Special Topics [4 additional papers, variously paginated]+2 transparencies [contained in back cover pocket].

Wray, P. and Martin, K. R. 1983. Historical whaling records from the western Indian Ocean. *Rep. int. Whal. Commn* (special issue 5): 213–41.

Notes to the Tables

Throughout the Tables, abbreviations of vessel names are used. In order to facilitate the reading of these Tables, the vessels are listed in alphabetical order by abbreviation below: AB = Abbie Bradford; AG = Ansel Gibbs; AL = Abbott Lawrence; AT = A. R. Tucker; BG = Bart Gosnold; Ca = Canton; CM = Charles W. Morse; DW = Daniel Webster; DS = D. A. Small; EC = E. B. Conwell; EH = E. H. Hatfield; EJ = Emma Jane; EN = E. Nickerson; Es = Eschol; FB = F. Bunchinia; GC = Golden City; Hu = Huntress; JD = J. H. Duvall; JE = John and Elizabeth; JR = John A. Ross; JS = John E. Smith; LA = Louisa A.; LB = Lewis Bruce; LC = Lottie E. Cook; Me = Messenger; Md = Medford; Mo = Montezuma; NC = N. D. Chase; OC = Olive Clark; Oh = Ohio; Pa = Palmetto; Ri = Richmond; Ro = Rothschild; SC = Silver Cloud; Sp = Spartan; SS = S. R. Soper; St = Stafford; Su = Surprise; SW = Sea Witch; TW = Thomas Winslow; Wa = Watchman; WD = William P. Dolliver; Wg = Washington; WG = William A. Grozier; WI = Walter Irving; WM = William Martin; WW = Water Witch; VH = Varnum H. Hill.

Table 1.

Data from a sample of eighteenth-century North Atlantic whaling logbooks and journals. Home port for all vessels was Nantucket apart from Reliance (Dartmouth). The type of vessel is also given. The first dates refer to the sailing and returning dates, the dates in parentheses to the period on the whaling grounds. * Includes time on Grand Bank, in "mouth" of Davis Strait, and between the two. ** Journal consists of only one entry.

Destination	Main activity	Lowerings for other species	Right whale encounters
1. Grampus, sloop, 1 May – 15 May 1751, (ca 4–10 May)			
Offshore	Sperm whaling.	Blackfish.	None recorded.
2. Grampus, sloop, 18 May – 18 June 1751, (unclear)			
Offshore	Sperm whaling.	None recorded.	None recorded.
3. Grampus, sloop, 23 June 1751 [only entry], (unclear)			
Offshore	Uncertain.	None recorded.	None recorded.
4. Grampus, sloop, 2 July – 20 July 1751, (ca. 6–14 July)			
Offshore	Sperm whaling.	None recorded.	None recorded.
5. Mary, sloop, 16 March – 12 April 1752, (28 March–?)			
Offshore	Sperm whaling.	Outbound, took 2 porpoises.	None recorded.
6. Mary, sloop, 15 April – 26 May 1752, (22 April–ca 21 May)			
Offshore	Sperm whaling.	None recorded.	None recorded.
7. Seaflower, sloop, 3 June – 26 August 1752, (12 June –14 August)			
Newfoundland	"We Shall Have a good time to Newfoundland to kill Some Humps" – humpbacking.	None recorded; Seaflower and 6 other vessels got "Something better than 100 barrels apiece of Humpback oyl."	None recorded.
8. Greyhound, sloop, 17 March – 10 April 1753 [incomplete], (unclear)			
Offshore	Apparently sperm whaling.	None recorded.	None recorded.
9. Greyhound, sloop, 7 May – 24 September 1753, (26 May–ca 28 August*)			
"Streights St Davis" [Davis Strait]	Sperm whaling and "right" (bowhead?) whaling.	Sighted finbacks, "Sulphur-Bottom" (blue whale), and humpback but lowered only for sperms and "rights" (bowheads?).	1. 20 June struck 2; one stove a boat, both "ran away." Position 18 June: "mouth" of Davis Strait, ca 60°22'N. 2. 21 June took one with 8ft 3in bone, "a very Large Deep whale" in heavy ice. Yielded only 68bbls, "the blubber not being so fat as we hop'd for." 3. 25 June chased "right" (bowhead?) whales and sperms. 4. 12 July saw "right whale" and "Sulphur-Bottom". 5. 13 July learned that Jonathan Coffin had 170 [?] bbls from "one Right whale the Bone 7 foot long." 6. 14 July took a large sperm; saw a "multitude of Ice Islands." Position 16 July: 61°02'N, in sight of 6 Dutch whalers.
10. Phebe, sloop, 9 March – 28 April 1754, (?–23 April)			
Offshore	Sperm whaling.	Caught 2 porpoises.	None recorded.
11. Phebe, sloop, 6 May – 30 May 1754 [incomplete], (21–30+ May)			
Offshore	Not stated, presumably sperm whaling.	None recorded.	None recorded.
12. Phebe, sloop, 11 July – 12 September 1754, (17 July–3 September)			
To "the Eastward of the Grand Bank of Newfoundland"	Sperm whaling.	Finbacks seen but not chased.	1. 23 July "Saw Several Right Whales & Chased them & Struck One who Shook out her Iron & then Ran away." Position 19 July: 49°19'N, 48°50'W; had seen "Icy Islands" 20 July. 2. 30 August "Saw a Noble Right Whale Close under Our Counter but it was so thick of Fog that We Could do nothing With however We hove Out Our Boats & Try'd to Strike her but She Soon Run us out of Sight in the fog." Position 28 Aug.: 45°24'N, E of Grand Bank. 3. 31 August chased 3 but "Could not Strike." Position 1 Sept.: 45°12'N. 31 Aug.: "We know not how far we are to the Eastward of the Grand Bank of Newfoundland."
13. Phebe, sloop, 20 April – 23 May 1757 [incomplete], (24 April–23 May)			
Offshore	Sperm whaling.	None recorded.	None recorded.
14. Union, sloop, 9 July – 4 September 1757 [nearly complete], (14 July–late August)			
Grand Bank	Sperm whaling.	Struck several porpoises; saw but did not chase finbacks.	None recorded.

Table 1 (*continued*)

Destination	Main activity	Lowerings for other species	Right whale encounters
15. Phebe, sloop, 28 May – 23 June 1757, (not noted)			
Offshore	Sperm whaling.	[not noted]	None recorded.
16. Phebe, sloop, ca 1 July – 10 August 1757** (early July–10 Aug.)			
Offshore	Sperm whaling.	None recorded.	None recorded.
17. Phebe, sloop, 22 August – 13 September 1757, (not noted)			
Offshore	Probably sperm whaling.	[not noted]	None recorded.
18. Francis, sloop, 28 June – 21 September 1758, (6 July–12 Sept.)			
"Ye Bank of Newfoundland"	Sperm whaling.	Took several porpoises; sighted "killers" and humpbacks but did not chase.	None recorded.
19. Jolly Nancy, sloop, 14 June – ca 2 July 1759**, (Unclear)			
Offshore	Sperm whaling.	None recorded.	None recorded.
20. Jolly Nancy, sloop, 4 July – 25 July 1759 [incomplete], (Unclear)			
Offshore	Probably sperm whaling.	None recorded.	None recorded.
21. Bristol, sloop, 4 July – 25 September 1759, (12 July–13 Sept.)			
"Banks of Newfoundland"	Sperm whaling.	None recorded.	None recorded.
22. Jolly Nancy, sloop, 18 August – 16 Sept. 1759 [incomplete], (Unclear)			
Offshore	Sperm whaling.	None recorded.	None recorded.
23. Enterprise, sloop, 13 March – 4 April 1760 [incomplete], (Unclear)			
Offshore	Probably sperm whaling.	None recorded.	None recorded.
24. Enterprise, sloop, Between April and July 1760, (Unclear)			
Probably offshore	Sperm whaling.	None recorded.	None recorded.
25. Enterprise, sloop, 1 July – 29 August 1760, (11 July–at least late August)			
"To the East-ward of the Grand Bank of Newfoundland"	Sperm whaling.	[not noted]	"Robert Hussey Told J.B. [James Bunker, who was spoken by <u>Enterprise</u> on 11 Aug. at 43°20'N] He Killed a Right Whale & She Sunk." On 12 Aug. Robert Hussey's vessel in sight of Enterprise at 42°46'N, ca 12–14 leagues [36–42nmi] E. of Grand Bank.
26. Bristol, sloop, 10 July – 2 September 1760 [incomplete], (17 July–at least 2 September)			
Grand Bank	Sperm whaling.	Saw a finback but did not chase.	None recorded.
27. Endeavor, sloop, 30 June – 8 August 1761 [incomplete], (16 July–at least 8 Aug.)			
Grand Bank	Sperm whaling.	Saw humpbacks and a finback but did not chase.	None recorded.
28. Endeavor, sloop, 7 July – 23 Sept. 1762, (Did not note)			
Grand Bank	Sperm whaling.	None recorded.	None recorded.
29. Dolphin, sloop, 5 July – 11 Oct. 1763, (11 July–24 Sept.)			
"Grand Bank of Newfound-land and East-ward"	Sperm whaling.	Saw humpbacks and finbacks several times but did not chase.	1. 5 August "Saw a Right Whale and hove out our Boats & Chased but could not Strike" at 47°46'N along or just E. of Grand Bank. 2. 7 August "Saw a Right Whale hove out our Boat & Chased her till Night but could not Strike" at 47°45'N. 3. 24 August at 46°52'N "Spoke with Thomas Jones with 60 Barrels a Cutting up told us he Left Bell Isl Ye 10 of this month told us Nath Woodbury William George Folger Richard Chadwick & Giles had got 200 Bbl & 4000 wt of Bone Each & Shubel Pinkham Isaac Myrick and Sundry others had got nothing."
30. Olive, sloop, 11 July – 10 October 1764, (21 July–29 Aug. and later)			
"The Grand Bank & East-ward"	Sperm whaling.	24 July E of Grand Bank at 43 50'N, chased "Humbacks".	None recorded.
31. Diamond, sloop, 6 July – 18 October 1765, (1 Aug.–1 Oct.)			
Grand Banks	Sperm whaling.	1. 1 Aug. chased humpbacks. 2. 11 Aug. chased humpbacks. 3. 15 Aug. at ca 48°29'N spoke vessel that had taken a humpback – icebergs in sight. 4. 3 Sept. chased humpbacks at 47°59'N.	1. 13 Sept. "saw too Right whails and wee hove out our Boats an gave them Chase. It was very Ruged whail weather…we Struck Both Ye Whails Rise under our Boate and Cut her In to." One of the whales was secured. Position 12 Sept.: 46 48'N apparently near E. edge of Grand Bank. 2. 14 Sept. cut in the whale – "She is But a Small one." 3. 20 Sept. finished trying the right whale – filled 19 casks.
32. Olive, sloop, 9 July – 5 October 1765, (21 July–ca 15 Sept.)			
"to Ye Grand Bank & East-ward"	Sperm whaling.	"Saw Humps Plenty" at 43°35'N on 12 Sept., but did not chase.	None recorded.
33. Reliance, sloop, 14 April – 15 October 1768, (27 May–24 Sept.)			
"the Straights of bellile"	Right (bow-head?) whal-ing.	Saw finbacks, humpbacks, and sperms frequently, but only chased sperms once – on 6 Oct. at 43°16'N, 62°41'W.	1. 27 May "We got Into braddore the Ice very thick Some Whales Run…." 2. 25 July "Saw a Rite Whale [bowhead?] bound to Nward gave her Chase 6 hours Could Not Strike her." Position 24 July: 60°06'N. 3. 26 July "Saw Rite Whales [bowheads?] Very Plenty Could Nots Strike them." 4. 28 July "Saw Whales plenty" at 61°N – "Judge We was in 62 yesterd." Position 29 July: 61°48'N, "Within 20 Leagues" of land – "Cald It Cape Dissolation." 5. 9 August "Saw a Rite Whale [bowhead?] gave her Chase Could Nots Strike her." Later, "Saw Rite Whales [bowheads?] Plenty Chasd them With the _____ Could Not Strik them." Latitude on 10 Aug.: ca 58°N. 6. 12 August "Lots Whalle"; spoke Capt Goodspeede who "told Us Whales Was plenty on the Coste" – 53°18'N. 7. 13 August "Saw Whales [balaenids?] Struck one Lost her Lost one Iron & 12 or fifteen fath. toeline." Later, "Saw Whales gave them Chase Could Nots Strike." 8. 14 August "Saw Whales Plenty" at 54°06'N. 9. 19 August "Saw Whales" at 51°05'N. 10. 20 August "Kild one Whale in Co with Capts Russell the Westher good the Sea bad Whale Sunken"; "our Whale Lost one Spade" – 51°16'N; 21 August "Cuting the head"; "Wents to trying"; 22 August "Rafts of bluber from Capts Russell"; 23 August "Stoed away our oyl"; apparently secured one balaenid.

Table 1 (continued)

Destination	Main activity	Lowerings for other species	Right whale encounters
34. Reliance, sloop, 22 April – 10 July 1769 [incomplete], (Before 16 June–9 July "bound toard the Western Islands [Azores]")			
"To the Straites of Bellile"	Probably balaenid whaling.	None recorded.	16 June "Killed one Whale [probably a balaenid] between Capts Russell & our Silves." No position given until 2 July when vessel "Saild for Newfound Land to git Wood."
35. Reliance, sloop, 27 April – 14 August 1771 [incomplete], (10 May "made the N shore"–14 Aug. & later)			
"the Straghts of Bellile"	Probably balaenid whaling.	None recorded.	1. 29 June "Killed on Whale [probably a balaenid]" at 55 15'N. 2. 4 August "Struck a Whale [probably a balaenid] Lost her." 3. 14 August "Struck a Whale [probably a balaenid] Lost her."
36. Lark, schooner, 24 November 1784 – 26 May 1785, (mid December 1784–May 1785)			
West Indies	Whaling for sperm, humpback and pilot whales.	Various.	None recorded.
37. Dolphin, sloop, 23 February – 5 October 1790 [incomplete], (Unclear)			
Bahamas	Apparently sperm whaling.	Blackfish only.	None recorded.

Table 2.

Data on right whaling on the Cape Farewell Ground during the nineteenth century. Home port for all vessels was New Bedford. The type of vessel and its tonnage are also given. The first dates refer to the sailing and returning dates, the dates in parentheses to the period on the Cape Farewell Ground. S = whales sighted, C = whales chased, S_1 = whales struck but lost, K_1 = whales killed but lost and Se = whales secured. Quantities of sperm oil (Sp) and whale oil (Wh) are in barrels while quantities of whalebone (Wb) are in pounds. Production data are from Starbuck (1878) or Hegarty (1959). Under 'Sources', WSL = Whalemen's Shipping List.

S	C	S_1	K_1	Se	Other vssls	Remarks on right whales	Sp	Wh	Wb	Sources
1. Ansel Gibbs [AG], bark, 303t, 3 June 1868 to 26 September 1869 (1–10 July 1868)										
–	–	–	1	1	None	Cow and calf killed 5 July (60°N, 34°W); cow sunk, calf produced 26bbls; vessel reached Resolution Is. by 29 July and wintered in Hudson Bay.	–	650	10,100	AG, 1868–9, Ms
2. Daniel Webster [DW], bark, 327t, 17 April 1877 to 23 October 1880 (Mid–28 June 1877)										
–	–	–	1	1	None	Calf taken 17 June, 20bbls; cow (est. 100bbls) escaped "spouting blood" same date. Three struck 8 May 1878 (49°N, 23°W). One seen 23 May 1878 (50 N, 23 W). Visited Commodore Morris Gd before and after C. Farewell.	200	530	2,400	DW, 1877–9, Ms
3. John A. Ross* [JR], brig, 197t, 17 July 1877 to 10 April 1878 (11 Aug.–early Sept. 1877)										
–	3+	–	–	4	None	Whale taken 13 Aug. produced 65bbls; 18 Aug., 75bbls; 22 and 24 Aug., 191bbls combined. Spent winter season in Cintra Bay but caught none there. Reptd at Madeira 26 Oct. with 240bbls whale oil, 2,400lbs bone, headed for Africa; "had experienced heavy weather and encountered quantities of ice, and lost one boat."	–	243	2,300	JR, 1877–8, Ms; Tilton, 1928, p.24–7; WSL, 15 Jan. 1878
4. Abbot Lawrence [AL], brig, 160t, 6 April 1880, condemned at Nfld (July 1880)										
–	–	–	–	–	AT	22 July 1880, A.R. Tucker sold a whaleboat to Abbot Lawrence.	–	30	–	AT, 1880–3, Ms
5. A.R. Tucker [AT], bark, 145t, 13 April 1880 to 24 May 1883 (5 June–early Aug. 1880)										
5	1	0	1	1	AL	Whale taken 23 June produced 69bbls; cow and calf seen 30 July.	405	245	–	AT, 1880–3, Ms
6. Bart. Gosnold [BG], bark, 365t, 23 April 1881 to 5 October 1885 (5–17 June 1881)										
–	–	–	–	–	None	"Right whaling of[f] Cape Farewell" en route to S. Atlantic and Indian O.	2,800	–	–	BG, 1881–3, Ms
7. Abbie Bradford [AB], schooner, 115t, 22 May 1884 to 29 September 1885 (20 June–2 July 1884)										
–	–	–	–	–	None	Visited C. Farewell Gd en route from New Bedford to Hudson Bay.	–	100	–	AB, 1884–5, Ms
8. Palmetto [Pa], bark, 215t, 24 June 1886 to 6 November 1886 (mid July–mid Aug. 1886)										
1+	7+	1	1	5	None	Whale taken 27 July produced 75bbls; 29 July, 75bbls; whalebone saved; darting gun in use.	–	–	–	Pa, 1886, Ms
9. Canton [Ca], bark, 238t, 1 May 1895 to 8 October 1896 (13 June–10 July 1895)										
–	–	–	–	–	AT	Visited C. Farewell Gd en route from Commodore Morris Gd to Hudson Bay; 4 June "Left for Greenland Right-whaling".	80	90	2,300	Ca, 1895–6, Ms a; Ca, 1895–6, Ms b
10. A.R. Tucker [AT], bark, 145t, 4 May 1895 to 7 October 1896 (early July 1895)										
3+	–	–	1	–	Ca	None.	35	50	1,450	Ca, 1895–6, Ms b
11. A.R. Tucker [AT], bark, 145t, 21 April 1897 to 11 October 1898 (June 1897)										
–	–	–	–	–	Ca	None.	35	20	520	Ca, 1897–8, Ms
12. Canton [Ca], bark, 238t, 8 May 1897 to 11 September 1898 (mid June–mid Aug. 1897)										
1	–	–	1	1	AT	Calf taken 1 July was discarded – "did not have any bone"; cow killed but sunk; two chased 30 May 1897 (46°30'N, 43°W) en route to C. Farewell Gd.	475	100	–	Ca, 1897–8, Ms

* Variously called A. T. Ross, A. J.Ross, J. A. Ross.

Table 3.

Data on right whaling on the Southeast U.S. Coast Ground during the 19th century. Home port for all vessels was New Bedford apart from *Emma Jane* and *E. H. Hatfield* (Edgartown). The type of vessel and its tonnage are also given. The first dates refer to the sailing and returning dates, the dates in parentheses to the period on the Southeast US Coast Ground. S = whales sighted, C = whales chased, S_1 = whales struck but lost, K_1 = whales killed but lost and Se = whales secured. Quantities of sperm oil (Sp) and whale oil (Wh) are in barrels while quantities of whalebone (Wb) are in pounds. Production data are from Starbuck (1878) or Hegarty (1959). Under 'Sources', NIM = Nantucket Inquirer and Mirror and WSL = Whalemen's Shipping List.

S	C	S_1	K_1	Se	Other vessels	Remarks on right whales	Sp	Wh	Wb	Sources
						**1. Golden City [GC], schooner, 89t, 9 December 1875 to 29 September 1876 (13 Feb.–18 March 1876)**				
–	2+	–	–	1	None	Whale taken 25 February off Fernandina, Florida; others chased on subsequent days.	440	40	–	GC, 1875–6, Ms; Earll, 1887b; Clark, 1887a; NIM56(37):11III1876; NIM56(35):26II1876.
						2. Golden City [GC], schooner, 84t, 19 June 1877 to 21 September 1878 (24 Jan.–at least 18 Feb. 1878)				
–	–	–	–	1	None	65bbl whale taken "off the bar" at Brunswick, 18 February 1878.	365	40	–	WSL36(3):5III1878; NIM58(35):2III1878; NIM58(31):2II1878.
						3. Golden City [GC], schooner, 8½t, 29 November 1878 to 18 March 1880 (30 Jan.–7 March 1879)				
3+	1	0	0	0	EC	Two seen 25 February were "going to the North fast".	340	60	500	GC, 1878–80, Ms; WSL37(42):2XII1879.
						4. Golden City [GC], schooner, 84t, 29 November 1878 to 18 March 1880 (at least early Feb.–7 March 1880)				
–	–	–	–	1	None	Whale taken off Brunswick before 8 February.	340	60	500	NIM60(33):14II1880; NIM60(39):27III1880.
						5. E.B. Conwell [EC], schooner, 91t, 6 May 1878 to 28 July 1879 (at least 31 Jan.–3 Feb. 1879)				
–	–	–	–	2	None	Chasing whales 31 January; cow and calf taken 3 February "just outside the bar."	610	100	880	GC, 1878–80, Ms; WSL37(1):18II1879; NIM59(33):15II1879.
						6. Charles W. Morse [CM], schooner, 112t, 14 May 1878 to 23 August 1879 (ca. Feb.–March 1879)				
–	–	–	–	1	None	Whale taken from "school" off Port Royal, est. 80–90bbls, 1,000–1,200 lbs bone; towed on 7 March by pilot boat Surprise.	290	60	750	Earll, 1887b; WSL37(2):25II1879; WSL37(6):25II1879.
						7. Charles W. Morse [CM], schooner, 112t, 30 October 1879 to 23 August 1881 (7 Feb.–17 March 1880)				
–	–	–	–	3½+	EC	First whale (35–40bbls) taken before 23 February; whale taken off Brunswick 23 February expected to produce 50bbls; one of others was a 30bbl whale; shipped 310bbls whale oil and 2,900lbs bone from Brunswick 13 April.	500	345	–	Earll, 1887b; WSL38(4):9III1880; WSL38(7):30III1880; WSL38(10):20IV1880; NIM60(39):27III1880; NIM60(38):2III1880; NIM60(37):13III1880; NIM60(36):6III1880.
						8. E.B. Conwell [EC], schooner, 91t, 13 October 1879 to 3 September 1880 (before 23 Feb.–ca. 1 April? 1880)				
–	–	–	–	½	CM	Whale taken before 23 February in company with Chas. W. Morse.	380	20	200	WSL38(4):9III1880; WSL38(15):25V1880; NIM60(36):6III1880.
						9. Emma Jane [EJ], schooner, 86t, 30 November 1879 to 31 October 1881 (at least 6 Jan.–19 Feb. 1880)				
–	–	–	–	½	Su	Whale taken near Brunswick, 15 February, in company with Surprise.	760	30	–	WSL37(49):20I1880; 38(3):2III1880; 38(18):15VI1880; Anon., 1832–1905, Ms., p.128; Townsend & Watson, n.d.
						10. Surprise [Su], schooner, 54t, 1 November 1879 to 24 August 1880 (at least 8 Jan.–19 Feb. 1880)				
–	–	–	–	1½	EJ	Whale taken off Brunswick 7 February; another (80bbls) taken in company with Emma Jane 15 February; shipped 1,077lbs bone to NY by steamer from Brunswick.	65	85	1,000	WSL37(49):20I1880; WSL38(3):2III1880; NIM60(35):28II1880; NIM60(33):14II1880.
						11. E.H. Hatfield [EH], schooner, 89t, 30 November 1880 to 19 August 1882 (5 Feb.–17 May 1881)				
0	0	0	0	0	EJ	Right whaling along coast from Morehead City, No. Carolina, to Macon, Georgia, in company with Emma Jane.	260	10	–	EH, 1880–2, Ms; NIM61(37):12III1881; NIM61(35):26II1881.
						12. Emma Jane [EJ], schooner, 86t, 30 November 1879 to 3 September 1881 (at least 14 Feb.–27 April 1881)				
–	–	–	–	–	EH	Right whaling in company with E.H. Hatfield; as of 30 March "had not seen a whale this season."	760	30	–	EH, 1880–2, Ms; NIM61(41):9IV1881; NIM61(35):26II1881.
						13. Golden City [GC], schooner, 84t, 2 June 1880 to 22 August 1881 (19 Jan.–14 Feb. 1881)				
0	0	0	0	0	None	Right whaling off Brunswick.	300	5	–	GC, 1880–81, Ms.
						14. Charles W. Morse [CM], schooner, 112t, 30 October 1879 to 26 August 1881 (13 Jan.–12 April 1881)				
–	2+	–	–	1+	None	As of 22 February "had seen but one whale on the grounds which was lost after being chased by six or eight boat crews"; at sea 28 February "with a 30bbl right whale alongside, and the boats chasing whales."	500	345	–	WSL38(50):25I1881; WSL39(4):8II1881; WSL39(5):15 III1881; WSL39(10):19IV1881; Earll, 1887b, p. 514; NIM61(37):12III1881.
						15. Lottie E. Cook [LC], schooner, 82t, 21 October 1880 to 21 May 1882 (at least 25 Feb. 1881)				
–	–	–	–	1	None	Arrived at Tybee Roads, So. Carolina, on 25 February with a large whale in tow, captured off Port Royal – had 100bbls oil on board.	85	125	–	NIM61(37):12III1881
						16. Golden City [GC], schooner, 84t, 13 October 1881 to 18 September 1882 (11 Jan.–6 March 1882)				
–	–	–	–	1	None	A 25bbl whale taken off Georgia 26 February; "Skraped and washed the Bone."	100	23	–	GC, 1881–2, Ms.; WSL40(2):21III1882; WSL40(4):7III1882; NIM62(38):11III1882; NIM62(35):18II1882.
						17. Lottie E. Cook [LC], schooner, 82t, 21 October 1880 to 2 April 1882 (at least 7 Feb.–9 March 1882)				
–	–	–	1	3	None	"Captured a right whale and calf, which had sunk" before 25 February; had "taken two right whales making 125bbls oil and 1,200lb bone – 85 bbls sperm 185 do. whale oil and 2,000lb bone all told" before 9 March.	85	125	–	WSL40(2):21III1882; WSL40(4):7III1882; WSL40(6):21III1882; NIM62(42):8IV1882; NIM62(35):18II1882.

Table 4.

Data on right whaling on the Cintra Bay Ground during the 19th century. The type of vessel, tonnage and home port are given. The first dates refer to the sailing and returning dates, the dates in parentheses to the period on the Cintra Bay Ground. S = whales sighted, C = whales chased, S_l = struck but lost, K_l = whales killed but lost and Se = whales secured. Quantities of sperm oil (Sp) and whale oil (Wh) are in barrels while quantities of whalebone (Wb) are in pounds. Production data are from Starbuck (1878) or Hegarty (1959). Under 'Sources', WSL = Whalemen's Shipping List.

S	C	S_l	K_l	Se	Other vessels	Remarks on right whales	Sp	Wh	Wb	Sources
1. N.D. Chase [NC], bark, 242t, Beverly, 21 December 1854 to 28 December 1856 (4 Dec.-ca 10 Dec. 1855)										
-	-	-	-	-	FB (1), 3 others	Sent home 25bbls sperm oil (Starbuck, 1878, p.521).	-	15	-	NC, 1855-6, Ms.
2. F. Bunchinia [FB], bark, 200t, Provincetown, 17 July 1855 to 16 September 1856 (at least 1 Dec. 1855-16 March 1856)										
-	-	-	-	1+	NC	Sent home 217bbls sperm oil (Starbuck, 1878, p.531). Took a whale on 4 December. At Oura River 1 Dec. with 50bbls sperm oil "and one large right whale since leaving Fayal [in September or October?]".	204	520	4,000	NC, 1855-6, Ms; Wood, n.d., Ms, Vol. III, p.651.
3. Walter Irving [WI], schooner, 133t, Provincetown, 9 November 1855 to 16 September 1856 (14 Dec. 1855-26 April 1856)										
2	15	1	-	9⅚	SS (1⅓); EN (2⅓); JS (2⅓); Sp, JE	80bbl whale taken 3 Jan.; another 25 Jan.; another 4 February in co. with EN and SS; another 8 February with JS; 2 on 9 February, one of which in co. with JS, the other of which produced 47bbls; others on 22 and 25 Feb. with SS; 2 killed on 6 March, one with JS and the other of which sunk and was recovered 8 March; struck/lost one 7 March (harpoon drew); took whale with EN 10 March; took a large cow with JS 20 March; took whale 11 April; took another with EN 18 April; killed/sunk whale with JS 18 April, recovered carcass next day.	40	150*	-	WI, 1855-6, Ms.
4. William Martin [WM], schooner, 134t, Orleans, 30 January 1856 to 28 September 1856 (8 March-at least 16 March 1856)										
-	-	-	-	+	None	Apparently took a whale on Cintra Bay Ground between 8 March and 1 May.	-	189	800	Wood, n.d., Ms, Vol. III, p.492.
5. Messenger [Me], bark, 216t, Salem, 14 June 1854 to 30 August 1856 (at least 3 Feb.-16 March 1856)										
-	-	-	-	+	None	Probably got all whale oil and bone from Cintra Bay Ground - at least 3 [right] whales.	231	216	1,200	Wood, n.d., Ms, Vol. III, p.499.
6. S.R. Soper [SS], schooner, 130t, Provincetown, 16 October 1855 to 11 September 1856 (4 Feb.-at least 25 Feb. 1856)										
-	-	-	-	1⅓	WI, EN	Whale taken 4 Feb. in co. with WI and EN; another in co. with WI 22 Feb.; another with WI 25 Feb.	42	152	-	WI, 1855-6, Ms.
7. E. Nickerson [EN], schooner, 132t, Provincetown, 24 August 1855 to 22 June 1856 (at least 4 Feb.-26 April 1856)										
-	-	-	-	2⅓	WI, SS	Whale taken 4 Feb. in co. with WI and SS; seen boiling 24 Feb.; another taken in co. with WI 10 March; received share of a whale (32bbls oil) from WI 15 April; whale taken with WI 18 April; delivered share of oil to WI 21 April.	178	325	-	WI, 1855-6, Ms.
8. John E. Smith [JS], schooner, 119t, New London, 18 September 1855 to 21 June 1856 (at least 8 Feb.-26 April 1856)										
-	-	-	-	2½	WI	Whales taken in co. with WI 8 and 9 Feb.; another with WI 6-7 March; a large cow taken in co. with WI 20 March; delivered 32bbls oil to WI 26 March; whale taken with WI 18-19 April.	-	365	3,000	WI, 1855-6, Ms.
9. Rothschild [Ro], bark, 261t, Orleans, 12 September 1855 to 30 September 1856 (at least 8 Feb.-ca 25 March 1856)										
-	-	-	-	+	None	May have taken as much as 260bbls oil from right whales on C. Bay Grd.	325	380	-	Wood, n.d., Ms, Vol. III, p.489.
10. Lewis Bruce [LB], brig, 135t, Orleans, 21 April 1855 to 25 April 1856 (at least 3 Feb.-8 March 1856)										
-	-	-	-	+	None	Apparently at least 275bbls oil from right whales on C. Bay Gd.	-	313	2,800	Wood, n.d., Ms, Vol. III, p.488.
11. Spartan [Sp], bark, 188t, Provincetown, 11 June 1855 to 6 September 1857 (3 Feb.-at least 22 April 1856)										
-	-	-	-	+	WI	Took at least 230bbls whale oil on C. Bay Gd. Starbuck gave destination for this voyage as "Ind. & Atlantic".	450	450	4,000	WI, 1855-6, Ms.; Wood, n.d., Ms.
12. John and Elizabeth [JE], ship, 296t, New London, 11 September 1855 to 11 June 1856 (at least 22 April 1856)										
-	-	-	-	-	WI	Arrived at Cintra or Goree Bay 22 April with 250bbls whale oil on board. No evidence of whaling this season on Cintra Bay Gd. Starbuck gave destination for this voyage as "Indian Ocean".	-	518	5,110	WI, 1855-6, Ms.
13. E. Nickerson [EN], schooner,. 132t, Provincetown, 22 August 1856 to 4 August 1857 (20 Nov. 1856-2 March 1857)										
9	4	3⅓		3⅚	Sp (+); Wa; Md (+); WD; WI; Mo (1); SC; OC; JD; St; SW.	Cow/calf pairs sighted 20 Nov., 12 Jan., 24 Jan. Whale taken 26 Nov. produced 80bbls. Cow/calf pair taken 22 Dec.; cow produced 85bbls; "let the calf go" (after killing it). Struck, then cut from, cow/calf pair 3 Feb. On 10 Feb., killed 75bbl cow and her calf, which sunk, in co. with Sp and Md. Small cow taken 14 Feb. in co. with Md produced 32bbls. EN was whaling in Gora Bay, Cintra Bay, in a "cove" in or near Gora Bay, "down the coast" 20-26mi to leeward of Gora Bay in 12fthms (ca 1mi offshore).	65	200	1,800	EN, 1856-7, Ms.
14. Spartan [Sp], bark, 188t, Provincetown, 11 June 1855 to 6 September 1857 (before 25 Nov. 1856-2 March 1857)										
-	1(+?)	1(+?)	⅓	⅓	EN; WI	Destination given by Starbuck as "Ind. & Atlantic". On 25 Nov., "from Cintra Bay" with 240bbls whale oil and 200 sperm on board. Second mate killed while attempting to capture a whale in Cintra Bay, 7 Jan. Mated with EN and Md; shared products of whale killed 10 Feb.	450	450	4,000	EN, 1856-7, Ms; WI, 1856-7, Ms.
15. Watchman [Wa], schooner, 140t, Nantucket, 23 September 1856 to 26 August 1858 (7 Dec. 1856-13 Feb. 1857)										
-	-	-	-	-	EN; WI	"Clean" on arrival in Gora Bay, 7 Dec. Mated with EN. By 27 Dec. reported in co. with WD, 2 mos out with 30bbls whale oil (both vessels combined?), in Cintra Bay.	44	386	1,350	EN, 1856-7, Ms, WI, 1856-7, Ms.
16. Medford [Md], brig, 108t, Orleans, 18 August 1856 to 7 September 1857 (12 Dec. 1856-2 March 1857)										
-	-	-	⅓	1⅓	EN; WI; St (½)	"Clean" on 7 Dec.; arrived Gora Bay 12 Dec.; by 19 Jan. had 160bbls whale oil on arrival in Cintra Bay; by 2 Feb., 200bbls. Mated with EN and Sp, and shared oil and bone from whales taken 10 and 14 Feb. Seen 3 Jan. boiling in co. with St. Had 240bbls whale oil and 2,000lb bone by 29 March. Had been "on coast of Africa" on 5 Nov. 1855, previous voyage (Wood).	55	285	2,100	EN, 1856-7, Ms; WI, 1856-7, Ms; Wood, n.d., Ms, Vol. III, p.643.
17. Sea Witch [SW], schooner, 109t, New London, 4 November 1856 to 19 July 1857 (14 Dec. 1856-13 Feb. 1857)										
-	-	-	-	-	EN	In addition to Cintra Bay right whale(s), may have taken Cape Verdes humpback(s).	-	130	600	EN, 1856-7, Ms; Wood, n.d., Ms, Vol. III, p.544.
18. William P. Dolliver [WD], schooner, 86t, Nantucket, 30 October 1856 to 20 October 1857 (15 Dec. 1856-22 Jan. 1857)										
-	-	-	-	-	EN; WI	Clean on arrival in Cintra Bay, 15 Dec. Reported in Cintra Bay on 27 Dec. in co. with Wa, 2 mos out with 30bbls whale oil (both vessels combined?).	20	66	-	EN, 1856-7, Ms; WI, 1856-7, Ms.
19. Montezuma [Mo], schooner, 92t, Provincetown, 12 November 1856 to 28 December 1856 [sic] (18 Dec. 1856-at least 19 Feb. 1857)										
-	-	-	-	1(+?)	EN; WI	Clean on arrival in Cintra Bay, 18 Dec. Took a 40-50bbl whale 20 Dec., possibly another on 21 Dec.	57	-	-	EN, 1856-7, Ms; WI, 1856-7, Ms.

Table 4 (*continued*)

S C S_1 K_1 Se	Other vessels	Remarks on right whales	Sp	Wh	Wb	Sources
20. Walter Irving [WI], schooner, 133t, Provincetown, 17 November 1856 to January 1858 (18 Dec. 1856–11 Jan. 1857)						
- 1 - - 1	Sp; EN (1); Mo (1); WD; Wa; SC; OC; JD; Md (½); St (½).	Whale taken 5 Jan., 20mi N of Cape Barbess [?] in ca 14fthms; made only 8 bbls.	-	50	-	EN, 1856–7, Ms; WI, 1856–7, Ms.
21. Silver Cloud [SC], bark, 451t, New Bedford, 12 November 1856 to 14 August 1860 (27–28 Dec. 1856)						
- - - - -	EN; WI	Sent home 305bbls sperm oil, 537 whale, and 22,352lbs whalebone (Starbuck). On 27 Dec. 1856, EN spoke "schr silver cloud" in Cintra Bay "2 months out clean", and on 28 Dec. WI spoke her there, 45 da out and clean; however, a journal of bark SC kept by Hiram Borden (SC, 1856–60, Ms.) indicates this vessel was in South Atlantic by this date.	840	1,475	-	EN, 1856–7, Ms; WI, 1856–7, Ms.
22. Washington [Wg], schooner, 160t, Edgartown, 31 September 1856 to 8 September 1857 (13 March 1857)						
- - - - -	None	None.	90	64	-	Wood, n.d., Ms, Vol. III, p.664.
23. Olive Clark [OC], schooner, 95t, Provincetown, 6 June 1856 to 23 May 1857 (28 Dec. 1856–2 Jan. 1857)						
- - - - -	EN; WI	Had 9bbls blackfish oil when spoken in Cintra Bay, 28 Dec.	-	105	-	EN, 1856–7, Ms; WI, 1856–7, Ms.
24. J.H. Duvall [JD], bark, 200t, Provincetown, 27 November 1856 to 27 April 1860 (28 Dec. 1856–1 Jan. 1857)						
- - - - -	EN; WI	Left Cintra Bay 1 [or 3?] Jan. "for the Indian ocean".	504	683	4,300	EN, 1856–7, Ms; WI, 1856–7, Ms.
25. Stafford [St], bark, 206t, New Bedford, 21 August 1854 to 23 June 1857 (at least 5–19 Jan. 1857)						
- - - - ½	EN; WI; Md (½)	Sent home 353bbls sperm oil; sailed for Atlantic and Indian oceans (Starbuck). Spoken in Cintra Bay 19 Jan. 1857, with 1,000bbls whale and sperm oil. Seen 5 Jan. boiling in co. with Md.	235	280	-	EN, 1856–7, Ms; WI, 1856–7, Ms.
26. Water Witch [WW], brig, Portuguese, (30 Nov. 1857–18 Feb. 1858)						
- - - - 1	Ri	Not listed in Starbuck. Mated with Ri for a short time.	-	-	-	Ri, 1857–60, Ms.
27. Huntress [Hu], bark, 383t, New Bedford, 27 September 1857 to 13 September 1861 (30 Nov. 1857–at least 27 March 1858)						
- 2⅔- - 5	Ri	Sent home 363bbls sperm oil, 450 whale, and 8,300lbs bone (Starbuck). Mated with Ri and shared oil and bone with her. Shipped 450bbls whale oil and 4,700lbs bone from Fayal, 13 May 1858, suggesting a large catch on Cintra Bay Ground.	684	313	-	Ri, 1857–60, Ms.
28. Rothschild [Ro], bark, 261t, Orleans, 6 January 1857 to 16 September 1858 (ca 15 Dec. 1857–at least 8 Jan. 1858)						
- - - - -	None	Apparently failed to catch any right whales; whale oil was from humpback(s) probably taken at Cape Verdes.	46	64	-	Wood, n.d., Ms, Vol. III, p.489.
29. Richmond [Ri], bark, 180t, New Bedford, 1 October 1857 to 24 March 1860 (30 Nov.–6 Dec. 1857; 8 Jan.–15 April 1858)						
- 13⅓- - 5	Hu; WW; SC; Es; VH; FB; Wa; NC; JS	Sent home 23bbls sperm, 161 whale, and 18,000lbs bone (Starbuck). Whale boiled 2 Dec. had "very dry" blubber; one boiled 19 March "blubber being young not yielding oil"; calf taken 27 Feb. produced 6.5bbls; Ri mated with Hu, WW, NC, and shared oil and bone with them. Cow/calf pairs taken 10 Jan. and 27 Feb. Landed 160bbls whale oil and 1,800lbs bone at Fayal, 5 June 1858 (Wood, n.d., Ms.).	156	134	600	Ri, 1857–60, Ms.
30. Silver Cloud [SC], schooner, 140t, New London, 26 October 1856 to 25 May 1858 [Wood, n.d., Ms.] (5 Dec. 1857–18 Feb. 1858)						
- - - - +	Ri	Had 150bbls whale oil by May 1857; by end of voyage, had 275bbls whale oil and 2,000lbs bone, suggesting catch of some right whales on Cintra Bay Gd. "Wrecked at sea September 25, 1862" (Starbuck).	-	-	-	Ri, 1857–60, Ms; Wood, n.d., Ms, Vol. III, p.533.
31. Eschol [Es], brig, 143t, Provincetown, 5 May 1857 to 19 May 1858 (11 Dec. 1857–Feb. 1858)						
- - - - +	Ri	Had 60bbls whale oil while "off Cintra Bay" on 11 Dec.; all 140bbls eventually secured may have been from right whales.	200	140	300	Ri, 1857–60, Ms; Wood, n.d., Ms, Vol. III, p.491.
32. N.D. Chase [NC], bark, 242t, Beverly, 8 June 1857 to 13 October 1859 (12 Dec. 1857–30 March 1858)						
- 1⅚- - +	Ri	Sent home 280bbls whale oil and 3,000lbs bone (Starbuck). Mated with Ri; reached Fayal, 15 June 1858, with 325bbls and 3,500lbs bone, all apparently from right whales taken on Cintra Bay Gd. The following 22 June (1859), arrived at Fayal with 250bbls and 2,300lbs, suggesting the 1858–9 season also may have been spent right whaling on Cintra Bay Gd.	140	575	5,500	Ri, 1857–60, Ms; Wood, n.d., Ms, Vol. III, p.497.
33. Watchman [Wa], schooner, 140t, Nantucket, 23 September 1856 to 26 August 1858 (at least 1 Jan.–15 Feb. 1858)						
- - - - +	Ri	At least 100bbls of whale oil was from humpbacks (Wood). Shipped 15 bundles of whalebone on brig Pilgrim at Cape Verdes. Following winter (1858–9) followed similar itinerary, returning 564bbls whale oil from a voyage of 8 mo 23 da. After following a similar itinerary in 1859–60, returned 400bbls humpback oil and 700lbs bone.	44	386	1,350	Ri, 1857–60, Ms; Wood, n.d., Ms, Vol. III, p.672.
34. Varnum H. Hill [VH], schooner, 155, Provincetown, 23 May 1857 to 15 September 1858 (at least 12 Jan.–6 March 1858)						
- - - - 1(+?)	Ri	Sent home 98 bbls sperm oil (Starbuck). Anchored in Cintra Bay and boiling a whale on 6 March.	230	120	-	Ri, 1857–60, Ms.
35. John E. Smith [JS], schooner, 119t, New London, 1 September 1857 to 5 September 1858 (19 Jan. 1858–?)						
- - - - +	Ri	Sent home 120bbls whale oil and 1,260lbs bone (Starbuck); returns suggest some catch of right whales. Note: JS's 1855–6 cruise to "Atlantic" of 9 mos 3 days' duration, returned 365bbls whale oil and 3,000lbs bone.	-	42	800	Ri, 1857–60, Ms; Wood, n.d., Ms.
36. William Martin [WM], schooner, 134t, Orleans, 26 December 1856 to 24 July 1858 (December 1857)						
- - - - -	None	Reported at Goree Bay on 12 December.	225	96	-	Wood, n.d., Ms, Vol. III, p.492.
37. F. Bunchinia [FB], bark, 200t, Provincetown, 26 December 1856 to 30 August 1858 (at least 12 Dec. 1857–16 Feb. 1858)						
- - - - -	Ri	Sent home 800lbs bone (Starbuck).	95	125	600	Ri, 1857–60, Ms.; Wood, n.d., Ms, Vol. III, p.651.
38. Watchman [Wa], schooner, 140t, Nantucket, 6 September 1859 to 23 September 1860 (ca Jan. 1860)						
- - - - +	None	Shipped 70bbls whale oil, 700lb bone from Cape Verdes, 30 Jan. 1860. Subsequently humpbacked there.	68	384	-	Wood, n.d., Ms., Vol. III, p.672.
39. Thomas Winslow [TW], bark, 136t, New Bedford, 15 March 1864 to 23 July 1865 (at least 17 Feb. 1865)						
- - - - -	None	At Goree Bay on 17 Feb., but returns indicate whale oil was from humpbacks (probably Cape Verdes).	200	300	-	Wood, n.d., Ms, Vol. IV, p.203
40. Ohio [Oh], bark, 363t, New Bedford, 6 July 1875 to 18 October 1878 (24 Jan.–5 Feb. 1876)						
0 0 0 0 0	A "fishing schooner"	One boat lost in unknown circumstances.	1,800	-	-	Oh, 1875–8, Ms.

Table 4 (*continued*)

S C S₁ K₁ Se	Other vessels	Remarks on right whales	Sp	Wh	Wb	Sources
41. John A. Ross [JR], brig, 197t, New Bedford, 17 July 1877 to 10 April 1878 (14 Nov. 1877–20 Jan. 1878)**						
1 3 – – 0	LA	Mated with LA. Cow and calf seen 30 Nov. At Madeira 26 Oct 1877, with 240bbls whale oil and 2,400lbs bone, "bound to the Coast of Africa right whaling" (WSL).	–	243	2,300	JR, 1877–8, Ms.; Tilton, 1928, p. 24–9; WSL: 15I 1878.
42. Louisa A. [LA], schooner, 122t, Boston, 29 June 1877 to 17 July 1879 (at least 24 Nov. 1877–20 Jan. 1878)						
1+ – – – –	JR	Mated with JR.	420	35	–	JR, 1877–8, Ms.
43. William A. Grozier [WG], schooner, 117t, Provincetown, 24 April 1879 to 12 July 1880 (at least 1 February 1880)						
– – – – ½	DS	85bbl whale taken 1 Feb. in co. with DS.	735	35	–	WSL 38(5):16III 1880.
44. D.A. Small [DS], brig, 119t, Provincetown, 7 May 1879 to 3 October 1880 (at least 1 Feb. 1880)						
– – – – ½	WG	85bbl whale taken 1 Feb. in co. with WG.	430	40	–	WSL 38(5):16III 1880.

* Wood, n.d., Ms., indicates 215bbls.
** Variously called A. T. Ross, A. J. Ross, J. A. Ross.

Table 5.

Hunting efficiency for a sample of nineteenth-century voyages to major right whaling grounds outside the North Atlantic. Home port for all vessels is New Bedford except *Triton* (Portsmouth) and *Mary* (Edgartown). Key (all values refer to right whales only): s = killed but lost, including those lost spouting blood; u = struck and lost but 'unspecified'; d = struck and lost because the iron drew; p = struck and lost carrying whaling gear; c = calves orphaned; T = whales secured including carcasses found and taken alongside, as well as those secured but not tried out because of low oil yield ('dry skins'). LRF is calculated loss rate factor, LRF = T+s+0.5(u)+0.5(d)+p+c / T.

Vessel	Ground	Dates on Ground	Lowerings**	Whales struck/lost					T	LRF
				s	u	d	p	c		
Ship Triton	S. Atlantic, ca 31–41°S, 01°W –11°E	9 Oct'34 – 29 Jan'35	75	6	0	6	3	0	19	1.63
Ship George Porter	S. Atlantic, Tristan	15 Oct'35 – 21 Jan'36	53	5	0	0	1	0	11	1.55
Ship India	S. Atlantic, Platte	20 Sep'59 – 24 Nov'59	38	2	1	2	5	0	4	3.13
Ship India	"to the East of Tristan d. Acunha"	11 Nov'60 – 4 Jan'61	8	0	0	0	0	0	1	1.00
Ship Cicero	S. Atlantic, ca 38–41°S	2 Nov'35 – 10 Jan'36	50	4	0	4	1	0	14	1.50
Ship Mary	N. Pacific, NW coast	1 June'46 – 8 Aug'46*	37	1	1	2	3	0	7	1.79
Ship John and Edward	Indian O., off Amsterdam I.	10 Aug'55 – 1 Jan'56	ns	0	2	2	2	0	5	1.80
Ship John and Edward	Indian O., Desolation	17 Jan'56 – 11 Mar'56	27	0	0	3	2	0	12	1.29
Ship John and Edward	Coast of New Holland	6 Aug'56 – late Dec'56	13	3	0	1	0	0	4	1.88
Bark A.R. Tucker	Pigeon, ca 37–42°S, 10–22°W	26 Nov'66 – 8 Jan'67	17	1	0	0	0	0	3	1.33
Bark Sea Ranger	Tristan	15 Nov'79 – ca 1 Feb'80	6	0	1	0	0	0	4	1.13
Ship Hunter	Tristan	21 Dec'63 – 8 Feb'64	17	0	0	3	0	0	9	1.17
Bark Tropic Bird	Tristan d'Acunha	27 Nov'52 – 16 Dec'52	ns	2	0	0	1	0	2	2.50
Ship Braganza	Northwest coast	30 May'41 – 17 Aug'41	44	8	3	2	8	0	17	2.09
Ship Braganza	Northwest coast	1 May'42 – 17 July'42	39	1	0	6	6	0	12	1.83
Totals			424	33	8	31	32	0	124	1.69

*incomplete.
**ns = not scored.

Table 6.

Estimated total fishing mortality of right whales on whaling grounds used by nineteenth-century American pelagic whalers. Number killed includes a correction for hunting loss in those instances where information on loss rate is available. See Section VIII of 'Results' for discussion. A dash denotes no information. Values for the SE US coast include a few kills made by shore-based whalers, but probably underestimates their contribution to total kill. * Mainly by modern Norwegian catcher-vessels based at Iceland.

Ground	Right whales killed					Ground	Right whales killed				
	1855–56	1866–75	1876–85	1886–95	1896–1905		1855–56	1866–75	1876–85	1886–95	1896–1905
Cape Farewell	–	2	9	9	5	Others	–	–	2	17(+)*	–
SE US Coast	–	1(+)	26–31	2(+)	1(+)						
Cintra Bay	65	–	1	–	–	Totals	65	3(+)	38–43	28(+)	6(+)

Notes on Nineteenth Century Catches of Southern Right Whales (*Eubalaena australis*) off the Southern Coasts of Western Australia

J. L. BANNISTER

The Western Australian Museum, Perth, Western Australia

ABSTRACT

An attempt has been made to estimate the total number of right whales taken by local bay whalers off the southern coasts of Western Australia in the nineteenth century. At least 266 whales may have been taken in a 30 year period from 1836. Estimations are complicated by lack of distinction between right whales and humpbacks in the records, and frequent references to annual yields rather than the total catch. Information is also summarised on the timing, catching strategy, catch rates and possible effect of whaling on whale behaviour, by American pelagic whalers between 1838 and 1849, a period during which pelagic fishing on this species seems to have reached an early peak and rapid decline, at least off this, the 'Coast of New Holland Ground'.

INTRODUCTION

Two main types of whaling activity occurred last century on and off the Western Australian coast: 'bay' and 'shore station' whaling by locals; and 'pelagic' whaling by vessels from several countries including the USA, France and Great Britain. The latter vessels also undertook some bay whaling.

Information on the catches of right whales in both the above operations has been sought from available records. It has been possible to construct an estimate of the total (local) bay whaling catch and to obtain information on catches for a limited number of pelagic vessels (out of a considerably greater number that must have operated in those waters). Estimates have also been made of catch rates, and of 'whales struck and lost', and of a 'mortality factor' from which to obtain an estimate of the maximum likely kill. Indications of changes in pelagic whaling strategy during the period examined have also been obtained.

BAY WHALING BY LOCALS

Two sources of information have been used.

(*a*) *Heppingstone* (1966). He reviews the history of bay whaling in Western Australia and describes activities over the period 1837 to 1879 from contemporary accounts including diaries, newspapers and other publications. His account includes details of whales caught by particular operations in particular years but does not address total catches for the period.

(*b*) *'Blue Books'*. These are the official statistical returns of the Colony compiled from records in the Colonial Secretary's Office and show (not necessarily consistently) for a given year:

(i) under 'Imports and Exports' – the amount of 'black' or 'whale' oil, 'sperm' oil and 'whalebone' imported and exported;

(ii) under 'Fisheries' – the number of ships and boats engaged in the local fishery, together with the number of whales caught and their products, usually in tuns of oil and tons (sometimes cwt or lbs) of whalebone, for particular localities or 'stations'.

The first whale product 'Blue Book' return under 'Imports and Exports' is for 1836, with information on the export of '13 tuns of whale oil, valued at £520, and 7 tons of whalebone and sealskins, £630' from Albany on the south coast. The last return is for 1880, when whale oil exports, valued in total at £4,238, were made to Victoria, South Australia and Tasmania. There are details of whale product imports for 1836 and 1838, but none thereafter.

Returns of some kind occur for each year between 1836 and 1880, except for 1840, when 'no Ships or Boats (were) employed...in Whaling', and 1841 and 1842 when no returns were possible through the 'absence of any Custom's House Establishment'.

Under 'Fisheries', the first whaling return is again for 1836, when 10 boats were recorded as bay whaling, with the annotation 'the Whale Fisheries are only recently established in preparation for the ensuing season'. The last return is for 1877. There are no returns under this heading from 1838 to 1843.

An example of a particularly comprehensive 'Fisheries' return is given in Fig. 1.

Using combinations of the above sources an attempt has been made to estimate the total catch of right whales in each year for the period during which bay whaling occurred, i.e. 1836–*ca* 1877. Where, as is generally the case, the total catch is not recorded in the 'Fisheries' returns, estimates have been made by converting tuns of oil to 'whales'. Where there are no fishery returns the export figures have been used, although these do not necessarily reflect that year's fishery exactly, since they are sometimes less (when, presumably, some of the product was retained for local consumption) and sometimes more (presumably augmented by pelagic vessel products or by products held over from the previous year).

In the above, where individual numbers of whales are not recorded but yields are, a conversion factor of five tuns of oil per right whale has been used. This is low by comparison with elsewhere, but the only data from Western Australian records (three instances: 24 tuns from 3 whales; $5\frac{1}{2}$ tuns from 2; 14 tuns from 3) average 4.8 tuns per whale. This conversion factor can be used where there is certainty that the 'whales' yielding the product were right whales, but the Western Australian picture is confused by the knowlege that humpback whales were

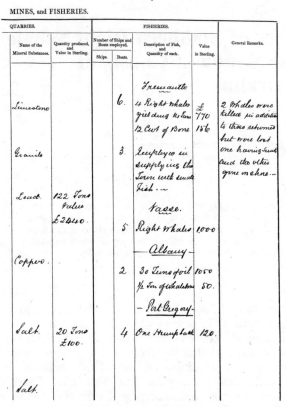

Fig. 1. Western Australia 'Blue Book' for 1854, page 195: annual 'Fisheries' return.

Table 1

Estimated 19th Century catch of right whales, "local" Bay whaling, Western Australia. Where the "Fishery" record reports what appears to be the total catch, a note also indicating a record in Heppingstone (1966) for that year will not appear.

[1]From Heppingstone (1966). [2]From "Fishery" records. [3]Estimated from export figures. [4]Estimated from "Fishery" records. *Includes 26 animals estimated for 1841 and 1842.

Year	Total	Total 5-yr group	Est. humpback catch	Year	Total	Total 5-yr group	Est. humpback catch
1836	3[3]			1858	18[4]		19
1837	23[3]		36	1859	0		29
1838	24[3]			1860	0	38	10
1839	0		9	1861	1[2]		11
1840	0	50		1862	2[4]		16
1841	?			1863	0		29
1842	?			1864	0		26
1843	3[3]			1865	1[1]	4	39
1844	16[4]			1866	7[4]		13
1845	20[4]	65*		1867	0		7
1846	32[3]		7	1868	0		10
1847	10[4]		44	1869	0		5
1848	14[4]		9	1870	0	7	27
1849	0		27	1871	0		30
1850	2[4]	58	27	1872	0		22
1851	8[4]		10	1873	0		15
1852	4[4]		16	1874	0		3
1853	5[2]		12	1875	0	0	11
1854	8[2]		11	1876	0		4
1855	19[4]	44	11	1877	0		3
1856	6[4]		25	1878	0		0
1857	14[4]		18	Total	266*		591

also taken during the period. They are first recorded in 1846: 'five humpbacks taken at Torbay' (Heppingstone, 1966). In 1850 the Blue Books record '14 cwt humper bone' at Albany (with a return of 16 cwt of whalebone also); in 1858 '37 right whales and humpbacks were taken at the five whaling stations'. Although humpback baleen is inferior to right whale baleen, there are certainly returns of the former. An attempt has therefore been made to determine, for those records where the species is not recorded, which species was likely to have been taken on the basis of the ratio tuns oil/tons whalebone, given that the yield of bone from humpbacks is likely to be relatively much less than from right whales. From the four records available where for a named species the yields of oil and bone are specified, a ratio of $\leq 25:1$ is taken to denote a right whale, and $> 25:1$ a humpback. (There are two records for right whales, 20:1, 23:1 and two for humpbacks, 27:1, 48:1. These are confirmed by two pelagic vessel records in 1837 – when humpbacks are extremely unlikely to have been taken – of 25:1 and 18:1. There are also records for Champion Bay and Port Gregory, both well north of Perth, where right whales are very unlikely to have been taken and bone yields are frequently not recorded, but where they are they give ratios of 32:1, 47.5:1, 66:1 and 112:1). For those records where oil and bone yields are available, but 'whale' is otherwise unspecified, determinations have been made using the above ratio.

The above have all been combined with information from Heppingstone (1966) for years where no additional catch data are recorded. Using an average figure for the two years (1841 and 1842) where no records appear at all, a total of 266 right whales is estimated as the total 'local'

bay whaling catch of this species off the Western Australian coast between 1836 and 1866 (Table 1). This is very probably a minimum estimate. If, indeed, no humpbacks were taken prior to the first available record of their capture (i.e. 1846), a further 45 animals could be added, making the total 311 right whales.

There seems no doubt that humpbacks were taken increasingly from the late 1850s. Whaling stations on the west coast north of Perth, on the northward migration route of humpbacks returning to winter breeding grounds from the Antarctic, feature in the returns from 1853 (Port Gregory) and 1871 (Champion Bay). In 1870 there was a move also to Malus Island in the Dampier Archipelago, i.e. off the northwest coast (Heppingstone, 1966), solely for humpbacks. That area ('Barrows Island', 'Rosemary Island' in pelagic logbooks) is the only, and very prominent, humpback ground off Western Australia on Townsend's 'humpback' chart (Townsend, 1935). The probable decline in right whale availability on the south coast from a peak in the earlier years (1836–1850) is reflected by the remarks of Nelson Cole Haley (quoted by Heppingstone, 1966) who, on the *Charles W. Morgan* at Two Peoples' Bay on the south coast in late 1849, states 'some years ago whale ships came here in certain seasons to catch right whales, but it has been abandoned now for that purpose'.

PELAGIC WHALING

Two main sources are again available.

(a) *Heppingstone* (1969). He records some details of vessels visiting the coast between 1833 and 1888, and describes interactions between locals and visiting whalers.

(b) *American whaling logbooks*. These are available on microfilm (Langdon, 1978).

At least in terms of numbers killed, pelagic whaling must have had a considerably greater effect on the stock of right whales off Western Australia than bay whaling, although this may have been counterbalanced to some extent by the killing of cows and calves by bay whalers.

In 1837, for example, the 'Blue Book' records show exports of 305 tuns whale oil, 15 tons bone, 100 tons oil and bone, from three whaling vessels. At five tuns of oil per whale, this would give a catch of 61 animals for two of those vessels alone. By contrast, for that year the estimate of the Western Australian bay whaling catch is only 23 animals (Table 1).

The first-known American whaler to visit the coast was the *Asia* in 1792. Whalers were probably present from then, but from at least 1837 to the 1850s they were a major feature of the local scene. Their presence, particularly in the early years of settlement, was not always welcome. Contemporary comments (see Heppingstone, 1969) include:

...much resentment was felt at the competition from American whalers;

...foreigners...infest our bays from the beginning of May to the end of October (1839);

...every year now at the end of December, during January, February and March the fleet could be expected (1840);

...a great number of whalers on the coast [in February]. 15...at Leschenault [Bunbury]...10 [at] Gage Roads [Fremantle] (1841);

...During the 1840s and 50s large numbers of whalers called for refreshment;

...no less than 260 American whaling ships are recorded as having visited these shores up to 1890.

There is, however, no readily available estimate of the total catch by these vessels off Western Australia, the 'Coast of New Holland Ground'.

To gain some indication of the likely extent of that catch, the American logbooks available on microfilm through the New England Microfilming Project (Langdon, 1978), have been examined for catch information. These had already been the subject of preliminary examination as part of an earlier exercise on sperm whaling (see Bannister, Taylor and Sutherland, 1981, Appendix A).

Of 146 logbooks indexed as 'Australia – Western Australia' in the 'Index to Places Visited', 111 are of ships visiting the area of study (taken as 90–140° E). Of those 111, at least 15 are 'good' logbooks with references to right whaling. A 'good' logbook is one where the writing is legible, most pages are present, basic data on position, weather, catch are recorded, and the vessel is present whaling on the ground and not just on passage through it.

Summarised results of the examination of these 15 logbooks, particularly to extract details of catch by date and position, are given in Table 2. Some generalisations which can be made from this rather small sample are given below.

(1) American vessels took right whales on the 'Coast of New Holland Ground', at least between 1838 and 1849, with a peak of activity in 1839 and 1940 (No. of vessels on ground: 1838 – 1; 1839 – 6; 1840 – 5; 1841 and 1842 – 3; 1843, 1845 and 1849 – 1; no vessel in 1844 or 1846–48).

(2) Vessels were present on the ground from late spring until summer, with a peak in November and December (no. of vessels: Sept. – 4; Oct. – 9; Nov. – 18; Dec. – 14; Jan. – 6; Feb. – 1).

(3) Some bay whaling by American vessels also occurred, but somewhat earlier in the year, from June to October (no. of vessels: June – 2; July – 3; Aug. – 3; Sept. – 2; Oct. – 1).

(4) The above differences in timing and location of the vessels' bay whaling operations – on the coast and mainly in winter and spring – by comparison with their activity 'on the ground' in late spring and summer, suggests a seasonal movement of whales from one location to the other. The positions of the catches during the 'on the ground' operations, virtually all at that time to the south or south west of the Continent, are consistent with a movement of animals away from the coast in early summer, generally towards the south.

(5) In the early years of the period, up to 1843, the operational pattern seems to have been a voyage from the North Atlantic round the Cape of Good Hope, to arrive on the ground (often right whaling in the South Atlantic and around St. Paul/Amsterdam *en route*) in late spring/early summer. Right whaling would then proceed from, say, October to December or January, when the vessel might then proceed northwestwards, sperm whaling in the eastern Indian Ocean, towards the East Indies. The following year, again after sperm whaling in the eastern Indian Ocean, the vessel might arrive off the Western Australian coast in June or July, and then undertake bay whaling from June or July to October. She would then proceed to sea again, right whaling or perhaps sperm whaling westwards, returning home whence she came, via the Cape of Good Hope.

After 1843 the pattern changes, with vessels passing eastwards through the New Holland ground rather rapidly, *en route* for Van Diemen's Land (Tasmania) or New Zealand, arriving there in January or February, and then sailing off 'to the Northwest', i.e. to the northeast Pacific 'Northwest Ground' in the Gulf of Alaska. There she would fish for right whales, and return home via Cape Horn.

(6) The number of right whales taken per vessel in one season on the 'Coast of New Holland Ground' ranges from 33 to 1; the number of days on the ground ranges from 104 to 8 per season, and the catch rate (whale per vessel day) from 0.47 to 0.02, with an average for 22 vessel-seasons of 0.22. Detailed extractions of six logs from 1838 and 1839 give a total of 152 right whales seen, of which 112 were 'struck' and 83 'tried out', giving a 'mortality factor' of 1.35.

(7) That right whales seem to have become increasingly shy of whaling vessels, if not indeed less numerous, by the mid-1840s in this area is exemplified by comments in the log of the *St. George*. On the ground between 20 October and 25 November 1845, she took three right whales, but on several occasions recorded seeing whales and not being able to take them. From 3–5 November, in six lowerings (for more than 10 whales) none was taken. Thus for 3 November the log reads '...at seven A.M. saw 2 rite whales lowered all four boats and persued without success...saw several more whales at ½ past ten lowered again could not get on...'. For 4 November: 'at one p.m. lowered all the boats persued several different whales without success...At five A.M. rose 2 rite whales lowered...could not get on...at eight A.M. raised several more...persued several without success the whale very wild and going quick...'. For 5 November: '...at one

Table 2.

Summarised results of examination of fifteen "good" logbooks from the Coast of New Holland ground, 1838–49. Figure in brackets following vessel name refers to PMB microfilm number.

[1] Duplicated in 573 and 847. [2] Incomplete log. [3] Log then missing.

Year	Date	Position	Catch etc.	Year	Date	Position	Catch etc.
Emerald (209)				**Phoenix** (250)			
1838	13 Oct–20 Dec	Off SW Cape New Holland	18 right whales (1 sunk); Av. bbls 66.3 "Plenty of whales"	1840/1841	17 Nov–4 Feb	S of New Holland (38–46 S, 102–132 E)	19 right
1839	1 July–5 Oct	Doubtful I. Bay, S. coast W. Australia	21 right – 4 cows and calves, 5 cows, 2 bulls, 1 "small", 1 dryskin, 4 unspecified. Av. bbls 74.1	1841	3 Nov–11 Dec	S of New Holland (38–41 S, 118–122 E)	14 right, incl. 1 "sunk", 1 "lost dead"
Huron (228)				**Mercator** (844)			
1839/1840	10 Nov–5 Jan	Off SW New Holland	10 right; returned home via C. Good Hope	1841	21 Oct–6 Dec (est.)	S of New Holland	2 right (initially sperm whaling on ground)
Maria Theresa (296)					23 Nov	40 16'S, 122 40'E (S of New Holland)	1 right
1839	13–29 Nov	Between 35–36 S and 97–92 E	8 right, incl. 1 "dryskin" ("took the head")	**Tuscarora** (846)			
1841	3 Oct–28 Dec	S. of New Holland to 41 S and 123 E	28 right	1842	14 July–6 Sept	Geographe Bay, SW coast of New Holland	14 right, incl. 1 cow and calf, 1 "smawl one".
Amazon (400)[1]				**Stephania** (268)			
1839	24 Nov–28 Dec	36 46'S, no long. (towards and near New Holland)	9 right	1842/1843	18 Sept–15 Jan	36–43 S, 116–138 E (S of New Holland)	17 right, incl. 1 lost, 1 sunk
1840	8 Jan	47 45'S, 123 15'E	1 right	**Europa** (840)			
	10 June–28 Aug	Fowler's Bay S. Australia	33 right, incl. 12 cows and calves, 2 "scrag", (also 8 humpback, incl. 3 cows and calves)	1842	28 Sept–28 Nov	36–40 S, 91–121 E (S of New Holland)	4 right, incl. 2 lost; Av. bbls 87.5
	29 Nov–27 Dec	Off SW New Holland	4 right	**Roman** (890)			
Montpelier (882)				1843	21–30 Nov	39 S, 123–130 E (S of New Holland)	3 right
1840	20 Sept–22 Nov	Cruising off and S. of New Holland	11 "whales" (only 5 specified as right) but presumably all right; incl. 1 sunk. "Saw plenty of whales"..."a number of whales in sight".	**St George** (692)			
				1845	20 Oct–25 Nov	Cruising off New Holland	3 right
Mayflower (219)				**Jasper**[2] (870)			
1839/1840	28 Dec–1 Jan	SW of New Holland	2 right	1847	6 Sept–9 Sept[3]	SW of New Holland	1 right
1840	23 Oct–9 Nov	SW of New Holland	4 right	**Betsy Williams** (577)			
Condor (273)				1849	6 Nov–28 Dec	SW of New Holland	1 right
1839/1840	25 Dec–18 Jan?	S of New Holland	1 right, 70 bbls.				
1840	19 Oct–21 Dec	S of New Holland (117–119 E, 36–40 S)	27 right incl. 3 "sunk", 1 "lost", 1 cow and calf; "Left calf, to small to save". "Struck 5, 3 parted".				

P.M. lowered again whales going quick chaced several whales without success...'. The vessel then sailed on for Van Diemen's Land and New Zealand. Off the latter she seems to have been more successful, operating around Stewart and Chatham Islands, before sailing to the North Pacific and the 'Northwest' (Coast of America) Ground in July and August 1846.

(8) The possibility that there may be segregation of sexual classes of right whales 'offshore' and 'on the coast' receives some confirmation from the small number of records of sexed animals in the catch. Only four vessels of those listed in Table 2 give the sex of any animals caught. Of the 27 records available from that source, all but two are from the coastal fishery, and were taken from June to September. Cows and calves comprise 18 of the 25, cows alone, 2, and bulls, 2. The two from the offshore fishery are both cows and calves, recorded southwest of the Continent in October and December.

Further evidence along these lines is provided by catch records in extracts of logbooks used by Townsend in drawing up his 1935 charts. The extracts available are only a subset of those he used, and only a small proportion of the catch is sexed. The instances of sexed catches are mainly from the 1830s, but range from 1827 to 1908. They were taken mostly in the South Atlantic and Indian Oceans, and from 32 to 51° S. Of the 73 animals sexed 44 were bulls (61%), 14 were cows (18%) and 15 cows and calves (21%). Only 11 of the 44 bulls (25%) were caught 'near land' (i.e. close to continental coasts or oceanic islands) whereas 9 of the 15 cows and calves (60%) but only two of the single cows (14%) were. Of the six cows and calves not 'near land', all but one were taken from spring to mid-summer (October–January); the exception was taken in late autumn (May).

The records confirm the generally held view that cows with calves occur close to the coast in winter and that bulls occur there less commonly. But a difficulty with these data is the extent to which cows and calves are likely to have been recorded by comparison with the other classes. The latter, i.e. bulls and non-suckling cows, seem to have been recorded when cows and calves were also being caught but not otherwise. There is a temptation to believe that most animals caught offshore in summer and not otherwise identified must have been bulls, but that does not explain where the cows that calve close to the coast in winter are to be found in summer. Neither 19th-century whalers nor 20th-century biologists would expect many, if any, right whales to remain near land in summer. Some proportion of the catch taken offshore in summer must therefore have been non-lactating cows and perhaps also sub-adults; unfortunately the present data do not help to distinguish between them.

ACKNOWLEDGEMENTS

Thanks are due for assistance from Dr W. H. Dawbin who advised on likely sources of data; to him and Mr I. D. Heppingstone for comments on a draft typescript, and to Ms Sandra Taylor whose earlier extracts of microfilmed logbooks provided the basis of the author's own foray into the field. Dr P. B. Best provided the data from the Townsend logbook extracts made available to him through the courtesy of Dr W. E. Schevill. These notes were produced in response to a request from the International Whaling Commission Boston Workshop on the Status of Right Whales for information on early catches of the species.

REFERENCES

Bannister, J. L., Taylor, S. and Sutherland, H. 1981. Logbook records of 19th century American sperm whaling: a report on the 12 month project, 1978–79. *Rep. int. Whal. Commn.* 31: 821–33.

Heppingstone, I. D. 1966. Bay whaling in Western Australia. Early days. *Early days. J. Proc. Roy. Western Australia Hist. Soc.* VI(V): 29–41.

Heppingstone, I. D. 1969. American whalers in Western Australian waters. *Early days. J. Proc. Roy. Western Australia Hist. Soc.* VII(I): 35–53.

Townsend, C. H. 1935. The distribution of certain whales as shown by logbook records of American whaleships. *Zoologica*, N.Y. 19(1): 1–50.

Langdon, R. (ed). 1978. *American Whalers and Traders in the Pacific: A Guide to Records on Microfilm*. Pacific Manuscripts Bureau, Research School of Pacific Studies, Australian National University, Canberra.

Right Whales Caught in Waters around South Eastern Australia and New Zealand during the Nineteenth and Early Twentieth Centuries

W. H. DAWBIN

P.O. Box A285, Department of Mammalogy, Australian Museum, Sydney, N.S.W. 2000, Australia

ABSTRACT

Estimates of right whale catches have been made mainly from Government documents and other sources listing amounts of 'black' oil and whalebone for the Australian and New Zealand colonies from 1827 to 1899, together with some catch data in the early 1900s. At least 26,000 right whales were caught in southwestern Pacific waters. More than two-thirds of these were taken by shore based operations from New Zealand and southeastern Australian stations and by bay whalers of Australian registry. The nature of the returns does not allow complete partitioning between these two or of the limited truly pelagic operations. Many American and French whalers obtained catches by bay whaling and others by pelagic operations in adjacent waters occupied presumably by the same right whale stocks. The significant British catches are incomplete and not included. Nearly three-quarters of all catches were made in the decade 1835–1844 followed by decline which seems to have been due largely to depletion of whale stocks.

INTRODUCTION

A good general background to Australasian whaling has been given by Dakin (1977). It also includes many references for further details on many localities around Tasmania and mainland Australia. Early records around New Zealand are well documented by Sherrin and Wallace (1890), Sherrin (1886) and McNab (1907 and 1913). The earliest whaleship listed as calling at New Zealand was the *William and Ann* in 1791. Four others returned to England from the Australian coast (New South Wales) in 1793 out of 20 that had engaged in the Pacific Ocean Fishery. In 1804 six British whalers were off northern New Zealand and from 1805 onwards, whalers were calling regularly at Bay of Islands. Other years listed include 1808 – 10 ships, 1814 – 6, 1820 – 10, 1821 – 14 including 2 American. From 1821 to 1830 only five American whalers appear to have operated in the area but there is frequent unspecific mention of considerable numbers of British vessels.

The detailed compilation by Cumpston (1977) gives a more complete picture at Sydney, N.S.W. where there were 170 visits by whaling vessels between 1791 and 1825. British vessels made at least 140 calls compared with only 14 by American whalers. Of all whalers whose cargo or type of fishery are listed, 118 were sperm whalers and only 11 had 'black' oil. This preference in catch is partly confirmed from Appendix III in Jenkins (1921) which shows that British vessels from 1823–1832 brought back a yearly average of 594 tons of 'common' oil compared with 5,069 tons of sperm oil from the whole southern whale fishery. It seems clear that right whales were not a major quarry for pelagic whalers in the southwest Pacific before the early 1830s.

In this paper an attempt is made to estimate the numbers of right whales killed in the waters around southeastern Australia and New Zealand from 1827 onwards. Some conclusions are drawn from the catch history about the migratory routes of right whales in this region.

MATERIALS AND METHODS

A full listing of all the historical sources consulted in this study is available from the Secretariat of the International Whaling Commission (The Red House, Station Road, Histon, Cambridge CB4 4NP, UK).

In order to reconstruct the landed catch of right whales, a number of different approaches have been used because of the lack of a consistent series of comprehensive catch or production data for most regions.

In a number of cases within the Colonial Secretary returns of the Colony (Blue Books), the number of 'black' (right) whales is listed by individual shore stations or by ships registered in local ports as well as giving oil and whalebone yields, their value and the number of men and boats employed. In other cases oil yield in barrels, gallons or tuns only may be given and has been converted to whales, by using 5 tuns (40 barrels) as an average per whale (since the average from 413 shore-caught whales was 4.18 tuns and pelagic yields *ca* 6 tuns) or by using whalebone at 600 lb per whale. In a few cases, value only has been given and these, of course, have been used and estimates made from oil and whalebone yields (occasionally value) for years for which actual counts are missing. This procedure has been followed for each of the east Australian States as well as New Zealand to give the detail contained in Table 1.

Shore-based whaling

The earliest definite reports of right whaling in Australia were catches in 1805 from shore-based whalers in the Derwent Estuary near present-day Hobart (Dakin, 1977). It is clear that there was some spread of shore-based whaling along the coast of Tasmania but details are sketchy and catches unrecorded in official records until 1822 and are then ambiguous until 1827 since elephant seal oil was usually included in returns of 'black' oil.

In the late 1830s, the number of shore stations peaked at about 50, the exact figure depending on whether temporary sites used for only one season are included.

Table 1.

Right whale catches, 1827–1930.

Column D' refers to catches from New Zealand included under (D) and thus not included again in the summation (see text).

The catches are estimated as described in the text using data listed in the following references. (A) South Australia: Borrow, 1947; Cumpston, 1970; GBP, 1801–57; Newland, 1920–21. (B) Victoria: GB BT, 1839–52; GB HC, 1801–65; NSW CS, 1822–57; Henty diaries. (C) Tasmania: GB BT, 1839–52; GB P, 1801–57; TCS, 1839–59. (D) New South Wales: Dakin, 1977; GB BT, 1839–52; GB HC, 1801–65; GB P, 1801–57; HA, 1914–25; H NSW, 1892–1901; NSW CS, 1822–57; NSW LC, 1847; NSW P, 1857; Thompson, 1893. (E) New Zealand: GB P, 1801–57; McNab, 1908–14; McNab, 1913; NZ, 1841–53; NZ, 1854–1900; Sherrin, 1886; Wakefield, 1848. (F) American pelagic: Starbuck, 1878. (G) French pelagic; Du Pasquier, 1986

No estimates have been included for British and German pelagic whaling or for pre-1827 catches from Tasmanian shore stations New Zealand returns 1830–1842 are from shore stations south of Banks Peninsula. No allowance has been made for the additional mortality of animals that were struck and lost. At many locations, this certainly exceeded the common estimate of 20% (examples in Sherrin, 1886)

Year	SA (A)	Vic (B)	Tas (C)	NSW (D)	D'	NZ (E)	Pelagic off NZ		Total
							American (F)	French (G)	
1827	–	–	64	–	–	–	–	–	64
1828	–	–	109	10	–	–	–	–	119
1829	–	–	131	9	–	–	–	–	140
1830	–	–	233	103	*	28	–	–	364
1831	–	–	195	201	*	30	–	–	426
1832	5	–	246	49	*	23	36	–	359
1833	–	–	346	94	62	56	–	–	496
1834	–	61	356	237	118	84	–	–	738
1835	–	170	409	279	271	98	156	85	1,197
1836	–	97	493	235	127	82	–	89	996
1837	55	142	815	401	198	72	689	901	3,075
1838	41	3	844	435	325	145	539	582	2,589
1839	60	60	1,064	539	390	128	1,194	1,066	4,111
1840	72	–	804	317	242	86	265	392[1]	1,936
1841	42	44	279	198	166	57	987	756	2,363
1842	28	5	167	320	249	25	97	–	642
1843	51	27	277	58	50	333	60	–	806
1844	–	35	241	114	85	316	214	–	920
1845	10	4	259	91	66	187	129	–	680
1846	–	21	85	140	54	151	44	–	441
1847	–	8	104	60	41	135	–	–	307
1848	4	3	70	77	23	95	42	–	291
1849	1	1	24	34	10	23	31	–	114
1850	–	1	46	76	15	17	–	–	140
1851	–	1	32	129	10	5	–	–	167
1852	–	–	13	24	21	17	–	–	54
1853	3	–	8	78	34	14	–	–	103
1854	3	–	–	27	1	11	–	–	41
1855	2	–	–	10	7	25	–	–	37
1856	2	–	–	23	10	30	–	–	55
1857	–	–	–	11	–	25	–	–	36
1858	–	–	–	5	–	35	–	–	40
1859	–	–	–	52	17	53	–	–	105
1860	–	–	–	42	11	5	–	–	47
1861	–	–	–	24	5	2	–	–	26
1862	–	–	–	57	5	6	–	–	63
1863	–	–	–	11	9	6	–	–	17
1864	–	–	–	22	7	10	–	–	32
1865	–	–	–	15	7	1	–	–	16
1866	–	–	–	12	–	7	–	–	19
1867	–	–	2	30	1	–	–	–	32
1868	–	–	6	45	1	–	–	–	51
1869	–	–	2	10	–	17	–	–	29
1870	–	–	1	28	–	18	–	–	47
1871–1900	–	–	20	136	–	168	4	–	328
1901–30	–	–	–	7	–	89[2]	–	–	96
Sum	379	683	7,745	4,875	2,638	2,715	4,487	3,871	24,755

The positions of the main sites used in Tasmania and mainland southeastern Australia are shown in Fig. 1. From then onwards, several official publications, referred to in the notes accompanying Table 1, start to give varying degrees of detail for Tasmania, New South Wales and New Zealand (they sometimes are very well itemized and at other times incomplete or ambiguous).

Australian whaling vessels

Table 1 not only includes shore station records but also those from vessels locally registered and usually built locally. Eventually more than 50 vessels were registered as operating from Hobart and Launceston in Tasmania and 40 from Sydney, N.S.W. The right-whaling vessels from all these ports operated in bays over a wide area and it is sometimes difficult to partition their catch or oil yield between New South Wales, Tasmania and New Zealand. The Board of Trade 'Tables of revenue....' itemize, in part, the years 1839 to 1852 but further searching may reveal more data that could change the partitioning of catches between these regions. There are cases of oil from vessels registered in Hobart, for example, that discharged their oil during a call at Sydney. Some of these may, therefore, be duplicated in two port lists and it is hoped that further searching will resolve such cases. The situation is further complicated by inconsistent itemizing of the oil sources that are listed from vessels that were registered locally. For example, Hobart and Sydney vessels often went bay-whaling off New Zealand and this is itemized in some cases but unclear in others.

The problem was recognized nearly a century ago when Sherrin (1886) commented on the table he had compiled for New Zealand from various governmental and other sources, stating

Prior to... 1868 – it is feared that little reliance can be placed on the figures in the foregoing table, as it is manifestly impossible that they can represent the full quality and value of the whaling products exported. Thus from 1841 to 1852, inclusive, the books of the Customhouse at Wellington alone show that no less than sixty-one vessels all laden with 'oil and bone' as it was then the custom to call such cargoes. Those vessels were of the tonnage from 50–580 tons, but chiefly from 200 to 400 tons each, of which twelve cleared for London, and most of the rest for Sydney and Hobart Town.

The further sources listed in the references to Table 1 are probably fairly complete in the quantities and values of the produce obtained by the efforts of each colony and in total they should represent the results for the southeastern Australian – New Zealand region as a whole.

New Zealand

New Zealand shore whaling did not commence until two stations began to operate in 1829, one in Cook Strait and the other at Preservation Inlet in the southwest corner of New Zealand. Yields from these and an increasing number of other shore stations, reaching a peak of about 80 establishments (or more if temporary sites are included) in 1843–1845, are well documented in the official records and by tables in Sherrin (1886) and Wakefield (1848) which were all used as the main sources for the present tabulation. Some additions have been made to include what is at present known of the New South Wales and Tasmanian whalers' additional catches around New Zealand. Locations of the main whaling sites are shown in Fig. 2.

Victoria and South Australia

Along Victoria, shore and some bay whaling occurred mainly near Portland and Port Fairy. In South Australia there was whaling at sites between Port Lincoln and Encounter Bay but in both areas the number of years of catching was relatively small. Catches are known in detail

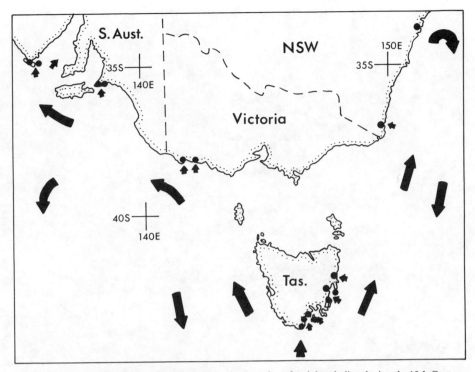

Fig. 1. Southeastern Australian sites of the main shore stations for right whaling during the 19th Century. Large arrows indicate the overall trend in whale movements and small arrows indicate the main movements of cows to calve near sheltered bays.

from Portland (diaries of the Henty family, Melbourne Public Library). Logs of bay whalers and station records in the South Australian Archives relate to the Encounter Bay region, Kangaroo Island and Sleaford. Interesting details of South Australian whaling are given by Newland (1920), Borrow (1947) and Cumpston (1970).

Pelagic whaling after 1830

Pelagic whaling in the area until the early 1830s was certainly dominated by British vessels but full details are unavailable. They were not overtaken by American and French whalers until the mid-1830s. Of vessels entering the Bay of Islands, New Zealand, in 1838, Sherrin (1886) stated that the number of whaleships included 36 American, 23 British, 21 French, 24 New South Wales, 6 New Zealand and 1 Bremen. Some recently located papers from the British Resident, Bay of Islands show a large number of American and New South Wales vessels and only 3 French vessels in 1836 but his table numbers vessels that called more than once as 'distinct vessels on each visit'. It is not clear whether Sherrin's figures refer to visits or the number of individual vessels that called one or more times in the year.

American bay whaling from pelagic vessels anchored in or operating near bays commenced with the *Erie* in New Zealand waters in 1832 and expanded very rapidly as shown by estimated catches in the table. The estimates are made from the returns specifically listing New Zealand in Starbuck (1878) which records them under the year of the vessel's departure. Such returns could be from catches over two, three or more years and should be partitioned further by estimates for each year or by supplementary data now available from many logs (it should be noted that these might contain oil from localities other than New Zealand). This has not been

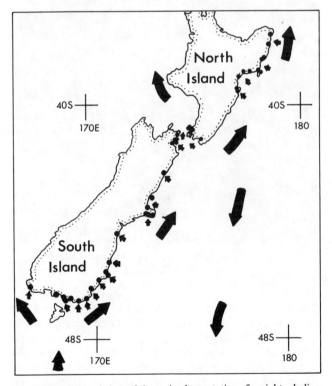

Fig. 2. New Zealand sites of the main shore stations for right whaling during the 19th and early-20th Centuries. Large arrows indicate the overall trend in whale movements and small arrows indicate the main movements of cows to calve near sheltered bays.

attempted for the present tabulation which is, therefore, an estimate for mixed years and should strictly be treated for the years grouped together in the present case. Other logs listed in Starbuck as 'Pacific Ocean' with no further details, may also have included some New Zealand oil.

Plate I. Right whale hunting off Twofold Bay, N.S.W. from an original painting by Oswald Brierly held by the National Library, Canberra.

Plate II. Right whale on slipway, Tory Channel, Cook Strait, New Zealand.

Plate III. Right whale on slipway, showing underside, Tory Channel, Cook Strait, New Zealand.

The estimates of French catches off New Zealand are from the data of Du Pasquier (1986) and greatly help to complete estimates of pelagic catches off New Zealand where such activity was much greater than around the coasts of eastern Australia. German pelagic catches are likely to have been small and Portuguese even smaller, but British returns are greatly needed to complete the estimates of total pelagic catches. It must be borne in mind that a significant but unknown proportion of 'pelagic' catches was made during bay whaling operations.

RESULTS AND CONCLUSIONS

In general, the data available from shore and pelagic operations combined are sufficient to estimate a total catch of more than 26,000 right whales from southeast Australian and New Zealand waters since 1822. Apart from some British pelagic catches, shore whalers from the coast of Tasmania were the first to harvest right whales, joined in 1828 by Sydney and Hobart vessels carrying on bay whaling. American whalers caught about 4,500 right whales in the 1835–46 period and nearly 4,000 were caught by French whalers 1835–41. The remaining two-thirds of the total catch were taken from shore stations and by Australian registered vessels operating mainly as bay whalers in the region from 1828 onwards. They therefore preceded and then coincided with the peak activities of the foreign fleets and continued operations at a declining rate for rather longer.

The results from all the whalers were greatest in the decade 1835–44 when nearly three-quarters of all the

Plate IV. Whalers on 'strag' of right whale, Kaikoura, New Zealand.

Plate V. (above and right) Whalers with adult right whale, Kaikoura, New Zealand, *circa* 1920.

catches were made. During this period the local right whale catch formed a major proportion of all those taken world wide, possibly one-third or more of the world right whale catches.

Along with the departure of foreign fleets following decreasing catches, shore station and local vessel activity gradually declined, with total annual catches of less than 300 after 1846 and less than 50 after 1862. The few Sydney and Hobart vessels operating in the 1860s were changing progressively to sperm whale hunting. Some Hobart vessels whaled until the end of the 19th century but their catches in the last three decades were almost exclusively sperm whales.

Much reduced and intermittent shore whaling continued longest from New Zealand and became combined with humpback whaling. The only exclusively right whale operation was at Campbell Island from 1909–1913 when 63 were caught. Shore whaling had ceased by 1880 in all eastern Australian states except New South Wales where a small station at Twofold Bay continued until 1930. Its small catches were mainly humpbacks but included an occasional right whale.

In the region as a whole, there was a more or less simultaneous peak period in the decade 1835–44 followed by a rapid decline in all regions. This also coincided with changes back to sperm whaling from pelagic vessels and to humpback whaling from shore, suggesting a real reduction in availability of right whales. Economic and other factors may have contributed to a change in preference by pelagic whalers, but there are also many contemporary comments on progressive scarcity of right

Plate VI. Cooking blubber at a temporary shore station, east coast of New Zealand.

Plate VII. Head of a right whale before removal of baleen, Campbell Island, *circa* 1911.

whales. Despite more than a century of zero catches in most parts of the region there was no firm evidence of significant recovery in local right whale stocks before 1982 (Bannister, 1986).

Note on migration routes

The distribution of right whales caught by American whaleships worldwide during the nineteenth century is well known from the charts of Townsend (1935). The monthly plottings are especially concentrated in the South Atlantic, parts of the southwest Indian Ocean and

off Chile, but in the southwest Pacific there are fewer plottings from the logbooks which he examined. Apart from a major concentration in October and November east of Kermadec Islands and a smaller concentration to the east and southeast of the South island of New Zealand the plottings of catches are relatively sparse. In particular there are very few for the waters around Tasmania and southeastern Australia where many whales were caught, however, by local whalers.

Cumpston (1970) has described many nineteenth century observations from South Australia in particular and the southeastern region in general and illustrated the results in a map showing 'the winter migration route of black whales about 1830.' Fig. 1 has been derived in part from this map with the addition of small arrows into bays where whaling stations had been sited to take advantage of the localized calving groups. The progression past western Tasmania and Victoria to approach South Australia from the east appears to be well corroborated but there is little indication of the routes followed on departing from the coast. Similarly, the northern route past eastern Tasmania and New South Wales up to the region of Sydney can be well documented. Very few right whales were observed north of Sydney and the routes followed on their departure from the coast are uncertain.

Seasonal movements around New Zealand in the early 1840s have been described by Wakefield (1908) from personal and other contemporary observations. These form the basis for the main trends of the winter migration shown in Figure 2. It should be noted that the description included by Sherrin (1886) is derived from an account by Dr E. Dieffenbach who describes the right whales as coming into Cook Strait from the north in May, i.e. the reverse of Wakefield's and other contemporary descriptions. There appears to be no other contemporary account that agrees with Dieffenbach's description. The route followed after right whales departed from New Zealand coastal regions is largely uncertain.

ACKNOWLEDGEMENTS

I wish to thank the librarians of Mitchell and Fisher Libraries in Sydney; Turnbull Library and the National Archives in Wellington, New Zealand; the Tasmanian State Library (State Archives and Crowther Library), Hobart; South Australian Archives, Adelaide and National Library, Canberra. Funds for periods of searching assistance provided by the Australian Conservation Foundation, Australian National Parks and Wildlife Service and Greenpeace (Australian) are gratefully acknowledged. Helpful discussions with Mr J. L. Bannister and the comments on the manuscript by Monsieur T. Du Pasquier and an anonymous reviewer are much appreciated. I am especially indebted to my wife Janet for great help in the searches.

REFERENCES

Bannister, J. L. 1986. Southern right whales: status off Australia from twentieth century 'incidental' sightings and aerial surveys. (Published in this volume.)

Borrow, K. T. 1947. *Whaling at Encounter Bay.* Pioneer's Association of South Australia, Adelaide. 8 pp.

Cumpston, J. S. 1970. *Kangaroo Island 1800–1836.* Roebuck, Canberra. 197 pp.

Cumpston, J. S. 1977. *Shipping Arrivals and Departures Sydney, 1788–1825.* Roebuck, Canberra. 2 parts, 210 pp.

Dakin, W. J. 1977. *Whalemen Adventurers in Southern Waters.* Rev. Ed. Angus and Robertson, Sydney. 252 pp.

Du Pasquier, T. 1986. Catch history of French right whaling mostly in the South Atlantic. (Published in this volume.)

Dunbabin, T. 1925. Whalers, sealers and buccaneers. *J. roy. Aust. Hist. Soc.* 11:1–32.

Great Britain and Ireland. Board of Trade. Statistical Department [GB BT] 1839–52. Tables of revenue, population, commerce etc. of the United Kingdom and its dependencies, compiled from official returns. London, H.M.S.O.

Great Britain and Ireland. House of Commons. [GB HC] 1801–65. Journals, 1801–1865. cl. 449. 1st April 1846: Southern whale fishery. c. 921. 10th–11th July 1845: A return...exports and imports of New South Wales 1836 to 1844. London, H.M.S.O.

Great Britain and Ireland. Parliament [GB P] 1801–57. Parliamentary Papers. xlv.183.1846: Account of ships employed in whale fishery. 1x.1847 Shipping. 1xv.843.1847: Statement of quantities of principal articles imported. liv. 1833: Statement of imports in New South Wales, Van Diemens Land and South Australia. xxiv.227. 1833: oil returns. 1844–1850: Papers relative to New Zealand. London, H.M.S.O.

Historical records of Australia. [HA] 1914–25. Series I.v. 1–26: Governor's despatches to and from England, 1788–1848. Series III.v. 1–6: Despatches and papers relating to the settlement of the state, 1803–1830. Library Committee of the Commonwealth Parliament, Sydney.

Historical records of New South Wales. [HNSW] 1892–1901. Govt. Pr., Sydney.

Jenkins, J. T. 1921. *A History of the Whale Fisheries.* Witherby, London. 336 pp.

McNab, R. 1908–14. *Historical Records of New Zealand.* Govt. Pr., Wellington. 2 v. 770 pp, 650 pp.

McNab, R. 1907. *Murihiku and the Southern Islands.* William Smith, Invercargill. xxiii + 337 pp.

McNab, R. 1913. *The Old Whaling Days: a history of southern New Zealand from 1830 to 1840.* Whitcombe & Tombs, Christchurch. xiii + 508 pp.

New South Wales. Colonial Secretary. [NSW CS] 1822–57. Returns of the colony, 1822–1857. Govt. Pr., Sydney.

New South Wales. Legislative Council. [NSW LC] 1847. Minutes of proceedings of the Legislative Council from 1824 to 1831, inclusive, and votes and proceedings of the Legislative Council from 1832 to 1837 inclusive in two parts. Govt. Pr., Sydney.

New South Wales. Parliament. [NSW P] 1857. Journal of the Legislative Council of New South Wales session 1856 to 1857. Govt. Pr., Sydney.

New Zealand. [NZ] 1841–53. Blue book of statistics, 1841–1853. Australian Joint Copying Project Colonial Office (CO213) PRO Reel 1502–1504.

New Zealand. [NZ] 1854–1900. *Statistics of New Zealand.* Govt. Pr., Wellington.

Newland, S. 1920–21. Whaling at Encounter Bay. *Proc. roy. Geogr. Soc. Aust., S. Aust. branch* 22:15–40.

Sherrin, R. A. A. 1886. *Handbook of the fishes of New Zealand.* 307 pp.

Sherrin, R. A. A. and Wallace, J. H. 1890. *Early history of New Zealand.* Brett, Auckland. 728 pp.

Starbuck, A. 1878. History of the American whale fishery from its earliest inception to the year 1876. *U.S. Comm. Fish and Fisheries. part IV. Rep. Commr 1875–76. Appendix A:* 779 pp.

Tasmania. Colonial Secretary. [TCS] 1839–59. Statistical returns 1804–1858. Govt. Pr., Hobart.

Thompson, L. G. 1893. *History of the Fisheries of New South Wales.* Govt. Pr., Sydney. 126 pp.

Townsend, C. H. 1935. The distribution of certain whales as shown by logbook records of American whaleships. *Zoologica N.Y.* 19:1–50.

Wakefield, E. J. 1848. *The Handbook for New Zealand.* John W. Parker, London, 493 pp.

Wakefield, E. J. 1908. *Adventure in New Zealand from 1839 to 1844.* Whitcombe & Tombs, Wellington, 735 pp.

Catch History of French Right Whaling Mainly in the South Atlantic

THIERRY DU PASQUIER

6 *Rue de la Mission, Marchand, 75016 Paris, France*

ABSTRACT

This paper shows how existing documents permit computation of the catch of right whales by French whalers. It sums up available data in French archives for all periods and all parts of the world. However the only time for which complete statistics can be accurately compiled is from the end of the 18th century to the mid 1830s, mostly in the South Atlantic. Between 1817 and 1868, about 11,000 right and bowhead whales are estimated to have been taken by French whalers worldwide.

I. THE BASQUE FISHERY

As early as the 12th century, the French and Spanish Basques were whaling in the Bay of Biscay, in which were found Biscayan right whales, which they called *Sarde* or *baleine de Sarde*. They later expanded their fishery to the north and discovered the bowhead whales which they called *Baleines de Grande Baie* (or *Grand Bay whales*) around Newfoundland and Labrador in the 16th century, and around Spitsbergen and Greenland at the beginning of the 17th century.

They taught their art to the Dutch, and when around 1635 they were expelled from the bays of Spitsbergen, they turned to whaling on the high seas, trying the blubber on board their vessels.

Whereas the Dutch and English seem to have mostly captured bowhead whales (also called Greenland whales), the Basques, in the 1670s were whaling among the icefloes, and if they did not make a complete catch, they went fishing the Sardes around Iceland on the return voyage.

Table 1 gives the number of French whalers known for each year during the 17th century, although the figures cannot be considered complete because of the sources used. From the beginning to 1669 we rely mostly on the notarial records from Bayonne and Saint-Jean de Luz. The figure of 20 vessels in 1664 is certain and complete, as Colbert ordered that a list be compiled of all vessels in every harbour of the Kingdom.

The number of whalers increased after 1665 when the Compagnie du Nord, which had a monopoly, was suppressed.

From 1669 to 1679, the main source is the insurance policies in the books of an insurance company established in Paris (Archives Nationales, Z[1D]). Whaling grew to a peak with over 35 whalers in 1672; but French shipping was a victim of Louis XIVth's wars with maritime powers.

In 1688, after the peace, the number of whalers climbed again to 37 units, but then fell back to a low level, due to the wars at the end of the century.

Table 1.

Number of French whalers known 1613–1700.

Main sources: Archives des Pyrénées Atlantiques, Pau, Notarial records of Saint-Jean de Luz, Série IIIE, Bibliothèque Nationale, Paris, Cinq Cents de Colbert 199 (List of vessels in 1664); Archives Nationales, Paris Z 1D 75–80, insurance policies 1669–1679. Archives de Seine Maritime, Rouen, Amirauté du Havre, série 216 BP.

Year	No.	Year	No.	Year	No.	Year	No.	Year	No.
1613	6	1641	3	1658	3	1673	9	1688	37
1615	3	1642	5	1659	3	1674	28	1689	13
1617	1	1643	6	1660	5	1675	17	1690	8
1622	2	1644	6	1661	6	1676	31	1691	6
1623	2	1645	14	1662	7	1677	19	1692	0
1625	4	1646	4	1663	10	1678	14	1693	3
1631	1	1647	1	1664	20	1679	15	1694	1
1632	5	1648	2	1665	8	1680	10	1695	7
1633	4	1649	1	1666	13	1681	8	1696	8
1634	6	1650	1	1667	4	1682	8	1697	11
1635	2	1653	6	1668	2	1683	15	1698	6
1636	14	1654	4	1669	11	1684	13	1699	6
1637	1	1655	1	1670	13	1685	20	1700	5
1639	2	1656	1	1671	25	1686	15		
1640	2	1657	2	1672	35	1687	6		

Table 2.

Number of Sardes (right whales) taken by whalers returning to Honfleur 1680–1687.

Source: Archives Municipales de Honfleur, Reports 1665–1688, 2 II 287–96.

	Number of vessels	Number of Sarde	Casks of oil
1680	1	5	
1681	1	5	120
1682	2	11	343
1683	2	3	90
1684	1	4	100
1685	1	1	0
1687	1	7	160

There are also other sources that give quantitative information on the catch of the whalers. Many Basque whalers returned to unload their cargo of oil and whalebone in Le Havre and Honfleur. These cargoes were later sent to Paris by barges on the river Seine. The masters had to make reports to the Amirauté when they arrived. They stated details on their campaigns as well as the number of whales taken and casks of oil brought back. Thus there are data for over 30 campaigns from 1667 to 1688. In several cases it is possible to identify the difference between the number of Sarde and of Grand Bay whales caught, and the amount of oil of each of the two species. (See Table 2 giving data on the whalers returning to Honfleur.) The last Sardes which we know to have been killed from shore stations in Biscay were chased in 1688.

As of 1701, it is possible to determine exactly the number of French whalers sailing each year (see Table 3), with about 30 ships yearly between 1725 and 1730. They were still going between Spitsbergen and Greenland, and after 1719 also in Davis Strait.

Table 3.

Number of French whalers 1701–1766.

Main source: Archives de la Marine, Rochefort, Inscription Maritime de Saint-Jean de Luz et Bayonne, Matricules 15 P 3, Rôles d'équipage 13 P 8, 15 P 4.

Year	No.	Year	No.	Year	No.	Year	No.
1701	11	1716	14	1731	27	1746	
1702	6	1717	15	1732	31	to	
1703	2	1718	16	1733	30	1749	0
1704	2	1719	12	1734	23	1750	4
1705	2	1720	11	1735	17	1751	4
1706	0	1721	13	1736	16	1752	4
1707	2	1722	17	1737	13	1753	?
1708	4	1723	18	1738	15	1754	5
1709	1	1724	23	1739	15	1755	4
1710	6	1725	24	1740	10	1756	
1711	7	1726	21	1741	10	to	
1712	8	1727	26	1742	6	1764	0
1713	10	1728	28	1743	8	1765	2
1714	17	1729	30	1744	5	1766	2
1715	15	1730	28	1745	1		

The main source for this list is the Archives of the Inscription Maritime of Bayonne and Saint-Jean de Luz, kept at the Navy Archives of Rochefort. There are statistics on the oil brought back by Bayonne whalers from 1725 to 1730, for Saint-Jean de Luz and Bayonne from 1732 to 1734, for Saint-Jean de Luz only in 1737 and a few isolated figures of the catch of certain vessels until 1755 (Table 4). As late as 1754, the last French whalers were still chasing Sardes or Biscayan right whales. French whaling was already declining when it was stopped by the war with England after 1744. Two unsuccessful attempts to revive it in 1750–1755 and 1765–1766 failed.

The fishery of the Basques will be the subject of a book I hope to publish within a few years.

Table 4.

Capture of Sarde in the 18th century.

Sources: Archives Nationales, Paris, Marine B 3 383 p. 578 (1737). Archives de la Marine, Rochefort, 13 P 8 94 (1740), 15 P 4 1 (1743), 15 P 4 5 (1754).

	Number of vessels	Number of Sardes	Casks of oil
1737	12	14	91
1740	1	1	
1743	2	2	
1754	3	5	

II. THE DUNKIRK WHALING OUTFITS FROM 1784 TO 1794 AND 1802 TO 1803

A whaling company was established in Dunkirk in 1784 with the help of the French Government. It sent 6 whalers both to the Northern and Southern whaling grounds, with little success, until 1788.

Table 5.

Number of French whalers 1784–1803.

Main source: Archives Nationales, Paris, F 12 1839 B.

Year	No.	Year	No.	Year	No.	Year	No.
1784	5	1787	17	1790	18	1793	8+
1785	4	1788	14	1791	21	1802	15
1786	7	1789	19	1792	38+	1803	4

But the Government then encouraged a colony of Nantucketers to settle at Dunkirk with their vessels. The number of whalers fitted out from Dunkirk and also from Lorient rose to over 30 units in 1792 (see Table 5).

There is a good series of reports by the masters on their returns, kept in the French Archives. They are fairly complete except for 1792 and 1793, when the French Revolution interrupted the keeping of good records.

The whalers were commanded and largely manned by inhabitants of the island of Nantucket. They went mostly to the South Atlantic, either to the coast of Africa (Tiger's Bay, Woolwich Bay, Saldana Bay, Saint-Helena Bay, Table Bay), or to the Brazil Banks and Falkland Islands.

Table 6 gives the number of right whales, barrels of oil and pounds of whalebone taken in the South Atlantic.

From 1784 to 1791–92, catches are known for 92.2% of the 64 whaling voyages, representing 870 whales and 40,000 barrels of oil. Only the result of a few of the whalers sailing in 1792 is known, but it seems to be the year when the greatest number of right whales were taken by French whalers: approximately 460 or even more. The total estimate for the period 1784–1793 is approximately 1,400 right whales caught by French whalers in the South Atlantic.

Certain reports are sufficiently precise for giving the number of whales struck and escaping, and the whales that were killed but sunk. Ten voyages from 1787 to 1792 give the following averages (see Table 7):

> struck: 294 whales   100%
> escaped: 70   23.8%
> sunk after killed: 41.5   14.1%
> processed: 182.5   62.1%

(One of the whales sunk after it was half cut.)

A certain number of the whales that escaped probably later died, but it is impossible to know how many. If 14% is added to the number of whales processed to see how many were actually killed, we arrive at approximately 1,600 right whales killed between 1784 and 1792.

No estimate has been made for 1793–1794 when most whalers returned to the United States or were taken by the British, and I have been unable to trace statistics relating to the short revival which took place in 1802–1803, after the peace of Amiens.

French whaling vessels also went sporadically to the Greenland fishery.

In 1788, two whalers went around Madagascar and to Delagoa Bay, which became an important whaling ground in the following years. Six whalers sailing in 1790 and 1791 went to the Pacific. Although statistics can be computed for these whaling grounds, it is not the main purpose of this paper, and it is a very long process, as each report must be analyzed in detail.

The author is presently finishing a book on French whaling from 1775 to 1815.

Table 6.

Right whale catch in South Atlantic, 1784–1804.

The destination of certain vessels is only indicated as "South Atlantic", which explains why the total is for some years higher than the addition of the figures for Brazil and Africa.

E: Indicates that the figures for a limited number of campaigns are estimates.

[E]: The number of whales for these years was not given, and has been computed approximately with about 45 to 50 barrels to a whale.

(1) The destination of 9 other ships is unknown.
(2) The destination of 10 more ships is not known.
(3) The destination of 2 ships is unknown.

Estimate of the catch, for 100% of the vessels:

1784–1792	945 whales
1792–93	460 whales
	1,405 whales

Main source: Archives Nationales, Paris, F 12 1839 B, reports of the masters.

	No. of vessels		Number of whales	Barrels of oil	Pounds of whalebone
	Total	Catch of which is known			
Brazil Bank					
1784–85	4	3	14E	562	>3,230
1785–86	2	1	5	293	2,500
1786–87	3	3	34E	1,786	13,650
1787–88	10	8	91 1/3	4,652	46,800
1788–89	3.5	3.5	33	1,523	16,000
1789–90	6	6	63.5	3,526	38,000
1790–91	1	1		450	9,000
1791–92	8	7		8,538	86,000
1792–93	3	1		200	3,000
1802–03	2	0			
1803–4	1	0			
Coast of Africa					
1784–87	0	0			
1787–88	3	3	43.5	2,440	22,000
1788–89	6.5	6.5	103.5	3,849	45,500
1789–90	10	10	165	7,005	75,200
1790–91	1	1	28	1,350	15,000
1791–92	3	3		2,600	29,000
1792–93	6	2		500	7,000E
Total catch, South Atlantic					
1784–85	4	3	14E	562	3,200
1785–86	2	1	5	293	2,500
1786–87	3	3	34E	1,786	13,650
1787–88	13	11	134.8	7,092	68,800
1788–89	10	10	136.5	5,372	61,500
1789–90	16	16	228.6	10,531	78,726
1790–91	3	3	[50E]	2,150	26,500
1791–92	13	12	[270E]	12,866	132,000
	64	59 92.2%	871.9	40,652	386,906
1792–93[1]	23	13 56.5%	[206E]	12,280	141,000
1793–94	3	0			
1802–03[2]	2	0			
1803–04[3]	1	0			

III. FRENCH WHALING, MOSTLY IN THE SOUTHERN ATLANTIC FROM 1817 TO 1837

The French Government, hoping for a new revival of whaling, allowed American whalers to come to France again, after the fall of Napoleon. The most important shipowner for whaling from 1817 to 1830 was Jeremiah Winslow (1780–1858) fitting out up to 8 whalers yearly from Le Havre.

Table 8 gives the number of whalers sailing each year from 1817 to 1868.

Table 9 gives the approximate number of whales and barrels of oil taken annually in the South Atlantic.

Table 7.

Statistics on certain whaling voyages 1787–1792.

		Number of whales				
		Struck	Escaped	Killed and sunk	Saved	% saved
Dauphin	1787–88	42	10	3	29	69.0
Nancy	1787–88	16	5	4	7	43.8
Dunkerque *	1787–88	22	2	6	14	63.6
Favorite *	1789–90	32	9	7.5	15.5	48.5
Judith	1789–90	43	13	3	27	63.0
Harmonie *	1789–90	19	2	1	16	84.2
Dunkerque	1789–90	17	3	6	8	47.0
Hébé	1789–90	32	7	1	25	78.1
Espérance	1789–90	31	6	1	23	74.1
Caton	1791–92	40	13	9	18	45.0
		294	70 23.8%	41.5 14.1%	182.5 62.1%	

* In company with other vessels.

Table 8.

Number of whalers fitted out from French ports. Source: Theirry Du Pasquier, *Les Baleiniers Francais au XIXe siecle*, Grenoble 1982, pp. 232–49.

	Southern fishery	Northern fishery		Southern fishery	Northern fishery		Southern fishery
1817	4	1	1833	33	–	1849	8
1818	15	1	1834	32	–	1850	8
1819	10	4	1835	34	1	1851	8
1820	13	1	1836	34	1	1852	5
1821	8	1	1837	40	1	1853	6
1822	7	1	1838	20	–	1854	7
1823	3	1	1839	31	–	1855	0
1824	7	1	1840	14	–	1856	7
1825	6	–	1841	28	–	1857	4
1826	8	–	1842	13		1858	2
1827	6	–	1843	19		1859	3
1828	8	–	1844	22		1860	2
1829	9	1	1845	10		1861	2
1830	17	3	1846	9		1862	1
1831	13	3	1847	7		1863	2
1832	25	2	1848	2		1864	1

Table 9.

Right whales taken in the South Atlantic.

(1) Including 1 lost. (2) Including 3 lost. (3) Including 2 lost. (4) Including 2 lost. (5) Including 1 lost. Main source: Archives Nationales, Paris, Marine CC[5] 594–595.

	Number of vessels				Catch of which		Barrels of oil
	Brazil bank	African coast	Tristan da Cunha	Total	known	Whales	
1817–18	1	1	–	2	2	60	4,000
1818–19	9	1	–	11	10	105.5	7,743
1819–20	12	–	–	16	15	181	12,813
1820–21	11	1	–	14	14	174	11,791
1821–22	6	1	–	9	9	118	7,482
1822–23	5.5	1.5	–	8	8	96	6,234
1823–24	5	2	–	7	7	109.5	7,705
1824–25	6	–	–	6	6	88.5	5,787
1825–26	5	–	–	9	9	210	12,951
1826–27	5	–	–	5	5	126	10,176
1827–28	7	–	–	7	7	115.5	8,229
1828–29	8	–	–	8	7	98.5	7,948
1829–30	7	–	–	7	7	131	11,831
1830–31	8	1.5	0.5	10	8	152	12,113
1831–32	4	1.5	5.6	11 (1)	8	188	13,831
1832–33	3.5	7	3.5	14 (2)	10	203	9,781
1833–34	7	12	6	26 (3)	21	226	16,577
1834–35	8	16	6	30 (4)	24	177.5	22,205
1835–36	9.5	4.5	1	12	7	71.5	5,359
1836–37	5	4.5	0.5	10	8	76.5	4,875
1837–38	0.5	2	0.5	3 (5)	1	9.5	660
				225	193	3,604	200,193

Plate I. Whaling scenes by Garnerey and Morel-Fatio, both eye-witnesses of whaling during the first half of the 19th century.

The ships used to fish from approximately September to May–June, and generally return after one whaling season. Sometimes, they did not succeed in filling the hold, especially when the crews were not very skilled, and after a call on one of the harbours of the South American coast, or at Capetown, they made a second cruise. In that case, the vessel is included in our statistics for two successive years. When the document does not give an account of the whales taken in each of the two successive seasons of a whaler, we have included one half of the whales and barrels of oil in each year.

In most cases we have been able to isolate the number of right whales from sperm whales taken. Although a few sperm whales may have been included in certain years, this cannot represent a great number as we have estimated that sperm whales comprised less than 10% of the total catch of French whalers.

For most campaigns some or all of the following data are available: number of whales, barrels of oil, kilograms of oil, kilograms of whalebone. If one of these indicators is missing, it has been estimated by comparison with other vessels of the same period. For instance, if only the number of barrels is known, the number of whales was estimated by taking the average number of barrels per whale for other vessels in the same year. Kilograms have been converted into barrels with about 100 kilograms net for a barrel.

It is interesting to see where the vessels went whaling in the South Atlantic. Table 9 indicates, when known, in which South Atlantic ground they went cruising. If in the same season they visited two different regions – for instance Brazil Bank and then the African coast – they have been put half on each ground.

At the beginning, from 1817 to 1830, the Brazil Banks were mostly visited. After 1831, for a few years, the waters around Tristan da Cunha, then again the African coast were highly frequented.

Later, many ships looked for whales on the Brazil Bank, and not finding many, went to the Pacific via Cape Horn. For instance, the *Bourbon* in 1835–36 caught 6 right whales on the Brazil Bank, then went to the Pacific, where she took 16 more whales. The *Courrier des Indes* (1836–1837) took only one whale on Brazil Bank, and then went to the coast of Chile. Several ships whaling unsuccessfully on the African coast would also go to the Indian Ocean. The table includes only ships known to have *caught* whales in the South Atlantic, although 3 more crossed these exhausted fields in 1834–35, 8 in 1835–36 and 7 in 1836–37. Others went directly to the Pacific without trying to take whales on the Brazil Bank.

In 1834–35 the French Navy sent the corvette *Circé*, especially to assist the whalers in the South Atlantic. She met 15 of them on the coast of Africa and around Tristan da Cunha.

The following year (1835–1836), another Navy corvette, the *Héroine* went in the same region, but met only 6 French whalers learning that most of them went to Chile. The commander Cécille wrote in his report:

For several years these regions have been exploited by a number of fishermen. The whales, overchased, and partly destroyed, leave these latitudes where they are no more quiet, for more calm regions.

Several years ago, one had to be cautious to go around Tristan in a boat, as there were such a great number of whales in the seaweeds surrounding this island. Then, within three to four months, a fisherman would load his vessel. Last year, one hundred whales were still taken around that island. This year, I saw only two, taken in a fortnight. It is exactly the same in the bays of the African coast.[1]

Thus, the right whales were not fished in the South Atlantic by French whalers after 1837.

It is interesting to compare the captures of the period 1784–1793 and of 1817–1837. One has to know that the vessels used prior to the French Revolution were smaller, with usually a crew of 22 or 23 men, with three whaleboats, whereas after 1817, the usual crew was around 30, with four whaleboats.

The average catch of a ship for a season was 14 whales for the first period and 18 for the second, but only 9 or 10 each season after 1834–35, which shows whales were becoming scarce.

For 48 of the campaigns between 1821 and 1837, we know the number of whales that were harpooned but could not be saved, whether because the harpoon did not hold, the line broke, or because the whale sunk after killed, or was lost after being killed, due to bad weather. 942 whales were saved, from a total of 1,330 struck, which makes a percentage of 70.8%, not very different from the 62.1% of the period 1784–1793.

[1] Archives Nationales, Marine BB⁴ 569.

In certain cases, whalers would have the good luck to find a dead whale. We have no complete statistics, but it is usually represented by only one or two whales for a campaign, or even zero. These dead whales should in most cases be deducted from the whales struck and lost, but the figures are too small to be really meaningful.

The catch of about 3,600 whales, by 86.5% of the vessels should make a total catch of over 4,100 whales. If we apply the same percentage of 14% whales killed that were not processed, we arrive at a total removal of over 4,700 right whales in 20 years by the French whalers.

During this period, the 'Northern' whale fishery continued sporadically, and with very low results.

A new ruling in 1829, followed by a law in 1832 favoured a new development of French whaling, with the greatest number of whalers being reached in 1837 with 41 vessels sailing and 55 already at sea.

IV. NEW WHALING GROUNDS (1837–1868)

(a) Coast of Chile

For several years, the French whalers went to the coast of Chile. Table 10 gives the number of whalers in the Pacific, with a rough estimate of right whale captures, mostly from 1832 to 1837. The vessels also sometimes fished in the Brazil Bank and around the Falkland Islands. A campaign would usually last around 18 months, with calls in different ports of this coast.

The figures in this table are only rough estimates, because each report was not analyzed in detail, and for many voyages it was considered that all whales were taken in the Pacific, although a few might have been taken in the South Atlantic. The whalers sailing one year were usually fishing the following year in the Pacific. Thus we can see from this table that the peak was attained after 1835, when whales were disappearing in the South Atlantic.

Table 10.

Rough estimate of right whales taken on the coast of Chile, 1817–1837 Notes: (1) Including 1 lost; (2) Including 1 lost; (3) Including 1 lost; (4) Including 2 lost; (5) Including 3 lost and 1 condemned; (6) 13 more whales called in Chilean ports, but their main whaling ground was New Zealand. Main source: Archives Nationales, Paris, Marine CC⁵ 594–595.

Year of sailing	Number of vessels	Catch of which is known	Whales	Barrels of oil
1817	1	1	31	1,937
1818	1	0	?	?
1819–23	0	–	–	–
1824	2	2	51E	2,500E
1825	1	0	?	?
1826	3	3	10	750E
1827	1	0	?	?
1828	0	–	–	–
1829	2	1	8	670E
1830	6	2	40	2,941E
1831	4 (1)	4	96	7,300E
1832	11 (2)	9	241E	15,900E
1833	5	5	69	4,500E
1834	12 (3)	11	416E	25,010
1835	21 (4)	19	515E	32,776E
1836	25 (5)	21	536E	35,940E
1837	13 (6)	13	298	18,400E
1841	3	3	46	3,500
1845–48	1	1	24E	1,261
	112	95 (84.8%)	2,372	153,385

Table 11.

Number of vessels (n) whaling near Southern Australia, Tasmania and New Zealand.

Year of sailing	n	Rough estimate of catch		Year of sailing	n	Rough estimate of catch	
		Whales	Barrels of oil			Whales	Barrels of oil
1835	2	85	4,210	1840	13 (1)	392	25,583
1836	2	89	5,005	1841	27 (2)	756	52,235
1837	24	901	55,904	1842	8 (3)	–	–
1838	19	582	36,155	1943	9 (3)	–	–
1839	30	1,066	68,688				

(1) Including one ship lost, catch unknown, and one vessel that fished both to New Zealand and in the North East, that took 19 whales, yielding 1,900 barrels. (2) Including 5 vessels that fished both around New Zealand and North of the Equator. Their total catch was 130 whales and 12,274 barrels. It we deduct the catch of these 5 ships, the catch of the 22 others was 626 whales and 39,961 barrels. The catch of one ship is unknown. (3) Figures for the following years are not meaningful, as most whalers also went to the North Pacific. Main source: Archives Nationales, Paris, Marine CC⁵ 595, 611.

(b) New Zealand, Southern Australia and Tasmania

Two ships, the *Mississippi* and the *Asia*, sailing in 1835 went to New Zealand via the Cape of Good Hope, and returned by Cape Horn with a full cargo. After this date, many French ships went to these new fields (see Table 11). They may also have captured a few whales on the coast of Chile, on the return trip. One of the reasons why French whalers went to New Zealand is that the master of a whaler purchased from the natives the Banks Peninsula, and the French Government stationed a Navy corvette from 1837 to 1846 at Akaroa, to protect a colony developing there. The French claim to sovereignty was later left to Britain. A complete study of each report would allow the determination of how many whales were caught each year in each region of this part of the world: South Indian Ocean, bays of South Australia, Tasmania, Chatham Islands, but mostly New Zealand in different bays and especially the bays of Banks Peninsula.

(c) Northern Pacific, Japan Sea, Okhotsk Sea, Arctic Ocean, Lower California (1842–1868)

In 1842, French whalers began to go to the northeast (Kodiak ground), calling at Honolulu, and soon after discovered the right and bowhead whales in the Sea of Okhotsk. Most of the whalers mentioned in New Zealand in 1842 and 1843 went also North of the Equator. The campaigns became longer and longer, with many successive cruises, and would last up to four years. The main ports of call were Honolulu, Sydney and Hong Kong. After 1849, whales were also fished in the Arctic.

It is more difficult to make statistics for this latest period, as it is not always known how many whales were taken in each cruise and often we only have an aggregate number for the whole campaign. No difference is usually made between right whales and bowheads, but it can be seen from the average number of barrels yielded by the whales that a great percentage of the captures were bowheads.[2] A few humpback whales and perhaps gray whales were also taken. The number of sperm whales in each cargo is usually known, as there was a special bonus on sperm oil, after 1841.

Although they received high bounties, the shipowners found it less and less profitable to send whalers. The economic crisis of 1848, and later the Crimean war accelerated the decline of the industry, and the last whaler was the *Winslow*, returning to Le Havre in 1868.

CONCLUSION

I have arrived at an estimate of about 11,000 right whales and bowheads taken by French whalers all over the world from 1817 to 1868. Considering the high number of American vessels employed for the whale fishery, French whalers were no longer an important factor in whaling after 1850.

The only periods and parts of the world where they had a significant impact on the stock of whales were in the South Atlantic from 1784 to 1793 and 1817 to 1837, the coast of Chile from 1833 to 1838, and New Zealand from 1837 to 1843.

[2] Thierry Du Pasquier, *Les baleiniers français au XIXᵉ siècle 1814–1868* p. 183.

Catches of Right Whales from Shore-based Establishments in Southern Africa, 1792–1975

PETER B. BEST[1]

Mammal Research Institute, University of Pretoria, Pretoria, South Africa

AND GRAHAM J. B. ROSS

Port Elizabeth Museum, Port Elizabeth, South Africa

ABSTRACT

From a combination of historical catch records and production figures, the total number of right whales landed in shore-based open boat whaling along the southern African coast between 1792 and 1912 is estimated as 1,580. Assuming a figure of 20% for the proportion of whales struck and lost that subsequently died, the total mortality inflicted by this fishery is estimated as 1,896. Modern whaling in the coastal waters of southern Africa accounted for at least 105 right whales between 1908 and 1975. The catch in both episodes of whaling was comprised mainly of adults, amongst which females predominated. An assessment of the pelagic catch of right whales from this stock by eighteenth and nineteenth century whalers is needed before original levels of abundance can be estimated.

INTRODUCTION

Shore-based whaling began in South Africa in about 1792 and continued more or less without interruption until 1975. For the first 116 years of this exploitation the principal target of the whalers was the southern right or black whale (*Eubalaena australis*).

In this paper an attempt is made to compile all known captures of right whales made by shore-based establishments in southern Africa (i.e. Africa south of the equator), and to estimate the size of these catches where direct evidence does not exist. A brief catch history for South Africa from 1789 to 1909 has already been published (Best, 1970), and this is revised and extended to cover modern whaling in southern Africa.

'Shore-based establishments' have been taken as including factory ships moored or operating in inshore waters in the early years of the modern fishery, but no attempt has been made to estimate the size of the (apparently) substantial catches made by the open-boat pelagic whalers from America, Britain, France, etc., that operated on and off the coast of southern Africa from about 1770 to the early 1900s (Best, 1970; 1981).

MATERIALS AND METHODS

Besides specific publications, the following general data sources were consulted: relevant abbreviations used in the text are placed in square brackets.

1. *Cape of Good Hope Blue Book and Statistical Registers, 1821–1909* Cape Archives [CO 5963–6053] From 1828 to 1848 this publication lists (at least partially) numbers of stations operating and numbers of whales landed each year; the species involved and their value are also sometimes included. Data on the amount of whalebone and/or whale oil produced in the Colony and exported and its value are given annually from 1822 to 1909.

2. (i) *Ledgers of imports under countries, 1809–1823* Public Records Office, Kew, England [CUST 4]

(ii) *Ledgers of imports under articles, 1792–1809* Public Records Office, Kew, England [CUST 5]

These compilations list total quantities of 'oil, train, not blubber or spermaceti of British fishery' and 'whale fins' (and their value) imported into Great Britain from the Cape of Good Hope. Data are missing for 1813 in CUST 4, and for 1793–1799, 1801–1805 and 1808 in CUST 5.

3. *Bills of Entry (A) Ships' reports 1817–1822* [ENT A] *Bills of Entry (B) Imports, Exports 1817–1822* [ENT B] Customs House, London

Daily reports of ships entering and clearing from London (and some other ports). Manifest of each vessel listed separately in Bill (A), giving countries visited. In Bill (B) exports and imports summarised daily under article, giving country of origin (e.g. Cape of Good Hope). Quantities usually given more accurately in Bill (A), e.g. 'A parcel', or 'A quantity' in Bill (B) frequently given as casks or lb in Bill (A). Bill (B) not available for 1820.

4. (i) *Archives of the Controller of Customs, Cape Colony: Import and Export papers, 1795–1816* Cape Archives [CCT 374]

(ii) *Archives of the Controller of Customs, Cape Colony: Import and Export papers, 1816–1827* Cape Archives [CCT 375]

Compilation of ships' manifests for vessels arriving at and departing from Table and Simons Bays. Very incomplete, with (*inter alia*) no data for June 1797 – December 1810 and March 1819 – March 1827.

5. *Fairbridge Index* 62:57–81 Cape Archives [FI] Chronology of whale occurrences, catches, etc. compiled by a journalist, Mr Charles Aken Fairbridge, for his personal use. Items recorded as handwritten notes on reference cards. Sometimes difficult to interpret abbreviations and/or handwriting. This has been used as reference when the original sources could not be checked.

6. *Whales and whaling. Cape Colony – analysis of statistics* 1918, 1920, 1922–29, 1937 [HSC] Unpublished statistics of whale catches from land stations in the Cape Colony compiled by Sir Sidney Harmer and lodged in the British Museum (Natural History). These analyses list the species, length, sex, date

[1] Postal address: c/o South African Museum, Box 61, Cape Town, South Africa.

of capture and name of catcher boat for each whale landed for those companies that sent in returns. Foetal lengths and sexes are also given in some cases.

7. *Whales and whaling. Natal – analysis of statistics 1918, 1920, 1922–28* [HSN]
Unpublished statistics of whale catches from land stations in Natal compiled by Sir Sidney Harmer and lodged in the British Museum (Natural History). Similar records to those in 6 above.

8. *Natal Fisheries Department. Annual Reports* for 1913–16, 1918–23, 1925–33 [NFD]
These include summaries of the numbers of whaling companies operating each year, the numbers of vessels and persons employed, the number of whales captured, the amount of oil, whalebone, fertiliser, boiled bone and whale finners produced and their value. Summaries are also given of the numbers of each species landed by sex, the maximum (sometimes minimum) and mean lengths of each species and their mean oil yields. A short report on the industry is also given.

9. *Cape Provincial Administration Nature Conservation Department files*, 1904–1930 Cape Archives [PAN]
Volumes 45–52, 83–84 include correspondence and statistics concerning the establishment, regulation, catch and production of the whaling industry in the Cape Province (including Walvis Bay).

10. *Thesen's Company Records*
The firm H. W. Thesen & Co of Knysna acted as agents for Harald Haarfarge Whaling Co., Plettenberg Bay, and also had a commercial interest in Hans Ellefsen Co. Ltd., Salamander Bay. Amongst the company records examined at Knysna the most important sources were:
(a) General Letter Books [TLB]
Outgoing correspondence from the Knysna office of Thesen and Co. Ltd contained in 58 volumes with separate index (compiled by T. P. Willis in 1968). Searched volumes 35 to 58 (covering 29 May 1907 to 30 June 1917), using index as far as volume 40 (ending 28 November 1911) but page-by-page thereafter.
(b) 'Shipping Clerk' Diaries [TD]
Handwritten entries on shipping movements in and out of Knysna, etc., contained in 37 diaries for 1878–83, 1887–89, 1892–3, 1895–1918, and 1924 (two for 1913). Not searched but important entries re whalers given in Willis' index (see above) checked and diaries consulted where index did not help.

11. *International Whaling Statistics* [BIWS]
Volumes published annually or biannually since 1930 by the Committee for Whaling Statistics, Oslo, containing details of whaling materials, catches and production worldwide.

12. *The following newspapers were also consulted:*
Luderitzbuchter Zeitung, 1913–14 [LZ]
Mossel Bay Advertiser, May to November 1907–10; May 1911 to January 1914 [MBA]
Natal Pictorial Mercury, 1905–1914 [NPM]
Eastern Province Herald, 1845–1897, June to Oct 1898–1905 [EPH]
Cape Times, 1907–1910, May to November only [CT]

References to other newspapers are given as follows:
Cape Argus [CA]
Cape Argus Weekly [CAW]
Cape Chronicle [CC]
Cape of Good Hope Government Gazette [CGHG]
Cape Monitor [CM]

Cape Mercantile Advertiser [CMA]
Cape Standard [CS]
Cape Times Weekly [CTW]
Cape Town Mail [CTM]
Cape Weekly Chronicle [CWC]
Graham's Town Journal [GJ]
King William's Town Gazette and Kaffrarian Banner [KWTG]
South African Commercial Advertiser [SACA]
Cape of Good Hope and Port Natal Shipping & Mercantile Gazette [SMG]

RESULTS

Shore-based whaling in southern Africa fell into two main categories. From about 1792 to 1912, whaling took place using open boats and hand-held implements (Fig. 1), while modern whaling (using Norwegian-type steam catchers with mounted harpoon guns) began in 1908 and lasted till 1975. The statistics for open-boat and modern whaling are considered separately. Towards the end of the open-boat whaling era, and before modern whaling proper began, some 'intermediate' technology was adopted, including the use of small, mounted harpoon guns and some powered craft such as launches (EPH 18.10.1893, 12.8.1896). Catches of such operations have been included with those of the open boat whalers.

Open-boat whaling

There is some confusion over the year in which organised shore-based whaling began on the South African coast. One early account states 'omtrent (about) 1780' (Anon, 1827), while another states 'about the year 1791' (Memorial from P. L. Cloete to the Governor at the Cape of Good Hope, September 1806 – Cape Archives no. CO 3859). Most recent authors (e.g. Best, 1970; de Jong, 1967) have followed the information contained in a letter from the Governor of the Cape to the Colonial Secretary (dated 15 June 1807) that

...about the year 1789 two Merchants of the Cape, Messrs Fehrson and Truter, began under the sanction of Government to kill Whales.

A statement from Truter enclosed with this letter gives the commencement as 'about the Year 1788 or 89' (Theal, 1900).

Capture of a "Right Whale."

Fig. 1. Capture of a right whale by open-boat whalers in Simon's Bay, date unknown (from Gillard, 1910).

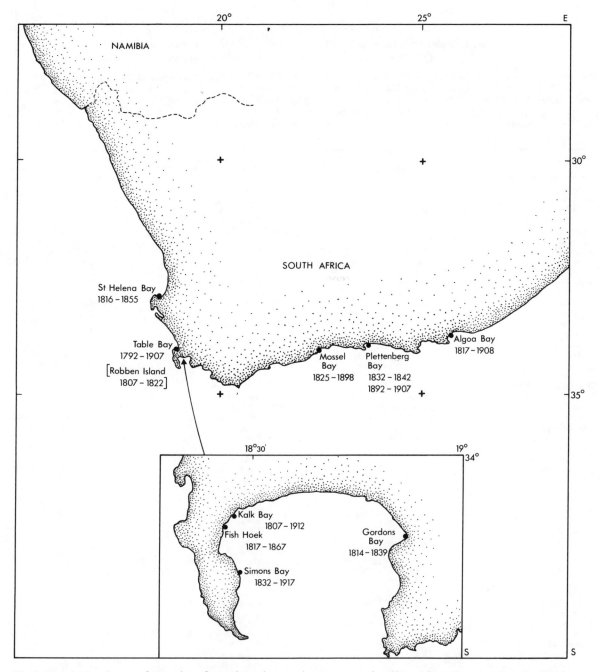

Fig. 2. Locations and years of operation of open-boat shore stations on coast of southern Africa. Some locations (e.g. Table Bay, Algoa Bay) may include a number of different stations in close proximity. Years shown indicate catches of first and last whales where known, and may not adequately reflect duration of effort.

However, Hendrik Johannes Fehrsen applied for (and received) permission to land and try-out right whales on the shores of Table, False (Simon's) and Saldanha Bay on 11 October 1791 (Cape Archives no. C 197), and from a subsequent letter to the Commissioners General Nederburg and Frykenius dated 31 July 1792 it seems that Fehrsen only began to build or acquire suitable boats and equipment for the fishery after October 1791. By July 1792 he had taken three whales (presumably in the 1792 season) the smallest of which gave six leggers of oil (Cape Archives no. C 675). We have therefore adopted this latter date (1792) as representing the onset of organised shore-based whaling at the Cape.

Operations were confined to Table Bay until 1807, when another establishment began at Kalk Bay. Thereafter stations opened at Gordons Bay (1814), St Helena Bay (1816), Algoa Bay and Fish Hoek (1817),

Mossel Bay (*ca.* 1825), Simons Town and Plettenberg Bay (1832) (Chapman, 1977; de Jong, 1967; Holman, 1834; Cape Almanac, 1833). Brief episodes of locally-based pelagic whaling also occurred in 1816/17 (brig *Good Hope*), 1831, 1834 (brig *Calypso*), and 1845/46 (bark *Vigilant*), and as these usually operated along the South African coast, their catches have been included here where known. To the best of our knowledge, no other shore-based open-boat whaling took place on the coast of southern Africa (Fig. 2). A record catch of 76 whales was supposedly achieved in 1817 (Anon, 1827). During most of this development and expansion, catch statistics are poor and definitely incomplete (Table 1).

This is particularly so for the earliest years of whaling.

[*Text continues on p. 280*]

Table 1.

Landed catches reported in open-boat whaling along the South African coast, 1792–1917
(figures within square brackets are included in preceding data).

[1]Another two struck and lost. [2]One other possibly struck and lost 29 Sep 1858. [3]One whale struck and lost 24 Aug 1862. [4]One whale struck and lost same day.[5]Whale struck and let go, spurting blood, 1 Oct (EPH 8 Oct). [6]Whale killed and anchored but lost (EPH 18 Jul). [7]Whale struck and line parted, 23 Jun (EPH 25 Jun), [8] Whale struck and cut loose, 1 whale killed and sank, 30 Aug (EPH 3 Sep). [9]Whale struck and broke loose (EPH 21 Jun). [10]Whale struck by boats from Simon's Town 10 Jul but harpoon drew (EPH 16 Jul). [11]Gave 600 gals oil and 90 lb bone. [12]In addition 1 right bull killed 26 Sep but lost. [13]Gave 1,200 gals oil and 360 lb bone. [14]One of these 43–44 ft female in PE Museum collection. [15]CA.

Year	Locality/ Owner	Number landed	Date of capture	Date of report	Notes and source	Year	Locality/ Owner	Number landed	Date of capture	Date of report	Notes and source
1792	Table Bay	14	–	–	(See text)	1833	George distr.	4	–	–	£1,000. (CO 5975)
1793	Table Bay	14	–	–	(See text)		[Mossel Bay]	[1]	–	15 Jun	SACA.
1794	Table Bay	14	–	–	(See text)		[Plett. Bay]	[1]	–	13 Jul	Gave 2,100 gals oil. (SACA)
1795	Table Bay	14	–	–	(See text)		Algoa Bay	21	–	–	£3,150. (CO 5975)
1796	Table Bay	14	–	–	(See text)	1834	Table Bay	5	–	–	Black whales, £1,000. (CO 5976)
1797	Table Bay	14	–	–	(See text)		"Calypso"	1	–	–	Black whale. Also 30 tons sperm oil. (CO 5976)
1798	Table Bay	22	–	–	(See text)						
1799	Table Bay	22	–	–	(See text)		Kalk Bay	7	–	–	£900. (CO 5976)
1800	Table Bay	22	–	–	(See text)		Mossel Bay	1	–	–	£200. (CO 5976)
1801	Table Bay	22	–	–	(See text)		Algoa Bay	9	–	–	£1,350. (CO 5976)
1802	Table Bay	22	–	–	(See text)	1835	Kalk Bay	4	–	–	£480. (CO 5977)
1803	Table Bay	43	–	–	Anon (1827)		Algoa Bay	3	–	–	Chase (1843)
1804	Table Bay	39	–	–	Theal (1900)	1836	Table Bay	4	–	–	£1,200. (CO 5978)
1805	Table Bay	11	–	–	Theal (1900)		Kalk Bay	7	–	–	Black whales–£350. (CO 5978)
1806	Table Bay	19	–	–	Theal (1900)		George dist.	2	–	–	£300. (CO 5978)
1810	Simons Bay	16	–	3 Sep	Prior (1820)		Algoa Bay	5	–	–	£660. (CO 5978)
1812	False Bay	21	–	–	15–18 leaguers oil per whale. Value 50Rds /£12 per leaguer. (Crowe, unpub.)	1837	Table Bay	3	–	–	£900. (CO 5979)
							Simonstown	4	–	–	£1,000. (CO 5979)
1817	Cape Colony	76	–	–	Anon (1827)		Gordons Bay	1	–	–	£200. (CO 5979)
1818	Simons Bay	25	–	–	Chapman (1977)		Mossel Bay	1	–	–	£150. (CO 5979)
1819	Algoa Bay	9	–	–	Chase (1843)	1838	Table Bay	4	–	–	£1,000. (CO 5980)
1820	Algoa Bay	20	–	–	Chase (1843)		Simonstown	2	–	–	Black whales, £300. (CO 5980)
1821	Cape Colony	37	–	–	Bird (1823)		Gordons Bay	1	–	–	£150. (CO 5980)
	[Algoa Bay]	[12]	–	–	Chase (1843)		Algoa Bay	5	–	–	3 valued at £612. (CO 5980; Chase, 1843)
1822	Algoa Bay	8	–	–	Chase (1843)						
1823	Algoa Bay	12	–	–	Chase (1843)	1839	Table Bay	4	–	–	£800. (CO 5981)
1824	St Helena Bay	7	–	–	Thompson (1827)		Simonstown	4	–	–	Black whales, £600. (CO 5981)
	Algoa Bay	6	–	–	Chase (1843)		Gordons Bay	1	–	–	£150. (CO 5981)
1827	Algoa Bay	3	–	–	Chase (1843)		Algoa Bay	1	–	–	Chase (1843)
1828	Table Bay	3	–	–	CO 5970	1840	Cape Division	3	–	–	Black whales, £450. (CO 5982)
	St Helena Bay	1	–	–	CO 5970		Algoa Bay	3	–	–	£450. (CO 5982)
	Simons Bay	4	–	–	Holman (1834)	1841	Table Bay/				
	Mossel Bay	2	–	–	Holman (1834)		Robben Island	5	–	–	CO 5983
	Algoa Bay	6	–	–	Chase (1843)		Cape Division	2	–	–	Black whales. (CO 5983)
1829	Table Bay	6	–	–	£1,500. One cow & calf. (CO 5972; Holman, 1834)		Mossel Bay	1	–	–	Black whale, £150. (CO 5983)
							Algoa Bay	4	–	–	Chase (1843)
	Simons Bay	18	–	–	£4,000. (CO 5972)		[Algoa Bay]	[1]	3 Aug	12 Aug	Very large. (GJ)
	[Fish Hoek] (Thwaites)	[6–7]	–	15 Jun	SACA		(Chase)				
	Mossel Bay	5	–	–	£650. (CO 5972)	1842	Table Bay/				
	Algoa Bay	18	–	–	£3,500. (CO 5972)		Robben Island	1	–	–	£300. (CO 5984)
1830	Table Bay	3	–	–	2 valued at £500. (FI 62: 62; CO 5973)		Cape Division	4	–	–	Black whales. (CO 5984)
							Mossel Bay	1	–	–	Black whale. (CO 5984)
	Simons Bay	20	–	–	£5,000. (CO 5973)		Plett. Bay	1	–	–	Black whale. (CO 5984)
	[Fish Hoek]	[9]	–	9 Oct	SACA		Algoa Bay	1	–	–	£150. (CO 5984)
	[Kalk Bay]	[3]	–	9 Oct	SACA	1843	Table Bay/				
	Mossel Bay	8	–	9 Oct	6 valued at £780. (SACA; CO 5973)		Robben Island	2	–	–	CO 5985.
							Cape Division	2	–	–	Black whales. (CO 5985)
	Algoa Bay	15	–	–	£2,820. (CO 5973)		[Kalk Bay]	[2]	–	–	Right whales. (Chapman, 1977)
1831	Table Bay	4	–	– ⎤	£1,350. (CO 5974)	1844	Table Bay/				
	"Calypso"	2	–	– ⎦			Robben Island	1	–	–	CO 5986.
	Kalk Bay	10 ⎤			£2,250. (CO 5974)		Cape Division	1	–	–	Black whale. (CO 5986)
	Fish Hoek	⎦					Mossel Bay	1	–	–	CO 5986.
	St Helena Bay	4	–	–	£900. (CO 5974)	1845	Kalk Bay	1	–	–	Black whale. (CO 5987)
	Mossel Bay	14	–	–	£3,150. (CO 5974)		Mossel Bay ("Vigilant")	4	–	–	CO 5987.
	Algoa Bay	12	–	–	9 valued at £2,025 (CO 5974; Chase, 1843)		George dist.	2	–	–	£300. (CO 5987)
							Algoa Bay	3	>4 Oct	25 Oct	First for 2 years. (CTM)
1832	Cape Colony	59	–	–	GH 23/10.	1846	Algoa Bay	2	–	–	£300. (CO 5988)
	[Kalk Bay]	[16]⎤	–	–	Cape Almanac, 1833.		"Vigilant"	3	–	–	CO 5988.
	[Fish Hoek]	⎦				1847	Cape Town	2	–	–	CO 5989.
	[Plettenberg Bay]	[5]	–	–	Cape Almanac, 1833.	1848	Cape Town	4	–	–	CO 5990.
	[Algoa Bay]	[12]	–	–	Cape Almanac, 1833.		Algoa Bay	1	30 Aug	2 Sep	£100 (CO 5990; EPH)
	[Algoa Bay] (Daniel)	[1]	30 Jun	6 Jul	GJ.	1851	Table Bay (Granger)	1[1]	26 Jul	31 Jul	Fine – £200. (CM)
	[Algoa Bay] (Korsten)	[1]	1 Jul	6 Jul	Cow. (GJ)		Simons Bay	1	15 Jul	31 Jul	CM
	[Algoa Bay]	[1]	1 Jul	6 Jul	Killer whale. Attacked calf of above whale – chunks of blubber found in gut. (GJ)		Table Bay (Granger)	2	–	15 Aug	CM
						1853	Simons Bay (Hoets)	1	–	30 Jul	Fine. (CM)
1833	Cape Town/						(Miller)	1	–	30 Jul	CM
	Cape District	15	–	–	£2,505. (CO 5975)		Table Bay (Granger)	1	26 Aug	3 Sep	Large–caught off Hout Bay. (CM)
	[Table Bay]	[3]	–	15 Jun	SACA.		Algoa Bay (Sterley)	1	29 Sep	8 Oct	CM.
	[Gordons Bay]	[1]	15 Jun	15 Jun	SACA		Algoa Bay	1	2 Oct	3 Oct	EPH.

Year	Locality/Owner	Number landed	Date of capture	Date of report	Notes and source
1854	Table Bay (Granger)	1	5 Sep	8 Sep	Large. (CGHG)
	Mossel Bay	1	1 Sep	8 Sep	Fine. (CGHG)
	Malmesbury district	1	-	-	CO 5996.
1855	St Helena Bay (Mclachlan & Bass)	1	3 Jun	-	Sulphurbottom 94ft yielded 25 leagues oil value £500. (FI 62:67)
	Mossel Bay	1	-	27 Jul	Large. (SMG)
	Kalk Bay (Zeeman/Hoets)	2	22 Jul	27 Jul	One 60-70ft est. 20 leaguers value £400, other small est. 6-7 leaguers. (SMG)
	Table Bay (Granger)	1	13 Aug	17 Aug	CGHG
1856	Cape Town	7	-	-	CO 5998.
	[Table Bay]	[1]	24 Aug	29 Aug	Black whale. Gave 1 ton. (SMG)
	[Table Bay] (Granger)	[1]	19 Sep	26 Sep	SMG
	Kalk Bay (Granger)	2	8 Jun	13 Jun	Right; "Fine". (SMG)
	Simons Bay (Hoets)	1	-	3 Oct	FI 62:69
	False Bay	1	3 Oct	10 Oct	Right. "Finest bull ever taken in that quarter". Expected yield 18-20 leagues oil. (SMG)
1857	Table Bay (Granger)	1	11 Jul	14 Jul	Right bull. (EPH)
	Table Bay (Granger/Roe)	1	26 Sep	30 Sep	CA
1858	Kalk Bay (Zeeman)	1	19 Aug	19 Aug	CA
	Algoa Bay	2[2]	28 Sep	29 Sep	Cow and calf. (EPH)
1859	Table Bay (W. Johnston)	1	29 Jul	5 Aug	Predicted value £300. (CWC)
1861	Algoa Bay	1	-	14 Jun	Young - ca. 28ft. (EPH)
	Algoa Bay	1	-	11 Oct	EPH
	Algoa Bay	1	11 Oct	18 Oct	EPH
1862	Algoa Bay	1	<7 Oct	11 Jul	Good, fat - oil est. £150. (CC)
	Algoa Bay (Watts)	2	11 Oct	14 Oct	Large cow and well grown calf. (EPH)
1863	Kalk Bay (M. Zeeman)	1	21 Jul	27 Jul	40ft long, 12ft broad. 1st whale at Kalk Bay for 3 or 4 yrs. Est. 10-12 leaguers. (CA)
	Table Bay (J. Zeeman)	1	1 Aug	4 Aug	36ft, blubber 10ins thick (CA)
	Algoa Bay (Watts)	1[3]	ca4 Sep	4 Sep	Calf. (EPH)
	Table Bay (John Roe)	1	7 Oct	8 Oct	Largest ever in Table Bay. (CA)
1864	Kalk Bay (Zeeman)	1	16 Jul	21 Jul	40ft, blubber 8-22ins thick - 12 tons oil. (CA)
	Algoa Bay	1	4 Sep	6 Sep	Large. (EPH)
1865	Simons Bay (Lesar)	1	4 Jul	5 Jul	Fine large. (SAAM)
1866	Algoa Bay (Malays)	1	22 Aug	24 Aug	EPH
	Algoa Bay (Fernandez?)	1	25 Aug	28 Aug	Struck and lost and then washed up dead. (EPH)
1867	Fish Hoek	1	19 Aug	-	Right. (Milner and Brierly, 1869)
	Kalk Bay (Lesar)	1	10 Jul	11 Jul	Fine. (CS)
	Mossel Bay (Munroe)	1	20 Sep	24 Sep	35ft. (CS)
	Algoa Bay (Watts)	2	25 Sep	26 Sep	56ft cow, 26ft calf. (CS)
1868	Table Bay	1	1 Aug	11 Aug	Found dead, apparently killed False Bay. (Black & Budge) (EPH)
	Table Bay	1	-	10 Aug	36ft. (KWTG)
	Mossel Bay (Munroe)	1	31 Jul	7 Aug	Fine. (EPH)
	Mossel Bay (Munroe)	1	-	15 Sep	60ft. (CS)
	Algoa Bay (Watts)	1	5 Aug	7 Aug	56ft bull. (EPH)
1894	("Harry Mundahl")		15 Sep	-	(Humpback. (EPH))
	False Bay	1	-	29 Oct	74ft (Fifth in as many weeks). (EPH)
	Plett. Bay	1	24 Jul	-	Sewell (unpub.)
	Plett. Bay	1	28 Aug	-	Right. (Sewell, unpub.)
	Algoa Bay	1	-	1 Jun	Humpback; Sunk and refloated. (EPH)
	Algoa Bay[7]	2	23 Sep	28 Sep	Right, cow and calf. (EPH)
1869	Algoa Bay (Watts)	1[4]	5 Jul	6 Jul	56ft bull (large cow CMA 12.7.69). (EPH)
	Kalk Bay (van Reenen)	1	26 Jul	-	Large. (FI 62:72)
1871	Mossel Bay (Munroe)	1	10 Aug	18 Aug	ca 50ft. (EPH)
	Algoa Bay (Kemsley)	1	25 Nov	28 Nov	26-28ft. (EPH)
	Algoa Bay	2	-	Dec	FI 62:73
1876	Simons Bay	1	-	29 Aug	Large. (FI 62:73)
1879	Kalk Bay	2	-	-	"Bottlenose whales" locally known as "keelers" - flesh poisonous - 28 people died. (FI 62:73)
1881	Table Bay (Kehoe)	1	3 Oct	4 Oct	"Fully 40ft" cow. (EPH)
1884	Algoa Bay (Malays)	2	28 Jul	29 Jul	Est. 2,000 gals oil, £300 value. (EPH)
	Table Bay	1	-	4 Aug	16ft calf. (FI 62:74)
				11 Aug	"Right" whale - cow escaped (EPH)
1885	Algoa Bay	-	-	2 Sep	One whale struck and lost. (EPH)
1886	Algoa Bay (St Frances)	2	-	9 Aug	Bull and cow. (EPH)
	Algoa Bay (St Frances)	2	-	13 Aug	EPH
1887	Kalk Bay	2	Oct	10 Oct	CMA
	Algoa Bay (Malays)	1	1 Oct	10 Oct	Humpback cow (tail 12ft wide, flippers 14ft long); (Calf (ca 25ft) escaped wounded). (EPH)
1888	Simon's Bay	1	- Aug	-	Right, adult. (Photo in Simonstown Museum, T.T.C. Purland Collection)
	Algoa Bay	2	29 Jun	2 Jul	Bull ca 50ft "Species most prized for oil & bone". (EPH)
	Algoa Bay	1	22 Sep	24 Sep	Cow 54ft 7ins, blubber up to 13in thick, gave 2,000 gals; Calf escaped. (EPH)
1890	Algoa Bay (Searle)	2	31 Jul	4 Aug	Cow and calf; "Cow enormous & of a valuable species". (EPH)
	Algoa Bay (Searle)	2	24 Sep	26 Sep	Cow and calf; "Cow larger than that killed a while ago". (EPH)
1891	Table Bay	1	12 Feb	12 Feb	12ft long calf, 2ins blubber (not in fishery?). (CA)
	Algoa Bay	1	-	27 Jul	EPH
	Algoa Bay	1	9 Aug	10 Aug	EPH
	Algoa Bay	2	10 Aug	12 Aug	Cow and calf. (EPH)
	Algoa Bay	1	20 Oct	21 Oct	EPH
	Algoa Bay	1	24 Oct	26 Oct	Young. (EPH)
	Algoa Bay(?)	1	-	11 Nov	Washed ashore dead Tsitsikama coast with two irons in side; 56ft. (EPH)
1892	Plett. Bay	1	6 Sep	-	Cow of good size. (Sewell, unpub.)
	Plett. Bay	1	5 Oct	-	Landed 10 Oct, 56ft. (Sewell, unpub.)
	Plett. Bay	2	17 Oct	-	Humpbacks, bull and cow. (Sewell, unpub.)
	Algoa Bay	2	7 Aug	8 Aug	Cow and calf; Both sank - recovered(?). (EPH)
1893	Plett. Bay	1	18 Aug	-	Finback. (Sewell, unpub.)
	Plett. Bay	1	25 Sep	-	Humpback, good-sized. (Sewell, unpub.)
	Algoa Bay (Schello & Peel)	1	28 Jul	31 Jul	Cow, ca 55ft; Calf killed and set adrift. (EPH)
	Algoa Bay	1	29 Oct	30 Oct	Black whale. (EPH)
				(2 Nov	Humpback, male. (EPH))
	Algoa Bay	2	1 Nov	2 Nov	Humpback, cow and calf. (EPH)
1894	Table Bay (Kinsley & Morgenrood)	1[5]	2 Mar	7 Mar	22-23ft. (EPH)
	Simonstown	1	24 Aug	29 Aug	Right, cow, 57ft, £1,000 (calf escaped). (CTW)
	Simons Bay	2[6]	13 Sep	15 Sep	CA
1900	Plett. Bay	1	26 Jul	-	Right calf; £120.[10] (Gilchrist, 1901)
	Plett. Bay	1	13 Oct	-	Humpback calf. £9. (Gilchrist, 1901)
	Plett. Bay[11]	1	18 Oct	-	Right bull; £300.[12] (Gilchrist, 1901)
	Simons Bay	1	5 Oct	7 Nov	Right, bull, 42ft. (CTW)
	Algoa Bay	1	11 Oct	13 Oct	Right. (EPH)

Year	Locality/ Owner	Number landed	Date of capture	Date of report	Notes and source	Year	Locality/ Owner	Number landed	Date of capture	Date of report	Notes and source
1895	Plett. Bay	1	10 Aug	–	Right, 1,600 gals oil, 600–700lb bone. (Sewell, unpub.)	1901	Simons Bay	1	15 Sep	–	Right; £200. (Gilchrist, 1902)
	Plett. Bay	1	31 Aug	–	Right, large bull. (Sewell, unpub.)		Kalk Bay	1	15 Oct	–	Right; £400. (Gilchrist, 1902)
	Plett. Bay	1	26 Sep	–	Right, 1,400 gals oil, 600lb bone. (Storrar, 1978)		Plett. Bay	1	18 Sep	–	Humpback; £40. (Gilchrist, 1902)
	Algoa Bay	1	9 Jan	11 Jan	Right, half grown. (EPH)		Algoa Bay	1	– Jul	–	Right; £600. (Gilchrist, 1902)
	Algoa Bay[8]	1	16 Sep	18 Sep	Calf (cow escaped). (EPH)		Algoa Bay[13]	1	– Aug	–	Right; £600. (Gilchrist, 1902)
1896	Plett. Bay	1	–	19 Jul	Sewell (unpub.)		Algoa Bay	1	10 Oct	11 Oct	Right, cow, calf escaped. (EPH)
	Algoa Bay	2	10 Aug	12 Aug	Right, cow and calf. (EPH)		Muizenberg	1	–	9 Oct	Right. (CAW)
1897	Table Bay	1	16 Jun	–	Humpback, 40ft, value £200. (FI 62:77)	1903	Table Bay	1	[17 Sep]	17 Sep]14	Gilchrist (1904)
	Table Bay	1	3 Sep	8 Sep	FI 62:78		Plett. Bay	1	11 Sep	–	Right; £400. (Gilchrist, 1904)
	Simons Bay	1	–	17 Mar	Ca 15ft. (EPH)	1904	Kalk Bay	1	26 Aug	–	Humpback. (Gilchrist, 1906a)
	Simons Bay	1	25 Jun	30 Jun	FI 62:77		Algoa Bay	1	18 Oct	–	Right; £500. (Gilchrist, 1906a)
	Simons Bay	1	16 Oct	20 Oct	Humback ("another"). (FI 62:78)	1905	Kalk Bay	1	25 Aug	–	Humpback; £20. (Gilchrist, 1906b)
	Plett. Bay	1	–	20 Oct	Humpback. Value ca £200. (GKH)		Algoa Bay	1	–	–	Gilchrist (1906b)
	Algoa Bay	1	15 May	19 May	Sperm, large. (FI 62:77)	1906	Simons Bay	1	– Jul	–	Right; £100. (Gilchrist, 1907)
	Algoa Bay	1	12 Oct	13 Oct	Right, 40–50ft. (EPH)		Kalk Bay	1	20 Aug	–	Right; £200. (Gilchrist, 1907)
1898	Kalk Bay[9] (Auret)	1	3 Jun	4 Jun	Right, cow, ca 60ft. Value £800–1,000 (calf escaped). (EPH)	1907	Table Bay	1	22 May	23 May	25ft. (CT)
	Mossel Bay	1	– Oct	–	Humpback, adult. (SAM photo files)		Mossel Bay	1	7 Jul	9 Jul	Right. 50–60ft. Found dead. (MBA)
	Plett. Bay	2	–	–	Right. (Gilchrist, 1899)		Table Bay (Zeeman)	1	12 Aug	13 Aug	Right cow, 60–70ft (calf killed and lost). (CT)
	Plett. Bay	1	–	–	Humpback. (Gilchrist, 1899)		Plett. Bay (Toplis)	1	– Sep	–	Right. (Storrar, 1978)
	Algoa Bay	1	15 Jun	16 Jun	Right. (EPH)	1908	Algoa Bay (Searle)	1	19 Jun	20 Jun	Right. (EPH) (40ft preg.). (NPM 2 July)
				17 Jun	45ft. (EPH)	1912	Muizenberg (Auret)	1	31 Oct		Right, large. (PAN 45 vol.1) (70ft – Anon, 1912)
				15 Jul	Fetched not more than £150. (EPH)	1917	Simons Town (Cotton)	1	12 Jan	–	Pygmy right, 3.39m male. (Ross et al., 1975)
	Algoa Bay	1	14 Jul	15 Jul	Right, 50ft. (EPH)						
	Algoa Bay	1	–	1 Sep	Right, cow, "quite 55ft." Calf killed but not landed. (EPH)						
1900	Simons Bay	1	12 Sep	–	Right; £200. (Gilchrist, 1901)						
	Muizenberg	1	6 Oct	–	Right; £200. (Gilchrist, 1901)						

The catches made by the Fehrsen Company were given as 'from 12 to 16 whales yearly' and '[on average] 12' in unsigned memoranda accompanying a letter from the Earl of Caledon dated 15 June 1807 (Theal, 1900). In an essay undated but believed to have been written in 1795, the statement appears that

> A Whale Fishery was established, some years past, at Cape Town, and though the vessels never went out of Table Bay, they made about 300 Tons of Oil. (Anon., c. 1795).

At an average 1,839 gallons (or 7.3 tons) of oil per whale (see below), this production would be equivalent to a landed catch of about 41 whales. If it is assumed that this was the accumulated production from 1792 to 1794, it would represent an average annual catch of between 13 and 14 whales. This accords with Theal's figures.

There is some suggestion from the remarks of Barrow (1801) and Cloete (Memorial to Governor of the Cape, September 1806; Cape Archives no. CO 3859) that Fehrsen's fishery began to run into difficulties in the late 1790s, forcing the sale to John Murray in 1798 (Theal, 1900). Without any indication of actual catches, however, the average value of 14 whales per year has been carried through from 1792 to 1797.

According to the same source that gave Fehrsen's catches as 12 to 16 yearly, John Murray 'generally caught from 15 to 30' whales per year (Theal, 1900). Initially his catches may have been low. According to the Cape Town Gazette and African Advertiser, 9 January 1802,

> Such a [soap] manufactory would be the means of reviving and encreasing [sic] the whale fishery lately carried on in Table Bay; and which has been relinquished, or nearly so, for no other reason than that of there being no demand for the oil.

In the absence of any definite catch figures, however, a median value of 22 within the given range of 15 to 30 whales has been used.

Specific catches made by Murray are given as 43 for 1803 (Anon, 1827) and 39 for 1804 (Theal, 1900). There is an apparent inconsistency here, for in 1802 the Batavian Republic awarded an exclusive right to whaling in Cape waters to a Dutch company, the Afrikaansche Visscherij Societeit, whose principals and equipment arrived at Cape Town in April 1803, when Murray was obliged to desist from whaling (de Jong, 1967). The Afrikaansche Visscherij Societeit is said to have fished from 1803 to 1805 with indifferent success (Anon, 1827). The source that gave Fehrsen's and Murray's earlier catches states that in their first year (1805) this Society took 11 whales and in their second year 19 (Theal, 1900). In an apparent attempt to reconcile these inconsistencies, de Jong (1967) has attributed Murray's catch of 39 whales to 1802 rather than 1804 and the Afrikaansche Visscherij Societeit's catches of 11 and 19 whales to 1803 and 1804, rather than 1805 and 1806. We have chosen not to follow this approach, as it seems unlikely that the dates could have been so mistaken in a document apparently written in 1807, although we recognize that this does not resolve the inconsistencies.

A description of the Table Bay fishery published in 1806 states that:

> The fishery is rather on the decline; but is still carried on with considerable success. The average fishing of a season is about sixteen whales,...(Anon, 1806).

This figure is close to the average (15) of the annual catches given for the Afrikaansche Visscherij Societeit.

Fig. 3. A right whale landed at Muizenberg in October, 1912 (from Anon, 1912).

Beginning in 1828, details of whaling in the Cape Colony began to appear regularly in the Cape of Good Hope Blue Book (later called Statistical Register), and until 1848 the coverage of annual landings seems adequate. Thereafter catch statistics from this source became irregular and sometimes unreliable (where, for instance, the same number of whales with exactly the same value of production is reported for four successive years). After 1868 they cease altogether.

As there appears to be no comprehensive and reliable set of catch statistics from 1849 to 1899, reliance has had to be placed on press reports. In several cases it has been possible to confirm the consistency of these reports from similar entries in different newspapers, but their accuracy (in terms of the real number of whales landed) remains unknown.

From 1900 to 1906 regular compilations of catch statistics were resumed and appeared in the Annual Reports of the Government Biologist (Gilchrist, 1901–1904; 1906–1907).

From 1907 catch statistics were no longer compiled for the open-boat fishery, so press reports have again been the only source available. They have been searched as far as 1910 for reports of catches in the last years of open-boat whaling.

The last capture of a right whale in this fishery that we have been able to trace occurred in 1912 (Fig. 3), but this obviously did not mark the end of the fishery. A pygmy right whale was harpooned off Simons Town in 1917, and Irvin and Johnson's factory at Donkergat purchased two whales 'caught in the vicinity of False Bay' in 1919 (PAN 48). The last recorded attempt to catch a whale using open boats probably occurred in August 1929, when a whale in False Bay was pursued by two boats from Kalk Bay in an endeavour to harpoon and kill it. The whale escaped, but all involved in the hunt were warned by the police that a licence was needed to pursue or kill whales (PAN 52). This incident may have discouraged further such attempts.

The total number of whales 'known' to have been taken in open-boat whaling on the South African coast from 1792 to 1917 is 1,106 (Table 1). This total includes

18 humpback whales, 2 'bottlenose' whales, 1 sperm whale, 1 blue ('sulphurbottom') whale, 1 finback whale, 1 pygmy right whale and 1 killer whale, while 81 kills were recorded as black or right whales. The remainder were unidentified, but it is believed that (until possibly the last few years of the fishery) the landings were essentially composed of right whales (Best, 1970). All references to humpback whales occurred after 1886, and it seems that this species was not an object of pursuit when right whales were more abundant.

> There are none of the spermaceti, but an abundance of those called hunchback, or the fin whale. These are so furious and active, that they are avoided by the harpooner, yielding each no more than about three or four leggers. (Bird, 1823).

This total must be considered a probable underestimate because of inadequate or missing catch statistics for several years. Best (1970) attempted to estimate the size of catches in such years by applying a mean yield of whalebone per whale to the total amount of whalebone exported from the Colony that year. A similar approach will be adopted here.

Systematic records of the export of whale products from the Cape Colony are only available from 1822, when publication of the Cape of Good Hope Blue Books started. Figures for whalebone exports run continuously from 1822 to 1908 (and thereafter, but then obviously include the products from modern whaling operations), while those for whale oil continue only as far as 1865 (Table 2). The figures given are those for products of the Colony. When whale oil or bone was shipped from the Cape to England, the proprietor of the whale fishery had to make an oath before the collector or controller of customs that the same were *bona fide* products from fish actually taken wholly by His Majesty's subjects usually residing in the Colony (Cape Almanac, 1832; Chapman, 1977). Consignments imported from ships calling at the Cape and then exported were recorded separately in the Blue Books as 'other produce' (and were not included here).

In the absence of systematic export figures prior to 1822, imports of whale products from the Cape of Good Hope into Great Britain have been investigated: these are

Table 2.

Whale oil and whalebone produced in and exported from the Cape Colony annually (from CO 5964–6052 except where indicated). Quantity of whale oil is given in gallons (unit value per 100 gals). Quantity of whalebone is in pounds (unit value per 100 lb).

[1]1822–24 In Rixdollars, rest in poinds sterling. [2]CO 3869 no. 275 – False Bay only. [3]Estimated catch for 1808 adjusted on pro-rata basis from ratio of oil produced in 1807 and 1808. [4]CO 4826: 30–31 – False Bay only. [5]Bird (1823) – Table Bay only. [6]Excluding casks. [7]Cape Almanac (1834). [8]Also 25 gals whale oil value at £8. [9]Also 49,763 gals whale oil valued at £1,500.

	Whale oil			Whalebone			Est. no.
Year	Quantity	Value[1]	Unit value	Quantity	Value[1]	Unit value	of whales
1807[2]	33,357	–	–	–	–	–	25[3]
1808[4]	28,609	–	–	13,440	–	–	21
1821[5]	6,600	5,690	86.2	4,600	450	9.8	8
1822	101,633	81,673	80.4	34,689	7,850	22.6	52
1823	91,050	72,135	79.2	29,140	12,270	42.1	44
1824	24,539	18,247	74.4	6,300	3,500	55.6	11
1825	41,201	2,717	6.6	14,602	430	2.9	23
1826	10,122	950	9.4	2,000	110	5.5	4
1827	24,693	2,177	8.8	9,150	585	6.4	15
1828	39,843	2,530	6.3	9,780	587	6.0	16
1829	34,662+ 90 cks	4,024	8.1[6]	23,034	1,392	6.0	35
1830	36,980+ 504 cks	7,079	8.5[6]	29,860	1,797	6.0	45
1831	72,248+ 142 cks	6,515	7.4[6]	28,134	1,619	5.8	43
1832[7]	117,324	9,385	8.0	47,187	2,163	4.6	70
1833	77,545	5,024	6.5	24,693	1,182	4.8	38
1834	90,940	7,082	7.8	14,351	686	4.8	22
1835	39,164	2,217	5.7	13,969	426	3.0	22
1836	31,331	2,952	9.4	14,807	638	4.3	23
1837	20,344	1,637	8.0	4,113	187	4.5	7
1838	10,133	959	9.5	6,851	314	4.6	11
1839	19,446	1,476	7.6	5,477	272	5.0	9
1840	8,977	634	7.1	4,017	246	6.1	7
1841	10,726	673	6.3	4,433	212	4.8	8
1842	15,443	1,220	7.9	9,906	493	5.0	16
1843	8,617	742	8.6	3,783	240	6.3	7
1844	2,906	320	11.0	2,695	150	5.6	5
1845	2,600	300	11.5	3,808	370	9.7	7
1846	2,584	211	8.2	3,851	264	6.9	7
1847	7,400	511	6.9	1,170	66	5.6	3
1848	4,604	355	7.7	2,852	141	4.9	6
1849	4,423	405	9.2	5,124	404	7.9	9
1850	2,402	146	6.1	418	26	6.2	2
1851	0	–	–	4,849	277	5.7	8
1852	7,388	1,025	13.9	5,304	380	7.2	9
1853	5,132	546	10.6	569	50	8.8	2
1854	0	–	–	2,134	65	3.0	4
1855	3,317	549	16.6	2,688	141	5.2	5
1856	2,660	327	12.3	1,982	102	5.1	4
1857	9,336	1,060	11.4	4,982	498	10.0	9
1858	900	150	16.7	3,487	105	3.0	6
1859	38	7	18.4	0	–	–	0
1860	120	20	16.7	112	5	4.5	1
1861	0	–	–	0	–	–	0
1862	128	50	39.1	1,331	115	8.6	3
1863	1,790	223	12.5	672	37	5.5	2
1864	8,523	1,335	15.7	1,290	150	11.6	3
1865	2,095	312	14.9	454	44	9.7	2
1866				409	32	7.8	2
1867				1,524	220	14.4	4
1868				2,266	235	10.4	5
1869				501	24	4.8	2
1870				0	–	–	0
1871				1,252	118	9.4	3
1872				0	–	–	0
1873				1,727	113	6.5	4
1874				182	8	4.4	2
1875				144	7	4.9	2
1876				466	20	4.3	2
1877				124	6	4.8	2
1878				0	–	–	0
1879				42	5	11.9	1
1880				0	–	–	0
1881				173	10	5.8	2
1882				0	–	–	0
1883				312	20	6.4	2
1884				720	100	13.9	2
1885				0	–	–	0
1886				429	51	11.9	2
1887				372	73	19.6	2
1888				1,574	789	50.1	4
1889				445	51	11.5	2
1890				1,800	800	44.4	4
1891				2,328	1,475	63.4	5
1892				1,206	575	47.7	3
1893				1,298	311	24.0	3
1894				2,328	1,204	51.7	5
1895				3,829	1,990	52.0	7
1896				428	210	49.1	2
1897				2,265	1,250	55.2	5
1898				1,423	1,060	74.5	3
1899				1,530	320	20.9	4
1900				208	120	57.7	2
1901				1,875	1,375	73.3	4
1902				295	369	125.1	2
1903				1,148	1,245	108.4	3
1904				1,163	602	51.8	3
1905				0	–	–	0
1906[8]				264	237	89.8	2
1907[9]				1,189	1,000	84.1	3
1908				0	16	–	0

available from 1809 (Table 3). No reliable source of production figures for this fishery prior to 1809 has yet been discovered.

Satisfactory catch and production data are available for the years 1817, 1828 to 1834 and 1836 to 1848, and from these the correlation between production and landings can be investigated (Figs 4 and 5). Correlation is high for both oil (r = 0.9237) and whalebone (r = 0.9753), with mean overall values of 1,839 gallons per whale and 641 1b per whale respectively. At 31.5 gallons per barrel, this is a ratio of 11 lb of bone per barrel of oil. Starbuck (1878) gives the average yield of whalebone for right whales as from 8 to 10 pounds per barrel of oil.

Although either product could be used to estimate landings, whalebone production has been preferred here because (a) whalebone from other species such as humpback probably made a minimal contribution, if it was collected at all, (b) no export figures are available for whale oil after 1865, and (c) whale oil was apparently exported in significant quantities to countries other than Great Britain, thus partly invalidating the use of British imports from 1809 to 1822.

From 1822 to 1834 (except 1832), the Cape of Good Hope Blue Book lists the values of whale products shipped each year to different destinations ('Great Britain', 'North America', 'West Indies', 'British Colonies elsewhere', 'USA', and 'Foreign States (not USA)'). Whalebone was exported almost entirely to Great Britain (annual figures ranging from 91.5 to 100% of production, mean 98.5%), with the remainder going to Foreign States. Whale oil was mainly exported to Great Britain, but in quite variable proportions from year to year (38.1 to 95.6%, mean 76.1%, with British Colonies elsewhere the next most important destination (0 to 40.1%, mean 16.1%), and some going to Foreign States (0 to 21.4%, mean 5.1%) or the West Indies (0 to 21.8%, mean 2.7%). It therefore seems preferable to use whalebone production as an index of catch, especially when considering imports into Great Britain.

Table 3.

Whale oil and whalebone imported into Great Britain from the Cape of Good Hope (from CUST 4.5–4.18)

[1] Assuming 1 tun = 4 hogsheads = 8 barrels = 252 gallons.
[2] Assuming 1 cwt = 4 quarters = 112 lb.
[3] Including "other parts of Africa".

Year imported	Train oil		Whale fins		Estimated no. of whales	Year killed
	Quantity[1] (gals)	Value (sterling)	Quantity[2] (lb)	Value (sterling)		
1809	7,254	374	5,050	361	9	1808
1810	42,979	2,217	27,568	1,969	42	1809
1811	49,518	2,538	11,825	845	19	1810
1812	28,265	1,458	26,592	1,899	40	1811
1813	–	–	–	–	–	1812
1814[3]	106,996	5,130	24,189	1,488	37	1813
1815	62,931	3,246	34,353	2,454	52	1814
1816	32,958	1,700	8,629	616	14	1815
1817	87,605	4,519	21,560	1,540	33	1816
1818	22,437	1,158	6,468	462	11	1817
1819	154,460	7,968	41,251	2,947	62	1818
1820	58,344	3,010	15,315	1,094	24	1819
1821	108,048	5,574	36,850	2,632	55	1820
1822	29,241	1,509	18,820	1,344	29	1821
1823	78,309	4,040	14,460	1,033	23	1822

A linear regression of whalebone production against landings (Fig. 5) gives an estimating equation of

$$y = 1.3324 + 0.0015\,x$$

where x = whalebone production in lb and y = number of whales landed. This equation has been used to estimate the number of whales landed each year from the trade figures for whalebone, but with the assumption that zero production represented zero catch (Tables 2 and 3). In the case of imports into the UK it is assumed that the figures refer to production in the year prior to importation.

In Fig. 6 the monthly distribution of quantities of whalebone exported from the Cape Colony between 1814 and 1818 (from CCT 374, 375) is compared with that for imports of whalebone from the Cape of Good Hope into Great Britain between 1817 and 1822 (from ENT A). Most bone was exported from the Cape between June and December, with a peak in September: this (together with the good correlation between the number of whales taken in any one year and the amount of whalebone exported the same year) suggests that whalebone was shipped very rapidly once it had been obtained. Supporting this, the mean time between capture and shipment of whalebone from Algoa Bay, where these can be linked with certainty, was 30 days (range 20–46 days, n = 7). Most bone arrived in Great Britain between January and May, with a peak in March: given the delay in transit from the Cape to England, this presumably refers to the previous seasons's production.

Because there is no single comprehensive set of catch statistics on this fishery, a composite has to be made from the 'actual' landings in Table 1 and the estimated landings in Tables 2 and 3. The principle adopted in compiling this list has been that 'actual' landings should be used whenever possible and when these were believed to be more comprehensive; estimated landings have been used where 'actual' landings were unavailable or less complete. All whales are assumed to be right whales except where stated (the whalebone from other species probably made an insignificant contribution, if any, to export figures). A figure of 1,580 right whales landed between 1790–9 and 1910–19 is obtained (Table 4).

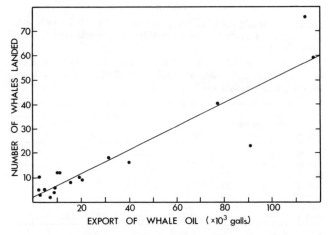

Fig. 4. Relationship between whale oil exported from Cape Colony and number of whales landed the same year, 1817, 1828, 1833–34, 1836–48.

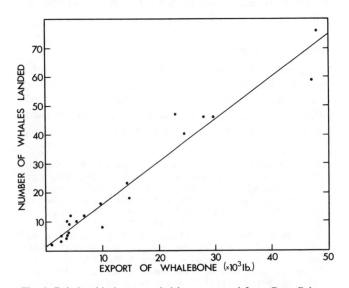

Fig. 5. Relationship between whalebone exported from Cape Colony and number of whales landed the same year, 1817, 1828–34, 1836–48.

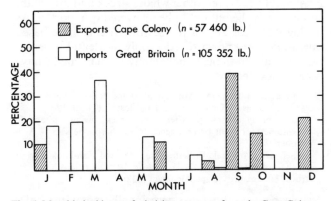

Fig. 6. Monthly incidence of whalebone exports from the Cape Colony (1814–18) and imports into Great Britain from the Cape of Good Hope (1817–22).

The accuracy of this figure is clearly affected by the scarcity of detailed landings or production figures prior to 1809. The reliability of whalebone exports as an indicator of the catch also depends critically on the assumptions (a) that production efficiency remained constant, and (b) that local consumption of whalebone

Table 4.

Total landings of right whales in open-boat whaling along the South African coast. Reported landings, see Table 1. Estimated landings, see Tables 2 and 3.

[1] Using data from Table 1 for 1792–1806, 1812, 1817, 1821–48, 1900 onwards, Table 2 for 1807–08, 1822–27, 1849–99, and Table 3 for 1809–11, 1813–16, 1818–20.

Decade	No. of reported landings	No. of estimated landings	Total[1]	Decade	No. of reported landings	No. of estimated landings	Total[1]
1790–99	128	–	128	1860–69	27	24	24
1800–09	178	88	266	1870–79	5	16	16
1810–19	147	292	378	1880–89	14	16	16
1820–29	156	284	304	1890–99	43	41	41
1830–39	270	290	270	1900–09	23	19	23
1840–49	55	75	64	1910–19	1	–	1
1850–59	34	49	49	Total	1,081	1,194	1,580

remained minimal, throughout the time series. The total of 1,580 whales should therefore be considered as preliminary.

Whales struck and lost

The figures for whales landed do not represent the total mortality inflicted by the fishery. As in other open-boat operations, a proportion of the whales struck escaped, sank and were lost, or were abandoned. Some of these might subsequently be recovered, and so would feature in the landings.

> The whale brought in as derelict on Friday by a Table Bay fisherman (John Wilson who sold it for £40) has rather an adventurous story connected with the close of its career. It appears that the brute was killed ten days ago by Messrs Black and Budge, of Simon's town, off Miller's Point in False Bay. With their boat they were tackled to it for ten hours, and were compelled to abandon it only as night set in. From there it has been drifted round by the current until it was observed on Friday by the *Hannibal*, off Mouille Point, at the entrance of Table Bay. On Friday evening Mr Black made an affidavit describing the appearance of the animal, the harpoon stabs it got, etc., which left no doubt of the identity. In drifting round for so many days the sharks fed liberally, and its appearance and odour at Granger's Bay, when being cut up, was anything but agreeable (EPH, 11 August 1868).

Presumably, however, other whales struck and lost might subsequently die but fail to be recovered or reported. As no logbooks for any of the South African shore-based operations are known to exist, only incidental observations remain to indicate how many animals might have been struck and lost.

> …in the year 1804 he [Mr Murray] killed and boiled the blubber of 39 Fish, besides 8 which were killed and lost;…(Theal, 1900)
> A good many fish escape after being struck, owing perhaps to unskilfulness or want of experience in the harpooners (SACA, 9 October 1830)
> …there are two Whale Fisheries, Kalk Bay and Fish-hook Bay, at which were caught during the last season, 10 whales; 15 others were struck, but escaped. (Cape Almanac, 1832).

Newspaper accounts also occasionally mention whales struck and lost, but these were probably considered of lesser interest than landings and so may have been under-reported. To make allowance for this, only those years in which at least one whale was reported to have been struck and lost have been used, and analyses have been confined to the fishery local to the newspaper concerned. For the Algoa Bay fishery, suitable data are available for 1848, 1858, 1862 and 1869 (Table 1): in these seasons seven whales were landed and a further five reported struck and lost (EPH).

Combining all data sources, the ratio of struck and lost whales to whales landed can be calculated as 20:17 (or about 1:1). The proportion of these that subsequently died is unknown, but from the data for Murray's operation in 1804, 8 out of 47 whales killed were lost. This implies an approximate ratio of 1 whale killed and lost for every 5 landed. Presumably this was a minimum figure, as it only included whales known to have died. Values for the landed catch can therefore be multiplied by 1.2 to correct (at least partially) for whales struck and lost that subsequently died.

However, this correction factor is based on a very small sample of unknown reliability. Loss rates in the fishery and their associated mortality may also have varied with time as gear technology changed – particularly after the introduction of explosives (the darting gun and bomb lance). This correction should therefore be considered as only a first approximation.

Its adoption would infer that a total of $1,580 \times 1.2 = 1,896$ right whales were killed as a result of shorebased open-boat whaling on the South African coast.

Seasonality of the catch

There were 131 whales taken in open-boat whaling for which the dates (or at least the months) of capture could be discovered (Table 5). With three exceptions these whales were taken between May and November, with the majority (85%) occurring between July and October. The 41 right whales for which dates of capture are known were taken over a similar period, as were the 15 humpbacks, although there seemed to be a tendency for the latter to be taken later in the season.

The seasonal distribution of catches may however, have been influenced by the distribution of effort. In the diaries of John Sewell, harbour-master at Plettenberg Bay from 1892 to 1897, some statements suggest that activities of the whalers were seasonally planned. On 27 October 1892, for instance, Sewell reports,

> Whalers now gone and will not be back for another 8 months.

and on 29 June 1893,

> The whalers brought their new boat down and got their license
> (Sewell, unpubl.)

It is not known how widespread such a seasonal restriction of effort may have been, or whether it applied equally throughout the history of the fishery.

Table 5.

Monthly distribution of catches of whales in open-boat fishery and of right whales in the modern fishery.

[1] One was a Pygmy right whale.
[2] Probably not in fishery.

Month	Open-boat (1832–1917)			Modern (1910–1963)
	Total	Humpback	Right	Right
January	2[1]		1	
February	1[2]			
March				
April				1
May	2			
June	11	1	5	3
July	26	–	6	8
August	31	2	12	16
September	26	3	7	16
October	29	7	10	2
November	3	2		2
December				
Total	131	15	41	48

Composition of the catch

The average whalebone yield calculated above (641 1b) agrees closely with published figures for adult right whales (550 to 726 1b – Collett, 1909), indicating that the catch must have contained a high proportion of adult animals.

Several contemporary accounts mention the apparent predominance of females amongst the right whales taken on the South African coast, and these have been discussed previously (Best, 1970; 1981). The present data set shows that male right whales were occasionally taken, and that these were not necessarily all juveniles: there are six unequivocal references to 'bull' right whales in Table 1, and from the size or description of oil and bone yield given for four of these it is clear that they were adults.

Omitting humpback whales, there are ten references in Table 1 to the landing of cows and calves (or animals of their size) together, another eight to the landing of only the cow from such a pair, and another four to the landing of only the calf. Because of their proximity to shore, and their tendency to surface more frequently than other classes (Best, 1981), it is possible that female right whales with calves were a prime target for the whalers. This was clearly the case for French right whalers operating on the African coast, where a common ploy was to harpoon the calf first (without killing it) so that the mother could be more easily secured. Separate whale lines were even rigged for cows and calves (Robineau, 1985).

MODERN WHALING

The first modern whaling operations in southern Africa commenced at Durban in 1908. Expansion (and subsequent partial collapse) was particularly rapid; by 1913 eleven floating factories and 17 land stations were operating at a number of localities along the coast of southern Africa between the French Congo (Gabon) and central Mozambique, but by 1918 these had been reduced to only 4 land stations (Fig. 7). Unfortunately systematic reporting of catches by the whaling companies was not universal during the early years of the modern fishery, and apart from the total number of whales caught and total production figures, no information on the species taken is available in the International Whaling Statistics for the Angolan coast 1913–1916, Walvis Bay 1912–1913, the Mozambique coast in 1911 and 1914–15, the coast of Congo 1912–14, Luderitz 1913–14, the Natal coast prior to 1912 and the Cape Colony prior to 1916. From other catches made at the first three of these localities prior to 1915 (a total of about 9,092 whales), it is known that the majority (97%) of the animals taken were humpback whales, with increasing numbers of blue, fin and sperm whales being taken latterly. Although no right whales are included amongst the catches listed in the BIWS for the coasts of west and east Africa during this period, Olsen (1914) mentions one right whale as being taken at Porto Alexandre in 1912, and it is possible that others were included in the large catches made at that time.

For the missing early years of the fishery in Natal and Cape Colony it has been possible to consult other sources, but almost certainly some right whale landings have gone undetected, particularly in the Cape Colony. At Donkergat, for instance, no right whale catches prior to 1911 have been traced, but when Wilson (1972) visited the station in August 1910 he was told by the owner that 'They get the Atlantic Right Whale but very rarely'.

According to a report on the Cape whaling industry dated 30 December 1913, right whales were valued (according to size) at £100–800 each, sperm whales at £30–800, and the rest (blue, humpback, fin and sei) at £150 or less (PAN 49). This high value must have encouraged the taking of right whales even if the animals were scarce. For instance lighthouse keepers at Cape Recife, Cape St Francis and Mossel Bay (and other interested parties) were requested to cable the manager of the Plettenberg Bay whaling station whenever right whales were seen, giving position and direction of movement. Honoraria were paid for such information, which resulted in the capture of at least three right whales in 1915, one of which was about 80 nmi. from the station (TLB 51, 52).

Further, the management of the whaling company at Mossel Bay included the following in a notice in the local newspaper on 5 December 1911:

'In less than three months during which the Company carried on its operations during the past season, 125 whales were successfully dealt with and this number included one right whale. It is confidently expected that during next season more right whales will be captured as this class of whale frequents these seas in the earlier part of the season (May) during which the Company was not established in the past year' (MBA).

Apart from the problem of missing data, the published statistics for right whale catches in the early years of the modern fishery are very unreliable. Tønnessen and Johnsen (1982) have published a revised list of world right whale catches from 1904 to 1918, and E. Vangstein has kindly supplied us with some other corrections for the African statistics after 1920 (Table 6).

Protection was eventually given to the right whale in terms of a League of Nations Convention for the Regulation of Whaling that came into force on 16 January 1935. Although South Africa signed and ratified this convention in January 1933, the ban on catching right whales does not seem to have been incorporated into national legislation until proclamation no. 159 of 1940 was promulgated (under the Sea Fisheries Act no. 10 of 1940). The 1935 catches at Durban and the 1937 catches at Donkergat were therefore not technically illegal, and were in fact reported to the Committee for Whaling Statistics in Oslo. While the animal taken in 1963 was an error of judgement (Best, 1981), and the circumstances of the two animals taken at Durban in 1951 are unknown, other right whales may have been taken after 1940 in deliberate violation of the ban and not reported. This was certainly the case for the female landed at Donkergat in 1953. From 1958, however, the level of national inspection and scientific monitoring of the catches was greatly increased, and it is highly unlikely that any further undeclared catches of right whales occurred from South African land stations. The 1951 capture of a right whale at Cap Lopez was recorded as an infraction (Budker and Collignon, 1952).

Modern whaling ceased in South Africa in October 1975 with the closure of the Durban whaling station. In all, 105–106 right whales are known to have been taken in modern whaling on the southern African coast between 1908 and 1975 (Table 5), though from the incomplete statistics of the earliest years (and the possibility of some undeclared catches after 1940) it is probable that this figure is an underestimate.

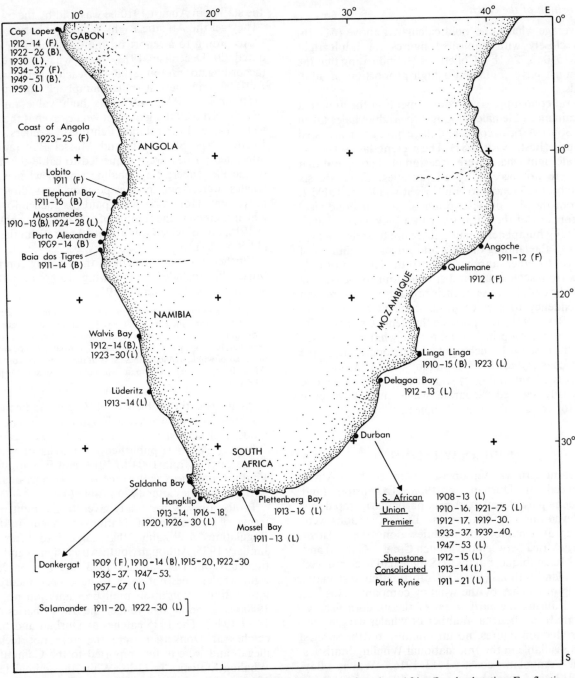

Fig. 7. Locations and years of operation of modern whaling stations on coast of southern Africa (L = land station, F = floating factory, B = both). Stations in Durban area identified by name of last company to operate them. Sources: Gambell (1971), Risting (1922), Strong (1915), Tønnessen (1967) and PAN files.

Seasonality of the catch

Modern whaling activities on the coast of southern Africa were usually seasonally restricted, either for logistical reasons (the same catcher boats or personnel being needed for the Antarctic summer season) or latterly because of a legally imposed catching season. The companies working in West Africa in 1913, for instance commenced operations in June and finished in either mid-October or mid-November (Strong, 1915). At Saldanha Bay in 1912, whaling was only carried out in the months March to November (Hjort, 1915), although Olsen (1914) shows catches of Bryde's whales being made there in December. At Plettenberg Bay in 1914, the catchers seemed to operate from March to October (Lea, unpubl.).

In Harmer's statistics from companies operating in the period 1918–28, whales were caught between the following months:-

Cape Colony		*Natal**	
March to December	1 season	March to December	1 season
April to December	2 ,,	April to December	2 ,,
April to November	13 ,,	April to September	1 ,,
April to October	4 ,,	May to December	1 ,,
May to November	1 ,,	May to October	7 ,,
May to October	1 ,,	May to September	2 ,,
May to September	1 ,,	June to November	1 ,,
June to October	1 ,,	June to September	1 ,,

* Also some whaling in January one season

In most years, therefore, the stations were operating throughout the majority of the period when right whales were likely to be abundant in coastal waters (Best, 1981).

Table 6.

Reported catches of right whales in modern whaling on the southern African coast, 1908–1975.

[1]Figures within brackets are taken as being included in preceding data. [2]The 14 animal listed for 1907/8 by Tonnessen were taken by an American open-boat whaler (Tonnessen, 1969). [3]Carl Ellefsen, manager of station, to Director of south African Museum, in litt. 21 October 1912; refers to catching a right whale of over 50 ft, and later to seeing a right whale foetus 15 ft long (SAM files). Probably more than one individual. [4]Pregnant with a foetus 14 ft long. [5]Right whale taken in Natal according to BIWS (1942) was actually a minke whale (NFD, 1915). [6]Although Anon (1922) lists a total of 9 right whales for the Cape Province in 1919, a perusal of the catch data sent by the companies to the Provincial Administration reveals only the two captures listed here (PAN 50, 51). [7]Although 2 right whales listed for Cape Colony in BIWS (1942), no whaling took place there in 1921 (Tonnessen and Johnsen, 1982). [8]Although 3 right whales listed for Cape Colony in BIWS (1942), none listed in HSC or by Tonnessen (1969). [9]Right whale taken in Natal according to BIWS (1942) was actually a Bryde's whale (E. Vangstein, in litt. 19 Aug 1985). [10]Dates obtained from platform records held in files of the Sea Fisheries Research Institute, Cape Town.

Year	Locality	Number landed	Length (feet)	Sex	Date landed	Source
1908–10[2]	Natal	7–8	–	–	–	NPM, 15.6.11
(1910)	(Natal)	(1)	–	–	22 Aug	Olsen, 1914
(1910)	(Natal)	(1)	(50)	–	15 Oct	NPM, 20.10.10
1911	Natal	1	–	–	21 Jun	Olsen, 1914
	Mossel Bay	2	54	F	8 Sep	MBA, 11.9.11
			Calf	–		
	Donkergat	1	–	–	27 Sep	Olsen, 1914
1912	Natal	2	–	–	–	NFD, 1913
	(Natal)	(1)	–	–	24 Jun	Olsen, 1914
	(Natal)	(1)	(Ad)	(F)	–	SAM photo files
1911–12	Salamander	1	Ad	F	–	Ellefsen[3]
1913	Natal	3	–	–	–	BIWS, 1942
	Plettenberg Bay	1	–	–	11 Jun	TD
	Hangklip	4	–	–	–	Lea, unpubl.
	Donkergat	1	Ad	F	18 Apr	Olsen, 1914; SAM photo files[4]
	Salamander	1	"large"	–	–	Olsen, 1914
	Porto Alexandre	1	–	–	–	Olsen, 1914
1914	Natal	3	–	–	–	BIWS, 1942
	Plett. Bay	1	–	–	–	Lea, unpubl.
1915[5]	Plett. Bay	2	Ad	F	10 Aug	TLB 51
			Calf	–		
		2	–	–	–	TLB 51
		1	–	–	11 Sep	TLB 52
	Salamander	2	–	–	–	PAN 49
1916	Natal	2	–	–	–	BIWS, 1942
	Plett. Bay	1	–	–	–	TLB 55
1917	Hangklip	2	–	–	–	Harmer, unpubl.
1918	Donkergat	1	40		8 Sep	HSC
	Natal	2	–	–	– Sep	NFD, 1919
1919[6]	Donkergat	1	–	M	– Sep	PAN 50
	Salamander	1	–	–	– Aug	PAN 51
1920	Donkergat	2	48.7	F	8 Nov	HSC
			28.3	M		
	Salamander	1	46.0	F	5 Aug	PAN 51
1921[7]	Natal	5	Av 46.4	–	–	NFD, 1921
			Max 48.0			
1922[8]	Natal	1	45.0	F	4 Oct	HSN
1923	Salamander	1	40	F	14 Aug	HSC
1924	Natal	2	48	F	30 Sep	HSN
			22	F		
1925	Coast of Angola (Fl.f.Esparanca)	17	–	–	–	BIWS (1942)
1926	Natal	1	45	F	6 Aug	HSN
	Salamander	1	50	F	26 Jul	HSC
	Donkergat	2	51.8	F	26 Aug	HSC
			22.2	M		
1927[9]	Hangklip	1	48.5	F	15 Aug	HSC
1928	Hangklip	1	50	F	25 Jul	HSC
		2	49.6	F	27 Sep	HSC
			30	F		
1929	Salamander	1	47	F	12 Aug	HSC
	Hangklip	1	53.7	F	12 Jul	HSC
1930	Hangklip	1	54.0	F	23 Aug	PAN 51
1932	Natal	1	–	F	– Sep	NFD, 1932
1933	Natal	2	45	F	– Jul	NFD, 1933
			47	F		
1934	Natal	2	–	–	–	BIWS (1942)
1935	Natal	2	–	–	–	BIWS (1942)

Table 6 (continued)

Year	Locality	Number	Length	Sex	Date	Source
1937	Donkergat	1	50.3	F	12 Jul	HSC
		1	51.3	F	22 Jul	HSC
		1	43.5	F	28 Jul	HSC
		1	46.2	F	13 Aug	HSC
		1	48.2	M	16 Sep	HSC
		1	43.7	F	21 Sep	HSC
		1	44.3	F	21 Sep	HSC
1951	Cap Lopez	1	49	F	–	BIWS (1953)
	Durban	1	44		10 Aug	BIWS (1953[10])
		1	47	F	11 Aug	BIWS (1953[10])
1953	Donkergat	1	Ad	F	–	C.E. Ash, in litt. 23.8.85
1963	Durban	1	43	M	14 Aug	Best (1981)

The 48 right whales for which at least the month of capture is known were taken between April and November, with the majority (83.3%) being killed from July to September (Table 5). This is a similar pattern to that seen for open-boat whaling.

Composition of the catch

From statistics sent by the whaling companies to the British Museum (Natural History), and some other sources, the sex and length of some of the animals taken have been established (Table 6). The accuracy of the lengths given is dubious as methods of measurement may not have been standardised. The two right whales taken at Donkergat in 1926, for instance, were measured as 15.23 m (50 ft) and 6.5 m (21.3 ft) in length by 'Discovery' scientists (Matthews, 1938), or somewhat shorter than the lengths sent to Harmer by the whaling company. There were 33 females and five males in the sample, and two distinct size categories: 30 large animals 40 to 54 ft (mean 47.5 ft) in length and four small animals 22.2 to 30 ft (mean 26.1 ft) in length. Two of the five males fell in the latter group. The catch therefore seemed to consist mainly of adult females with some calves or yearlings. Adult males were however taken on occasion (Fig. 8).

The composition of the catch in modern whaling therefore seems to have been very similar to that in the earlier open-boat whaling. This suggests either that similar selectivity was operating in both fisheries, or that both were accurate representations of the composition of the inshore population.

DISCUSSION

The availability of right whales to the open-boat whalers seemed to decline markedly in the 1830s (Best, 1970). Remarks associated with the annual statistics in the Cape of Good Hope Blue Books are valuable as contemporary comment.

(1828) There has been a whale fishery at St. Helena Bay for some years but no Fish have been killed there during the last three seasons. (CO 5970)
(1829) The whale fishery was last season particularly fortunate throughout the Colony but it is probable that few will be taken next season, as they are invariably found to desert, for a time, places where they are molested. (CO 5971)
(1830) The whale fishery in Table Bay was last season not so successful as in the preceding year, but the number (36) killed throughout the Colony has been upon the whole favourable. (CO 5973)

Fig. 8. Adult male right whale landed at Cape whaling station (probably Hangklip), date unknown. (SAM photo files).

(1831) The number of whales taken in Table Bay, although double that of the preceding year, was, in the opinion of persons well qualified to judge, much less than it would have been had the Fishery been confined to one Establishment as was previously the case, many of the Fish having been disturbed by the opposition of the three different parties. (CO 5974)

(1835) No whales have been caught in Table Bay this season. Not less than 30 American whale ships have fished successfully along and in the neighbourhood of the coasts of this Colony during the Whaling season in the years 1833 and 1834. A great number of American vessels have (it is reported) been on the same grounds during the whaling season of the year 1835 but have not been so successful; it is probable that the whales have been so chased and destroyed for the last 3 or 4 years that they have deserted the coast. It is certain that they have not been seen in such numbers lately. Only 5 were observed in Table Bay last season and they were so wild that not one of them was taken. (CO 5977)

(1836) Very few whales entered Table Bay during this year. (George District) But few whales have been taken this year. This is ascribed by the proprietors of the Fisheries with great reason to the number of American Vessels, constantly fishing on our coasts. (CO 5978)

(1837) Few whales have been seen in Table Bay since the whaling season of 1833–1834, when a large number of American whalers fished, with great success off and along the west coast of the Colony. (CO 5979)

(1840: George district) The whale fisheries have not been carried on during 1840, although whales were plentiful during the season, both in Mossel and Plettenberg's Bays. (CO 5982)

(1841) Whales are plentiful in Mossel Bay during the season, and the small number taken can only be attributed to the want of experience in the persons employed. (CO 5983)

(1842) Whales visit Plettenberg's Bay and Mossel Bay annually. One has been killed in each Bay this year, and more might have been obtained at the latter had there been any establishment for that purpose. (CO 5984)

(1843) Many whales have visited Plettenberg's Bay and Mossel Bay this year, but no attempts have been made to kill them. (CO 5985)

(1844–1848) Whales visit Plettenberg's Bay and Mossel Bay annually. (CO 5986–5990)

(1848: Port Elizabeth) The whale fishery of late years has been unsuccessful. (CO 5990).

These comments suggest a declining abundance of whales firstly in St Helena Bay, then Table Bay and finally in Algoa Bay. It is interesting to note that (at least up to 1843) there did not appear to be a reduction in the availability of whales on the south coast (around Mossel and Plettenberg Bays). If these observations were accurate, they would suggest a contraction of range as the population declined. This contraction might still have existed when modern whaling started. According to Thompson (1913), visits by right whales to the South African coast had become less frequent year by year,

except perhaps in the vicinity of Plettenberg Bay, and were comparatively rare in Algoa, False and Table Bays. Furthermore, although catch records are very incomplete, there are no known instances of right whales being taken at the Luderitz or Walvis Bay whaling stations, both of which were situated in areas of high right whale catches in the late eighteenth and early nineteenth centuries (Best, 1981). Certainly the distribution of right whales along the southern African coast today is still much reduced from what it was historically, the main focus of abundance being on the south coast (Best, 1981).

The size of the take in open-boat whaling (an estimated) total of 1,894 animals in 120 years) may have been relatively insignificant compared to the catches taken by foreign pelagic whalers, both on the South African coast and elsewhere from the same stock. In order to establish the original level of abundance of right whales in this area, some assessment of the size of this pelagic take is urgently needed.

The composition of the catch in both open-boat and modern whaling indicates that exploitation in coastal waters may have been especially damaging to the reproductive potential of the stock. Thus while the original depletion of the right whale population off southern Africa might be attributed mainly to the activities of foreign whalers, the continued taking of animals in open-boat whaling along the southern African coast in the latter half of the nineteenth century (and particularly by modern whaling in the twentieth century) may have been sufficient to retard or prevent the subsequent recovery of the population until all catching ceased.

ACKNOWLEDGEMENTS

The late F. P. Chapman provided a complete listing of his references on the history of South African whaling: this proved to be invaluable. C. de Jong (University of South Africa) and S. G. Brown (Sea Mammal Research Unit, UK) assisted in the search for archival material. Permission to consult the Thesen Company archives at Knysna was given by S. B. Thesen to whom we are greatly indebted, and Mrs P. Storrar kindly drew our attention to these records.

REFERENCES

Anon. c. 1795. *Sketches of the Political and Commercial History of the Cape of Good Hope.* 440 pp. Cape Archives microfilm no. ZK 3/24.

Anon. 1806. *Gleanings in Africa: exhibiting a faithful and correct view of the manners and customs of the inhabitants of the Cape of Good Hope, and surrounding country.* London, James Cundee, 320 pp.

Anon. 1827. Zuid-Afrikaansche Walvisch-vangst. *Het Nederduitsch Zuid-Afrikaansch Tydschrift* 4(5): 342–3.

Anon. 1912. Photograph with caption 'Een onzaglik Walvis, te Muizenburg gevangen door de heer Auret. Het dier is 70 voet lang.' *De Goede Hoop,* 11 (5), facing page 128.

Anon. 1922. The fishing industry of the Cape coast. Facts and figures from the Provincial Administration's report. *S. Afr. J. Ind.* July: 1–4.

Barrow, J. 1801. *An Account of Travels into the Interior of Southern Africa, in the Years 1797 and 1798: etc.* London T. Cadell and W. Davies, 2 vols., 418 and 452 pp.

Best, P. B. 1970. Exploitation and recovery of right whales *Eubalaena australis* off the Cape Province. *Investl Rep. Div. Sea Fish. S. Afr.* 80: 1–20.

Best, P. B. 1981. The status of right whales (*Eubalaena glacialis*) off South Africa, 1969–1979. *Investl Rep. Sea Fish. Inst. S.Afr.* 123: 1–44.

Bird, W. 1823. *State of the Cape of Good Hope, in 1822.* London, John Murray, 377 pp.

Budker, P., and Collignon, J. 1952. Trois campagnes baleinieres au Gabon (1949–1950–1951). *Bull. Inst. Centrafr.* (3): 75–100.

Cape Almanac. 1832. *The South African Almanac and Directory for 1832.* Cape Town, George Greig, 350 pp.

Cape Almanac. 1833. *The South African Almanac and Directory for 1833.* Cape Town, George Greig, 292 pp.

Cape Almanac. 1834. *The South African Directory and Almanac for 1834.* Cape Town, George Greig, 280 pp.

Chapman, F. P. 1977. Some notes on early whaling in False Bay. *Bull. Simon's Town Hist. Soc.* 9(4): 132–60.

Chase, J. C. 1843. *The Cape of Good Hope and the Eastern Province of Algoa Bay, &c. &c. with statistics of the colony.* London, Pelham Richardson, 338 pp.

Collett, R. 1909. A few notes on the whale *Balaena glacialis* and its capture in recent years in the North Atlantic by Norwegian whalers. *Proc. zool. Soc. Lond.* : 91–98.

Crowe, J. Unpublished MS. *The diary of Joseph Crowe, covering the period 1811–1866.* Jagger Library, University of Cape Town; Bain and Lister family papers BC 543 (original in possession of Miss M. Lister, of Wynberg, Cape Town).

De Jong, C. 1967. Walvisvangst bij Kaap de Goede Hoop tijdens de Bataafse Republiek. *Historia* 12(3): 171–198.

Gambell, R. 1971. A short history of modern whaling off Natal. *Mercurius* 14: 37–48.

Gilchrist, J. D. F. 1899. *Report of the Marine Biologist for the year 1898.* Cape of Good Hope, Dept. of Agriculture, 362 pp.

Gilchrist, J. D. F. 1901. *Report of the Government Biologist for the year 1900.* Cape of Good Hope, Dept. of Agriculture, 180 pp.

Gilchrist, J. D. F. 1902. *Report of the Government Biologist for the year 1901.* Cape of Good Hope, Dept. of Agriculture, 104 pp., 2 charts.

Gilchrist, J. D. F. 1903. Report of the Government Biologist for the year 1902. Cape of Good Hope, Dept. of Agriculture, 283 pp.

Gilchrist, J. D. F. 1904. *Report of the Government Biologist for the year 1903.* Cape of Good Hope, Dept. of Agriculture, 194 pp.

Gilchrist, J. D. F. 1906a. *Report of the Government Biologist for the year 1904.* Cape of Good Hope, Dept. of Agriculture, 40 pp.

Gilchrist, J. D. F. 1906b. *Report of the Government Biologist for the year 1905.* Cape of Good Hope, Dept. of Agriculture, 42 pp.

Gilchrist, J. D. F. 1907. *Report of the Government Biologist for the year 1906.* Cape of Good Hope, Dept. of Agriculture, 44 pp.

Gillard, W. S. 1910. *A souvenir of Simonstown, being an historical and pictorial guide to Simonstown and the neighbourhood.* 80 pp + i–viii.

Harmer, S. F. Unpublished. Report to Trustees of British Museum (Natural History), June 10, 1918. In 'Harmer Whaling Reports 1910–1920 and 1912–18', British Museum (Natural History), London.

Hjort, J. 1915. Memorandum on the distribution of the whales in the waters about the Antarctic Continent. *In: Interdepartmental committee on whaling and the protection of whales. Minutes of evidence, etc.* Colonial Office Confidential Print Misc. 298.

Holman, J. 1834. *A Voyage Round the World, Including Travels in Africa, Asia, Australasia, America, etc., etc., from 1827 to 1832.* London, Smith, Elder & Co., vol. 2, 492 pp.

Lea, E. Unpublished. Studies of the modern whale fishery in the Southern Hemisphere. Type-written MS, 95 pp, 47 tables, 23 figs., annotated in pencil '1919 [Received by the Falklands Islands Committee]'. In Harmer's files, British Museum (Natural History), London.

Matthews, L. H. 1938. Notes on the southern right whale, *Eubalaena australis.* '*Discovery' Rep.* 17: 169–182.

Milner, J., and Brierly, O. W. 1869. *The Cruise of H.M.S. Galatea, Captain H.R.H. The Duke of Edinburgh, K.G., in 1867–1868.* London, W. H. Allen & Co., 488 pp.

Olsen, Ø. 1914. Hvaler og hvalfangst i Sydafrika. *Bergens Museums Aarbok 1914–1915* 5: 1–56.

Prior, J. 1820. *Voyage in the Indian Seas, in the Nisus frigate, to the Cape of Good Hope, Isles of Bourbon, France, and Seychelles; to Madras; and the Isles of Java, St Paul, and Amsterdam, during the years 1810 and 1811.* London, Sir Richard Phillips & Co., 114 pp.

Risting, S. 1922. *Av Hvalfangstens Historie.* Christiana, J. W. Cappelens Forlag. i–xvi + 625 pp + i–v.

Robineau, D. 1985. Relation de la pêche de la baleine à la côte d'Afrique. *Ann. Soc. Sci. nat. Charente–Maritime* 7(3): 365–76.

Ross, G. J. B., Best, P. B. and Donnelly, B. G. 1975. New records of the pygmy right whale (*Caperea marginata*) from South Africa, with comments on distribution, migration, appearance and behaviour. *J. Fish. Res. Bd Can.* 32 (7): 1005–17.

Sewell, J. F. Unpublished. *Journal and log of John Fisher Sewell, Harbour Master, Plettenberg Bay.* S.A. Library, Rex Collection cat. no. MSC9, microfiche MF31.

Starbuck, A. 1878. History of the American whale fishery from its earliest inception to the year 1876. *U.S. Comm. Fish & Fisheries. Part IV. Rep. Commnr 1875–1876* Appendix A. 779 pp.

Storrar, P. 1978. *Portrait of Plettenberg Bay.* Cape Town, Centaur publishers, i–x + 242pp.

Strong, F. E. K. 1915. Report on whaling stations on the west coast of Africa. *In: Further Correspondence (January 1914 – March 1915) relating to whaling and the protection of whales.* Colonial Office Confidential Print Misc. 300.

Theal, G. M. 1900. *Records of the Cape Colony from July 1806 to May 1909.* Vol. 6, London, Government of Cape Colony, 511 pp.

Thompson, W. W. 1913. *The Sea Fisheries of the Cape Colony from Van Riebeeck's Days to the Eve of the Union.* Cape Town, Maskew Miller, 163 pp.

Thompson, G. 1827. *Travels and Adventures in Southern Africa.* London, Henry Colburn. Van Riebeeck Society edition (V. S. Forbes, ed.), 1968: Cape Town, The Van Riebeeck Society, Parts 2 and 3, 277 pp.

Tønnessen, J. N. 1967. *Den Moderne Hvalfangsts Historie. Opprinnelse og utvikling. 2. Verdensfangsten 1883–1924 Del I 1883–1914.* Sandefjord, Norges Hvalfangstforbund, i–xv + 619 pp.

Tønnessen, J. N. 1969. *Den Moderne Hvalfangsts Historie. Opprinnelse og utvikling. 3. Verdensfangsten 1883–1924 Del II 1914–1924. Den pelagiske fangst 1924–1937.* Sandefjord, Norges Hvalfangstforbund, i–xi + 648 pp.

Tønnessen, J. N. and Johnsen, A. O. 1982. *The History of Modern Whaling.* London, C. Hurst & Co; Canberra, Australian National University Press: i–xx + 798 pp.

Wilson, E. 1972. *Diary of the 'Terra Nova' expedition to the Antarctic 1910–1912. An account of Scott's last expedition edited from the original mss in the Scott Polar Research Institute and the British Museum by H. G. R. King.* London, Blandford Press. i–xxiii + 279 pp.